W9-BUI-583

HISTORICAL TABLES

58 BC-AD 1985

BY

S. H. STEINBERG

ELEVENTH EDITION UPDATED BY

JOHN PAXTON

FOREWORD BY

G. P. GOOCH

Garland Publishing, Inc.
New York

Library of Congress Cataloging-in-Publication Data

Steinberg, S. H. (Sigfrid Henry), 1899-1969.
  Historical tables, 58 BC-AD 1985.

    Rev. ed. of: Historical tables, 58 B.C.-A.D. 10th ed. 1979.
    1. Chronology, Historical—Tables. I. Paxton, John.
II. Steinberg, S.H. (Sigfrid Henry), 1899-1969.
Historical tables, 58 B.C.-A.D. 1978. III. Title.
D11.S83   1986   902'.02   86-18326
ISBN 0-8240-8951-0

Published by Garland Publishing, Inc.
136 Madison Avenue, New York, New York 10016

Printed in Great Britain

TO THE MEMORY OF

THE RIGHT REVEREND BISHOP G. K. A. BELL

(4 FEBRUARY 1883 — 3 OCTOBER 1958)

WHO, WHILE HE HAD TIME, DID GOOD UNTO ALL MEN;

AND ESPECIALLY UNTO THEM THAT ARE OF

THE HOUSEHOLD OF FAITH

FOREWORD

FORTY years ago Lord Acton wrote a Foreword to my *Annals of Politics and Culture, 1492-1899*, a work now out of print. Public events, he declared, were the foundation of history ; but it derived its best virtue from regions beyond the sphere of State. Justice, he continued, must be done to its several elements, to thought as well as action, to the mass of influences which constitute opinion and govern the life of nations and the progress of civilization. His writings, fragmentary though they are, breathe the same conviction that history is the record and interpretation of the life of humanity. Goethe, declared Matthew Arnold in a celebrated phrase, saw life steadily and saw it whole. The historian must try to follow his example. *Homo sum : humani nihil a me alienum puto.* Though we all have our preferences and scholars must specialise, we must never forget that the stuff of history is the whole field of human experience. Its subject is the making of civilization, the ascent of man.

How it is to be interpreted is a problem that each of us must decide for himself. History, as Froude used to say, is a child's box of letters : you can spell with them any word you will. The best preparation for the task is the recognition that it must be studied in all its length, in all its breadth, in all its depth. Nothing less will give us the perspective and the insight we need. Dr. Steinberg has compiled this extremely useful work in the belief that civilization is a co-operative achievement and a common heritage. To cast one's eye down the column headed Cultural Life is to realise the width of his studies and interests. Peoples are connected with one another by a network of contacts and obligations, visible and invisible. The older the world grows, the greater the debt of each to all and of all to each. Every one of us is a citizen of the world : each nation is a branch of the human tree. Geographical, racial and linguistic barriers blur but cannot destroy the fundamental unity of mankind.

In presenting the life of man as a whole in so far as this is possible in the bare bones of historical tables, the author is merely holding up the mirror to the past. The flesh to cover the bones is conveniently supplied by the Cambridge Ancient, Medieval, and Modern Histories, happily completed at last. There is no propaganda either in the selection of his material or in the recesses of his mind. He has written history elsewhere, but he is not writing it here. He is merely aiding teachers, students and the general reader to discover or recall what was going on in a given age in various parts of the world and in different fields of activity. It is not a book to be read through and put back on our shelves, but an indispensable companion to be kept on the table. It should prove of the greatest value in schools and colleges, and when the days of examinations are over it will remain within reach. For who can keep in mind the dates, the details and the sequences even of the most important transactions from the rise of the Roman Empire to the end of 1945? No work of precisely this character, so far as I am aware, is available for English readers. In my opinion the author has successfully achieved his purpose of filling the gap.

G. P. GOOCH

PREFACE

TO THE FIRST EDITION

THE Foreword by Dr. G. P. Gooch has introduced the reader to the general aims of the present book, so that the author can confine himself to a few notes on some technical details.

As the Historical Tables will probably be used chiefly by Anglo-Saxon students, the history of the British Commonwealth and that of the United States have been given a slight predominance, without, however, upsetting the balance, and distorting the relative importance, of historical facts. It need scarcely be emphasized that the author could not go back to the primary sources in each instance; but he has always tried to avail himself of the best authorities.

Apart from the sections dealing with the world wars, six columns have been provided for every period. For the greater part of the book, the left-hand pages deal chiefly with the relations of the Powers. The three columns on the right-hand pages are given to what may be described as home affairs and the history of civilization; i.e. constitutional, economic, spiritual, and intellectual activities. All entries which do not expressly mention another country refer to England or, after 1707, Great Britain. This arrangement is, of course, open to criticism in many cases, since political, constitutional, and economic events have always influenced each other. The author therefore asks the reader always to regard the six columns as a unit which has been broken up only for convenience sake.

The arrangement of the first ten or twelve pages has been made on different lines. It is meant to show the gradual absorption of the Roman Empire by the Papacy, the Islamic states, and the Teutonic tribes, up to the revival of the Western Empire under Charlemagne, and the first shaping of what was to become the kingdom of England, under Egbert of Wessex. Similarly the period following the Great War has been presented in a way different from that used for the bulk of the book. Since it is as yet impossible to pass a fair judgement on the greater or lesser importance of contemporary events, the author has confined himself to the rôle of an annalist who simply enumerates the major occurrences as he sees them.

Other changes of smaller significance explain themselves as being necessitated by the historical development itself; e.g. the change of the heading 'Islam and Asia' to 'Countries Oversea', from the age of discovery onward ; and the abandonment of a special section for 'Ecclesiastical History' after the close of the Thirty Years' War.

The New Style has been uniformly adopted for all dates after its introduction by Pope Gregory XIII in 1582, regardless of its reluctant acceptance in non-Roman countries which extended over almost two centuries. Two exceptions, however, have been deliberately conceded. as their dates are commonly known in the Old Style, namely, the deaths of Mary Queen of Scots and Queen Elizabeth. Should there be found other deviations from the above rule, the benevolent critic will perhaps attribute them to the negligence of some authors who omitted to mention which style they had adopted.

In the eighteenth and nineteenth centuries, inventions and discoveries in the sphere of Natural Science which have more or less immediately influenced economic, and sometimes even political, history, have been brought under the heading of 'Economic History', whereas scientific progress on purely philosophical or academic lines has been kept under 'Cultural Life' as before.

It is with great pleasure that I here acknowledge my profound gratitude to all those friends who unhesitatingly gave much time and thought to assist me in rendering the present work as reliable and useful as possible. The responsibility for its shortcomings must rest with me alone.

The first edition was published a few weeks after the outbreak of the second world war. A new edition was called for immediately after the end of the 'emergency'. The author took this opportunity to revise the portions up to 1914 and to rewrite and extend the latter part from 1914 onward. In the third and later editions further corrections and insertions have been made, for which the author is once more indebted to many friends and critics.

S. H. S.

PREFACE

TO THE ELEVENTH EDITION

Dr. S. H. Steinberg died in 1969 but fortunately he left detailed revisions for the ninth edition and his notes only ceased a few weeks before his death.

The period 1969-78 was brought up-to-date by Christine Steinberg and myself and for the tenth edition the opportunity was taken to re-arrange the tables from 1945.

Christine Steinberg died in 1985 and so I was deprived of her help in revising the eleventh edition. For this new edition I've re-assessed some of the entries for the period 1972-78 and extended the chronologies to the end of 1985. I also took the opportunity to 'fatten' the entries in the medieval period in the light of recent scholarship.

Bruton, Somerset   JOHN PAXTON
January 1986

ix

HISTORICAL TABLES

I. ROMAN EMPIRE	II. ASIA AND AFRICA	III. BRITAIN
58-51 B.C. Caesar subdues Gaul.	**56-37** B.C. Orodes I of Parthia; defeats Romans at Carrhae (**53**).	**55-54** B.C. Caesar twice invades Britain.
44 B.C. *Mar. 15:* Caesar murdered. **30** B.C. Octavianus Augustus becomes virtual monarch (-A.D. **14**).	**51-30.** B.C. Cleopatra VII, last Queen of Egypt.	
		A.D. **5-40.** Cymbeline, King of the Catuvellauni, 'Rex Brittonum.'
A.D. **14-37.** Emperor Tiberius; **25-30.** Pontius Pilate, procurator of Judaea.	A.D. **25-220.** Later or Eastern Han dynasty in China.	
41-54. Emperor Claudius; numerous non-Italians enfranchised. **54-68.** Emperor Nero; **64.** First persecution of Christians. **69-79.** Emperor Vespasian.	**41-42.** Romans annex Mauretania. **58-76.** Ming-ti, Emperor of China; introduces Buddhism. **70.** Titus destroys Jerusalem.	**43.** Romans begin conquest of Britain. **61.** British rebellion under Queen Boadicea (Boudicca).
79-81. Emperor Titus. **81-96.** Emperor Domitian. **96-98.** Emperor Nerva. **98-117.** Emperor Trajan; Roman Empire reaches its widest limits.		**78-85.** Agricola, governor of Britain, completes Roman conquest as far as Clyde and Firth of Forth.
117-138. Emperor Hadrian; reorganizes army and civil service with provincials.	**114-116.** War against Parthians. **123.** Hadrian renounces all territories across Euphrates. **132-135.** Jewish rising under Bar Kokba.	**122.** Hadrian's wall from Tyne to Solway. **140-142.** Antonine's wall from Forth to Clyde.
161. Marcus Aurelius (-**180**) and Verus (-**169**) reign together; beginning of partition of Empire. **193-211.** Emperor Septimius Severus. **212.** *Constitutio Antoniniana* bestows Roman citizenship upon every freeborn subject. **222-235.** Emperor Alexander Severus; tries in vain to check Vandals and Langobards.	**195-199.** Septimius Severus conquers Mesopotamia. **226.** Ardashir I overthrows Artabanus V, last Arsacid, and founds Neo-Persian Empire under Sassanid dynasty.	*ca.* **185.** Antonine wall abandoned. **208.** Emperor Septimius Severus rebuilds Hadrian's wall; dies at York (**211**).
251. Emperor Decius defeated and killed by Goths at Silistria. **254-257.** Pope Stephen I. **257-258.** Pope Sixtus II. **259-267.** Pope Dionysius.	**260.** Shapur I of Persia captures Emperor Valerian.	

IV. WEST TEUTONIC TRIBES	V. EAST TEUTONIC TRIBES	VI. CULTURAL LIFE
55 B.C. Caesar crosses the Rhine.		**54-51** B.C. Cicero: *De Re Publica*.
		51 B.C. Caesar: *De Bello Gallico*.
12 B.C.-A.D. **6.** Drusus and Tiberius subdue Germany.		**30** B.C. - A.D. **14.** Augustan age: Vergil, Horace, Ovid, poets; Livy, historian; Strabo, geographer; Labeo, Capito, jurists.
A.D. **9.** Arminius defeats Romans in Teutoburg Forest. **14.** Campaign of Germanicus in Northern Germany.	A.D. **1-50.** Formation of a Gothic kingdom on the lower Vistula.	
		A.D. **28-29.** Preaching of St. John the Baptist. **30** or **33.** Crucifixion of Jesus.
69-71. Batavian rising under Claudius Civilis.		**51-57.** Missionary travels of St. Paul. *ca.* **65.** Gospel according to St. Mark. *ca.* **80.** Gospel according to St. Luke.
96. Roman conquest of West and South Germany completed by finishing the Limes (fortified frontier-road).		**80.** Colosseum, Rome, completed. *ca.* **85.** Gospel according to St. Matthew. *ca.* **90-95.** Gospel according to St. John. **98-118.** Tacitus: *Germania, Agricola, Annales, Historiae*. **106.** Column of Trajan, Rome, erected.
	150. Goths migrate to the Black Sea.	*ca.* **150.** Ptolemy, geographer.
		161. Gaius: *Institutiones*.
		200-230. Clement and Origen of Alexandria.
	220. Goths begin to threaten Balkans and Asia Minor. **238.** Goths begin to invade the Eastern Empire.	
		244-270. Plotinus in Rome. **248.** Millenary of Rome. **250.** Persecution of Christians by Decius; Pope Fabian martyred.
	257. Goths occupy Dacia; Ostrogoths and Visigoths split. **258.** Goths invade Asia Minor.	**258.** Cyprian of Carthage, originator of the Catholic conception of the Church, executed.
260. Alamanni settle between Limes and Rhine. Franks advance towards lower Rhine.		

I. ROMAN EMPIRE	II. ASIA AND AFRICA	III. BRITAIN
269. Emperor Claudius defeats Goths at Nish. **270-275.** Emperor Aurelianus, *restitutor orbis*. **276-282.** Emperor Probus; defeats Vandals, Alamanni, Franks, and Burgundians. **284-305.** Emperor Diocletian. **285.** Partition of the Empire into Western and Eastern Empires. **293-306.** Emperor Constantius I Chlorus.	**268-273.** Zenobia, Queen of Palmyra; conquers Syria, Mesopotamia, and parts of Egypt. **273.** Emperor Aurelian overthrows kingdom of Palmyra. **280.** Emperor Wu-ti reunites China. **293-302.** Narses of Persia; loses Armenia to the Romans (**297**).	 **286-293.** Independent British kingdom under Carausius, and **293-296** under Allectus. **296.** Emperor Constantius I recovers Britain.
306-337. Constantine the Great, son of Constantius, proclaimed Emperor at York. **313.** Milan Edict recognizes Christianity as a legal religion. **311-314.** Pope Miltiades. **314-335.** Pope Silvester I.	**310-379.** Shapur II of Persia; recovers Armenia. **318.** China divided into Northern and Southern realms. *ca.* **320.** Chandragupta I establishes Gupta empire in India.	**305.** Emperor Constantius I defeats Picts and Scots.
323. Constantine overthrows Licinius, his co-regent, and becomes absolute monarch.	**330-375.** Samudragupta, Indian Emperor.	
332. Constantine defeats Goths; afterwards hires Gothic auxiliaries. **337-352.** Pope Julius I.		
352-366. Pope Liberius.	*ca.* **350.** Huns invade Europe.	
361-363. Emperor Julian. **366-384.** Pope Damasus I.	**375-413.** Chandragupta II; conquers Ujjain.	**360-367.** Picts, Irish, and Saxons invade Britain.
378. *Aug. 9:* Emperor Valens defeated and killed by Visigoths at Adrianople. **379-395.** Emperor Theodosius I; resettles Visigoths in the Empire (**382**). **384-399.** Pope Siricius.	**386-636.** Dynasty of Yüan Wei in Northern China. **387.** Theodosius I and Shapur III of Persia partition Armenia.	**383-407.** Roman legions evacuate Britain.

IV. WEST TEUTONIC TRIBES	V. EAST TEUTONIC TRIBES	VI. CULTURAL LIFE
270. Marcomanni advance from Bohemia across the Danube.	**268.** Goths sack Athens, Corinth, and Sparta.	**268.** Synod of Antioch condemns heresy of Paul of Samosata.
		277. Mani, founder of the Gnostic sect of Manichaeism, *d.*
		ca. **280.** Armenia christianized.
286-288. Alamanni, Franks, and Burgundians cross the Rhine.		*ca.* **285.** Beginning of monastic life in Egypt.
295. Caesar Galerius defeats Marcomanni.		
298. Caesar Constantius defeats Alamanni.		
307. Emperor Constantine I defeats Alamanni and Franks.		**305-311.** Persecution of Christians by Diocletian and Galerius.
		311. Galerius, Licinius, and Constantine issue Toleration Edict.
		311-411. Donatist struggle.
		321-381. Arian struggle.
		325. Council of Nicaea decides the Arian question in favour of Athanasius (*d.* **373**).
		330. *May 11*: Constantinople (Byzantium) made capital of the Empire.
	334. Vandals settle in Pannonia.	**341.** Synod of Antioch deposes Athanasius.
	341. Wulfila begins christianizing Visigoths.	**343.** Synod of Sardica confirms jurisdiction of Roman see.
	348. Visigoths persecute Christians; Constantius II settles Visigothic Christians in the Balkans.	
350. Alamanni occupy Alsace.		
357. Caesar Julian defeats Alamanni at Strasbourg.		
358. Salian Franks settle in Northern Brabant.		*ca.* **370.** Beginning of monastic life in Occident.
	375. Huns overthrow Ostrogothic kingdom in South Russia.	
	376. Visigoths, pressed by Huns, settle in Transylvania and Thrace.	
	380. Ostrogoths settle in Pannonia.	**380.** *Feb. 27*: Theodosius' edict on the catholic faith.

I. ROMAN EMPIRE	II. ASIA AND AFRICA	III. BRITAIN
395. Definite partition of Eastern and Western Empires. Arcadius, Eastern Emperor (**-408**); Honorius, Western Emperor (**-423**), under guardianship of the Teuton Stilicho (murdered **408**).		
	399-420. Yazdegerd I of Persia; tolerates Christianity.	
401-403. Visigoths invade Italy; imperial residence moved to Ravenna (**402**).		
406. Stilicho checks Ostrogothic invasion at Fiesole.		
408-450. Theodosius II, Eastern Emperor.		
408-410. Second Visigothic invasion of Italy.		
410. *Aug. 24*: Alaric sacks Rome.		
	413-455. Kumaragupta I, Indian Emperor.	
	420-439. Bahram V of Persia; persecutes Christians; attacked by White Huns.	
422-432. Pope Celestine I.	**420-479.** Sung dynasty in Southern China.	
425-455. Valentinian III, Western Emperor; **429-454.** Aetius, virtual ruler.	**428-633.** Armenia under Persian rule.	
	433-453. Attila, ruler of the Huns.	
438. *Codex Theodosianus*, legal separation of Eastern and Western sections of the Empire.		
440-461. Pope Leo I the Great.		
		449. Angles, Saxons, and Jutes begin the conquest of Britain.
450-457. Marcian, Eastern Emperor.		
451. Aetius defeats the Huns under Attila on the Mauriac Plains near Châlons.		
452. Attila invades Northern Italy; turned back by Pope Leo I.		
455. *June*: Vandals sack Rome.	**455-467.** Skandagupta, Indian Emperor.	**457.** Anglo-Saxons defeat Britons at Crayford.
456-472. The Teuton Ricimer, virtual ruler of the Western Empire.		
457-471. Leo I, Eastern Emperor.		
460 and **468.** Vandals destroy Roman fleets off Cartagena and Cape Bon.	*ca.* **470.** Huns disappear from Europe. White Huns break up the Gupta empire.	
474-491. Zeno, Eastern Emperor.		

IV. WEST TEUTONIC TRIBES	V. EAST TEUTONIC TRIBES	VI. CULTURAL LIFE
	395-410. Alaric, King of Visigoths.	**396-430.** St. Augustine, Bishop of Hippo.
	395-398. Alaric pillages Balkans and Greece.	**397.** *Apr. 4*: Ambrose, Bishop of Milan, *d.* *ca.* **400.** Hieronymus translates Scriptures into Latin. **401-417.** Innocent I, Bishop of Rome; establishes primacy of Rome.
406. Salian Franks occupy Flanders, Ripuarian Franks occupy the district of Cologne.	**406.** Burgundians found kingdom on the middle Rhine (capital, Worms). **406-428.** Gunderic, King of Vandals. **409.** Vandals, Alani, and Suevi overrun Spain. **413-436.** Gundecar, Burgundian King. **415.** Wallia establishes Visigothic kingdom of Toulouse. **416-418.** Visigoths conquer Vandal kingdom in Spain. **418-451.** Theodoric I, King of Visigoths.	**411-431.** Pelagian struggle; Pelagius, British theologian, affirms freedom of will. **413-426.** St. Augustine: *Civitas Dei.* **420.** Hieronymus *d.* at Bethlehem.
436. Alamannian realm established on Upper and Middle Rhine.	**428-477.** Genseric, King of Vandals. **429.** Genseric founds Vandal kingdom in Northern Africa; Suevi remain in Northern Spain. **436.** Huns destroy Burgundian kingdom of Worms. **442.** Genseric takes last Roman possessions and establishes absolute monarchy. **443.** Burgundians settle in the districts of Geneva and Grenoble.	**431.** Third Council of Ephesus, condemns Pelagianism. **432-461.** St. Patrick's mission in Ireland.
	451. Ostrogoths support, Visigoths and Burgundians defy, Huns; Theodoric I killed in battle. **453-466.** Theodoric II, King of Visigoths.	**451.** *Oct.*: Council of Chalcedon. **451-680.** Monophysite struggle in the Eastern Church.
ca. **460.** Franks take Cologne.	**461.** Lyons made capital of Burgundy. **466.** Theodoric II murdered by his brother, Euric (reigns till **484**). **471-526.** Theodoric the Great, King of Ostrogoths.	

I. ROMAN EMPIRE	II. ASIA AND AFRICA	III. BRITAIN
476. Odovacar deposes Romulus Augustulus, last western emperor.		
	479-502. Chi dynasty in Southern China.	**477** (?). Kingdom of Sussex founded.
491-518. Anastasius I, eastern emperor. **492-496.** Pope Gelasius I.		**491.** Saxons storm Anderida near Pevensey.
496-498. Pope Anastasius II.		**495** (?). Kingdom of Wessex founded.
514-523. Pope Hormisdas.		
523-526. Pope John I.	**525.** Abyssinians conquer Yemen.	
526-530. Pope Felix IV. **527-565.** Emperor Justinian I, reunites the empire. **533-534.** Belisarius overthrows Vandal kingdom and makes northern Africa a Byzantine province. **535-540.** Belisarius occupies Gothic kingdom in Italy. **537-555.** Pope Vigilius.	**531-579.** Chosroes I of Persia; political and cultural prime. **539-562.** War between Persia and the eastern empire. **550.** Migration of Turks begins.	**537** (?). Arthur, king of Britons, killed in the battle of Camlan. **547** (?) Kingdom of Bernicia founded.
552-555. Narses destroys Gothic kingdom in Italy, and makes Italy a Byzantine province. **556-561.** Pope Pelagius I. **561-574.** Pope John III.		**560-616.** Ethelbert, king of Kent. **563.** Columba (*d.* **597**) goes to Iona and begins to convert the Picts.
565-578. Emperor Justin II.		
578-582. Emperor Tiberius II. **582-602.** Emperor Maurice.	**572-591.** War between Persia and the eastern empire. **575.** Persians overthrow Abyssinian rule over Yemen.	**577.** The English of Wessex defeat Welsh at Deorham, Glos. **584** (?). Kingdom of Mercia founded.

IV. WEST TEUTONIC TRIBES	V. EAST TEUTONIC TRIBES	VI. CULTURAL LIFE
	476. Genseric sells Eastern Sicily to Theodoric.	
	477-484. Hunneric, King of Vandals; persecutes Roman Catholics.	
481-511. Clovis, King of Franks.	**484-496.** Gunthamund, King of Vandals.	**484-519.** First schism between Western and Eastern Churches.
	484-507. Alaric II, King of Visigoths.	
	487-493. Theodoric conquers Italy.	**491.** Armenian Church secedes from Byzantium and Rome.
486. Clovis defeats Syagrius, last Roman governor of Gaul.	**493.** *Mar. 5*: Odovacar capitulates at Ravenna, is murdered by Theodoric, who marries Clovis's sister.	
496. Clovis defeats Alamanni at Strasbourg.	**496-523.** Thrasamund, King of Vandals.	
		499. *Mar.*: Synod of Rome, issues first decree on papal election.
503. *Dec. 25:* Baptism of Clovis.	**500.** Thrasamund obtains Western Sicily as dowry of Theodoric's sister.	*ca.* **500.** Neo-Platonic writings of so-called Dionysius the Areopagite.
507. Clovis annexes Visigothic kingdom of Toulouse.	**506.** *Lex Romana Visigothorum*, law-code of Alaric II.	
511. Partition of Frankish kingdom between Clovis's sons Theuderic I (-534), Clodomir (-524), Childebert I (-558), Clotaire I (-561).		*ca.* **520.** Systematic grammar of Priscian.
	516-523. Sigmund, King of Burgundy; later canonized.	**523-524.** Boethius: *Consolatio Philosophiae*.
	523-532. Godomar II, last King of Burgundy.	
	523-530. Hilderic, King of Vandals.	**529.** Justinian closes Athens University. Benedict of Nursia founds monastery of Montecassino.
531. Franks overthrow kingdom of Thuringia.	**526-534.** Amalaswintha, daughter of Theodoric, regent of Italy.	
532-534. Franks overthrow kingdom of Burgundy.	**530-534.** Gelimer, last King of Vandals.	**529-534.** *Institutes, Digests,* and *Codex Justinianus* issued.
	540. Badwila (Totila) re-establishes Gothic rule in Italy.	**547.** Gildas: *De Excidio Britanniae*.
	552. Badwila killed at Taginae.	
558-561. Clotaire I reunites Frankish kingdom.	**552-553.** Teias, last King of Ostrogoths.	**553-555.** Fifth Council of Constantinople.
561. Partition of Frankish kingdom between Clotaire's sons Charibert (-567), Guntram (-592), Sigebert (-575), Chilperic (-584).		
567. Partition of Frankish kingdom into Austrasia, Neustria, and Burgundy.	**567-586.** Leovigild, King of Visigoths.	**563.** *Dec. 24*: Cathedral of Hagia Sophia, Constantinople, consecrated.
575-613. Queen Brunhild, regent of Austrasia.	**568.** Langobards invade Northern Italy.	
584-628. Clotaire II, alleged son of Chilperic, King of Neustria.	**584-590.** Authari, first King of Langobards.	
	585. Leovigild overthrows the Suevic kingdom.	
	586-601. Reccared, King of Visigoths.	
	589. Visigoths converted to Roman Catholicism.	

I. ROMAN EMPIRE	II. ASIA AND AFRICA	III. BRITAIN
590-604. Pope Gregory I.	**589-605.** Emperor Yang-kien, founder of the Suy dynasty in China.	**592** (or **593**)**-616.** Ethelfrith, king of Bernicia.
		596. Pope Gregory I dispatches Augustine as missionary to Britain.
		597-616. Supremacy of Kent.
602-610. Emperor Phocas.	**604.** Constitution of 17 articles in Japan.	**602.** Augustine establishes archiepiscopal see at Canterbury.
	606-647. Harsha, ruler of Northern India.	**604.** St Paul's, London, founded; *May 26*; Augustine *d.*
610-641. Emperor Heraclius.	**608-642.** Pulakesin II Chalukya, ruler of the Deccan.	**613.** Northumbrians defeat Welsh near Chester.
610-638. Sergius, patriarch of Constantinople.	**614.** Persians take Damascus and Jerusalem.	**615.** Columban the Younger, founder of Luxeuil and Bobbio, *d.*
	618-619. Persians conquer Egypt.	**617-685.** Supremacy of Northumbria.
619-625. Pope Boniface V.	**622.** Mohammed flees from Mecca to Medina (the Hegira).	
625-638. Pope Honorius I.		**627.** Christianization of Northumbria begins.
629. Heraclius recovers Jerusalem.	**632.** *June 8*: Mohammed *d.*; succeeded by caliph Abu Bekr (-**634**).	**632.** Christianization of East Anglia begins.
	634-644. Caliph Omar; takes Damascus (**635**), Ctesiphon (**637**), Jerusalem (**638**), conquers Mesopotamia (**639-641**), Egypt (**640-642**), Persia (**641-643**).	**633-641.** Oswald, king of Northumbria and Bernicia.
636. *Aug. 20*: Byzantines defeated at Yarmuk, lose Syria to Arabs.		**635.** Christianization of Wessex begins.
	644-656. Caliph Othman.	**636.** Southern Irish church submits to papacy.
640-642. Pope John IV.		**641-670.** Oswiu, king of Northumbria and Bernicia.
641-668. Constans II, eastern emperor.	**647.** Arabs conquer Tripoli.	
642-649. Pope Theodore I.	**649.** Arabs conquer Cyprus.	
649-655. Pope Martin I.	**652.** Arabs raid Syracuse.	
	654-661. Arabs subdue Armenia.	**654.** Penda, heathen king of Mercia, defeated and killed by Oswiu.
654-657. Pope Eugenius I.	**656.** *June 17*: Caliph Othman murdered; succeeded by Ali.	
657-672. Pope Vitalian.	**658.** Moawiya sets up Omayyad dynasty at Damascus.	**658-675.** Wulfhere, Penda's son, king of Mercia.
	661. *Jan. 24*: Caliph Ali murdered; succeeded by Moawiya.	**664.** Oswiu of Northumbria adopts Roman ritual.
663. Last visit to Rome by an emperor.	**664.** Arabs invade the Punjab.	**664-673.** Egbert of Kent (and Surrey).
		669-690. Theodore, archbishop of Canterbury.
668-685. Emperor Constantine IV.	**670.** Arabs begin conquering North Africa.	**673.** *Sept. 24*: First synod of the English church, at Hertford.
669. Arabs besiege Constantinople.		**673-685.** Hlothhere of Kent.
674-680. Arabs besiege Constantinople.	**680.** *Oct. 10*: Husain, son of Ali, killed when fighting against caliph Yezid I.	**685-704.** Aldfrith of Northumbria.
678-681. Pope Agatho.	**685-705.** Caliph Abdalmalik.	**686.** Sussex, last heathen kingdom, converted.
682-683. Pope Leo II.		**688-726.** Ine, king of Wessex; subdues Essex and Kent.
685-695, 705-711. Emperor Justinian II.		**690-725.** Wihtred, king of Kent.
687-701. Pope Sergius I.	**693-862.** Armenia under Arab rule.	**695.** Wihtred's law code.
695-698. Emperor Leontius.	**695.** First Arab coinage.	**697.** Northern Irish church submits to papacy.

IV. WEST TEUTONIC TRIBES	V. EAST TEUTONIC TRIBES	VI. CULTURAL LIFE
	590-616. Agilulf, King of Langobards.	**594.** Gregory of Tours *d.*, author of *Historiae Francorum.*
	603. Langobards converted to Roman Catholicism.	**603.** Bishopric of Rochester founded.
		609. Pantheon, Rome, consecrated as Christian church.
613. Austrasia and Burgundy united.		
614. *Oct. 18: Edictum Chlotacharii II*, defines rights of king, nobles and Church.	**616-626.** Adalwald, King of Langobards; murdered.	
		622. Isidore, Bishop of Seville: *Etymologiae.*
623-639. Dagobert I; Pepin the Elder, Mayor of the Palace.		**622-680.** Monothelete controversy.
	633. Visigothic Spain becomes elective kingdom.	
638-657. Clovis II, King of Neustria and Burgundy.	**636-652.** Rothari, King of Langobards.	
	641-652. Chindaswinth, King of Visigoths.	**641-661.** Prime of Armenian architecture under Patriarch Nerses III.
643-656. Grimoald, son of Pepin, Mayor of the Palace in Austrasia.		**649.** *Oct. 5-31:* Lateran Synod condemns Monotheletism.
	653-672. Recceswinth, King of Visigoths.	**653.** Caliph Othman edits Koran.
		656. Monastery of Peterborough founded.
657-673. Clotaire III, King of the whole kingdom till **663,** and afterwards of Neustria.		**657.** Streoneshalh (Whitby) monastery founded.
663-675. Childeric II, King of Austrasia, and of the whole kingdom after **673.**		
	672-680. Wamba, King of Visigoths.	**674-682.** Wearmouth and Jarrow monasteries founded.
		680. Caedmon, first English Christian poet, *d.*
		680 *Nov. 7-681 Sept. 16:* Sixth Council of Constantinople, condemns Monophysitism and Monotheletism.
687. Pepin II subdues Neustria, becomes Mayor of the Palace of the whole kingdom.	**687-701.** Egica, King of Visigoths.	**692.** *Concilium Quinisextum*, settles the Biblical Canon of the Eastern Church.

I. ROMAN EMPIRE	II. ASIA AND AFRICA	III. BRITAIN
698-705. Emperor Tiberius III.	**701.** Codification of Japanese law.	
	705-715. Caliph Welid I.	**705.** Diocese of Sherborne established; moved to Salisbury in 1078.
708-715. Pope Constantine I; last pope to call on the emperor in Constantinople.	**712.** Muhammad ibn Kasim establishes a Moslem state in Sind.	**705-716.** Osred of Northumbria.
715-731. Pope Gregory II; dispatches Wynfrith-Boniface as missionary to Germany.	**715-717.** Caliph Soliman I.	
716, *Aug.-***717,** *Sept.* Arabs besiege Constantinople.		**716-757.** Ethelbald of Mercia, virtual lord of all England except Northumbria.
717-741. Emperor Leo III; prohibits image-worship (**726**).	**717-720.** Caliph Omar II; grants immunity from taxes to all believers.	
	720-724. Caliph Yezid II.	
	724-743. Caliph Hisham; reforms taxation.	**729-737.** Ceolwulf of Northumbria.
731-741. Pope Gregory III.		**731-734.** Tatwine, archbishop of Canterbury.
		735-766. Egbert, first archbishop of York.
741-775. Emperor Constantine V; renews prohibition of image-worship (**754**).	**744-750.** Caliph Mervan II, last of the Omayyad caliphs.	
741-752. Pope Zacharias.	**750-754.** Caliph Abul Abbas, founder of Abbaside dynasty.	
752-757. Pope Stephen II.	**754-775.** Abu Jafar al Mansur, caliph.	**752.** Cuthred of Wessex defeats Ethelbald at Burford.
	755. The Omayyad Abderrahman founds the caliphate of Cordoba.	
757-767. Pope Paul I, brother of Stephen II.	**762.** Baghdad founded as capital of the caliphs.	**757-796.** Offa, king of Mercia.
768-772. Pope Stephen III.		**765-774.** Alhred of Northumbria.
772-795. Pope Hadrian I.		
		774. Offa subdues Kent.
775-780. Emperor Leo IV.	**775-785.** Caliph Mahdi; institutes Inquisition.	**777.** Offa subdues Wessex.
780-802. Irene, virtual ruler of the eastern empire (**780-790.** Constantine VI; **790-797.** Constantine VII).	**782.** Arabs raid Constantinople.	**784.** Offa's Dyke, marks frontier between Mercia and Wales.
	786-809. Caliph Harun al Rashid; **786-803.** Yahya, vizir (*d.* **805**).	**787.** Offa establishes Archbishopric of Lichfield; has his son Egfrith anointed king (**-796**).
	788. Idris establishes a Shiite kingdom in Morocco.	**789-820.** Constantine I, Scots king.
	788-796. Caliph Hisham I of Cordoba.	**790.** Offa founds St Alban's abbey.
		793. Offa annexes East Anglia. Danes destroy Lindisfarne monastery.
	794. Japanese capital moved from Nara to Kyoto.	**796.** Commercial agreement between Charlemagne and Offa.
		796-821. Cenwulf, king of Mercia.
795-816. Pope Leo III.	**796-822.** Caliph Hakam I of Cordoba.	**796-810.** Eardwulf of Northumbria.
		798. Cenwulf subdues Kent.

IV. WEST TEUTONIC TRIBES	V. EAST TEUTONIC TRIBES	VI. CULTURAL LIFE
		700-730. *Beowulf* epic.
709-710. Pepin subdues Alamanni.		**709.** *May 25*: Aldhelm, bishop of Sherborne, *d.*
	711-713. Arabs overthrow Visigothic kingdom.	
	712-744. Liutprand, king of Langobards.	
716-719. Duke Lantfrid issues *Lex Alamannorum.*		
717-741. Charles Martel, mayor of the palace.		**719-754.** Wynfrith-Boniface, 'apostle of the Germans', christianizes central Germany.
	720. Arabs seize Visigothic kingdom of Septimania.	**724.** Reichenau abbey founded.
		725. Image-worship controversy begins. Bede: *De Temporum Ratione.*
		731. Bede: *Historia Ecclesiastica gentis Anglorum.*
732. *Oct. 25*: Charles Martel defeats Arabs at Poitiers.		
735. Charles Martel subdues Burgundy.	**739.** Pope Gregory III asks Charles Martel for help against Langobards, Greeks and Arabs.	**744.** Fulda abbey founded.
748-788. Tassilo, last independent duke of Bavaria.	**749-757.** Aistulf, king of Langobards.	
751. Pepin III the Younger deposes Childeric III, and is elected king (-768).	**751.** Aistulf takes Ravenna from Byzantium.	*ca.* **750-800.** Cynewulf: *Elene, Juliana, The Ascension, Fates of the Apostles.*
754. Pepin's donation to papacy, creates papal state.	**754-756.** Pepin wars against Langobards; Aistulf made Frankish vassal.	
	757-774. Desiderius, last king of Langobards.	
768-814. Charlemagne; **768-771.** Carloman, his brother, co-regent.		**766-782.** Aethelbert and Alcuin make York a centre of learning.
772-804. Charlemagne subdues Saxony.	**773.** Pope Hadrian I appeals to Charlemagne for help against the Langobards.	
774 and **781.** Charlemagne confirms and enlarges Pepin's donation.	**773-774.** Charlemagne annexes Langobardian kingdom.	
782. Charlemagne issues *Capitulatio de partibus Saxoniae.*		
785. Widukind, Saxon duke, baptized.	**787.** Charlemagne annexes Langobardian duchy of Beneventum.	**787.** *Sept. 24-Oct. 23*: Seventh council of Nicaea, regulates image-worship.
788. Charlemagne annexes Bavaria.		**790.** *Libri Carolini*, memorandum of Carolingian divines on image-worship. Alcuin appointed principal of Frankish court school.
		794. State paper mill set up in Baghdad.
797. Charlemagne issues *Capitulare Saxonicum.*		**799.** Paul the Deacon, *d.,* author of *Historia Langobardorum.*

I. WESTERN EUROPE	II. CENTRAL EUROPE	III. EASTERN EUROPE, ISLAM, ASIA
802-839. Egbert of Wessex, first ' king of the English ' **802-825.** Vikings dominate Ireland. **810-841.** Eanred of Northumbria.	**800.** *Dec. 25*: Charlemagne crowned emperor by Leo III at Rome. **812.** Charles's title of emperor recognized by Byzantium. **814-840.** Emperor Louis I, the Pious.	**802-811.** Nicephorus I, eastern emperor. **809-813.** Caliph Emin. **811-813.** Michael I Rhangabe, eastern emperor. **813-820.** Leo V the Armenian, eastern emperor. **813-833.** Caliph Mamun. **818.** Cordoba rebellion against Arabs. **820-829.** Michael II, eastern emperor.
821. Cenwulf of Mercia, *d.*; end of Mercian supremacy. **825.** Egbert conquers Kent and defeats Beornwulf of Mercia at Ellendun.	**824.** *Constitutio Romana*, confirms imperial control of Rome.	**822-852.** Abd-er-Rahman II, caliph of Cordoba. **826.** Arabs take Crete. **827.** Arabs begin the conquest of Sicily.
829. Egbert annexes Mercia; Eanred of Northumbria does homage to Egbert. **832-860.** Kenneth MacAlpin, king of Kintyre, of the Scots (**839**), and of the Picts (**844**). **835.** Danes raid England (Sheppey). **836.** Danes sack London. **839-858.** Ethelwulf, king of England.	**833.** *June 20*: Louis I deposed by his sons. **834.** *Feb.*: Louis I restored by his younger sons. **840-855.** Emperor Lothair I. **841.** *June 25*: Lothair defeated by his brothers at Fontenoy.	**829-842.** Theophilus, eastern emperor; persecutes image-worshippers. **833-842.** Caliph Mutasim. **838.** Arabs sack Marseilles and settle in southern Italy. **842-847.** Caliph Wathik.
843. *Aug.*: Treaty of Verdun; divides the Carolingian empire; Charles (the Bald), king of France (**-877**).	**843.** Treaty of Verdun; Lewis the German obtains Germany (**-876**) Lothair keeps Lotharingia and Italy. **846.** Arabs pillage Rome. Lewis defeats Moimir, prince of Moravia.	**842-867.** Michael III, eastern emperor. **847-860.** Caliph Mutawakkil.
851. Danes take Canterbury and burn London; defeated by Ethelwulf at Oakley. **856.** Rebellion of Ethelbald, son of Ethelwulf; reigns till **860**. **860-866.** Ethelbert, king of England. **860-863.** Donald, brother of Kenneth, king of Scots. **863-877.** Constantine II, son of Kenneth, king of Scots. **866-871.** Ethelred I, king of England. Danes occupy Northumbria (**866**) and East Anglia (**870**) and attack Wessex (**870**). **871-899.** Alfred the Great, king of England. **877-879.** Louis II, king of France.	**855-875.** Louis II, king of Italy and emperor. **870.** *Aug. 9*: Treaty of Mersen; Lotharingia divided between Germany and France. **875.** *Dec. 17*: Charles II (the Bald) crowned emperor. **876-887.** Charles III, the Fat.	**852-886.** Mahomet I, caliph of Cordoba. **858-859.** Vikings sack Algeciras, are expelled by Moslems. **859-890.** Ashot I founds Bagratide dynasty of Armenia. **867-886.** Basil I, eastern emperor; recovers southern Italy from the Arabs. **868-905.** Independent Tulunid dynasty in Egypt and Syria. **869.** Arabs capture Malta. **870-892.** Caliph al-Mutamid. **874-999.** Samanid dynasty in Persia.

IV. ECCLESIASTICAL HISTORY	V. CONSTITUTIONAL AND ECONOMIC HISTORY	VI. CULTURAL LIFE
803. End of the archbishopric of Lichfield; Canterbury restored as metropolitan see. **805-832.** Wulfred, archbishop of Canterbury.	**802.** Germanic tribal laws codified by order of Charlemagne.	*ca.* **800.** *Hildebrandslied.* **804.** *May 19:* Alcuin, scholar and reformer of learning, *d.*
816-817. Pope Stephen V. **817-824.** Pope Paschal I. **817.** *Pactum Hludovicianum,* confirms papal territory. **824-827.** Pope Eugene II. **827.** Pope Valentine. **827-844.** Pope Gregory IV. **831.** Bishopric of Hamburg founded; made archbishopric (**832**).		*ca.* **820.** The *Heliand* epic. **822.** Hrabanus Maurus becomes abbot of Fulda (**847**, archbishop of Mainz, *d.* **856**). **829.** End of the *Annales Regni Francorum* (official chronicle). **840.** Einhard, biographer of Charlemagne, *d.*
844-847. Pope Sergius II. **847-855.** Pope Leo IV; fortifies Rome (Leonine city). *ca.* **850.** Pseudo-Isidorian decretals forged in France. **855-858.** Pope Benedict III. **858-867.** Pope Nicholas I.		**842.** *Feb. 14:* Oaths of Strasbourg, first record of final separation of French and German languages. **849.** Walahfrid Strabo *d.: Glossa ordinaria* (patristic commentaries on the Bible). **851.** Johannes Scotus Eriugena: *De Praedestinatione.* **858-860.** Johannes Scotus's Latin translation of Dionysius the Areopagite. **862.** Servatus Lupus, abbot of Ferrières, philologist, *d.* *ca.* **865.** Otfrid of Weissenburg: *Diatessaron* in German verse.
864. Constantine (Cyril) and Methodius christianize Moravia and Bulgaria. **867-872.** Pope Hadrian II. **872-882.** Pope John VIII, murdered by Roman nobles.	**877.** *June 14:* Edict of Quierzy, renders fiefs hereditary in France.	**867.** Johannes Scotus: *Peri physeon merismou.*

I. WESTERN EUROPE	II. CENTRAL EUROPE	III. EASTERN EUROPE, ISLAM, ASIA
878. Danes invade Wessex, defeated by Alfred at Edington. Treaty of Wedmore: Danes keep East Anglia, Essex and part of Mercia.		
879-882. Louis III, king of northern France; **879-884.** Carloman, king of southern France.	**880.** Treaty of Ribemont: Charles III cedes Lorraine to Lewis II.	**879.** Nepal gains its independence of Tibet.
881. *Aug. 3*: Louis III defeats Normans at Saucourt.	**881.** *Feb. 12*: Charles III crowned emperor.	
881-889. Eocha, king of Scots.	**882.** Normans sack Cologne, Aix-la-Chapelle and Prüm.	
884. Emperor Charles III elected king of France (-888).		**885.** Ashot I of Armenia assumes title of king.
885-886. Normans besiege Paris, defended by Odo.		**886-912.** Leo VI the Wise, eastern emperor.
888-898. Odo, count of Paris.	**887-899.** Arnulf, German king.	**888-912.** Abdallah, caliph of Cordoba.
889-900. Donald I, king of Scots.	**888-924.** Berengar of Friuli, king of Italy.	**888.** Arabs occupy Garde-Freinet on the coast of Provence.
	891. *Feb. 21*: Wido of Spoleto crowned emperor and king of Italy. *Sept. 1*: Arnulf defeats Normans at Louvain.	
	892. Lambert of Spoleto crowned emperor.	
893. Danish invasion of Kent fails.	**894.** Arnulf marches to Italy. emperor Wido *d.*	
893-929. Charles the Simple, king of France.	**896.** Second expedition of Arnulf to Italy; crowned emperor.	
899-925. Edward the Elder, king of England.	**898.** *Oct. 15*: Emperor Lambert *d.*	
900-935. Gorm, founder of the Danish kingdom.	**899-911.** Lewis III the Child, German king.	**902.** *Aug. 1*: Arabs take Taormina, last Byzantine place in Sicily.
900-942. Constantine III of Scots.	**901-905.** Emperor Louis III, the Blind, king of Lower Burgundy.	**904.** Saracens seize Salonika.
910. *Aug. 5*: Wessex victory at Tettenhall over Northumbrian Danes.	**906-955.** Magyars continually invade Germany.	**907-960.** Epoch of the five dynasties in China.
910-924. Ordoño II of Asturia (Leon); futile attacks on Moslems.	**911-918.** Conrad I, duke of Franconia, German king.	**909-1171.** Caliphate of the Fatimids in Tunisia and, from **969**, Egypt.
911. Treaty of St Clair-sur-Epte establishes the dukedom of Normandy.	**911.** Lorraine transfers allegiance from Germany to France.	**912-961.** Abd-er-Rahman III, Caliph of Cordoba; Omayyad rule in Spain at zenith.
911-931. Rollo, duke of Normandy.	**915.** Berengar of Friuli crowned emperor.	**913-959.** Constantine VII Porphyrogenitus, eastern emperor.
911-918. Ethelflaed, Alfred's daughter, Lady of the Mercians.	**916.** Synod of Hohenaltheim under presidency of papal legate.	
917. Edward subdues Danes of East Anglia.	**919-936.** Henry I, duke of Saxony, German king.	**919-944.** Romanus I Lecapenus, co-regent with Constantine VII; extension of the Byzantine empire to Euphrates and Tigris.
922-923. Robert, duke of Francia, anti-king in France.		

IV. ECCLESIASTICAL HISTORY	V. CONSTITUTIONAL AND ECONOMIC HISTORY	VI. CULTURAL LIFE
880. Montserrat monastery founded.		
		881. *Ludwigslied* in praise of Louis of Bavaria. The first historical ballad in German literature. **883.** Notker Balbulus: *Gesta Karoli.*
882-884. Pope Marinus I (formerly bishop of Caere; first bishop to become pope). **884-885.** Pope Hadrian III.		
885-891. Pope Stephen VI.		**886.** Alfred rebuilds London.
890-914. Plegmund, archbishop of Canterbury. **891-896.** Pope Formosus.		*ca.* **890.** *Cantilène de Ste. Eulalie,* first French poem. **891.** *Anglo-Saxon Chronicle* begun.
896. Pope Boniface VI. **896-897.** Pope Stephen VII. **897.** Pope Romanus; pope Theodore II. **898-900.** Pope John IX.		**894.** King Alfred's translation of Gregory's *Cura Pastoralis.*
900-903. Pope Benedict IV. **904-963.** Era of pornocracy in Rome (Theodora and her daughters Marozia and Theodora). **904-911.** Pope Serguis III.	**905.** County of Navarre made kingdom.	
910. Cluny abbey founded by William, duke of Aquitaine.		
911-913. Pope Anastasius III.	**911.** Treaty of commerce between Russia and Byzantium.	
913-914. Pope Lando.		**912.** Notker Balbulus, author of *Gesta Karoli Magni,* d.
914-928. Pope John X, paramour of Theodora. **916.** Arabs expelled from central Italy.		

I. WESTERN EUROPE	II. CENTRAL EUROPE	III. EASTERN EUROPE, ISLAM, ASIA
923-936. Rudolf II of Upper Burgundy, anti-king in France. **924-939.** Aethelstan of England.	**924.** Nine years' truce with Magyars. **925.** Lorraine definitely sides with Germany. **926-945.** Hugh of Vienne, king of Italy. **928-929.** Henry I subdues Slavs on the Havel. **929.** *Sept. 28*: Wenceslas of Bohemia murdered by Boleslav I, his brother. **932.** King Hugh of Italy marries Marozia.	**922.** Cordoba becomes autonomous caliphate. **923-936.** Dynasty of Hou-T'ang in China. **927-968.** Peter, tsar of Bulgaria.
931. Rudolf of Upper Burgundy acquires Vienne and Lyon. **931-942.** William Longsword, duke of Normandy.	**933.** *Mar. 15*: Henry I defeats Magyars at Riade near Merseburg. **934.** Henry I acquires Slesvig Marches.	**931.** Abd-er-Rahman takes Ceuta from the Berbers. **932.** Abd-er-Rahman takes Toledo.
935-970. Fernan Gonzalez, count of Castile. **936-986.** Harold Bluetooth of Denmark. **936-954.** Louis IV of France.	**936-973.** Otto I the Great, German king.	**935-969.** Ikhshidid dynasty in Egypt, Syria and Arabia. **935.** Wang Chien establishes central monarchy in China. **936-947.** Dynasty of Hou-Chin in China. **937.** Navarre recognises Abd-er-Rahman as suzerain.
937. Aethelstan defeats Kelts and Vikings at Brunanburh. **938.** Louis IV fails to invade Lorraine.	**938-941.** Rebellions in Franconia, Bavaria and Lorraine against Otto I. **941-945.** Berengar of Ivrea as refugee at Otto's court.	
939-946. Edmund I of England, half-brother to Aethelstan. **942-996.** Richard the Fearless, duke of Normandy. **942-954.** Malcolm I, king of Scots. **945.** Scots acquire Cumberland and Westmorland. Louis IV taken prisoner by duke Hugh of Francia. **946.** Otto I supports Louis IV, and advances to Rouen and Paris. **946-955.** Edred, brother to Edmund, king of England.	**945-950.** Lothair III, king of Italy.	**942.** Pilgrim, bishop of Passau, begins christianizing Hungary. **945-1055.** The Buyides rule over Baghdad.
950. Otto I mediates peace between Louis IV and Hugh (*d. June 16*, 956).	**947.** Otto I consolidates Slesvig. **950.** Berengar and his son Adalbert crowned kings of Italy.	**947-951.** Dynasty of Hou-Han in China.
954-962. Indulf, king of Scots. **954-986.** Lothair, king of France.	**951.** Otto's first expedition to Italy against Berengar. **953-955.** Rebellions in Germany against Otto I.	**951-960.** Dynasty of Hou-Chou in China.
955-959. Edwy, son of Edmund, king of England. **957-966.** Sancho I of Leon.	**955.** *Aug. 10*: Otto defeats Magyars at Augsburg; *Oct. 16*: Slavs in Mecklenburg.	**955.** The Russian grand duchess, Olga, christened at Byzantium.
959-975. Edgar the Peaceable, brother to Edwy, king of England.		**959-963.** Romanus II, eastern emperor.

IV. ECCLESIASTICAL HISTORY	V. CONSTITUTIONAL AND ECONOMIC HISTORY	VI. CULTURAL LIFE
924-942. Odo, Abbot of Cluny; extension of the Reform movement in France and (from **933**) Lorraine. **928-929.** Pope Leo VI. **929-931.** Pope Stephen VIII. **931.** Papal charter for Cluny. **931-936.** Pope John XI, son of Marozia. **932-954.** Count Alberic of Tusculum, son of Marozia, governor of Rome. **936-939.** Pope Leo VII. **939-942.** Pope Stephen IX. **942-946.** Pope Marinus II. **942-958.** Oda, Archbishop of Canterbury. **946-955.** Pope Agapetus II. **948.** Bishoprics of Brandenburg and Havelberg established. Ecclesiastical organisation of Jutland by Adaldag, Archbishop of Hamburg. **954-994.** Mayeul, Abbot of Cluny, in close alliance with Otto I and Otto II. **955-963.** Pope John XII, son of Alberic (Octavianus, first Pope to change his name). **959-988.** Dunstan, Archbishop of Canterbury.	**948-953.** Struggle of Milanese citizens in support of their archbishop against the candidate of king and nobles. **951.** Otto I assumes title of " king of the Franks and Lombards ". **953-965.** Brun I, brother of Otto I, Archbishop of Cologne and (from **959**) Duke of Lorraine. **958.** Berengar confirms privileges of Genoa.	*ca.* **930.** Ekkehard of St. Gallen: *Walter of Aquitaine* (epic poem).

I. WESTERN EUROPE	II. CENTRAL EUROPE	III. EASTERN EUROPE, ISLAM, ASIA
		960-992. Misika I of Poland.
		960-1280. Dynasty of Sung in China.
		961. Byzantines reconquer Crete from the Arabs.
	961-965. Otto's second expedition to Italy against Berengar.	**961-976.** Hakam II, caliph of Cordoba.
	962. *Feb. 2*: Otto I crowned emperor at Rome.	**962.** Alptigin founds Turkish principality at Ghazni, Afghanistan.
	963. Otto I takes Berengar prisoner.	**963-969.** Nicephorus II Phocas, eastern emperor.
		964-966. Nicephorus conquers Cyprus.
965. The English invade Gwynedd (North Wales).	**965.** Harold Bluetooth of Denmark baptized.	**965.** Fatimide Arabs conquer Sicily.
	966-972. Otto I's third expedition to Italy against Byzantines in Apulia.	
967-971. Cuilean, king of Scots.	**967.** *Dec. 25*: Otto II crowned emperor in Rome.	
	967-999. Boleslav II, duke of Bohemia.	**969.** Fatimide Arabs conquer Egypt. *Dec.*: Nicephorus II murdered by John Zimisces who succeeds as emperor (-976).
970-1035. Sancho, king of Navarre.		
971-995. Kenneth II, king of Scots.		**971.** John Zimisces subdues Bulgaria and defeats Sviatoslav of Russia.
	972. Otto II marries Theophano, daughter of Romanus II; Byzantium keeps Apulia and Calabria.	**972.** North Africa frees herself from Egypt.
	973-983. Otto II emperor.	
973. *May 11*: Edgar crowned at Bath.	**974.** Otto II defeats Harold Bluetooth of Denmark.	**975-996.** Caliph Al-Aziz of Egypt.
975. William, count of Arles, takes Garde-Freinet from Arabs.		**976-1025.** Basil II Bulgaroktonos, eastern emperor.
975-979. Edward the Martyr, king of England.	**976.** Henry of Bavaria dethroned; Carinthia becomes independent of Bavaria.	**976-1014.** Samuel, tsar of Bulgaria.
978. Lothair of France sacks Aix-la-Chapelle; Germans advance to Paris.		**977.** Arabs begin invading southern Italy.
979. Louis V, co-regent of France. *Mar. 14*: Edward murdered at Corfe castle. *Apr. 14*: Ethelred II crowned at Kingston.		**977-1002.** Al-Mansur, virtual ruler of Cordoba.
980. Vikings attack Chester, Southampton and Thanet.		**980-1015.** Vladimir, grand prince of Kiev.
981. Hugh Capet makes agreement with Otto II.	**981-983.** Otto II wars against Saracens in south Italy.	**981.** Hisham II of Cordoba (Al-Mansur) makes Leon tributary.
981-982. Vikings ravage Devonshire and South Wales.	**982.** *July 15*: Otto II defeated by Saracens.	
982. Eric the Red begins to colonize Greenland.	**983.** Otto III elected king. Rebellion of Danes and Wends; German colonization east of the Elbe breaks down.	

IV. ECCLESIASTICAL HISTORY	V. CONSTITUTIONAL AND ECONOMIC HISTORY	VI. CULTURAL LIFE
960. John XII asks for Otto I's support against Berengar, and promises him imperial crown.		*ca.* **960-980.** Hrotsvit of Gandersheim: 6 Christian plays.
962. *Feb. 13:* Otto I's privilege for the Roman Church. **963.** *Dec. 4:* Roman synod deposes John XII (*d.* **964**). **963-965.** Pope Leo VIII.		**961-971.** Liutprand, Bishop of Cremona: *Antapodosis,* and *History of Otto I.*
964. Anti-pope Benedict V, carried off by Otto II. **965-972.** Pope John XIII.	**964-969.** Working of mines (copper, silver) at Goslar (Harz) begun.	**963-984.** Ethelwold, Bishop of Winchester: translator of the Rule of St. Benedict. **965-967.** Widukind of Corvey: *Saxon History.* **966.** Flodoard of Reims *d.* (*Annals, History of Reims Church*).
968. Archbishopric of Magdeburg established.		**970.** St. Ethelwold of Winchester, *Regularis Concordia.* Rules for English monastic life. **971.** Blickling Homilies.
973-974. Pope Benedict VI. **974.** *June-Aug.:* Pope Boniface VII. **974-983.** Pope Benedict VII. **975.** Bishoprics of Prague and Olomuc established.		**978.** Mainz Cathedral begun.
980. The rule of the nobles breaks down in Rome. **981.** Bishopric of Merseburg abolished.	**983.** Otto grants city of Lazise on Lake Garda right to levy tolls and dues.	

I. WESTERN EUROPE	II. CENTRAL EUROPE	III. EASTERN EUROPE, ISLAM, ASIA
	983-1002. Otto III, under guardianship of his mother Theophano (*d.* **991**) and, till **995**, his grandmother Adelheid (*d.* **999**).	
985-1014. Svein, King of Denmark and (from **995**) of Sweden.	**985.** Bavaria restored to Duke Henry.	**985.** *July 1*: Almanzor takes Barcelona. Eric the Red founds a Scandinavian settlement in Greenland.
986-987. Louis V, King of France.		**986.** Sabuktagin, Amir of Ghazni, invades Punjab.
987. Hugh Capet becomes King of France (-**996**; Capetian dynasty rules till **1328**).		
988. *Jan. 1*: Robert, son of Hugh Capet, co-regent. Vikings attack Devon and Somerset; Irish Danes raid Wales.	**988.** Empress Theophano conducts government of Italy, at Rome.	
990-1029. William V, Duke of Aquitaine.	**989.** Carinthia reunited with Bavaria (-**996**).	**989.** Vladimir of Kiev baptised.
991. After battle of Maldon, Essex, Ethelred buys Vikings off.	**991.** *June 15*: Empress Theophano *d.*	**990.** Yantu (Pekin) made capital of Northern China.
992. Charles of Lorraine, the last Carolingian *d.*	**992-1025.** Boleslav Chrobry, Duke of Poland.	
993. Vikings sack Yorkshire.		
994. Olaf of Norway and Svein of Denmark besiege London.	**994.** Vikings ravage Hadeland and Friesland.	
995-997. Constantine IV of Scotland.		
995-1000. Olaf Tryggveson, King of Norway; introduces Christianity.		
996. *Oct. 24*: Hugh Capet *d.*, succeeded by Robert II (-**1031**).	**996.** *May 21*: Otto III crowned Emperor at Rome.	
996-1026. Richard II the Good, Duke of Normandy.	**997.** Gerbert of Reims joins court of Otto III.	
997-999. Vikings renew attacks on Dorset, Hants, Sussex, and Kent.	**997-1038.** Stephen I of Hungary.	**997-1030.** Mahmud, son of Sabuktagin, Sultan of Ghazni.
997-1005. Kenneth III of Scotland.	**997-998.** Second expedition of Otto III to Italy; Crescentius beheaded.	
999-1027. Alfonso V, King of Leon.	**999.** Boleslav Chrobry acquires Cracow, Silesia, and Slovakia.	**999.** Armenia reunited with Eastern Empire.
1000. Ethelred II ravages Cumberland and Isle of Man. Sancho of Navarre acquires Aragon. Vikings attack Normandy. Svein of Denmark conquers Norway and kills Olaf at Swold.	**1000.** Otto III visits tombs of St. Adalbert at Gnesen and of Charlemagne at Aix-la-Chapelle; makes Rome permanent residence.	**1000.** Leif Ericsson, son of Eric the Red, discovers America (Nova Scotia). Chinese first make gunpowder.
	1001. Romans rebel against Emperor and Pope. Stephen I of Hungary made King by Pope.	**1001.** *Nov. 27*: Mahmud of Ghazni defeats Jaipal, Raja of the Punjab, at Peshawar, and annexes his territory.

IV. ECCLESIASTICAL HISTORY	V. CONSTITUTIONAL AND ECONOMIC HISTORY	VI. CULTURAL LIFE
983-984. Pope John XIV, previously Peter of Pavia, imperial chancellor. **984-985.** Second pontificate of Boniface VII. **985-996.** Pope John XV; Crescentius the Younger assumes powers of patrician in Rome.	**985.** Quarrel between Ethelred II and the Witan begins.	
990-992. Poland submits to the Holy See. **991.** Arnulf, archbishop of Reims, deposed in favour of Gerbert. **991-996.** Gerbert leads Gallican opposition to Rome. **993.** Ulric, bishop of Augsburg (d. 973) canonized; first canonization by pope. **994-1048.** Odilo, abbot of Cluny; Cluniac movement at its prime. **995.** John XV deposes Gerbert of Reims.		**989.** Novgorod Cathedral begun. *ca.* **990-1020.** Aelfric the Grammarian, abbot of Eynsham: *Homilies, Latin Grammar* and *Glossary*, **993-1022.** Bernward, bishop of Hildesheim, patron of art and learning. **995.** Durham cathedral begun. Aelfric, *Lives of the Saints.*
996-999. Pope Gregory V (Brun, nephew of Otto III, first German pope). **997.** *Apr. 23*: Adalbert of Prague, missionary to Prussia, slain. **997-998.** Anti-pope John XVI (John Philagathos), deposed by Otto III. **998.** Feast of All Souls first celebrated at Cluny. **999-1003.** Pope Silvester II (Gerbert of Reims, first French pope). **1000.** Archbishopric of Gnesen established.		**1000-1010.** *Chanson de Roland.*
1001. Reorganization of Fécamp abbey, Normandy.		**1001.** Cathedral of Ani, Armenia, completed; destroyed by Seljuks, **1064.**

I. WESTERN EUROPE	II. CENTRAL EUROPE	III. EASTERN EUROPE, ISLAM, ASIA
1002. *Nov. 13:* Massacre of St Brice (Danes in England murdered). **1003-1014.** Almost annual Danish invasions in England.	**1002-1024:** Henry II, formerly duke of Bavaria, German king. **1002-1015.** Ardoin, marquis of Ivrea, anti-king in Italy. **1002-1004.** Bohemia under Polish rule. **1004.** Henry II defeats Ardoin. *May 15:* Henry crowned king of Lombardy at Pavia. War against Boleslav Chrobry begins (**-1018**).	**1002-1008.** Muzaffar, ruler of Cordoba. **1003.** Arabs ravage Leon. **1004.** Arabs sack Pisa. Rule of Samanides overthrown in Persia. China becomes tributary of the Tungusic Khitans.
1005-1034. Malcolm II of Scotland. **1006.** Robert II of France allies with Henry II against Baldwin of Flanders. **1007.** Ethelred buys two years' peace from Danes. **1009.** Danes attack London.	**1006.** Rudolf III of Burgundy appoints Henry II his heir. **1009.** Brun of Querfurt martyred by Prussians. **1011-1013.** Slav rebellion in Northalbingia and Northern March.	**1006.** Mohammedans settle in north-west India. **1008.** Mahmud of Ghazni defeats Hindu league at Peshawar. **1009.** Mohammedans profane Holy Sepulchre at Jerusalem. **1011.** Arabs sack Pisa.
1011. Ethelred invades south Wales. Danes take Canterbury. **1012.** *Apr. 19:* Danes murder archbishop Elfheah, and are again bought off by Ethelred. **1013.** Danes conquer Northumbria, Wessex, London; Ethelred flees to Normandy.		
1014. *Feb. 3:* Svein *d.*, succeeded by Cnut. Ethelred returns on the English leaders' terms; Cnut withdraws to Denmark. **1015.** Wessex submits to Cnut. **1015-1030.** Olaf II the Saint, king of Norway. **1016.** *Apr. 23:* Ethelred II *d. Oct.:* Edmund Ironside and Cnut divide England among themselves. *Nov. 30:* Edmund Ironside *d.*; Cnut recognized as king of England. **1018.** Malcolm II conquers all Lothian.	**1014.** Second expedition of Henry II to Italy; Ardoin submits. *Feb. 14:* Henry crowned emperor. **1016.** Norman knights arrive in southern Italy. **1018.** *Jan. 30:* Peace of Bautzen between Henry II and Boleslav, who keeps Lusatia. **1020.** Rebellion of Bernard II, duke of Saxony. **1021-1022.** Third expedition of Henry II to Italy against Byzantines.	**1015.** Arabs conquer Sardinia. **1015-1054.** Jaroslav, prince of Kiev. **1016.** The pope, Pisa and Genoa rescue Sardinia from Mujahid of Denia. **1018.** Basil II subdues Bulgaria. Byzantines defeat Lombards and Normans at Cannae. **1019.** Mahmud of Ghazni conquers Kanauj. **1021-1022.** Basil II's campaign against Armenia.
1023. Robert II of France and emperor Henry II meet at Ivry.	**1024-1039.** Conrad II, formerly duke of Franconia, German king.	

IV. ECCLESIASTICAL HISTORY	V. CONSTITUTIONAL AND ECONOMIC HISTORY	VI. CULTURAL LIFE
1003. Pope John XVII. **1003-1009.** Pope John XVIII. **1004.** Bishopric of Merseburg re-established.		
1005. St Nilus *d.* **1005-1012.** Ælfheah, archbishop of Canterbury.		**1005.** Aelfric appointed as the first abbot of Eynsham.
1007. Bishopric of Bamberg established. **1009-1012.** Pope Sergius IV. **1010.** Robert II of France proclaims peace of God.	**1008.** Ethelred II organizes English fleet.	**1009-1018.** Thietmar, bishop of Merseburg: *Chronicle.* **1010.** Richer of St Remy *d.*, author of *Historia Remensis Ecclesiae.*
1012. Counts of Tusculum overthrow Crescentius family in Rome; Benedict VIII, count of Tusculum, made pope (**-1024**). First persecution of heretics in Germany.	**1012.** *Decretum* of Burchard, bishop of Worms—Levy of heregeld for payment of royal retainers in England.	**1014.** Archbishop Wulfstan: *Sermo Lupi ad Anglos.*
	1015. First '*communitas*' (municipal self-government) at Benevento.	
1016. Benedict VIII calls Normans to aid against Arabs and Byzantines.		
	1017. Cnut divides England into 4 earldoms. **1018.** Assembly of Oxford: Danes and English to live under English laws.	
1019. Synod of Goslar decides against marriage of priests.	**1020.** Alfonso V issues the *fuero* (statutes) of Leon and charters in favour of the cities.	**1020.** Bamberg cathedral consecrated by Benedict VIII.
1022. Synod of Pavia insists on celibacy of higher clergy. **1024-1032.** Pope John XIX, brother of Benedict VIII.		**1022.** *June 29*: Notker Teutonicus, monk of St Gall, translator of Boethius, Martianus Capella, Aristotle and the Psalter, *d.* **1023.** Wulfstan, archbishop of York, *d.* (*Homilies*).

I. WESTERN EUROPE	II. CENTRAL EUROPE	III. EASTERN EUROPE, ISLAM, ASIA
1026. Cnut defeated by Swedes and Norwegians on Helge river.	**1025.** Boleslav of Poland assumes title of king; *d. June 17.*	**1025-1026.** Mahmud conquers Gujarat.
	1025-1030. Rebellion of Ernest, duke of Swabia.	**1025-1028.** Constantine VIII. eastern emperor.
1026-1027. Richard III, duke of Normandy.	**1026-1027.** First expedition of Conrad II to Italy.	
1027. Malcolm II does homage to Cnut. *May 14:* Henry I becomes co-regent with Robert II.	**1027.** Henry III, Conrad's son, invested with Bavaria. Treaty of succession between Conrad and Rudolf, king of Burgundy. *Mar. 26:* Conrad crowned emperor.	**1027-1031.** Hisham III, caliph of Cordoba.
1027-1035. Robert the Devil, duke of Normandy.		
1028. Cnut conquers Norway. Sancho of Navarre acquires Castile.	**1028.** *Apr. 14:* Henry III elected king.	
1028-1037. Bermudo III, king of Leon.		**1028-1034.** Romanus III, eastern emperor.
1030. *July 29:* Olaf Haraldson, Norwegian pretender, defeated at Stiklestad.	**1030.** Normans settle **at** Aversa near Naples.	**1030.** Seljuks advance in Asia Minor. Jaroslav of Kiev founds Dorpat.
1031-1060. Henry I, king of France.	**1031.** Poland cedes Lusatia to Conrad. Frontier treaty with Hungary.	**1031.** *Dec.:* Caliphate of Cordoba abolished by viziers.
1032. Henry I subdues his seditious brother, Robert.	**1032.** *Sept. 6:* Rudolf III of Burgundy *d.*; Conrad unites Burgundy with the empire.	
	1033. Poland becomes fief of the empire. Upper and Lower Lorraine united.	
1034. *Nov. 25:* Malcolm II murdered, succeeded by Duncan, his grandson (**-1040**).	**1034-1055.** Bratislav, duke of Bohemia.	**1034.** Genoa and Pisa take Bona (Tunis).
		1034-1042. Michael IV, eastern emperor.
1035. Sancho III of Spain *d.*; partition of his kingdom into Castile, Navarre, Aragon. *July 2:* Robert of Normandy dies on pilgrimage at Nicaea; succeeded by illegitimate son William. *Nov. 12:* Cnut *d.*; his kingdoms divided between his 3 sons; Harold Harefoot obtains England (**-1040**), Sweyn, Norway (**-1036**), Hardacnut, Denmark.		
1035-1065. Ferdinand I of Castile; conquers Portugal.		
1036. Harold defeats Alfred, son of Ethelred II. Sweyn expelled from Norway.	**1036.** Conrad subdues Lyutitzi Slavs.	
1037. Union of Castile and Leon.	**1036-1038.** Second expedition of Conrad to Italy.	
1038. Agreement between Hardacnut of Denmark and Magnus of Norway.	**1038.** Henry III invested with Swabia. Conrad II recognizes Norman county of Aversa. *Aug. 15:* Stephen of Hungary *d.* ; Abo usurps throne. Peter, legal heir, flees to Germany.	

IV. ECCLESIASTICAL HISTORY	V. CONSTITUTIONAL AND ECONOMIC HISTORY	VI. CULTURAL LIFE
		1030. Moveable wooden characters used in printing in China.
1032-1045. Pope Benedict IX, nephew of Benedict VIII.		**1032.** Canute completes restoration of St. Edmunds Bury.
		1033. Anselm *b*.
	1035-1037. War between citizens of Milan and minor nobles.	
	1036. Jaroslav the Wise revises *Pravda Russkaia*.	**1036.** Avicenna, Arab philosopher, *d*.
1038. Order of Vallombrosa founded.	**1037.** *May 28:* Conrad II issues *Constitutio de feudis* which makes fiefs of small holders (valvassores) hereditary in Italy.	**1037.** Cathedral of St. Sophia, Kiev begun, completed 1046 and later altered.

I. WESTERN EUROPE	II. CENTRAL EUROPE	III. EASTERN EUROPE, ISLAM, ASIA
1039. Gruffyd ap Llywelyn, king of Gwynedd and Powys, defeats English.	**1039.** *June 4*: Conrad II *d.*; succeeded by Henry III (**-1056**). Henry III seizes duchy of Carinthia.	
1040. *March 17*: Harold I of England *d.*; *June 17*: succeeded by Hardacnut (**-1042**). *Aug. 14*: Duncan slain by Macbeth, who becomes king of Scots (**-1057**).		
1041. Siward murders Eardwulf, earl of Bernicia, and becomes ruler of whole of Northumbria.	**1041.** *May 4*: Lombards and Normans defeat Greeks at Montemaggiore. Bohemia submits to Henry III.	
	1041-1058. Casimir I, duke of Poland.	
1042. *June 8*: Hardacnut *d.*; succeeded by Edward the Confessor, son of Ethelred (**-1066**).	**1042-1047.** Magnus, king of Denmark.	**1042.** Michael V, eastern emperor, deposed by his wife Zoe.
		1042-1055. Constantine IX Monomachos, eastern emperor.
1043. *Nov.*: Agnes of Poitou married to Henry III.		**1043.** Rebellion of George Maniakes, Byzantine commander.
1044. Gruffyd defeats Danish invaders from Ireland. Geoffrey of Anjou takes Tours.	**1044.** Henry III wars against Abo of Hungary. Godfrey of Lorraine loses Lower Lorraine.	
1045. Harold, son of Godwin, and brother-in-law of king Edward, made earl of East Anglia.	**1045.** Henry III restores Peter in Hungary, who does homage.	**1045.** Byzantines conquer Armenia.
	1046. *Dec. 25*: Henry III crowned emperor at Rome.	
1047. William of Normandy, aided by Henry I, defeats rebellious nobles at Val-des-Dunes.	**1047.** Henry III re-establishes duchies of Carinthia, Bavaria, and Swabia. Henry negotiates peace between Bohemia, Poland, and Pomerania. Henry invests Norman princes with Aversa and Apulia. Godfrey of Upper Lorraine loses his duchy.	
1047-1066. Harald Hardrada, king of Norway.		
1047-1076. Svein Estrithson, king of Denmark.	**1047-1060.** Andrew I, king of Hungary.	
1048. William of Normandy defeats Geoffrey of Anjou and takes Domfront and Alençon.		
1049. William begins to annex Maine.	**1049.** Henry III aided by English and Danish ships, wars against Flanders.	

IV. ECCLESIASTICAL HISTORY	V. CONSTITUTIONAL AND ECONOMIC HISTORY	VI. CULTURAL LIFE
	1040. Truce of God proclaimed in Aquitaine.	**1040.** *La Vie de Saint Alexis*, Anonymous. Considered to be the beginning of French literature.
	1042. Truce of God proclaimed in Normandy. Milanese drive out nobles.	
1043-1072. Adalbert, Archbishop of Bremen; plans a Nordic Patriarchate including Scandinavia, under German influence.		
1044-1051. Robert of Jumièges, Bishop of London (first Norman bishop in England).	**1044.** Nobles return to Milan on harsh conditions.	
1045. *May 1*: Benedict IX sells Papacy to Gregory VI (John Gratianus); Silvester III (Crescentius) elected anti-pope.	**1045.** Earliest dated use in China of (earthenware) moveable type for printing, initiated by Pi Sheng. Constantine IX re-founds the University of Constantinople, establishing faculties of Law and Philosophy.	
1046. *Dec. 20*: Synod of Sutri: Henry III deposes Silvester III and Gregory VI. *Dec. 24*: Synod of Rome. Clement II (Suidger, Bishop of Bamberg) elected Pope.		**1046.** Richard of St. Vannes ecclesiastical writer, *d.*
1047. *Jan.*: Synod of Rome against simony. *Oct. 9*: Clement II *d.*; Benedict IX returns; Damasus II (Poppo, Bishop of Brixen) elected Pope.		
1048. *July 16*: Benedict IX definitely resigns. *Aug. 9*: Damasus II *d.*; Leo IX (Bruno of Egisheim, Bishop of Toul) elected Pope.		
1049. *Oct. 3*: Council of Reims, regulates elections of bishops and abbots.		
1049-1109. Hugh, Abbot of Cluny.		

I. WESTERN EUROPE	II. CENTRAL EUROPE	III. EASTERN EUROPE, ISLAM, ASIA
1051. William visits Edward; receives promise of succession to English throne.		**1050-1084.** Michael of Serbia; receives title of king from Gregory VII.
1051-1052. Robert de Jumièges, Archbishop of Canterbury.	**1051-1052.** Unsuccessful expedition of Henry III against Hungary.	
1052-1070. Stigand, Archbishop of Canterbury.	**1052.** Rebellion of Conrad, duke of Bavaria; deposed in **1053.**	
1053. *Apr. 15*: Godwin *d.*; Harold succeeds as earl of Wessex. Archbishop of Rouen excommunicates William who deposes him.	**1053.** *June 18*: Normans defeat and capture Leo IX at Civitate. Henry III makes peace with Hungary.	
1054. *July 27*: Siward of Northumbria and Malcolm defeat Macbeth at Dunsinane. William defeats Henry I at Mortemer.	**1054.** *July 17*: Henry IV elected king. Godfrey of Lorraine marries Matilda, marchioness of Tuscany.	**1054.** Jaroslav of Kiev *d.*; subsequent decline of his empire.
1055. Siward of Northumbria *d.*; succeeded by Tostig, son of Godwin. Gruffyd sacks Herefordshire.	**1055.** Second expedition of Henry III to Italy.	**1055.** Seljuks take Baghdad.
	1055-1061. Spitigniev II of Bohemia.	
1056. Harold of Wessex and Leofric of Mercia force Gruffyd to do homage.	**1056.** *Oct. 5*: Henry III *d.*; succeeded by Henry IV, till **1062** under guardianship of empress Agnes.	**1056-1057.** Michael VI, eastern emperor.
1057. *Aug. 15*: Malcolm kills Macbeth, whose stepson Lulach succeeds him. *Aug. 31*: Leofric of Mercia *d.*, succeeded by Alfgar.		**1057-1059.** Isaac Comnenus, eastern emperor.
1058. *Mar. 17*: Malcolm slays Lulach and becomes king of Scots (**-1093**). *Aug.*: William of Normandy defeats Geoffrey of Anjou at Varaville.	**1058.** Richard of Aversa becomes prince of Capua.	
	1058-1081. Boleslav II, duke of Poland.	
1059. *May 23*: Philip I made co-regent of France. Lanfranc reconciles William of Normandy with the church.	**1059.** *Aug.*: Treaty of Melfi; Robert Guiscard, duke of Apulia, and Richard of Aversa become papal vassals.	**1059-1067.** Constantine X Ducas, eastern emperor.
1060. *Aug. 4*: Henry I of France *d.*, succeeded by Philip I (**-1108**).	**1060-1063.** Bela I, king of Hungary.	
1061. Malcolm of Scotland invades Northumberland.	**1061.** Normans conquer Messina. Otto of Nordheim created duke of Bavaria.	
	1062. *Apr.*: *Coup d'état* of Kaiserswerth: Anno, archbishop of Cologne, seizes Henry IV; Anno and Adalbert, archbishop of Bremen, co-regents (**-1065**).	
1063. Harold and Tostig subdue Wales. William of Normandy conquers Maine.	**1063.** Victorious German expedition against Hungary.	**1063-1072.** Alp Arslan, ruler of Seljuks.
1064. *Aug. 5*: Gruffyd ap Llywelyn *d.* Harold visits Normandy and does homage to William.	**1063-1074.** Solomon, king of Hungary (*d.* **1087**).	**1064.** Seljuks conquer Armenia. German pilgrimage to Jerusalem.

IV. ECCLESIASTICAL HISTORY	V. CONSTITUTIONAL AND ECONOMIC HISTORY	VI. CULTURAL LIFE
1050-1080. Dispute about transubstantiation between Berengar of Tours and Lanfranc, Archbishop of Canterbury.	**1051.** Edward abolishes heregeld.	**1050.** Radulfus Glaber *d.*, author of *Historiae sui Temporis. Ruodlieb*, first German novel of chivalry.
		1052. Westminster Abbey begun.
1053. *Jan. 6*: Adalbert of Bremen appointed Papal Vicar of Northern Europe.		
1054. *July 16*: Reciprocal excommunication of the Roman and Greek Churches; repealed *7 Dec. 1965.*		
1054-1057. Pope Victor II (Gebhard, Bishop of Eichstätt).		
	1056. Outbreak of the Pataria (democratic movement) at Milan.	
1057-1072. Peter Damiani, Cardinal Bishop of Ostia.		
1057-1058. Pope Stephen IX (Frederick of Lorraine).		
1058. Cardinal Humbert: *Adversus Simoniacos.*		
1058-1060. Pope Benedict X (John, Bishop of Velletri).		
1059-1061. Pope Nicholas II (Gerard, Bishop of Florence).		
1059. *Apr. 13*: Decree establishing papal election by Cardinals only. Hildebrand appointed Archdeacon of the Roman Church.		
1060. Bishoprics of Mecklenburg and Ratzeburg established.		**1060.** Ekkehard IV of St. Gall, author of *Casus Sancti Galli, d.*
1061-1073. Pope Alexander II (Anselm, Bishop of Lucca).		
1061-1064. Imperial anti-pope Honorius II (Cadalus, Bishop of Parma).		
1063. Bishopric of Olomuc reestablished. First mention of Rule of St. Augustine.		**1063-1118.** Pisa Cathedral built.
1064. Council of Mantua declares Alexander II lawful Pope.	**1064-1069.** Promulgation of *Usages* of Raymond Berengar I, earliest feudal code.	**1064.** *Ezzolied*, German crusaders' song.

I. WESTERN EUROPE	II. CENTRAL EUROPE	III. EASTERN EUROPE, ISLAM, ASIA
1065. Tostig expelled from Northumberland, succeeded by Morcar, son of Alfgar. **1065-1072.** Sancho II, King of Castile. **1065-1109.** Alfonso VI, King of Leon and (from **1072**) Castile. **1066.** *Jan. 5:* Edward the Confessor *d. Jan. 6:* Harold crowned. *Sept. 20:* Harald Hardrada of Norway and Tostig defeat Morcar at Fulford. *Sept. 25:* Harold defeats invaders at Stamford Bridge. *Sept. 28:* William of Normandy lands at Pevensey. *Oct. 14:* Harold defeated and killed at Hastings. *Dec. 25:* William I crowned.	**1065.** *Mar. 29:* Henry IV comes of age. Lorraine, undivided, given to Duke Godfrey.	**1065.** Seljuks invade Asia Minor.
1068. William conquers Western and Northern England. **1069.** William subdues rising in the North and expels Danish invaders. **1070.** Rising in Ely under Hereward. Malcolm of Scotland invades Northumberland. **1071.** Philip I attacks Robert, Count of Flanders; *Feb. 22:* is defeated at Cassel. William I suppresses the last risings in England. **1072.** Malcolm of Scotland acknowledges William's suzerainty. Hereward submits.	**1066.** *Jan.:* Adalbert of Bremen overthrown by princes. *June:* Rising of Slavs. **1066-1090.** Halstan, King of Sweden. **1069.** *Dec. 24:* Godfrey, Duke of Lorraine, *d.* **1070.** *Aug. 2:* Otto of Nordheim dispossessed of Bavaria, which is bestowed upon Guelph IV. **1071.** *Apr.:* Normans conquer Bari and Brindisi, last Byzantine possessions in Italy. **1072.** Normans conquer Palermo.	**1068-1071.** Romanus IV Diogenes, Eastern Emperor. **1068-1086.** Shen-tsung, Emperor of China; China disorganized by State interference in economics. **1071.** Seljuks take Jerusalem. *Aug. 26:* Romanus IV defeated and captured by Seljuks at Manzikert. **1071-1078.** Michael VII Parapinaces, Eastern Emperor. **1072-1073.** Michael VII appeals in vain to Pope and Robert Guiscard for assistance.
1073. William I suppresses municipal movement in Maine.	**1073.** *Aug.:* Revolt of the Saxons under Otto of Nordheim against Henry IV. Gregory VII excommunicates Henry's Counsellors. Union of Savoy territories.	
1074. First rebellion of Norman barons against William.	**1074.** *Feb. 2:* Peace of Gerstungen between Henry IV and the Saxons, who subsequently revolt again. Robert Guiscard excommunicated by Gregory VII. **1074-1077.** Geiza I, King of Hungary. **1075.** *June 9:* Henry IV defeats Saxons at Homburg-on-Unstrut.	
1076. Philip I defeats Normans. Navarre divided between Aragon and Castile.	**1076.** *Jan. 24:* Synod of Worms; German bishops challenge Gregory VII, who dethrones and excommunicates Henry IV. *Feb. 26:* Godfrey, Duke of Lower Lorraine, assassinated. *Oct. 16:* Trebur meeting of princes who oppose Henry IV.	**1076.** Seljuks conquer Damascus.

IV. ECCLESIASTICAL HISTORY	V. CONSTITUTIONAL AND ECONOMIC HISTORY	VI. CULTURAL LIFE
		1065. Consecration of St. Peter's, Westminster (Westminster Abbey).
1066. Alexander II supports William's attack on England.		
1069-1091. William, Abbot of Hirsau.		
1070-1089. Lanfranc, Archbishop of Canterbury.		
1072. Bishopric of Gurk, Carinthia, established.	**1072.** Commune formed at Le Mans.	
1073. Reorganization of the English Church; York subordinated to Canterbury; ecclesiastical courts established.		**1073.** Abbey of St. Augustine, Canterbury, begun.
1073-1085. Pope Gregory VII (Hildebrand).		
1074. *Mar. 1*: Gregory VII announces a crusade. *Mar. 9*: Excommunication of married priests.	**1074.** *Jan. 18*: Imperial charter for city of Worms.	
1075. *Dictatus Papae*, outlines papal world dominance.		**1075.** Adam of Bremen: *History of the Hamburg Church.*
1076. Roman ritual introduced in Navarre and Castile. Order of Grandmont founded by St. Stephen.		

I. WESTERN EUROPE	II. CENTRAL EUROPE	III. EASTERN EUROPE, ISLAM, ASIA
1077. Second rebellion of Norman barons, headed by Robert, William's son, and aided by Philip.	**1077.** *Jan. 28:* Henry IV goes as penitent to Canossa; absolved by Gregory VII. *Mar. 15:* Rudolf, Duke of Swabia, elected anti-king. *Dec. 14:* Empress Agnes *d.*	
1078. Philip of France aids Rudolf, German anti-king.	**1077–1095.** Vladislav I, King of Hungary.	**1078–1081.** Nicephorus III, Eastern Emperor.
1079. William defeats Robert at Gerberoi. Malcolm ravages Northumberland.	**1079.** Frederick of Staufen marries Henry IV's daughter and is created Duke of Swabia.	
1080. Robert invades Scotland and builds Newcastle-upon-Tyne.	**1080.** *Mar. 7:* Gregory VII again deposes and excommunicates Henry IV. *Oct. 15:* Henry IV defeated, Rudolf killed at Pegau. Gregory VII and Robert Guiscard reconciled.	**1080.** Armenian state established in Cilicia (Armenia Minor).
1080–1086. Canute IV (the Saint), King of Denmark.		
1081. William makes an expedition into Wales.	**1081.** Henry IV marches to Italy. *Aug. 9:* Hermann, Count of Salm, elected anti-king.	**1081–1118.** Alexius Comnenus, Eastern Emperor.
		1081. Robert Guiscard invades Balkan Peninsula.
1082. Odo, Bishop of Bayeux and Earl of Kent, William's brother, imprisoned (**-1087**).	**1081–1102.** Vladislav I, Duke of Poland.	**1082.** Robert Guiscard defeats Alexius at Durazzo.
1083–1086. New rebellion in Maine against William.	**1083.** *Jan. 11:* Otto of Nordheim *d. June 3:* Henry IV storms Rome.	**1083.** Alexius defeats Normans at Larissa.
	1084. *Mar. 31:* Clement III crowns Henry IV Emperor.	
1085. *May 25:* Alfonso VI of Castile captures Toledo. Denmark, Norway, and Flanders prepare to invade England.	**1085.** Henry IV reconciles Saxony. *June 15:* Vratislav, Duke of Bohemia, crowned King. *July 17:* Robert Guiscard *d.*	**1085.** Normans evacuate Balkan Peninsula, after Guiscard's death.
1086–1095. Olaf, King of Denmark.		**1086.** Almoravide dynasty revives Mohammedan rule in Spain.
1087. Philip's invasion of Normandy repelled by William. *Sept. 9:* William I *d.,* succeeded by Robert in Normandy (**-1106**), by William II (Rufus) in England (**-1100**).	**1087.** *May 30:* Conrad, Henry IV's eldest son, crowned King. *Dec. 27:* Empress Bertha *d.*	**1087.** Pisa and Genoa capture Mahdiyah in Barbary.
1088. Odo of Bayeux revolts against William II in favour of Robert.	**1088.** *Sept. 28:* Hermann of Salm *d.*	**1088–1090.** Patzinaks, Turkish tribes, settle between Danube and Balkans.
	1089. Guelph V marries Matilda of Tuscany; Henry IV marries Praxedis (Adelaide) of Kiev.	**1089–1125.** David III, King of Georgia.
1090–1112. Ingo I, King of Sweden.	**1090–1097.** Henry IV wages war in Italy.	
1091. Treaty of Caen between William and Robert. Malcolm invades England.	**1091.** Norman conquest of Sicily completed. Vladislav of Hungary subdues Croatia.	**1091.** *Apr. 29:* Alexius defeats Patzinaks by river Leburnium.

IV. ECCLESIASTICAL HISTORY	V. CONSTITUTIONAL AND ECONOMIC HISTORY	VI. CULTURAL LIFE
1077. First English Cluniac monastery founded at Lewes.		**1077.** Lampert of Hersfeld *d.*, author of *Annals*.
		1077-1115. St. Albans Abbey built.
1079. Manasse, Archbishop of Reims, reprimanded by Gregory VII.		**1079-1093.** Winchester Cathedral built.
1080. *June 25*: Synod of Brixen, elects imperial anti-pope Clement III (Wibert, Archbishop of Ravenna; **-1100**). William I of England refuses to do homage as papal vassal.	**1080.** First mention of autonomous Consuls at Lucca.	
	1081. Alexius grants commercial privileges to Venice. Consular constitution in Milan.	**1081.** Mayence Cathedral rebuilt. **1081-1090.** Bishop Gundulf builds Tower of London.
		1083-1189. Ely Cathedral built.
1084. *May*: Normans sack Rome; Gregory VII flees with them to Salerno. **1085.** *May 25*: Gregory VII *d.* at Salerno.	**1084.** First mention of Consuls at Pisa. **1085.** Henry IV extends Peace of God over the whole Empire.	
1086. Bruno of Cologne founds Carthusian Order. **1086-1087.** Pope Victor III (Desiderius, Abbot of Montecassino).	**1086.** Compilation of *Domesday Book* (inventory and assessment of landed property); all English vassals made dependent on the King.	
		1087. Constantinus Africanus *d.*, at Montecassino.
1088-1099. Pope Urban II (Odo of Chatillon).		
1089. Sancho Ramirez, King of Aragon, does homage as papal vassal. *May 28*: Lanfranc *d.*; Canterbury vacant four years. **1090.** Berengar II, Count of Barcelona, does homage as papal vassal. **1090-1116.** Ivo, Bishop of Chartres.		**1089.** Gloucester Abbey Church, since 1539 the Cathedral, begun. **1089-1130.** Abbey Church of Cluny rebuilt. **1090-1100.** Vault of Spires Cathedral built.

I. WESTERN EUROPE	II. CENTRAL EUROPE	III. EASTERN EUROPE, ISLAM, ASIA
1092. William conquers Cumberland and Westmorland; *Nov. 13*: Malcolm III defeated and killed near Alnwick.	**1092.** *Jan. 14*: Vratislav II of Bohemia *d.*; internal strife **-1140**.	**1092.** Malek Shah, Seljuk Sultan, *d.*; capital moved from Iconium to Smyrna.
1093. *Apr. 17-23*: The Welsh prince, Rhys ap Tewdwr, *d.*; South Wales conquered by English. *Nov. 13*: Malcolm of Scotland killed when invading England; succeeded by Donald Bane, his brother, who expels all English.	**1093.** King Conrad deserts Henry IV, is crowned King of Italy, supported by Urban II and Matilda.	
1094. William wars against Robert in Normandy. Welsh reconquer Angelsey. Donald Bane and Edmund divide Scotland. Henry of Burgundy becomes Margrave of Portugal.	**1094.** Empress Praxedis deserts Henry IV.	**1094-1095.** Alexius repels attacks of the Cumans, Turkish tribes, at Adrianople.
1095. Conspiracy of Robert of Mowbray, Earl of Northumberland, against William II put down. Philip I of France excommunicated for adultery.	**1095.** Guelph V divorces Matilda. **1095-1114.** Koloman, King of Hungary; conquers Dalmatia and Herzegovina.	**1095.** Alexius calls on Urban II for help against the Turks. *Nov. 27*: Council of Clermont determines on a Crusade.
1095-1103. Eric I, King of Denmark.		
1096. Robert mortgages Normandy to William. English recover Anglesey. The Cid conquers Valencia. Peter I of Aragon defeats Moors at Alcaraz.	**1096.** Henry IV and Guelph IV reconciled.	**1096-1099.** First Crusade. **1096.** Disorganized crusaders led by Peter the Hermit perish in Asia Minor. *Aug.*: Godfrey of Bouillon, Duke of Lorraine, sets out with Crusaders.
1097. War between William and Philip. William II makes Edgar, son of Malcolm, King of Scotland (**-1107**).	**1097.** Henry IV returns to Germany.	**1097.** *June 19*: Crusaders take Nicaea. *July 1*: Crusaders defeat Turks at Dorylaeum.
1098. Louis VI made co-regent of Philip I of France. Magnus of Norway seizes Orkneys, Hebrides and Isle of Man.		**1098.** *June 3*: Crusaders take Antioch. *June 28*: Crusaders defeat Turks at Antioch.
1099. William II subdues Maine. After death of the Cid, Moors recover Valencia.	**1099.** *Jan. 6*: Henry V elected King.	**1099.** *July 15*: Crusaders take Jerusalem. *July 22*: Godfrey of Bouillon elected Defender of the Holy Sepulchre. *Aug. 12*: Crusaders defeat Egyptians at Ascalon.
		1100. David III of Georgia expels Arabs from Tiflis.
1100. *Aug. 2*: William II shot in New Forest, succeeded by Henry I (**-1135**), who marries (*Nov. 11*) Matilda, daughter of Malcolm of Scotland.		**1100-1118.** Baldwin I, King of Jerusalem.
1101. *July 19*: Robert of Normandy invades England, is bought off (Treaty of Alton).	**1101.** *July 27*: King Conrad *d.* **1101-1154.** Roger II, King of Sicily.	
1102. Revolt of Robert of Belesme and the Montgomerys against Henry I suppressed.	**1102-1138.** Boleslav III, Duke of Poland; conquers Pomerania and Rügen.	
1103. Magnus III of Norway invades Ireland; killed *Aug. 24*.		

IV. ECCLESIASTICAL HISTORY	V. CONSTITUTIONAL AND ECONOMIC HISTORY	VI. CULTURAL LIFE
1092. Vladislav, King of Hungary, allows marriage of priests.		**1092.** Roscelin recants his nominalistic philosophical doctrines.
1093. Urban II recovers Rome from the Germans. **1093-1109.** Anselm, Archbishop of Canterbury; pioneer of scholasticism.		**1093-1133.** Durham Cathedral built. **1093-1156.** Abbey Church of Maria Laach built.
1094. Quarrel between William II and Anselm begins.		
1095. Clergymen forbidden to take oath of fealty to laymen.	**1095.** King Conrad acts as Marshal to the Pope.	**1095.** Urban II consecrates rebuilt Abbey Church of Cluny.
		1096-1117. Crypt of Canterbury Cathedral built. **1096-1145.** Nave of Norwich Cathedral built.
1097-1100. Archbishop Anselm in exile at Rome and Cluny.		**1097.** Westminster Hall built.
1098. *Mar. 21*: Citeaux monastery founded. *July 5*: Roger I of Sicily appointed permanent papal legate. Order of St. John founded. **1099-1118.** Pope Paschal II (Cardinal Rainer).	**1099.** First mention of Consuls at Genoa. Assize of Jerusalem; organization of kingdom of Jerusalem.	**1098.** *Mar. 21*: Robert of Molesme founds Citeaux Abbey and the Cistercian Order.
1100-1107. Ranulf, Bishop of Durham, imprisoned in Tower by Henry I.	**1100.** Henry I issues Charter of Liberties.	**1100.** *Gesta Francorum et aliorum Hierosolimitanorum*, Anonymous. Chronicle of the First Crusade, **1096-99**.
	1102-1139. Roger, Bishop of Salisbury, chancellor and justiciar under Henry I and Stephen, establishes the Exchequer.	
1103-1105. Second exile of Archbishop Anselm in Rome.	**1103.** Public peace of Mayence for the Empire, for 4 years.	

I. WESTERN EUROPE	II. CENTRAL EUROPE	III. EASTERN EUROPE, ISLAM, ASIA
1104. Philip I absolved by Pope. **1104-1134.** Alfonso I of Aragon. **1104-1134.** Nicholas, King of Denmark. **1105.** War between Henry and Robert in Normandy. **1106.** *Sept. 28:* Henry I defeats Robert at Tinchebrai, imprisons him at Cardiff until his death (**1134**), and takes Normandy; William Clito, Robert's son, hostile to Henry. **1107.** *Jan. 8:* Edgar of Scotland *d.*, succeeded by his brother, Alexander I (**-1124**). **1108.** *July 29:* Philip I of France *d.*, succeeded by Louis VI (**-1137**). **1109-1113.** Anglo-French war. **1109-1127.** Alfonso I of Aragon also ruler of Castile and Leon. **1112.** Rebellion in Eastern Normandy; Henry imprisons Robert of Belesme. **1112-1118.** Philip, King of Sweden. **1113-1115.** Balearic Islands conquered by Pisa. **1114.** David, brother of Alexander I of Scotland, obtains Earldom of Huntingdon. **1117-1120.** Henry I wars against William Clito, who is assisted by France, Flanders, and Anjou. **1118.** Alfonso I of Aragon takes Saragossa. Rebellion in Eastern Normandy. **1118-1129.** Ingo II, King of Sweden. **1119.** *Aug. 20:* Henry I defeats Louis VI and William Clito at Brémule.	**1104.** Henry V deserts his father. **1105.** Henry IV captured by his son; abdicates. **1106.** Henry IV flees; *d. Aug. 7.* **1106-1125.** Lothair of Supplinburg, Duke of Saxony. **1110.** Henry V marches to Italy. **1111.** *Apr. 13:* Henry V crowned Emperor in Rome. Matilda of Tuscany appoints Henry her heir. **1112.** *Sept.:* Synod of Vienne excommunicates Henry V. **1114.** *Jan. 7:* Henry V marries Matilda, daughter of Henry I of England. Rebellion in Saxony. **1115.** *Feb. 11:* Lothair of Saxony defeats imperial troops at Welfesholz. *July 24:* Matilda of Tuscany *d.* **1115-1131.** Stephen II, King of Hungary. **1116.** Henry V occupies Tuscany. **1117.** *Mar. 25:* Henry V crowned Emperor. **1118.** *Apr. 7:* Gelasius II excommunicates Henry V. **1119-1127.** Charles the Good, Count of Flanders.	**1104-1108.** Bohemond, Prince of Antioch, wages war in Epirus against Byzantium. **1109.** Tripoli made independent principality under Count of Toulouse. **1110.** Crusade of Sigurd, King of Norway. **1113-1125.** Vladimir II Monomach, Grand Duke of Kiev. **1115.** State of Chin established in Northern China. **1118-1131.** Baldwin II, King of Jerusalem. **1118-1143.** John II Comnenus, Eastern Emperor.

IV. ECCLESIASTICAL HISTORY	V. CONSTITUTIONAL AND ECONOMIC HISTORY	VI. CULTURAL LIFE
1104. Bishopric of Lund separated from Hamburg and made archbishopric.		**1104-1108.** Simeon of Durham: *Historia Dunelmensis Ecclesiae.*
	1105. Colonization of Eastern Germany begins.	
1106. End of investiture strife in France. Paschal II approves Order of Fontevrault.		
1107. *Aug.*: Anselm of Canterbury and Henry I compromise over investiture.		
1109. Creation of diocese of Ely. *Apr. 21*: Anselm *d.*; Canterbury vacant five years.	**1109-1111.** Ordinance of Henry I regulates and strengthens shire and hundred courts.	**1109.** Anselm of Canterbury, author of *Cur Deus Homo, Monologion, Proslogion, d.*
1109-1122. Pontius, Abbot of Cluny.		
ca. **1110.** Bishopric of Greenland established.	**1111.** Alexius grants commercial privileges to Pisa. *Aug. 14*: Imperial Charter for city of Speier.	**1110.** Henry of Maine, *De Imagini Mundi.* Theobald of Etampes known as the first teacher at Oxford. Nestor of Kiev *d.*, author of the first Russian chronicle.
1111. *Feb. 4*: Treaty of Sutri; Henry V renounces investiture, Paschal II surrenders regalia. *Feb. 12*: Henry V imprisons Paschal. *Apr. 12*: Paschal concedes investiture to Henry V.		
1113. St. Bernard joins Cistercian Order. Scone monastery founded by Alexander I.	**1113-1118.** Compilation of *Leges Henrici.*	**1113.** St. Bernard enters the convent of Citeaux. Peter Abelard opens a school for rhetoric, philosophy and theology at Paris.
1114-1123. Ralf of Escures, Archbishop of Canterbury.		
1115. *June 25*: Foundation of Clairvaux; St. Bernard first Abbot (**-1153**).		**1115.** Chancellor Bernard reorganizes Chartres school.
1116. Paschal II withdraws concessions to Henry V.		
1118. Order of Templars founded. Jedburgh monastery founded by Earl David.		
1118-1119. Pope Gelasius II (John of Gaeta); **1118-1121.** Imperial anti-pope Gregory VIII (Maurice, Archbishop of Braga).		
1119-1124. Pope Calixtus II (Guy, Archbishop of Vienne).		**1119.** Guido the Geographer, *Geographia*, an encyclopaedia, with two maps of Italy and of the world.
1119. *Dec. 23*: Calixtus II confirms Cistercian *Carta Caritatis.*		

I. WESTERN EUROPE	II. CENTRAL EUROPE	III. EASTERN EUROPE, ISLAM, ASIA
1120. Peace between Henry I and Louis VI. *Nov. 25:* Henry I's sons drowned off Harfleur.		
	1121. Würzburg meeting of German princes to effect a compromise between Emperor and Pope.	
1122-1152. Suger, Abbot of St. Denis, leading French statesman.	**1122.** *Sept. 23:* Concordat of Worms ends German Investiture struggle; Henry V absolved.	**1122.** Byzantines exterminate Patzinaks.
1123-1125. Last rebellion in Normandy, headed by William Clito.	**1123.** Conrad of Wettin created Margrave of Meissen.	**1123.** John II defeats Serbians.
1123-1139. William of Corbeuil, Archbishop of Canterbury.		
1124. *Apr. 22:* Alexander I of Scotland *d.;* succeeded by David I (-**1153**).	**1124.** Henry V aids Henry I of England in his French campaign.	**1124.** Christians capture Tyre. John II defeats Hungarians.
	1125. *May 23:* Henry V *d. Aug. 30:* Lothair of Saxony elected King (-**1137**).	**1125.** Almohades conquer Morocco.
1126. *Dec. 25:* English barons accept Matilda as future sovereign.	**1126-1139.** Henry the Proud, Duke of Bavaria, son-in-law of Lothair.	
1126-1157. Alfonso VII, King of Castile and Leon.	**1127.** *Mar. 2:* Charles of Flanders murdered. *Dec. 18:* Conrad, Duke of Swabia, elected antiking.	**1127 - 1146.** Imadeddin Zengi, ruler of Mosul.
1128. *June 17:* Empress Matilda marries Geoffrey of Anjou. *Aug.:* William Clito of Normandy *d.*	**1128.** *Aug. 22:* Honorius II invests Roger II with Apulia.	
1128-1185. Alfonso I, King of Portugal.	**1128-1130.** Conrad, crowned King of Italy (*June 29*), reigns in Italy.	
1129-1155. Swerker I, King of Sweden.	**1128-1168.** Thierry of Alsace, Count of Flanders.	
1130. Henry I and Louis VI support Innocent II at instigation of St. Bernard.	**1130.** *Sept. 27:* Anacletus II invests Roger II with Sicily. *Dec. 25:* Roger crowned King.	
1131. *Sept. 8:* English barons renew oath of succession to Matilda. *Oct. 13:* Philip, heir to French throne, *d. Oct. 25:* Louis VII made co-regent.	**1131-1141.** Bela II, King of Hungary.	**1131-1143.** Fulk of Anjou, King of Jerusalem.
	1132. Lothair conducts Innocent II to Rome, at St. Bernard's instigation.	
	1133. *June 4:* Lothair crowned Emperor and invested with Tuscany by Innocent II. Sardinia and half Corsica assigned to Pisa, other half of Corsica to Genoa, by Innocent II.	
1134. *Sept. 7:* Moors defeat and kill Alfonso of Aragon at Fraga.	**1134.** Lothair invests Albert the Bear with Nordmark.	
1135. Alfonso VII of Castile assumes title of Emperor. *Dec. 1:* Henry I *d.;* succeeded by Stephen of Blois, his nephew (-**1154**).	**1135.** Frederick of Swabia and King Conrad submit to Lothair. King of Denmark and Duke of Poland do homage to Lothair.	

IV. ECCLESIASTICAL HISTORY	V. CONSTITUTIONAL AND ECONOMIC HISTORY	VI. CULTURAL LIFE
1120. Norbert, Count of Xanten, founds Prémontré monastery. Earl David consecrated Bishop of Bangor. **1121.** Gregory VIII imprisoned and put into a monastery.	**1120.** Freiburg, Breisgau, founded.	**1121.** Synod of Soissons condemns Abelard's philosophy.
1122. Pontius, Abbot of Cluny, deposed; succeeded by Peter the Venerable (**-1156**). **1123.** *Mar.*: First Lateran Council; confirms Worms Concordat; suppresses simony and marriage of priests. **1124-1130.** Pope Honorius II (Lambert de Fagniano). **1124.** Otto, Bishop of Bamberg, begins to christianize Pomerania.	**1122.** Henry I creates Earldom of Gloucester for his son, Robert of Caen. **1123.** Louis VI establishes a commune at Corbie.	**1123.** Foundation of the priory and hospital of St. Bartholomew, Smithfield, London.
1126-1134. Norbert of Xanten, Archbishop of Magdeburg.	**1126.** Venetian commercial privileges in Eastern Empire renewed. Louis VI establishes a commune at St. Riquier.	**1126.** Bernard of Clairvaux, *On the Love of God.*
1128. Abbey of Holyrood founded by David I.		**1128-1133.** Vault over the nave of Durham Cathedral built.
	1129-1130. First Pipe Roll.	**1129.** Simeon of Durham, *Historia Regum.*
1130-1143. Pope Innocent II (Cardinal Deacon Gregory); expelled from Rome by Roger II. **1130-1138.** Anti-pope Anacletus II (Cardinal Priest Peter Pierleoni). **1131.** Gilbertine Order founded at Sempringham.	**1130-1133.** Henry I gives a Charter to London. **1131.** Lothair acts as Marshal to the Pope.	
1132-1169. Gerhoh, Provost of Reichersberg. **1133.** Creation of diocese of Carlisle.		**1133.** Robert Pullus teaches at Oxford. Foundation of St. Bartholomew's Fair, London.
1135. *May 30-June 6*: Council of Pisa: St. Bernard successfully pleads cause of Innocent II.		**1134-1150.** Western façade of Chartres Cathedral built.

I. WESTERN EUROPE	II. CENTRAL EUROPE	III. EASTERN EUROPE, ISLAM, ASIA
1136. *Jan. 1:* General rising in South Wales under Gruffyd ap Cynan. *Feb.*: Agreement of Durham: David of Scotland acknowledges Stephen as King.	**1136-1137.** Second Italian expedition of Lothair; conquest of Apulia.	
1137. Successful expedition of Stephen against Geoffrey of Anjou. Gruffyd *d.*; succeeded by Owain the Great (**-1170**). *Aug. 1:* Louis VI *d.*; succeeded by Louis VII (**-1180**), married to Eleanor of Aquitaine. Union of Aragon and Catalonia.	**1137.** Pisans sack Amalfi. *Dec. 4:* Lothair *d.*	**1137.** Raymond of Antioch becomes Byzantine vassal. John II defeats Armenians.
1137-1146. Eric III, King of Denmark.		
1138. *Aug. 22:* Stephen defeats David of Scotland near Northallerton (Battle of the Standard).	**1138.** *Mar. 7:* Conrad III elected King, opposed by Henry the Proud, who loses Saxony to Albert the Bear.	
1139. *Sept. 30:* Matilda lands at Arundel; civil war breaks out. Geoffrey of Anjou begins conquest of Normandy. Alfonso I of Portugal (**1139-1185**) becomes papal vassal.	**1139.** Henry the Proud loses Bavaria to Leopold, Margrave of Austria. *Oct. 20:* Henry the Proud *d.*, leaving Henry the Lion his heir.	
1140. Navarre made vassalage of Aragon.	**1140-1197.** Vladislav II of Bohemia.	
1141. *Feb. 2:* Stephen captured at Lincoln. *Mar. 3:* Matilda proclaimed Queen at Winchester. *Dec. 25:* Stephen, exchanged for Robert of Gloucester, crowned at Canterbury.	**1141-1161.** Geiza II, King of Hungary.	**1141-1143.** Abbot of Cluny sponsors first Latin translation of the Koran.
1142. Henry, son of Matilda, comes to England.	**1142.** Saxony restored to Henry the Lion, Bavaria to Henry Jasomirgott, husband of the widow of Henry the Proud.	**1142.** Manuel I allies with Conrad III. China made tributary to Chin.
1143. Portugal made kingdom, with papal consent.	**1143.** Eastern Holsatia Germanized; Count Adolf founds Lübeck.	**1143-1180.** Manuel I, Eastern Emperor.
1144. Geoffrey of Anjou created Duke of Normandy.		**1144-1163.** Baldwin III, King of Jerusalem.
		1144. *Dec. 25:* Zengi takes Edessa.
1146. Alfonso VII of Castile takes Cordoba.	**1146-1173.** Boleslav IV, Duke of Poland.	**1146-1174.** Nureddin, Sultan of Syria.
1147. Louis VII joins the Crusade. *Oct. 25:* Alfonso I of Portugal takes Lisbon. Matilda leaves England.	**1147.** Conrad III joins the Crusade, has his son Henry elected King. Henry the Lion conquers Mecklenburg.	**1147-1149.** Second Crusade.
1148. Raymond Berengar IV of Catalonia takes Tortosa.	**1148-1150.** Guelph VI, brother of Henry the Proud, rebels.	**1147.** Crusaders perish in Asia Minor. First mention of Moscow.
		1148. *July:* Crusaders defeated before Damascus. Normans subdue Tunis and Tripoli.

IV. ECCLESIASTICAL HISTORY	V. CONSTITUTIONAL AND ECONOMIC HISTORY	VI. CULTURAL LIFE
1136. David I founds Melrose Abbey.		**1136.** Hospital of St. Cross, Winchester, founded.
1137. Creation of bishopric of Aberdeen.		**1137.** Mayence Cathedral completed. **1137-1144.** Suger builds Abbey Church of St. Denis. **1137-1158.** Otto, Bishop of Freising (half-brother of Conrad III), author of *De duabus civitatibus* and *Gesta Friderici I.*
1138-1161. Theobald, Archbishop of Canterbury.		
1139. *Apr.*: Second Lateran Council: ends schism, condemns Arnold of Brescia. *July 22*: Innocent II captured by Roger II; recognizes Norman kingdom. **1140.** Creation of the exempt diocese of Wollin (*ca.* **1180** moved to Cammin). **1141.** Hugh of St. Victor, ecclesiastical writer, *d.*	**1140.** Assizes of Ariano, Sicilian law-code.	**1140.** Synod of Sens condemns Abelard. Western façade of Rochester Cathedral begun. **1141.** Thierry, brother of Bernard, appointed Chancellor of Chartres school; establishes scientific and classical studies. Ordericus Vitalis: *Historia Ecclesiastica.*
1142-1154. Gilbert de la Porrée, Bishop of Poitiers.		**1142.** *Apr. 21*: Peter Abelard, author of *Sic et non* and *Historia Calamitatum, d.*
1143-1144. Pope Celestine II (Guido de Castello). **1144-1145.** Pope Lucius II (Gerard). **1144.** *Oct.*: Republican regime established in Rome, under Arnold of Brescia. **1145-1153.** Pope Eugene III (Petrus Bernardus), pupil of St. Bernard. **1145.** *Dec. 1*: Eugene III proclaims a crusade. **1146.** *Mar. 31*: St. Bernard preaches crusade at Vezelay. **1147.** *June 20*: Eugene III decides against claim of Bishop of St. David's to be independent of Canterbury. **1148.** Council of Reims; Gilbert de la Porrée recants his doctrines.	**1143.** First foundation of Lübeck.	**1143.** William of Malmesbury, author of *Gesta Pontificum Anglorum* and *Gesta Regum Anglorum, d.* **1146-1148.** Nivardus of Ghent: *Ysengrinus.* **1147.** Geoffrey of Monmouth: *Historia Regum Britanniae.* **1148.** *Landnámabók*, Icelandic chronicle, family saga.

I. WESTERN EUROPE	II. CENTRAL EUROPE	III. EASTERN EUROPE, ISLAM, ASIA
1149. Louis VII allies with Roger II and returns to France. Raymond Berengar takes Lerida. **1150-1160.** Eric the Saint, King of Sweden. **1151.** *Sept. 7:* Geoffrey of Anjou *d.*; Henry succeeds to Anjou and Touraine. **1152.** *Jan. 13:* Suger, Abbot of St. Denis, *d. Mar.:* Louis VII divorces Eleanor. *May:* Henry of Anjou marries Eleanor and renews war against Stephen. **1153.** *May 24:* David I of Scotland *d.*; succeeded by his grandson, Malcolm IV (**-1165**). *Aug. 18:* Eustace, son of Stephen, *d. Nov. 7:* Treaty of Wallingford: Stephen recognizes Henry as successor. **1154.** *Oct. 25:* Stephen *d. Dec. 19:* Henry II crowned (**-1189**); Thomas Becket, Chancellor. **1155.** Hadrian IV bestows Ireland on Henry II. **1156.** Henry II suppresses revolt of his brother, Geoffrey, in Anjou and Touraine. **1157.** Successful expeditions of Henry II against Owain and Malcolm IV, who cedes Northumberland, Cumberland, and Westmorland. Castile and Leon separated. **1157-1182.** Valdemar I the Great, King of Denmark. **1158.** Second Welsh expedition of Henry II, who gains overlordship of Deheubarth and Gwynedd. On death of Geoffrey of Anjou, Henry II gains overlordship of Brittany. **1159.** Louis VII defends Toulouse against Henry II and Malcolm IV. **1160.** Malcolm IV finally subdues Galloway.	**1149.** Conrad III returns from the Crusade. **1150.** Albert the Bear inherits Brandenburg. King Henry *d.* **1152.** *Feb. 15:* Conrad III *d. Mar. 4:* Frederick I Barbarossa, nephew of Conrad III, elected King (**-1190**). Guelph VI obtains Tuscany and Spoleto. **1153.** *Mar. 23:* Treaty of Constance: Frederick I and Eugene III ally against Roger II and Arnold of Brescia. **1154.** Frederick I recognizes Henry the Lion as Duke of Bavaria and marches to Italy. **1154-1166.** William I, King of Sicily. **1155.** Arnold of Brescia hanged. *June 18:* Frederick I crowned Emperor. **1156.** Conrad, Frederick's brother, invested with the Palatinate. *June:* Frederick marries Beatrice, heiress of Upper Burgundy. *Sept. 17:* Austria made a Duchy with special privileges. **1157.** Poland subdued, loses Pomerania. *Oct.:* Diet of Besançon; political defeat of Papacy. Eric of Sweden conquers Finland. **1158.** *Jan. 11:* Frederick I creates Ladislaus II King of Bohemia. Frederick's second Italian expedition against cities of Lombardy. **1160.** *Jan.:* Frederick I captures Crema. **1160-1162.** Henry the Lion subdues Wends.	**1149.** Normans attack Byzantine Empire, lose Corfu. **1150.** Alauddin Husain, Sultan of Ghor, destroys Empire of Ghazni. **1153.** Normans take Bona, Tunis. **1154.** Nureddin takes Damascus **1154-1184.** George III, King of Georgia; Georgian power and civilization at their height. **1155.** Manuel I attacks Normans in Southern Italy. **1156.** *May 28:* Normans take Brindisi. *Sept.:* Hungary recognizes Byzantine overlordship. **1157-1174.** Andrew Bogoljubsky, Prince of Suzdal. **1158.** Peace between Manuel I and William I of Sicily. **1160.** *Jan.:* Normans expelled from North Africa.

IV. ECCLESIASTICAL HISTORY	V. CONSTITUTIONAL AND ECONOMIC HISTORY	VI. CULTURAL LIFE
1150. Compilation of *Decretum Gratiani*. Bishoprics of Dunblane and Brechin founded.		
1152. Archbishopric of Nidaros established in Norway.		
1153-1154. Pope Anastasius IV (Conrad de Suburra). **1153.** *Aug. 20*: Bernard of Clairvaux *d*.		
1154-1159. Pope Hadrian IV (Nicholas Breakspeare, only English Pope); quarrel between Emperor and Pope renewed.		**1154.** Edrisi: *Geography*. End of the *Anglo-Saxon Chronicle*. **1154-1181.** Ripon Cathedral built.
	1155. Henry II abolishes fiscal earldoms and resumes royal demesnes. **1156.** Rainald of Dassel appointed Imperial Chancellor.	**1155.** Wace: *Roman de Brut*.
1156. Carmelite Order and Order of the Knights of Alcantara founded.		
	1157. Privileges granted to German merchants in England.	
1158. Order of the Knights of Calatrava founded.	**1158.** *Nov.*: Diet of Roncaglia, defines Imperial rights in Italy. Henry the Lion founds Munich and Lübeck.	
1159-1181. Pope Alexander III (Cardinal Chancellor Roland of Siena). **1159-1164.** Imperial anti-pope Victor IV (Cardinal Octavian of Tusculum). **1159-1167.** Rainald of Dassel, Archbishop of Cologne. **1160.** Imperial Council at Pavia; Papal Synod at Toulouse. France sides with Alexander III.	**1159.** Henry II accepts scutage (shield money) in place of feudal military service.	**1159.** John of Salisbury: *Policraticus* (on statesmanship, dedicated to Thomas Becket). **1159-1160.** Peter Lombard, Bishop of Paris; from **1140** teacher at Paris University. *ca.* **1160.** *Ludus de Antichristo*, Tegernsee. Benoit de St. Maur: *Roman de Troie*. **1160-1170.** Walter Map, Anglo-Latin lyrical poet.

I. WESTERN EUROPE	II. CENTRAL EUROPE	III. EASTERN EUROPE, ISLAM, ASIA
1161-1184. Magnus VI, King of Norway.		
1162-1170. Thomas Becket, Archbishop of Canterbury. **1162-1196.** Alfonso II of Aragon. **1163.** Quarrel between Henry II and Thomas Becket. **1164.** *Nov. 2*: Becket flees to France.	**1162.** *Mar.* : Frederick I destroys Milan and returns to Germany. **1163.** Third expedition of Frederick I to Italy. Peace with Poland. **1164.** *July 6*: Adolf II, Count of Holstein, killed in victorious campaign against Slavs.	**1162-1173.** Amalric I, King of Jerusalem.
1165. Great invasion of Wales by Henry II fails. *Dec. 9*: Malcolm IV *d.*; succeeded by his brother, William the Lion (**-1214**). **1166.** Brittany does homage to Henry II. Dermot, King of Leinster, appeals to Henry II for help against his Irish rivals.	**1165.** *May*: Diet of Würzburg; Frederick I definitely declares against Alexander. Alliance between Henry II and Frederick I. **1166.** Fourth Italian expedition of Frederick I. War between Henry the Lion and Albert the Bear. **1166-1189.** William II, King of Sicily. **1167.** *May 28*: Frederick I defeats Romans at Tusculum. *Aug. 1*: Frederick crowned Emperor. *Aug. 2*: Plague in Frederick's army; Rainald and Guelph VII *d. Dec.*: Rising of Lombard League compels Frederick to return. **1168.** Milan rebuilt. Alessandria founded. Frederick reconciles Henry the Lion and Albert. Valdemar I subdues Rügen. Henry the Lion marries Matilda, daughter of Henry II of England.	**1165.** Byzantium allies with Venice against Frederick I.
1169. *Jan. 6*: Peace between Henry II and Louis VII. Norman nobles begin conquest of Ireland. **1170.** *July 22*: Henry II and Becket formally reconciled. *Nov. 23*: Owain *d. Dec. 3*: Becket returns to Canterbury. *Dec. 29*: Becket murdered by 4 Norman knights. **1171.** *Oct. 16*: Henry II lands in Ireland. *Nov. 12*: Henry II acknowledged Lord of Ireland. **1172.** Queen Eleanor raises Aquitaine against Henry II.	**1169.** *Aug. 15*: Henry VI elected King of the Romans. **1170.** *Nov. 18*: Albert the Bear *d.* **1172.** Pilgrimage of Henry the Lion to Palestine.	**1169.** Nureddin of Damascus invades Egypt. Kiev incorporated in Suzdal. **1169-1193.** Saladin of Damascus. **1171.** Saladin subdues Egypt.

IV. ECCLESIASTICAL HISTORY	V. CONSTITUTIONAL AND ECONOMIC HISTORY	VI. CULTURAL LIFE
1161. Canonization of Edward the Confessor. (Translation *Oct. 13, 1163*). **1161-1165.** Alexander III expelled from Rome, goes to France. **1162.** *Aug.*: German-French agreement on schism fails.	**1162-1179.** Richard de Lucy, Justiciar of England.	**1161-1165.** The German Archipoeta.
		1163-1235. Notre Dame, Paris, built.
1164. Alexander III approves Order of Calatrava. Norwegian Church organized (clergy privileged). Archbishopric of Upsala established in Sweden. **1164-1168.** Imperial anti-pope Paschal III (Guy, Bishop of Crema). **1165.** *Nov. 23*: Normans conduct Alexander III back to Rome. *Dec. 29*: Canonization of Charlemagne.	**1164.** *Jan.*: Constitutions of Clarendon; limitation of ecclesiastical jurisdiction. **1166.** Assize of Clarendon, establishes the Grand Jury.	**1164.** Gautier d'Arras: *Eracle.* **1165-1175.** Marie de France: *Lais.*
1167. Council of Albigenses at Toulouse.		**1167-1168.** Oxford University founded.
1168-1178. Imperial anti-pope Calixtus III.		
	1169. Towns represented in the Cortes of Castile.	
1170. Alexander III establishes rules for canonization of Saints.	**1170.** 'Inquest of Sheriffs', financial inquiry, results in strengthening the Exchequer.	*c.* **1170.** Thomas of Brittany: *Roman de Tristan.*
1171. *Jan. 25*: Interdict on Henry II's continental possessions. **1172.** *May 21*: Henry II reconciled with Papacy (right of appeal to Rome conceded). Council of Cashel: Irish clergy brought under authority of Rome.	**1171.** *Mar. 12*: Manuel I confiscates goods of Venetian merchants.	**1172.** Wace: *Roman de Rou.* **1172-1219.** Palazzo della Ragione built at Padua.

I. WESTERN EUROPE	II. CENTRAL EUROPE	III. EASTERN EUROPE, ISLAM, ASIA
1173. *Jan.*: Henry II arbitrates between Aragon and Toulouse; Toulouse becomes dependent on him. Henry's sons rebel against their father in alliance with France and Scotland. Queen Eleanor imprisoned (**-1189**).	**1173-1196.** Belą III, King of Hungary.	**1173-1185.** Baldwin IV, King of Jerusalem.
1174. *July 12*: Henry II does penance at Canterbury. *July 13*: William the Lion captured, does homage to Henry. *Sept. 30*: Treaty of Montlouis between Henry II and Louis VII ends conspiracy against Henry.	**1174.** Fifth Italian expedition of Frederick I, who buys Tuscany, Spoleto, Sardinia, and Corsica from Guelph VI. **1175.** *Apr. 16*: Treaty of Montebello between Frederick I and Lombard League; jeopardized by Alexander III. **1176.** Henry the Lion refuses to help Frederick. *May 29*: Lombards defeat Frederick at Legnano. *Nov.*: Preliminary peace of Anagni between Emperor and Pope.	**1175.** Muhammad of Ghor begins to invade India. **1176.** Saladin conquers Syria. Manuel I defeated by Seljuks at Myriokephalon.
1177. Henry II arbitrates between Kings of Castile and Navarre. Prince John made Lord of Ireland. Treaty of Ivry between Henry II and Louis VII. **1177-1202.** Sverrir, King of Norway; period of civil war. **1178.** Henry II and Louis VII meet and arrange a crusade.	**1177.** *July 22*: Peace of Venice between Emperor and Pope.	
1179. *Nov. 1*: Philip, Louis VII's son, appointed co-regent.	**1178.** *July 30*: Frederick I crowned King of Burgundy. Trial of Henry the Lion. **1179.** Guelph VI sells his Swabian territories to Frederick.	
1180. *June 28*: Treaty of Gisors between Henry II and Philip. *Sept. 18*: Louis VII *d.*; succeeded by Philip II Augustus (**-1223**).	**1180.** *Jan.*: Henry the Lion outlawed, loses his imperial fiefs. *Apr. 13*: Westphalia given to Cologne, Saxony to Bernard of Anhalt; *Sept.*: Bavaria, from which Styria is separated, to Otto of Wittelsbach.	**1180-1183.** Alexius II Comnenus, Eastern Emperor.
1181. Second rebellion of Henry II's sons.	**1181.** Henry the Lion submits, keeps Brunswick, is exiled for 3 years, goes to England.	
1182. Jews expelled from France. **1182-1202.** Canute VI, King of Denmark. **1183.** *June 11*: Prince Henry, eldest son of Henry II, *d.*; end of rebellion.	**1182.** Florentines acquire Empoli. **1183.** *June 25*: Peace of Constance; Lombard League recognized under imperial overlordship.	**1183.** Saladin takes Aleppo. Alexius II murdered. **1183-1185.** Andronicus I Comnenus, Eastern Emperor. **1184.** Cyprus frees herself from Byzantium.
1184. Third rebellion of Henry II's sons.	**1184.** *May*: Diet of Mayence; Frederick's power at its height.	**1184-1212.** Tamara, Queen of Georgia.

IV. ECCLESIASTICAL HISTORY	V. CONSTITUTIONAL AND ECONOMIC HISTORY	VI. CULTURAL LIFE
1173. *Feb. 21*: Canonization of Thomas Becket. Waldensian movement begins.		**1173.** Chrestien de Troyes: *Yvain.*
		1174. Choir of Canterbury Cathedral built by William of Sens. Campanile of Pisa built.
		1174-1226. Laon Cathedral built.
1175. Order of the Knights of St. James of Compostela founded. Archbishop of York claims obedience from Scottish bishops.	**1175.** Treaty of Windsor: Rory O'Connor acknowledges Henry II as lord of Ireland.	**1175.** Latin translation of Avicenna.
1176. *Jan. 25*: Scottish bishops assert independence of jurisdiction of York. Petrus Waldes begins preaching at Lyons.	**1176.** Assize of Northampton; organization of judicial districts. First Eisteddfod (?).	**1176-1209.** London Bridge built (stood till **1832**).
		1176. Eisteddfod held at Cardigan Castle, Wales.
	1178-1179. Richard Fitznigel: *Dialogus de Scaccario*, system of English financial administration.	
1179. *Mar.*: Third Lateran Council: decrees on elections of Popes and Bishops. *Sept. 17*: Hildegard of Bingen, mystic nun, *d.*	**1179.** Grand Assize of Windsor, checks feudal courts in favour of King's court. Venetian privileges in Eastern Empire again confirmed.	
	1180. Ranulf de Glanville appointed Chief Justiciar of England; judicial reforms.	**1180.** John of Salisbury, Bishop of Chartres, *d.*
		c. **1180.** Chrestien de Troyes: *Conte del graal.*
1181-1185. Pope Lucius III (Cardinal Bishop Ubald of Ostia).	**1181.** Assize of Arms; reorganizes militia.	
1181. First Carthusian monastery in England, at Witham. Crusade against Albigenses.		
1182. St. Francis of Assisi born.	**1182.** Jews banished from France.	
1184. Negotiations between Emperor and Pope at Verona fail.	**1184.** Assize of Woodstock concerning royal forests.	

I. WESTERN EUROPE

1185-1211. Sancho I, King of Portugal.
1185. Philip II wars against Flanders; gains Amiens and Vermandois.

1186. *Aug. 19:* Geoffrey of Brittany, younger son of Henry II, *d.*

1187. Richard and John rebel against their father.

1188. *Nov. 18:* Richard allies with Philip II and does homage to him for Aquitaine.
1189. Henry II loses Berry to Philip II. *July 6:* Henry II *d.*; succeeded by Richard I (-1199). *Dec. 5:* Richard I acknowledges independence of Scotland; sells Roxburgh and Berwick to William the Lion.
1190. *July 1:* Richard and Philip start on the Third Crusade. *Oct. 4:* Richard storms Messina.

1191. *Apr.:* Richard conquers Cyprus and sells it to Templars. *June:* Philip returns to France and annexes Péronne.
1192. *Oct.:* Richard returns from Palestine. *Dec. 21:* Richard captured by Leopold, Duke of Austria.

1193. *Feb. 14:* Richard surrendered to Henry VI; imprisoned at Trifels. Philip II attacks Normandy.
1194. *Feb. 3:* Richard released. *Apr. 17:* Second coronation of Richard I. *July 22:* Richard defeats Philip at Fréteval.
1194-1240. Llywelyn Fawr the Great, prince of Gwynnedd.

II. CENTRAL EUROPE

1185. Quarrel between Emperor and Pope renewed.

1186. *Jan. 27:* Henry VI marries Constance, heiress of Sicily, and assumes title of Caesar.

1188. *Aug.:* Henry the Lion exiled again.

1189. *Apr. 3:* Peace of Strasbourg between Emperor and Pope. *May:* Frederick sets out on Third Crusade. *Nov. 18:* William II of Sicily *d.*; succeeded by Tancred the Bastard.

1190. *June 10:* Frederick I drowned in river Saleph in Cilicia. Henry the Lion returns to Germany. *July:* Henry VI makes peace with Henry the Lion.
1191. *Apr. 14:* Henry VI crowned Emperor. Expedition against Sicily fails.

1192. Albert, bishop elect of Liége, murdered by Imperial Knights. Alliance of the Guelphs, Brabant and Cologne against Henry VI. Styria united with Austria.

1194. *Feb. 20:* Tancred *d.* Henry VI conquers Sicily. *Dec. 25:* Henry VI crowned King of Sicily. *Dec. 26:* Frederick II born.
1194-1227. Lesko V, the White, Duke of Poland.
1195. Henry VI seizes Meissen. *Aug. 6:* Henry the Lion *d.*

III. EASTERN EUROPE, ISLAM, ASIA

1185. Norman invasion of Eastern Empire fails.
1185-1195. Isaac II Angelus, Eastern Emperor.
1185-1186. Baldwin V, King of Jerusalem.
1186-1188. Bulgaria frees herself from Byzantium.
1186-1333. Kamakura Era in Japan.
1186-1187. Guy of Lusignan, King of Jerusalem.
1187. *July 4:* Saladin defeats Christians at Hittin. *Oct. 2:* Saladin takes Jerusalem. Muhammad of Ghor conquers Punjab.

1189-1193. Third Crusade.

1190. Frederick I conquers Iconium.

1191. *July 12:* Crusaders take Acre.
1191-1192. Conrad of Montferrat, King of Jerusalem.
1192. King Conrad murdered; succeeded by Henry II (-1198). *Sept. 1:* Truce between Richard I and Saladin. Muhammad of Ghor defeats Hindu League at Tarain.
1192-1219. Shogunate of Minamoto family in Japan (Yoritomo, first Shogun).
1193. *Mar. 4:* Saladin *d.* Zen order founded in Japan.

1195. Armenia and Cyprus recognise Henry VI as their overlord. Isaac II deposed by his brother Alexius.

IV. ECCLESIASTICAL HISTORY	V. CONSTITUTIONAL AND ECONOMIC HISTORY	VI. CULTURAL LIFE
1185-1187. Pope Urban III (Hubert Crivelli).		**1185 - 1200.** Lincoln Cathedral built. *Igor's Campaign*, Russian epic.
1186. Livonia christianized.		**1186.** Chichester Cathedral begun.
1187. Pope Gregory VIII (Albert of Morra). Welsh Church placed under authority of Canterbury. **1187 - 1191.** Pope Clement III (Paul Scolari).		**1187-1230.** Walter von der Vogelweide, lyrical and political poet.
	1188. *Sept. 19*: Frederick I's Charter for Lübeck. Saladin tithe in England. **1189-1212.** Henry Fitzaylwin, first Mayor of London. **1189.** Commercial treaty between Novgorod and German merchants.	
1190. Order of German Hospitallers founded (**1198** transformed into Teutonic Order).		*ca.* **1190.** Chrestien de Troyes, author of *Lancelot, Yvain, Guillaume d'Angleterre, Perceval, d.*
1191 - 1198. Pope Celestine III (Jacinto Bobo).	**1191.** *Oct. 8*: King John grants the Commune of London.	**1191-1204.** *Nibelungenlied.*
1192. Cencius, Papal Chamberlain, begins *Liber Censuum*, record of papal administration.		
	1193-1198. Hubert Walter, Chief Justiciar of England (*d.* **1205**).	**1193.** Benedict of Peterborough *d.*; author of *Gesta Henrici II*. Richard of Devizes: *Gesta Ricardi I.*
	1194. Privileges granted to German merchants in England.	
		1195-1196. Ambrose: *L'estoire de la guerre sainte.*

I. WESTERN EUROPE	II. CENTRAL, NORTHERN AND EASTERN EUROPE	III. ISLAM AND ASIA
1196. William the Lion defeats Harold, Earl of Orkney. Philip II obtains Gisors, Vexin and Auvergne from Richard I. **1196-1213.** Peter II, King of Aragon.	**1196.** *Apr.*: Henry VI attempts to make kingship hereditary. *Dec. 25*: Frederick II elected King. **1196-1204.** Emeric I, King of Hungary.	**1195-1203.** Alexius III, Eastern Emperor. **1196.** Alexius III pays tribute to Henry VI. Muhammad of Ghor conquers Gwalior and Gujarat.
1198. War between Richard and Philip renewed.	**1197-1230.** Otakar I of Bohemia. **1197.** Henry VI puts down a rebellion in Sicily. *Sept. 28*: Henry VI d. **1198.** *Mar. 8*: Philip, Duke of Swabia, brother of Henry VI, *June 9*: Otto, Duke of Saxony, son of Henry the Lion, elected Kings. Civil war in Germany. *May 17*: Frederick II crowned King of Sicily, under guardianship of Innocent III.	**1197.** Henry VI's crusaders take Beirut. Muhammad of Ghor takes Anhilwara. **1198.** *June*: Maluk el Adil makes truce with Christians till **1204**.
1199. *Apr. 6*: Richard d.; succeeded by his brother, John (-1216). Arthur, son of Geoffrey of Brittany, flees to Philip II. **1200.** *May 22*: Peace of Le Goulet between John and Philip II. Llywelyn the Great seizes Anglesey. *Nov. 22*: William the Lion does homage for his English possessions. **1201.** Rebellion in Poitou, supported by Philip, against John. Llywelyn swears fealty to John. **1202.** War breaks out between John and Philip.	**1199-1210.** Swerker II, King of Sweden. **1201.** Albert, Bishop of Livonia, founds Riga. **1202.** *Jan.*: Hohenstaufen partisans protest against papal interference, at Halle. **1202-1241.** Valdemar II of Denmark.	**1202-1204.** Fourth Crusade, directed against Constantinople by Venice.
1203. *Apr. 3* (?): John murders Arthur of Brittany.		**1203.** Jenghiz Khan defeats his rival, Ongkhan. Muhammad of Ghor completes subjection of Upper India.
1204. Philip conquers Normandy, Maine, Anjou, and Touraine; Poitou submits to Philip; Gascony remains faithful to John.	**1205.** *Jan. 6*: Philip crowned at Aix-la-Chapelle. **1205-1235.** Andrew II of Hungary. **1206.** *July 27*: Philip defeats Otto IV at Wassenberg.	**1204.** *Apr. 12*: Crusaders take Constantinople and establish Latin Empire. **1206.** *Mar.*: Muhammad of Ghor murdered; his general, Kutbuddin Ibak, establishes a Muhammedan Sultanate at Delhi (-1526). **1206-1227.** Jenghiz Khan, Emperor of the Mongols.

IV. ECCLESIASTICAL HISTORY	V. CONSTITUTIONAL AND ECONOMIC HISTORY	VI. CULTURAL LIFE
	1196. English crown lays down standards for size and quality of woollen cloth.	**1196.** Bertran de Born, Gascon poet, *d.*
1197 *Oct.*-**1198** *Feb.*: Cencius compiles Order of Coronation, programme of papal world policy. **1198.** *Jan. 8*: Lothair of Segni elected Pope Innocent III (-**1216**).	**1198.** Venetian merchants freed from customs duties in Eastern Empire.	**1198.** *Dec. 12*: Averroes, Arab philosopher, *d.* William of Newburgh: *Historia Rerum Anglicarum.*
	1199. *May 28*: Declaration of Spires: German princes confirm right of free election of King.	
1200. Innocent III claims decision between Otto IV and Philip of Germany.		**1200.** Drapers' Hall at Ypres begun. Hartmann von Aue: *Der arme Heinrich* (epic).
1201. *Mar.*: Innocent decides to support Otto IV. **1202.** Decretal *Venerabilem* asserts superiority of papacy over Empire. Albert, Bishop of Livonia, founds Order of Brethren of the Sword. Joachim, Abbot of Fiore, *d.*	**1201.** English Barons require confirmation of privileges before following John to France. **1202.** First trial of a Peer (King John) in France.	**1201.** Hartmann von Aue: *Iwein.* Roger of Hoveden: *Chronica.* **1202-1233.** Church of Heisterbach monastery built.
		1203. Wolfram of Eschenbach: *Parcival.* Siena University founded.
1204. Peter II of Aragon accepts his territory as papal fief.		**1204.** *Dec. 13*: Mose ben Maimon (Maimonides), Jewish philosopher, *d.*
1205. *Dec. 11*: John de Gray elected Archbishop of Canterbury, but refused by Innocent III. **1206.** Amalric of Bena, pantheistic mystic, *d. Dec.*: Stephen Langton elected Archbishop of Canterbury.	**1206.** Council of 24 men elected in London.	**1205.** Peire Vidal, Provençal troubadour, *d.*

I. WESTERN EUROPE	II. CENTRAL, NORTHERN, AND EASTERN EUROPE	III. ISLAM AND ASIA
1208. Llywelyn seizes Powys.	**1208.** *June 21:* Philip murdered by Otto of Wittelsbach, at Bamberg.	**1208.** Theodore Laskaris founds Empire of Nicaea.
1209. *July:* John invades Scotland. *Aug. 4:* Peace between John and William the Lion. *Oct.:* Welsh Princes do homage to John at Woodstock. Simon de Montfort overruns Languedoc.	**1209.** *Oct. 4:* Otto IV crowned Emperor at Rome.	
1210. *June:* Expedition of John to Ireland.		
1211. *May:* War between John and Llywelyn.	**1211.** Andrew of Hungary appeals to Teutonic Order for protection of Transylvania. Frederick of Sicily set up as anti-king by opposition princes and Pope.	**1211-1215.** Jenghiz Khan invades China.
1211-1223. Alfonso II of Portugal.		**1211-1236.** Iltutmish, Sultan of Delhi.
1212. *July 16:* Kings of Castile, Aragon, and Navarre defeat Moors at Navas de Tolosa.	**1212.** Venice conquers Candia (Crete). *Dec. 5:* Frederick II elected German King.	
1213. *June 3:* Truce between John and Llywelyn. *Sept. 12:* Albigenses decisively defeated at Muret, Peter II of Aragon killed; Raymond VI of Toulouse makes peace.	**1213.** *July 12:* Frederick II grants Charter of Eger to Pope. *Sept. 28:* Queen Gertrude of Hungary murdered by Magyar magnates.	
1213-1276. James I of Aragon.		
1214. *July 27:* Philip II defeats Otto IV and the English at Bouvines. English barons make truce with Philip. *Dec. 4:* William the Lion *d.*; succeeded by Alexander II (**-1249**).	**1214.** *May:* Frederick II assigns Northalbingia to Denmark. Frederick II invests Wittelsbachs with Palatinate.	
1215. *Jan. 8:* Council of Montpellier elects Simon de Montfort lord of Languedoc. John cedes Poitou, Anjou, and Brittany to France, keeping Guienne and Gascony.	**1215.** *July 25:* Frederick II generally recognized as King and crowned at Aix-la-Chapelle; vows Crusade.	
1216. *Jan.:* French aid English barons. *May:* Prince Louis of France enters London. *Oct. 19:* John *d.* at Newark. *Oct. 28:* Henry III crowned at Gloucester (reigns till **1272**).	**1216-1225.** Engelbert I, Archbishop of Cologne, leading statesman.	
1217. *May 20:* French defeat at Lincoln. *Aug. 24:* French defeat off Sandwich. *Sept. 11:* Treaty of Lambeth; French leave England.	**1217-1263.** Haakon IV of Norway.	**1217-1221.** Crusade against Egypt fails.
1217-1252. Ferdinand III of Castile.		

IV. ECCLESIASTICAL HISTORY	V. CONSTITUTIONAL AND ECONOMIC HISTORY	VI. CULTURAL LIFE
1207. King John resists election of Langton. Innocent III sides with Philip of Germany. **1208.** *Mar. 23*: England and Wales laid under interdict. Innocent III regulates public peace in Sicily. **1209.** *Nov.*: King John excommunicated. Francis of Assisi issues first rule for his brotherhood. Albigensian Crusade begins in Southern France. **1210.** *Nov. 18*: Innocent III excommunicates Otto IV.		**1207.** Reinmar the Old of Hagenau, minnesinger, *d.* **1209-1235.** Nave of Lincoln Cathedral built. *ca.* **1210.** Epic of Gudrun. Hartmann von Aue, epic poet, *d.* Gotfrid von Strassburg: *Tristan und Isolt.* **1210-1221.** North transept of Chartres Cathedral built. **1211-1241.** Reims Cathedral rebuilt.
1212. Innocent III absolves England from allegiance to John. Children's Crusade. Clara degli Scifi founds Second Order. **1213.** *May 15*: John submits to Pope, making England and Ireland papal fiefs. Philip II submits to Pope in his matrimonial dispute.	**1212.** *Sept. 26*: **Frederick II makes Bohemia a hereditary Kingdom.** **1213.** *Aug. 4*: Council of St. Albans (precursor of Parliament). *Oct.*: Peter des Roches, Chief Justiciar.	**1212.** Gervase of Tilbury: *Otia Imperialia.* Arnold of Lübeck, historiographer, *d.* **1213.** Godfrey of Villehardouin *d.*, author of *La Conqueste de Constantinople.*
		1214-1235. Nave of Wells Cathedral built.
1215. *Nov.*: Fourth Lateran Council, establishes doctrine of transubstantiation, regulates auricular confession and inquisition, prohibits trial by ordeal. **1216-1227.** Pope Honorius III (Cencius Savelli). **1216.** *Dec. 22*: Honorius confirms Dominican Order.	**1215.** *June 19*: John seals *Magna Carta,* at Runnymede. *Aug. 24*: Innocent III annuls *Magna Carta* in favour of John. *Oct.*: Barons begin civil war.	**1215.** Robert de Courçon, papal legate, issues first statutes of Paris University. **1216.** Saxo Grammaticus, Danish historiographer, *d.*
1217. Honorius regulates Beguine communities. Dominicans (Black Friars) come to England.	**1217.** *Sept. 23*: Re-issue of *Magna Carta* at Merton. *Nov. 6*: Forest Charter, mitigates Henry II's Assize of the Forest.	

I. WESTERN EUROPE	II. CENTRAL, NORTHERN, AND EASTERN EUROPE	III. ISLAM AND ASIA
1218. *Mar.*: Peace of Worcester between Henry III and Wales. *June 25*: Simon de Montfort the elder *d.*	**1218.** *May* 19: Otto IV *d.*	**1218-1224.** Jenghiz Khan conquers Khwarazm, Transoxania (**1219**), Samarkand, Bokhara, and Persia.
1219. Albigensian War renewed. William Marshal, Regent of England, *d.*	**1219.** Valdemar of Denmark conquers Estonia. Reval founded.	
1220. *May 17*: Henry III crowned at Westminster.	**1220.** Henry (VII), regent of Germany under guardianship of Engelbert of Cologne. *Nov. 22*: Frederick II crowned Emperor at Rome.	
	1221-1288. Henry the Illustrious, Margrave of Meissen.	**1221.** Mongols invade sultanate of Delhi.
		1222-1254. Nicholas Vatatzes, emperor of Nicaea.
1223. *Apr.*: Honorius III declares Henry III competent to rule. *July 14*: Philip II Augustus of France *d.*; succeeded by Louis VIII.	**1223.** *May 6-7*: Henry of Schwerin captures Valdemar of Denmark.	**1223.** *June 16*: Mongols defeat Russians at River Kalka.
1223-1245. Sancho II of Portugal.		
1224. *May 4*: France declares war on England. Louis VIII conquers Poitou.		**1224.** Vatatzes of Nicaea expels Latins from Asia Minor.
1225. *Mar.*: English secure Gascony.	**1225.** *Nov. 7*: Engelbert of Cologne murdered. Valdemar obtains release by renouncing North-albingia.	
1226. Louis VIII fails to take Avignon or Toulouse. *Nov.*: Louis VIII *d.*; succeeded by Louis IX (**-1270**; until **1236** under regency of Blanche of Castile).	**1226.** Frederick II authorizes Teutonic Order to conquer Prussia, and makes Hermann of Salza Prince of the Empire. Lombard League renewed.	
1227. *Jan. 8*: Henry III declares himself of age. Truce between France and England.	**1227.** *July 22*: Valdemar defeated by Germans at Bornhöved.	**1227.** Jenghiz Khan *d.*
1228-1232. James I of Aragon conquers Balearic Islands.		**1228.** *Sept. 7*: Frederick II lands at Acre. Civil war between Saladin's heirs.
1229. Treaty of Meaux, brings district between Rhone and Narbonne under French crown.	**1229.** *June 10*: Frederick II defeats papal troops.	**1229.** *Feb. 18*: Treaty between Frederick II and Sultan of Egypt. *Mar. 18*: Frederick crowns himself King of Jerusalem.
		1229-1241. Ughetai, Khan of Mongols.
1230. *May-Oct.*: Campaign of Henry III in France. Ferdinand III unites Leon to Castile.	**1230.** Frederick II makes peace with Pope at San Germano, and is absolved from excommunication at Ceprano.	
1231. *July 4*: 3 years' truce between England, France, and Brittany.	**1230-1253.** Wenceslas I of Bohemia.	**1231-1288.** Ertogrul, chieftain of Turks.

IV. ECCLESIASTICAL HISTORY	V. CONSTITUTIONAL AND ECONOMIC HISTORY	VI. CULTURAL LIFE
1218. Bishopric of Seckau, Styria, established.		**1218.** Amiens Cathedral begun.
1220. *Sept. 22*: Franciscans put on same basis as older monastic orders (*Cum secundum*).	**1219.** Clash between Hubert de Burgh, Justiciar since 1215, and the Poitevins. **1220.** *Apr. 26*: Frederick II issues *Confoederatio cum principibus ecclesiasticis*. Assizes of Capua and Messina reorganize Sicily.	**1220.** Nôtre Dame Cathedral, Paris, completed according to the plan of **1163**. Wolfram of Eschenbach, epic poet, *d*. Brussels Cathedral begun. **1220-1258.** Salisbury Cathedral built.
1221. *Aug. 6*: Dominic *d*. Archbishop of Canterbury appointed *Legatus Natus* of Holy See. **1222.** Constitutions of Stephen Langton promulgated at Osney. **1223.** *Nov. 29*: Honorius confirms Franciscan rule of 1221 (*Solet annuere*).	**1222.** Andrew II of Hungary issues *Golden Bull* in favour of nobles.	**1221.** Burgos Cathedral begun. **1222.** Padua University founded. **1222-1224.** Eike of Repgow: *Saxon Law-Code*. **1223.** Gerald de Barry *d*., author of *Topographia Hibernica, Expugnatio Hibernica, Itinerarium Cambriae, Gemma Ecclesiastica*. **1223-1224.** Caesarius of Heisterbach: *Dialogus Miraculorum*. **1224.** Naples University founded by Emperor Frederick II.
1224. *Sept. 10*: Franciscans (Grey Friars) come to England.	**1224.** Henry (VII) proclaims Public Peace (*Treuga Heinrici*) at Würzburg. **1225.** *Feb. 25*: Third re-issue of *Magna Carta* (this the lasting form).	**1225.** Guillaume de Loris: *Roman de la Rose*. **1225-1230.** Bartholomaeus Anglicus: *De proprietatibus rerum*.
1226. *Oct. 3*: Francis of Assisi *d*. Carmelite Order confirmed.	**1226.** Pass over St. Gotthard opened. Lübeck made Free City of Empire.	**1226.** Laon Cathedral completed.
1227-1241. Pope Gregory IX (Hugo of Segni); excommunicates Frederick II, in **1227**.	**1227.** Gold coinage resumed, in Marseilles.	**1227.** Toledo Cathedral begun.
1228. *July 9*: Stephen Langton *d*. *July 16*: Francis of Assisi canonized. **1229.** *Jan. 17*: Albert, Bishop of Riga, missionary to Baltic countries, *d*. Carmelites (White Friars) come to England.	**1228.** Fondaco dei Tedeschi built at Venice. **1229.** First commercial treaty between German merchants and Grand Duke of Smolensk.	**1228-1253.** St. Francis's Church, Assisi, built. **1229.** Toulouse University founded. Guido Faba: *Doctrina ad inveniendas materias*.
1230. *Sept. 28*: Gregory IX interprets Franciscan rule, chiefly concerning poverty (*Quo elongati*). **1231.** *June 13*: Anthony of Padua *d*. Gregory IX issues new laws against heretics. **1231-1234.** General persecution of heretics.	**1230.** Heller first coined, at Hall, Swabia. **1231.** *May 1*: *Statutum in favorem principum* checks Henry (VII)'s policy in favour of towns and constitutes German principalities. Frederick II's legislation for Sicily (Constitutions of Melfi).	**1230.** Walter von der Vogelweide, minnesinger and political poet, *d*.

I. WESTERN EUROPE	II. CENTRAL, NORTHERN, AND EASTERN EUROPE	III. ISLAM AND ASIA
	1232-1259. Ezzelino da Romano, lord of Verona, Vicenza (**1236**), Padua and Treviso (**1237**).	**1232-1272.** Muhammad I, founder of Nasrid dynasty at Granada.
1233. *Oct.*: Rebellion of Earl of Pembroke, aided by Welsh.		
1234. Theobald of Champagne cedes Chartres, Blois, and Sancerre to French crown.	**1234.** Crusade against peasants in Stedingen near Bremen. (*May 27*: battle of Altenesch.)	
	1235. Rebellion of Henry (VII) subdued ; Henry imprisoned (*d.* **1242**). Dukedom of Brunswick-Luneburg established. Frederick II declares war on Lombard League.	
1236. *Apr. 25*: Louis IX comes of age. *June 29*: Ferdinand III of Castile conquers Cordoba.	**1236 - 1263.** Alexander Nevski, Grand Duke of Novgorod and (from **1252**) Vladimir.	
1237-1238. James I of Aragon annexes Valencia and Murcia.	**1237.** *Feb.*: Conrad IV elected 'Roman King and future Emperor'. *Nov. 27*: Frederick II defeats Lombard League at Cortenuova. Teutonic Order and Knights of the Sword in Livonia united.	**1237-1240.** Mongols conquer Russia.
	1238. Enzio, Frederick II's son, made King of Sardinia. Pope, Venice, and Genoa ally against Frederick.	**1238.** Mongols take Moscow.
1239. Louis IX buys Macon; refuses papal offer to attack Emperor.	**1239.** *Mar. 20*: Gregory IX again excommunicates Frederick II.	**1239.** Mongols sack Ani, capital of Armenia.
1240-1246. Dafydd ap Llywelyn, Prince of Snowdon.	**1240.** Gregory IX proclaims Crusade against Frederick.	**1240.** Crusade of Richard of Cornwall and Simon de Montfort to Jaffa.
1241. Dafydd of Snowdon submits to Henry III. Alfonse, brother of Louis IX, invested with Poitou and Auvergne.	**1241.** *Apr. 9*: Mongols defeat Germans at Liegnitz, Silesia. *May 3*: Imperial fleet defeats Genoese off Monte Cristo.	**1241.** Ughetai, Khan of Mongols, *d.* Mongols invade Poland and Hungary.
1242. *Mar.-July*: Campaign of Henry III in Poitou; Henry defeated at Taillebourg and Saintes.		**1242.** Batu, Jenghiz Khan's grandson, establishes realm of the Golden Horde in Russia.
1243. *Apr. 7*: 5 years' truce between England and France. *Sept.*: Henry resigns claims to Poitou and cedes Isle of Rhé to France. Treaty of Lorris renews treaty of Meaux between France and Toulouse.		

IV. ECCLESIASTICAL HISTORY	V. CONSTITUTIONAL AND ECONOMIC HISTORY	VI. CULTURAL LIFE
1232. *May 20*: Anthony of Padua canonized.	**1232.** *May*: Frederick II confirms *Statutum in favorem*, at Cividale. *July 29*: Hubert de Burgh dismissed; Peter des Roches, Henry III's chief adviser.	
1233. Penitentiary movement (*Great Hallelujah*) in Upper Italy. *July 20*: Gregory entrusts Dominicans with inquisition. *July 30*: Conrad of Marburg, inquisitor, murdered.	**1233.** *Dec. 28*: Herman of Salza, Master of Teutonic Order, issues Constitution of Kulm.	**1233.** Western façades of Peterborough and Ripon Cathedrals built.
1234. *July 12*: Dominic canonized. *Sept. 5*: Gregory issues Decretals *Liber extra* (*Rex pacificus*).	**1234.** *Apr. 9*: Fall of Peter des Roches.	
1235. *May 27*: Elizabeth, Landgravine of Hesse, canonized (*d.* **1231**).	**1235.** *Aug. 15*: Mayence Public Peace, first Imperial law in German language.	**1235.** St. Elizabeth's Church, Marburg, begun. Omar ibn al Fârid, Arabian poet, *d.*
1235-1253. Robert Grosseteste, Bishop of Lincoln.		
	1236. Declaration *Nolumus leges Angliae mutari* against Church Courts.	
		1237. Bamberg Cathedral consecrated.
1239. *Mar. 20*: Hermann of Salza, Master of Teutonic Order, *d.*	**1239.** Alexander II opposes attempts to extend papal jurisdiction to Scotland.	**1239.** Mayence Cathedral consecrated.
		ca. **1240.** Thomas de Chantimpré: *Liber de natura rerum.*
1241. *Aug. 21*: Gregory IX *d.*; succeeded by Celestine IV, who reigns 18 days; vacancy of 20 months follows.	**1241.** First commercial alliance between Lübeck and Hamburg.	**1241.** *Sept. 22*: Snorri Sturlason, Icelandic poet, *d.* Choir of Reims Cathedral completed.
		ca. **1241-1260.** Sculptures at Mayence, Naumburg, and Meissen by the Master of Naumburg.
1243-1254. Pope Innocent IV (Sinibald Fieschi).		**1243.** Ferdinand III of Castile confirms Salamanca University.

I. WESTERN EUROPE	II. CENTRAL, NORTHERN, AND EASTERN EUROPE	III. ISLAM AND ASIA
1244. End of persecution of Albigenses.		**1244.** *Aug. 23:* Egyptian Khwarazmi take Jerusalem.
1245. Innocent IV declares Sancho II of Portugal dethroned, and his brother Alfonso III successor (**-1279**).	**1245.** *July 17:* Innocent IV declares Frederick II dethroned, at Lyons Council.	
1246. Charles of Anjou, brother of Louis IX, marries heiress of Provence.	**1246.** *May 22:* Henry Raspe, landgrave of Thuringia, set up as anti-king. Frederick II seizes vacant Dukedoms of Austria and Styria.	**1246.** Vatatzes of Nicaea conquers Salonika.
1246-1282. Llywelyn ap Gruffydd, Prince of Snowdon.		**1246-1266.** Nasiruddin Mahmud, Sultan of Delhi.
1247. Alfonse of Poitou succeeds to Toulouse, after the death of Count Raymond VII.	**1247.** *Feb. 16:* Henry Raspe d. *Oct. 3:* William, Count of Holland, elected anti-king.	**1247.** Georgia reduced to Persian vassalage.
1248. *Nov. 22:* Ferdinand III of Castile conquers Seville. Simon de Montfort appointed Seneschal of Gascony.	**1248.** *Feb. 18:* Lombards defeat Frederick II at Parma.	**1248.** Genoese take Rhodes.
		1248-1254. Sixth Crusade, led to Egypt by Louis IX.
1249. Truce between England and France renewed.	**1249.** *May 26:* Enzio captured by Bolognese (*d.* **1272**). Birger Jarl extends Swedish rule in Finland.	**1249.** *June 4:* Louis IX lands in Egypt.
1249-1286. Alexander III of Scotland.		
1250. Gascony rebels against Simon de Montfort.	**1250.** *Dec. 13:* Frederick II *d.*; succeeded by Conrad IV (*d.* **1254**).	**1250.** Saracens capture Louis IX, who restores Damietta. Beginning of Mameluke rule in Egypt, after murder of the last Ayyubid.
	1250-1275. Valdemar I, King of Sweden, till **1266** under regency of Birger Jarl, his father.	
1251. *May:* De Montfort subdues Gascony. Alfonso III of Portugal conquers Algarve.	**1251.** Otakar of Bohemia seizes Austria.	
1252-1282. Alfonso X, the Wise, of Castile (*d.* **1284**).		**1252-1255.** William of Rubruque's journey to Central Asia.
1253. De Montfort secures Gascony for England. Anglo-French truce renewed.	**1253-1278.** Otakar II of Bohemia.	
	1253. Innocent IV offers Sicily to Richard of Cornwall, who refuses.	
	1253-1294. Lewis II, Duke of Bavaria and Count Palatine, guardian and heir of Conradin, son of Conrad IV.	
1254. *Apr.:* Treaty between Henry III and Alfonso of Castile.	**1254.** *Dec. 2:* Manfred, illegitimate son of Frederick II, keeps Sicily through his victory at Foggia.	**1254.** *Apr. 24:* Louis IX leaves Palestine and returns to France.
	1255. *Oct.:* Henry III of England accepts Sicily for his son, Edmund.	
	1256. *Jan. 28:* King William killed in skirmish against rebellious Frisians.	

IV. ECCLESIASTICAL HISTORY	V. CONSTITUTIONAL AND ECONOMIC HISTORY	VI. CULTURAL LIFE
1244. Innocent flees to Lyons.	**1244.** Innocent IV sends Master Martin to England to raise money.	
1245. First Council of Lyons. *Nov. 14*: Innocent seizes property of Franciscan Order (*Ordinem vestrum*).	**1245.** *July*: Master Martin expelled from England by joint action of king, clergy, and barons.	**1245.** Alexander of Hales, schoolman, *d.* Johannes Zemecke Teutonicus, author of *Glossa ordinaria* to *Decretum Gratiani*, *d.* **1245-1270.** Choir and cloisters of Westminster Abbey built.
1247. Innocent transforms Carmelites into mendicant friars.		**1247.** Gautier de Metz: *Image du Monde.*
		1248. *Aug. 15*: Cologne Cathedral begun. **1248-1252.** Alfonso X of Castile has *Tabulae Alfonsinae* drawn up by astronomers.
	1249. Fall of Peter de Vinea, protonotary of Frederick II.	**1249.** University College, Oxford, founded.
	1250. First statute of German factory at Novgorod.	*ca.* **1250.** *The Harrowing of Hell*, earliest extant English play. **1250.** Neithard of Reuenthal, lyrical poet, *d.* **1250-1275.** Nave of Strasbourg Minster built.
1251. *July*: Innocent returns to Italy.		**1251.** St. Mary's Church, Lübeck, begun.
	1252. First privileges for German merchants at Bruges. Florin first coined, at Florence.	
1253. *Aug. 11*: Clara of Assisi *d.* Innocent returns to Rome.		**1253.** *Oct. 9*: Robert Grosseteste, Bishop of Lincoln, philosopher and ecclesiastical politician, *d.*
1254-1261. Pope Alexander IV (Rainald of Segni).	**1254.** League of Rhenish Towns formed to maintain public peace. Representatives of towns sit in Portuguese Cortes for the first time.	**1254.** Rudolf of Ems, author of a World-Chronicle, *d.* Peire de Corbiac: *Tezaur.*
1255. Archbishopric of Riga established. *Sept. 26*: Clara of Assisi canonized. **1256.** *May 4*: Alexander IV founds Order of Augustine Hermits (*Licet ecclesiae catholicae*).	**1256-1263.** Alfonso X of Castile draws up *Siete Partidas.*	**1255.** Ulrich of Lichtenstein: *Frauendienst.* Thomas of Celano, biographer of St. Francis and author of *Dies irae*, *d.*

I. WESTERN EUROPE	II. CENTRAL, NORTHERN, AND EASTERN EUROPE	III. ISLAM AND ASIA
1257. Llywelyn styles himself Prince of Wales, after having obtained Anglesey, Snowdon, and Powys. Louis IX unites Perche to the crown.	**1257.** *Jan. 13*: Richard of Cornwall elected King of the Romans by 4 Electors. *Apr. 1*: Alfonso X of Castile elected by 3 Electors. *May 17*: Richard crowned at Aix-la-Chapelle.	
1258. *May 11*: Treaty of Corbeil between Louis IX and James of Aragon, regulates Pyrenees frontier.	**1258.** *Aug. 10*: Manfred crowned King of Sicily at Palermo. Alexander IV cancels grant of Sicily to Prince Edmund.	**1258.** *Jan. 17*: Mongols take Bagdad and overthrow Caliphate.
1259. *Aug. 1*: Peace between England and Wales. *Nov.*: Treaty of Paris defines extent of English possessions in France for which Henry III does homage.		**1259-1282.** Michael Palaeologus, emperor of Nicaea.
	1260. *July 12*: Otakar of Bohemia defeats Hungarians at Croissenbrunn. *Sept. 4*: Florentine Ghibellines defeat Guelphs at Montaperti.	**1260.** *Sept. 3*: Kotuz, Sultan of Egypt, compels Mongols to retreat behind Euphrates. **1260-1294.** Kublai Khan, founder of Mongol Yuan dynasty in China.
	1261. Otakar of Bohemia obtains Styria. Urban IV offers Sicily to Charles of Anjou.	**1261.** *July 4*: Baibars establishes Sultanate of Egypt. *July 25*: Michael VIII Palaeologus recovers Constantinople and overthrows Latin Empire.
1262. Llywelyn begins successful border warfare against English. *Sept. 14*: Alfonso X of Castile takes Cadiz. Louis IX unites Arles, Foix, and Calais to the crown.	**1262.** Otakar recognizes King Richard and is invested with Austria and Styria. Iceland comes under Norwegian rule.	
1263. *Oct. 2*: Scots defeat Haakon of Norway at Largs; Norway cedes Hebrides.	**1263-1280.** Magnus VI of Norway.	
1264. *May 14*: De Montfort defeats Henry III at Lewes.	**1264.** Venetians defeat Genoese off Trapani. **1264-1293.** Obizzo II, Marquis of Este, lord of Ferrara, Modena (**1288**), and Reggio (**1289**).	
1265. *Aug. 4*: Prince Edward defeats De Montfort, who is killed, at Evesham.	**1265.** *June 21*: Charles of Anjou invested with Naples and Sicily by Clement IV.	
1266. *July 2*: Treaty of Perth; Haakon of Norway cedes Suderies and Isle of Man to Scotland.	**1266.** *Jan. 6*: Charles of Anjou crowned. *Feb. 26*: Manfred defeated and killed by Charles of Anjou, at Benevento.	**1266-1287.** Balban, Sultan of Delhi.

IV. ECCLESIASTICAL HISTORY	V. CONSTITUTIONAL AND ECONOMIC HISTORY	VI. CULTURAL LIFE
1257. Bonaventura becomes Franciscan General.		**1257.** Robert de Sorbon, chaplain to Louis IX, founds Sorbonne, Paris.
	1258. *June 11*: English Barons headed by Simon de Montfort extort Provisions of Oxford from Henry III (Committee for political and economic affairs, three Parliaments every year, aliens expelled from office).	
	1259. Provisions of Westminster, complete the reforms promised in Provisions of Oxford. Commercial union between Lübeck, Rostock, and Wismar.	**1259.** Matthew Paris, English chronicler, *d.* Vincent of Beauvais: *Speculum Triplex* completed.
1260-1261. First Flagellant movements in Upper Italy and South Germany.		**1260.** *Oct. 24*: Chartres Cathedral consecrated. Cimabue: *Madonna* for Trinità, Florence. Niccolò Pisano: Pulpit in Pisa Baptistery. Accursius, author of *Glossa ordinaria* to *Corpus iuris civilis, d.*
		1260-1280. Nave and East End of Lincoln Cathedral built.
1261-1264. Pope Urban IV (Jacques Pantaleon).	**1261.** Alexander IV frees Henry III from Provisions of Oxford and Westminster.	
	1262. Strasbourg frees itself from episcopal overlordship.	
1263. Urban issues *Qui celum* on the right of electing the German King.		
1264. *Corpus Christi Day* made official feast (*Transiturus*).	**1264.** *Jan. 23*: Louis IX arbitrates between Henry III and Barons, and annuls Provisions of Oxford (Mise of Amiens).	**1264.** Merton College, Oxford, founded. Vincent of Beauvais *d.*
1265-1268. Pope Clement IV (Guido Fulcodi).	**1265.** *Jan. 20*: Parliament, representing shires, cities, and boroughs, summoned by Simon de Montfort.	**1265.** Dante Alighieri born in Florence.
	1266. *Oct. 31*: *Dictum de Kenilworth* confirms Charters. Louis IX reforms French coinage, creating *Gros Tournois*.	**1266.** Roger Bacon: *Opus Maius.*

I. WESTERN EUROPE	II. CENTRAL, NORTHERN, AND EASTERN EUROPE	III. ISLAM AND ASIA
1267. *Sept. 29*: Treaty of Shrewsbury (or Montgomery) between Henry III and Llywelyn, who is recognized as Prince of Wales. Portuguese finally annex Algarve.	**1268.** *Aug. 23*: Conradin defeated by Charles of Anjou, at Tagliacozzo ; *Oct. 29*: beheaded at Naples.	**1268.** Christians lose Antioch to Baibars of Egypt.
	1269. Otakar acquires Carinthia and Carniola.	**1268-1272.** Crusade of Prince Edward to Palestine.
1270. *Aug. 25*: Louis IX *d.*; succeeded by Philip III (-**1285**).	**1270-1272.** Stephen V of Hungary.	**1270.** Seventh (last) Crusade, led by Louis IX to Tunis, where he dies (*Aug. 25*). Philip III makes treaty with Sultan.
1271. Toulouse and Poitou united to French crown. *Mar. 13*: Henry of Almaine, son of Richard of Cornwall, murdered by De Montforts at Viterbo.		**1271-1295.** Marco Polo of Venice travels through Asia to China
1272. *Nov. 16*: Henry III *d.*; succeeded by Edward I (-**1307**). *Dec.*: Archbishop of Lyons takes oath of fealty to Philip III.	**1272.** *Apr. 2*: King Richard of Cornwall *d.*	
	1272-1290. Ladislaus of Hungary.	
	1273. *Oct. 1*: Rudolf, Count of Hapsburg, elected king. *Oct. 24*: Rudolf crowned at Aix-la-Chapelle.	
1274. *Aug. 19*: Edward I crowned at Westminster.	**1274.** *Sept. 26*: Pope recognizes King Rudolf.	**1274.** Kublai Khan fails to conquer Japan.
	1275-1290. Magnus I of Sweden.	**1275-1292.** Marco Polo in service of Kublai Khan.
1276. *Nov.*: First Welsh War begins.	**1276.** *June 24:* Otakar outlawed by Rudolf. *Nov. 21*: Otakar submits to Rudolf and keeps only Bohemia and Moravia.	
1276-1285. Peter III of Aragon.		
1277. *Nov. 9-10*: Treaty of Conway, reduces Llywelyn's power.	**1277.** Otto Visconti, Archbishop of Milan, obtains Signoria of Milan.	
	1278. Otakar takes up arms. *Aug. 26*: Otakar defeated by Rudolf, and killed, at Dürnkrut, Marchfeld.	
	1278-1305. Wenceslas II of Bohemia; under guardianship till **1290**.	
1279. Edward seizes Ponthieu. *May 23*: Philip III recognizes English claims to Ponthieu and Agenais.		**1279-1368.** Mongol dynasty rules China.
1279-1325. Diniz the Husbandman, King of Portugal.		
	1280-1299. Eric II of Norway.	

IV. ECCLESIASTICAL HISTORY	V. CONSTITUTIONAL AND ECONOMIC HISTORY	VI. CULTURAL LIFE
1268-1271. Vacancy in the papacy.	**1267.** Statute of Marlborough re-enacts chief Provisions of Westminster.	**1267.** Brunetto Latini: *Tresor* and *Tesoretto* completed. **1268.** Henry de Bracton, English jurist, *d.* Balliol College, Oxford, founded.
1271-1276. Pope Gregory X (Tedaldo Visconti).		
1272. *Dec. 13:* Bertold of Ratisbon, popular preacher, *d.*		
1273. Gregory buys County of Venaissin.	**1273.** *Summer:* First league of Uri, Schwyz and Nidwalden.	**1273.** Djelaleddin Rumi, Persian mystic poet and founder of Order of Dancing Dervishes, *d.*
1274. *Mar. 7:* Thomas Aquinas d. *May-July:* Second Council of Lyons, regulates papal election (*Ubi periculum maius*) and carries out reunion with Orthodox Church. *July 15:* Johannes Fidanza Bonaventura *d.* **1276.** *Jan. 21-June 22:* Pope Innocent V (Peter of Tarentaise); *July 11-Aug. 18:* Pope Hadrian V (Ottoboni Fieschi); *Sept. 15-* **1277.** *May 20:* Pope John XXI (Peter Juliani).	**1274.** *July 28:* Treaty of commerce between England and Flanders. **1275.** Statute of Westminster I, grants duty on wool to the king.	**1274.** *May.* Dante meets Beatrice. Arnold Fitz-Thedmar: *De Antiquis Legibus Liber* (London City Chronicle). **1275.** Swabian Law Code finished. Ratisbon Cathedral begun.
1277-1280. Pope Nicholas III (John Orsini).		**1277.** Archbishop of Canterbury and Bishop of Paris condemn philosophy of Averroes.
1278-1279. King Rudolf renounces Romagna.	**1278.** Statute of Gloucester restricts feudal jurisdiction by writs *Quo Warranto.* Special liberties granted to Cinque Ports.	**1278.** Martin of Troppau, chronicler, *d.* **1278-1283.** Campo Santo, Pisa, built. **1278-1350.** S. Maria Novella, Florence, built.
1279. *Aug. 14:* Nicholas III forbids controversy concerning apostolic poverty (*Exiit qui seminat*).	**1279.** Statute of Mortmain forbids grants of land to Corporations.	
1280. *Nov. 15:* Albert the Great, scientist and philosopher, *d.*	**1280.** German merchants in England form a Hansa. Glass mirror invented.	*ca.* **1280.** Niccolò Pisano *d.* Mathilda of Magdeburg, mystic, *d.* **1280-1330.** Lichfield Cathedral built.
1281-1285. Pope Martin IV (Simon de Brion).		**1281.** Alexander of Roes: *Tractatus de translatione Imperii.*

I. WESTERN EUROPE	II. CENTRAL, NORTHERN, AND EASTERN EUROPE	III. ISLAM AND ASIA
1282. Second Welsh War. *Dec. 11*: Llywelyn *d.* Alfonso X of Castile deposed by his son, Sancho IV (**-1295**).	**1282.** *Mar. 30*: Sicilian Vespers; French expelled from Sicily, which passes to Peter III of Aragon. *Dec. 27*: Rudolf invests his sons, Albert and Rudolf, with Austria, Styria, and Carniola.	
1283. *Oct. 1*: David, Llywelyn's brother, executed at Shrewsbury.	**1283.** Teutonic Order completes subjection of Prussia. The false Frederick II in Germany (**-1285**).	
1284. *Mar.*: Statute of Wales, issued at Rhuddlan, establishes English county administration.	**1284.** Genoese defeat Pisans off Meloria; beginning of the decline of Pisa.	
1285. *Oct. 5*: Philip III *d.*; succeeded by Philip IV the Fair (**-1314**).		**1285-1291.** Henry II, last King of Jerusalem.
1286. *Mar. 19*: Margaret, 'Maid of Norway', becomes Queen of Scots, under six guardians. Truce between France and Aragon.	**1286-1319.** Eric VI Menved of Denmark.	
1287. *July 15*: Treaty of Oléron between Edward I and Alfonso of Aragon.		
	1288. *June 5*: Battle of Worringen, decides Limburg war of succession in favour of Brabant.	**1288-1326.** Osman I, son of Ertogrul, founder of Ottoman Empire.
1289. *Nov. 6*: Treaty of Salisbury between England, Scotland, and Norway; Scotland under English influence.	**1289.** Rudolf I subdues Otto of Burgundy.	
1290. *Mar. 10*: Treaty of Brigham; Margaret of Scotland to marry Edward, son of Edward I. *Sept. 26*: Margaret of Scotland *d.* Edward I annexes Isle of Man.	**1290-1318.** Birger of Sweden, till 1306 under regency of Torkil Knutson.	**1290.** Kaikobad, Sultan of Delhi, murdered and succeeded by Jalaluddin.
1291. *May 10*: Meeting at Norham; Edward I to decide among 13 claimants to Scottish throne. Peace of Tarascon between Aragon and papacy.	**1290-1301.** Andrew III of Hungary.	
1291-1327. James II of Aragon.	**1291.** *July 15*: Rudolf I *d. Aug. 1*: Everlasting League between Uri, Schwyz, and Unterwalden.	**1291.** *May 18*: Mamelukes conquer Acre; end of Christian rule in the East.
1292. *Nov. 17*: Edward I awards the Scottish throne to John Baliol.	**1292.** *May 5*: Adolf, Count of Nassau, elected German King. *June 24*: Adolf crowned at Aix-la-Chapelle.	
1293. Edward restores Isle of Man to Scotland. *May 15*: Battle off St. Mahé between English merchant fleet and French fleet. Gascons attack French.	**1293.** Torkil Knutson conquers Karelia and founds Viborg.	**1293.** First Christian missionaries in China.
	1293-1295. Adolf seizes Thuringia and Meissen.	

IV. ECCLESIASTICAL HISTORY	V. CONSTITUTIONAL AND ECONOMIC HISTORY	VI. CULTURAL LIFE
1282. Andronicus II repeals Union of Eastern and Western Churches.	**1282.** Lübeck, Riga, and Visby ally to safeguard Baltic trade.	**1282.** Siger of Brabant, Aristotelian philosopher, *d.*
	1283. *Jan.*: Edward calls two provincial councils at York and Canterbury. *Oct. 3*: Peter III of Aragon grants General Privilege to Estates. *June 14*: Rostock alliance of Baltic towns headed by Lübeck with several princes for the protection of peace.	**1283.** Philip de Beaumanoir: *Coutumes de Beauvoisis.*
	1284. Sequins first coined at Venice.	**1284.** Peterhouse, Cambridge, founded.
		1284-1298. Giovanni Pisano: Sculptures on facade of Siena Cathedral.
1285-1287. Pope Honorius IV (Jacopo Savelli).	**1285.** Statute of Westminster II, to preserve public order. Statute of Winchester concerning police.	
	1286. Edward I issues writ *Circumspecte agatis.*	**1286.** Giovanni Balbi: *Catholicon.*
1287. German National Council at Würzburg.	**1287.** Alfonso of Portugal issues Privilege of Union, establishing right of resistance. Rudolf I proclaims Public Peace of Würzburg.	**1287.** Conrad of Würzburg, poet, *d.*
		1288. Matfré de Bezier: *Breviari d'amor.*
1288-1292. Pope Nicholas IV (Hieronimus of Ascoli).		**1288-1309.** Palazzo Communale, Siena, built.
1289. Nicholas IV cedes half of all income of Papal See to College of Cardinals. Concordat with Portugal.		**1289.** *Oct. 26*: Nicholas IV confirms Montpellier University. Worcester College, Oxford, founded.
	1290. Statute of Westminster III (*Quia emptores*). *July*: Jews expelled from England.	**1290.** Lisbon University founded.
1291. Knights of St. John take up residence in Cyprus.		**1291.** Sa'adi, Persian poet, *d.*
		1291-1324. Nave of York Minster built.
1292-1295. Guilelmus Durandus: *Pontificale.*		**1292.** Dante: *La vita nuova.* Roger Bacon, schoolman, *d.* (*Opus Tertium, Compendium Studii Philosophiae*).
	1293. *Ordinamenti della giustizia* exclude nobles from Florence government.	**1293.** Henry of Ghent, schoolman, *d.*
	1293-1295. Hansa Towns recognize Lübeck as their capital.	

I. WESTERN EUROPE	II. CENTRAL, NORTHERN, AND EASTERN EUROPE	III. ISLAM AND ASIA
1294. *Jan.*: Philip IV summons Edward I to Paris. Parlement of Paris declares that Edward has forfeited Gascony. *June*: England declares war on France. Rebellion in Wales.	**1294.** Adolf allies with Edward I against France.	
1295. *Jan. 22*: Welsh defeat at Conway. *July 1*: Alliance between France and Scotland.	**1295.** Matteo Visconti becomes tyrant of Milan.	
1296. *Apr. 27*: Edward defeats Scots at Dunbar. *July 10*: John Baliol resigns his crown to Edward I.	**1296–1337.** Frederick II, brother of James II of Aragon, King of Sicily.	**1296.** *July*: Jalaluddin of Delhi murdered and succeeded by Alauddin Khilji.
1297. *Apr.*: Truce between England and France, which keeps nearly all Gascony. *May*: Scottish rebellion under William Wallace. *Sept. 11*: Scots defeat English at Stirling Bridge.	**1297.** Genoese defeat Venetians off Curzola.	
1298. *Jan. 31*: Anglo-French truce at Tournai. *July 22*: Edward I defeats Wallace at Falkirk.	**1298.** *June 23*: Electors dethrone King Adolf. *July 2*: Adolf killed in battle of Göllheim. *July 27*: Albert I of Austria elected King.	
1299. *June 19*: Anglo-French truce at Montreuil. *Nov.*: Scots take Stirling Castle.	**1299.** *Dec. 8*: Albert I and Philip IV of France ally. **1299–1319.** Haakon V of Norway.	**1299.** Treaty between Venice and Turks.
1300. *July–Aug.*: War between Edward and the Scots.	**1300.** Wenceslas II of Bohemia becomes King of Poland.	
1301. Philip IV acquires part of county of Bar.	**1301.** *Jan. 14*: Andrew III of Hungary, last of Arpads, d. Charles of Valois subdues Florentine Ghibellines.	**1301.** Osman defeats Byzantines at Baphaion.
1302. *Jan.*: Anglo-Scots truce. *July 11*: Philip IV defeated by Flemings at Courtrai. *Dec.*: Bordeaux expels the French and calls in the English.	**1302.** Albert I subdues Electors of Mayence, Cologne, Treves, and Palatinate.	**1302–1311.** Malik Kafur, general of Alauddin Khilji, conquers Southern India.
1303. *May 20*: Treaty of Paris restores Gascony to England. *Sept.*: Edward I conquers Scotland again.	**1303.** Albert I recognizes papal supremacy and cancels alliance with Philip IV.	**1303.** Emperor Andronicus hires services of the Catalan Grand Company against Turks.
1304. *July 20*: Edward retakes Stirling Castle, Wallace made prisoner. Philip IV defeats Flemings by land and by sea.		
1305. *July*: Treaty of Athis between Philip IV and Flemings (Philip gets Lille, Douai, Béthune, Orchies). *Aug. 23*: Wallace executed at Smithfield.	**1305.** *June 21*: Wenceslas II of Bohemia, Poland, and Hungary, d.	
1306. *Mar. 25*: Robert Bruce crowned King of Scotland. *June 26*: English defeat Bruce at Methuen. *Aug. 11*: Defeat of Bruce at Dalry.	**1306.** *Aug. 4*: Wenceslas III of Bohemia, last of Przemysls, d. Albert I invests Rudolf, his son, with Bohemia. Vladislav I Lokietek succeeds in Poland (**-1333**).	

IV. ECCLESIASTICAL HISTORY	V. CONSTITUTIONAL AND ECONOMIC HISTORY	VI. CULTURAL LIFE
1294. *June 5-Dec. 13:* Pope Celestine V (Peter of Murrone; abdicates, *d.* **1296**). **1294-1303.** Pope Boniface VIII (Benedict Gaetani). **1294-1313.** Robert Winchelsey, Archibishop of Canterbury.	**1294.** Peace of Tonsberg confirms economic control of Norway by German Hanse.	**1294.** Arnolfo di Cambio begins S. Croce, Florence.
1296. *Feb. 25:* Bull *Clericis laicos* forbids ecclesiastics to pay taxes to temporal powers. Philip IV and Edward I oppose it.	**1295.** *Nov. 27:* 'Model Parliament' meets, grants money for French and Scottish wars. **1296.** *Aug. 8:* Scottish Coronation Stone moved from Scone to Westminster. **1297.** *Oct. 12: Confirmatio Cartarum,* incl. *Statutum de Tallagio non concedendo,* further limits royal power to raise taxes. Great Council of Venice definitely formed.	**1296.** Arnolfo di Cambio begins Florence Cathedral. Philip de Beaumanoir, French jurist, *d.*
1298. *Mar. 3: Liber Sextus* of the Decretals issued (*Sacrosanctae*).		**1298.** Jacobus de Varagine, author of *The Golden Legend, d.*
1299. *June 27:* Boniface VIII claims Scotland (*Scimus, fili*). **1300.** *Feb. 22:* Jubilee Year proclaimed (*Antiquorum habet fide*). **1301.** *Dec. 5:* Bull *Ausculta fili* against Philip IV of France.	**1299.** Act to repress bad coinage in England. **1300.** *March: Articuli super cartas,* supplementing Magna Carta and Forest Charter. **1301.** *Jan. 20:* Parliament of Lincoln rejects papal claims on Scotland. *Feb. 14:* Confirmation of the Charters. Edward I's son created Prince of Wales.	**1299-1301.** Palazzo Vecchio, Florence, built. **1300.** Guido Cavalcanti, representative of the *dolce stil nuovo, d.* **1301-1311.** Giovanni Pisano: Pulpit in Pisa Cathedral.
1302. *Nov. 18:* Bull *Unam sanctam* pronounces highest papal claims to supremacy.	**1302.** *Apr. 10:* First meeting of French States General.	**1302.** *July 11:* Pierre Flotte, French jurist, killed at Courtrai. Dante exiled from Florence.
1303. *Sept. 7:* William of Nogaret and Sciarra Colonna take Boniface VIII prisoner at Anagni. *Oct. 11:* Boniface VIII *d.* **1304.** Pope Benedict XI (Nicholas Bocasini).	**1303.** *June 13:* French States General support king against the Pope. *Carta mercatoria* of Edward I grants privileges to foreign merchants.	**1303.** Rome University founded. Peter of Abano: *Conciliator.* Cimabue *d.* **1304.** Rüdeger Manesse, connoisseur of the minnesingers, *d.*
1305. *June 5:* Bertrand de Got elected Pope Clement V; continues to reside in France.		**1305.** Giotto di Bondone: Frescoes in S. Maria dell' Arena, Padua.
1306. *Feb. 1:* Bull *Meruit* declares *Unam Sanctam* invalid for France.	**1306.** Philip IV expels Jews from France.	**1306.** *Dec. 25:* Jacopone da Todi. author of *Stabat Mater, d.*

I. WESTERN EUROPE	II. CENTRAL, NORTHERN, AND EASTERN EUROPE	III. ISLAM AND ASIA
1307. *May 10 and 13*: Bruce defeats English in Ayrshire. *July 7*: Edward I *d.* at Burgh-on-Sands; succeeded by Edward II (**-1327**). *Dec. 25*: Bruce defeats Earl of Buchan at Staines.	**1307.** *May*: Frederick of Meissen defeats Albert I at Lucka. *Aug. 15*: After Rudolf's death, Bohemians elect Henry of Carinthia king (**-1310**; *d.* **1335**). Albert invades Bohemia. **1307-1342.** Charles I Robert of Anjou, King of Hungary.	**1307.** Alauddin III, Sultan of Roum, *d.*; break-up of the power of Roum.
1308. *Feb. 25*: Coronation of Edward II. *May 22 and Aug. 22*: Bruce defeats his Scottish adversaries.	**1308.** *May 1*: Albert I murdered while advancing against Swiss League. *Nov. 27*: Henry VII, Count of Luxemburg, elected German King.	
1309. Permanent union of Aragon and Valencia.	**1309.** *June 3*: Henry VII recognizes Swiss League. Grand Master of Teutonic Order moves to Marienburg, Prussia. **1309-1343.** Robert of Anjou, King of Naples.	
1310. *Feb. 24*: Scottish clergy accept Bruce as king.	**1310.** *Aug. 31*: John, Henry VII's son, becomes King of Bohemia. Teutonic Order acquires Danzig and Pomerellen. Expedition of Henry VII to Italy.	**1310.** Moslems capture Dwarasamudra, capital of Mysore.
1311. Scots ravage North of England.	**1311.** Matteo Visconti made Imperial Vicar of Milan.	**1311.** Moslems capture Madura, Pandya capital.
1312. Treaty of Vienne (Lyons incorporated in France). Scots ravage Durham. **1312-1350.** Alfonso XI of Castile.	**1312.** Can Grande della Scala made Imperial Vicar of Verona and Vicenza (**-1329**). *June 29*: Henry VII crowned Emperor at Rome ; subsequently quarrels with Pope and Naples.	
1313. *Jan. 13*: Scots take Perth.	**1313.** *Aug. 24*: Henry VII *d.* while advancing against Naples.	
1314. *June 24*: Robert Bruce defeats Edward II at Bannockburn. *Nov. 29*: Philip IV *d.*; succeeded by Louis X (**-1316**).	**1314.** *Oct. 19-20*: Double election of Frederick of Austria and Lewis IV of Bavaria.	
1315. *May 25*: Edward Bruce, brother of King Robert, lands in Ulster.	**1315.** *Nov. 15*: Swiss defeat Leopold of Austria at Morgarten. *Dec. 9*: Swiss League renewed.	**1315.** *Jan. 2*: Alauddin Khilji of Delhi *d.*; Malik Kafur murdered.
1316. *May 2*: Edward Bruce crowned King of Ireland. *June 4*: Louis X *d.*; succeeded by Philip V (**-1322**).	**1316.** *Mar. 29*: Lewis IV confirms and extends Swiss privileges. **1316-1341.** Grand Duke Gedimin, founder of Lithuanian Empire.	**1316-1320.** Mubarak, last of the Khilji rulers of Delhi.

IV. ECCLESIASTICAL HISTORY	V. CONSTITUTIONAL AND ECONOMIC HISTORY	VI. CULTURAL LIFE
1307. Archbishopric of Pekin (Cambalu) established. **1307-1314.** Trial of Order of Templars at instigation of Philip IV of France.	**1307-1354.** Baldwin of Luxemburg, Archbishop of Treves, leading German statesman.	
	1308. *Apr.*: English barons insist on exiling Piers Gaveston, favourite of Edward II.	**1308.** Lisbon University moved to Coimbra. *Nov. 8*: John Duns Scotus, schoolman, *d.*
1309. Clement V fixes his residence at Avignon ('Babylonian captivity').	**1309.** *July*: Gaveston returns to England.	**1309.** Orleans University founded (privilege by Clement V, **1305**). **1309-1313.** Dante Alighieri: *De Monarchia.*
1310. Knights of St. John move from Cyprus to Rhodes.	**1310.** *Mar.*: Thomas of Lancaster and 20 other Lords Ordainers appointed by Parliament. Council of Ten established at Venice.	**1310-1340.** Palace of the Doges built at Venice. **1310.** 'Sumer is icomen in', English round-song.
1311-1312. Council of Vienne reprimands Beguines and Begards. **1312.** *Mar. 22*: Clement V suppresses Order of Templars. *May 6:* Decretal *Exivi de Paradiso* on Franciscan poverty.	**1311.** Lords Ordainers issue Ordinances, transferring government from king to barons. **1312.** *June 19*: Piers Gaveston executed.	**1311.** Duccio di Buoninsegna: *Maestà* in Siena Cathedral. Frauenlob (Henry of Meissen), founds the Mastersingers at Mainz.
1313-1327. Walter Reynolds, Archbishop of Canterbury. **1314.** *Mar. 11*: Jacques de Molay, Grand Master of Templars, burnt in Paris. *Apr. 14:* Clement V *d.*; Holy See vacant for 27 months. **1315.** Brethren and Sisters of the Free Spirit, pantheistic sect, in Upper Rhineland.	**1313.** *Oct.*: Edward II reconciled with nobles. **1314.** *Sept.*: Edward II confirms Ordinances. French nobles oppose the Crown. **1315.** *Feb.*: Ordinances make barons administrators of royal revenues; Despensers removed from the Council. Louis X gives charters to French provinces. Golden Book of patrician families in Venice closed.	**1313.** Berthold Schwarz, German Grey Friar, invents gunpowder. **1314.** Exeter College, Oxford, founded. **1314-1321.** Dante Alighieri: *La (Divina) Commedia.* **1315.** *Sept. 30*: Raymond Lull, schoolman and alchemist, *d.*
1316. *Dec. 22*: Aegidius Colonna (Romanus), Archbishop of Bourges, *d.* **1316-1334.** Pope John XXII (Jacques Duèse).	**1316.** *Jan.*: Edward II confirms Ordinances of 1315. Lancaster made chief of Council.	

I. WESTERN. EUROPE	II. CENTRAL, NORTHERN, AND EASTERN EUROPE	III. ISLAM AND ASIA
	1317. *Mar. 31*: John XXII claims Imperial rights in Italy.	
1318. *Mar. 28*: Robert Bruce captures Berwick. *Oct. 14*: Edward Bruce killed in battle of Faughart near Dundalk.	**1318.** Truce between Swiss League and Hapsburgs.	**1318.** Mohammedans defeat Harapala, ruler of West Deccan. **1318-1346.** George V of Georgia.
1319. *Sept. 20*: Scots defeat English at Myton.	**1319.** *Aug. 14*: Waldemar of Brandenburg, last of Brandenburg Ascanians, *d.* **1319-1363.** Magnus II Smek, King of Sweden and Norway.	
1320. *May 5*: Peace of Paris between France and Flanders.	**1320.** Gedimin of Lithuania conquers Kiev. **1320-1326, 1330-1331.** Christopher II of Denmark.	**1320.** Kutbuddin Mubarak, Sultan of Delhi, murdered; Ghazi Khan, governor of the Punjab, succeeds.
1322. *Jan. 3*: Philip V *d.*; succeeded by Charles IV (**-1328**). *Oct. 14*: Robert Bruce defeats Edward II at Byland.	**1322.** *Sept. 28*: Frederick of Austria defeated, and taken prisoner by Lewis IV, at Mühldorf.	
1323. Robert Bruce recognized as king by the Pope. Truce between England and Scotland for 13 years. James I of Aragon takes Sardinia from Pisa.	**1323.** *Dec. 18*: Nuremberg Diet rejects papal claim of approbation.	
1324. Charles IV sequesters Gascony. Moors recover Baza from Castile.	**1324.** *Jan. 5*: Frankfort Appellation against papal claims. *May 22*: Sachsenhausen Appellation of Lewis IV against the Pope. *June 24*: Lewis IV invests his son, Lewis, with Brandenburg.	
1325-1357. Alfonso IV of Portugal.	**1325.** *Sept. 5*: Lewis IV accepts Frederick of Austria as co-regent. **1326.** *Aug. 15*: Valdemar III of Denmark invests Gerard III of Holstein with Slesvig.	**1325-1351.** Muhammad Adil, Sultan of Delhi. **1326.** *Nov.*: Osman takes Brussa; succeeded by Orkhan (**-1359**).

IV. ECCLESIASTICAL HISTORY	V. CONSTITUTIONAL AND ECONOMIC HISTORY	VI. CULTURAL LIFE
1317. *Oct. 25*: *Clementinae Constitutiones* issued (Bull *Quoniam nulla*).	**1317.** *Feb.*: Salic Law, excluding women from succession to throne, adopted in France. *Apr. 7*: Philip V promises reforms to representatives of the towns. *Dec. 7*: Edward II confines privileges of German merchants to members of the Hansa.	**1317.** Jean de Joinville, French chronicler, *d.*
	1318. *Aug. 9*: Treaty of Leek between Edward II and the factions of the barons.	**1318.** *Nov. 29*: Heinrich Frauenlob, minnesinger, *d.*
	1318-1320. Philip V tries in vain to establish uniform coinage, weights and measures in France.	
	1319. Rise of the Despensers.	**1319.** Chapter house of Wells Cathedral completed.
1320. *Apr. 6*: Declaration of Arbroath. Augustinus Triumphus: *Summa de potestate ecclesiastica*.	**1320.** Lords form League against the Despensers. *Aug.*: 'Black Parliament' at Scone tries 70 persons for conspiracy against King Robert. Christopher II of Denmark compelled to renounce many royal prerogatives in favour of the Estates.	
	1321. *July*: Despensers banished.	**1321.** *Sept. 14*: Dante Alighieri *d.* at Ravenna. Pierre Dubois *d.*
1322. *Mar. 26*: Decretal *Quia nonnunquam* renews dispute on Franciscan poverty.	**1322.** *Feb.*: Edward II recalls Despensers. *Mar. 16*: Edward II defeats Lancaster at Boroughbridge. *Mar. 22*: Lancaster executed. *May 2*: Parliament at York repeals Ordinances and enacts that legislation demands consent of King and Parliament.	**1322.** Alan of Walsingham finishes octagon of Ely Cathedral. Master John finishes choir of Cologne Cathedral.
1323. *July 18*: Thomas Aquinas canonized. *Oct. 8*: First trial of Lewis IV by John XXII. *Nov. 12*: Bull *Cum inter nonnullos* declares Franciscan doctrine of Christ's poverty heretical.	**1323.** Charles IV abolishes the Commune of Laon.	
1324. *Jan. 7*: Second trial of Lewis IV by John XXII. *Mar. 23*: John XXII excommunicates Lewis IV.		**1324.** Dino Compagni, Florentine chronicler, *d.* Burgos Cathedral consecrated.
		1324-1327. Marsilius of Padua and John of Jandun: *Defensor Pacis*.
		1325. Johann von Buch: Glosses to Saxon Law-Code.
	1326. *Sept. 24*: Queen Isabella and Roger Mortimer raise rebellion against Edward II. *Oct. 26*: Elder Despenser executed. *Nov. 16*: Edward II captured. *Nov. 20*: Death of younger Despenser.	**1326.** University Hall (Clare College), Cambridge, and Oriel College, Oxford, founded.

I. WESTERN EUROPE	II. CENTRAL, NORTHERN, AND EASTERN EUROPE	III. ISLAM AND ASIA
1327. *Jan. 20*: Edward II resigns throne; succeeded by Edward III (**-1377**). *June-Aug.*: Scots invade England. *Sept. 21*: Edward II murdered. Charles IV restores Guienne to England, but keeps Agen.	**1327.** Lewis IV goes to Italy; Galeazzo Visconti of Milan submits to him. **1327-1331.** John of Bohemia acquires Silesia.	
1328. *Feb. 1*: Charles IV, last of the Capets, *d.*; succeeded by Philip VI of Valois. *May 4*: Treaty of Northampton between England and Scotland; Robert Bruce recognized king. *Aug. 23*: Philip VI defeats Flemings at Cassel.	**1328.** *Jan. 17*: Lewis IV crowned Emperor at Rome, according to doctrines of sovereignty of the people expressed in *Defensor Pacis*. Louis Gonzaga establishes his dynasty at Mantua. **1328-1340.** Ivan I Kalita, Grand Duke of Vladimir and Novgorod. **1329.** *Dec.*: Lewis IV returns to Germany.	
1329. *June 6*: Edward III does homage to Philip VI for Guienne and Ponthieu, at Amiens. *June 7*: Robert Bruce *d.*; succeeded by David II (**-1371**).		**1329.** Indecisive battle between Andronicus and Orkhan at Pelekanon; Orkhan takes Nicaea.
1330. *May 1*: Convention of Vincennes concerning homage and Aquitaine.	**1330.** *Jan. 13*: Frederick of Austria *d. Aug. 6*: Treaty of Hagenau; Hapsburgs recognize Lewis IV. **1331.** Gerard the Great of Holstein defeats Danes at Danewerk. **1331-1355.** Stephen IV Dushan, founder of Greater Serbia.	
1331. *Mar. 30*: Edward III ratifies Treaty of St. Germain concerning Aquitaine. *Mar. 31*: Edward III once more does homage to Philip.		
1332. *Aug. 12*: Edward Baliol defeats David II's troops at Dupplin Moor. *Sept. 24*: Baliol crowned king. *Nov. 23*: Treaty of Roxburgh; Baliol recognizes Edward III as overlord. *Dec. 16*: Baliol flees to England.	**1332.** *Nov. 7:* Lucerne joins Swiss League. Sweden takes Schonen from Denmark.	
1333. *July 19*: Edward III defeats Scots at Halidon Hill. Moors recapture Gibraltar from Castile.	**1333-1370.** Casimir III, the Great, of Poland.	**1333.** Alauddin, brother of Orkhan and organizer of the Turkish Empire, *d.* **1333-1354.** Yussuf I, Khalif of Granada.
1334. *May 14*: David II flees to France. *June 12*: Treaty of Newcastle; Baliol submits completely to Edward and cedes Berwick.		
1335. Edward III invades Scotland.	**1335.** *May*: Lewis IV invests Hapsburgs with Carinthia.	
1336. Edward III continues to occupy Scotland. Philip VI attacks Isle of Wight and Channel Islands. **1336-1387.** Peter IV, the Ceremonious, of Aragon.	**1336.** James van Artevelde, head of popular party, rebels against Louis II, Count of Flanders.	

IV. ECCLESIASTICAL HISTORY	V. CONSTITUTIONAL AND ECONOMIC HISTORY	VI. CULTURAL LIFE
1327. Oct. 23: Bull *Licet iuxta doctrinam* condemns some paragraphs of *Defensor Pacis*.		*1327.* Master Eckhart, philosopher, *d.* Tolomeo of Lucca, Bishop of Torcello, chronicler, *d.* The 'Chester Cycle' of mystery plays.
1328. Apr. 18: Emperor Lewis declares John XXII deposed for heresy and lèse-majesté. **1328-1330.** Anti-pope Nicholas V (Peter of Corbara; resigns; *d.* **1333**).	*1328. Oct*: Mortimer created Earl of March.	*1328.* Giovanni Pisano *d.* Heinrich Suso: *Büchlein der Wahrheit*.
1329. Mar. 27: John XXII condemns some opinions of Master Eckhart (*In agro dominico*).	*1329. Aug. 4*: Wittelsbach family compact of Pavia separates Bavaria and Palatinate. *1330. Nov. 29*: Mortimer executed.	*1329. May 31*: Albertino Mussato, chronicler and poet, *d.* *1330.* 'I Fioretti di San Francisco' ('The Little Flowers of Saint Francis'). Abbey Church of Ettal founded by Emperor Lewis. **1330-1336.** Andrea Pisano: South door of Baptistery, Florence.
1331. *Nov. 16*: Papal *Rota* constituted (*Ratio iuris*).		
	1332. First division of Parliament into two Houses recorded.	**1332.** Company of meistersingers formed at Toulouse.
1333. Annual English tribute to Rome, promised in 1213, falls into arrears. **1333-1348.** John Stratford, Archbishop of Canterbury. **1334-1342.** Pope Benedict XII (Jacques Fournier).		**1333-1391.** Zenith of Arabic civilization in Granada under Yussuf I and his son Muhammad V.
		1335. Matthew Blastares: *Syntagma Canonum et Legum*; compilation of Greek canon and civil law.
1336. *Jan. 29*: Bull *Benedictus Deus* decides dispute about the Beatific Vision. *June 20*: Reorganization of Benedictine Order (*Summi magistri*).	**1336.** Count of Flanders prohibits commerce with England. *Aug. 12*: Edward III prohibits export of wool to Flanders and moves staple from Bruges to Antwerp.	

I. WESTERN EUROPE	II. CENTRAL, NORTHERN, AND EASTERN EUROPE	III. ISLAM AND ASIA
1337. *Oct.*: Edward III claims French crown. *Nov.*: English defeat Count of Flanders, Philip VI's ally, at Cadsand; beginning of Hundred Years' War, **1337-1453.**		**1337.** Orkhan takes Nicomedia.
1338. *June*: French burn Portsmouth. *July*: Edward lands in Flanders and allies with Artevelde and Flemish towns.	**1338.** *Sept. 5:* Lewis IV and Edward III conclude alliance at Coblentz.	
1339. *Oct.*: Edward invades France from Flanders.	**1339.** Venice conquers Treviso, her first mainland possession.	
1340. *Jan. 25*: Edward assumes title of King of France, at Ghent. *June 24*: English defeat French off Sluys. French occupy Guienne. *Sept. 25*: Truce of Esplechin between Edward and Philip. *Oct. 30*: Alfonso XI of Castile defeats Moors at River Salado.	**1340.** *Apr. 1:* Gerard of Holstein murdered by Danish nobles. *Dec. 20*: Union of Upper and Lower Bavaria (**-1349**). **1340-1375.** Valdemar IV Atterdag of Denmark.	
1341. *Apr. 30*: John III of Britanny *d.* War of succession between John de Montfort and Charles of Blois. *June*: David II returns to Scotland; Baliol finally takes refuge in England.	**1341.** *Mar. 15:* Alliance between Lewis IV and Philip VI of France.	**1341-1347, 1354-1376, 1379-1391.** John V Palaeologus, Eastern Emperor.
1342. *Aug.*: De Montfort and the English defeat Charles of Blois at Morlaix.	**1342.** *Feb. 11:* Lewis IV invests his son, Lewis, with Tyrol and Carinthia. **1342-1382.** Louis II, the Great, of Hungary.	
1343. *Jan. 19:* Truce of Malestroit between Edward and Philip. Aragon conquers Mallorca.	**1343.** Peace of Kalisz; Poland cedes Pomerellen and Kulm to Teutonic Order. **1343-1381.** Joan I, Queen of Naples. **1343-1380.** Haakon VI of Norway.	
1344. Earl of Derby successful in Guienne. Philip VI invests his son Philip with the newly created dukedom of Orleans.	**1344.** Electors desert Lewis IV in favour of Charles of Moravia, son of John of Bohemia.	
1345. *Oct. 21*: Earl of Derby defeats French at Auberoche.	**1345.** Lewis IV obtains Holland, Zeeland, Frisia, and Hainault. *July 24*: James van Artevelde murdered.	
1346. *Aug. 26*: Edward defeats French at Crecy. Derby takes Poitiers. *Oct. 17*: Edward's Queen Philippa defeats and captures David II at Neville's Cross.	**1346.** *July 11:* Charles of Moravia elected German King (**-1378**). Valdemar IV of Denmark sells Estonia to Teutonic Order. Stephen IV of Serbia crowns himself emperor.	

IV. ECCLESIASTICAL HISTORY	V. CONSTITUTIONAL AND ECONOMIC HISTORY	VI. CULTURAL LIFE
		1337. *Jan. 8*: Giotto di Bondone *d.* **1337-1339.** Ambrogio Lorenzetti: Fresco in Palazzo Communale, Siena.
1338. *Sept. 5*: Emperor Lewis annuls all papal verdicts against himself.	**1338.** *July 16*: Electoral Union of Rense (a legally elected king does not need papal confirmation). *Aug. 6*: Lewis IV issues decree *Licet iuris* against papal interference.	
	1340. Robert de Bourchier appointed first lay Chancellor of England. First European paper mill set up at Fabriano, Italy.	**1339.** Grenoble University founded. **1340.** Queen's College, Oxford, founded. **1340-1341.** Lupold of Bebenburg: *Tractatus de iure regni et imperii.*
	1341. *Jan. 15*: Edward III removes all sheriffs. *Feb. 10*: Edward III issues *Libellus famosus* against Archbishop Stratford. *Apr.*: Parliament enforces reconciliation between Edward and Stratford.	**1341.** *Apr. 8*: Petrarch crowned poet on the Capitol, Rome.
1342-1352. Pope Clement VI (Peter Roger).		**1342.** Marsilius of Padua *d.*
1343. *Jan. 27*: Bull *Unigenitus Dei Filius* enacts Jubilee Year to be kept every 50th year.	**1343.** *Apr.*: Parliament revokes Royal Acts of **1341**. Constitution of Florence changed in favour of the lower guilds. *Sept. 9*: Magnus of Norway gives privileges to German merchants at Bergen.	
1344. *Apr. 30*: Archbishopric of Prague established (*Pro parte carissimi*). German Electors reject any papal interference in electing German king. **1344-1347.** Richard Fitz Ralph: *Summa contra Armenos.*		**1344.** St. Guy's Cathedral, Prague, begun by Matthew of Arras (-**1352**).
	1345. Harmenopulos: *Hexabiblos,* Byzantine adaptation of Roman civil law.	
1346. *Apr. 13*: Clement VI excommunicates and dethrones Lewis IV.	**1346.** *Jan. 7*: Emperor Lewis issues Law Code for Upper Bavaria. Bankruptcy of Florentine bankers Bardi and Peruzzi.	**1346.** Pembroke College, Cambridge, and Valladolid University founded.

I. WESTERN EUROPE	II. CENTRAL, NORTHERN, AND EASTERN EUROPE	III. ISLAM AND ASIA
1347. *June 19*: English defeat and capture Charles of Blois at La Roche. *Aug. 3*: Calais surrenders to Edward. *Sept. 28*: Anglo-French truce at Calais.	**1347.** *Oct. 11*: Lewis IV *d.* Louis of Hungary invades Naples to revenge murder of King Andrew, his brother (*Nov. 18*, **1345**). **1348.** *July 8*: Charles IV confers title of Dukes upon Princes of Mecklenburg. **1348-1350.** The false Valdemar in Brandenburg.	**1347.** Hasan Bahmani establishes kingdom of Kulbarga in the Deccan. **1347-1354.** John VI Cantacuzene, anti-emperor of Byzantium, aided by Turks.
1349. Philip VI gains Dauphiné and Montpellier for French crown.	**1349.** *Jan. 30-June 14*: Anti-king Gunther, Count of Schwarzburg. **1349-1352.** Casimir of Poland acquires Galicia.	
1350. *Aug. 22*: Philip VI *d.*, succeeded by John II (**-1364**). *Aug. 29*: English defeat Spaniards off Winchelsea. **1350-1369.** Peter the Cruel, of Castile.	**1350.** *Feb. 14*: Treaty of Bautzen; Charles IV cedes Brandenburg and Tyrol to the Wittelsbachs for their recognition of him. **1351.** Zurich joins Swiss League. **1351-1382.** Winrich of Kniprode, Grand Master of Teutonic Order; the Order at its zenith.	**1351-1388.** Firoz Shah, Sultan of Delhi.
1352. English capture Guisnes. French defeated in Brittany.	**1352.** Glarus and Zug join Swiss League. Austria wars against Zurich. *Jan. 14*: Peace between Louis of Hungary and Joan of Naples.	
	1353. Berne joins Swiss League, which now consists of ' the 8 old Cantons.' **1353-1390.** Rupert I, Elector Palatine.	**1353.** Turks begin to invade Europe by settling at Tzympe.
1354. Scots ally with France.	**1354.** Charles IV grants ducal rank to his brother, Wenzel of Luxemburg.	**1354.** Turks take Gallipoli.
1355. *Aug.*: Scots defeat English at Nesbit.	**1355.** *Apr. 5*: Charles IV crowned Emperor in Rome. Conspiracy and (*Apr. 17*) execution of Marino Falieri at Venice. *Dec. 20*: Stephen Dushan of Serbia *d.*	**1355.** Iliyas Shah establishes independent kingdom of Bengal.
1356. English raid Scottish Border (Burnt Candlemas). *Sept. 19*: Black Prince defeats French at Maupertuis; John II and his son Philip taken prisoners.	**1356.** Peace between Austria and Zurich. War between Venice and Hungary. Margravate of Jülich raised to a dukedom.	

IV. ECCLESIASTICAL HISTORY	V. CONSTITUTIONAL AND ECONOMIC HISTORY	VI. CULTURAL LIFE
1347. *Apr.-Dec.* Nicola di Rienzi, tribune of the people, rules Rome.	**1347.** Organization of Hanseatic merchants at Bruges. King Magnus introduces national law code in Sweden. **1347-1351.** Black Death devastates Europe.	
1348. Clement VI purchases town of Avignon.	**1348.** *July 21:* Peter IV of Aragon breaks power of Estates by his victory at Epila.	**1348.** *Apr. 7:* Prague University founded by Charles IV. Gonville College, Cambridge, founded. Giovanni Villani, Florentine chronicler, *d.* **1348-1353.** Giovanni Boccaccio: *Decamerone.*
1349. *Oct. 20:* Clement VI forbids Flagellant movement. **1349-1366.** Simon Islip, Archbishop of Canterbury. **1350.** Charles IV imprisons Rienzi at Prague.	**1349.** Great persecution of Jews in Germany. Edward III establishes Order of the Garter. Stephen Dushan issues Serbian law code.	**1349-1370.** Choir and staircase of St. Mary's, Erfurt, built. **1349.** *Apr. 10:* William of Occam *d. Sept. 29:* Richard Rolle of Hampole, mystic, *d.* **1350.** Trinity Hall, Cambridge, founded. Frescoes in Campo Santo of Pisa (*Triumph of Death*) begun.
1351. Statute of *Provisions* forbids papal provisions and reservations.	**1351.** Statute of Labourers regulates wages. *June 21:* First coinage of groats (4d.).	**1351.** *June 20:* Margaret Ebner, mystic, *d.*
1352. Charles IV extradites Rienzi to the Holy See. *Jan. 25:* Alvarez Pelayo, advocate of papal omnipotence, *d.* **1352-1362.** Pope Innocent VI (Stephen Aubert); restores discipline in the papal courts.	**1352.** Statute of Treasons defines the nature of treason.	**1352.** Corpus Christi College, Cambridge, founded. Ranulph Higden: *Polychronicon* (historical standard work in 14th and 15th centuries). Antwerp cathedral begun.
1353. Statute of *Praemunire* forbids appeals of English clergy to Holy See. **1353-1357.** Aegidius Albornoz, Cardinal legate, re-establishes papal authority in papal State. **1354.** Rienzi re-establishes his tyranny at Rome. *Oct. 8:* Rienzi murdered.	**1353.** Edward III moves wool staple from Bruges to England (*Ordinatio stapularum*).	**1353.** Boccaccio, *Decameron.* **1354-1357.** Andrea di Cione, called Orcagna: Altar of the Strozzi Chapel in S. Maria Novella, Florence. **1355.** St. Mary's, Nuremberg, endowed by Charles IV, begun.
	1356. *Jan. 3:* Wenzel of Luxemburg grants *Joyeuse Entrée* to Estates of Brabant. *Jan. 10 and Dec. 25:* Charles IV issues Golden Bull at Nuremberg and Metz (settles election of German king, and constitution of Empire till **1806**). *Sept.:* French States-General meet under Étienne Marcel and demand reforms.	**1356.** *Dec. 27:* Christina Ebner, mystic, *d.* **1356-1363.** Sultan Hassan mosque, Cairo, built. **1356-1364.** Papal Palace built at Avignon. **1356-1397.** Peter Parler of Gmünd, architect of Prague Cathedral.

I. WESTERN EUROPE	II. CENTRAL, NORTHERN, AND EASTERN EUROPE	III. ISLAM AND ASIA
1357. *Mar. 23:* 2 years' truce of Bordeaux. *July:* De Montfort established as duke of Brittany by the English. *Oct. 3:* Treaty of Berwick; David II released from captivity. **1357-1367.** Peter I, the Cruel, of Portugal.		**1357.** Turks take Adrianople.
1358. *Jan.:* Preliminary peace between Edward III and John II.	**1358.** The Hapsburgs, twice defeated at Zurich, make peace with Swiss league. Venetians, defeated by Genoese off Sapienza, cede Dalmatia to Hungary. **1358-1365.** Rudolf IV of Austria, styles himself (Palatine) archduke.	**1358-1389.** Sikandar Shah, king of Bengal.
1359. *Mar. 24:* Peace treaty of London, restoring Henry II's French possessions to England; rejected by French Estates. *Nov.:* Edward invades northern France, Champagne and Burgundy.		**1359-1389.** Murad 1, emir of Turks.
1360. *Jan. 11:* Treaty of Guillon between Edward III and Philip of Burgundy. *May 8:* Preliminary peace of Brétigny. *Oct. 24:* Final peace of Calais; Edward keeps Calais, Guisnes, Ponthieu, Guienne, Gascony, Poitou, Saintonge, La Rochelle, Limousin, Angoulême, Channel Islands.	**1360.** Valdemar IV of Denmark wins Schonen back from Sweden.	**1360.** Firoz Shah founds city of Jaunpur.
	1361. *July 27:* Valdemar IV takes Visby, Gotland.	**1361.** Murad takes Demotika and Seres.
1362. *Apr. 6:* Disbanded companies defeat royal French army at Brignais.	**1362.** *July:* Valdemar IV defeats Hanse off Helsingborg. **1362-1389.** Dmitri IV Donskoi, grand duke of Moscow.	
1363. John II invests his younger son, Philip, with dukedom of Burgundy (-**1404**).	**1363.** Rudolf IV of Austria obtains Tirol. Magnus II of Sweden dethroned (*d.* **1374**) and succeeded by Albert of Mecklenburg (-**1389**; *d.* **1412**).	**1363.** Timur begins conquest of Asia.
1364. *Apr. 8:* John II *d.* in England; succeeded by Charles V (-**1380**). *May 16:* French defeat Charles of Navarre at Cocherel. *Sept. 29:* French defeat Anglo-Breton army at Auray; Charles of Blois killed.	**1364.** *Feb. 10:* Family pact of succession between the Luxemburgs and Hapsburgs at Brünn.	**1364.** Revolt of Crete against Venice.

IV. ECCLESIASTICAL HISTORY	V. CONSTITUTIONAL AND ECONOMIC HISTORY	VI. CULTURAL LIFE
1357. Albornoz issues *Constitutiones Aegidianae* (Law-code of the Pontifical State, valid till **1816**).	**1357.** Revolution at Paris under Marcel and Robert Le Coq against Dauphin.	**1357.** Thomas of Strasbourg, schoolman, *d.* Bartholus, chief jurist of the Post-glossators, *d.*
1358-1367. Second legation of Cardinal Albornoz.	**1358.** Revolt of French peasants (Jacquerie); this, and revolution at Paris, subdued by Dauphin; Marcel killed. **1358-1360.** *Sept. 29*: Hanseatic embargo on Flanders.	**1358.** John Buridan, schoolman and scientist, *d.*
	1359. Edward III grants self-government to English merchants in Netherlands.	**1359.** Nave of St. Stephen's, Vienna, begun.
		1360-1402. Alcazar of Seville built.
	1361. Reappearance of Black Death in England.	**1361.** Pavia University refounded. *June 16*: John Tauler of Strasbourg, mystic, *d.*
1362-1370. Pope Urban V (William Grimoard).	**1362.** English Staple fixed at Calais.	**1362.** William Langland: *Piers Plowman*. English used henceforth instead of French in parliamentary proceedings and in law courts. **1363.** Magdeburg Cathedral consecrated.
1363. *Aug. 4*: Urban V extends papal right of reservation to all bishoprics and monasteries.		
		1364. Cracow University founded by Casimir III.

I. WESTERN EUROPE	II. CENTRAL, NORTHERN, AND EASTERN EUROPE	III. ISLAM AND ASIA
1365. *Apr. 12*: Treaty of Guérande; John IV de Montfort recognized as Duke of Brittany. Sir Owen ap Thomas allies with France. **1366.** French expel Peter the Cruel from Castile, and install Henry Trastamare as king.	**1365.** *June 4*: Charles IV crowned King of Burgundy at Arles; allies with France and appoints Dauphin, Imperial Vicar. **1366.** Casimir III of Poland acquires Volhynia.	**1365.** Peter I of Cyprus takes Alexandria, but fails to keep it. **1366.** Adrianople made Turkish capital. Amadeus VI of Savoy takes Gallipoli from Turks and Varna from Bulgarians, but fails to keep them.
1367. *Feb.*: Black Prince makes expedition to Spain to assist Peter. *Apr. 3*: Black Prince defeats Henry of Trastamara at Najara, and restores Peter. **1367-1383.** Ferdinand I of Portugal.	**1367.** *Nov. 19*: Confederation of Hanse towns against Valdemar of Denmark, at Cologne. Formation of Grisons League of God's House. **1368.** Charles IV obtains by treaty Schweidnitz-Jauer, last independent Silesian duchy, and Lower Lusatia. Hapsburgs gain Breisgau. Charles IV's second expedition to Italy. **1369.** Charles IV returns to Germany. Venice repels Hungarian invasion.	**1368.** Mongol Yuan dynasty in China overthrown by national Ming dynasty (-1644). **1369.** John V Palaeologus visits Pope, Venice and France to obtain aid against Turks. **1369-1405.** Timur Lenk (Tamerlane), ruler of Mongols.
1369. *Mar. 23*: Henry of Trastamara secures Castile by Peter's defeat at Montiel. *May 21*: Charles V declares war on England. *June 3*: Edward III resumes title of King of France. Anglo-Scottish truce for 14 years. **1370.** French successes over English near Paris (*Sept.*), in Gascony and Maine (*Dec.*). *Sept. 19*: Black Prince sacks Limoges. Owen ap Thomas styles himself Prince of Wales. **1371.** English defeat Flemings off Bourgneuf. **1371-1390.** Robert II Stewart, King of Scotland. **1372.** *June*: Owen of Wales takes Guernsey and aids French. *June 23*: French and Castilians defeat English off La Rochelle. *Aug. 7*: French take Poitiers. *Sept.*: French take Angoulême and La Rochelle. Treaty of Vincennes between Scotland and France. **1373.** Duke of Lancaster invades France from Calais to Bordeaux. Brittany sides with France. Anglo-Portuguese treaty of friendship. **1374.** Peace between Aragon and Castile.	**1370.** *Feb. 17*: Teutonic Order defeats Lithuanians at Rudau. *May 24*: Peace of Stralsund between Hansa and Denmark-Norway, secures Hanseatic predominance in Northern Europe. **1372.** War between Venice and Genoa. *Aug. 27*: Sicily, under Frederick III of Aragon, separated from Naples. **1373.** *Aug. 15*: Treaty of Fürstenwalde; Charles IV gains Brandenburg from the Wittelsbachs.	**1371.** *Sept. 26*: Turks defeat Serbians at Chirmen.

IV. ECCLESIASTICAL HISTORY	V. CONSTITUTIONAL AND ECONOMIC HISTORY	VI. CULTURAL LIFE
1365. New English statute of *Praemunire* passed.		**1365.** Vienna University founded by Rudolf IV.
1366. English Parliament refuses to pay feudal tribute to Pope.	**1366.** Statute of Kilkenny, forbids Anglo-Irish intermarriage and Irish laws and customs.	**1366.** *Jan. 25*: Henry Suso, mystic, *d.*
1367. *Oct. 16*: Urban V enters Rome. Militch of Kremsier, Czech reformer: *Prophecia de Antichristo.*	**1367.** Scottish Parliament first sets up a Committee.	
1368. Edward III deposes Simon Langham, Archbishop of Canterbury (*d.* **1376**).	**1368.** Casimir III issues Statute of Wislica (central law-code for Poland).	
		1369. Chaucer: *Boke of the Duchesse.*
1370. *Aug. 5*: Urban V confirms Order of Bridgittines. Urban V returns to Avignon. **1370-1378.** Pope Gregory XI (Peter Roger de Beaufort).	**1370.** *Nov. 17*: Casimir III *d.*; Louis of Hungary elected King of Poland (beginning of elective Polish monarchy).	
	1371. *Nov. 25*: By Westphalian Public Peace, Charles IV transfers jurisdiction to Vehmic courts.	
1373. *July 23*: Bridget of Sweden, founder of Order of Bridgittines, *d.* **1374.** Bull *Salvator generis humani* condemns 14 paragraphs of Saxon law-code of Eike of Repgow.	**1373.** Tunnage and poundage imposed on English and foreign merchants. **1374.** *Sept. 17*: Treaty of Kaschau: Louis I grants Polish nobles immunity from taxes.	**1373.** Boccaccio accepts newly established chair for explanation of the *Divine Comedy*, at Florence. **1374.** *July 18*: Petrarch *d.* Mohammed ibn al Chatîb, Arabian poet, historian and physician, *d.*

I. WESTERN EUROPE	II. CENTRAL, NORTHERN, AND EASTERN EUROPE	III. ISLAM AND ASIA
1375. *June 27*: Anglo-French truce of Bruges, confines English to Bordeaux, Bayonne, and Calais. **1376.** *June 8*: Black Prince *d*.	**1375.** English, Welsh and French mercenaries invade Switzerland (' War of the Hooded Men '). **1376.** *June 10*: Wenceslas, Charles IV's son, elected, and (*July 6*) crowned king of the Romans. **1376-1387.** Olaf V, King of Denmark and (from **1380**) Norway.	**1375.** Mamelukes take Sis, capital of Armenia Minor; end of Armenian independence.
1377. *June 21*: Edward III *d*.; succeeded by his grandson Richard II (-**1399**). French attack English coast. **1378.** Owen of Wales slain. Scots recover Berwick. English acquire Brest and Cherbourg.	**1377.** *May 21*. Swabian Towns defeat Ulrich of Württemberg at Reutlingen. **1378.** *Nov. 29*: Charles IV *d*.; succeeded by Wenceslas (-**1400**). **1378-1381.** Victorious war of Chioggia, of Venice against Genoa.	
1379. Rising in Brittany against Charles V. English recover Berwick. **1379-1390.** John I of Castile. **1380.** *June*: English defeat Franco-Castilian fleet off Ireland. *Sept. 16*: Charles V *d*.; succeeded by Charles VI (-**1422**).	**1379.** *Sept. 25*: Albert III and Leopold III divide Hapsburg territories between them (Treaty of Neuberg). **1380.** *May 24*: County of Berg and Ravensberg raised to a dukedom by Wenceslas.	**1380.** *Sept. 8*: Dmitri IV of Moscow defeats Mongols at Kulikov.
1381. Anglo-French truce for 6 years (English keep Calais, Cherbourg, Bordeaux, and Bayonne).	**1381.** *Jan. 20*: Rhenish Town-League formed; *June 17*: allies with Swabian Town-League.	**1381.** Timur conquers Herat.
1382. *Nov. 27*: Flemish nobles and French defeat citizens of Ghent at Roosebeke.	**1382.** Leopold III of Austria acquires Trieste. *June 27*: Joan I of Naples *d*.; succeeded by Charles III of Durazzo (-**1386**). *Sept. 11*: Lewis I of Hungary and Poland *d*.	**1382.** Turks capture Sofia.
1383-1433. John I, illegitimate son of Peter I, Regent and (from **1385**) King of Portugal. **1384.** *Feb.*: Anglo-Scottish war renewed. Philip of Burgundy gains Flanders, Artois, and Franche Comté through his wife. **1385.** *May 1*: Anglo-French war renewed. *Aug. 14*: John I of Portugal defeats John I of Castile at Aljubarotta.	**1384.** Jadviga, daughter of Louis I (*d.* **1382**), crowned ' King ' of Poland. **1385.** *Feb. 21*: Rhenish and Swabian Towns ally with Swiss League, at Constance.	

IV. ECCLESIASTICAL HISTORY	V. CONSTITUTIONAL AND ECONOMIC HISTORY	VI. CULTURAL LIFE
	1376. Good Parliament: Commons make first impeachments before Lords. *June 4*: Swabian Town-League founded.	**1375.** *Dec. 21*: Giovanni Boccaccio *d.* Coluccio Salutati appointed Latin Secretary of Florence. John Barbour: *Brus.* **1376-1382.** Loggia dei Lanzi, Florence, built. **1376-1421.** Bruges town hall built.
1377. *Jan. 17*: Gregory XI enters Rome; end of Babylonian captivity. *Feb. 15*: Concordat with England.	**1377.** Parliament passes a poll-tax. Richard II confirms Hanse privileges.	**1377.** Guillaume de Machaut, French poet, *d.* Cloisters of Gloucester Cathedral built. Ulm Cathedral and the Court of Lions of the Alhambra begun.
1378. Great Schism begins: Urban VI (Bartolomeo Prignano) elected Pope at Rome (*Apr. 8*), Clement VII (Robert of Geneva) at Fondi (*Sept. 20*). England, Italy, Austria, Bohemia, Hungary recognize Urban; France, Spain, Sicily, Scotland, Cyprus recognize Clement.	**1378.** Rising of Ciompi (cloth-weavers) at Florence.	**1378.** William of Cologne, painter, *d.* **1378-1411.** Nave of Canterbury Cathedral rebuilt.
1379. Urban VI institutes feast of Visitation of the Virgin. Clement VII moves to Avignon.	**1379.** Imposition of a graduated poll-tax in England.	**1379.** William of Wykeham founds New College, Oxford. Master Bertram: Grabow Altar paintings.
1380. *Apr. 29*: Catherine of Siena *d.* Gerard Groote establishes Brotherhood of Common Life. Wycliffe begins to translate New Testament.	**1380.** *Jan.*: Parliament declares Richard II of age. *Nov.*: Parliament imposes additional graduated poll-tax. Great Ravensburg Trading Company established.	**1380-1400.** *Theologia Deutsch*, by a Teutonic Knight of Frankfort.
1381. Paris University suggests General Council to remove Schism. *June 14*: Simon Sudbury, Archbishop of Canterbury, beheaded by insurgents.	**1381.** *June-July*: Peasants' Revolt under Wat Tyler.	**1381.** *Dec. 2*: John of Ruysbroek, Dutch mystic, *d.*
1382. Wycliffe expelled from Oxford University; his doctrines condemned by London Synod; persecutions of Wycliffites and Lollards begin.	**1382.** Rising of Maillotins in Rouen and Paris.	**1382.** William of Wykeham founds Winchester College. *July 11*: Nicholas d'Oresme, French political economist and Bishop of Lisieux, *d.* *July 18*: Rulman Merswin, Swabian mystic, *d.*
	1383. *Mar. 11*: Wenceslas proclaims Nuremberg Public Peace for the Empire.	
1384. *Aug. 20*: Gerard Groote *d.* *Dec. 31*: John Wycliffe *d.*	**1384.** *July 26*: Heidelberg Agreement among German Estates.	**1384.** Chaucer: *House of Fame.*
1385. First French Pragmatic Sanction against papal interference.		**1385.** Chaucer: *Troilus and Cryseide.* Altichiero da Zevio, Italian painter, *d.*

I. WESTERN EUROPE	II. CENTRAL, NORTHERN, AND EASTERN EUROPE	III. ISLAM AND ASIA
1386-1388. John of Gaunt supports Portugal against Castile.	**1386.** *Feb. 27:* Charles III of Naples *d.*; war of succession between his son, Ladislaus, and Louis II of Anjou. Jagiello of Lithuania marries Jadviga, heiress to the Polish throne, and becomes King Vladislav II of Poland (**-1434**). *July 9:* Leopold III of Austria defeated and killed by Swiss at Sempach. *Aug. 15:* Gerard IV of Holstein obtains dukedom of Slesvig as hereditary Danish fief, by treaty of Nyborg.	
1387-1395. John I of Aragon.	**1387.** *Mar. 31:* Sigmund of Brandenburg, son of Charles IV, becomes King of Hungary, by marriage. Gian Galeazzo Visconti of Milan expels the Della Scalas from Verona.	
	1387-1412. Margaret, daughter of Valdemar IV, Queen of Denmark and (from **1388**) Norway.	
1388. *Aug. 19:* Scots defeat English at Otterburn (Chevy Chase).	**1388.** *Apr. 9:* Swiss defeat Leopold IV of Austria at Näfels. *Aug. 23:* Count of Württemberg defeats Swabian Towns at Döffingen. *Nov. 6:* Rupert, Elector Palatine, defeats Rhenish Towns at Worms.	
1389. Truce of Boulogne between England, France, and Scotland, for 3 years.	**1389.** *Feb. 24:* Danes defeat Albert of Sweden at Falköping; personal union of Sweden, Denmark and Norway.	**1389.** *June 15:* Turks defeat Serbians at Kossovo; Murad I murdered.
1390. Philip of Burgundy acquires county of Charolais.	**1389-1425.** Vassili II, Grand Duke of Moscow.	**1389-1403.** Bajazet I, Emir of Turks.
1390-1406. Robert (Stewart) III, King of Scots.		**1390.** Byzantines lose last possessions in Asia Minor to Turks.
1390-1406. Henry III of Castile.		**1391-1425.** Manuel II, Eastern Emperor.
1392. Louis, brother of Charles VI, becomes Duke of Orleans. Charles VI seized with madness.	**1392.** *Nov. 19:* Third partition of Bavaria.	**1392.** Timur sacks Baghdad.
	1392-1430. Vitold, Grand Prince of Lithuania.	**1393.** Bajazet subdues Bulgaria.
1394. Anglo-French truce for 4 years. *Sept. 29:* Richard II starts on expedition to Ireland.	**1394.** *May 8:* Wenceslas taken prisoner by his cousin, Jobst of Moravia, and rebellious Bohemian barons.	
1395. Principal Irish chiefs do homage to Richard.	**1395.** *Feb. 14:* Upper or Grey League (Grisons) formed. *Sept.:* Wenceslas appoints Gian Galeazzo Visconti Duke of Milan.	
1395-1410. Martin I of Aragon.		

IV. ECCLESIASTICAL HISTORY	V. CONSTITUTIONAL AND ECONOMIC HISTORY	VI. CULTURAL LIFE
1386-1387. Windesheim near Zwolle founded as abbey of Augustine Canons; becomes nucleus of *devotio moderna*.	**1386.** *Oct.*: Parliament appoints Council of Eleven.	**1386.** Heidelberg University founded by Rupert I, Elector Palatinate.
	1387. *Nov.*: Lords Appellant restrict authority of Richard II	**1387.** Milan Cathedral begun. **1387-1400.** Geoffrey Chaucer: *Canterbury Tales.*
1388. Severe persecution of Lollards in England.	**1388.** *Feb. 3 - June 4*: Merciless Parliament opposes Richard II. *July 15-***1392.** *Dec. 13*: Hanseatic embargo on Flanders.	**1388.** Cologne University founded. **1388-1440.** Nave of S. Petronio, Bologna, built.
1389. *Apr. 14*: Urban VI orders Jubilee Year to be celebrated every 33rd year (*Salvator Noster*). *Nov. 2*: Boniface IX (Peter Tomacelli) elected Pope at Rome (**-1404**). **1390.** Wycliffe's writings begin to circulate in Bohemia. **1391.** *Oct. 7*: Bridget of Sweden canonized.	**1389.** *May*: Richard II appoints Bishop Wykeham chancellor. *May 5*: Public Peace of Eger forbids Leagues of Towns in the Empire. **1391.** *Sept.*: Bishop Arundel succeeds Wykeham as chancellor. Statute of Provisors re-enacted. **1392.** Statute forbidding aliens to sell by retail. Commercial treaty between German Hansa and Novgorod.	**1389.** Hâfiz, Persian lyrical poet, d. **1389-1404.** Claus Sluter: Portal and Well of Moses at Champmol Charterhouse near Dijon. **1390-1393.** John Gower: *Confessio Amantis.* **1392.** Erfurt University founded.
1393. *Mar. 20*: King Wenzel murders St. John of Nepomuk, at Prague. **1394.** *June 6*: Nicholas de Clémanges, of Paris University, issues Memorandum on convocation of Council. *Sept. 28*: Benedict XIII (Peter of Luna) elected Pope at Avignon (**-1424**). **1395.** *May 16*: Boniface IX confirms reformatory activities of Windesheim Congregation.	**1393.** *July 10*: Sempach Letter, first military organization of Swiss League. Statute of *Praemunire* re-enacted. **1394.** Arundel disgraced. Court of Chancery made permanent. **1395.** Richard II publishes amnesty in Ireland.	**1394-1486.** Nave of Winchester Cathedral rebuilt.

1396–1406

I. WESTERN EUROPE	II. CENTRAL, NORTHERN, AND EASTERN EUROPE	III. ISLAM AND ASIA
1396. *Oct. 25:* Charles VI of France becomes overlord of Genoa. *Nov. 4:* Richard II marries Isabella of France at Calais; truce extended to 28 years.		**1396.** *Sept. 27:* Bajazet defeats Christian army at Nicopolis.
1397. *Sept. 9:* Duke of Gloucester murdered. *Sept. 21:* Earl of Arundel executed.	**1397.** *July 20:* Union of Kalmar between Sweden, Denmark, and Norway.	
	1398. *Apr. 5:* Teutonic Order conquers Visby, Gotland.	**1398.** *Dec. 18:* Timur conquers Delhi.
1399. *Sept. 29:* Richard II deposed. *Sept. 30:* Henry IV, of Lancaster, son of John of Gaunt, succeeds to throne.	**1399.** *Aug. 5:* Mongols defeat Vitold of Lithuania at the River Vorskla.	
1400. *Jan.:* Henry IV suppresses rebellion of barons. *Feb. 14:* Richard II murdered. *Sept.:* Rebellion of Owain Glyndwr in Wales, lasts till 1415.	**1400.** *Aug. 20:* Rhenish Electors depose Wenceslas and (*Aug. 21*) elect Rupert III of the Palatinate king.	**1400.** Emperor Manuel II visits France and England to obtain aid against Turks. **1400-1440.** Ibrahim, King of Jaunpur.
	1401. *Jan. 18:* Poland and Lithuania formally united. Rupert makes inglorious expedition to Italy.	**1401.** *Mar. 24:* Timur conquers Damascus. *July 22:* Timur conquers Baghdad.
1402. *June 22:* English defeat Scots at Nesbit Moor. *Sept. 14:* Percies defeat Scots at Homildon Hill.	**1402.** Teutonic Order acquires Neumark from Brandenburg. *Sept. 3:* Gian Galeazzo Visconti *d.*	**1402.** *July 20:* Timur defeats Bajazet I at Ankara and takes him prisoner.
1403. *July 21:* Henry IV defeats rebellious Percies at Shrewsbury and subdues Northumberland.	**1403.** *June 3:* Valais joins Swiss League.	**1403.** *Mar. 8:* Bajazet I *d.*; Manuel II makes advantageous treaty with Soliman, one of his sons, who quarrel about succession. **1403-1411.** Soliman I, Emir of Turks.
1404. *Apr. 27:* Philip of Burgundy *d.*; succeeded by John the Fearless (**-1419**). *July 14:* Owain Glyndwr allies with France.	**1404.** *Aug. 4:* Dithmarschen peasants defeat Count of Holstein. Venice acquires Verona and Vicenza.	
1405. *Aug.:* French land in South Wales to aid Glyndwr.	**1405.** *Sept. 14:* Alliance of Marbach against King Rupert, headed by John, Archbishop of Mayence.	**1405.** *Feb. 18:* Timur *d.*; succeeded by Shah Rokh (**-1447**). **1405-1432.** Hoshang Shah, King of Malwa.
1406. *Feb. 28:* Treaty of Aberdaron between Percies, Mortimer, and Glyndwr aiming at partition of England. *Apr. 4:* Robert III of Scotland *d.*; James I a prisoner in England (**1405-1424**). Anthony, son of Philip of Burgundy, inherits Brabant and Limburg. **1406-1454.** John II of Castile.	**1406.** Venice acquires Padua. Florentines subdue Pisa.	

IV. ECCLESIASTICAL HISTORY	V. CONSTITUTIONAL AND ECONOMIC HISTORY	VI. CULTURAL LIFE
1396-1414. Thomas Arundel, Archbishop of Canterbury.		**1396.** Carthusian Convent of Pavia founded by Gian Galeazzo Visconti. *Aug. 20*: Marsilius of Inghen, schoolman, *d.*
1397. *Feb. 11*: Heinrich Heimbuch of Langenstein, advocate of General Council, *d.*	**1397.** Commons claim right of impeachment.	**1397.** Wilton Diptych painted.
1398-1399. Archbishop Arundel banished by Richard II.	**1398.** *Jan. 31*: Parliament of Shrewsbury gives Richard II income for life. *Apr. 1*: Robert III creates first Scottish Dukes.	**1398.** Confrérie de la Passion formed at Paris to perform religious plays (-**1548**).
	1399. *Sept. 30*: Parliament accepts resignation of Richard II and deposes him. *Oct. 15*: Acts of last Parliament of Richard II annulled.	**1399.** Johann von Saaz: *Der Ackermann aus Böhmen*.
		1399-1419. Tower of Strasbourg Minster built by Ulric of Ensingen.
		1400. *Oct. 25*: Geoffrey Chaucer *d. Apr. 28*: Baldus de Ubaldis, Italian jurist, *d.*
1401. Statute *De Heretico Comburendo* against Lollard heresies (repealed **1677**).	**1401.** Klaus Störtebeker, pirate, executed at Hamburg.	
		1402-1454. Brussels town hall built.
		1402-1517. Seville Cathedral built.
1403. Wycliffism spreads in Bohemia, preached by John Huss.	**1403.** Henry Beaufort, Henry IV's half-brother, appointed chancellor.	**1403-1502.** St. Mary's, Danzig, rebuilt.
		1403-1452. Lorenzo Ghiberti: Northern and Eastern Porches of the Baptistery, Florence.
1404. Sigmund of Hungary issues *Placitum Regium* against ecclesiastical courts. *Oct. 6*: 'Unlearned Parliament' of Coventry demands appropriation of all Church property.		**1404.** Conrad of Soest: Altar painting at Niederwildungen.
1404-1406. Pope Innocent VII (Cosimo de' Migliorati) at Rome.		
	1405. *June 6*: Archbishop Scrope of York and Thomas Mowbray Earl of Nottingham executed as rebels.	**1405.** Eustache Deschamps, French poet, *d.*
1406-1415. Pope Gregory XII (Angelo Correr) at Rome.	**1406.** *Feb.-Dec.*: Long Parliament reorganizes finances, reforms county elections, regulates succession to Crown, controls Privy Council.	**1406.** *Jan.*: Claus Sluter, sculptor, *d. May 4*: Coluccio Salutati, humanist, *d.* Abd er Rahmân ibn Chaldûn, Arabian historian, *d.*

I. WESTERN EUROPE	II. CENTRAL, NORTHERN, AND EASTERN EUROPE	III. ISLAM AND ASIA
1407. *Nov. 23:* Louis, Duke of Orleans, murdered by Burgundian agents.		
1408. *Feb. 19:* Rebel Earl of Northumberland killed at Bramham Moor. **1409.** Martin of Aragon obtains Sicily by marriage.	**1408.** *Apr. 21:* Ladislaus of Naples seizes Rome. **1409.** Venice wars against Sigmund of Hungary; *July 9:* recovers Dalmatia.	
1410. Civil war in France between followers of Dukes of Orleans and Burgundy. *May 31:* Martin, king of Aragon and Sicily, *d.*	**1410.** *May 18:* King Rupert *d.*; Wenceslas, Sigmund of Hungary, Jobst of Moravia, candidates. *July 15:* Vladislav II of Poland defeats Teutonic Order at Tannenberg.	
1411. Rebellion of the Cabochiens (guilds supporting Burgundy) at Paris. *Oct. 31:* Peace between Castile and Portugal. *Nov.:* English and Burgundians defeat Orleanists at St. Cloud.	**1411.** *Jan. 18:* Jobst of Moravia *d.* *Feb. 1:* First Peace of Thorn (Teutonic Order loses Samogitia). *May 19:* Louis of Anjou defeats Ladislaus of Naples at Rocca Secca. *July 21:* Sigmund elected German King (**-1437**). Appenzell allies with Swiss League.	**1411-1443.** Ahmad Shah, King of Gujarat; founder of Ahmadabad.
1412. *May 18:* Henry IV abandons Burgundy and allies with Orleans. Aragon Estates elect Prince Ferdinand of Castile king (**-1416**). **1413.** *Mar. 20:* Henry IV *d.* *Apr. 9:* Coronation of Henry V.	**1412-1439.** Eric of Pomerania, King of Denmark, Norway, and Sweden. **1412-1447.** Philip Maria, last Visconti Duke of Milan. **1413.** *Oct. 14:* Henry of Plauen, Grand Master of Teutonic Order, deposed.	**1413-1421.** Mohammed I, Emir of Turks.
1414. *May 23:* Henry V and Burgundy ally. *Sept. 29:* New Anglo-Burgundian treaty.	**1414-1435.** Joan II, Queen of Naples.	
1415. *Sept. 22:* Henry V takes Harfleur. *Oct. 25:* Henry V defeats French at Agincourt.	**1415.** *Apr. 30:* Sigmund gives Frederick VI, Burgrave of Nuremberg, Electorate of Brandenburg. Swiss take Aargau from Hapsburgs.	**1415.** *Aug. 21:* Portuguese conquer Ceuta.
1416. *Aug. 15:* Treaty of Canterbury between Henry V and the Emperor. *Oct. 8:* Treaty of Calais between Henry V, Emperor, and Burgundy. Owain Glyndwr *d.* **1416-1458.** Alfonso V of Aragon and Sicily and (from **1435**) of Naples.	**1416.** *Feb. 19:* Sigmund creates Amadeo VIII, Count of Savoy, a duke.	**1416.** Venetians defeat Turks off Gallipoli.

IV. ECCLESIASTICAL HISTORY	V. CONSTITUTIONAL AND ECONOMIC HISTORY	VI. CULTURAL LIFE
1407. *Feb. 18*: Ordinance on ' Old liberties of the Gallican Church '; published *May 15*, **1408.**	**1407.** First charter granted to Merchant Adventurers by Henry IV. *Oct.*: Parliament of Gloucester vindicates right of Commons to originate all money grants. St. George's Bank, Genoa, founded.	
1408. *June 29*: 13 Cardinals of both parties summon Council to end Schism. **1409.** Council of Pisa meets: Benedict XIII and Gregory XII deposed. *June 26*: Alexander V (Peter Philargi) elected Pope; rivalry of three Popes. **1410.** *May 3*: Alexander V *d.* Pisa Council elects John XXIII (Balthasar Cossa). *July 18*: Archbishop of Prague excommunicates Huss and his followers.	**1409.** *Sept. 4*: Commercial Treaty between England and Teutonic Order.	**1408.** Andrew Rublev: Holy Trinity (painting) at Troiza Sergius Monastery near Moscow. **1409.** Leipzig University founded by German émigrés from Prague.
	1410. *Jan.*: Sir Thomas Beaufort appointed chancellor.	**1410.** Jean Froissart, poet and chronicler, *d.* Paul, Hans, and Hermann of Limburg: *Les très riches heures du Duc de Berry.*
1411. John XXIII excommunicates Huss, who had refused to obey his summons.	**1411.** *Nov.*: Beauforts, aided by Prince of Wales, aim at deposing Henry IV.	**1411-1412.** Thomas Occleve: *De Regimine Principum.* **1411-1426.** London Guildhall built.
1412. Huss: *Adversus indulgentias; Contra bullam pape.*	**1412.** *Jan. 5*: Arundel appointed chancellor, Prince of Wales removed from Council.	**1412.** St. Andrews University founded.
1413. *Feb. 8*: John XXIII condemns Wycliff's writings. Huss: *De ecclesia.* **1414 - 1443.** Henry Chicheley, Archbishop of Canterbury. **1414-1418.** Council of Constance, to settle *causa unionis, reformationis, fidei.*	**1413.** *Mar. 21*: Henry Beaufort appointed chancellor. **1414.** *May*: Parliament passes Statute against Lollards.	**1413.** André Beauneveu, miniaturist and sculptor, *d.*
1415. *May 29*: John XXIII deposed. *July 4*: Gregory XII resigns. *July 6*: Huss burnt as heretic. Council condemns doctrine of tyrannicide as advocated by Jean Petit, of Paris University. **1416.** *May 30*: Jerome of Prague, follower of Huss, burnt.	**1415.** *Nov.*: Parliament grants Henry V customs on wool, tunnage, and poundage for life.	**1415.** Thomas à Kempis: *De Imitatione Christi. Apr. 15*: Manuel Chrysoloras *d.* at Constance.
		1416. Donatello: St. George (sculpture). Alain Chartier: *Livre de quatre dames.*

I. WESTERN EUROPE	II. CENTRAL, NORTHERN, AND EASTERN EUROPE	III. ISLAM AND ASIA
1417. *Sept. 20*: Henry V takes Caen. *Dec. 12*: Sir John Oldcastle, Lord Cobham, leader of Lollards, burnt.	**1417.** Sigmund creates Adolf II, Count of Cleves-Mark-Ravensberg, a duke.	
1418. *May*: Paris receives John of Burgundy.	**1418.** Venice takes Friuli from Sigmund.	
1419. *Jan. 19*: Rouen capitulates to Henry V. *July 29*: Peace of Melun between Dauphin and Burgundy. *Sept. 10*: John of Burgundy murdered by agents of the Dauphin, at Montereau. *Dec. 2*: Philip II of Burgundy (**-1467**) allies with Henry V.	**1419.** *Aug. 16*: Ex-King Wenceslas *d.*; Sigmund obtains Bohemia. **1419-1436.** War between Empire and Bohemian Hussites.	
1420. *May 21*: Treaty of Troyes; Charles VI recognizes Henry V as Regent and heir apparent. *June 2*: Henry V marries Catherine of France. *Dec. 1*: Henry V enters Paris.	**1420.** *Nov. 1*: Hussites defeat Sigmund at Vysehrad. Venice acquires Friuli and Belluno.	
	1421. *Oct. 2*: Hussites defeat Sigmund at Saaz. Florence acquires Leghorn.	**1421.** Pekin made capital of China. **1421-1451.** Murad II, Emir of Turks.
1422. *Aug. 31*: Henry V *d.*; succeeded by Henry VI, 9 months old (**-1461**). *Oct. 21*: Charles VI *d.*; succeeded by Charles VII (**-1461**).	**1422.** *Jan. 8*: Hussites defeat Sigmund at Deutschbrod.	**1422.** First siege of Constantinople by Turks.
1423. *Aug. 1*: Salisbury defeats French at Cravant. *Nov. 21*: James I of Scotland released.	**1423.** *Jan. 6*: Sigmund gives Frederick V, Margrave of Meissen, Electorate of Saxony.	
1424. *Aug. 17*: Bedford defeats French and Scots at Verneuil. *Oct.-Nov.*: Gloucester invades Burgundian Hainault.	**1424.** *Oct. 11*: Zizka, Hussite leader, *d.* of plague.	**1424.** Turks conquer Smyrna.
1425. *Aug. 2*: Salisbury takes Le Mans.	**1425-1462.** Vassili III of Moscow.	**1425-1448.** John VIII, Eastern Emperor.
1426. *Jan. 19*: Philip of Burgundy defeats Gloucester's army.	**1426.** *June 6*: Hussites win battle of Aussig.	
1427. *Sept. 5*: Dunois defeats English at Montargis.	**1427.** *July 11*: Danes defeat Hansa off Copenhagen. *Aug. 3*: Hussites win battle of Mies.	
1428. *July 3*: Treaty of Delft: Philip the Good acquires Holland, Zeeland, and Hainault. *Oct.*: Salisbury besieges Orleans.	**1428.** *Apr. 19*: Peace of Ferrara; Milan cedes Brescia and Bergamo to Venice.	
1429. *May 1-3*: Jeanne d'Arc raises siege of Orleans. *July 17*: Charles VII crowned at Reims. *Nov. 6*: Henry VI crowned at Westminster.		**1429.** *Mar.*: Turks take Salonika.

IV. ECCLESIASTICAL HISTORY	V. CONSTITUTIONAL AND ECONOMIC HISTORY	VI. CULTURAL LIFE
1417. *July 26*: Benedict XIII deposed. *Oct. 9*: Council issues 5 decrees of reform. *Nov. 11*: Martin V (Otto Colonna) elected Pope (**-1431**).		
1418. *Feb. 22*: Martin V condemns doctrines of Wycliffe and Huss (*Inter cunctas*). *Mar. 21*: Council issues 7 more decrees of reform. *May 2*: Concordats with France and Germany, *May 13*: with Castile, *July 21*: with England.	**1418.** *June 24*: Constitution of German Hansa.	
1419. *Apr. 5*: Vincent Ferrer, preacher of penitence, *d.* *July 30*: Hussite revolt in Prague.		**1419.** Rostock University founded. Filippo Brunelleschi: Foundling hospital, Florence. *Feb. 0*: Ulric of Ensingen, architect of Ulm and Strasbourg Minsters, *d.*
1420. *July*: Four articles of Prague, common confession of Hussites. *Aug. 9*: Peter of Ailli, conciliar theologian, *d.*		**1420-1434.** Brunelleschi: Cupola of Cathedral, Florence.
		1421. Brunelleschi begins rebuilding S. Lorenzo, Florence.
		1422. Thomas Walsingham: *Historia Anglicana*. William Caxton *b.*
1423-1424. Council of Pavia and Siena.		**1423.** James I of Scotland: *Kingis Quair*.
		1423-1438. Doges' Palace, Venice, enlarged.
1424-1429. Anti-pope Clement VIII (Egidius Muñoz; resigns; *d.* **1446**).	**1424.** *Jan. 17*: Meeting of Electors at Bingen. Scottish Parliament constitutes Committee of the Articles.	**1424.** Master Franke (John of Strasbourg?) paints St. Thomas' Altar for the Hamburg merchants trading with England.
		1425. Thomas à Kempis, *De imitatione Christi*. Alain Chartier: *La belle dame sans merci*.
	1426. Denmark imposes the Sound toll (until **1857**).	**1426.** Louvain University founded.
1427. *Aug. 30*: John I of Portugal issues *Concordia*.	**1427.** *Dec. 2*: Frankfort Diet votes a general and direct tax throughout the Empire, to continue Hussite war.	**1427.** Lincoln College, Oxford, founded.
		1428. Masaccio, painter, *d.*
1429. *July 12*: Jean Le Charlier de Gerson, conciliar theologian, *d.*	**1429.** *Jan. 10*: Philip of Burgundy creates Order of Golden Fleece.	

I. WESTERN EUROPE	II. CENTRAL, NORTHERN, AND EASTERN EUROPE	III. COUNTRIES OVERSEA
1430. *May 23*: Jeanne d'Arc captured by Burgundians at Compiègne. Philip of Burgundy inherits Brabant and Limburg.	**1430.** *Nov. 10*: Union of East Frisia under Cirksena chieftains.	
1431. *May 30*: Jeanne d'Arc burnt at Rouen. *Dec. 16*: Henry VI crowned at Paris. René, Duke of Bar, inherits Lorraine.	**1431.** *Aug. 14*: Hussites defeat Crusaders at Taus.	**1431-1432.** Portuguese discover Azores.
1433-1438. Edward of Portugal.	**1433.** *May 31*: Sigmund crowned Emperor by Eugene IV.	
1434. René of Lorraine inherits Provence and claim to Naples.	**1434.** *May 30*: Radical Hussites (Taborites) defeated at Lipan; Procop, their leader, killed. **1434-1444.** Vladislav III, King of Poland and (from **1440**) Hungary. **1434-1464.** Cosimo de' Medici, founder of Medicean rule over Florence.	
1435. *Sept. 15*: Duke of Bedford *d.* at Rouen. *Sept. 21*: Peace of Arras between Charles VII and Philip of Burgundy, who obtains Macon, Auxerre and part of Picardy. **1436.** *Apr. 13*: French recover Paris. **1437.** *Feb. 21*: James I murdered at Perth; succeeded by James II (-**1460**).	**1435.** *July 17*: Peace of Vordingborg; Eric of Denmark cedes Slesvig to Adolf VIII of Holstein. *Dec. 31*: Peace of Brest; Teutonic Order cedes Samogitia and Sudauen to Poland. **1437.** Venetians gain Dalmatian coast from Sigmund. *Dec. 9*: Sigmund *d*. *Dec. 18*: Albert V of Austria becomes King of Hungary and (*Dec. 27*) Bohemia.	
1438. *July 1*: Anglo-Scottish truce for 9 years. **1438-1481.** Alfonso V of Portugal.	**1438.** *Mar. 18*: Albert of Austria, Sigmund's son-in-law, elected German King. Swedish Diet appoints Charles Knutson regent.	
1439. *Sept. 28*: Anglo-Burgundian truce of Calais, for **3** years.	**1439.** Danish and Swedish Diets depose Eric and elect Christopher of Bavaria, his nephew (-**1448**). Armagnacs invade Alsace. *Oct. 27*: King Albert II *d*.	

IV. ECCLESIASTICAL HISTORY	V. CONSTITUTIONAL AND ECONOMIC HISTORY	VI. CULTURAL LIFE
	1430. First Disfranchising Statute, fixes 40s. freehold as qualification for voting. *Libel of English Policie* first shows importance to England of commerce and sea power.	**1430-1443.** Brunelleschi: Pazzi Chapel near S. Croce, Florence.
1431-1447. Pope Eugene IV (Gabriel Condulmer). **1431-1449.** Council of Basle.	**1431-1433.** First German peasant revolt near Worms.	**1431.** Henry VI founds Caen University; Charles VII of France, Poitiers University. **1432.** *May 6:* Jan van Eyck finishes altarpiece, St. John's, Ghent.
1433. *Nov. 30:* Prague Compact, placates Utraquists. Nicholas of Cues: *Concordantia Catholica.* **1434.** *May 29:* Revolt in Rome; Eugene IV flees to Florence.	**1433.** *Jan. 9:* Vladislav II grants Polish noblemen *Habeas Corpus* Constitution of Cracow.	
1435. *June 9:* Basle Council abolishes annates, payment for pallia, and other taxes.	**1435.** *July 17:* Peace of Vordingborg; Eric of Denmark confirming all privileges of the Hansa. First Swedish Riksdag, at Arboga. *ca.* **1435.** *Reformatio Sigismundi,* treatise on political and social reforms.	**1435.** Upsala Cathedral consecrated. L. B. Alberti: *Treatise on the art of painting.*
1436. *July 5:* Iglau Compact; peace with Hussites. **1437.** *Jan. 15:* Council ratifies Iglau Compact. *Sept. 18:* Eugene moves Council to Ferrara. Nicholas of Clémanges, conciliar theologian, *d.* **1438.** *July 7:* Pragmatic Sanction of Bourges, asserts Gallican liberties against papacy.	**1437.** *Mar. 22:* Henry VI confirms privileges of Hansa. Arnsberg reform of Vehmic courts. **1438.** Diet of Nuremberg begins to reform the Empire. **1438-1441.** Trade-war between Hansa and Holland.	**1438.** *Oct. 20:* Jacopo della Quercia, sculptor, *d.* All Souls College, Oxford founded.
1439. *Mar. 26:* German Diet accepts reform decrees of Basle Council. *May 16:* Basle Council makes authority of Council a dogma. *June 25:* Basle Council deposes Eugene IV. *July 6:* Union with Greek Church (*Laetentur coeli*). *Sept. 4:* Eugene IV condemns reform decrees and excommunicates Basle Council (*Moyses*). *Nov. 5:* Basle Council elects Amadeo VIII of Savoy Pope (Felix V). *Nov. 22:* Union with Armenian Church. Number of Seven Sacraments fixed (*Exultate Deo*). Eugene IV moves Ferrara Council to Florence.	**1439.** *Nov. 2:* Charles VII establishes permanent tax (*Taille*).	**1439.** Nicholas de Werwe, sculptor, *d.*

I. WESTERN EUROPE	II. CENTRAL, NORTHERN AND EASTERN EUROPE	III. COUNTRIES OVERSEA
1440. French Praguerie, headed by Dauphin, suppressed.	**1440.** *Feb. 1:* Frederick V, duke of Styria, elected German king (Frederick III; **-1493**). **1440-1457.** Vladislav Posthumus, son of king Albert II, succeeds in Hungary and Bohemia. **1441.** Venice acquires Ravenna. **1442.** Norwegians expel Eric (*d. 1459*), who is succeeded by Christopher of Denmark. *June 14:* Zurich allies with Frederick III against Swiss league.	
1443. *Feb. 26:* Alfonso V of Aragon enters Naples. *Dec. 23:* Philip II of Burgundy obtains Luxemburg.		**1443.** *Nov. 3:* Hunyady Janos defeats Turks at Nish.
1444. *May 28:* Anglo-French truce of Tours, for 2 years.	**1444.** *Aug. 26:* Armagnacs defeat Swiss at St Jacob, near Basle.	**1444.** *Nov. 10:* Vladislav III of Poland and Hungary killed in battle of Varna against Turks.
1445. *Apr. 22:* Henry VI marries Margaret of Anjou.		**1445.** Diniz Diaz discovers Cape Verde.
	1446. *Jan. 24:* Eugene IV deposes archbishops of Cologne and Trier for their opposition to Frederick III.	**1446.** Hunyady Janos elected regent of Hungary.
1447. *Aug. 13:* Filippo Maria Visconti *d.*; Alfonso of Naples and house of Orleans claim Milan.	**1447-1492.** Casimir IV of Poland and Lithuania.	**1447.** Scanderbeg defeats Murad II. India, Persia, Afghanistan, gain independence after breakup of Timur's empire.
1448. *May:* Anglo-Scottish war renewed. French recover Maine and Anjou.	**1448.** *Sept. 28:* Christian, count of Oldenburg, elected king of Denmark (**-1481**). Knutson Bonde elected king Charles VIII of Sweden (**-1470**). **1449-1453.** War between towns and princes in south Germany.	**1448.** *Oct. 19:* Murad II defeats Hunyady Janos at Kossovo. **1448-1453.** Constantine XI, eastern emperor.
1449. *Mar. 24:* English break truce, capturing Fougères. French recover Normandy. **1450.** *Feb. 26:* Francesco Sforza enters Milan and assumes title of duke (**-1466**). *Apr. 15:* French defeat English at Formigny. *May 2:* Suffolk murdered. *Aug. 12:* French recover Cherbourg.	**1450.** *July 13:* Zurich rejoins Swiss league. *Aug. 1:* Christian of Denmark becomes king of Norway. *Oct. 22:* Frederick III recognizes Hunyady Janos as regent of Hungary.	
1451. French conquer Guienne.	**1451.** St Gall allies with Swiss league.	**1451-1489.** Bahlol Lodi, first Pathan king of Delhi. **1451-1481.** Mohammed II, emir of the Turks.
1452. *May 18:* Frederick III creates Borso, marquis of Este, duke of Modena and Reggio. *Oct. 23:* English recapture Bordeaux.	**1452.** *Mar. 19:* Frederick III crowned emperor. *Apr. 27:* George Podiebrad elected regent of Bohemia.	

IV. ECCLESIASTICAL HISTORY	V. CONSTITUTIONAL AND ECONOMIC HISTORY	VI. CULTURAL LIFE
		1440. Johann Gensfleisch (Gutenberg) invents art of printing by movable type. Platonic Academy formed at Florence.
1441. *Feb. 4:* Eugene IV ascribes monopoly of all means of grace to Roman Catholic Church (*Cantate Domino*).	**1441.** *Sept. 6:* Peace of Copenhagen between Hansa and Holland.	**1441.** Jan van Eyck *d.* King's College, Cambridge, and Eton founded by Henry VI.
		1441-1447. Gürzenich (public dancing hall) built at Cologne.
	1442. *Aug. 14:* Reformation of Frederick III (Public Peace of Frankfort).	**1442-1458.** John of Cologne builds western towers of Burgos Cathedral.
1443. *Sept. 28:* Eugene IV returns to Rome, and moves Florence Council to Rome.	**1443.** *Aug. 15:* Commercial treaty between John II of Castile and Hansa.	**1443-1453.** Palace of Jacques Coeur built at Bourges.
1443-1452. John Stafford, Archbishop of Canterbury.		
1444. *May 20:* Bernardin of Siena *d.*		**1444.** *Mar. 9:* Leonardo Bruni, humanist, *d. Apr. 26:* Robert Campin ('Master of Flémalle'), painter, *d.* Enea Silvio: *Euryalus and Lucretia.*
1445. Rome Council dissolved.	**1445.** *Feb.-Mar.:* Charles VII creates standing army in France.	**1445-1471.** Choir of St. Lawrence's, Nuremberg, built.
1446. Joh. Hagen, Abbot of Bursfelde, establishes Bursfelde Congregation of German Benedictine monasteries.	**1446.** *Mar. 21:* Frankfort Agreement of Electors against papal interference in Empire affairs.	**1446-1515.** King's College Chapel, Cambridge, built.
1447. *Feb. 5-7:* Concordats with several German princes. *Feb. 23:* Eugene IV *d.; Mar. 6:* succeeded by Nicholas V (Thomas Parentucelli; **-1455**).		**1446.** *Apr. 15:* Brunelleschi *d.* Konrad Witz *d.*
		1447. Queens' College, Cambridge, founded. *Feb. 28:* Humphrey, Duke of Gloucester, humanist, *d.*
1448. *Feb. 17:* Vienna Concordat with Emperor Frederick III; final failure of conciliar movement. *July:* Basle Council moves to Lausanne.	**1448.** Frederick of Brandenburg subdues Berlin, Hansa town, and makes it capital.	**1447-1453.** Donatello: Gattamelata monument at Padua.
1449. *Apr. 7:* Felix V, last antipope, resigns (*d.* **1451**). *Apr. 25:* Lausanne Council dissolved.		
1450. Bohemian and Moravian Communion of Brethren (*Unitas fratrum*) formed.	**1450.** *May-July:* Rebellion of Jack Cade in Kent.	**1450.** Nicholas V forms Vatican Library. Nicholas of Cues: *Idiota de Sapientia.* Georgios Gemisthos Plethon, Greek philosopher and philologist, *d.*
1451-1452. Legation of Cardinal Nicholas of Cues to promote Church reform in Germany.	**1451.** Jacques Coeur, French financier, disgraced.	**1451.** *Jan. 7:* Glasgow University founded. Stephen Lochner, Cologne painter, *d.*
1452 (*or* **1453**). Agreement between ecclesiastical Electors to remedy abuses.	**1451.** *July 14-***1457.** *Aug.:* Commercial war between Hansa and Flanders-Burgundy.	
1452-1454. John Kemp, Archbishop of Canterbury.		

I. WESTERN EUROPE	II. CENTRAL, NORTHERN, AND EASTERN EUROPE	III. COUNTRIES OVERSEA
1453. *July 17*: French defeat English at Castillon. *Oct. 19*: Bordeaux surrenders to the French ; English hold only Calais and Channel Islands.	**1453.** *Apr. 27*: Peace of Lauf between Nuremberg and Albert Achilles of Brandenburg-Kulmbach.	**1453.** *May 29*: Turks capture Constantinople.
1454. *Mar. 27*: Richard duke of York made protector by parliament.	**1454.** *Apr. 9*: Peace of Lodi between Venice and Milan ; Venice secures Brescia, Bergamo, Crema, and Treviglio.	
1454-1474. Henry IV of Castile.		
1455. *Feb.*: York excluded from council. *May 22*: York defeats royal forces at St Albans (beginning of the Wars of the Roses). *Nov. 12*: York again becomes protector.	**1455.** *Feb. 25*: Italian league under protectorate of Nicholas V.	
1456. *Feb. 25*: York removed from protectorship. *July 7*: Trial of Joan of Arc annulled.	**1456.** *Aug. 8*: Hunyady *d.*	**1456.** Turks conquer Athens except the Acropolis. *July*: Hunyady successfully defends Belgrade.
	1457. *June 6*: Poles conquer Marienburg; grand master of Teutonic Order moves to Königsberg. *July 2*: Christian of Denmark and Norway crowned king of Sweden.	**1457.** Papal navy defeats Turks off Metelino.
		1457-1504. Stephen the Great, prince of Moldavia.
1458-1479. John II of Aragon and Sicily; Naples becomes separate kingdom under Ferdinand I, illegitimate son of Alfonso V (**-1494**).	**1458.** *Jan. 24*: Mathias Hunyady Corvinus elected king of Hungary (**-1490**). *Mar. 2*: George Podiebrad elected king of Bohemia (**-1471**).	**1458.** *June*: Turks take Acropolis of Athens.
1459. *Sept.-Oct.*: Henry VI subdues rebellion of Yorkist lords.	**1459-1463.** The Wittelsbachers (Palatinate and Bavaria) successfully defy the Emperor and Albrecht Achilles.	**1459.** Turks conquer Serbia.
		1459-1511. Mahmud Shah Bigarha, king of Gujarat.
1460. *July 10*: Richard of York defeats Henry VI at Northampton and takes him prisoner. *Aug. 3*: James II killed at Roxburgh; succeeded by James III (**-1488**). *Dec. 30*: Queen Margaret defeats and kills York at Wakefield.	**1460.** *Mar. 5*: Christian I of Denmark becomes duke of Slesvig and Holstein, which are declared indivisible for ever.	**1460.** Turks conquer Morea. *Nov. 13*: Henry the Navigator, infante of Portugal, *d.*
1461. *Feb. 2*: Edward of York wins battle of Mortimer's Cross. *Feb. 17*: Queen Margaret defeats Warwick at St Albans. *Mar. 4*: Henry VI deposed. *Mar. 29*: Edward IV defeats Henry VI at Towton; Henry flees to Scotland. *June 28*: Edward IV crowned. *July 22*: Charles VII *d.*; succeeded by Louis XI (**-1483**).	**1461-1463.** Dieter of Isenburg and Adolf of Nassau rivals for archbishopric of Mainz.	**1461.** Turks conquer Trebizond.
	1461. *Aug. 21*: Pius II deposes Dieter of Mainz. War between Frederick III and his brother, Albert VI (*d. Dec 2*, **1463**).	
1462. *June 28*: Queen Margaret allies with France. *Sept.-Dec.*: Warwick defeats queen and French. Louis XI acquires Roussillon from Aragon.	**1462.** *June 30*: Elector Palatine and archbishop Dieter defeat Adolf at Seckenheim.	**1462.** Castilians take Gibraltar from Arabs.
	1462-1505. Ivan III of Moscow.	

IV. ECCLESIASTICAL HISTORY	V. CONSTITUTIONAL AND ECONOMIC HISTORY	VI. CULTURAL LIFE
1453. Republican conspiracy in Rome, led by Stefano Porcaro, against papal rule.	**1453.** *Jan. 6*: Frederick III confirms forged *Privilegium Maius* in favour of the Hapsburgs. Polish Diet of Petrikau divided into Upper and Lower Houses.	**1453-1455.** Gutenberg and Fust print the 42-line (Mazarin) Bible, at Mayence.
1454-1486. Thomas Bourchier, Archbishop of Canterbury.		
1455-1458. Pope Calixtus III (Alfonso Borgia).		**1455.** *Mar. 18*: Antonio Pisanello *d. Dec. 1*: Lorenzo Ghiberti *d.* Fra Giovanni Angelico da Fiesole *d.*
1455. *May 15*: Crusade against Turks proclaimed (*Ad summi apostolatus apicem*).		
1456. Frankfort meeting of German princes, issue *Gravamina Nationis Germanicae*. *Oct. 23*: John of Capistrano *d.*		
		1457. Freiburg University founded. *Aug. 1*: Lorenzo Valla, humanist, *d.*
1458. John of Segovia, conciliar theologian and historian, *d.*		**1458.** Magdalen College, Oxford, founded.
1458-1464. Pope Pius II (Enea Silvio Piccolomini).		
1459-1460. Congress of Mantua, presided over by Pius II, decides upon Crusade against Turks.	**1459.** *Nov.*: First Bill of Attainder passed by Parliament, against Yorkist leaders.	**1459.** *Oct. 30*: Giovanni Francesco Poggio Bracciolini, humanist, *d.*
1460. *Jan. 18*: All appeals from the Pope to a Council forbidden (*Execrabilis*).		**1459-1460.** Basle University founded.
		1460. Hans Rosenplüt, Nuremberg meistersinger, *d.* Palazzo Pitti, Florence, begun.
		1460-1483. St. George's Chapel, Windsor Castle, built.
1461. *June 29*: Catherine of Siena canonized. *Nov. 27*: Louis XI temporarily annuls Pragmatic Sanction of Bourges.		
1462. *Mar. 31*: Pius II annuls Prague Compact and forbids chalice to the laity.	**1462.** *Oct. 20*: Louis XI diverts French commerce from Geneva to Lyons Fairs. John de Castro discovers alum-mines of Tolfa, Papal State.	

I. WESTERN EUROPE

1463. *Oct. 8*: Truce of Hesdin between Edward IV and Louis XI.

1464. *June 1*: Peace between Edward IV and Scots; Henry VI brought to London.

1465. Formation of the French League of Public Weal. *July 16*: Burgundy and rebels defeat Louis XI at Montlhéry. *Oct. 29*: Peace of St. Maur; Louis yields to League.

1466. Louis XI allies with Earl of Warwick.

1467. *June 15*: Philip II of Burgundy *d.*; succeeded by Charles the Bold (**-1477**). Liége submits to Charles the Bold.

1468. *Oct. 9*: Meeting of Louis XI and Charles the Bold at Péronne.

1469. *July 26*: Warwick defeats Edward IV at Edgecote. Charles the Bold acquires Alsace, Breisgau, and Ghent. *Oct. 19*: Ferdinand of Aragon marries Isabel of Castile.

1470. *Oct. 3*: Edward IV flees to Flanders. Warwick restores Henry VI.

1471. *Feb.*: Louis XI takes Amiens from Charles the Bold. *Feb. 20*: James III annexes Orkney and Shetland. *Apr. 14*: Warwick defeated and killed by Edward IV at Barnet. *May 4*: Edward IV defeats Queen Margaret and kills Prince Edward at Tewkesbury. *May 21*: Edward IV enters London; Henry VI murdered.

1472. Louis XI subdues a new League and checks Burgundy and Aragon.

1473. Charles the Bold acquires Gelderland and Zutphen.

1474. *July 27*: Treaty between Edward IV and Charles the Bold. *Nov.*: Louis XI occupies Franche-Comté.

1474-1504. Isabella, Queen of Castile.

II. CENTRAL, NORTHERN, AND EASTERN EUROPE

1463. *July 24*: Frederick III recognizes Mathias of Hungary, who recognizes Hapsburg claims to succession.

1464. *Dec. 23*: Ulric Cirksena created Count of East Frisia.

1465-1508. Albert IV the Wise, Duke of Bavaria.

1466. *Oct. 19*: Second Peace of Thorn; Teutonic Order cedes Pomerellen, Ermland, and Kulmerland to Poland; East Prussia made Polish fief.

1468. Christian I of Denmark pawns Orkney and (**1469**) Shetland islands to Scotland.

1469. *May 9*: Sigmund of Tyrol pawns Upper Alsace to Charles the Bold, by treaty of St. Omer.

1469-1492. Lorenzo de' Medici, il Magnifico, ruler of Florence.

1471. *May 27*: Vladislav, son of Casimir IV of Poland, becomes King of Bohemia and (**1490**) Hungary (**-1516**). *Oct. 10*: Swedes under Sten Sture defeat Christian of Denmark at Brunkeberg.

1471-1473. Naval war of Hansa towns with England.

1473. *Sept. 29*: Frederick III and Charles the Bold meet at Treves.

1474. *Mar. 30-June 11*: Hapsburgs recognize independence of Swiss League.

III. COUNTRIES OVERSEA

1463. Turks conquer Bosnia.

1463-1479. War between Venice and Turks.

1467. Turks conquer Herzegovina.

1468. *Jan. 17*: George Kastriota, called Skanderbeg, Prince of Albania, *d.*

1470. Turks take Negroponte (Euboea) from Venice.

1471. *Aug.*: Portuguese conquer Tangier.

1472. Dietrich Pining, Danish admiral, discovers Newfoundland.

1473. Mohammed II styles himself Sultan. Cyprus comes under Venetian rule.

IV. ECCLESIASTICAL HISTORY	V. CONSTITUTIONAL AND ECONOMIC HISTORY	VI. CULTURAL LIFE
1463. *Oct. 22*: Pius II proclaims crusade under his own control against Turks.		**1463.** François Villon, French lyrical poet, *d.*
		1463-1470. Sultan Mohammed II's mosque built at Constantinople.
1464-1471. Pope Paul II (Peter Barbo).	**1464.** *June 19*: Louis XI establishes French Royal Mail.	**1464.** *June 16*: Rogier van der Weyden *d. Aug. 11*: Cardinal Nicholas Krebs of Cues, German philosopher and ecclesiastical politician, *d.*
	1465. *Jan.*: Parliament grants Edward IV tunnage and poundage. Edward IV first coins the Angel-Noble (6s. 8d.).	**1465.** *Jan. 4*: Charles, Duke of Orleans, French poet, *d.* Sweynheym and Pannartz set up first printing press in Italy, at Subiaco.
1466. *Dec. 23*: Paul II deposes and excommunicates George Podiebrad of Bohemia.		**1466.** *Dec. 13*: Donatello *d.* Johann Mentel prints first German Bible at Strasbourg.
1468. Paul II abolishes Roman Academy. *Sept. 26*: Cardinal Juan de Torquemada, advocate of papalism, *d.* Bishopric of Vienna established.		**1468.** George Ganghofer begins building St. Mary's, Munich. *Feb. 3*: Johann Gutenberg *d.*
		1469. *Oct. 9*: Fra Filippo Lippi, painter, *d.*
1470. *Apr. 19*: Jubilee Year to be commemorated every 25th year.		**1470-1480.** Tomb of Frederick III, by Nicholas of Leyden, at St. Stephen's, Vienna.
1471. *Apr. 14*: Paul II creates Borso of Este, Duke of Ferrara.	**1471-1476.** Sir John Fortescue: *The Governance of England.*	**1471.** *July 25*: Thomas Hamerken of Kempen (Thomas à Kempis), religious writer, *d.*
1471-1484. Pope Sixtus IV (Francesco della Rovere).		**1471-1480.** Arnold of Westphalia builds Albrechtsburg at Meissen.
1472. *Aug. 17*: St. Andrews made archbishopric. Gregory Heimburg, German ecclesiastical politician, *d.*		**1472.** Ingolstadt University founded. *Apr. 25*: Leon Battista Alberti *d. Nov. 18*: Cardinal John Bessarion, Greek humanist, *d.*
	1473. Albert Achilles decrees indivisibility of Brandenburg Electorate (*Dispositio Achillea*). Fuggers begin business dealings with Hapsburgs.	**1473.** St Catharine's College, Cambridge, and Buda university founded.
1474. *May 23*: Sixtus IV confirms Order of the Hermits of St. Francis of Assisi, founded by Francis of Paula.	**1474.** *Feb. 28*: Peace of Utrecht between Hansa and England; Edward IV confirms all privileges. Three Fugger brothers transform their family business into a private company.	**1474.** Andrea Mantegna: Frescoes in Camera degli Sposi, Mantua. *Nov. 27*: Guillaume Dufay, French composer, *d.* Caxton prints first book in English (*Histories of Troy*), at Bruges.

I. WESTERN EUROPE	II. CENTRAL, NORTHERN, AND EASTERN EUROPE	III. COUNTRIES OVERSEA
1475. *July*: Edward IV invades France. *Aug. 29*: Peace of Picquigny between Edward and Louis. *Nov.*: Charles the Bold conquers Lorraine.	**1475.** *June 24*: An Imperial army relieves Neuss besieged by Charles the Bold.	
1476. *Mar. 2*: Swiss defeat Charles the Bold at Grandson and (*June 22*) Morat.		**1476.** Bahlol Lodi expels Husain, last King of Jaunpur.
1477. *Jan. 5*: Charles the Bold killed at Nancy. Louis XI seizes Burgundy and Artois; René II recovers Lorraine.	**1477.** *Aug. 19*: Maximilian, son of Frederick III, marries Mary of Burgundy.	
1478. Treaty between France and Castile.	**1478.** Ivan III of Moscow subdues Novgorod.	
1479. *Jan. 19*: Union of Aragon and Castile under Ferdinand the Catholic (**-1516**) and Isabella.	**1479.** *Aug. 7*: Maximilian defeats French at Guinegate.	**1479.** *Jan. 26*: Peace of Constantinople between Mohammed II and Venice, which cedes Lemnos and her possessions in Albania.
1480. *Mar. 6*: Treaty of Toledo; Spain recognizes conquest of Morocco by Portugal, Portugal cedes claims to Canaries. *July 10*: René of Lorraine, *d.*; Louis XI acquires Anjou, Bar, Maine, and Provence.	**1480.** Ivan III throws off Mongol rule and styles himself Tsar. **1480-1499.** Ludovico Sforza the Moor, Regent (from **1494** Duke) of Milan (*d.* **1508** imprisoned in France).	**1480.** *Aug. 11*: Turks take Otranto, and besiege Rhodes.
1481. *Apr.*: War breaks out between England and Scotland. **1481-1495.** John II of Portugal.	**1481.** *Dec. 22*: Fribourg and Solothurn join Swiss League. **1481-1513.** John of Denmark and (from **1483**) Norway.	**1481.** Turks evacuate Otranto. **1481-1512.** Bajazet II, Sultan of the Turks.
1482. *Dec. 23*: Peace of Arras divides Burgundy; Maximilian obtains Netherlands, Luxemburg, and Franche-Comté.	**1482.** War between Alfonso of Naples, Ferrara, Venice, and the Pope.	**1482.** End of Bahmani kingdom in the Deccan. Portuguese settle on Gold Coast.
1483. *Apr. 9*: Edward IV *d.*; succeeded by Edward V. *June 26*: Richard of Gloucester usurps the throne. *July*: Edward V and his brother murdered. *Aug. 30*: Louis XI *d.*; succeeded by Charles VIII (**-1498**).		
1484. *Sept. 20*: Anglo-Scottish truce for 3 years.	**1484.** *Aug. 7*: Peace of Bagnolo; Ferrara cedes the Polesina to Venice.	

IV. ECCLESIASTICAL HISTORY	V. CONSTITUTIONAL AND ECONOMIC HISTORY	VI. CULTURAL LIFE
1475. *Mar. 28*: Johann Pupper of Goch, Dutch church reformer, *d*.		**1475-1479.** Aristotle Fioravanti, of Florence, builds Uspensky cathedral in the Kremlin, Moscow.
	1476. Constabulary (*Santa Hermandad*) reorganized in Castile and Aragon.	**1476.** Caxton establishes printing press at Westminster. *July 6*: Johann Müller Regiomontanus, astronomer *d*. Uppsala University founded.
	1477. *Feb. 11*: Mary of Burgundy grants Great Privilege to Estates of Netherlands.	**1477.** Mainz and Tübingen universities founded.
		1477-1481. Michael Pacher: altar at St Wolfgang, Austria.
		1477-1489. Veit Stoss: carved altar in St Mary's, Cracow.
1478. Johann Geiler von Kaysersberg appointed preacher in Strasbourg cathedral.	**1478.** *Apr.*: Conspiracy of the Pazzi against Medici rule at Florence. *May 2*: Giuliano de' Medici assassinated.	
1479-1480. Johann Busch, German church reformer, *d*.		**1479.** Copenhagen university founded. Hans Memling: altarpiece in St John's hospital, Bruges.
1480. Ferdinand and Isabella of Spain authorized by the pope to appoint inquisitors against heresy chiefly among converted Jews.		**1480.** *Mar. 5*: Peter of Andlau, German constitutional jurist, *d*. Leonardo da Vinci invents parachute. Caxton prints *The Chronicles of England*.
1481. *Mar. 21*: Nicholas von der Flüe (Brother Claus) *d*. Johann Ruchrad of Wesel, church reformer, *d*.		**1481.** Verrocchio: statue of Bartolommeo Colleoni at Venice (cast by Leopardi in **1493**).
		1481-1483. Botticelli, Ghirlandaio, Perugino, Pinturicchio, Signorelli and others paint frescoes in Sistine chapel, Rome.
1482. Ferdinand and Isabella of Spain compel Sixtus IV to make a concordat.	**1482.** *Dec. 14*: Eberhard the Bearded unites Württemberg territories.	**1482.** *Feb. 2*: Luca della Robbia *d*. Hugh van de Goes *d*.
1483. *Oct. 17*: Spanish inquisition comes under joint direction of state and church. *Nov. 10*: Martin Luther *b*.	**1483.** Royal College of Arms, London, established.	
1484-1492. Pope Innocent VIII (John Baptist Cibò).	**1484.** Parliament passes reform acts on law, trade, and tax-collecting.	**1484.** Luigi Pulci, poet, *d*.
1484. *Dec. 5*: Bull *Summis desiderantes* against witchcraft and sorcery.	**1484-1504.** Bertold of Henneberg, archbishop of Mainz, leader of political reform movement in the empire.	

I. WESTERN AND SOUTHERN EUROPE	II. CENTRAL, NORTHERN, AND EASTERN EUROPE	III. COUNTRIES OVERSEA
1485. *Aug. 7:* Henry of Richmond lands at Milford Haven. *Aug. 22:* Richard III defeated and killed at Bosworth. *Nov. 7:* Henry VII crowned. Brittany revolts against Charles VIII.	**1485.** *May 22:* Matthias of Hungary captures Vienna. *Aug. 26:* Ernest and Albert of Saxony divide Wettin territories.	
1486. *Jan. 17:* 3 years' truce between England and France.	**1486.** *Feb. 16:* Maximilian I elected King of the Romans. **1486-1525.** Frederick the Wise, Elector of Saxony.	
1487. *May 5:* Rebellion of Yorkists. *May 24:* Lambert Simnel, pretender, crowned king in Dublin. *June 16:* Rebels defeated at Stoke-on-Trent.	**1487.** Tsar Ivan III subdues Kazan.	**1487.** Diaz rounds Cape of Good Hope.
1488. *June 11:* James III murdered; succeeded by James IV (**-1513**). *July 14:* Anglo-French truce renewed. *July 28:* Bretons defeated at St. Aubin. *Oct. 5:* 2 years' truce between England and Scotland.	**1488.** *Feb. 14:* Swabian League formed in South Germany. *Nov. 17:* Agreement of Reval between Teutonic Order and Sweden. **1488-1489.** Revolt of Flemish towns against Maximilian.	
1489. *Feb. 10:* Alliance of Redon between England and Brittany. *Aug. 18:* Ferdinand of Aragon captures Malaga.	**1489.** *Feb. 14:* Treaty of Dordrecht between Emperor and England. *Apr. 6:* Hans Waldmann, Burgomaster of Zurich, executed for his dictatorial proclivities.	**1489.** *Mar. 14:* Catherine Cornaro, Queen of Cyprus, cedes her kingdom to Venice. **1489-1517.** Sikandar Lodi Shah, Sultan of Delhi.
1490. *Jan. 20:* Peace between England and Denmark. *July 27:* Treaty between England and Ludovico Sforza of Milan.	**1490.** *Mar. 16:* Sigmund of Tyrol cedes lands to Maximilian. *Apr. 4:* Matthias Corvinus d. Hungarians elect Vladislav of Bohemia king.	
1491. *Dec. 6:* Charles VIII marries Anne, heiress of Brittany. *Dec. 21:* 5 years' truce of Coldstream between England and Scotland.	**1491.** *Nov. 7:* Treaty of Pressburg; Vladislav of Bohemia and Hungary acknowledges Hapsburgs' right of succession.	**1491.** Portuguese expedition to Angola.
1492. *Jan. 2:* Spaniards conquer Granada. *Apr. 8:* Lorenzo de' Medici d. *Oct. 2:* Henry VII lands in France. *Nov. 3:* Peace of Étaples between England and France; France abandons the Pretender, Perkin Warbeck; Henry is bought off.	**1492.** Albert IV of Bavaria makes treaty of friendship with Swabian League. *June 7:* Casimir IV of Poland d.; succeeded in Poland by John Albert (**-1501**), in Lithuania by Alexander (**-1506**).	**1492.** *Aug. 3:* Columbus sails from Palos. *Oct. 12:* Columbus discovers San Salvador.
1493. *Jan. 19:* Peace of Barcelona between France and Spain; France cedes Roussillon and Cerdagne. *May 23:* Peace of Senlis between France and Emperor; France renounces Netherlands and Burgundy.	**1493.** *Aug. 19:* Emperor Frederick III d.; succeeded by Maximilian I (**-1519**).	**1493.** *May 4:* Alexander VI divides New World between Spain and Portugal (*Inter cetera divina*). Columbus discovers Jamaica. **1493-1518.** Husain Shah, King of Bengal.
1494. *Sept. 1:* Charles VIII invades Italy. *Nov. 17:* Charles enters Florence and expels Medicis.	**1494.** Warbeck recognized as King of England by Maximilian. **1494-1535.** Walter of Plettenberg, Land Master of Teutonic Order in Livonia.	**1494.** *June 7:* Treaty of Tordesillas; Spain and Portugal divide New World between themselves. Babar succeeds to throne of Ferghana.

IV. ECCLESIASTICAL HISTORY	V. CONSTITUTIONAL AND ECONOMIC HISTORY	VI. CULTURAL LIFE
1485. Diet of Kuttenberg grants equal rights to Roman Catholics and Utraquists in Bohemia. *Sept. 15*: Pedro de Arbues, Spanish inquisitor, murdered.	**1485.** Henry VII renews privileges of German Hansa in England. Importation of Bordeaux wines limited to English ships.	**1485.** Sir Thos. Malory: *Morte d'Arthur*, printed by Caxton. *Oct. 28*: Rudolf Agricola, humanist, *d.*
1486-1500. Cardinal Morton, Archbishop of Canterbury.	**1486.** *Mar. 17*: Diet of Frankfort proclaims public peace for 10 years.	**1486.** *Paston Letters* come to a close (from **1440**). H. Institoris and J. Sprenger: *Malleolus Maleficarum*.
	1487. *Apr. 17*: Commercial treaty of Novgorod between Russia and Hansa. *Nov.*: Parliament entrusts wider powers to Court of Star Chamber.	
	1488. Henry VII grants concessions to Italian merchants.	**1488.** Duke Humphrey's Library, Oxford, opened. Giov. Bellini: Altar-piece in S. Maria dei Frari, Venice.
1489. *Oct. 4*: Wessel Gansfort, church reformer, *d.* Ferdinand of Aragon unites to the crown Grand Mastership of Order of Calatrava; **1494**, that of Alcantara ; **1497**, that of St. James.	**1489.** *Mar. 27*: Commercial treaty between England and Spain. Act concerning importation of Bordeaux wines made permanent.	**1489.** Poliziano: *Miscellanea*. Palazzo Strozzi, Florence, begun by Benedetto da Maiano.
1490. *June 3-July 30*: Congress in Rome decides upon crusade against Turks.	**1490.** Anglo-Danish treaty admits English shipping to Iceland.	**1489-1498.** Philip of Commines: *Memoirs*. **1490.** Giuliano da Maiano *d.*
		1491. William Caxton *d.* *Feb. 2*: Martin Schongauer *d.*
1492. *Jan. 9*: Glasgow elevated to an archbishopric. **1492-1503.** Pope Alexander VI (Roderigo Borgia).	**1492.** *Mar. 31*: Jews expelled from Spain. Peasants' rebellion in Allgäu.	**1492.** Lebrija: *Arte de la Lingua Castellana*. *Oct. 12*: Piero della Francesca *d.* **1492-1498.** Bramante builds choir and cupola of S. Maria delle Grazie, Milan.
	1493. Commercial war between England and Flanders; *Sept.* 18: Flemings banished from England; Merchant Adventurers move from Antwerp to Calais. First *Bundschuh* (peasants' revolt) in Alsace.	**1493.** *July 12* and *Dec. 23*: Latin and German versions of Hartmann Schedel's *World Chronicle*, published by Anton Koburger at Nuremberg.
1494. Disputation of Cardinal Cajetano with Pico della Mirandola.	**1494.** *Dec.*: Poynings' Laws, make Irish legislature dependent on England. *Nov. 6*: Ivan III closes Hanseatic counter at Novgorod.	**1494.** Seb. Brant: *Ship of Fools*; Engl. transl. **1509**. *Aug. 11*: Hans Memling *d.* *Nov. 17*: Giov. Pico della Mirandola *d.* Venetian press of Aldus Manutius issues its first book.

I. WESTERN AND SOUTHERN EUROPE	II. CENTRAL, NORTHERN, AND EASTERN EUROPE	III. COUNTRIES OVERSEA
1495. *Feb. 22*: Charles VIII enters Naples. *Mar. 31*: Holy League of Emperor, Pope, Spain, Venice, and Milan against Charles, who leaves Italy (*Nov.*). *July 3*: Warbeck fails to land at Deal; goes to Scotland.	**1495.** *July 21*: Württemberg raised to a dukedom.	
1495-1521. Emmanuel the Fortunate of Portugal.		
1496. *July 18*: England joins Holy League against France; *Sept.*: Scots invade England.	**1496.** *Oct. 21*: Philip, son of Maximilian, marries Joan, heiress of Spain.	**1496.** *Mar. 5*: Henry VII gives his patronage to Cabot's voyages to North America.
1497. *July-Sept.*: Rebellion of Perkin Warbeck in England. *Sept. 30*: Truce between England and Scotland.	**1497.** *Oct. 28*: John II of Denmark defeats Swedes at Brunkeberg, revives Scandinavian Union.	**1497.** *Nov. 22*: Vasco da Gama rounds Cape.
1498. *Apr. 7*: Charles VIII *d.*; succeeded by Louis XII of Orleans (-**1515**). *June 15*: Macchiavelli appointed Florentine Secretary (-*Nov.7*,**1512**). *July 14*: Peace of Étaples renewed at Paris.	**1498.** Grisons join Swiss League.	**1498.** *May 27*: Vasco da Gama reaches Calicut. Columbus discovers Trinidad and mainland of South America. Cabot discovers Labrador and east coast of North America.
1499. *Sept. 11*: French expel Ludovico Sforza from Milan. *Nov. 23* and *28*: Warbeck and Edward Earl of Warwick beheaded as Pretenders.	**1499.** 'Swabian War' of Maximilian against Swiss League. *Sept. 22*: Peace of Basle establishes Swiss independence of Empire.	**1499.** Amerigo Vespucci and Alonso Hojeda discover Guiana and Venezuela.
1500. *Nov. 11*: Treaty of Granada between France and Spain concerning partition of Italy.	**1500.** *Feb. 17*: Dithmarschen peasants defeat Danes at Hemmingstedt and maintain their independence. *Apr. 12*: Maximilian inherits county of Gorizia.	**1500.** *May 3*: Cabral discovers Brazilian coast and secures it for Portugal.
1501. *July-Aug.*: Louis XII and Ferdinand conquer Naples. *Oct. 13*: Peace of Trento between France and Emperor who recognizes French conquests in Upper Italy.	**1501.** Basle and Schaffhausen join Swiss League. Alexander of Lithuania succeeds to the Polish throne.	**1501.** First voyage of Anglo-Portuguese Syndicate to North America. Turks take Durazzo from Venice.
1502. War breaks out between France and Spain. *Apr. 2*: Arthur, Prince of Wales, *d.* *Aug. 8*: James IV marries Margaret Tudor, daughter of Henry VII.		**1502.** Fourth voyage of Columbus. Second voyage of Anglo-Portuguese Syndicate to Newfoundland. Ismail establishes Safavid dynasty in Persia (-**1736**).
1503. Spaniards expel French from Naples; *Dec. 29*: Battle of river Garigliano.	**1503.** *Dec. 1*: George, Duke of Bavaria-Landshut, *d.*; war of succession between Bavaria and Palatinate.	**1503.** Third Anglo-Portuguese expedition to Newfoundland.
1504. *Jan. 31* and *Mar. 31*: Treaty of Lyons; France cedes Naples to Aragon (-**1713**). *Sept. 22*: Treaty of Blois between Maximilian and Louis XII. *Nov. 26*: Queen Isabel of Castile *d.*	**1504.** Albert IV of Bavaria defeats Rupert, Count Palatine (*d. Aug. 20*) and re-unites the Bavarian duchies.	**1504.** Fourth Anglo-Portuguese expedition to Newfoundland. Babar occupies Kabul.

IV. ECCLESIASTICAL HISTORY	V. CONSTITUTIONAL AND ECONOMIC HISTORY	VI. CULTURAL LIFE
1495. Girolamo Savonarola, preacher of penitence at Florence, summoned to Rome, refuses to obey. **1495-1517.** Cardinal Francisco de Ximenes, Archbishop of Toledo, reforms Spanish Church.	**1495.** *Aug. 7:* Diet of Worms proclaims Perpetual Peace, sets up Imperial Chamber as Court of Appeal, and imposes general tax (Common Penny). Jews expelled from Portugal.	**1495.** *Feb. 10:* Aberdeen University founded. Reuchlin: *De Verbo Mirifico.* Boiardo: *Orlando Innamorato.* **1495-1497.** Leonardo da Vinci *Last Supper* in S. Maria delle Grazie, Milan.
	1496. *Feb. 24: Magnus Intercursus* between England and Flanders settles commercial dispute; English merchants return from Calais to Antwerp.	**1496.** Colet begins to lecture in Oxford. Cancelleria, Rome, completed; begun in **1486.**
1497. Alexander VI confers title of ' Catholic Majesties ' on Spanish King and Queen.	**1497.** Monopoly for Netherlands granted to Merchant Adventurers.	**1497.** Jesus College, Cambridge, founded. Conrad Celtis introduces Humanism at Vienna, Bebel at Tübingen, Mutianus Rufus at Erfurt.
1498. *May 23:* Savonarola burnt at Florence. *Oct. 16:* Thomas de Torquemada, Inquisitor General, *d.*	**1498.** *Feb. 13:* Maximilian I establishes Imperial Council, Chancery, and Chamber.	**1498.** Erasmus settles in Oxford. Reuchlin: *Henno,* creates Latin play in Germany. Dürer: *Apocalypse. Dec. 7:* Alex. Hegius, educationist, *d.*
1499-1501. Caesar Borgia, son of Alexander VI, conquers Romagna.		**1499.** Alcalá University founded. *Oct. 1:* Marsilio Ficino *d.* **1499-1504.** Luca Signorelli: Frescoes in Orvieto Cathedral.
1500. Great Jubilee Year. *June 1:* Alexander VI imposes general tithe and proclaims crusade against Turks.	**1500.** *July 2:* Diet of Augsburg establishes Council of Regency for Empire administration.	**1500.** Erasmus: *Adagia.* First edition of *Till Owlglass;* Engl. transl. **1528.** Aldus founds Venice Academy for study of Greek classics, and invents *italics.*
1501. Persecution of Moors in Spain.		**1501.** Erasmus: *Enchiridion Militis Christiani.* Gawain Douglas: *Palace of Honour.* **1501-1504.** Michelangelo: Statue of *David.*
	1502. Peasants' rebellion (*Bundschuh*) in bishopric of Spires.	**1502.** Wittenberg University founded.
1503. *Sept. 22-Oct. 18:* Pope Pius III (Francesco Todeschini). **1503-1513.** Pope Julius II (Giuliano della Rovere).	**1503.** Parliament passes Statute of Retainers.	**1503.** Leonardo da Vinci: *Monna Lisa.* **1503-1519.** Henry VII's Chapel in Westminster Abbey built.
	1504. Henry VII places guilds and companies under State supervision.	**1504.** Sannazaro: *Arcadia,* pastoral romance. Giorgione: *Madonna* at Castelfranco.

I. WESTERN AND SOUTHERN EUROPE	II. CENTRAL, NORTHERN, AND EASTERN EUROPE	III. COUNTRIES OVERSEA
1505. *Oct. 10*: Treaty of Blois; France and Spain agree over Naples.	**1505-1533.** Vassili III, Grand Duke of Moscow.	**1505.** Fifth Anglo-Portuguese expedition to Newfoundland. **1505-1507.** Portuguese establish factories on east coast of Africa.
	1506. *Sept. 25*: Philip, son of Maximilian, *d.* at Burgos. **1506-1548.** Sigmund I, King of Poland.	**1506.** *May 21*: Columbus *d.*
1507. *Mar. 12*: Cesare Borgia *d.* *May 11*: France annexes Genoa.	**1507-1530.** Margaret, daughter of Maximilian, Governor of Netherlands.	**1507.** Waldseemüller names New World 'America' after Amerigo Vespucci.
1508. *Dec. 10*: League of Cambrai between Maximilian I, Louis XII, and Ferdinand of Aragon, against Venice.	**1508.** *Feb. 6*: Maximilian assumes title of emperor without being crowned. **1508-1544.** Lewis V, Elector Palatine; **1508-1550.** William IV, Duke of Bavaria.	
1509. *Mar. 23*: Julius II joins League of Cambrai. *Apr. 21*: Henry VII *d.*; succeeded by Henry VIII (-**1547**). *May 14*: Venetians defeated at Agnadello. Julius II annexes Faenza, Rimini, Ravenna; Ferdinand annexes Otranto and Brindisi. **1510.** *Feb. 24*: Agreement between Julius II and Venice.		**1509.** *Feb. 2*: Portuguese defeat fleets of Egypt and Gujarat off Diu. *May*: Spaniards conquer Oran. **1510.** *Mar. 4*: Albuquerque annexes Goa for Portugal.
1511. *Oct. 4*: League between Julius II, Ferdinand, Henry VIII (*Nov. 17*), and Venice against France. **1512.** *Apr. 11*: Battle of Ravenna; French expelled from Italy. Spaniards invade Navarre.	**1511.** *Feb. 13*: Albert of Hohenzollern elected Grand Master of Teutonic Order. **1512-1522.** War between Poland and Russia.	**1511.** *June*: Albuquerque annexes Malacca for Portugal. **1512-1520.** Sultan Selim I.
1513. French invade Milan; *June 6*: defeated at Novara. *Sept. 9*: Scots allied with France, defeated at Flodden; James IV killed, succeeded by James V (-**1542**).	**1513.** *Apr. 5*: Treaty of Mechlin between Maximilian I, Henry VIII, Ferdinand of Aragon, and Leo X. *Aug. 16*: Maximilian and Henry VIII defeat French at Guinegate (Battle of Spurs).	**1513.** Balboa crosses Isthmus of Panama and reaches Pacific. Ponce de Leon discovers Florida. Portuguese factory established at Diu.
1514. *Aug. 6*: Peace between England and France.	**1514.** Princedom of Moldavia comes under Turkish sovereignty. *Aug. 4*: Alliance of Gmunden between Maximilian I and Vassilij III.	**1514-1516.** Turks wage war against Persia; Selim I settles Kurds in Armenia.

IV. ECCLESIASTICAL HISTORY	V. CONSTITUTIONAL AND ECONOMIC HISTORY	VI. CULTURAL LIFE
1505. *July 17:* Luther enters Augustinian friary at Erfurt.	**1505.** Henry VII gives new Charter to Merchant Adventurers. Francis of Taxis establishes first regular mail, between Vienna and Brussels.	**1505.** Christ's College, Cambridge, founded. Wimpfeling: *Epitome Rerum Germanicarum*, first German history.
	1506. *Apr. 30:* Commercial treaty (*Malus intercursus*) between England and Netherlands. *Dec. 6:* Macchiavelli creates Florentine militia, first national Italian troops.	**1505–1507.** Dürer's journey to Italy.
		1506. Bramante begins to rebuild St. Peter's, Rome. Laocoön group found in Rome. Reuchlin: *Hebrew Grammar* and *Dictionary*. Frankfort-on-the-Oder University founded.
1507. Julius II proclaims indulgence for helping the rebuilding of St. Peter's.	**1507.** *Apr.-May:* Diet of Constance, establishes Imperial Chamber and territorial taxation according to a fixed Roll.	**1507.** Giorgione and Titian paint Fondaco dei Tedeschi, Venice.
1508. Luther becomes Professor of Divinity at Wittenberg.	**1508.** Jacob Fugger knighted by Maximilian I.	**1508.** *Apr. 4:* First book printed in Scotland (*Chaucer*). Julius II calls Raphael to Rome.
		1508–1512. Michelangelo paints roof of Sistine Chapel, Rome.
1509. Pfefferkorn, baptized Jew, obtains Imperial order to destroy Jewish books; Reuchlin opposes persecution.	**1509.** Peter Henle, of Nuremberg, invents watch (*Nuremberg Egg*).	**1509.** St. John's, Cambridge, and Brasenose, Oxford, founded. Erasmus: *Encomium Moriae*.
		ca. **1509.** Matthias Grünewald paints Isenheim Triptych.
1510. *Mar. 10:* Johann Geiler von Kaysersberg, preacher, *d.*	**1510.** *Jan. 21-Feb. 23:* Parliament grants Henry VIII tonnage, poundage, and wool duties during life-time. *Aug. 17:* Empson and Dudley, tax-collectors of Henry VII, executed.	**1510.** Erasmus: *Institutio Christiani Principis*, political science. Roger Ascham: *Schoolmaster*. St. Paul's School, London, founded by Colet.
1510–1511. Luther in Rome as delegate of his Order.		**1510–1514.** Erasmus, Professor of Greek in Cambridge.
1511. Vassili III appoints Patriarch of Moscow on his own authority.		
1512. Luther lectures on Epistles to Romans and Galatians.	**1512.** Diet of Cologne, divides Empire into ten Circles, issues Acts against monopolies. *Sept. 6:* Florentine constitution altered; Medicis restored.	**1512.** Erasmus: *De Ratione Studii et Instituendi Pueros*. Stobnicza: *Introductio in Ptolemaei Cosmographiam*.
1512–1517. Fifth Lateran Council.		**1512–1518.** P. Torrigiano: Henry VII's tomb, Westminster Abbey.
1513. Albert of Brandenburg becomes Archbishop of Magdeburg. Inquisition introduced in Sicily.	**1513.** Peasants' rebellion in Breisgau.	**1513.** Cardinal Bibbiena: *Calandria*, Italian comedy, performed at Urbino. Marx Treizsaurwein: *Weisskunig*, with woodcuts by H. Burgkmair. Macchiavelli: *Il Principe*.
1513–1521. Pope Leo X (Giovanni de' Medici).		
1514. Albert of Brandenburg becomes Archbishop of Mayence in return for 30,000 ducats. Johann Tetzel begins sale of indulgences.	**1514.** Fuggers secure right of selling papal indulgences in Germany.	**1514.** Dürer: *Melencholia*. *Mar. 11:* Bramante *d.*

I. WESTERN AND SOUTHERN EUROPE	II. CENTRAL, NORTHERN, AND EASTERN EUROPE	III. COUNTRIES OVERSEA
1515. *Jan. 1:* Louis XII *d.*; succeeded by Francis I (**-1547**). Francis invades Italy. *Sept. 13-14:* Francis defeats Swiss mercenaries at Marignano, and conquers Milan. Navarre incorporated with Castile.	**1515.** *July-Aug.:* Vienna treaties between Maximilian, Sigmund of Poland, and Vladislav of Hungary, concerning mutual succession of Hapsburgs and Jagellons.	**1515.** Diaz de Salis reaches mouth of River Plate.
1516. *Jan. 23:* Ferdinand of Aragon *d.*; succeeded by Charles, his grandson and Maximilian's (**-1556**). *Aug. 13:* Peace of Noyon between France and Spain. *Dec. 3:* Peace of Brussels between France and Empire; Emperor keeps South Tyrol, cedes Verona to Venice.	**1516.** *Mar. 13:* Vladislav II of Bohemia and Hungary *d.*; succeeded by Louis II under regency of Maximilian I and Sigmund of Poland.	**1516.** Portuguese enter upon commerce with China.
		1517. Turks conquer Egypt and intercept traffic route to India. **1517-1526.** Ibrahim, Sultan of Delhi.
1518. *Oct. 2:* Peace of London between England, Empire, France, Spain, and Pope; diplomatic triumph of Wolsey.	**1518.** Diet of Augsburg refuses subsidies against Turks.	**1518.** Barbary States in North Africa founded. Grijalva discovers mainland opposite Cuba. **1518-1532.** Nasrat Shah, King of Bengal.
1519. Henry VIII and Francis I, candidates for the Imperial crown.	**1519.** *Jan. 12:* Maximilian I *d.* *June 28:* Charles of Spain elected emperor. Ulric of Württemberg raids Free City of Reutlingen; subsequently expelled from his dukedom by Swabian League.	**1519-1521.** Cortez conquers Mexico. **1519-1522.** First circumnavigation of the world by Magellan.
1520. *May 26-29:* Charles V visits Henry VIII at Dover and Canterbury. *June 4-24:* Henry VIII and Francis I meet on the Field of Cloth of Gold. *July 10:* Henry VIII visits Charles V at Gravelines. *July 14:* Secret treaty between Henry VIII and Charles V at Calais.	**1520.** *Feb. 6:* Swabian League sells Württemberg to Charles V. Christian II of Denmark invades Sweden. *Oct. 23:* Charles V crowned at Aix-la-Chapelle. *Nov. 7:* 'Blood Bath of Stockholm' by Christian II.	**1520-1566.** Sultan Suleiman I the Magnificent.
1521. *Aug. 25:* Secret treaty between Charles V and Wolsey against France, at Bruges. **1521-1557.** John III of Portugal; abandons North African possessions.	**1521.** *Apr. 28:* Ferdinand, brother of Charles V, obtains Austrian dominions of the Hapsburgs. *May 28:* Treaty between Charles V and Leo X against France.	**1521.** Portuguese reach Molucca Islands. *Apr. 27:* Magellan killed on Philippine Islands. *Aug. 29:* Suleiman conquers Belgrade.

IV. ECCLESIASTICAL HISTORY	V. CONSTITUTIONAL AND ECONOMIC HISTORY	VI. CULTURAL LIFE
1515. *Dec. 11-14*: Treaty of Bologna; Leo X surrenders Parma and Piacenza to France.	**1515.** *Oct. 10*: Commercial treaty between England and Spain. *Dec. 24*: Wolsey, created Cardinal (*Sept. 10*), becomes Lord Chancellor. Ulric Zasius: *Commentaries on Roman Law*.	**1515.** Trissino: *Sofonisba*; first play in blank verse. Correggio: *Virgin with St. Francis*. **1515-1516.** Michelangelo: Statue of *Moses*. **1515-1517.** *Epistolae Obscurorum Virorum*, by Mutianus Rufus, Hutten, and other German humanists. **1515-1530.** Hampton Court built. **1516.** Thos. More: *Utopia*. Ariosto: *Orlando Furioso*. Corpus Christi College, Oxford, founded. Raphael: *Sistine Madonna*. Macchiavelli: *Discorsi* and *La Mandragola*.
1516. *Aug. 18*: French Concordat; substantially maintains Gallican privileges of Pragmatic Sanction of Bourges, 1438. Erasmus edits New Testament. *Dec. 19*: Leo X reaffirms bull *Unam Sanctam* (Bull *Pastor Aeternus*). **1517.** *Oct. 31*: Luther affixes 95 theses against sale of indulgences to door of Wittenberg Palace Church. *Nov. 8*: Cardinal Ximenes, Inquisitor-General, d. **1518.** Melanchthon appointed Professor at Wittenberg. *Oct. 12*: Luther interrogated by Cardinal-legate Cajetanus, at Augsburg, refuses to recant. **1519.** *Jan.*: Disputation between Luther and Miltitz at Altenburg. *June 27-July 16*: Disputation between Luther and Eck at Leipzig. Zwingli begins Protestant preaching in Zurich.	**1517.** Privileges granted to English merchants in Andalusia. Coffee first imported into Europe. Verböczy: *Tripartitum*, codifies Hungarian constitution. **1518.** *June 1*: Agreement between English merchants and Antwerp. **1519.** ' *Fuggerei* ', settlement for the poor, established at Augsburg.	**1517.** Reuchlin: *De Arte Cabbalistica*. **1518.** Erasmus: *Colloquia Familiaria*. Royal College of Physicians founded by Linacre. Titian: *Assumption of the Virgin*. **1519.** Beatus Rhenanus: *Commentary on Tacitus's Germania*. *May 2*: Leonardo da Vinci d. at St. Cloud.
1520. *June 15*: Pope declares Luther a heretic (*Exsurge*). *Dec. 10*: Luther burns bull of excommunication. Luther's reform pamphlets: *To the Christian Nobility*; *De Captivitate Babylonica Ecclesiae*; *On the Freedom of a Christian*. Reformation movement in Netherlands. **1521.** *Apr. 17-18*: Luther cross-examined by Papal Nuncio Aleander at Diet of Worms. *May 20*: Loyola wounded and converted. *May 26*: Edict of Worms outlaws Luther and his followers. Luther on the Wartburg, translates New Testament. Anabaptist movement at Wittenberg. Melanchthon: *Loci Communes*; systematizes Luther's doctrine. *Aug.*: Henry VIII's *Golden Book* refutes Luther's *Babylonish Captivity*.	**1520.** *July 14*: Commercial treaty between England and Emperor. Rebellion of Spanish communities on behalf of their privileges. Chocolate first imported from Mexico into Europe. **1521.** *Apr. 24*: Spanish insurgents defeated at Vilhalar. Manufacture of silk introduced into France. Eberlin of Günzburg: *The Fifteen Allies*, programme of social reform, dedicated to Charles V.	**1520.** Scottish New Testament. *Apr. 6*: Raphael d. Macchiavelli: *Arte della Guerra*. **1520-1534.** Michelangelo builds Tomb Chapel of Medici, Florence. **1521.** Major: *History of Scotland*.

I. WESTERN AND SOUTHERN EUROPE	II. CENTRAL, NORTHERN, AND EASTERN EUROPE	III. COUNTRIES OVERSEA
1522. *Apr. 27*: Spaniards and Germans defeat French and Swiss at Bicocca. Francesco Sforza restored to Milan. *May*: England declares war on France. Alliance between France and Scotland.	**1522.** *Jan. 30* and *Feb. 7*: Treaties of Brussels between Charles V and Ferdinand concerning partition of Hapsburg territories. German knights under Francis of Sickingen attack Treves, but fail.	**1522.** *Dec.*: Turks capture Rhodes.
1523. Charles of Bourbon, Constable of France, joins Charles V; concentric invasion of France by Allies.	**1523.** *May 7*: Sickingen killed; end of activities of knights in Germany. *June 15*: Gustavus Vasa proclaimed King of Sweden (**-1560**); end of Scandinavian Union. Christian II of Denmark deposed; succeeded by Frederick of Holstein, his uncle (**-1533**).	**1523.** Europeans expelled from China.
1524. *July-Aug.*: Germans and Spaniards besiege Marseilles; disastrous retreat.		
1525. *Feb. 24*: Germans and Spaniards defeat French and Swiss at Pavia; Francis I taken prisoner. *Aug. 30*: Peace between England and France.	**1525.** *Apr. 10*: **Grand** Master Albert transforms Prussia into a secular duchy under Polish suzerainty. *May 5*: Frederick the Wise of Saxony *d.*; succeeded by John the Steadfast, his brother (**-1532**).	**1525.** Babar conquers the Punjab.
1526. *Jan. 14*: Peace of Madrid between Charles V and Francis I. *May 22*: League of Cognac between Pope, France, Venice, Florence, and Milan against Charles V.	**1526.** *Feb. 27*: Alliance of Gotha and (*May 2*) Torgau between John of Saxony and Philip of Hesse. *Aug. 29*: Louis II of Hungary defeated and killed by Turks at Mohacs. *Oct. 23*: Ferdinand of Austria elected King of Bohemia. *Nov. 11*: John Zapolya and (*Dec. 16*) Ferdinand elected Kings of Hungary.	**1526.** *Apr. 21*: Babar defeats and kills Ibrahim at Panipat; establishes Mogul dynasty at Delhi (**-1761**). Sebastian Cabot sails to River Plate.
1527. *Apr. 30*: Anglo-French alliance of Amiens. *May 6*: Sack of Rome by Germans and Spaniards under Charles of Bourbon, who is killed. *May 16*: Republic restored at Florence.	**1527.** *Aug.*: Ferdinand defeats Zapolya at Tokay.	**1527.** John Rut's voyage to find North-West Passage. *Mar. 16*: Babar defeats Hindu Confederacy at Kanwaha.
1528. *Jan. 21*: England declares war on Charles V. *Aug. 30*: French defeat at Aversa. *Sept. 12*: Genoa regains independence under Imperial protection.	**1528.** *Feb. 24*: Zapolya makes treaty with Suleiman. *Aug. 20*: George of Frundsberg, organizer of lansquenets, *d. Oct. 23*: Treaty of John Zapolya with France.	**1528.** German merchants of Augsburg attempt to colonize Venezuela.

IV. ECCLESIASTICAL HISTORY	V. CONSTITUTIONAL AND ECONOMIC HISTORY	VI. CULTURAL LIFE
1522. *Feb. 2*: Leo X bestows title of *Fidei Defensor* upon Henry VIII. *Mar. 9-16*: Luther preaches against fanatics and iconoclasts at Wittenberg. *Sept.*: First edition of Luther's New Testament.		**1522.** Sannazaro: *De Partu Virginis*; amalgamates Christian and pagan ideas. *June 30*: Reuchlin *d*.
1522-1523. Pope Hadrian VI (Adrian Florent; last non-Italian Pope).		
1523. Diet of Nuremberg; Pope promises to remove abuses; Diet demands Council to be summoned in Germany within a year. Philip, Landgrave of Hesse, joins Reformation. Zwingli reforms Zurich.	**1523.** John Fitzherbert, *Husbandry*, first English agricultural handbook.	**1523.** Hans Sachs: *Nightingale of Wittenberg*. *Aug. 29*: Ulric v. Hutten *d*.
1523-1534. Pope Clement VII (Giulio de' Medici).		
1524. Thomas Müntzer libels Luther. Diet of Nuremberg orders Edict of Worms to be carried out ' as far as possible '. Luther's first German Hymn Book.	**1524.** *Aug.*: Peasants' rebellion begins in South Germany. Esslingen regulation of coinage, attempts to unify German monetary system.	**1524.** Erasmus: *Diatribe de Libero Arbitrio*. Hans Holbein the Elder *d*.
		1524-1525. Holbein: *Dance of Death*.
1525. Wm. Tyndale translates New Testament. Matteo di Bassi founds Capuchin Order. *May 27*: Müntzer beheaded. *June 13*: Luther marries Catherine von Bora.	**1525.** Great Peasants' War in South Germany, Thuringia, Alsace; violently suppressed; end of free peasantry in Germany. *Dec. 30*: Jacob Fugger the Wealthy *d*.	**1524-1534.** Biblioteca Laurenziana, Florence, built by Michelangelo.
		1525. Wolsey founds Cardinal College, Oxford; **1546,** re-endowed as Christ Church. Holbein: *St. Mary with Burgomaster Meier*. Macchiavelli: *Florentine Histories*.
1526. *June*: First Diet of Spires, advises every Estate to so conduct itself ' as it should answer for it towards God and H.I.M.' First Evangelical Church constitution in Hesse. Anabaptists spread throughout South Germany. Luther: *German Mass and Order of Service*.	**1526.** *Mar.*: Rebellion of Austrian peasants quickly suppressed.	**1526.** Luther: *De Servo Arbitrio*, against Erasmus. Dürer: *Four Apostles*. Holbein goes to England. Hector Boece: *History of Scotland*.
1527. Sweden, Denmark and Luneburg reformed. Evangelical Church in Saxon Electorate established after general visitation of schools and churches.	**1527.** *Jan. 1*: Reorganization of Austrian administration; in force till 1848. *June 24*: Västerås Recess and Ordinances, regulate Swedish landed properties and religious questions in favour of Royal power.	**1527.** Colet: *Æditio*. Bald. di Castiglione: *Il Cortegiano*. *June 22*: Macchiavelli *d*.
1528. ' Pack Quarrels ', forged documents, improve Catholic position in Germany. *Mar. 10*: Hubmaier, leader of Austrian Anabaptists, burnt at the stake in Vienna. *Dec. 11*: Luke of Prague, refounder of Bohemian Brethren, *d*.	**1528.** *Mar.*: Arrest of English merchants in Spain and Flanders, reprisal against Wolsey's policy in wool trade. Cocoa beans first imported into Europe.	**1528.** Erasmus: *Ciceronianus sive de Optimo Genere Dicendi*; against dominance of Ciceronian style; *De Recta Latini Graecique Sermonis Pronuntiatione*. Marburg University founded by Philip of Hesse. *Apr. 6*: Dürer *d*.

I. WESTERN AND SOUTHERN EUROPE	II. CENTRAL, NORTHERN, AND EASTERN EUROPE	III. COUNTRIES OVERSEA
1529. *June 29*: Treaty of Barcelona, reconciles Emperor and Pope. *Aug. 5*: Peace of Cambrai between Charles V and Francis I; Francis renounces claims in Italy, Charles in Burgundy. *Aug. 27*: Henry VIII accedes to treaty of Cambrai. **1530.** *Aug. 12*: Imperial troops restore Medicis at Florence. Knights Hospitallers established in Malta by Charles V.	**1529.** *Sept. 21-Oct. 14*: First siege of Vienna by Turks. First civil war between Protestant and Catholic Swiss Cantons; Catholic party defeated. **1530.** *Feb. 24*: Charles V crowned Emperor by Clement VII at Bologna; last imperial coronation by a Pope. *Dec. 31*: Protestants form League of Schmalkalden.	**1529.** *Apr. 22*: Treaty of Saragossa defines Spanish-Portuguese frontier in Pacific; Spain gives up Moluccas. *May 6*: Babar defeats Hindus on the Gogra. **1530.** Fuggers attempt colonization in Sunda Archipelago and on west coast of South America. Portuguese definitely begin colonization of Brazil. **1530-1532.** Three expeditions to Brazil by William Hawkins. **1530-1556.** Humayun, son of Babar, Sultan of Delhi.
1531. Francis I allies with Zapolya. *Dec. 17*: Inquisition established in Portugal.	**1531.** *Jan. 5*: Ferdinand of Bohemia elected King of the Romans. *Jan. 31*: Truce between Ferdinand and Zapolya. Second civil war in Switzerland; *Oct. 11*: Protestants defeated at Kappel. *Oct. 24*: Bavaria, though Roman Catholic, joins League of Schmalkalden, at Saalfeld.	**1531.** Villegagnon discovers Rio de Janeiro. Bahadur Shah of Gujarat conquers Malwa.
1532. *May 26*: Alliance of Scheyern between Francis I, Bavaria, Saxony, and Hesse against Ferdinand.	**1532.** Christian II of Denmark fails to conquer Norway, is taken prisoner. League of Schmalkalden adopts 'defensive organization'. **1532-1554.** John Frederick, Elector of Saxony.	**1532.** *June*: Suleiman invades Hungary; *Aug.*: fails before Güns. **1532-1534.** Pizarro conquers Peru.
1533. *Jan. 25*: Secret marriage of Henry VIII with Anne Boleyn. *Apr. 23*: Henry VIII's marriage to Catherine of Aragon declared void.	**1533.** *June 22*: Peace between Ferdinand and Suleiman. **1533-1559.** Christian III of Denmark. **1533-1584.** Ivan IV the Terrible of Russia; autocrat from **1544**.	
1534. *Mar. 23*: Henry's marriage to Catherine declared valid by papal decree.	**1534.** *June 29*: Ulric of Württemberg restored by Philip of Hesse with French support. **1534-1535.** 'Count's War': Lübeck and Holstein against Denmark and Sweden.	**1534.** *Apr. 20*: Cartier reaches Labrador. Humayun conquers Gujarat and Malwa.
1535. *Feb.*: Defensive and offensive alliance between France and Turkey. *Nov. 1*: Francesco II Sforza *d.*; Charles V occupies Milan.	**1535.** *June*: Lübeck navy defeated by Danes and Swedes; end of Hanseatic League **as a great** power.	**1535.** *June*: Successful expedition of Charles V to Tunis. Buenos Aires and Lima founded. Cartier discovers St. Lawrence River.

IV. ECCLESIASTICAL HISTORY	V. CONSTITUTIONAL AND ECONOMIC HISTORY	VI. CULTURAL LIFE
1529. Second Diet of Spires. *Apr. 19*: Evangelical Estates 'protest' against validity of majority resolutions in religious affairs. *Oct. 1-4*: Disputation between Luther and Zwingli at Marburg; controversy about Eucharist hinders union. Sweden definitely Evangelical. **1530.** *June 25*: *Confessio Augustana* read before Diet of Augsburg. *Aug. 3*: *Confutatio*, by Roman Catholics. Melanchthon: *Apologia*.	**1529.** Jurisdiction of Star Chamber confirmed. *Oct. 17*: Fall of Lord Chancellor Wolsey; *Oct. 25*: succeeded by Thomas More. **1529-1536.** Reformation Parliament in England. **1530.** English merchants in Spain formed into a company. *Nov. 29*: Wolsey d. Police Regulations for Empire. Criminal Code (*Carolina*) for Empire, put into operation in **1532.** Antwerp Exchange built.	**1529.** Guevara: *Libro Aureo de Marco Aurelio.* Budaeus: *Commentarii Linguae Graecae.* **1530.** Geo. Agricola: *De Re Metallica*, first systematic mineralogy. Correggio: *Adoration of the Shepherds.*
1531. *Feb.*: Henry VIII recognized as supreme head of English Church. Strasbourg and South German Free Cities join League of Schmalkalden. *Oct. 11*: Zwingli killed at Kappel. Charles V prohibits Reformation doctrines in Netherlands.	**1531-1535.** Democratic revolution in Lübeck, headed by Geo. Wullenwever.	**1531.** First complete edition of Aristotle by Erasmus. Sir Thomas Elyot: *The Governor*; Ludovicus Vives: *De disciplinis*, treatises on education. *July 7*: Tilman Riemenschneider d. Hans Burgkmair d.
1532. *July 23*: Religious Peace of Nuremberg, caused by Turkish invasion. Calvin begins work for Reformation in Paris.	**1532.** *May 13*: Scottish College of Justice established. *May 16*: Thomas More resigns. Cultivation of sugar-cane in Brazil begins.	**1532.** First edition of Chaucer's complete works. Rabelais: *Pantagruel.* Joh. Cario: *Chronica*; first Protestant world-history. Rob. Etienne: *Thesaurus Linguae Latinae.* Holbein settles in England.
1533. *Mar. 30*: Cranmer becomes Archbishop of Canterbury. *July 11*: Clement VII excommunicates Henry VIII.	**1533.** *Apr. 12*: Thomas Cromwell appointed Privy Councillor and Secretary of State.	**1533.** *July 6*: Ariosto d. Veit Stoss d.
1534. *Aug. 15*: Jesuit Order founded at Paris. Act of Supremacy: severance of Church in England from Rome: Restraint of Annates, abolition of Peter's Pence; submission of the clergy to the king. Württemberg and Pomerania become Protestant. Luther's translation of whole Bible completed. **1534-1549.** Pope Paul III (Alexander Farnese). **1535.** *Jan.*: English bishops abjure papal authority. *Jan. 21*: Visitation of English churches and monasteries ordered. *June 22*: Bishop Fisher of Rochester, and, *July 6*, Sir Thomas More beheaded; both canonised in **1935**.	**1534-1535.** Anabaptist rule at Münster, Westphalia; puts into practice communistic ideals; violently suppressed by Protestant and Catholic princes. **1535.** Statute of Uses, restricts testamentary power of landowners. France makes first capitulation to Turkey.	**1534.** Rabelais: *Gargantua.* *Mar. 5*: Correggio d. **1534-1541.** Michelangelo: *Last Judgment*, Sistine Chapel. **1535.** John Bellenden: *Chronicles of Scotland.*

I. WESTERN AND SOUTHERN EUROPE	II. CENTRAL, NORTHERN, AND EASTERN EUROPE	III. COUNTRIES OVERSEA
1536. *Feb.–Apr.*: French conquer Savoy and Piedmont. *May 19*: Anne Boleyn beheaded. *May 30*: Henry VIII marries Jane Seymour. *July 14*: Naval treaty of Lyons between France and Portugal against Spain. *July*: Charles V invades Provence. *Sept.*: Disastrous retreat of Charles V from siege of Marseilles.		**1536.** Gujarat and Malwa regain their independence. Asuncion, Paraguay, founded.
1537. Francis I and Suleiman act in concert against Charles, in Italy and the Mediterranean. *Oct. 24*: Queen Jane Seymour *d.*	**1537.** *Oct. 18*: Mutual agreement of succession between Hohenzollerns and Piasts of Silesia.	
1538. *June 18*: Truce of Nice between Charles V and Francis I.	**1538.** *Feb. 24*: Peace of Grosswardein between Ferdinand and Zapolya. *June 10*: League of Nuremberg of Catholic German princes.	**1538.** Turks capture Aden.
1539. *Feb. 1*: Treaty of Toledo between Charles V and Francis I. *Mar.*: Truce between Venice and Turkey.	**1539.** *Apr. 19*: Truce of Frankfort between Charles V and Protestants.	**1539.** Spain annexes Cuba. Afghans defeat Humayun at Chausa.
1540. *Jan. 6*: Henry VIII marries Anne of Cleves. *July 6*: Henry's marriage declared void. *July 28*: Henry marries Catherine Howard. *Oct. 11*: Charles V invests his son Philip with Milan.	**1540.** *July 22*: John Zapolya *d.*; succeeded by his son John Sigmund.	**1540.** *May 17*: Humayun defeated at Kanauj and driven out of India by Sher Shah.
1541. Expedition of Charles V to Algeria fails.	**1541.** *Aug. 26*: Turks conquer Buda; Hungary becomes Turkish province (-**1688**). *Dec. 29*: Treaty of Gyalu: Zapolya's widow cedes Hungary to Ferdinand.	**1541.** Third voyage of Cartier to Canada.
1542. *Feb. 13*: Catherine Howard beheaded. *July 12*: Henry marries Catherine Parr. *July*: Wars between Charles V and Francis I, and between England and Scotland. *Nov. 24*: Scots defeated at Solway Moss. *Dec. 8*: Mary (Queen of Scots) born. *Dec. 14*: James V *d.*; Arran appointed Regent for Mary.	**1542.** *Sept.*: Imperial expedition against Turks in Hungary fails. League of Schmalkalden expels Henry of Brunswick, whose country turns Protestant.	**1542.** 'New Laws' issued for Spanish colonies in America, abolish Indian slavery. **1542-1552.** Francis Xavier's missionary activity in Japan.

IV. ECCLESIASTICAL HISTORY	V. CONSTITUTIONAL AND ECONOMIC HISTORY	VI. CULTURAL LIFE
1536. Dissolution of the lesser English monasteries; reform of Universities. Calvin goes to Geneva. *Mar. 27*: Swiss Protestants, Strasbourg, and Constance issue first Helvetian Confession. *May 29*: Wittenberg *Concordia* of Lutherans. *July 18*: Authority of Bishop of Rome declared void for England. Calvin: *Institutio Religionis Christianae.* **1537.** Paul III receives *Consilium de Emendanda Ecclesia.* Christian III issues Danish Church Order. First Roman Catholic Hymn Book by M. Vehe. **1538.** Destruction of Becket's Shrine at Canterbury, and of other shrines and relics. **1538-1541.** Calvin exiled from Geneva, lives at Strasbourg. **1539.** *Apr.*: Greater English monasteries dissolved. *May*: Henry VIII issues Six Articles. Saxon duchy and Brandenburg become Protestant. Consistory Court established at Wittenberg to be supreme Church office in Saxony. **1540.** *July 29*: Thomas Cromwell beheaded. Six new bishoprics created. *Sept. 27*: Paul III confirms Jesuit Order. Conflict among German Protestants caused by bigamy of Philip of Hesse. Cardinal Contarini tries to reconcile Protestants and Roman Catholics. **1541.** *Apr. 4*: Ignatius Loyola elected first General of Jesuit Order. *Nov. 20*: Calvin organizes Church at Geneva; Presbyterian Constitution. Knox begins reformation in Scotland. **1542.** Hermann von Wied, Archbishop of Cologne, tries to introduce Reformation into Cologne; is deposed. Cardinal Carafa reorganizes Inquisition on Spanish model.	**1536.** Unification of English and Welsh systems of government. *July 2*: Cromwell appointed Lord Privy Seal. **1536-1537.** Pilgrimage of Grace: religious and social rebellions in Lincolnshire, Yorks, Cumberland, Westmorland. **1537.** *Sept. 24*: Wullenwever, burgomaster of Lübeck, beheaded. **1539.** *Feb.*: England grants merchants free trade for 7 years. **1539-1592.** Trade war between Brandenburg and Pomerania. **1540.** Statute of Wills modifies Statute of Uses. *Feb.*: Charles V destroys liberties of Ghent. **1541.** *June*: Henry VIII assumes titles of King of Ireland and Head of the Irish Church. Wales obtains Parliamentary representation.	**1536.** *July 12*: Erasmus *d.* at Basle. Dolet: *Commentarii Linguae Latinae.* *Oct. 8*: Joh. Secundus (Jan Everaerts) *d.*, author of *Basia.* **1536-1553.** Sansovino builds St. Mark's Library, Venice. **1538.** Melanchthon: *Ethicae Doctrinae Elementa.* Joh. Sturm opens public school at Strasbourg. **1540.** Michael Servetus discovers the 'lesser circulation' of blood. Pietro Aretino: *Orazia*, comedy. *May 23*: Francesco Guicciardini, Italian historian, *d.* Sir David Lindsay: *Satyre of the Three Estaits.* **1541.** French translation of Psalms by Clément Marot, Protestant poet. *Sept. 24*: Theophrastus Paracelsus, physician and scientist, *d.* **1542.** Magdalene College, Cambridge, founded. Pisa University refounded.

I. WESTERN AND SOUTHERN EUROPE	II. CENTRAL, NORTHERN, AND EASTERN EUROPE	III. COUNTRIES OVERSEA
1543. *Feb.*: Henry VIII allies with Charles V against Francis I. *July 1*: Peace of Greenwich between England and Scotland; Prince Edward to marry Mary. *Dec. 11*: Scots Parliament repudiates Greenwich Treaty.	**1543.** *Sept. 7*: Charles V forces Duke of Cleves, ally of Francis I, to yield Guelderland and Zutphen to Netherlands.	**1543.** Fourth voyage of Cartier to Canada.
1544. *May*: English invade Scotland, take Leith and Edinburgh. *July*: Charles V and Henry VIII take St. Dizier and threaten Paris. *Sept. 14*: Henry takes Boulogne. *Sept. 18*: Peace of Crépy between Charles and Francis.	**1544.** *Feb.-Apr.*: Diet of Spires; Empire assists Charles against France and Turkey.	
1545. *Feb. 25*: Scots defeat English at Ancrum Moor. *Aug. 26*: Pier Luigi Farnese becomes Duke of Parma and Piacenza. *Sept.*: English again invade Scotland.	**1545.** *Nov.*: Truce of Adrianople between Charles and Suleiman.	**1545.** Humayun captures Kandahar.
1546. *June 7*: Peace of Ardres between England and France; Boulogne to remain English for 8 years.	**1546.** *June 19*: Maurice of Saxony allies with Charles V. *July 20*: John Frederick, Elector of Saxony, and Philip of Hesse outlawed by the Emperor. *Dec.*: Maurice occupies Saxon Electorate.	
1547. *Jan. 28*: Henry VIII *d.*; succeeded by Edward VI (**-1553**). *Jan. 31*: Somerset made protector. *Mar. 31*: Francis I *d.*; succeeded by Henry II (**-1559**). *Sept. 10*: Scots defeated at Pinkie.	**1547.** *Apr. 24*: League of Schmalkalden defeated by Charles V at Mühlberg, John Frederick and Philip taken prisoners. *May 19*: Saxon Electorate given to Maurice. *June 19*: 5 years' truce with Suleiman. *July*: Duke Henry restored to Brunswick.	**1547.** Humayun captures Kabul.
	1548. *June 26*: Administration of Netherlands made independent of Empire. **1548-1572.** Sigmund II Augustus, King of Poland.	
1549. *Aug. 9*: England declares war on France.	**1549.** *Feb. 14*: Maximilian (II), son of Ferdinand, recognized future King of Bohemia.	**1549.** First Jesuit missionaries in South America.
1550. *Jan.*: Somerset deposed; succeeded by Northumberland. *Mar. 24*: Peace of Boulogne between England and France, and England and Scotland; England cedes Boulogne.	**1550.** *Oct.*-**1551.** *Nov.*: Maurice of Saxony besieges Magdeburg.	

IV. ECCLESIASTICAL HISTORY	V. CONSTITUTIONAL AND ECONOMIC HISTORY	VI. CULTURAL LIFE
		1543. Nich. Copernicus (*d. Mar. 24*): *De Revolutione Orbium Celestium*; system of heliocentric astronomy. Hartmann, of Nuremberg, discovers declination of magnetic needle. Andreas Vesalius: *De Humani Corporis Fabrica*; anatomy. *Oct.-Nov.*: Holbein *d.* in London.
1544. Diet of Spires legalizes secularizations effected before **1541.**	**1544.** Silver mines of Potosi, Peru, discovered.	**1544.** Königsberg University founded. Margaret of Navarre: *Heptameron.*
1545. Palatinate becomes Protestant. *Dec. 13*: Council of Trent opened.	**1545.** Hansa counter at Bruges removed to Antwerp.	**1545.** First complete edition of Luther's writings. Paré: *Manière de traiter les Plaies*; modern surgery. R. Ascham: *Toxophilus.*
1546. *Feb. 18*: Luther *d. May 29*: Cardinal Beaton murdered; Scottish revolt from Rome begins. *June 6-7*: Charles V allies with Paul III against Protestants.	**1546.** English Navy Board established. Exchanges established at Lyons and Toulouse.	**1546.** Trinity College, Cambridge, and Christ Church, Oxford, founded. Farnese Bull found in Thermae of Caracalla, Rome. La Boétie: *Sur la Servitude Volontaire.* First book in Welsh (*Yny Lhyvyr hwnn*) printed.
1547. Council of Trent transferred to Bologna. Six Articles repealed. Wendish translation of New Testament. Knox exiled to France.	**1547.** First poor-rate levied in London. *Jan. 16*: Ivan IV crowned first Russian Tsar at Moscow.	**1547.** *Jan. 1*: Michelangelo appointed chief architect of St. Peter's. *June 21*: Sebastiano del Piombo *d.*
1548. *May 15*: Augsburg *Interim* concedes chalice to laity and matrimony to priests until final decision of General Council. Loyola: *Exercitia Spiritualia.*	**1548.** Chantries Act, abolishes religious guilds and chantries. Silver mines of Zacatecar, Mexico, discovered.	
1549. *June 9*: First Act of Uniformity; First Prayer Book. *June*: *Consensus Tigurinus*; Agreement between Calvin and followers of Zwingli about Holy Communion. *Sept. 13*: Paul III closes Council of Bologna.	**1549.** *June - Sept.*: Social and religious risings in Devon, Cornwall, Norfolk, Yorks. Enclosures legalized. Provision-dealers forbidden to combine to keep up prices.	**1549.** Joachim du Bellay, leader of the poetic group La Pléiade: *Défense et Illustration de la Langue Française*; theory and programme of French classicism.
1550-1555. Pope Julius III (Giov. Maria del Monte).		**1550.** Pierre de Ronsard: *Odes.* Udall: *Ralph Roister Doister.* Vasari: *Lives of the Painters.* Seb. Münster: *Cosmographia*; scientific geography.

I. WESTERN AND SOUTHERN EUROPE	II. CENTRAL, NORTHERN, AND EASTERN EUROPE	III. COUNTRIES OVERSEA
	1551. *Mar. 9:* Hapsburg family treaty makes Philip II sole heir of Charles V. *July 19:* Treaty of Karlsburg reaffirms Ferdinand's rights to Hungary and Transylvania.	
1552. *Jan. 15:* Treaty of Chambord between Henry II and German Protestants, who cede Metz, Toul, and Verdun to France. *Jan. 22:* Somerset beheaded.	**1552.** *May:* Maurice of Saxony secedes from Charles V, takes Augsburg, and almost captures Charles at Innsbruck. *Aug. 2:* Treaty of Passau; John Frederick and Philip released.	
1553. *Jan.:* Charles V fails to take Metz. *July 6:* Edward VI *d.*; succeeded by Mary I (**-1558**). **1553-1580.** Emanuel Philibert of Savoy.	**1553.** *July 9:* Maurice of Saxony killed at Sievershausen, while defeating Albert Alcibiades of Kulmbach.	**1553-1554.** Chancellor's expedition to Russia via Archangel. Willoughby discovers Nova Zembla.
1554. *Feb. 12:* Jane Grey beheaded. *Apr. 12:* Mary of Lorraine succeeds Arran as Scots Regent. *July 25:* Queen Mary I marries Philip (later II of Spain).	**1554.** Ivan IV of Russia conquers Astrakhan. Henry II of France invades Netherlands.	**1554.** John Locke's voyage to Guinea.
1555. *Oct. 25:* Charles V resigns Italy and Netherlands to Philip. *Apr. 17:* Spaniards take Siena and sell it to Cosimo de' Medici.	**1555.** *Sept.:* Diet of Augsburg, returns to Public Peace of 1495 as basis of Empire organization. Philip of Spain renounces his claim to the German crown in favour of Maximilian.	**1555.** Chancellor's second voyage to Archangel. Humayun regains his Indian Empire.
1556. *Jan. 16:* Charles V resigns Spain to Philip II (**-1598**). *Feb. 5:* Truce of Vaucelles between Henry II and Philip II. **1557.** *June 7:* England declares war on France. *Aug. 10:* English and Spaniards defeat French at St. Quentin. **1557-1578.** Sebastian, King of Portugal.	**1556.** *Sept. 7:* Charles V resigns Empire to his brother, Ferdinand I (**-1564**).	**1556-1605.** Akbar the Great, Great Mogul. **1556.** *Nov. 5:* Akbar defeats Hindus at Panipat. **1557.** Portuguese settlement at Macao.
1558. *Jan. 20:* French take Calais and (*June 22*) Thionville. *Apr. 24:* Mary Queen of Scots marries Dauphin Francis. *July 13:* Egmont defeats French at Gravelines. *Nov. 17:* Mary I *d.*; succeeded by Elizabeth (**-1603**).	**1558.** *Jan. 9:* Geneva becomes independent of Berne. *Mar. 14:* Ferdinand I assumes title of Emperor without being crowned by Pope. *Sept. 21:* Charles V *d.* Russians invade Livonia.	**1558.** Akbar conquers Gwalior.

IV. ECCLESIASTICAL HISTORY	V. CONSTITUTIONAL AND ECONOMIC HISTORY	VI. CULTURAL LIFE
1551. *Jan.*: Second session of Council of Trent (-**1552**). Rob. Estienne issues first Bible divided into verses. Bishop Hosius re-catholicizes Ermland (-**1569**).		**1551.** Gessner: *Historia Animalium;* first zoological work since the ancients. Palestrina appointed conductor at St. Peter's, Rome. Dedekind: *Grobianus;* mirror of morals.
1552. *Jan.*: Second Act of Uniformity; Second Prayer Book. *Aug. 2:* Treaty of Passau, annuls Augsburg *Interim* and grants Lutherans free exercise of religion. *Aug. 31:* *Collegium Germanicum* founded at Rome for education of German clergy. Calvin: *De Praedestinatione.*	**1552.** *Feb. 24:* Hansa privileges in England abolished.	**1552.** Bart. Eustachio: *Tabulae Anatomicae;* discovers Eustachian tube and Eustachian valve.
1553. *Aug.-Sept.*: Arrest of Protestant bishops and restoration of Roman Catholic bishops in England. Mich. Servetus: *Christianismi Restitutio. Oct. 27:* Servetus burnt at Geneva.		**1553.** *Apr. 9:* Rabelais *d. Oct. 16:* Lucas Cranach *d.*
1554. *Nov. 30:* England reconciled with Rome; full restoration of Roman Catholicism.	**1554.** State regulations for mines and forges in Saxony.	**1554.** Trinity College, Oxford, and Dillingen University founded. Bandello: *Novelle.* Antonio Moro appointed Court painter to Queen Mary. Cardano produces absolute alcohol.
1555. *May:* Knox returns to Scotland and unites Scots Protestants. *Sept. 25:* Religious Peace of Augsburg; Lutheran states permitted, Imperial Chamber to be composed equally of Protestants and Catholics. *Oct. 16:* Bishops Ridley and Latimer burnt at Oxford. Petrus Canisius: *Summa Doctrinae Christianae.*	**1555.** Charter for Muscovy Company. Commercial treaty between France and Turkey.	**1555.** St. John's, Oxford, founded. Ronsard: *Hymnes.* Sleidanus: *De Statu Religionis et Reipublicae Carolo V Caesare;* first contemporary history based on documents. **1555-1560.** Gray's Inn Hall, London, built.
1555-1559. Pope Paul IV (Gian Pietro Carafa). **1556.** *Mar. 21:* Archbishop Cranmer burnt. *Mar. 22:* Cardinal Pole becomes Archbishop of Canterbury. *July 31:* Loyola *d.*	**1556.** *Nov. 17:* Ferdinand I forms military council for German possessions of Hapsburgs.	**1556.** Matthias Flacius Illyricus: *Catalogus Testium Veritatis;* collection of pre-Lutheran writings against Roman Catholicism.
1557. *Sept. 11-Nov. 28:* Disputation at Worms; last attempt at reconciliation on part of Empire. *Dec. 3:* First Covenant signed in Scotland.	**1557.** First national bankruptcies in France and Spain. Stationers' Company incorporated.	**1557.** Gonville College, Cambridge, refounded by Dr. Caius. Repton School founded. Ronsard: *Amours.* Geo. Wickram: *Der Goldfaden,* first German novel.
1558. Fruitless attempt at unification among German Protestants at Diet of Frankfort. *Nov. 17:* Cardinal Pole *d.* Knox: *First Blast of the Trumpet against the Monstrous Regiment of Women.*	**1558.** *Nov. 20:* William Cecil appointed Chief Secretary of State. Hamburg Exchange established. Manufacture of firearms begins at Ferlach, Carinthia.	**1558.** Jena University founded.

I. WESTERN AND SOUTHERN EUROPE	II. CENTRAL, NORTHERN, AND EASTERN EUROPE	III. COUNTRIES OVERSEA
1559. *Apr. 3:* Peace of Câteau-Cambrésis between Philip II and Henry II; France restores Savoy and Piedmont, keeps Saluzzo. *July 10:* Henry II killed in tournament; the Guises seize government for Francis II. *Oct. 21:* Scots Regent deposed.	**1559.** *June 20:* Denmark conquers peasants' republic of Dithmarschen. **1559–1567.** Margaret of Parma, sister of Philip II, Regent in Netherlands. **1559–1588.** Frederick II, King of Denmark.	
1560. *Feb. 27:* Treaty of Berwick between Scots Lords and Elizabeth. *June 10:* Mary, Dowager Queen of Scotland, *d. July 6:* Treaty of Edinburgh between England and Scotland; Council of Regents established, French troops evacuated; treaty refused by Francis II and Mary. *Dec. 5:* Francis II *d.;* succeeded by Charles IX, his brother (**-1574**), under regency of Catherine de' Medici, his mother. **1561.** *Aug. 19:* Mary Queen of Scots lands in Scotland.	**1560–1568.** Eric XIV, King of Sweden. **1561.** Baltic States of Teutonic Order secularized; Courland becomes duchy, Estonia Swedish, Livonia Polish.	
1562. *Jan. 6:* Shane O'Neill, Irish rebel, surrenders to Elizabeth. *Mar. 1:* Massacre of French Protestants at Vassy; outbreak of Huguenot Wars. *Sept. 20:* Treaty of Hampton Court between Elizabeth and Huguenots. *Oct.:* English occupy Havre. **1563.** *Feb. 18:* Francis Duke of Guise murdered. *Mar. 19:* Peace of Amboise ends first Huguenot War. *July 28:* French regain Havre.	**1562.** *June 1:* Truce between Ferdinand and Turks for 8 years. *Sept. 20:* Maximilian, son of Ferdinand, crowned as King of Bohemia; *Nov. 24:* elected King of the Romans. **1563.** *Sept. 8:* Maximilian elected King of Hungary. Treaty between Brandenburg and Poland concerning Brandenburg succession in Prussia. **1563–1570.** War between Denmark and Sweden.	**1562.** John Hawkins starts slave trade between Africa and America. French attempt to colonize Florida. The Rajah of Jaipur submits to Akbar.
1564. *Mar. 13:* Philip II recalls Granvela from Netherlands. *Apr. 11:* Anglo-French peace at Troyes.	**1564.** *May 31:* Lübeck and Denmark defeat Swedes off Gotland. *July 25:* Emperor Ferdinand I *d.;* succeeded by Maximilian II (**-1576**).	**1564.** Akbar annexes Malwa. Spaniards occupy Philippines and build Manila. **1564–1565.** Second voyage of Hawkins to South America.

IV. ECCLESIASTICAL HISTORY	V. CONSTITUTIONAL AND ECONOMIC HISTORY	VI. CULTURAL LIFE
1559. *Jan. 13*: Menno Simons, organiser of Anabaptists, *d. May 8*: Elizabeth assents to Act of Supremacy. *May*: General Synod of French Calvinists at Paris; *Confessio Gallicana* on Geneva model. *June 22*: Elizabeth's Prayer Book issued. *Aug. 1*: Parker made Archbishop of Canterbury. **1559-1565.** Pope Pius IV (Giovanni Medici). **1560.** *Aug.*: Scots Parliament abolishes papal jurisdiction and adopts Calvinistic Confession. Crypto-Calvinists expelled from Saxony. First permanent Nunciature, at Vienna.	**1559.** High Commission Court established. Ferdinand I tries to standardize coinage in Empire. **1560.** Currency reform in England; relation of gold to silver 1 : 15½. Jean Nicot imports tobacco into France.	**1559.** Amyot's French translation of Plutarch. Geneva University founded. *Mar. 30*: Adam Riese, mathematician, *d.* T. Sackville: *Mirror for Magistrates.* **1559-1574.** *The Magdeburg Centuries*; Church history, written by orthodox Lutherans under Matth. Flacius. **1560.** Westminster School founded. *Apr. 19*: Philip Melanchthon *d.*
1561. Knox: Book of Discipline, establishes Scottish Church Constitution. *Feb. 1*: Ferdinand I compels his son, Maximilian, to renounce Protestant inclinations. Schwenckfeld, founder of the sect of Schwenckfeldians, *d.* **1562.** *Jan. 17*: Edict of St. Germain formally recognizes French Protestantism. *Jan. 18*: Council of Trent re-opened.		**1561.** J. C. Scaliger: *Poetics*; establishes modern literary criticism. **1561-1565.** Antwerp town hall built by Cornelius Floris. **1562.** Sackville and Norton: *Gorboduc*; first English tragedy in blank verse. **1562-1572.** Hall of Middle Temple, London, built.
1563. *Jan. 19*: Calvinistic Heidelberg Catechism introduced in Palatinate. *Mar. 19*: Edict of Amboise grants Huguenots some toleration. *Dec.*: Council of Trent ends. Organization of Calvinism in Netherlands. Counter-reformation begins in Bavaria. **1564.** *May 27*: Calvin *d.* Puritan opposition to Anglicanism begins. Counter-reformation begins in Poland. *Nov. 13*: *Professio Fidei*, final definition of Roman Catholic faith. *Nov. 24*: First *Index Librorum Prohibitorum.*	**1563.** Acts for relief of poor, and concerning labourers and apprentices; valid till **1814**. **1564.** Trade war between England and Spain; Philip II confiscates English ships; mutual embargo. English factory established at Emden. New Charter for Merchant Adventurers.	**1563.** John Shute: *First and Chief Groundes of Architecture.* Escorial begun. Jesuits take possession of Ingolstadt and Dillingen Universities. John Foxe: *Book of Martyrs.* **1564.** Adrien Turnebus: *Adversaria.* Bart. Eustachio: *Opuscula Anatomica. Feb. 18*: Michelangelo *d.* Philibert Delorme begins building Tuileries, Paris.

I. WESTERN AND SOUTHERN EUROPE	II. CENTRAL, NORTHERN, AND EASTERN EUROPE	III. COUNTRIES OVERSEA
1565. *June 14-July 2*: Alba and Queen Catherine meet at Bayonne. *July 29*: Mary Queen of Scots marries Darnley.	**1565.** *May-Sept.*: La Valette defends Malta successfully against Turks.	**1565.** Spaniards destroy Huguenot colony in Florida.
1566. *Mar. 9*: Murder of Rizzio. Beginning of unrest in Netherlands. Rebellion and suppression of Christianized Moors in Spain.	**1566.** Suleiman takes Chios from Genoa, invades Hungary, fails before Sziget.	**1566.** *Sept. 6*: Sultan Suleiman *d.*; succeeded by Selim II (**-1574**).
1567. *Feb. 10*: Murder of Darnley. *May 15:* Mary Queen of Scots marries Bothwell. *July 24*: Mary forced to abdicate. *Aug. 8:* Alba arrives in Netherlands. *Sept. 29*: Huguenot conspiracy of Meaux leads to Second Civil War.		**1567.** Akbar conquers Chitor. Nobunaga becomes supreme in Japan, deposes the Shogun, centralizes government.
1568. *Mar. 23*: Treaty of Longjumeau confirms Edict of Amboise. *May 13*: Mary Queen of Scots defeated at Langside. *May 19*: Mary flees to England. *June 5*: Egmont and Hoorne beheaded. *July 24*: Don Carlos of Spain *d. Aug.*: Third Civil War in France.	**1568.** *Feb. 17*: Maximilian II yields parts of Hungary to Selim II. *Sept.*: Swedish Estates dethrone Eric XIV (*d.* **1577**). **1568-1592.** John III, King of Sweden.	**1567-1568.** Third voyage of Hawkins, to Guinea and the West Indies. **1568.** *Sept.*: Spaniards defeat English off Mexican coast.
1569. Fitzmaurice's rebellion in Ireland (**-1574**). Rising of Northern Earls in England. Pope creates Cosimo de' Medici, Grand Duke of Tuscany.	**1569.** *July 1*: Union of Lublin establishes political unity of Poland.	
1570. *Jan. 23*: Scottish Regent Moray assassinated. *Jan. 27*: Matthew, Earl of Lennox, becomes Regent of Scotland. *Aug. 8*: Peace of St. Germain, grants Huguenots general amnesty.	**1570.** *Aug. 16*: Treaty of Speyer; Zapolya renounces Hungary, keeps Transylvania. *Dec. 13*: Peace of Stettin between Sweden and Denmark.	
1571. *May 20*: League of Pope, Spain, and Venice against Turks. *Sept. 4*: Regent Lennox *d.*; succeeded by John, Earl of Mar, (*Sept. 5*). *Oct. 7*: Don John of Austria defeats Turks off Lepanto; end of Turkish naval power.	**1571.** *Mar. 14*: John Sigmund of Transylvania *d.*; Transylvania elects Stephen Bathory prince. *July 30*: Treaty of mutual succession between Brandenburg and Pomerania.	**1571.** Turks take Cyprus from Venice, and Tunis from Spain.
1572. Dutch war of liberation begins. *July 18*: William of Orange elected Stadholder. *Oct. 29*: Regent Mar *d. Nov. 24*: James, Earl of Morton, becomes Regent of Scotland.	**1572.** *July 7*: Sigmund II of Poland *d.*; end of Jagellon dynasty; Poland becomes elective kingdom.	**1572.** Francis Drake begins attacks on Spanish harbours in America.

IV. ECCLESIASTICAL HISTORY	V. CONSTITUTIONAL AND ECONOMIC HISTORY	VI. CULTURAL LIFE
1565. Philip II issues religious edict in Netherlands; opposed by William of Orange, Egmont, and Admiral Hoorne.	**1565.** Manufacture of pencils begins in England.	**1565.** Jacobus Acontius, Italian living in England: *Stratagemata Satanae*; advocates religious toleration. Cinthio: *Hecatomiti*, collection of love stories.
1566. *Mar.*: Second Helvetian Confession, by Bullinger; basis of Reformed Churches. *Catechismus Romanus. Confessio Belgica*, issued by Synod of Antwerp. **1566-1572.** Pope Pius V (Mich. Ghislieri; formerly Grand Inquisitor). **1567.** Nonconformists begin to meet secretly in London. **1567-1568.** Maximilian II establishes Monastery Council to superintend clergy and enforce State control.	**1566.** Exchanges established in Rouen and Cologne. **1567.** English factory established in Hamburg, breaks Hansa monopoly of trade.	**1566.** Jean Bodin: *Methodus ad Facilem Historiarum Cognitionem*; positivistic methodology of history. *July 2*: Mich. Nostradamus, French Court Astrologer, *d.* **1567.** Rugby School and Helmstedt University founded. Matth. Flacius: *Clavis Scripturae*; dictionary and hermeneutics of Scripture.
1568. English College for education of Catholic priests established at Douai. Brunswick becomes Protestant. Czech translation of Bible. *Aug. 18* and *Dec. 7*: Maximilian II grants religious concessions to Austrian Protestant nobility.		**1568.** Fernandez de Navarrete appointed Court Painter to Philip II of Spain. **1568-1575.** Tomb of Christian II of Denmark, at Roskild, by Corn. Floris.
1569. Albert V of Bavaria issues school regulations to bring religious education under Catholic State control.	**1569.** Gerard Mercator's map of the World; founds modern cartography.	**1569.** John Heywood: *The Four P.'s*; interlude. *Sept. 5*: Peter Breughel the Elder *d.*
1570. *Feb. 25*: Bull *Regnans in Excelsis* excommunicates Elizabeth. *Apr. 14*: Consensus of Sendomir unifies Lutherans, Calvinists and Moravian Brethren in Poland.		**1570.** Maximilian II crowns Geo. Fabricius Poet Laureate. Palladio: *Treatise on Architecture*. Tomb of Albert of Prussia, at Königsberg, by Corn. Floris. *Sept. 27*: Jacopo Sansovino *d.*
1571. *Jan. 14*: Religious Assurance for Austrian nobility. *Apr.-May*: Parliament forbids importation of Papal Bulls into England. Convocation sanctions 39 Articles.	**1571.** *Feb. 25*: Cecil created Lord Burghley. Royal Exchange, London, opened. Acts promoting exportation of grain and prohibiting export of wool. Embargo against England by Spanish Netherlands.	**1571.** Jesus College, Oxford, and Harrow School founded. *Feb. 14*: Benevenuto Cellini *d.* R. Edwards: *Damon and Pithias*.
1572. *Aug. 23-24*: St. Bartholomew Massacre of French Protestants at Paris. *Nov. 24*: Knox *d.* Mennonites tolerated in Netherlands. **1572-1585.** Pope Gregory XIII (Ugo Buoncompagni).	**1572.** *July*: Burghley appointed Lord High Treasurer. Great land-owners in Brandenburg allowed to expropriate their peasants.	**1572.** Ronsard: *La Franciade*. Camoens: *The Lusiads*. Etienne: *Thesaurus Linguae Graecae*. **1572-1575.** Annibale Caro: *Lettere Familiari*; victory of Tuscan literary language in Italy.

I. WESTERN AND SOUTHERN EUROPE	II. CENTRAL, NORTHERN, AND EASTERN EUROPE	III. COUNTRIES OVERSEA
1573. *July 6:* Pacification of Boulogne ends fourth Huguenot War. *Sept.:* Alba recalled from Netherlands; succeeded by Requesens (*d. Mar. 5,* **1576**).	**1573.** *Mar. 7:* Peace of Constantinople between Turkey and Venice. *May 9:* Henry of Anjou elected King of Poland.	**1573.** *Feb. 11:* Drake sees Pacific from Isthmus of Panama. Akbar annexes Gujarat.
1574. Fifth war of religion in France. *May 30:* Charles IX *d.*; succeeded by Henry III (-**1589**).	**1574.** *June 18:* Henry leaves Poland for France, where he becomes King Henry III.	**1574.** Portuguese colonize Angola and found San Paulo. **1574-1595.** Sultan Murad III.
1575. *Nov. 14:* Elizabeth declines sovereignty of Netherlands.	**1575.** *Dec. 14:* Stephen Bathory elected King of Poland (-**1586**).	**1575.** Sir Humphrey Gilbert: *Discourse,* advocates English colonization. Akbar conquers Bengal.
1576. *May 6:* Edict of Beaulieu, allows reformed religion in France, except in Paris. *Nov. 4:* Spaniards sack Antwerp. *Nov. 8:* Pacification of Ghent unites all Dutch provinces against Spain.	**1576.** *Oct. 12:* Emperor Maximilian II *d.*; succeeded by his brother, Rudolf II (-**1612**).	**1576.** *July:* Frobisher annexes Frobisher Bay.
1577. *Feb. 12:* Don Juan issues Perpetual Edict to settle Dutch war; refused by William of Orange. *Mar.-Sept.:* Sixth war of religion in France. *Sept. 17:* Peace of Bergerac confirms peace of Beaulieu.		**1577.** Frobisher's second voyage. General patent of colonization granted to Sir H. Gilbert. **1577.** *Nov. 15* - **1580.** *Nov. 30:* Francis Drake circumnavigates the world.
1578. *Mar. 12:* James VI takes over government. *Aug. 13:* Duke of Anjou declared Defender of Dutch Liberties. *Oct. 1:* Don John of Austria *d.*; succeeded by Alexander Farnese, Duke of Parma, as governor of Netherlands.		**1578.** Sebastian of Portugal invades Morocco; is defeated and slain at Alcazar. Russians cross Urals. Frobisher's third voyage.
1579. *Jan. 23:* Union of Utrecht, of the seven Northern provinces. *May 17:* Peace of Arras; Southern Netherlands recognize Philip II. Desmond revolts in Ireland (-**1583**).	**1579-1597.** William V, Duke of Bavaria; strong supporter of Jesuits.	**1579.** Gilbert's expedition to the West Indies fails. *June 17:* Drake proclaims English sovereignty over New Albion (California). Portuguese trading station in Bengal.
1580. Seventh war of religion in France, ended by peace of Fleix (*Nov. 26*). Philip II conquers Portugal.		
1581. *July 26:* Northern Netherlands renounce allegiance to Spain. Marriage negotiations between Francis, Duke of Anjou, and Queen Elizabeth.		**1581.** Russians begin conquest of Siberia. Akbar subdues Afghanistan (formally annexed **1585**).

IV. ECCLESIASTICAL HISTORY	V. CONSTITUTIONAL AND ECONOMIC HISTORY	VI. CULTURAL LIFE
1573. Jesuits begin counter-reformation in Fulda.		**1573.** Fr. Hotman: *Francogallia*; political theory of Monarchomachism. Tasso: *Aminta*. Fischart: *Flöhhatz*.
1574. Roman Catholic activities in England. Crypto-Calvinism suppressed in Saxony.		
1575. *May 18*: *Confessio Bohemica* of all non-Roman denominations in Bohemia.	**1575.** Second national bankruptcy in Spain. Child labour abolished in Hungarian mines.	**1575.** Leiden University founded. Wm. Stevenson (?): *Gammer Gurton's Needle*. Turberville: *Book of Falconrie*.
1576. *May-June*: Torgau articles drawn up by Lutheran theologians.	**1576.** *Feb.-Mar*: Poor Relief Act.	**1576.** Warsaw University founded. Jean Bodin: *De la République*; theory of absolutism, advocates religious toleration. Three theatres built in London. Vieta introduces decimal fractions. Fischart: *Lucky Ship of Zurich*. *Jan. 19*: Hans Sachs, Meistersinger of Nuremberg, *d*. *Aug. 27*: Titian *d*.
1577. *May 28*: *Formula Concordiae*, final confession of Lutheranism. Greek College founded at Rome.	**1577.** *Mar. 1*: State monopoly of colonial trade abolished in Portugal.	**1577.** Raphael Holinshed: *Chronicles*.
1578. English College removed from Douai to Rheims. Protestant preachers expelled from Vienna.		**1578.** Wilna and Altdorf universities founded. Du Bartas: *La Semaine*, Christian epic. John Lyly: *Euphues, the Anatomy of Wit*.
1579. *May 1*: English College founded at Rome. Sozzini (Socinus) founds Socinian sect in Poland.	**1579.** Charter for Fellowship of Eastland Merchants for trading in Scandinavia and the Baltic. English privileges to Hansa merchants withdrawn.	**1579.** North's translation of Plutarch's Lives. Geo. Buchanan: *De jure regni apud Scotos*. Edmund Spenser: *Shepherd's Calendar*. *Vindiciae contra Tyrannos*; political theory of Huguenots.
1580. *June 25*: *Book of Concord*, official collection of Lutheran confessional treatises.	**1580.** First commercial treaty between England and Turkey. Venetians import coffee into Italy.	**1580.** Lyly: *Euphues and his England*. Bodin: *Démonomanie*. Montaigne: *Essais*, vol. i-ii. Last Miracle play performed at Coventry. Jan Kochanowski: *Treny* (Dirges).
1581. *Jan. 28*: James VI signs second Scottish Confession of Faith. English Act imposing heavy fines for Catholic recusancy. *Harmonia Confessionum Fidei*, collection of Calvinistic confessional treatises. Claudius Aquaviva becomes General of Jesuits.	**1581.** Levant or Turkey Company formed. Wm. Strafford (?): *Compendious or Brief Examination of Certain Ordinary Complaints of Our Countrymen*; standard work of English mercantilism. Franco-Turkish commercial treaty renewed, including French protectorate over Oriental Christians.	**1581.** Tasso: *Gerusalemme Liberata*. Sidney: *Defence of Poesy*; and *Arcadia*. Cervantes: *Galatea*.
1581-1582. Gregory XIII tries in vain to reconcile Russian Church.		

I. WESTERN AND SOUTHERN EUROPE	II. CENTRAL, NORTHERN, AND EASTERN EUROPE	III. COUNTRIES OVERSEA
1582. *Aug. 22*: Raid of Ruthven; James VI in hands of English party in Scotland.	**1582.** *Jan. 15*: Peace of Jam-Zapolski between Russia and Poland: Russia cut off from the Baltic.	**1582.** Hakluyt's *Voyages* published. Hideyoshi succeeds Nobunaga as supreme in Japan. Todar Mal's revenue settlement, the Mogul Domesday Book.
1583. *Jan. 7*: Anjou sacks Antwerp; *June*: Anjou leaves Netherlands.		**1583.** *Aug.*: Gilbert founds first English colony in Newfoundland.
1584. *July 10*: William of Orange assassinated; succeeded by his son, Maurice. *Dec. 31*: The Guises and Philip II form League of Joinville against Huguenots.	**1584-1598.** Theodore, Tsar of Russia, last of Rurik dynasty; from **1588** under regency of Boris Godunov.	**1584.** Raleigh discovers and annexes Virginia.
1585. *Feb.*: Henry III of France refuses sovereignty of Netherlands. *Aug. 17*: Alexander of Parma takes Antwerp, and regains Flanders and Brabant. *Dec.*: English auxiliary corps under Leicester supports the Dutch.		**1585.** *Apr.*: Raleigh begins to colonize Virginia; abandoned in **1586.** **1585-1587.** John Davis tries to find North-West Passage; discovers Davis Straits.
1586. War of the three Henrys in France (Henry III, Henry of Navarre, Henry of Guise). *Aug.*: Babington's conspiracy discovered. *Oct. 14-15*: Trial of Mary Queen of Scots.	**1586.** *Dec. 12*: Stephen Bathory, King of Poland, *d.*	**1586-1588.** Third circumnavigation of the world, by Cavendish. **1586-1628.** Abbas the Great, Shah of Persia.
1587. *Feb. 8*: Mary Queen of Scots beheaded at Fotheringhay. *Apr. 19*: English expedition under Drake attacks Cadiz. *Aug.*: Leicester fails in Dutch expedition, returns to England.	**1587.** *Aug. 19*: Sigismund III, son of John of Sweden, elected King of Poland (-**1632**).	**1587.** Second English settlement in Virginia, fails in **1591.** Akbar annexes Kashmir.
1588. *May 12*: Barricade-fighting in Paris; Henry III forced to flee, calls States-General to Blois (*Oct.*). *July 31-Aug. 8*: Defeat of Spanish Armada; decline of Spain begins. *Dec. 23 and 24*: Duke Henry and Cardinal Louis of Guise assassinated.	**1588-1648.** Christian IV, King of Denmark.	**1588.** Charter to English Guinea Company.
1589. *Jan. 5*: Catherine de' Medici *d. Apr. 3*: Peace between Henry III and Henry of Navarre. *Aug. 2*: Henry III murdered; house of Valois extinct; Henry of Navarre claims the crown.	**1589.** *Mar. 9*: Peace of Beuthen; Archduke Maximilian renounces claims to Polish crown.	

IV. ECCLESIASTICAL HISTORY	V. CONSTITUTIONAL AND ECONOMIC HISTORY	VI. CULTURAL LIFE
1582. Jesuit mission in China begins. *Oct. 4*: St. Teresa de Jesus, Spanish mystic, *d.*	**1582.** *Oct. 4-15*: Gregorian Calendar introduced, at first in Roman Catholic countries only. First waterworks in London. Venetian constitution altered; power of Council of Ten restricted.	**1582.** Edinburgh and Würzburg Universities, and Accademia della Crusca, Florence, founded. Buchanan: *Rerum Scoticarum Historiae.*
1583-1584. ' Cologne War ' between Catholics and Calvinists for possession of Cologne Archbishopric; Roman Catholic party victorious.		**1583.** J. Scaliger: *De Emendatione Temporum*; criticizes sources of ancient history. Sir Thos. Smith: *De Republica Anglorum; the Manner of Government of England.*
1584. *Nov.*: Parliament passes bills against plotters, expels Jesuits and seminary priests. *Nov. 3*: Cardinal Carlo Borromeo, champion of Counter-reformation, *d.*	**1584.** Potatoes first imported into Europe.	**1584.** Emmanuel College, Cambridge, founded. Green: *Myrror of Modestie.* Justus Lipsius : *De Constantia*; revival of stoicism.
1584-1602. Struggle in Strasbourg Chapter; Roman Catholic party victorious.		**1584-1585.** Giordano Bruno: *Spaccio della Bestia Trionfante; Della Causa, Principio ed Uno; Degli Eroici Furori* (published in England).
1585. *Mar.*: Parliament passes Acts for security of the Queen, against Jesuits, priests, etc.	**1585.** *Aug. 17*: Antwerp, sacked by Spaniards, loses its importance in international trade to Amsterdam.	**1585.** Shakespeare leaves Stratford for London. Jesuit University of Graz founded. Guarini: *Pastor Fido.* Quirinale Palace, Rome, built by Dom. Fontana.
1585-1590. Pope Sixtus V (Felix Peretti).		
1586. Sixtus V fixes number of Cardinals at 70. Giordano Bruno at Wittenberg (**-1588**).		**1586.** Camden: *Britannia.* Warner: *Albion's England. Oct. 17*: Sir Philip Sidney *d.*
1586-1593. Cardinal Rob. Bellarmin, S.J.: *De Controversiis Christianae Fidei adversus huius Temporis Haereticos.*		**1586-1593.** Cesar Baronius: *Annales Ecclesiastici*; standard work of Roman Catholic history.
1587. *Mar. 1*: Peter Wentworth, M.P., challenges Elizabeth's absolutism in Church affairs. Recatholicization of bishopric of Würzburg completed.		**1587.** Knox: *History of the Reformation in Scotland.* First German book on Dr. Faustus published at Frankfort; Engl. transl. **1588.**
		1587-1591. Rialto Bridge, Venice, built.
1588. Welsh translation of Bible by Wm. Morgan. Penry: *Martin Marprelate Tracts*, attack English Church system. Luis de Molina, S.J.: *Concordia Liberi Arbitrii cum Gratiae Donis*, attacks Thomism; causes dispute between Jesuits and Dominicans.		**1588.** Montaigne: *Essais*, vol. iii. *Apr. 19*: Paolo Veronese *d.*
		1588-1590. Cupola and lantern of St. Peter's, Rome, finished by Fontana.
1589. Metropolitan of Moscow becomes Patriarch and independent of Constantinople. *Dec.*: Sixtus V clears way for reconciliation of Henry IV of France.	**1589.** Standing Committee for Privileges first appointed.	**1589.** Sidney Sussex College, Cambridge, and Academy of Kiev founded.

I. WESTERN AND SOUTHERN EUROPE	II. CENTRAL, NORTHERN, AND EASTERN EUROPE	III. COUNTRIES OVERSEA
1590. *Mar. 14*: Henry IV defeats League at Ivry. *Sept.*: Alexander of Parma attacks Henry IV of France.	**1590.** *July 10*: Charles of Inner Austria *d.*; succeeded by Ferdinand III (Emperor Ferdinand II).	**1590.** Emperor of Morocco annexes Timbuctoo and Upper Niger. Akbar conquers Orissa.
1591. English and German troops assist Henry IV.	**1591.** *Feb. 3*: German Protestant League of Torgau. *May 15*: Dmitri, son of Ivan the Terrible, *d.*	**1591.** Lancaster makes first English voyage to East Indies.
1592. *Dec. 3*: Alexander of Parma *d.*	**1592.** *Nov. 27*: John III of Sweden *d.*; succeeded by Sigmund of Poland (-**1604**).	**1592.** Japanese begin to conquer Korea. Portuguese settle at Mombasa. Akbar conquers Sind.
1593. *July 25*: Henry IV of France becomes a Roman Catholic.	**1593.** Renewal of war with Turks in Hungary. Michael the Brave becomes Prince of Wallachia; wins independence from Turks.	
1594. *Mar. 22*: Henry IV enters Paris. Earl of Tyrone's revolt in Ireland.	**1594.** Turks capture Raab fortress.	**1594.** Lancaster breaks Portuguese monopoly in India. Akbar takes Kandahar. *Nov. 22*: Frobisher *d.*
1595. *Jan. 17*: Henry IV declares war on Spain.	**1595.** *Oct. 28*: Sigmund Bathory defeats Turks at Giurgevo, and subdues Wallachia. *Oct.*: The Protestant Charles IX made Lieutenant-Governor of Sweden, in defiance of his Catholic nephew Sigmund.	**1595.** Dutch begin to colonize East Indies and Sunda Islands. *Jan. 28*: Drake *d. Nov. 12*: Hawkins *d.* **1595-1603.** Sultan Muhammad III.
1596. *Jan.*: End of French League. *Apr.*: Spaniards take Calais. *June 30-July 1*: English sack Cadiz. England, France, and Netherlands ally against Spain. **1597.** Spanish naval expeditions against England fail.	**1596.** Turks conquer Erlau. *Oct. 23-26*: Turkish victory at Keresztes. **1597.** *Dec.*: Sigmund Bathory cedes Transylvania to Rudolf II. **1597-1651.** Maximilian I of Bavaria.	**1597.** Chinese expel Japanese from Korea.
1598. *May 2*: Peace of Vervins between France and Spain. Tyrone victorious in Ireland. *Sept. 13*: Philip II of Spain *d.*; succeeded by Philip III (-**1621**).	**1598.** *Sept. 25*: Charles IX of Sweden defeats Sigmund of Poland at Stangebro. **1598-1605.** Boris Godunov, Tsar of Russia.	**1598.** Hideyoshi *d.*; Jeyasu Tokugawa restores Shogunate. **1598-1601.** Fourth circumnavigation of the world, by van Noort.

IV. ECCLESIASTICAL HISTORY	V. CONSTITUTIONAL AND ECONOMIC HISTORY	VI. CULTURAL LIFE
1590. *Sept. 15-27:* Pope Urban VII (Giov. Batt. Castagna). Bishop Khlesl becomes president of Reformation Committee in Austria; favours Counter-reformation. **1590-1591.** Pope Gregory XIV (Niccolò Sfondrato). **1591.** *Oct. 29-Dec. 30:* Pope Innocent IX (Ant. Facchinetti). *Dec. 14:* John of the Cross, Spanish mystic, d. **1592.** Presbyterian system established in Scotland. Definitive edition of *Vulgate.* **1592-1605.** Pope Clement VIII (Ippolito Aldobrandini). **1593.** *Feb.:* Parliament passes Act against 'seditious sectaries and disloyal persons'. *May 29:* John Penry and other opponents of royal supremacy executed. **1594.** Hooker: *Ecclesiastical Polity,* I-IV, defends Anglican system; book V published in **1597.** **1595.** *Feb. 21:* Rob. Southwell, Jesuit poet, hanged. Vadstena monastery, Sweden, destroyed. *May 26:* Filippo Neri, mystic, d. *Sept. 17:* Pope absolves Henry IV. **1597.** *Dec. 21:* Peter Canisius, first German Jesuit and intellectual head of German Counter-reformation, d. *Dec. 22:* Cesare, Duke of Este-Ferrara, excommunicated. **1597-1602.** Upper Austria, Styria, Carinthia, and Carniola recatholicized by force. **1598.** *Jan. 12:* Pope seizes Duchy of Ferrara. *Apr. 13:* Edict of Nantes grants toleration to Huguenots.	**1590.** Coal-mining begun in Ruhr district. Zach. Janssen invents microscope. **1591.** Philip II suppresses liberties of Aragon. **1595-1597.** Peasants' rising in Upper Austria. **1596.** Third national bankruptcy in Spain. Enno III of East Frisia plans Imperial Navy. **1597.** *Aug. 1:* Hansa secures Act banishing English merchants and goods from Empire. Acts for erection of workhouses and punishment of beggars; valid till **1834.** **1598.** *Aug. 4:* Hanseatic Steel-yard, London, closed. *Aug. 4:* Lord Burghley d.	**1590.** Edmund Spenser: *Faery Queene,* i-iii. Sidney: *Arcadia.* Marlowe: *Tamburlaine; Jew of Malta.* **1591.** Shakespeare: *Henry VI.* Sidney: *Astrophel and Stella.* Vieta popularizes alphabetical symbols in algebra. Trinity College, Dublin, founded. **1592.** Bodin: *Colloquium heptaplomeres;* advocates toleration of all denominations. Remains of Pompeii discovered. *Sept. 13:* Montaigne d. T. Kyd: *Spanish Tragedy.* Marlowe: *Dr. Faustus.* **1593.** Shakespeare: *Richard III; Comedy of Errors; Venus and Adonis.* Pierre Leroy a.o.: *Satyre Ménippée. May 30:* Marlowe murdered. **1594.** Shakespeare: *Titus Andronicus; Taming of the Shrew. Feb. 2:* Palestrina d. *June 14:* Orlando di Lasso d. **1595.** Shakespeare: *Two Gentlemen of Verona; Love's Labour's Lost.* Spenser: *Amoretti.* P. Charron: *De la vraie Sagesse* (moral philosophy). **1596.** Shakespeare: *Midsummer Night's Dream.* Joh. Kepler: *De Admirabili Proportione Coelestium Orbium.* Galileo invents thermometer. **1597.** Shakespeare: *King John; Merchant of Venice; Richard II; Romeo and Juliet.* Francis Bacon's first *Essays.* James VI: *Demonologie.* **1598.** Shakespeare: *Henry IV.* Francis Mere: *Palladis Tamia.* Abr. Scultetus: *Medulla Theologiae Patrum;* Protestant dissertation on Patristic writers. John Stow, *A Survey of London.*

I. WESTERN AND SOUTHERN EUROPE	II. CENTRAL, NORTHERN, AND EASTERN EUROPE	III. COUNTRIES OVERSEA
1599. *Sept. 8*: Essex, appointed Deputy in Ireland, makes unfavourable treaty with Tyrone.	**1599.** *Apr. 29*: Arrangement of Gera between the branches of the Hohenzollern family concerning mutual succession. Michael of Wallachia conquers Transylvania.	**1599.** Akbar begins to subdue Deccan.
1600. *Jan.*: New rising of Tyrone.	**1600.** *Feb.*: Charles IX of Sweden has leaders of pro-Polish party beheaded at Linköping.	**1600.** *Apr.*: William Adams lands in Japan.
1601. *Jan. 17*: Treaty of Lyons between France and Savoy; France gains Bresse, Bugey, Valromey, and Gex. *Feb. 25*: Essex beheaded for attempted rebellion. *July 15*: Spaniards begin siege of Ostend. *Sept.*: Spaniards land at Kinsale, Ireland.	**1601.** *Aug. 19*: Michael of Wallachia murdered by Hungarians. **1601-1606.** Pseudo-Demetrius in Russia.	**1601.** *Feb. 13*: First voyage of East India Company ships under Lancaster. Akbar annexes Khandesh.
1602. *Jan. 2*: Spaniards capitulate at Kinsale.	**1602.** *Dec.*: Duke of Savoy fails to conquer Geneva.	**1602.** Dutch East India Company ejects Portuguese from Moluccas.
1603. *Mar. 20 (O.S.)*: Tyrone submits. *Mar. 24 (O.S.)*: Elizabeth *d.* *Apr. 10 (O.S.)*: James VI proclaimed King of England, Scotland, France, and Ireland, as James I (**-1625**). **1604.** *Aug. 19*: Peace between England and Spain. *Sept. 25*: Spaniards capture Ostend.	**1604.** *Jan. 21*: Pseudo-Demetrius defeated by Tsar Boris. Successful rising of Hungarian Protestants under Stephen Bocskai. *Mar. 20*: Charles IX assumes title of King of Sweden.	**1603.** Tokugawa family obtains Shogunate (**-1867**). **1603-1604.** Champlain's expedition to Canada. **1603-1617.** Sultan Ahmed I. **1604.** French settlement in Acadia (Nova Scotia). Sir Henry Middleton leads second voyage of East India Company to Java and Moluccas.
1605. *Nov. 5 (O.S.)*: Gunpowder Plot discovered.	**1605.** *Apr.*: Stephen Bocskai elected Prince of Transylvania. *Apr. 23*: Tsar Boris *d.* *June 20*: Tsar Theodore II, son of Boris, murdered.	**1605.** *Oct.*: Jehangir succeeds Akbar. James I proclaimed King of Barbadoes. *Dec. 29*: John Davis killed by Japanese near Singapore.
1606. Henry IV occupies Sedan, capital of the rebellious Duke of Bouillon.	**1606.** *Apr.*: Archdukes rebel against Rudolf II, who resigns his possessions, except Bohemia and Tyrol, to Matthias. *June 23*: Peace of Vienna between Hapsburgs and Hungary; religious toleration granted, Bocskai acknowledged. *Nov. 11*: Peace of Zsitva-Torok with Turkey.	**1606.** *Apr. 10*: First Charter of Virginia for London and Plymouth Companies.

IV. ECCLESIASTICAL HISTORY	V. CONSTITUTIONAL AND ECONOMIC HISTORY	VI. CULTURAL LIFE
1599. James VI: *Basilikon Doron*, condemns Presbyterianism and asserts Divine Right of Kings.	**1599.** First postal rates fixed in Germany.	**1599.** Shakespeare: *Julius Caesar*. Juan de Mariana: *De Rege et Regis Institutione*, justifies tyrannicide.
1600. *Nov.*: James VI appoints three titular bishops in Scotland. *Dec. 5*: Scottish College founded in Rome.	**1600.** *Dec. 31*: East India Company established (*The Governor and Company of Merchants of London trading into the East Indies*). Amsterdam Bank founded. First endorsed bill of exchange, at Naples.	**1600.** Shakespeare: *Henry V*; *As You Like It*; *Much Ado*. Jonson: *Every Man out of His Humour*. William Gilbert discovers terrestrial magnetism. *Feb. 17*: Giordano Bruno burnt at Rome.
1601. Disputation between Protestants and Jesuits at Ratisbon.	**1601.** Postal agreement between Germany and France. John Wheeler, Secretary of the Merchant Adventurers: *A Treatise of Commerce*.	**1601.** Shakespeare: *Twelfth Night*; *Troilus and Cressida*. Jonson: *Every Man in His Humour*. *Oct. 24*: Tycho de Brahe, astronomer, *d.*
1602. Persecution of Protestants in Bohemia and Hungary begins. **1602–1603.** Violent recatholicization of Lower Austria.	**1602.** *Mar. 20*: Dutch East India Company established.	**1602.** Shakespeare: *Merry Wives of Windsor*. Bodleian Library opened. Tommaso Campanella: *Civitas Solis* (publ. **1620**). **1602–1604.** Galileo discovers laws of gravitation and oscillation.
1603. *July 17*: James I grants toleration to Roman Catholics. *Sept.*: Henry IV calls Jesuits back to France.		**1603.** Shakespeare: *All's Well That Ends Well*; *Hamlet*. Accademia dei Lincei, Rome, founded. Joh. Althusius: *Politica Methodice Digesta*; theory of Monarchomachism.
1604. *Mar. 3*: Fausto Sozzini *d.* **1604–1619.** Arminians attack doctrine of predestination in Netherlands.	**1604.** French East India Company established.	**1604.** Shakespeare: *Othello*; *Measure for Measure*. Rob. Cawdrey: *Table Alphabetical*, first English dictionary. J.-A. De Thou: *Historiae sui Temporis*. J. V. Andreae: *Rosicrucian Writings* (anonymously publ. **1614**).
1605. Pope Leo XI (Alexander de' Medici). Maurice of Hesse-Cassel converted to Calvinism. **1605–1621.** Pope Paul V (Camillo Borghese).	**1605.** Dutch Calvinists admitted to Hamburg.	**1605.** Shakespeare: *King Lear*; *Macbeth*. Bacon: *Advancement of Learning*. Cervantes: *Don Quixote*, pt. i (Engl. transl. **1612**).
1606. Increase of titular bishops in Scotland; many Presbyterian ministers banished. Protestant church at Cracow demolished.	**1606.** Commercial treaty between England and France.	**1606.** J. Scaliger: *Thesaurus Temporum*. Galileo invents proportional compass. Shakespeare: *Antony and Cleopatra*. *Nov.*: John Lyly *d.*

I. WESTERN AND SOUTHERN EUROPE	II. CENTRAL, NORTHERN, AND EASTERN EUROPE	III. COUNTRIES OVERSEA
1607. Ulster estates confiscated and given to English and Scottish settlers. Tyrone flees to Rome.	**1607.** *Mar. 15:* Charles IX crowned King of Sweden.	**1607.** English settlements in Virginia; *May 13:* Jamestown founded.
1608. *June:* Treaty for mutual defence between England and Netherlands.	**1608.** *Apr. 27:* Diet of Ratisbon broken up by Protestants. *June 25:* Rudolf II cedes Hungary, Austria, and Moravia to his brother Matthias. **1608-1619.** John Sigmund, Elector of Brandenburg.	**1608.** Jesuit State of Paraguay established. *July:* Champlain founds Quebec.
1609. *Apr. 9:* 12 years' truce between Spain and Netherlands. *June 17:* Netherlands ally with England and France for 12 years. *Sept. 22:* Moors expelled from Spain. **1610.** *Feb. 12:* Henry IV allies with German Protestant Union. *May 14:* Henry IV assassinated; succeeded by Louis XIII (-**1643**), under regency of Mary de' Medici, his mother, until **1617.** *June 9:* Arbella Stuart imprisoned for marrying Wm. Seymour.	**1609.** *Mar. 25:* Last Duke of Jülich-Cleves *d.*; quarrel about succession between Brandenburg and Palatinate-Neuburg. **1610.** *Sept. 1:* Archduke Leopold driven out of Jülich by Brandenburg, Neuburg, English, and Dutch. *Sept. 19:* Frederick V becomes Elector Palatine. Poles invade Moscow.	**1609.** Charter of East India Company renewed. New Charter for Virginia. *Apr. 16-Nov. 2,* **1611:** Hawkins, first British envoy to Great Mogul. **1610-1611.** Henry Hudson explores Hudson Bay.
	1611. *May 23:* Matthias becomes King of Bohemia. *Apr. 4:* Denmark declares war on Sweden. *Oct. 30:* Charles IX *d.*; succeeded by Gustavus II Adolphus (-**1632**).	**1611.** Dutch allowed to trade with Japan. **1611-1616.** Sir Thomas Dale, governor of Virginia, consolidates colony.
1612. *May 24:* Robert Cecil *d. Nov. 5:* Henry, Prince of Wales, *d.*	**1612.** *Jan. 20:* Emperor Rudolf II *d.*; succeeded by Matthias (-**1619**).	**1612.** Bermudas colonized from Virginia.
1613. *Feb. 14:* Elizabeth, daughter of James I, marries Frederick V, Elector Palatine.	**1613.** *Jan. 20:* Peace of Knaeroed between Sweden and Denmark. *Feb. 21:* Michael Romanov elected Tsar (-**1645**). *Oct. 24:* Gabriel Bethlen becomes Prince of Transylvania.	**1613.** Jehangir permits English settlement at Surat.
1614. Civil war in France, begun by Condé (*Feb. 19*); ended by peace of St. Menehould (*May 15*). War between Spain and Savoy.	**1614.** *Nov. 12:* Treaty of Xanten; Jülich-Cleves divided between Brandenburg and Neuburg.	**1614.** Virginian colonists prevent French settlements in Maine and Nova Scotia. United New Netherland Company establishes colony at mouth of Hudson.
1615. *Aug. 9:* Second Civil War in France. *Sept. 27:* Arbella Stuart *d.*	**1615.** *May 6:* Peace of Tyrnau; Matthias acknowledges Bethlen.	**1615.** Dutch seize Moluccas from Portuguese. England claims Spitzbergen. **1615-1618.** Sir Thomas Roe, British ambassador to Jehangir.
1616. *May 3:* Treaty of Loudun ends rebellion of Condé. *July 20:* Tyrone *d.*, at Rome. *Nov. 25:* Richelieu becomes Secretary of State.	**1616.** Archdukes Maximilian and Albert renounce their claims to the Empire in favour of Ferdinand of Styria.	**1616.** Manchu Tartars invade China.

IV. ECCLESIASTICAL HISTORY	V. CONSTITUTIONAL AND ECONOMIC HISTORY	VI. CULTURAL LIFE
1607. *Dec. 17*: Maximilian of Bavaria occupies Protestant town of Donauwörth.	**1607.** Emperor Rudolf II confirms English factory at Stade. Fourth national bankruptcy in Spain. Parliament rejects real Union with Scotland.	**1607.** Shakespeare: *Timon of Athens*. Jonson: *Volpone*. Monteverdi: *Orfeo* (opera). Giessen University founded. **1607-1611.** Hatfield House, Herts, built by John Thorpe.
1608. *May 12-14*: Protestant Union under leadership of Palatinate formed at Auhausen. Francis of Sales: *Introduction à la Vie Dévote*.	**1608.** First mention of the use of forks, in Italy.	**1608.** Shakespeare: *Coriolanus*. Lippersheim invents telescope.
1609. *July 9*: Royal Charter issued by Rudolf II, allows freedom of conscience in Bohemia. *July 10*: Catholic League under Bavarian leadership formed at Munich. **1610.** Full restoration of Episcopacy in Scotland. *Apr. 15*: Robert Parsons, leader of English Jesuits, *d.*	**1609.** Charter of East India Company renewed. Hugo Grotius: *Mare Liberum*, advocates freedom of the sea on behalf of Netherlands. **1610.** Dutch East India Company introduces the term *share*. Tea first imported into Netherlands.	**1609.** Shakespeare: *Sonnets*. Kepler: *Astronomia Nova*; laws of the orbits of planets. First regular newspapers in Germany, at Strasbourg and Wolfenbüttel. **1610.** Shakespeare: *Cymbeline*. D'Urfé: *Astrée*; pastoral novel.
1611. *Authorized Version* of Bible issued.	**1611.** Order of Baronets instituted. Permanent settlement of Merchant Adventurers at Hamburg.	**1611.** Shakespeare: *Winter's Tale*. Beaumont and Fletcher: *Philaster*. Kepler invents astronomical telescope. Chapman's translation of *Iliad* completed (from **1598**).
1612. Scots Parliament confirms restoration of Episcopacy. Two Unitarians burnt in England; last time heretics were burnt. **1613.** *May 16*: Protestant Union allies with Netherlands. *July*: Wolfgang Wilhelm of Palatinate-Neuburg converted to Roman Catholicism. *Dec. 25*: John Sigmund of Brandenburg converted to Calvinism. Fr. Suarez, S.J.: *Defensio Fidei Catholicae adversus Anglicanae Sectae Errores*. **1614.** John Sigmund of Brandenburg prohibits clergy abusing and slandering in pulpits.	**1613.** Amsterdam Exchange built.	**1612.** Shakespeare: *Tempest*. Jacob Böhme: *Aurora*; mystical philosophy. Rubens: *Descent from the Cross*. **1613.** Shakespeare: *Henry VIII*. Cervantes: *Novelas Ejemplares*. Erpenius: *Arabic Grammar*. *Apr. 7*: Domenico Theotocopoulos (El Greco) *d.* Beaumont and Fletcher: *Knight of the Burning Pestle*. **1613-1618.** Bodleian Library, Oxford, built by Thos. Holt. **1614.** Napier invents logarithms. Chapman's translation of *Odyssey*, i-xii (completed **1615**). **1614-1628.** Salzburg Cathedral built by Santino Solari.
1615. David Pareus: *Irenicum*, attempts to reconcile Protestants.	**1614.** Bankruptcy of commercial firm of Welsers, Augsburg. *Oct.*: Last session of French Estates-General before 1789. Danish East India Company formed. **1615.** Montchrétien: *Traité de l'économie politique*; system of mercantilism.	**1615.** Wm. Camden: *Annales*, pt. i (completed **1627**). Cervantes: *Don Quixote*, pt. ii. **1615-1620.** Elias Holl builds town hall of Augsburg.
1616. Protestant churches at Posen, Poland, demolished. Francis of Sales: *Traité de l'Amour de Dieu*.	**1616.** Dutch-Japanese commercial treaty. Serfdom of peasants established in Pomerania.	**1616.** *Apr. 23*: Shakespeare *d.* at Stratford; Cervantes *d.* in Madrid. Snellius discovers law of refraction. Bernini: *Apollo and Daphne*; his first work.

I. WESTERN AND SOUTHERN EUROPE

1617. *Apr.*: Richelieu dismissed. *June 6* and *July 29*: Treaty of succession between Austrian and Spanish Hapsburgs. *Oct. 9*: Peace between Spain and Savoy.

1618. *Feb.*: Peace of Madrid between Venice and Austria.

1619. *Mar. 13*: Oldenbarnevelt, Dutch Secretary of State, executed. James refuses to assist Frederick of Bohemia.

1620. *May-Aug.*: Rising of French nobles and Huguenots suppressed; Béarn and Navarre united with France.

1621. *Mar. 31*: Philip III *d.*; succeeded by Philip IV (**-1665**); who renews war with Netherlands.

1622. *Jan.*: Richelieu re-enters Royal Council. *Oct. 18*: Treaty of Montpellier, confirms Edict of Nantes, leaves La Rochelle and Montauban to Huguenots.
1623. *Mar. 7 - Aug. 30*: Charles, Prince of Wales, at Madrid; fails to secure betrothal to Spanish princess.

1624. *Mar. 10*: England declares war on France. *June 20*: Treaty of Compiègne between France and Netherlands. *Aug. 13*: Richelieu becomes First Minister (**-1642**).

II. CENTRAL, NORTHERN, AND EASTERN EUROPE

1617. *Feb. 27*: Peace of Stolbova between Russia and Sweden; Sweden obtains Karelia and Ingria. *June 29*: Archduke Ferdinand crowned King of Bohemia. War between Sweden and Poland.
1618. Rebellion in Bohemia because of breach of Royal Charter. *May 23*: 'Defenestration' of Prague. *July 1*: Ferdinand crowned King of Hungary. *Dec. 24*: Poland makes truces with Sweden and Turkey. Brandenburg obtains Prussia as Polish fief.

1619. *Mar. 20*: Emperor Matthias *d. Aug. 26*: Bohemians depose Ferdinand and elect Frederick V of Palatinate king. *Aug. 28*: Ferdinand elected emperor (**-1637**). Bethlen besieges Vienna.
1620. *July 3*: Agreement between Protestant Union and Catholic League at Ulm. *Sept. 20*: Turks defeat Poles at Jassy. *Nov. 8*: League under Tilly defeats Frederick of Bohemia at the White Hill near Prague.
1621. *Jan. 22*: Frederick V outlawed. *Apr.*: Protestant Union dissolved. Gustavus Adolphus conquers Livonia.

1622. *Jan. 7*: Peace between Ferdinand and Bethlen. Tilly defeats George Frederick of Baden, Christian of Halberstadt, and Ernest of Mansfeld.
1623. *Feb. 25*: Maximilian of Bavaria obtains electorate of Palatinate.

1624. *May 11*: Treaty of Düsseldorf between Brandenburg and Neuburg. *Nov.*: French, allied with Venice and Savoy, occupy Valtellina.

III. COUNTRIES OVERSEA

1617. Raleigh's last expedition to Guiana. Dutch settle on island of Goree.

1618. *Oct. 29*: Raleigh beheaded. English West Africa Company founded; occupies Gambia and Gold Coast.

1619. Dutch found Batavia, Java. *July 30*: First American Parliament meets in Jamestown, Virginia.

1620. *Sept. 17*: Pilgrim Fathers leave Plymouth in the *Mayflower*. *Dec. 22*: *Mayflower* lands; New Plymouth founded. Negro slaves first imported to North America (Jamestown).

1621. Conflict between English and Dutch East India Companies. Scottish settlement in Acadia (Nova Scotia) fails.

1622. First English ambassador to Turkey. English capture Ormuz. Jehangir loses Kandahar to Persia.

1623. *Feb.*: Dutch massacre English colonists at Amboina, Molucca Islands. English and French settlements in St. Kitts.
1623-1640. Sultan Murad IV.
1624. First English settlement in East India. Dutch found New Amsterdam (New York). England effectively occupies Barbadoes. Charter of London Company revoked; Virginia made a crown colony.

IV. ECCLESIASTICAL HISTORY	V. CONSTITUTIONAL AND ECONOMIC HISTORY	VI. CULTURAL LIFE
1617. *June 15*: Church lands in Béarn restored to Roman Catholics. *Sept. 25*: Francis Suarez, S.J., Spanish theologian, *d*.	**1617.** *Mar. 7*: Bacon appointed Lord Keeper. Snellius invents triangulation.	**1617.** *Aug. 24*: *Fruchtbringende Gesellschaft* founded at Weimar, on the model of Accademia della Crusca. *Oct. 2*: Isaac Oliver, miniaturist, *d*.
1618. *Aug. 27*: Five Articles of Perth enacted; victory of episcopal party. Benedictine Congregation of St. Maur, at St. Germain, founded; beginning of Patristic studies. **1618-1619.** General Synod of Calvinists at Dordrecht; victory of strict Calvinists (Gomarists), condemnation of Arminians (Remonstrants). **1619.** Hugo Grotius: *De Veritate Religionis Christianae.* J. Böhme: *On the three Principles of Christianity.*	**1618.** *Jan. 7*: Bacon appointed Lord Chancellor. Declaration of Sports issued. **1619.** Hamburg and Venice Banks founded.	**1618.** G. R. Weckherlin: *Odes and Hymns.* **1619.** Dulwich College founded by Edw. Alleyn. Beaumont and Fletcher: *A King and No King.* *Jan. 7*: Nich. Hilliard *d*.
1620. *June 19*: Massacre of Protestants in Valtellina. Bohemia, Palatinate, and Béarn recatholicized by force.	**1620-1623.** Great currency inflation in Germany.	**1620.** Francis Bacon: *Novum Organum Scientiarum.*
1621-1623. Pope Gregory XV (Alexander Ludovisi). **1621.** *Nov. 16*: Gregory XV settles papal election (*Aeterni Patris*). Papal Chancery first adopts January 1 as beginning of the year; definitely adopted **1691**. **1622.** *Apr. 17*: French Huguenots placed under Royal Commissioners.	**1621.** *Apr.-May*: Bacon impeached and deprived of Great Seal. Dutch West India Company founded. **1622.** *Feb. 8*: James I dissolves Parliament after 2 meetings. Hamburg creates currency of Mark Banko.	**1621.** Rob. Burton: *Anatomy of Melancholy.* J. Barclay: *Argenis.* *June 6*: *Corante*, first English newspaper (-**1641**). **1622.** Benedictine University of Salzburg founded. Asellius discovers lacteal vessels.
1623-1644. Pope Urban VIII (Maffeo Barberini). **1623.** *Nov. 11*: Philippe Duplessis-Mornay, ' Pope of Huguenots', *d*. **1624.** Lazarus Order founded.	**1623.** Dutch-Persian commercial treaty. **1624.** Parliament declares monopolies illegal.	**1623.** First Folio edition of Shakespeare's plays. Massinger: *Duke of Milan.* Ch. Sorel: *Francion.* **1624.** Herbert of Cherbury: *De Veritate*; standard work on Deism. Martin Opitz: *Buch von der deutschen Poeterey.* Helmont introduces the term *gas*.

I. WESTERN AND SOUTHERN EUROPE	II. CENTRAL, NORTHERN, AND EASTERN EUROPE	III. COUNTRIES OVERSEA
1625. *Mar. 27:* James I and VI *d.*; succeeded by Charles I (-**1649**). *Apr. 23:* Maurice of Nassau *d.*; succeeded by Frederick Henry as Stadholder. *May 11:* Charles I marries Henrietta Maria of France. *Sept. 15:* Defeat of Huguenots under Soubise, who flees to England.	**1625.** *Apr. 7:* Wallenstein appointed Imperial generalissimo. *June 13:* Wallenstein created Duke of Friedland. *Dec. 9:* Treaty of the Hague; England and Netherlands subsidize Denmark against Emperor.	**1625.** French occupy Antilles and Cayenne. Colonial Office established in London.
1626. *Feb. 6:* Peace of La Rochelle ends Huguenot revolt. *Mar. 5:* Treaty of Monzon between France and Spain confirms independence of Grisons.	**1626.** *Apr. 25:* Wallenstein defeats Ernest of Mansfeld at Dessau, and occupies Pomerania. *Aug. 27:* Tilly defeats Christian IV of Denmark at Lutter. *Dec. 20:* Treaty of Pressburg between Emperor and Bethlen.	**1626.** English occupy St. Kitts.
1627. Huguenots revolt again. *Aug. 10:* Richelieu begins siege of La Rochelle, which the English fail to relieve. *Dec. 26:* Duke of Mantua *d.*; war of succession between Emperor and France.	**1627.** Wallenstein and Tilly occupy Silesia, Holstein, and Jutland.	**1627.** English occupy Nova Scotia. Korea becomes tributary of China. Japan excludes all foreigners (-**1852**).
1628. *Aug. 23:* Duke of Buckingham assassinated. *Oct. 28:* La Rochelle capitulates.	**1628.** *Jan. 26:* Wallenstein obtains duchy of Mecklenburg. *Apr. 21:* Wallenstein appointed Admiral of the Baltic. *June 9:* Dukes of Mecklenburg outlawed by Emperor. *Aug.:* Wallenstein fails to take Stralsund.	**1628.** England acquires Nevis. Dutch conquer Java and Malacca. **1628-1658.** Shah Jahan, Great Mogul.
1629. *Apr. 14:* Peace of Susa between England and France. *June 28:* Peace of Alais ends Huguenot wars; Huguenots obtain religious freedom, dissolve their political organization.	**1629.** *May 22:* Peace of Lübeck between Emperor and Denmark; Christian renounces intervention in Empire. *June 16:* Wallenstein created duke of Mecklenburg. *Sept. 25:* Truce of Altmark between Sweden and Poland; Sweden obtains Livonia and parts of Prussia.	**1629.** English settlements in Massachusetts.
1630. *Nov. 5:* Treaty of Madrid ends war between England and Spain. *Nov. 10:* Richelieu overthrows dangerous conspiracy (Day of Dupes). **1630-1637.** Victor Amadeus I of Savoy.	**1630.** *July 6:* Gustavus Adolphus lands in Pomerania. *July:* Electors, backed by France, meet at Ratisbon to defy Emperor and Wallenstein. *Aug. 13:* Wallenstein dismissed.	**1630.** Buccaneers settle in Tortuga, off Hispaniola. **1630-1635.** Dutch take Pernambuco from Portuguese.
1631. *Jan. 23:* Treaty of Bärwalde between France and Sweden. *June 19:* Treaty of Cherasco; Mantua given to Charles of Nevers. Urban VIII annexes Urbino. Savoy cedes Pinerolo to France.	**1631.** *May 20:* Tilly sacks Magdeburg. *June 20:* Brandenburg allies with Sweden. *Sept. 11:* Saxony allies with Sweden. *Sept. 17:* Gustavus Adolphus defeats Tilly at Breitenfeld. *Nov. 15:* Saxons take Prague.	**1631.** English colonize Leeward Islands.

IV. ECCLESIASTICAL HISTORY	V. CONSTITUTIONAL AND ECONOMIC HISTORY	VI. CULTURAL LIFE
1625. Vincent de Paul founds Order of Sisters of Mercy. Act of Revocation, to recover church property in Scotland for national use.	**1625.** *June:* Parliament grants tonnage and poundage to Charles I for one year.	**1625.** Bacon: *Essays*. Grotius: *De Jure Belli ac Pacis;* pioneer work of international law. Racan: *Les Bergeries.*
1626. Irish College founded at Rome. **1626-1628.** Rebellion of Protestant peasants in Austria.	**1626.** *Feb. 6 - June 15:* Second Parliament; Charles continues to levy tonnage and poundage, and collects Forced Loan.	**1626.** Sandys's translation of Ovid's *Metamorphoses;* first literary work undertaken in America. Quevedo Villegas: *Vida del gran Tacaño.*
1627. *Aug. 8: Collegium de Propaganda Fide* founded at Rome.	**1627.** Bohemian Government moved to Vienna. Swedish South Sea Company founded.	**1627.** Bacon: *New Atlantis. Daphne,* first German opera, written by Opitz, composed by H. Schütz, performed at Torgau.
1628. David Blondel proves Decretals of Isidore to be forged.	**1628.** *June 7:* Petition of Right, against arbitrary imprisonment, martial law, forced loans, billeting of soldiers and sailors. Richelieu founds Canada and Senegal Companies. First port equipped with sluices, at Le Havre.	**1628.** Wm. Harvey: *De Motu Cordis et Sanguinis;* discovers double circulation of blood. *Oct. 16:* Malherbe, Court poet of Henry IV, d. Taj Mahal built at Agra. **1628-1631.** Amos Comenius: *Informatorium der Mutterschul,* principles of primary education.
1629. *Mar. 6:* Edict of Restitution orders all Church property secularized since **1552** to be restored to the Roman Church, and excludes Calvinists from religious peace.	**1629.** *Mar. 2:* Parliament dissolved, having voted the Three Resolutions.	**1629.** Corneille: *Mélite.* Carlo Maderna *d.;* Bernini appointed architect of St. Peter's, Rome. A. Girard introduces brackets and imaginary roots in algebra.
1630. *Jan. 13:* Pope dissolves Congregation of Female Jesuits, founded in **1609.** Congregation of English Ladies founded at Munich.	**1630.** *Jan.:* Distraint of Knighthood. Thomas Mun: *England's Treasure by Forraign Trade;* theory of Mercantilism; printed in **1664.** *Feb. 24:* Confederation of Hamburg, Bremen, and Lübeck as assigns of Hansa.	**1630.** Arrebo: *Hexameron;* initiates modern Danish literature. *Nov. 15:* Kepler *d.*
1631. *Feb. 20 - Apr. 12:* Leipzig Convention of German Protestants to prevent Catholic attacks.	**1631.** Wm. Petty: *Political Arithmetic;* advocates State regulation of economic policy.	**1631.** *Gazette de France* appears. Fr. v. Spee: *Cautio Criminalis;* against trials for witchcraft.

I. WESTERN AND SOUTHERN EUROPE	II. CENTRAL, NORTHERN, AND EASTERN EUROPE	III. COUNTRIES OVERSEA
1632. Richelieu suppresses insurrection headed by Gaston of Orleans, heir presumptive to the throne, and Montmorency, who is beheaded (*Oct. 30*).	**1632.** *Apr. 15:* Gustavus Adolphus defeats Tilly on the Lech, (*May 17*) enters Munich. *Apr. 13:* Wallenstein reinstated in command, drives Saxons out of Bohemia. *Sept. 3-4:* Battle of Nuremberg between Gustavus Adolphus and Wallenstein. *Nov. 16:* Defeat of Wallenstein, death of Gustavus Adolphus at Lützen; succeeded by Christina (**-1654**).	**1632.** English colonies in Antigua and Montserrat. Portuguese expelled from Bengal.
1633. French occupy Lorraine (**-1659**). *June 18:* Charles I crowned King of Scotland at Edinburgh.	**1632-1648.** Vladislav IV of Poland. **1633.** *Apr. 23:* League of Heilbronn, of South German Protestants with Sweden and France. *Oct. 12:* Wallenstein defeats Swedes in Silesia. *Nov. 14:* Bernard of Weimar seizes Ratisbon.	**1633.** First English factory in Bengal.
	1634. *Feb. 25:* Wallenstein murdered at Eger. *Sept. 5-6:* Bernard of Weimar and Swedes defeated at Nördlingen.	**1634.** Lord Baltimore founds Maryland for Roman Catholic settlers. Dutch take island of Curaçao.
1635. *Apr. 28:* France allies with Sweden. *May 19:* France declares war on Spain. *Oct. 27:* Bernard of Weimar in pay of France.	**1635.** *May 30:* Peace of Prague between Emperor and Saxony; Saxony obtains Lusatia. *Sept. 12:* Truce of Stuhmsdorf between Sweden and Poland for 20 years.	**1635.** English colonize Virgin Islands. French occupy Martinique and Guadeloupe. Dutch occupy Formosa. Persians take Erivan from Turks.
1636. *July:* Piccolomini invades France.	**1636.** *Oct. 4:* Swedes defeat Saxons at Wittstock. *Dec. 22:* Ferdinand III elected king.	**1636.** Dutch occupy Ceylon. Bijapur becomes tributary to Delhi. English settlements in Rhode Island and Connecticut.
1637. French begin to conquer Artois; completed in **1640**. *Oct. 10:* Dutch recapture Breda, last Spanish stronghold. **1637-1675.** Charles Emanuel II of Savoy. **1638.** *Feb. 27 - Mar. 9:* National Covenant of Scots, protest against church policy of Charles I.	**1637.** *Feb. 15:* Emperor Ferdinand II *d.*; succeeded by Ferdinand III (**-1657**). *Mar. 20:* Bogislav XIV, last duke of Pomerania, *d.* **1638.** *Dec. 17:* Bernard of Weimar takes Breisach.	**1637.** English factory at Canton. Dutch expel Portuguese from Gold Coast. French traders found St. Louis at mouth of Senegal. Portugese expelled from Japan. **1637-1644.** John Maurice of Nassau, Dutch governor of Brazil. **1638.** Swedes settle on Delaware (New Sweden). French take Réunion. Turks take Baghdad back from Persia.
1639. French begin to occupy Alsace. *May 24:* Skirmish of Turriff, first bloodshed in Scottish Civil War. *Oct. 21:* Dutch defeat Spaniards off Downs.	**1639.** *Jan. 24:* George Jenatsch, leader of Grisons, murdered. *July 18:* Bernard of Weimar *d.*	**1639.** English factory at Madras. Turkey and Persia settle Armenian frontier.

IV. ECCLESIASTICAL HISTORY	V. CONSTITUTIONAL AND ECONOMIC HISTORY	VI. CULTURAL LIFE
1632. Jean Daillé: *Traité de l'Emploi des Saints Pères*, against authority of Patristic writers.	**1632.** Export of grain from England without Royal licence forbidden. **1632-1644.** Oxenstierna, Swedish chancellor.	**1632.** Galileo Galilei: *Dialogo sopra i due massimi sistemi del mondo*. Rembrandt: *The Lesson in Anatomy*. Van Dyck settles in England as Court painter.
1633. *Aug. 6*: Laud becomes Archbishop of Canterbury. Edition of Bible (*Textus Receptus*) by Elzevir, Leiden.	**1633.** *Oct. 18*: Declaration of Sports on Sundays re-issued.	**1633.** Wm. Prynne: *Histriomastix*; against stage-plays. Rob. Fludd: *Clavis Philosophiae et Alchymiae*. Abr. Cowley: *Poetical Blossoms*. John Donne: *Poems*. Geo. Herbert: *The Temple*. J. Callot: *Misères et Malheurs de la Guerre*; engravings. *June 22*: Galilei forced by Inquisition to abjure theories of Copernicus.
1634. Panzani, Italian priest, allowed to enter England. First performance of Passion-Play at Oberammergau. **1635.** *May*: Charles authorizes new Book of Canons for Scotland.	**1634.** *Oct. 20*: First writ of ship-money in London, to make the king independent of Parliament. **1635.** *Aug. 4*: Second writ of ship-money, extended to the whole kingdom. Enlargement of Royal forests.	**1634.** Milton: *Comus*. Corneille: *La Veuve*; *La Suivante*. **1635.** Sir Thos. Browne: *Religio Medici*; publ. **1642**. *Jan. 29*: Richelieu founds Académie Française. First vol. of Calderon's Comedies published. *Aug. 27*: Lope de Vega *d*.
1636. Pope sends agent to Queen of England. *Dec.*: Scottish Council orders use of new Service Book. **1637.** Charles attempts to introduce new Prayer Book into Scotland. Outbreak of religious rebellion in Scotland. *Aug. 17*: Joh. Gerhard, champion of Lutheran orthodoxy, *d*. at Jena.	**1636.** *Oct. 9*: Third writ of ship-money. Creation of new monopolies and augmentation of taxation. Tea first introduced into Paris. **1637.** Speculation in tulips collapses in Holland. **1637-1638.** Ship-money case of John Hampden.	**1636.** Corneille: *Le Cid*. Harvard College founded as seminary for clergy. Utrecht University founded. **1637.** Descartes: *Discours de la Méthode*. First public opera house, at Venice. Milton: *Lycidas*.
1638. *May 6*: Cornelius Jansen, originator of Jansenism, *d. Nov. 21-Dec. 20*: General Assembly at Glasgow restores state of Scottish Kirk as before **1580**.		**1638.** Thos. Shelton: *Tachygraphy*. Descartes invents analytical geometry.
1639. *Aug.*: General Assembly abolishes Episcopacy in Scotland. Common activity of Lutheran and Calvinistic theologians at Frankfort University.	**1639.** Last writ of ship-money. 'Fundamental Orders' of Connecticut, first written constitution in America.	**1639.** First printing press established in America. Poussin appointed French Court painter.

I. WESTERN AND SOUTHERN EUROPE	II. CENTRAL, NORTHERN, AND EASTERN EUROPE	III. COUNTRIES OVERSEA
1640. *May 12*: Revolts in Catalonia and (*Dec. 1*) Portugal; Portugal becomes independent under dynasty of Braganza (**-1910**). **1640-1656.** John IV of Portugal.	**1640-1688.** Frederick William of Brandenburg, the Great Elector.	**1640.** Final English settlement in Bengal. Dutch monopoly of trade in Japan. Dutch destroy Malacca. **1640-1649.** Sultan Ibrahim.
1641. *June 1*: France and Portugal ally against Spain. *Aug.*: Treaty of friendship and commerce between Portugal and Sweden. *Oct.*: Outbreak of Irish rebellion.	**1641.** *July 24*: Truce between Sweden and Brandenburg.	**1641.** *Jan.*: Portuguese surrender Malacca to the Dutch.
1642. *Aug. 22*: Royal standard raised at Nottingham; beginning of English Civil War. *Dec. 4*: Richelieu *d*; Cardinal Mazarin becomes First Minister (**-1661**).	**1642.** *Mar.*: Turks renew peace with Emperor. *Nov. 2*: Swedes defeat Imperial army at Breitenfeld.	**1642.** Tasman discovers Tasmania (*Nov. 24*) and New Zealand (*Dec. 13*).
1643. *May 14*: Louis XIII *d*.; succeeded by Louis XIV (**-1715**). *May 19*: French defeat Spaniards at Rocroi. *Sept. 15*: 'First Cessation' ends Irish rebellion. *Sept. 25*: Solemn League and Covenant between Parliament and Scots.		**1643.** Confederation of united colonies of New England; dissolved **1698**.
1644. *July 2*: Royalists defeated at Marston Moor. *Sept. 2*: Essex's army surrenders to Charles at Lostwithiel. French driven out of Aragon.	**1644.** *Jan.*: Sweden declares war on Denmark. *Nov. 23* and *Dec. 4*: Peace Conferences at Münster and Osnabrück opened.	**1644.** End of the Ming and beginning of the Manchu dynasties in China (**-1912**). Dutch settlement in Mauritius.
1645. *June 14*: Cromwell defeats Royalists at Naseby. *Aug. 25*: Treaty of Glamorgan (concessions to Irish Roman Catholics). *Sept.*: Bristol. *Sept. 24*: Montrose defeated at Philiphaugh.	**1645.** *Mar. 7*: Swedes defeat Imperial army at Jankau. *Aug. 23*: Peace of Brömsebro between Sweden and Denmark; Denmark loses her possessions in Sweden. Turks begin conquest of Crete (**-1669**). **1645-1676.** Alexis, Tsar of Russia.	**1645.** Portuguese in Brazil rebel against Dutch.
1646. *May 5*: Charles I surrenders to Scottish army at Newark. *June 5*: Victory of Irish Catholics at Benburb.	**1646.** *July*: French and Swedes invade Bavaria.	**1646.** English occupy the Bahamas.
1647. *Feb. 3*: Scots sell Charles to Parliament for £400,000. *Mar. 14*: Frederick Henry, Dutch Stadholder, *d*.; succeeded by William II. *Aug. 8*: Parliamentary army defeats Irish at Dangan Hill.	**1647.** *Mar. 14*: Treaty of neutrality between Bavaria, France, and Sweden, at Ulm. Austria cedes Burgenland to Hungary (**-1919**). *Sept. 2*: Bavaria sides again with Emperor.	
1648. *Apr.*: Scots begin Second Civil War. *Aug. 17*: Cromwell defeats Scots at Preston. *Aug.*: Outbreak of the Fronde in France (**-1653**).	**1648.** *Jan. 30*: Peace between Spain and Netherlands. *July 26*: Swedes take Prague. *Oct. 24*: Peace of Westphalia, at Münster and Osnabrück; France obtains Alsace, Sweden obtains mouths of Oder, Elbe, and Weser, independence of Switzerland, Netherlands, and all German states guaranteed. **1648-1668.** John II Casimir, King of Poland.	**1648.** Arabs capture Muscat from Portuguese.

IV. ECCLESIASTICAL HISTORY	V. CONSTITUTIONAL AND ECONOMIC HISTORY	VI. CULTURAL LIFE
1640. Jansen: *Augustinus*, published.	**1640.** *Apr. 13–May 5*: Short Parliament. *Aug. 28*: Petition of 12 Peers for new Parliament. *Nov. 3*: Long Parliament meets. *Dec. 11*: Root and Branch Petition. Louis d'or first coined.	**1640.** Hobbes: *Elements of Law, Natural and Politique* (publ. **1650**). Corneille: *Polyeucte; Horace; Cinna.* Moscherosch: *Visions of Philander of Sittewald.* Abo University founded. *May 30*: Rubens *d.*
1641. *Oct.*: Massacre of Protestants in Ulster.	**1641.** *May 12*: Lord Strafford beheaded. Star Chamber and High Commission Court abolished. *Nov. 22*: Grand Remonstrance.	**1641.** Descartes: *Meditationes de Prima Philosophia.* Guevara: *El Diabolo Cojuelo.* Lely comes to England. *Dec. 9*: Van Dyck *d.*
1642. *Dec. 22*: Urban VIII reduces annual feast-days to 32 (*Universa per Orbem*). Urban condemns Jansen's *Augustinus* at instigation of Jesuits. **1643.** *Sept. 25*: Assembly of Westminster adopts Presbyterianism.	**1642.** *Jan. 4*: Charles attempts to arrest Five Members. *Sept. 10*: Essex in command of Parliamentary armies. *Sept.*: Deflation of Spanish currency. **1643.** *June 24*: Hampden defeated and killed at Chalgrove Field. *Dec. 3*: Pym *d.* First subscription loan in Austria.	**1642.** Hobbes: *De Cive.* Theatres closed in England, till **1660**. Rembrandt: *Night Watch. Jan. 8*: Galileo *d. Aug. 8*: Guido Reni *d.* **1643.** Joh. Bollandus, S.J., begins to edit *Acta Sanctorum.* Torricelli invents barometer. Herm. Conring: *On the Origin of German Law*; against Roman law.
1644. Antonio Escobar: *Liber Theologiae Moralis*; standard work of Jesuit moral theology. **1644-1655.** Pope Innocent X (Giambattista Pamfili). **1645.** Synchretistic dispute between Geo. Calixtus, who advocates religious reunion, and Lutheran orthodoxists.	**1645.** *Jan. 10*: Archbishop Laud beheaded. *Jan. 21*: Sir Thomas Fairfax appointed commander of Parliamentary army. *Apr. 3*: Self-denying Ordinance passed by Lords.	**1644.** Milton: *Areopagitica.* Descartes: *Principia Philosophiae. Pegnitzischer Blumenorden*, poetical society, founded at Nuremberg. **1645.** Lord Herbert of Cherbury: *De Religione Gentilium Errorumque apud eos Causis.* Edm. Waller: *Poems.* Comenius: *Panergesia.* Philipp von Zesen: *Adriatische Rosemund. Aug. 28*: Grotius *d.*
		1646. Henry Vaughan: *Poems.* Rich. Crashaw: *Steps to the Temple.*
1647. *Nov. 11*: Lutherans acknowledge Calvinists as co-religionists.	**1647.** Swedish African Company founded.	**1647.** La Calprenède: *Cléopâtre.* Corneille: *Rodogune.* A. Cowley: *The Mistress.*
1648. *Nov. 20*: Innocent X condemns Peace of Westphalia (*Zelo Domus Dei*; published in **1651**). George Fox founds Society of Friends.	**1648.** *Dec. 6*: Pride's Purge of House of Commons. Charles Louis, son of Frederick V of Palatinate, created eighth Elector.	**1648.** Royal Academy of Arts founded at Paris. Herrick: *Hesperides.* **1648-1650.** Cyrano de Bergerac: *Histoire comique des états de la lune.*

I. WESTERN AND SOUTHERN EUROPE

1649. *Jan. 30*: Charles I beheaded. *Apr.*: Cromwell suppresses revolt of Levellers. *Sept. 11*: Cromwell sacks Drogheda and (*Oct. 11*) Wexford, Ireland.

1650. *Sept. 3*: Cromwell defeats Scots at Dunbar. *Nov. 6*: William II of the Netherlands *d.* *Dec. 19*: Edinburgh Castle surrenders to Cromwell.

1651. *Jan. 1*: Charles II crowned at Scone. *Sept. 3*: Cromwell defeats Charles at Worcester. *Oct. 17*: Charles escapes to France. *Oct. 27*: Limerick surrenders.

1652. *June 30*: England declares war on Holland. *Sept.*: Spaniards take Dunkirk. *Nov.*: Fronde ally with Spain.

1653. *July 31*: Bordeaux surrenders; end of Fronde. *Aug 9*: Dutch defeated by English off Texel.

1654. *Apr. 5*: Peace of Westminster between England and Holland which recognizes Navigation Act. *June 7*: Coronation of Louis XIV. *July 10*: Treaty between England and Portugal establishes English control over Portugal. *Aug. 5*: French take Stenay.

1655. *Aug.*: French successes in Spanish Netherlands.

1656. *Feb.*: Spain declares war on England. *Apr.*: Treaty between Philip IV and the exiled Charles II. *Sept. 5*: Treaty of friendship between England and France.
1656–1683. Alfonso VI, King of Portugal.

II. CENTRAL, NORTHERN, AND EASTERN EUROPE

1648–1670. Frederick III, King of Denmark.

1650. *June 26*: Exchange of peace treaties between Emperor and Sweden at Nuremberg.

1651. Formation of Catholic and Protestant Leagues in Germany for carrying out Peace of Westphalia.

1652. *Feb.*: Alliance of Hildesheim between North German Protestants and Sweden. *July 20*: Electorate of Saxony divided in four parts (**-1746**).
1653. *May 24*: Ferdinand IV elected King of the Romans (*d. July 9*, **1654**).

1654. *June 6*: Christina of Sweden abdicates in favour of Charles X of Zweibrücken (**-1660**). War between Russia and Poland; *Sept. 10*: Tsar takes Smolensk.

1655. *July*: Charles X invades Poland, takes Warsaw (*Aug. 30*) and Cracow (*Oct. 8*). *July 27*: Defensive treaty between Brandenburg and Netherlands.

1656. *Jan. 17*: Alliance between Brandenburg and Sweden; Prussia becomes Swedish fief. *June*: Russians invade Swedish territories in the Baltic. *July 28-30*: Swedes and Brandenburgers defeat Poles at Warsaw. *Nov. 3*: Treaty of Vilna between Russia and Poland. *Nov. 20*: Treaty of Labiau between Brandenburg and Sweden; Sweden renounces sovereignty over Prussia.

III. COUNTRIES OVERSEA

1649. *Aug.*: Sultan Ibrahim deposed and murdered; succeeded by Muhammad IV (**-1687**). Persians recapture Kandahar.

1650. Frontier between English and Dutch colonies in North America defined.

1651. East India Company occupy St. Helena.

1652. Dutch found Cape Town.

1654. Dutch finally lose Brazil to Portugal.
1654–1658. Gambia, colony of James, Duke of Courland.

1655. *May*: England occupies Jamaica. Dutch annex New Sweden. Russians build forts on the Amur. Blake destroys pirate fleet of Bey of Tunis.

1656. Dutch enter upon trade with China. Dutch take Colombo from the Portuguese.

IV. ECCLESIASTICAL HISTORY	V. CONSTITUTIONAL AND ECONOMIC HISTORY	VI. CULTURAL LIFE
1649. Richard Baxter: *The Saints' Everlasting Rest*; devotional book of Independents. Maryland assembly passes Toleration Act.	**1649.** *May 29:* England declared Free Commonwealth. Russia abolishes English trade privileges. Standing army established in Austria.	**1649.** *Oct. 6:* Milton: *Eikonoklastes.* Andreas Gryphius: *Carolus Stuardus;* play. Fr. v. Spee: *Trutznachtigall;* lyrical poems.
1650. Calixtus: *Judicium de Controversiis,* to reconcile Lutherans and Calvinists.	**1650.** *Aug. 1:* Permanent economic council formed by Cromwell. Tea first imported into England. First coffee-house opened in Oxford.	**1650.** Joost van den Vondel: *Manual of Dutch Poetry. Mar.:* Milton: *Pro Populo Anglicano Defensio.*
	1651. *Oct. 9:* First Navigation Act; monopoly for English shipping in foreign trade.	**1651.** Hobbes: *Leviathan, or, the Matter, Form and Authority of Government.* Scarron: *Roman Comique.*
1652. *Jan. 6:* Ernest, Landgrave of Hesse, turns Roman Catholic.	**1652.** *Feb.:* Act of Pardon and Oblivion, to reconcile Royalists. *Aug. 12:* Army rejects Perpetuation Bill.	**1652.** Winstanley: *Law of Freedom;* communist theory. Otto von Guericke invents air-pump at Magdeburg. *June 21:* Inigo Jones d. *Sept. 2:* Jusepe di Ribera *d.*
1653. Blaise Pascal joins Jansenists at Port Royal. *July 22: Corpus Evangelicorum* formed at Diet of Ratisbon.	**1653.** *Mar. 10:* Commercial treaty between England and Portugal. *Apr. 20:* Cromwell expels Long Parliament for attempting to pass Perpetuation Bill. *July 4-Dec. 12:* Little or Barebones Parliament. *Aug. 5:* Standing army in Brandenburg. *Dec. 16:* Instrument of Government; Cromwell made Lord Protector with a Council of State.	**1653.** Izaak Walton: *Compleate Angler.* Gracián: *Oráculo Manual.* Mme de Scudéry: *Le Grand Cyrus.* Lauremberg: *Comic Poems,* in Low-German dialect.
1654. *Aug. 22:* Commissioners ('Ejectors') appointed to remove incapable clergymen. **1654-1657.** Bishop Walton of Chester publishes *Polyglot Bible.*	**1654.** *Apr. 11:* Commercial treaty between England and Sweden. *Apr. 12:* Scotland and Ireland united with England. *Sept. 3:* First Protectorate Parliament meets. *Sept. 11:* Exclusion of irreconcilable republicans. *Sept. 14:* Commercial treaty between England and Denmark.	**1654.** Comenius: *Orbis Pictus,* first picture-book for children. Cyr. de Bergerac: *Le Pédant Joué.* Fr. v. Logau: *Epigrams.* Duisburg University founded.
1655. *Apr.:* Massacre of Protestants in Savoy. *Nov. 3:* Christina of Sweden turns Roman Catholic. *Nov. 24:* Cromwell prohibits Anglican services. **1655-1667.** Pope Alexander VII (Fabio Chigi). **1656-1657.** Pascal: *Lettres Provinciales,* against Jesuits.	**1655.** *Jan. 22:* Parliament dissolved. *Aug.:* Eleven major-generals appointed for the 11 districts into which England was divided. *Oct. 24:* Commercial treaty between England and France. **1656.** *June:* Commercial treaty between England and Sweden. *Sept. 17:* Second Protectorate Parliament meets. Hôpital Général opened in Paris, combines poor-house and factory. First manufacture of stockings in Paris.	**1655.** Dugdale: *Monasticon Anglicanum* (-1673). John Wallis: *Arithmetica Infinitorum.* Hobbes: *De Corpore.* Huyghens invents pendulum-clock. First newspaper at Berlin. **1656.** James Harrington: *Oceana;* political romance. J. Clauberg: *Ontosophia.*

I. WESTERN AND SOUTHERN EUROPE	II. CENTRAL, NORTHERN, AND EASTERN EUROPE	III. COUNTRIES OVERSEA
1657. *Mar. 23*: Treaty of Paris between England and France against Spain. *Apr. 20*: English destroy a Spanish fleet off Santa Cruz. *Oct. 3*: French capture Mardyke.	**1657.** *Apr. 2*: Emperor Ferdinand III *d.* *Sept. 19*: Treaty of Wehlau; Poland renounces sovereignty of Prussia on behalf of Brandenburg. *Nov. 6*: Brandenburg allies with Poland against Sweden.	**1657.** Turks capture Tenedos **and** Lemnos from Venice.
1658. *June 13*: English and French defeat Spaniards at Dunes, take Dunkirk (*June 25*) and Gravelines (*Aug. 24*). *Sept. 3*: Oliver Cromwell *d.*; succeeded by his son Richard.	**1658.** *Mar. 8*: Treaty of Roskild between Sweden and Denmark. *Aug. 1*: Leopold I elected Emperor (**-1705**). *Aug. 15*: Rhenish League founded under French protectorate. *Aug.-Nov.*: Charles X besieges Copenhagen.	**1658.** Dutch take Jaffnapatam, last Portuguese possession in Ceylon. *June 7*: Aurangzeb, son of Shah Jahan, secures the succession, through his victory at Samgarh. *June 18*: Shah Jahan imprisoned by Aurangzeb (*d.* **1666**).
1659. *May 21*: England, France, and Holland agree at the Hague, to force Denmark and Sweden to make peace. *Nov. 7*: Peace of the Pyrenees between France and Spain; France obtains Roussillon, Cerdagne, Artois, and fortresses in Flanders, Luxemburg, and Hainault; Spain resigns her claims to Alsace.	**1659.** The Great Elector drives Swedes out of Pomerania and Prussia.	**1659.** *May 26*: Aurangzeb formally ascends the throne (**-1707**).
1660-1685. Charles II King of England. **1660-1673.** James Duke of York, Lord High Admiral of England.	**1660.** *Feb. 23*: Charles X of Sweden *d.*; succeeded by Charles XI (**-1697**). *May 3*: Peace of Oliva finishes 1st Northern War between Brandenburg, Poland, Austria, Sweden. *June 6*: Peace of Copenhagen between Sweden and Denmark. Turks attack Transylvania.	**1660-1669.** Dutch subdue Celebes. **1660.** *Dec. 18*: Royal African Company founded.
1661. *Mar. 9*: Mazarin *d.*; personal rule of Louis XIV (**-1715**).	**1661.** *June 21*: Peace of Kardis between Sweden and Russia. *Nov.*: Ahmad Kiuprili becomes Grand Vizier.	**1661.** *June 23*: Portugal cedes Tangier and Bombay to Charles II as dowry of his queen. Autonomy of Formosa (till **1683**). *Aug. 6*: Portuguese retain Brazil, the Dutch Ceylon, by English mediation.
1662. *Oct. 27*: Charles II sells Dunkirk to France for 2½ million livres.	**1662.** *Apr.*: County of East Frisia becomes a hereditary principality.	**1662.** English Guinea Company incorporated. Liberal Charter for Connecticut. **1662-1723.** K'ang-hsi Emperor of China.

IV. CONSTITUTIONAL HISTORY	V. ECONOMIC HISTORY AND NATURAL SCIENCE	VI. CULTURAL LIFE
1657. *Mar. 31:* Humble Petition and Advice, offers title of king to Cromwell. *May 25:* New Humble Petition and Advice, creates new House of Lords and increases Cromwell's power. *June 26:* Additional Petition and Advice, enhances power of Parliament.	**1657.** Fountain pens manufactured in Paris.	**1657.** Durham University founded by Cromwell (suppressed **1660**). Angelus Silesius: *Sinn- und Schlussreime;* later called *Der Cherubinische Wandersmann.*
1658. *Feb. 4:* Parliament dissolved.		**1658.** Socinians expelled from Poland. Dryden: *Heroic Stanzas* (on Cromwell's Death).
1659. *May 7:* Long Parliament restored. *May 25:* Richard Cromwell resigns (*d.* **1712**). *Oct. 12:* Army expels Long (Rump) Parliament. *Nov.:* Monk calls Convention in Scotland. *Dec. 26:* Long Parliament meets again.	**1659.** Ordinance for protection of peasants' land in France.	**1659.** Corneille: *Oedipe.* Molière: *Les Précieuses Ridicules.* Samuel Pepys begins his diaries. Last National Synod of French Protestants at Loudun. Hobbes: *De Homine.*
1660. *Feb. 3:* General Monk enters London and proclaims a free Parliament. *Apr. 15 - Dec. 29:* Convention Parliament. *May 29:* Charles II re-enters London. **1660-1667.** Sir Edward Hyde (**1661,** Earl of Clarendon) Lord Chancellor.	**1660.** Navigation Act re-enacted. *Nov. 7:* Council of Trade; *Dec. 1:* Council for Foreign Plantations appointed. Organization of Brandenburg postal service between Cleves and Memel.	**1660.** Dryden: *Astraea redux.* Mme de Scudéry: *Clélie;* novel. *Aug. 6:* Velasquez *d.*
1661. *Apr.:* English Coronation of Charles II. *Dec.:* Corporation Act (renunciation of Covenant). **1661.** *May 8 -* **1679.** *Jan:* Cavalier Parliament. **1661-1683.** Colbert Controller-General of French Treasury.	**1661.** Huyghens invents manometer.	**1661.** Translation of New Testament into Algonquin dialect by John Eliot (first American Bible edition). Rembrandt: *The Syndics of the Cloth Hall.* Rob. Boyle: *Sceptical Chemist;* founds modern chemistry.
1662. *May 19:* Press Act (rigid censorship). *May 19:* Act of Uniformity (consent to revised Prayer Book). Louvois appointed French Secretary of State.	**1662.** Act of Settlement. Exportation of leather, skins, and wool, importation of laces and embroideries prohibited. *Mar.:* Hearth-tax revived. Sir William Petty: *Treatise of Taxes and Contributions.*	**1662.** *July 15:* Royal Society founded. Mich. Wigglesworth: *The Day of Doom;* poem characteristic of New England Puritanism. Molière: *Ecole des Femmes.* Versailles Palace begun. Thos. Fuller: *Worthies of England.*

I. WESTERN AND SOUTHERN EUROPE	II. CENTRAL, NORTHERN, AND EASTERN EUROPE	III. COUNTRIES OVERSEA
1663. French alliance with Denmark. *June 8:* English and Portuguese defeat Spaniards at Ameixial.	**1663.** *Apr. 18:* Turkey declares war on Austria. *Sept. 25:* Surrender of Neuhäusel.	**1663.** *June 10:* Charter for Royal African Company. Royal Charter for Rhode Island.
1664. French alliance with Brandenburg and Saxony.	**1664.** *Aug. 1:* Turkish defeat at St. Gotthard-on-the-Raab. *Aug. 10:* Peace of Eisenburg between Emperor and Turks.	**1664.** *Aug. 29:* English annex New Netherland. *Aug.:* Colbert establishes French East India Company, and reorganizes West India Company. **1664-1667.** Dutch buy Swedish colonies on Gold Coast.
1665-1667. Second naval war between England and Holland. **1665.** *June 17:* Spaniards defeated by Portuguese and English at Montes Claros. *Sept. 17:* Philip IV of Spain *d.*; succeeded by Charles II (**-1700**).	**1665.** *June:* Extinction of last Hapsburg collateral line (Tyrol).	**1665.** English privateers capture St. Eustatius, Saba, and Tobago.
1666. *June 11-14:* Albemarle defeated by De Ruyter off Dunkirk. *Aug. 4:* Albemarle defeats De Ruyter off North Foreland. *Oct. 25:* Quadruple alliance between Netherlands, Brandenburg, Brunswick, and Denmark. **1667.** *Mar. 31:* Secret treaty between Charles II and Louis XIV. *June:* De Ruyter enters mouth of Thames; fails to land at Harwich. *July 31:* Peace of Breda between England and Holland. **1667-1668.** French war of Devolution against Spain in the Netherlands.	**1666.** *Feb. 2:* Danish-Dutch alliance. *Feb. 16:* Brandenburgian-Dutch alliance. The Raskol (Great Schism) breaks out in the Russian Church. **1666-1667.** War between Turkey and Poland. **1667.** *June 9:* Oldenburg united with Denmark. *Jan. 20:* Truce of Andrussov between Russia and Poland, which cedes Smolensk and Kiev. *Aug.:* Rhenish Confederation of **1658** dissolved.	**1666.** Antigua, Montserrat, and St. Christopher captured by French, Surinam by Dutch. *Jan. 22:* Shah Jahan *d.* **1667.** *July 31:* Peace of Breda: England obtains Cape Coast Castle, Holland keeps only Guiana. *Oct.:* New Amsterdam renamed New York.
1668. *Jan. 23:* Alliance of the Hague; England and Holland against France. *Feb.:* France occupies Franche-Comté. *Feb. 13:* Spain recognizes independence of Portugal. *Apr.:* Sweden joins Anglo-Dutch alliance. *May 2:* Peace of Aix-la-Chapelle; France obtains 12 Flemish fortresses.	**1668.** *Sept. 19:* John Casimir of Poland abdicates (*d.* **1672** *Dec. 16*).	**1668.** Fort William near Calcutta founded. Bombay made over to East India Company. First French trading station in India.
	1669. *June 19:* Michael Wisniowiecki elected King of Poland (**-1673**). *Sept.:* Turks conquer Crete. *Dec. 31:* Secret treaty between Brandenburg and France. **1670.** Conspiracy of Hungarian magnates against Hapsburgs, suppressed.	**1669.** Dutch conquer Macassar in Celebes. South Carolina founded.
1670. *June 1:* Secret Anglo-French treaty of Dover; France gets hands free in Holland, England receives subsidies from France. *Aug.:* France occupies Lorraine.	**1670-1699.** Christian V, King of Denmark.	**1670.** John Locke draws up Constitution of Carolina. Charleston, Ca., founded. Hudson's Bay Company formed by Prince Rupert.

IV. CONSTITUTIONAL HISTORY	V. ECONOMIC HISTORY AND NATURAL SCIENCE	VI. CULTURAL LIFE
1663. German Diet at Ratisbon becomes a permanent institution.	**1663.** Irish shipping excluded from colonial trade. Turnpike Act introduces turnpike-tolls. Importation of linen and curtains prohibited. The guinea first minted.	**1663.** Leibniz: *De principiis individui.* Gryphius: *Peter Squentz.* **1663-1678.** Sam. Butler: *Hudibras.*
1664. *July:* Conventicle Act; against meetings of Nonconformists.	**1664.** Colbert's tariff-reform abolishes French inland duties.	**1664.** Lord Orrery: *Mustapha.* George Etherege: *Love in a Tub.* Molière: *Tartuffe.* Order of La Trappe founded. Francisco Zurbarán *d.*
1665. *Oct.:* Five Mile Act; restrictions on Nonconformist ministers. *Nov. 14:* Lex Regia introduces absolutism in Denmark.	**1665.** Navigation Act again enforced. *June-Sept.:* Great Plague in London. Robert Hooke: *Micrographia,* describes microscope.	**1665.** Beginning of *London Gazette* and the *Journal des Savants.* Dryden: *The Indian Emperor.* La Rochefoucauld: *Réflexions et maximes.* Lafontaine: *Contes* (-**1674**). *Nov. 19:* Nic. Poussin *d.*
1666. Treaty of Cleves divides Jülich-Cleves territories between Brandenburg and Neuburg. Louvois appointed French Minister of War.	**1666.** Importation of Irish cattle, sheep, and swine to England prohibited. *Sept. 2-7:* Great Fire of London.	**1666.** Dryden: *Annus Mirabilis.* Molière: *Le Misanthrope.* Newton uses infinitesimal calculus (published in **1692**). *Aug. 26:* Frans Hals *d. Sept. 23:* François Mansard, French architect, *d.*
1667. *Aug. 30:* Fall and banishment of Clarendon (*d.* **1674** at Rouen); Cabal Ministry (Clifford, Arlington, Buckingham, Ashley, Lauderdale; till **1673**).	**1667.** Protectionist tariff in France. Excise in Brandenburg towns. Monetary convention of Zinna between Brandenburg, Saxony, Hanover, and Brunswick. First public observatory in Paris.	**1667.** Milton: *Paradise Lost* (2nd enlarged edition, **1674**). Pufendorf: *De Statu Imperii Germanici.* Complete edition of religious lyrics of Paulus Gerhardt. Racine: *Andromaque.*
	1668. Colbert introduces provisioning of troops from depots. Oder-Spree Canal, begun in **1661**, completed. Leeuwenhoek discovers red blood corpuscles.	**1668.** Dryden: *Essay of Dramatick Poesy.* Etherege: *She Would If She Could.* La Fontaine: *Fables.* Grimmelshausen: *Simplicius Simplicissimus. Giornale de Letterati,* first Italian periodical.
1669. Duke of York proclaims himself Roman Catholic. Colbert appointed French Secretary of State for Navy.	**1669.** Phosphorus discovered. Sir Josiah Child, Director of East India Company: *A New Discourse of Trade,* from mercantilist point of view.	**1669.** W. Penn: *No Cross, No Crown. Oct. 4:* Rembrandt *d.* Mariana Alcoforado: *Lettres Portugaises.* Dryden: *Conquest of Granada.* Racine: *Britannicus.*
1670. Duke of Monmouth appointed Captain General of the Army.	**1670.** Louvois introduces uniforms and paper cartridges in French army.	**1670.** Dryden appointed Poet Laureate and Royal Historiographer. Spinoza: *Tractatus theologico-politicus.* Pascal: *Pensées.*

I. WESTERN AND SOUTHERN EUROPE	II. CENTRAL, NORTHERN, AND EASTERN EUROPE	III. COUNTRIES OVERSEA
1671. Philip of Orleans, brother of Louis XIV, marries Liselotte, heiress of the Palatinate. *Nov. 1:* Treaty of neutrality between France and Emperor.	**1671.** *Feb.*: Treaty of assistance between Brandenburg and Netherlands; effective *May 6,* **1672.**	**1671.** Danes take St. Thomas. English West Indies organized (Barbadoes, Leeward and Windward Islands). *Jan.*: Buccaneers destroy Panama.
1672. *Mar.*: British navy attacks Dutch ships in Atlantic. *Apr. 7:* England and France declare war on Holland. *July 4:* William III becomes Stadholder (-**1702**). *Aug. 20:* De Witt brothers, leading republican Dutch statesmen, assassinated. **1672-1678.** Second war of Louis XIV against Netherlands. **1673.** *Aug. 30:* Alliance of the Hapsburgs with Holland and Lorraine against France. *Sept. 16:* Emperor declares war on France.	**1672.** *Apr. 14:* Alliance between France and Sweden. *June 23:* Alliance between Emperor and Brandenburg; *July 25:* between Emperor and Holland. *Oct. 18:* Treaty of Buczácz; Poland cedes Podolia to Turkey. **1672-1676.** Turks attack Poland.	**1672.** French occupy Pondicherry and Coromandel Coast. English Guinea Company merged in Royal African Company, which obtains monopoly of slave trade till **1698.**
1674. *Feb. 19:* England withdraws from war against Holland; Spain, Empire, and Pope ally against France. *June-Oct.*: French successes in Franche-Comté, Flanders, and Western Germany.	**1673.** *June 6:* Peace of Vossem between Brandenburg and France; Elector promises not to support any enemy of Louis XIV. *Nov. 11:* Sobieski defeats Kiuprili at Khoczim. **1674.** John III Sobieski elected King of Poland (-**1696**). *May 24:* German Diet votes war against France. *Dec.*: Swedes invade Brandenburg and Prussia.	**1673.** French take Chandarnagar on the Ganges. French Senegal Company formed. Frontenac, Governor of Canada, conciliates Iroquois.
1675. *July 27:* Turenne killed at Sassbach; end of great French victories. **1675-1730.** Victor Amadeus II, Duke of Savoy. **1676.** *Feb. 17:* Secret alliance between Charles II and Louis XIV. *Apr. 22:* Defeat of De Ruyter off Messina. *Apr. 29:* De Ruyter *d.*	**1675.** *June 11:* Alliance between France and Poland. *June 25:* Great Elector defeats Swedes at Rathenow and (*June 28*) Fehrbellin. **1676.** Denmark declares war on Sweden. *Oct. 27:* Peace of Zurawna between Turkey and Poland, who divide Podolia. **1676-1682.** Theodore III, Tsar of Russia.	**1674.** Sivaji, founder of Mahratta State, declares himself independent of Aurangzeb. French expelled from Madagascar by natives. *Feb. 9:* Peace of Westminster between England and Holland: New Netherland and New Sweden definitely English. French Guiana organized. **1675-1676.** War with Red Indians in New England. **1675-1708.** Guru Gobind Singh, organizer of political power of Sikhs. **1676.** Nathaniel Bacon heads rebellion of Virginians against governor.
1677. *Apr. 11:* William of Orange defeated at Cassel. *Nov. 17:* French take Freiburg.	**1677-1679.** Great Elector conquers Hither Pomerania and Rügen, pursues Swedes up to Riga. **1677-1682.** Hungarians under Count Tököly rebel against Hapsburgs.	
1678. *Aug. 10:* Peace of Nijmegen between France and Holland; *Status quo. Sept. 17:* Peace of Nijmegen between France and Spain which cedes Franche-Comté and 16 Flemish towns.		**1678.** Holland cedes Goree to France.

IV. CONSTITUTIONAL HISTORY	V. ECONOMIC HISTORY AND NATURAL SCIENCE	VI. CULTURAL LIFE
1671. Free City of Brunswick subdued by Duke of Wolfenbüttel and subsequently made capital.	**1671.** Newton constructs reflecting telescope. Malpighi: *Anatome Plantarum*, histology of plants.	**1671.** Milton: *Paradise Regained; Samson Agonistes.* Wycherley: *Love in a Wood.* Duke of Buckingham: *The Rehearsal;* satire against Dryden. Académie de Musique founded at Paris, under Lully. Skinner: *Etymologicon Linguae Anglicanae.* **1671–1676.** The Monument erected in London.
1672. *Mar. 15* (*O.S.*): Declaration of Indulgence, towards Nonconformists. *Nov. 8:* Colonel Kalckstein, leader of Prussian Estates, beheaded. *Nov. 17:* Ashley (Earl of Shaftsbury) appointed Lord Chancellor (**-1673**).	**1672.** *Jan. 2:* Stop of Exchequer, suspends payment for 12 months. thousands of business men bankrupt. Economic Council reorganized under Shaftesbury as president and Locke as secretary. Newton's law of gravitation.	**1672.** Wycherley: *The Gentleman Dancing Master.* Tsar becomes Protector of all Greek Orthodox Christians. *May 5:* Samuel Cooper *d. Nov. 6:* Heinrich Schütz, composer, *d. Mercure galant*, first journal for light reading.
1673. *Mar. 22:* Test Act, excludes Roman Catholics from office under the Crown; Duke of York retires as Lord High Admiral. Abrogation of French Parlement's Right of raising objections to royal edicts. **1673–1678.** Earl of Danby, chief minister.	**1673.** Huyghens: *Horologium oscillatorium* (determination of centrifugal force).	**1673.** Molière: *Le Malade Imaginaire; Feb. 17:* Molière *d.* during rehearsal. Dryden: *Amboyna.*
	1674. Earl of Danby, Lord Treasurer, reorganizes English finances.	**1674.** Wycherley: *The Country Wife; The Plain Dealer.* Boileau: *Art Poétique. Nov. 8:* Milton *d.* Kneller settles in England. **1674–1678.** Nic. Malebranche: *De la recherche de la vérité.*
1675. Last Piast of Silesia dies; in spite of Brandenburgian claims, Emperor seizes Silesia as Bohemian fief.	**1675.** Royal Observatory instituted at Greenwich. Leibniz invents differential calculus (published **1684**).	**1675.** Dryden: *Aurangzebe.* Jacob Spener: *Pia Desideria;* beginning of Pietism. Chr. Wren: St. Paul's Cathedral; completed in **1710.**
1676. *Oct.:* Ahmad Kiuprili, Turkish Grand Vizier, *d.;* succeeded by Kara Mustafa.	**1676.** Barlow invents repeating clocks and watches. Wiseman: *Seven Chirurgical Treatises;* modern surgery. Olaus Römer's observations on velocity of light.	**1676.** Thos. Otway: *Don Carlos.* Etherege: *The Man of Mode.* Ben. Thompson (first poet born in America): *New England's Crisis.*
1677. *Nov. 15:* William of Orange marries Princess Mary, daughter of James, Duke of York.		**1677.** Racine: *Phèdre.* Spinoza: *Ethics. Feb. 21:* Spinoza *d.* Innsbruck University founded.
1678. Roman Catholic conspiracy falsely alleged by Titus Oates; persecution of Roman Catholics in England. Roman Catholics excluded from Parliament.	**1678–1685.** Importation of all French goods into England prohibited.	**1678.** Bunyan: *Pilgrim's Progress* (2nd part, **1684**). Dryden: *All for Love.* Thos. Corneille: *Earl of Essex.* First permanent German opera house at Hamburg.

I. WESTERN AND SOUTHERN EUROPE	II. CENTRAL, NORTHERN, AND EASTERN EUROPE	III. COUNTRIES OVERSEA
1679. *Feb. 5*: Peace of Nijmegen between France and the Empire, which cedes Freiburg and Breisach. *Oct.*: Chambers of Reunion installed at Metz, Breisach, Besançon, and Tournai.	**1679.** *June 29*: Peace of St. Germain between Brandenburg and Sweden; Brandenburg loses all her conquests. *Sept. 2*: Peace of Fontainebleau between Denmark and Sweden: Denmark restores all her conquests. **1679-1726.** Maximilian II Emanuel, Elector of Bavaria.	**1679.** *Sept. 18*: New Hampshire created a province separate from Massachusetts.
	1680-1682. Charles XI transforms Sweden into absolute monarchy.	**1680.** First Brandenburgian expedition to West Africa. **1680-1682.** French colonial empire from Quebec to mouth of Mississippi organized.
1681. *Sept. 30*: French take Strasbourg and Casale in time of peace.	**1681.** *Jan. 11*: Defensive alliance between Brandenburg and France.	**1681.** *Mar. 14*: Royal Charter for Pennsylvania. **1681-1690.** Tobago, colony of James, Duke of Courland.
1682. Conflict between France and Pope about Gallicanism. French Protestants excluded from guilds, civil service, and the king's household.	**1682-1689.** Tsaritza Sophia, Regent of Russia. **1682.** Turks proclaim Tököly King of Hungary.	**1682.** La Salle founds St. Louis. Danes settle on Gold Coast. *July*: Philadelphia, Pa., laid out. **1682-1690.** Sir John Child, Governor of Bombay.
1683. Association of the Hague against France. *July 30*: Maria Theresa, Queen of Louis XIV, *d.*; he then marries Mme de Maintenon. *Dec.*: War between France and Spain. **1683-1706.** Peter II of Portugal. **1684.** *June*: French take Treves and Luxembourg. *Aug. 15*: Truce of Ratisbon between Empire and France for 20 years. **1685.** *Feb. 6*: Charles II *d.*; succeeded by James II (-1688).	**1683-1699.** Austria and Poland at war with Turkey. **1683.** Prince Eugene of Savoy enters Imperial army. *July 14-Sept. 12*: Turks besiege Vienna. *Sept. 12*: Charles of Lorraine defeats Turks at the Kahlenberg near Vienna. **1684.** *Mar. 5*: Holy League of Linz between Austria, Poland, and Venice against Turkey. **1685.** *May 26*: Charles, Elector Palatine, *d.*; Louis XIV claims Palatinate for his sister-in-law, Liselotte. **1685-1690.** Venetians conquer Athens and the Morea.	**1683.** Manchus conquer isle of Formosa (Chinese possession till **1895**). Brandenburgian factories on Gold Coast. Dutch traders admitted at Canton. **1684.** Charter of Massachusetts annulled. French Mississippi Company formed. English lose Tangier to Morocco. **1685.** French Guinea Company formed. K'ang-hsi opens all Chinese ports to foreign trade. French embassy sent to Siam.
1686. *July 9*: League of Augsburg between Emperor, Spain, Sweden, Saxony, Palatinate, etc., against Louis XIV. *Dec. 11*: Prince de Condé *d.*	**1686.** *Apr. 1*: Alliance between Emperor and Great Elector, who obtains Schwiebus and renounces claims to Silesia. *Sept. 2*: Charles of Lorraine takes Buda.	**1686.** Siamese embassy sent to France. Aurangzeb annexes kingdom of Bijapur.

IV. CONSTITUTIONAL HISTORY

1679. *Feb. 28*: Duke of York banished to Brussels (-1680). Two general elections; party names of Whig and Tory come into use. *May 26*: Habeas Corpus Act. Halifax chief Minister. *June 22*: Battle of Bothwell Bridge; Monmouth subdues insurrection of Scottish Covenanters.

1680. *May 21*: Exclusion Bill, against succession of Duke of York, passes Commons, rejected by Lords. Archbishopric of Magdeburg incorporated with Brandenburg.

1681. *Mar. 19-28*: Parliament of Oxford. *Nov. 9*: Religious toleration granted to Hungarian Protestants.

1682. Plot of radical Whigs under Shaftesbury. *Mar.*: French Assembly of Clergy defines liberties of Gallican Church. Pennsylvania assembly issues constitution (Great Charter).

1683. *Jan. 21*: Shaftesbury *d*. *June*: Rye House Plot discovered; Monmouth exiled to Holland; Lord Wm. Russell (*July 21*) and Algernon Sidney (*Dec. 7*) beheaded.

1684. Charters of London and 65 Whig cities remodelled.

1685. *May 20*: James II's Parliament meets. *May-June*: Argyll's rebellion in Scotland. *June 11*: Rebellion of Duke of Monmouth; defeated at Sedgemoor (*July 6*) and beheaded (*July 15*). *Sept.*: Bloody Assizes; Jeffreys appointed Lord Chancellor.

1686. *July*: Court of Ecclesiastical Commission created.

V. ECONOMIC HISTORY AND NATURAL SCIENCE

1679. Sir Wm. Petty: *A Treatise on Taxes and Contributions*. Newton's calculations of the lunar orbit. Colbert's decree to examine every merchant in bookkeeping, commercial law, and knowledge of mercantile wares.

1680. Dockwra institutes penny post in London.

1681. *May*: Canal du Midi, begun in **1664,** opened.

1682. Sir Wm. Petty: *Quantulumcunque, or, a Tract concerning Money*. Pierre Baille establishes weaving mill with 100 looms at Amsterdam.

1683. *Sept. 6*: Colbert *d*.

1684. Portugal prohibits importation of woollen goods. First attempt to light London streets. Hooke invents optical telegraph.

1685. Entails introduced in Scotland. *Oct. 18*: Louis XIV revokes edict of Nantes; thousands of French refugees arrive in England, Netherlands, and Brandenburg, where they introduce many new industries.

1686. Willoughby and Ray: *Historia Piscium*.

VI. CULTURAL LIFE

1679. Gilbert Burnet: *History of the English Reformation*. Lee and Dryden: *Oedipus King of Thebes*. *Feb. 2*: Jan Steen *d*.

1680. Bunyan: *Life and Death of Mr. Badman*. Otway: *The Orphan of China*. Fléchier: *Oraisons Funèbres*. Comédie Française established. Purcell: *Dido and Aeneas*. *Sept. 25*: Samuel Butler *d*. *Nov. 30*: Peter Lely *d*.

1681. Dryden: *Absalom and Achitophel*; *Religio Laici* (2nd part **1684**). Bossuet: *Treatise on Universal History*. Mabillon: *De Re Diplomatica*; standard work on diplomatics.

1682-1776. *Acta Eruditorum*; first German learned periodical.

1682. Otway: *Venice Preserved*. Dryden: *The Medal, a Satire against Sedition*. Complete edition of Pierre Corneille. *Mar. 13*: J. van Ruisdael *d*. *Apr. 3*: Murillo *d*. *Nov. 23*: Claude Lorrain *d*.

1683. Wm. Penn: *General Description of Pennsylvania*.

1684. Thos. Burnet: *Theory of Earth*. Ph. W. von Hörnigk: *Österreich über alles wenn es nur will*.

1685. Dryden: *Albion and Albinus*. M. van Coehoorn: *Nieuwe Vestingsbouw*; theory of fortification.

1686. Mme de Maintenon founds Maison de St. Cyr for poor noble girls. Pufendorf appointed court-historiographer of Brandenburg.

I. WESTERN AND SOUTHERN EUROPE	II. CENTRAL, NORTHERN, AND EASTERN EUROPE	III. COUNTRIES OVERSEA
1687. *July 3*: James II receives papal nuncio.	**1687.** *Aug. 18*: Turkish defeat at Mohács. *Sept. 26*: Venetians bombard Athens and destroy Parthenon and Propylaea. *Nov. 2*: Mohammed IV deposed; succeeded by Suleiman III; Mustafa Kiuprili, Grand Vizier.	**1687.** Arguin, Guinea, established as Brandenburgian colony. French build Fort Niagara against English. Aurangzeb conquers Golkonda.
1688. James II recalls British troops from Holland. *Sept. 24*: Louis XIV begins war against Empire without declaration. *Nov. 15*: William of Orange lands at Torbay. *Nov. 26*: Louis XIV declares war on Holland. *Dec. 25*: James II escapes to France. *Dec. 28*: William enters London. **1688-1697.** War of League of Augsburg. **1689-1694.** Mary II; **1689-1702,** William III, Queen and King of England. **1689.** *May 12*: England and Holland join League of Augsburg. Rising of Protestants in Cevennes.	**1688.** *May 9*: Frederick William, the Great Elector, *d.*; succeeded by Frederick III (**-1713**). *Sept. 6*: Turks lose Belgrade. *Sept. 25*: French invade Palatinate. *Oct. 22*: Magdeburg Convention against Louis XIV. *Oct. 24*: French take Heidelberg. **1689.** *Jan.-June*: Mélac devastates Palatinate. Russia joins war against Turkey. **1689-1725.** Peter I, Tsar of Russia.	**1687-1689.** French Huguenots settle at Cape of Good Hope. **1688.** Dutch found Fort Vreedenburg, Gold Coast. Revolution in Siam against French influence. French bomb Algiers and subsequently make treaty. James II revokes Charters of Connecticut and Rhode Island. **1689.** Natal becomes Dutch colony. Boundary convention of Nerchinsk between Russia and China. William and Mary recognize old Charters of colonies.
1690. *June 6*: Spain joins Great Alliance. *July 1*: Allies defeated at Fleurus. *Aug. 18*: Piedmontese defeated at Staffarda. *Oct. 20*: Savoy joins Great Alliance. **1691.** *July 6*: Louvois *d.*	**1690.** *Apr. 18*: Charles of Lorraine, Imperial generalissimo, *d. Oct. 8*: Turks reconquer Belgrade. **1691.** *Aug. 19*: Louis of Baden, imperial generalissimo, defeats Turks at Szlankamen; Mustafa Kiuprili killed in action. **1691-1695.** Sultan Ahmad II. **1692.** *June 5*: Louis of Baden takes Grosswardein.	**1690.** English factory at Calcutta established. **1691.** New East India Company formed. Massachusetts receives new Charter. **1692.** K'ang hsi grants free exercise of religion to Jesuits.
1692. *May 29*: English defeat French off La Hogue. *Aug. 3*: William III defeated at Steenkerke. **1693.** *July 29*: William III defeated at Neerwinden.	**1693.** *May 22*: French again destroy Heidelberg. **1693-1747.** Leopold I, Prince of Anhalt, organizer of Prussian army.	**1693.** Carolina divided into North and South Carolina; constitution on the model of Virginia. Dutch take Pondicherry.
1694. *Dec. 28*: Queen Mary II *d.*	**1694-1733.** Augustus the Strong, Elector of Saxony. **1694.** *Dec. 20*: Frederick of Brandenburg restores Schwiebus to Austria, thereby reviving claims to Silesia.	**1694.** Venetians attack Chios, defeated by Turks. **1694-1721.** Husain, Shah of Persia.

IV. CONSTITUTIONAL HISTORY	V. ECONOMIC HISTORY AND NATURAL SCIENCE	VI. CULTURAL LIFE
1687. *Jan.*: Tyrconnel appointed Viceroy of Ireland. *Apr. 2*: Declaration of Indulgence. *July 2*: Parliament dissolved. Dispute between Louis XIV and Pope (-1689). *Oct.*: Hungarian Diet renounces right of resistance. **1688.** *May 4*: Declaration of Indulgence reissued. *June 29-30*: Trial and acquittal of the Seven Bishops opposing Declaration. *June 30*: Seven Lords invite William of Orange to England.	**1687.** Newton: *Philosophiae Naturalis Principia Mathematica.* **1688.** Abraham Thevart first casts plate-glass.	**1687.** Dryden: *The Hind and the Panther.* Fénelon: *De l'éducation des filles.* Thomasius lectures for the first time in German, at Leipzig University. **1688.** Thomas Shadwell: *The Squire of Alsatia.* Boileau: *Les Héros de Roman.* Ziegler: *Asiatische Banise.* *Aug. 31*: John Bunyan d. La Bruyère: *Caractères.* **1688-1703.** Prime of Japanese art and science in the Genroku era.
1689. *Feb. 12*: Declaration of Rights. *Mar. 12*: James II arrives in Ireland. *Apr. 20-Aug. 1*: Siege of Londonderry. *May 24*: Toleration Act. *July 27*: Scottish Jacobites defeated at Killiecrankie. *Oct.*: Bill of Rights. Reich Law Court established at Wetzlar. **1690.** *July 11*: William defeats James II at the Boyne.	**1689.** Export duties on corn abolished in England. **1690.** Huyghens's theory of undulation of light.	**1689.** John Locke: *On Civil Government.* Casper von Lohenstein: *Arminius and Thusnelda.* **1690.** Locke: *Essay Concerning Human Understanding.* Nath. Lee: *Massacre of St. Bartholomew.* Poetical circle of Arcadia formed in Rome.
1691. *July*: Limerick capitulates; Protestant farmers settled in Ireland. *Dec. 4*: Diploma Leopoldinum confirms political and religious liberties of Transylvania. **1692.** *Feb. 13*: Massacre of Highlanders at Glencoe. *Dec. 19*: Duke Ernest Augustus of Hanover made ninth Elector. **1693.** *Mar. 14*: William vetoes bill for Triennial Parliaments. Charles XI of Sweden formally declares himself absolute monarch. Gallican Church reconciled with Papacy.	**1691.** Sir Wm. Petty: *Political Survey, or, Anatomy of Ireland; Essays in Political Arithmetic.* **1692.** Lloyd's coffee-house becomes office for marine insurance. **1693.** New Charter for Old East India Company. National Debt established. Halley composes first scientific astronomical tables.	**1691.** Claude Fleury: *Histoire de l'église;* from the Gallican point of view. C. Stieler: *Treasure of German Language;* grammar and dictionary. Purcell: *King Arthur.* **1692.** Purcell: *Fairy Queen.* **1693.** Locke: *Ideas on Education.* Pufendorf: *The Achievements of the Great Elector.* W. Penn: *Essay on the Present and Future Peace of Europe;* suggests European federation.
1694. *Dec. 3*: Triennial Bill becomes law.	**1694.** *July 27*: Bank of England established.	**1694.** Halle University founded. Purcell: *Te Deum* and *Jubilate.*

I. WESTERN AND SOUTHERN EUROPE	II. CENTRAL, NORTHERN, AND EASTERN EUROPE	III. COUNTRIES OVERSEA
1695. *Jan. 4*: Marshal Luxembourg *d.* *Sept. 1*: William III takes Namur.	**1695-1703.** Sultan Mustafa II.	
1696. *Oct. 6*: Savoy withdraws from Great Alliance; obtains Pinerolo back from France.	**1696.** *July 29*: Peter of Russia takes Azoff from Turks.	**1696.** Fort William, Calcutta, built. **1696-1706.** Russians conquer Kamchatka.
1697. *Sept. 20*: Treaty of Ryswyck between France, England, Holland, and Spain; France recognizes William III as king, and Anne as his heir presumptive.	**1697.** *June 27*: Augustus of Saxony elected King of Poland. *Sept. 11*: Prince Eugene defeats Turks at Zenta. *Oct. 30*: Peace of Ryswyck between France and Empire; France restores right bank of Rhine, and is bought off as regards her claims to Palatinate. **1697-1718.** Charles XII, King of Sweden.	**1697.** *Sept. 20*: Peace of Ryswyck; Fort Albany restored to Hudson's Bay Company; Pondicherry and Acadia to France; Spain keeps in the West Indies only East San Domingo, Cuba, and Porto Rico. China conquers Western Mongolia. **1697-1702** and **1714-1720.** Governor De Brue attempts to establish French colonial empire in West Africa.
1698. *Oct. 11*: First Partition Treaty regarding Spain; Spanish possessions to be divided between Electoral Prince of Bavaria, Dauphin, and Archduke Charles.	**1698.** *Sept.-Oct.*: Peter of Russia executes rebel musketeers (Strieltzy). **1698-1727.** George Lewis, Elector of Hanover.	**1698.** African trade opened to all British subjects. Scottish colony established on Isthmus of Darien. **1698-1700.** First French legation to China.
1699. *Feb. 6*: Josef Ferdinand, Electoral Prince of Bavaria, *d.*	**1699.** *Jan. 26*: Peace of Karlowitz between Austria-Hungary, Poland, Venice, and Turkey, which cedes Hungary, Transylvania, Croatia, Slavonia to the Hapsburgs, Podolia and Ukraine to Poland, and Morea to Venice. **1699-1730.** Frederick IV of Denmark.	**1699.** Scottish settlement in Darien fails. Dampier explores N.W. coast of Australia.
1700. *Mar. 25*: Second Partition Treaty; Archduke Charles to have Spain, her colonies, the Netherlands, and Sardinia; Dauphin, Italian territories. *Oct. 3*: Charles II of Spain appoints Philip of Anjou, grandson of Louis XIV, his only heir. *Nov. 1*: Charles II *d.*	**1700-1721.** Second Northern War. **1700.** *June 23*: Truce between Russia and Turkey, which cedes Azov. *Aug. 9*: Peter invades Livonia. *Aug. 18*: Charles XII enforces peace of Travendal on Denmark. *Nov. 30*: Charles XII defeats Peter at Narva.	**1700.** Administrative organization of Bengal under Sir Charles Eyre.

IV. CONSTITUTIONAL HISTORY	V. ECONOMIC HISTORY AND NATURAL SCIENCE	VI. CULTURAL LIFE
1695. End of Press censorship in England.	**1695.** Window tax imposed in England.	**1695.** Congreve: *Love for Love.* Leibniz: *Système nouveau de la nature.* Purcell: *Indian Queen* Quesnel: *Moral Reflexions on the New Testament.* Fénelon made Archbishop of Cambrai; controversy with Boileau. Breslau University founded. *Nov. 21:* Henry Purcell *d.* **1695-1697.** Pierre Bayle: *Dictionnaire historique et critique.*
1696. Habeas Corpus Act suspended. Board of Trade and Plantations established. **1697.** *June 2:* Augustus of Saxony turns Roman Catholic. *Dec. 4:* Fall of E. von Danckelmann, Brandenburg Chancellor. Somers appointed Lord Chancellor of a wholly Whig Ministry.	**1696.** English currency restored under direction of Locke and Newton. **1697.** *Mar.* - **1698.** *Sept.* First visit of Peter I of Russia to Prussia, Holland, England, and Vienna.	**1696.** Academy of Arts established at Berlin. Christian Reuter: *Schelmuffsky.* Vanbrugh: *The Relapse.* **1697.** Leibniz: *Thoughts on Improving German Language.* D'Herbelot: *Bibliothèque Orientale.*
	1698. Charter for New East India Company. First Eddystone lighthouse.	**1698.** Fénelon: *Télémaque* (published and immediately suppressed in **1699**). Francke endowments at Halle founded by H. A. Francke. New Palace, Bamberg, finished. **1698-1706.** Berlin Palace built by Andreas Schlüter.
1699. Administrative reforms of Peter the Great begin.		**1699.** Innocent XII condemns Fénelon's *Maximes des Saints.* *Apr. 22:* Racine *d.* G. Farquhar: *Love and a Bottle.* Richard Bentley: *Phalaris.*
1700. Resumption Bill. *Nov. 16:* Crown Treaty between Emperor and Elector of Brandenburg.	**1700.** Sewall: *Selling of Joseph;* first American protest against slavery. Sauveur measures and explains musical vibrations.	**1700.** German Protestants adopt Gregorian Calendar. *Apr. 30:* Dryden *d.*

I. WESTERN AND SOUTHERN EUROPE	II. CENTRAL, NORTHERN, AND EASTERN EUROPE	III. COUNTRIES OVERSEA
1701-1714. War of the Spanish Succession. **1701.** *Feb.*: Philip enters Madrid; French occupy southern Spanish Netherlands. *Apr.-Sept.*: Prince Eugene defeats French in Lombardy. *Sept. 16*: James II *d.*; Louis XIV recognizes Old Pretender as James III. *Sept. 17*: England, Holland, and the Emperor ally against France. **1702.** *Mar. 19*: William III *d.*; succeeded by Queen Anne (**-1714**) in England; no Stadholder in Holland. *May 4*: England, Holland, and the Emperor declare war on France. Marlborough victorious in Netherlands, French in Lombardy. Rebellion of Protestant Camisards in Cevennes (**-1705**). **1703.** *May 26*: Portugal joins Great Alliance. Marlborough occupies Electorate of Cologne. *Nov. 4*: Savoy joins Great Alliance. **1704.** *Aug. 4*: English take Gibraltar. *Aug. 13*: Marlborough and Prince Eugene defeat French and Bavarians at Blenheim. **1705.** *Oct. 14*: English navy takes Barcelona; Charles (III) recognized in Catalonia, Valencia, and Aragon. **1706.** *May 22*: English raise siege of Barcelona by the French. *May 23*: Marlborough defeats French at Ramillies, and conquers Spanish Netherlands. *June 27*: English and Portuguese enter Madrid. *Sept. 7*: Prince Eugene defeats French at Torino. **1707.** *Apr. 25*: English defeat at Almanza. *Aug.* Unsuccessful siege of Toulon by Allies; Imperial troops take Naples. **1708.** *Mar.*: Unsuccessful expedition of Old Pretender to Scotland. *July 11*: Marlborough and Prince Eugene defeat French at Oudenarde. *Aug.*: English take Sardinia. *Sept.*: English capture Minorca. *Oct. 21*: Allies take Lille.	**1701.** *Jan. 18*: Frederick of Brandenburg crowned king in Prussia, as Frederick I. *Mar. 9*: Electors of Bavaria and Cologne side with France. *June-July*: Charles XII occupies Livonia and Courland, and invades Poland. **1702.** *May 14*: Charles XII takes Warsaw. *July 19*: Charles XII defeats Poles at Klissow; seizes Cracow. Frederick I of Prussia acquires countships of Lingen and Mörs. *Sept 28*: Imperial Diet decides on war against France. **1703.** *May 1*: Charles XII defeats Peter at Pultusk. Hungarians, supported by France, revolt against Emperor. *May 27*: St. Petersburg founded. Campaign in Rhineland and South Germany. **1704.** *July 15*: Stanislas Leszczinski elected King of Poland at Charles XII's instigation. Peter fortifies Kronstadt and takes Dorpat and Narva. **1705.** *May 5*: Emperor Leopold I *d.*, succeeded by Josef I. **1706.** *Feb. 13*: Charles XII defeats Russians and Saxons at Fraustadt. *Sept. 24*: Peace of Altranstädt between Sweden and Saxony: Augustus renounces Polish crown. **1707.** *Jan. 4*: Louis of Baden *d.* Prussia acquires principality of Neuchâtel and countship of Tecklenburg. Charles XII takes Vilna, and allies with Cossacks under Mazeppa. **1708.** Charles XII takes Mohilev and invades Ukraine. Hungarian rebels defeated by Austrians. Emperor claims reversion of Duchy of Mantua.	**1703.** Delaware becomes a separate colony. **1705.** Husseinite dynasty of Beys become rulers of Tunis. **1706.** Successful defence of Charleston, S.C., against French and Spaniards. **1707.** *Mar. 3*: Aurangzeb *d.*; succeeded by Bahadur (**-1712**).

IV. CONSTITUTIONAL HISTORY	V. ECONOMIC HISTORY AND NATURAL SCIENCE	VI. CULTURAL LIFE
1701. *Mar. 8*: Mecklenburg divided into Schwerin and Strelitz (**-1934**). *June 12*: Act of Settlement, provides for Protestant succession of house of Hanover.		**1701.** Steele: *The Christian Hero.* Yale College, Newhaven, Conn., founded. Russian Patriarchate abolished. Society for Propagation of the Gospel in Foreign Parts founded.
	1702. Asiento Guinea Company formed to transport negroes to America. Serfdom abolished on royal estates in Denmark.	**1702.** *Daily Courant*, first English daily newspaper. J. Kersey: *New English Dictionary.* **1702-1714.** Vanbrugh builds Castle Howard, Yorks.
	1703. *May 16*: Methuen Treaty between England and Portugal.	**1703.** Schlüter's statue of the Great Elector, Berlin. *Vyedomosti*, first Russian newspaper.
1704. *Apr.*: Harley and St. John, moderate Tories, join Ministry.	**1704.** Newton: *Optics*; corpuscular theory of light. Newcomen erects first steam-engine.	**1704.** Swift: *Tale of a Tub.* Defoe starts *Weekly Review*, first American newspaper, at Boston. *Oct. 28*: John Locke *d. Oct. 29*: *Vossische Zeitung* first published at Berlin (**-1933**).
1705. *Aug. 28*: George William, Duke of Lüneburg-Celle, *d.*; his country united with Hanover. *Oct. 25*: Parliament with Whig majority meets; Cowper appointed Lord Chancellor.		**1705.** B. de Mandeville: *Fable of the Bees*; political satire. Vanbrugh builds Blenheim Palace, Oxfordshire. Peter the Great founds Moscow University.
1706. *Apr. 29*: Electors of Bavaria and Cologne outlawed by the Emperor. *Dec. 3*: Sunderland appointed Secretary of State.	**1706.** Mill invents carriage-springs.	**1706.** Excavations begun at Pompeii and Herculaneum. G. Farquhar: *The Recruiting Officer.*
1707. *May 1*: Union between England and Scotland. Union between Castile and Aragon.	**1707.** Vauban: *Projet d'une Dîme Royale*, on social and economic defects of France; burnt by command of king. Denis Papin invents steamboat; destroyed by mob.	**1707.** Fénelon exiled from French court. G. Farquhar: *The Beaux' Stratagem.* Isaac Watts: *Hymns and Spiritual Songs.* Society of Antiquaries, London, founded.
1708. *Feb.*: Ministry made wholly Whig. *Oct. 28*: Prince Consort, George of Denmark *d.* Russia divided into 8 governments.	**1708.** East India and New East India Companies merged.	**1708.** Handel: *Agrippina.* Montfaucon: *Palaeographia Graeca.* First permanent German theatre at Vienna.

I. WESTERN AND SOUTHERN EUROPE	II. CENTRAL, NORTHERN, AND EASTERN EUROPE	III. COUNTRIES OVERSEA
1709. *July 30:* Marlborough and Prince Eugene take Tournai, defeat French at Malplaquet (*Sept. 11*), and take Mons (*Oct. 20*).	**1709.** *July 8:* Peter I defeats Charles XII at Poltava (Pultowa). Charles flees to Turkey. Augustus of Poland expels Stanislas.	**1709.** First mass emigration of Germans to America, from Palatinate to Pennsylvania. Russian prisoners first sent to Siberia.
1710. *July 27:* English victories at Almenara and (*Aug. 20*) at Saragossa. *Sept. 28:* Charles (III) enters Madrid. *Dec. 9:* Defeat of English at Brihuega. *Dec. 10:* French defeat Austrians at Villa Viciosa; Philip V master of Spain.	**1710.** *Mar. 31* and *May 4:* Alliance of the Hague, establishes neutrality of Swedish possessions in Germany. *Nov. 30:* Turkey declares war on Russia, at Charles XII's instigation.	**1710.** Mauritius becomes French. English take Port Royal (Annapolis), Acadia.
1711. *Apr. 13:* Dauphin *d. Sept. 27:* Charles (III) leaves Spain.	**1711.** *Apr. 17:* Josef I *d.;* succeeded by Charles III of Spain, as Charles VI (**-1740**). *Apr. 29:* Agreement between Emperor and Hungarian rebels. *July 21:* Peter I, surrounded by Turks at the Pruth, makes peace and restores Azov.	**1711.** *May-Oct.:* Unsuccessful English expedition to Canada. English South Sea Company formed.
1712. *Jan. 12:* Peace Congress opened at Utrecht. *Feb. 18:* Louis, Duke of Burgundy, heir apparent to Louis XIV, *d. Mar. 8:* Duke of Brittany, next heir, *d. July 16:* English-French truce. *July 24:* Dutch defeat at Denain; Holland joins truce with France.	**1712.** Russians and Danes defeat Swedes in Baltic and Scandinavia.	**1712.** War of succession between Bahadur's 4 sons.
1713. *Apr. 11:* Peace of Utrecht between France and Britain, Holland, Savoy, and Portugal; France dismantles Dunkirk, recognizes Protestant succession in Britain; France gains fortresses on northern frontier, Holland establishes barrier against France, Sicily to be ceded to Savoy as kingdom. *June 13:* Peace of Utrecht between England and Spain; Spain cedes Gibraltar and Minorca.	**1713.** *Apr. 11:* Peace of Utrecht between France and Prussia, which obtains Upper Gelderland and Neuchâtel. *Apr. 19:* Charles VI issues Pragmatic Sanction (female right of succession in Hapsburg possessions). Charles XII prisoner of Turks. **1713-1740.** Frederick William I, King of Prussia.	**1713.** *Mar. 21:* Spain grants England privileges in slave-trading, by Asiento Treaty. *Apr. 11:* Peace of Utrecht; France cedes Newfoundland, Acadia, and Hudson Bay to England; Spain cedes San Sacramento, north of River Plate, to Portugal.
1714. *June 26:* Peace of Utrecht between Spain and Holland. *Aug. 1:* Queen Anne *d.;* succeeded by George Lewis, Elector of Hanover, as George I (**-1727**). *Sept. 11:* Duke of Berwick storms Barcelona, last stronghold of partisans of Charles (III). *Sept. 16:* Philip V of Spain marries Elizabeth Farnese; Alberoni, leading Minister.	**1714.** *Mar. 7:* Peace of Rastatt between France and Emperor; France recognizes Italian possessions of Hapsburgs, Electors of Bavaria and Cologne are restored. *Sept. 7:* Peace of Baden between France and Empire; France keeps Alsace with Strasbourg. *Nov. 22:* Charles XII arrives at Stralsund after 16 days' ride from Adrianople.	**1714.** Tripoli becomes independent of Constantinople.

IV. CONSTITUTIONAL HISTORY	V. ECONOMIC HISTORY AND NATURAL SCIENCE	VI. CULTURAL LIFE
	1709. Böttger produces first European porcelain at Meissen. Abraham Darby produces coke and uses it to smelt iron.	**1709.** Berkeley: *New Theory of Vision.* First Copyright Act. **1709-1711.** Richard Steele: *The Tatler.*
1710. *June 14:* Sunderland dismissed. *Aug. 8:* Fall of Whig Ministry; Harley and St. John form Tory Ministry. *Sept. 28:* Parliament dissolved. *Nov. 25:* Parliament with Tory majority meets.	**1710.** English South Sea Company formed. Le Blon invents three-colour printing. *Jan. 27:* First budget in Russia.	**1710.** Leibniz: *Théodicée.* Handel: *Rinaldo.* Berkeley: *Principle of Human Knowledge.*
1711. *Feb. 22:* Administrative Senate formed in Russia. *May 23:* Harley created Earl of Oxford. *Dec. 31:* Marlborough dismissed from office.	**1711.** Partels constructs first ventilator, John Shore first tuning-fork. Queen Anne establishes Ascot races.	**1711.** Alex. Pope: *Essay on Criticism.* Shaftesbury: *Philosophical Writings.* London Academy of Arts opened under Kneller. Berlin Academy established, Leibniz president. **1711-1712.** Steele and Addison: *The Spectator.* **1711-1722.** The Zwinger, Dresden, built by Pöppelmann.
1712. *Jan. 17:* Walpole sent to Tower. *July 7:* St. John created Viscount Bolingbroke. *Nov. 5:* Philip V of Spain renounces claims to French throne.	**1712.** Newspaper Stamp Act. Last execution for witchcraft in England. Jan Kruse begins cultivation of moorlands in East Friesland.	**1712.** Pope: *The Rape of the Lock.* John Arbuthnot: *History of John Bull.*
1713. *Mar.:* Dukes of Berry and Orleans renounce claims to Spanish throne.		**1713.** Addison: *Cato.* Steele and Addison: *The Guardian.* Abbé de St. Pierre: *Projet de paix perpétuelle.* Gravina: *Della Tragedia.* Clement XI condemns Quesnel's Jansenist *Moral Reflections* (Bull *Unigenitus*). **1713-1716.** Prince Eugene's Belvedere palace, Vienna, built.
1714. *Feb. 14:* Paris Parlement registers Bull *Unigenitus.* *July 27:* Lord Oxford dismissed. *Sept.:* Whig Ministry under Townshend, including Walpole, Sunderland, Orford, Halifax.	**1714.** Fahrenheit constructs mercury thermometer.	**1714.** Leibniz: *Monadology.* Spanish Academy of Science founded. G. Arnold: *Impartial History of Church and Heresy.* Worcester College, Oxford, founded.

I. WESTERN AND SOUTHERN EUROPE	II. CENTRAL, NORTHERN, AND EASTERN EUROPE	III. COUNTRIES OVERSEA
1715. *Feb. 6*: Peace of Madrid between Spain and Portugal. *Sept. 1*: Louis XIV *d.*; succeeded by Louis XV, his great-grandson (-**1774**), till **1723** under regency of Philip, Duke of Orleans. *Sept. 6*: Jacobite rising in Scotland. *Nov. 13*: Defeat of Jacobites at Preston and Sheriffmuir.	**1715.** *May*: Alliance between Prussia, Denmark, Hanover, Saxony, and Poland against Sweden completed; *May 1*: Declaration of war. *Nov. 15*: Barrier Treaty between Austria and Holland; Austria obtains Spanish Netherlands; 8 fortresses occupied by Dutch garrisons. !*Dec. 24*: Prussians take Stralsund from Swedes. Charles XII attacks Norway.	**1715.** Turks expel Venetians from the Morea.
1716. *Jan. 2-Feb. 4*: James (III) in Scotland. *May 25*: Treaty of Westminster between England and Austria for mutual defence. *Nov. 28*: Defensive alliance at the Hague between England and France.	**1716.** *Apr. 13*: Emperor declares war on Turkey. *Aug. 5*: Prince Eugene defeats Turks at Peterwardein. *Oct.*: Russians occupy Mecklenburg.	
1717. *Jan. 4*: Triple alliance between England, France, and Holland. *Aug. 17*: Convention of Amsterdam between France, Russia, and Prussia, to maintain treaties of Utrecht and Baden. *Aug. 22*: Spain attacks Sardinia.	**1717.** *Aug. 18*: Prince Eugene captures Belgrade.	**1717.** *Dec. 18*: Prussian colonies in Africa sold to Dutch.
1718. *Aug. 2*: Quadruple alliance between the Emperor, England, France, and Holland against Spain. *Aug. 11*: Byng defeats Spaniards off Cape Passaro. *Dec. 28*: England declares war on Spain.	**1718.** *June 26*: Tsarevitch Alexis *d.* *July 21*: Peace of Passarowitz between Austria and Turkey; Austria obtains Belgrade, the Banat, and part of Serbia; Turkey keeps Morea. *Dec. 11*: Charles XII killed before Frederikshall; succeeded by his sister, Ulrica Eleanor.	**1718.** New Orleans founded. Law's scheme to exploit Mississippi regions.
1719. *Jan. 9*: France declares war on Spain. *Apr. 13-June 10*: Spanish invasion of Scotland fails. *Dec. 5*: Fall of Alberoni.	**1719.** *Jan. 5*: Alliance of Vienna between Emperor, Saxony-Poland, and England-Hanover against Russia and Prussia. *Nov. 20*: Peace between Sweden and Hanover, which buys Bremen and Verden for 1 million thalers.	**1719.** Muhammad Shah, grandson of Bahadur, Great Mogul (-**1748**).
1720. *Feb. 17*: Peace between Quadruple Alliance and Spain; Savoy obtains Sardinia from Austria in exchange for Sicily.	**1720.** *Feb. 1*: Treaty of Stockholm between Sweden and Prussia, which obtains Pomerania between Oder and Peene including Stettin. *July 3*: Treaty of Frederiksborg between Sweden and Denmark, which is exempted from Sund duties.	**1720.** Tibet becomes tributary to China. First settlement in Vermont.
1721. *June 21*: Defensive alliance between England, France, and Spain.	**1721.** *Sept. 10*: Treaty of Nystad between Sweden and Russia, which obtains Livonia, Estonia, Ingria, and Eastern Karelia.	**1721.** Holland buys last Prussian factories in Africa. French occupy Mauritius.

IV. CONSTITUTIONAL HISTORY	V. ECONOMIC HISTORY AND NATURAL SCIENCE	VI. CULTURAL LIFE
1715. *Mar. 28*: Bolingbroke flees to France. *July 16*: Oxford imprisoned; Habeas Corpus Act suspended; Riot Act passed. *Oct. 11*: Walpole appointed Chancellor of the Exchequer.	**1715.** First dock opened at Liverpool.	**1715.** Le Sage: *Gil Blas*. *Jan. 7*: Fénelon *d.* The diocese of Karlsburg established to re-catholicize Transylvania. **1715-1720.** Pope's translation of Homer's *Iliad*.
1716. *May 7*: Septennial Act passed. *Dec. 15*: Townshend dismissed.	**1716.** John Law founds joint-stock bank in Paris. **1716-1717.** Second visit of Tsar Peter to Western Europe.	**1716.** J. B. Homann: *World Atlas*. *Nov. 14*: Leibniz *d*.
1717. *Apr. 10*: Walpole resigns. Stanhope appointed First Lord of the Treasury. *Sept. 24*: Dubois appointed French Foreign Secretary. Four Jansenist bishops appeal from Bull *Unigenitus* to a General Council. **1718.** *Mar.*: Reconstruction of Cabinet by Earl of Sunderland, with Stanhope as Secretary of State (*d.* **1721** *Feb. 4*).	**1718.** Lady Mary Wortley Montagu introduces inoculation against smallpox. Halley discovers independent movement of fixed stars. Leopold of Dessau invents iron ramrod, thereby increasing speed and accuracy of fire of Prussian infantry. *Dec.*: Law's bank made Royal bank.	**1717.** Union of the English Freemasons Grand Lodge inaugurated. Fénelon: *Télémaque*. Compulsory school-attendance in Prussia. Watteau: *Embarkation for Cythera*. St. Mary le Strand, London, built by James Gibbs. **1718.** Voltaire: *Édipe*. *Jan.*: London Society of Antiquaries founded.
1719. *Sept. 23*: Liechtenstein becomes independent principality of Empire. Peerage Bill, to close House of Lords, rejected by Commons.	**1719.** *May 27*: Emperor founds Oriental Company at Vienna. Law forms French Mississippi Company.	**1719.** Defoe: *Robinson Crusoe*.
1720. *Feb. 29*: Ulrica Eleanor, Swedish Queen abdicates in favour of her husband, Frederick I, prince of Hesse-Cassel (-**1751**). *June:* Townshend and Walpole recalled to office.	**1720.** Law appointed Controller-General of France. *Oct.-Dec.*: South Sea Bubble bursts. *Dec.*: National bankruptcy in France; Law flees. Austrian East India Company formed at Ostend.	**1720.** Handel: *Esther*. Christian Wolff: *Rational Thoughts on God, the World, and the Human Soul*. **1720-1744.** Würzburg Residency built by B. Neumann.
1721. *Apr. 3*: Robert Walpole appointed First Lord of the Treasury and Chancellor of the Exchequer (-**1742**). *Oct. 22*: Peter I proclaimed Emperor of All the Russias.	**1721.** Walpole restores public credit. Geo. Graham invents compensator pendulum.	**1721.** Nathan Bailey: *Universal Etymological English Dictionary*. Montesquieu: *Lettres Persanes*. Watteau: *Gersaint's Signboard*. **1721-1726.** St. Martin in the Fields built by J. Gibbs. **1721-1723.** Bodmer and Breitinger, Zurich: *Discourses of the Painters*.

I. WESTERN AND SOUTHERN EUROPE	II. CENTRAL, NORTHERN, AND EASTERN EUROPE	III. COUNTRIES OVERSEA
1722. *June 16:* Marlborough *d.*	**1722.** Hungary agrees to Pragmatic Sanction.	**1722.** *Sept. 12:* Russia takes Baku and Derbent from Persia.
		1722-1736. Persia under Afghan rule.
1723. *Feb. 16:* Louis XV attains majority. *Oct. 12:* Treaty of Charlottenburg between England and Prussia.		**1723.** Nizam of the Deccan becomes independent of Moghul. Turkey attacks Persia.
		1723-1736. Yungchen Emperor of China.
1724. *Jan. 14:* Philip V of Spain abdicates in favour of Don Luis, who dies *Aug. 31;* Philip returns.	**1724.** *Feb. 22:* Treaty of assistance between Russia and Sweden, at Stockholm.	**1724.** *June 23:* Treaty of Constantinople between Russia and Turkey against Persia. Turks take Erivan from Persia.
1725. *May 1:* Treaty of Vienna between Austria and Spain; Spain guarantees Pragmatic Sanction, Austria to aid Spain to recover Gibraltar. *Sept. 23:* Treaty of Herrenhausen between England, France, and Prussia; mutual guarantee of integrity; Prussia's claims to Jülich-Berg recognized.	**1725.** *Feb. 8:* Peter the Great of Russia *d.;* succeeded by Catherine I, his Empress (**-1727**).	
	1726. *Aug.:* Austria and Palatinate agree on succession of Elector to Jülich and Berg. *Aug. 6:* Treaty between Russia and Austria against Turkey. *Oct. 12:* Treaty of Wusterhausen between Austria and Prussia.	
1727. *Feb.:* War between England and Spain; siege of Gibraltar. *June 12:* George I *d.;* succeeded by George II (**-1760**). *Nov. 12:* Secret treaty of 1714 between France and Bavaria renewed.	**1727.** *Apr. 16:* Denmark joins Hanoverian Alliance.	**1727.** Amur frontier between Russia and China rectified.
	1727-1730. Peter II, grandson of Peter I, Tsar of Russia.	
1728. *Mar. 6:* Convention of the Prado ends war between England and Spain.	**1728.** *Dec. 23:* Treaty of Berlin between Emperor and Prussia; Prussia guarantees Pragmatic Sanction; Charles recognizes Prussia's claims to Jülich and Berg.	
1729. *Nov. 9:* Treaty of Seville between England and Spain; joined by France and Holland; ends Austro-Spanish alliance.	**1729.** *Nov. 21:* Holland joins treaty of Seville. Corsica becomes independent of Genoa.	**1729.** North and South Carolina become Crown colonies. Baltimore founded.
1730. *Sept. 30:* Victor Amadeus II of Savoy abdicates; succeeded by Charles Emanuel I (**-1773**).	**1730.** *Feb. 11:* Peter II of Russia *d.;* Anne, daughter of Ivan V, succeeds (**-1747**). *Sept. 17:* Ahmad III deposed and succeeded by Mahmoud I.	**1730.** Kuli Khan expels Afghans from Persia.
	1730-1746. Christian VI, King of Denmark.	
1731. *Jan. 10:* Farnese line extinct in Parma and Piacenza. *July 22:* Treaty of Vienna between England, Holland, Spain, and Austria; Maritime Powers guarantee Pragmatic Sanction; Spain obtains Parma and Piacenza.		
	1732. *Jan.:* Empire except Saxony, Bavaria and Palatinate guarantees Pragmatic Sanction.	**1732.** James Oglethorpe founds colony of Georgia.

IV. CONSTITUTIONAL HISTORY	V. ECONOMIC HISTORY AND NATURAL SCIENCE	VI. CULTURAL LIFE
1722. *Oct.*: Habeas Corpus Act suspended. *Dec.*: General Directory of War, Finance, and Domains established in Prussia. **1723.** *June*: Bolingbroke returns from exile.	**1722.** *June 16*: Austrian East India Company established at Ostend. Prussian Seehandelsgesellschaft established. Workhouse Test Act. **1723.** Duty on tea reduced in England.	**1722.** J. S. Bach: *Wohltemperiertes Klavier*: Herrnhut founded as a Moravian settlement in Saxony. **1723.** Voltaire: *Henriade. Feb. 25*: Sir Christopher Wren *d. Oct. 19*: Sir Godfrey Kneller *d.* **1723-1751.** L. A. Muratori: *Rerum Italicarum Scriptores.*
1724. *Apr. 1*: Carteret appointed Lord Lieutenant of Ireland; pacifies country. **1725.** Louis XV marries Maria Leszczinska of Poland.	**1724.** Swift: *Drapier's Letters*, against Wood's contract for supplying copper coinage in Ireland. **1725.** Behring discovers Behring Straits. Guy's Hospital founded.	**1725.** Pope's edition of Shakespeare. G. B. Vico: *Scienza Nuova intorno alla Natura.* Academy of Science founded at St. Petersburg. **1725-1726.** Pope's translation of Homer's *Odyssey.* **1726.** Swift: *Gulliver's Travels.* Allan Ramsay opens first circulating library, at Edinburgh. *Mar. 26*: Sir John Vanbrugh *d.*
1726-1743. Cardinal Fleury, Chief Minister in France.		
1727. Chauvelin, head of anti-English party, appointed French Foreign Secretary.	**1727.** *May 31*: Austrian East India Company dissolved.	**1727.** German Society, Leipzig, founded by Gottsched. *Mar. 31*: Newton *d.*
1728. Foreign Ministry established in Prussia.		**1728.** John Gay: *Beggar's Opera.* Pope: *Dunciad.*
	1729. Hall constructs achromatic lens. Bradley discovers aberration of light.	**1729.** J. S. Bach: *St. Matthew Passion.* Haller: *The Alps.*
1730. *May 15*: Quarrel between Walpole and Townshend, who resigns. *Aug. 4*: Frederick, Crown Prince of Prussia, tries to flee to England, but is imprisoned by his father. **1731.** *Sept.*: Paris Parlement declares temporal power independent of all other powers, and places clergy under jurisdiction of Crown. **1732.** *July-Dec.*: 139 members of Paris Parlement exiled; eventual triumph over Crown.	**1730.** Réaumur's thermometer scale. Townshend begins four-crop system of agriculture. **1731.** Harley invents quadrant for use at sea. Attempt to abolish compulsory guild system in German Empire. *Oct. 31*: Protestants expelled from Archbishopric of Salzburg. **1732.** 20,000 Salzburg Protestants settled in Eastern Prussia. Boerhaave: *Elements of Chemistry*; founds organic chemistry.	**1730.** Thomson: *The Seasons.* Lillo: *London Merchant.* Gottsched: *Critical Art of Poetry for the Germans.* Senate House, Cambridge, built by J. Gibbs. **1731.** *Gentlemen's Magazine* appears. *Apr. 26*: Defoe *d.* **1731-1743.** Schnabel: *Island of Felsenburg*, imitation of *Robinson Crusoe.* **1732.** Voltaire: *Zaïre.* Gottsched: *Dying Cato*; after Addison. **1732-1734.** Pope: *Essay on Man.*

I. WESTERN AND SOUTHERN EUROPE	II. CENTRAL, NORTHERN, AND EASTERN EUROPE	III. COUNTRIES OVERSEA
1733. *Nov. 7*: Treaty of the Escorial between France and Spain against Britain (First 'Family Compact').	**1733–1735.** War of Polish succession; Russia and Austria recognize Augustus III of Saxony against Stanislas Leszczinski.	**1733.** Oglethorpe founds Savannah. St. Thomas, St. Croix, and St. John in the West Indies become Danish (**-1917**).
1734. French, Sardinian, and Spanish troops defeat Austrians throughout Italy.	**1734.** *Jan. 1*: Empire declares war on France. *June 30*: Russians take Danzig and expel Stanislas from Poland.	**1734.** 8000 Protestants emigrate from Salzburg to Georgia. Persians recapture Erivan from Turks.
	1735. *Oct. 3*: Peace of Vienna; Stanislas obtains Lorraine, Duke of Lorraine to obtain Tuscany on Grand Duke's death, Austria obtains Parma and Piacenza; Don Carlos, Naples and Sicily; France guarantees Pragmatic Sanction.	**1735.** French East India Company establishes sugar industry in Mauritius and Réunion
1736. *May 18*: Spain accedes to treaty of Vienna.	**1736.** *Feb. 12*: Maria Theresa marries Francis Stephen of Lorraine. *Apr. 21*: Prince Eugene d. *May*: War of Turkey with Austria and Russia. *Apr. 15*: Baron Theodore of Neuhof elected King of Corsica (**-1738**).	**1736.** Kuli Khan becomes Shah of Persia, as Nadir Khan (**-1747**). **1736–1796.** Chienlung, Emperor of China.
1737. *Feb. 20*: Fall of Chauvelin, French Foreign Secretary and leader of war party.	**1737.** *July 9*: Death of last Medici Grand Duke of Tuscany, which goes to Francis Stephen of Lorraine. *May 4*: Kettelers extinct in Courland; Count Ernest John of Biron elected Duke.	**1737.** Richmond, Virginia, founded.
1738. *Oct.*: Alliance between France and Sweden. *Nov. 18*: France recognizes Pragmatic Sanction.	**1738.** *May 27*: Turks take Orsova. *Nov. 18*: Definitive peace treaty of Vienna.	
1739. *Oct. 19*: England declares war on Spain.	**1739.** *Jan.*: Secret treaty between Austria and France to guarantee Wittelsbach claims to Jülich-Berg. *Apr. 5*: Secret treaty between Prussia and France to divide Jülich-Berg. *Sept. 18*: Peace of Belgrade between Austria and Turkey; Austria cedes Orsova, Belgrade, and Serbia. *Sept. 23*: Treaty of Belgrade between Russia and Turkey; Russia restores her conquests except Azoff.	**1739.** War between English and Spaniards in West Indies. Viceroyalty of New Granada separated from Peru. Nadir sacks Delhi and conquers Punjab.
	1740. *May 31*: Frederick William I of Prussia d.; succeeded by Frederick II (**-1786**). *Oct. 20*: Charles VI, last Hapsburg Emperor, d.; succeeded by his daughter Maria Theresa, Queen of Bohemia and Hungary. (**-1780**). *Dec. 16*: Frederick II enters Silesia.	**1740–1756.** Bengal independent under Alivardi Khan.

IV. CONSTITUTIONAL HISTORY	V. ECONOMIC HISTORY AND NATURAL SCIENCE	VI. CULTURAL LIFE
1733. Conscription introduced in Prussia. Non-Catholics excluded from office in Poland.	**1733.** Molasses Act forbids American colonies to trade with French West Indies.	**1733.** Prévost: *Manon Lescaut*. Bach: *B-minor Mass*. First German Masonic Lodge at Hamburg (closed **1933**).
	1734. Anglo-Russian commercial treaty (**-1786**).	**1734.** Voltaire: *Lettres sur les Anglais*. Bach: *Christmas Oratorio*. Pitaval: *Causes Célèbres*.
1735. Zenger case establishes freedom of the Press in New England.	**1735.** Berkeley: *Querist*; on true nature of money. Linnaeus: *Systema Naturae*.	
1736. *Sept. 7:* Porteous Riots in Edinburgh. English Statutes against witchcraft repealed.	**1736.** Harrison invents chronometer. Euler establishes analytical mechanics.	
1737. *Nov. 1:* Cocceji appointed Prussian Minister of Justice. All plays subjected to censorship of Lord Chamberlain.		**1737.** Göttingen University founded by George II. Gottsched abolishes clown on German stage.
		1737-1749. J. Gibbs builds Radcliffe Library, Oxford.
	1738. First spinning machines patented in England. Daniel Bernoulli's kinetic theory of gases. John Kay invents flyshuttle.	**1738.** Handel: *Saul*. John Wesley starts Methodist revival. *Apr. 28:* Clement XII's bull against Freemasonry (*In Eminenti*). M. Bouquet: *Recueil des historiens*.
		1739. D. Hume: *Treatise of Human Nature*. Charter for Foundling Hospital, London. *Göttingische Anzeigen von Gelehrten Sachen* appears. Voltaire: *La Pucelle* (published **1755**).
1740. Frederick II abolishes torture and introduces liberty of Press and of worship in Prussia.	**1740.** Huntsman, of Sheffield, produces crucible steel.	**1740.** Thomson: *Rule Britania*. Richardson: *Pamela*. University of Pennsylvania founded.

I. WESTERN AND SOUTHERN EUROPE	II. CENTRAL, NORTHERN, AND EASTERN EUROPE	III. COUNTRIES OVERSEA
1741. *May 28:* Treaty between Spain and Bavaria. *June 5:* Treaty between France and Prussia against Austria. *Aug. 15:* French invade South Germany, Austria, and Bohemia. *Sept. 27:* George II secures neutrality of Hanover from France.	**1741.** *Apr. 10:* Frederick defeats Austrians at Mollwitz, and conquers Silesia. *Nov. 26:* French, Bavarians, and Saxons conquer Prague. **1741-1762.** Elizabeth, Empress of Russia.	**1741-1754.** J. Fr. Dupleix, Governor-General of French possessions in India.
1742. English navy prevents Neapolitans from joining Spaniards in Lombardy. *Nov. 29:* Anglo-Prussian alliance. *Dec. 12:* French evacuate Prague and return to France. **1743.** *June 27:* George II defeats French at Dettingen. *Sept. 13:* Treaty of Worms between Austria, England, and Sardinia. *Oct. 25:* Offensive and defensive alliance of Fontainebleau between France and Spain (Second ' Family Compact ').	**1742.** *Jan. 24:* Charles Albert, Elector of Bavaria, elected Emperor (Charles VII). *July 28:* Peace of Berlin between Austria and Prussia, which obtains Silesia and Glatz. **1743.** *Aug. 17:* Peace of Abo between Russia and Sweden, which cedes Southern Finland.	
1744. *Mar. 15:* France declares war on England. *June 5:* Alliance between France and Prussia.	**1744.** *May 25:* Prussia acquires East Friesland on death of her last prince. *Aug. 15:* Frederick II invades Saxony and enters Bohemia.	**1744.** Clive arrives at Madras. **1744-1762.** Teymuras II, King of Southern Georgia.
1745. *Jan. 8:* Quadruple alliance of Maritime Powers with Austria and Saxony. *May 11:* French defeat Duke of Cumberland at Fontenoy. *Aug. 2:* Charles Edward lands in Scotland, victorious at Gladsmuir (Prestonpans) (*Nov. 20*), advances to Derby (*Dec. 4*).	**1745.** *Jan. 20:* Charles VII *d.* *Apr. 22:* Peace of Füssen between Austria and Bavaria, which renounces its claims. *June 4:* Frederick defeats Austrians at Hohenfriedberg. *Sept. 13:* Francis Stephen elected Emperor (**-1765**). *Dec. 15:* Frederick's victory at Kesselsdorf. *Dec. 25:* Peace of Dresden; Prussia keeps Silesia, recognizes Pragmatic Sanction.	**1745.** *May:* British conquer Louisburg. Behring discovers Aleutian Islands. *June:* British take Cape Breton Island.
1746. *Jan. 17:* Charles Edward victorious at Falkirk. *Apr. 16:* Final defeat of Jacobites at Culloden. *Oct. 11:* French victory at Rocoux over Austrians, who lose Netherlands. **1746-1759.** Ferdinand VI of Spain. **1747.** *July 2:* French defeat Duke of Cumberland at Lauffeld. *Dec. 9:* Convention of St. Petersburg between England, Holland, and Russia, whose troops are allowed to pass through Germany. **1748.** *Apr. 30:* Preliminary Peace of Aix-la-Chapelle between France and Maritime Powers.	**1746.** *June 2:* Austro-Russian alliance against Prussia. **1746-1766.** Frederick V, King of Denmark. **1747.** *May 29:* Prusso-Swedish alliance of Stockholm. **1748.** *Oct. 18:* Peace of Aix-la-Chapelle; general recognition of Pragmatic Sanction and conquest of Silesia.	**1746.** *Sept.:* French conquer Madras. **1746-1784.** Persecution of Christians in China. **1747.** Afghanistan becomes independent of Persia after the murder of Nadir. **1748.** English surrender Cape Breton to French. Ahmad Shah invades Punjab. Ohio Company founded in Virginia and Maryland.

IV. CONSTITUTIONAL HISTORY	V. ECONOMIC HISTORY AND NATURAL SCIENCE	VI. CULTURAL LIFE
1741. *Dec. 19*: Charles Albert of Bavaria receives homage as King of Bohemia at Prague.	**1741.** Highway Act, improves English roads.	**1741.** Handel: *Messiah*. Voltaire: *Mahomet*. First German translation of a Shakespeare play (*Julius Caesar*, by von Borcke).
1742. *Feb. 2*: Walpole resigns; succeeded by Wilmington; Carteret, Secretary of State.	**1742.** Celsius's thermometer scale. Canal between Elbe and Havel.	**1742.** *Apr. 13*: First performance of Handel's *Messiah* at Dublin. Edward Young: *Night Thoughts* (-**1746**).
1743. *July 2*: Wilmington *d.*; succeeded by Pelham as First Lord of the Treasury.	**1743.** Clairaut: *Théorie de la figure de la terre*; measures length of a meridian degree.	**1743.** Handel: *Samson*. Voltaire: *Mérope*. Erlangen University founded. *Oct. 20*: Michael Dahl *d.* **1743-1772.** B. Neumann builds Vierzehnheiligen Church.
1744. *Nov. 24*: Fall of Carteret, Secretary of State; reconstruction of Cabinet.	**1744.** India-rubber becomes familiar in Europe. First cotton factory in Berlin.	**1744.** Hogarth: *Marriage à la Mode*. **1744-1748.** *Bremer Beiträge*; periodical. **1744-1766.** J. M. Fischer builds Ottobeuren Church.
1745-1755. Cocceji reforms Prussian law-courts.	**1745.** W. Cooke invents heating by steam. Bakewell, of Leicestershire, reforms breeding of sheep. E. J. von Kleist, of Cammin, invents Leyden jar.	**1745.** Lamettrie: *Histoire naturelle de l'âme*; publicly burnt. *Oct. 19*: Swift *d.* **1745-1747.** Knobelsdorff builds Sanssouci Palace, Potsdam.
1746. *Feb. 14*: Reconstruction of Pelham Ministry, with Pitt. Abolition of Scottish clan organization by 'Butcher' Cumberland.		**1746.** Handel: *Judas Maccabeus*.
	1747. Marggraf discovers sugar in beetroot. Swinemünde harbour founded.	**1747.** Frauen-Kirche, Dresden, completed by Baehr (since **1727**).
	1748. Paul invents wool-carding machine. First silk factory at Berlin.	**1748.** Richardson: *Clarissa*. T. Smollett: *Roderick Random*. Montesquieu: *Esprit des lois*. Gozzi: *Turandot*. Gellert: *Fables*. Voltaire: *Sémiramis*. Klopstock: *Messiah*, i-iii.

I. WESTERN AND SOUTHERN EUROPE	II. CENTRAL. NORTHERN, AND EASTERN EUROPE	III. COUNTRIES OVERSEA
1749. *Oct. 5*: Treaty of Aquisgran; Britain secures confirmation of commercial rights from Spain. **1750-1777.** Joseph I of Portugal; Pombal, chief minister.		**1749.** *Mar. 16*: Ohio Company obtains royal charter. *June 23*: Georgia becomes Crown colony. Halifax, Nova Scotia, founded.
1751. *Mar. 20*: Frederick Lewis, Prince of Wales, *d. Sept. 13*: England accedes to Austro-Russian alliance of 1746.	**1751-1771.** Adolphus Frederick of Holstein-Gottorp, brother-in-law of Frederick II, King of Sweden.	**1751.** Clive takes Arcot, and defeats French.
1752. *June 14*: Treaty of Aranjuez between Spain and Austria; mutual guarantee. **1753.** Spanish concordat, enhances rights of Crown over clergy.		**1752.** *June 9*: Trichinopoly surrenders to Clive. **1753.** Duquesne, French Governor of Canada, seizes Ohio valley, and builds Fort Duquesne. **1754.** Outbreak of Anglo-French war in North America. *Dec. 26*: Dupleix's successor, Godeheu, abandons French conquests in India.
1755. *Aug.*: End of British alliance with Austria. Corsican rising, led by Paoli, against Genoa.		**1755.** *July 9*: English defeated near Fort Duquesne. French settlers deported from Nova Scotia.
1756. *Jan. 16*: Treaty of Westminster between England and Prussia. *May 1*: Alliance of Versailles between France and Austria, reverses French policy. *May 15*: England declares war on France. *June 28*: French take Minorca (*Mar. 14*, **1757**: Admiral Byng shot). **1757.** *May 1*: Second treaty of Versailles between France and Austria; Prussia to be divided. *July 26*: French defeat English at Hastenbeck. *Sept. 8*: English capitulate at Kloster Zeven.	**1756.** *Aug. 29*: Frederick II invades Saxony; outbreak of Seven Years' War. *Oct. 1*: Frederick defeats Austrians at Lobositz. *Oct. 15*: Saxon army capitulates at Pirna. **1757.** *Jan. 10*: Empire declares war on Prussia. Russia, Poland, and Sweden join war against Prussia. *May 6*: Frederick's victory at Prague. *June 18*: Austrians defeat Frederick at Kolin. *Aug. 30*: Russian victory at Gross Jägersdorf; Russians occupy East Prussia. *Sept.*: Swedes invade Pomerania. *Nov. 5*: Frederick defeats French and Imperial troops at Rossbach. *Dec. 5*: Frederick defeats Austrians at Leuthen.	**1756.** *June*: Massacre of Black Hole of Calcutta. *Aug. 14*: Montcalm takes Oswego. **1757.** *Jan. 2*: Clive takes Calcutta. *June 23*: Clive wins battle of Plassey.

IV. CONSTITUTIONAL HISTORY	V. ECONOMIC HISTORY AND NATURAL SCIENCE	VI. CULTURAL LIFE
1749. Administrative and economic reforms in Spain. Consolidation Act concerning British navy.	**1749.** Buffon: *Histoire Naturelle.* **1749-1753.** Drainage of the Oder moorlands.	**1749.** H. Fielding: *Tom Jones.* Bach: *Art of the Fugue.*
	1750. *Oct. 5:* England renounces Asiento of negroes. Westminster Bridge completed. Muschenbroek constructs the pyrometer.	**1750.** Frederick the Great: *Oeuvres du Philosophe de Sanssouci.* Rousseau: *Discours sur les arts et les sciences. July 28:* J. S. Bach d.
1751. *June:* Reconstruction of Cabinet; Grenville, President of Council.	**1751.** Chamette invents breechloader. Frederick II founds Emden Trading Company.	**1751.** Voltaire: *Siècle de Louis XIV.* Linné (Linnaeus): *Philosophia Botanica.* Thomas Gray: *Elegy written in a Country Churchyard.* **1751-1772.** The French *Encyclopédie,* edited by Diderot and d'Alembert.
	1752. Franklin invents lightning-rod.	**1752.** Hume: *Political Discourses. Sept. 2-14:* Gregorian Calendar adopted by Great Britain.
1753. Hardwicke's Marriage Act, for prevention of clandestine marriages.	**1753.** Second national bankruptcy in France.	**1753.** British Museum founded. Richardson: *Sir Charles Grandison* (-**1754**). Horace Walpole begins Strawberry Hill.
1754. *Mar. 6:* Pelham *d.;* Newcastle, Prime Minister. *June 19:* Albany Congress of New England colonies rejects Franklin's scheme of American union.	**1754.** Cort erects first iron-rolling mill near Fareham.	**1754.** Rousseau: *L'inégalité parmi les hommes.* Hume: *English History* (-**1762**). Society for the Encouragement of Arts founded.
1755. *Nov. 20:* Pitt, Legge, and Grenville dismissed. *Apr. 18:* Privileges of the Estates confirmed in Mecklenburg (valid till **1918**). **1756.** *Nov.:* Fall of Newcastle Ministry; succeeded by Devonshire and (*Dec. 4*) Pitt. Codex Maximilianeus, Bavarian civil code.	**1755.** *Nov. 1:* Earthquake at Lisbon; 30,000 people killed. **1756.** First chocolate factory in Germany.	**1755.** Hume: *Natural History of Religion.* Lessing: *Miss Sara Sampson.* Samuel Johnson: *Dictionary of the English Language.* **1756.** Holberg: *Le Christianisme dévoilé.* L. Walter: *Lexicon Diplomaticum.* Gessner: *Idyls.* Geo. Stubbs: *Anatomy of the Horse* (-**1760**).
1757. *Apr. 5:* Fall of Devonshire-Pitt Cabinet. *June 29:* Coalition between Pitt and Newcastle. Organization of Militia.		**1757.** *Nibelungenlied* edited by Bodmer. G. D. Mansi: *Conciliorum Collectio* (-**1798**). Diderot: *Le Fils Naturel.*

I. WESTERN AND SOUTHERN EUROPE	II. CENTRAL, NORTHERN, AND EASTERN EUROPE	III. COUNTRIES OVERSEA
1758. *Apr. 11:* London Convention; English subsidies for Prussia. *June 23:* French defeat at Crefeld.	**1758.** *Aug. 25:* Frederick defeats Russians at Zorndorf. *Oct. 14:* Austrian victory at Hochkirch. **1758-1828.** Charles Augustus, Duke of Weimar; till **1775** under regency of his mother, Amalia.	**1758.** *July 24:* British take Louisburg. *Nov. 25:* Washington takes Fort Duquesne (Pittsburg). English conquer French Senegal. Dutch capitulate to Clive at Chinsura. **1758-1759.** China conquers Eastern Turkestan.
1759. *Apr. 13:* French victory at Bergen near Frankfort. *Aug. 1:* French defeat at Minden. *Aug. 10:* Ferdinand VI of Spain *d.*; succeeded by Charles III, King of Naples (-**1788**). *Sept.:* Expulsion of Jesuits from Portugal. *Nov. 20:* English defeat French off Quiberon. **1760.** *Oct. 25:* George II *d.*; succeeded by George III, his grandson (-**1820**).	**1759.** *Aug. 12:* Russians and Austrians defeat Frederick at Kunersdorf. *Nov. 21:* Prussian army capitulates at Maxen. **1760.** *June 23:* Prussian defeat at Landshut. *Aug. 15:* Frederick defeats Austrians at Liegnitz and (*Nov. 3*) Torgau.	**1759.** *Apr. 7:* Coote takes Masulipatam. *Sept. 18:* English win battle of Quebec; Montcalm and Wolfe killed. **1760.** *Jan. 22:* French defeat at Wandewash. *Sept. 8:* English take Montreal. Clive returns to England. *Sept. 27:* Secret treaty between East India Company and Mir Kasim who becomes Nawab of Bengal.
1761. *Aug. 15:* Alliance between France and Spain (Third 'Family Compact ').	**1761.** *Oct. 1:* Austrians take Schweidnitz and blockade Frederick at Bunzelwitz. *Dec. 16:* Russians take Kolberg.	**1761.** *Jan. 14:* Afghans defeat Mahrattas at Panipat. *Jan. 15:* English defeat Shah Alam at Patna. *Jan. 16:* Coote takes Pondicherry. English conquer Cuba and Antilles.
1762. *Jan. 4:* England declares war on Spain and Naples. *Apr.:* England ceases to subsidize Prussia. *Nov. 1:* French capitulate at Cassel, and evacuate right bank of Rhine.	**1762.** *Jan. 5:* Elizabeth of Russia *d.*; succeeded by Peter III. *May 5:* Peace between Russia and Prussia. *May 22:* Peace between Prussia and Sweden. *July 17:* Peter III assassinated; succeeded by Catherine II (-**1796**). *July 21:* Frederick defeats Austrians at Burkersdorf. *Nov. 24:* Truce between Prussia, Austria, and Saxony.	**1762.** English take St. Vincent, Grenada, Martinique, Havana, and Philippines. **1762-1798.** Heraclius II, reunites Southern and Eastern Georgia.
1763. *Feb. 10:* Peace of Paris between England, France, Spain, and Portugal; England and France retire from German war; England recovers Minorca. **1764.** *Apr. 15:* Marquise de Pompadour *d.* *Nov. 26:* Suppression of Jesuits in France.	**1763.** *Feb. 15:* Peace of Hubertusburg between Prussia and Austria, which definitely cedes Silesia. *Oct. 5:* Augustus III of Saxony and Poland *d.* **1764.** *Apr. 11:* Treaty between Russia and Prussia to control Poland. *Sept. 7:* Stanislas Poniatowski elected King of Poland.	**1763.** *Feb. 10:* Peace of Paris; England secures St. Vincent, Tobago, Dominica, Grenada, Senegal, Canada, Nova Scotia, Cape Breton, Florida. **1764.** *Oct. 23:* English defeat Nawab of Oudh at Buxar. Hyder Ali usurps sovereignty of Mysore.
1765-1790. Leopold, brother of Josef II, Grand Duke of Tuscany.	**1765.** *Aug. 18:* Emperor Francis I *d.*; succeeded by Josef II (-**1790**).	**1765-1767.** Clive reforms Indian administration.

IV. CONSTITUTIONAL HISTORY	V. ECONOMIC HISTORY AND NATURAL SCIENCE	VI. CULTURAL LIFE
1758. *Oct. 9:* Choiseul appointed French Foreign Secretary.	**1758.** Bridgewater Canal from Liverpool to Leeds begun. Quesnay: *Tableau économique;* origin of Physiocratic school. Threshing machine invented.	**1758.** Helvétius: *De l'Esprit,* publicly burnt in Paris, **1759.** Diderot: *Le Père de famille.* Gleim: *Songs of a Prussian Grenadier.*
	1759. Frederick II leases Prussian coinage to Jewish company of Ephraim and Itzig.	**1759.** British Museum opened. Voltaire: *Candide.* Haydn: *First Symphony.* Lessing: *Letters concerning modern literature* (in collaboration with Nicolai and Mendelssohn). Bavarian Academy of Science founded. *Apr. 14:* Handel d.
	1760. Wedgwood establishes pottery works at Etruria, Staffs. Lambert invents photometry.	**1760.** Macpherson: *Fragments of Ancient Poetry. May 9:* Count Zinzendorf d. Israel ben Eliezer, founder of Jewish mystical movement of Chassidism, d.
1761. *Mar. 25:* Bute appointed Secretary of State. *Oct. 5:* Pitt resigns. Choiseul appointed Minister for War and Navy.	**1761.** Trade treaty between Prussia and Turkey.	**1761.** Rousseau: *Julie ou la Nouvelle Héloïse.* G. B. Morgagni: *On the Causes of diseases, based on anatomical reasons.*
1762. Social reforms of Peter III of Russia, cut short by his murder. *May 26:* Newcastle resigns; Bute, First Lord of the Treasury.		**1762.** Macpherson: *Fingal.* Rousseau: *Emile; Contrat Social.* Clavigo: *El Pensador,* rationalist periodical, Madrid. Gluck: *Orfeo.* Trial of Jean Calas at Toulouse. Wieland's translation of Shakespeare (**-1766**).
1763. *April 7:* Grenville succeeds Bute. Wilkes case arises. *Oct.:* Proclamation of George III promising administrative reforms in New England.		**1763.** Voltaire: *Treatise on Tolerance.* Justinus Febronius (Von Hontheim, Bishop of Treves): *De Statu Ecclesiae.*
1764. *Jan. 19:* Wilkes expelled from House of Commons.	**1764.** Watt invents condenser, first step towards steam-engine. Hargreaves invents spinning-jenny. Sugar Act reinforces Molasses Act of 1733.	**1764.** Beccaria: *Dei Delitti e delle Pene.* Winckelmann: *History of Ancient Art. Oct. 25:* Hogarth d. Pantheon built in Paris (**-1790**). H. Walpole: *Castle of Otranto.*
1765. *Mar. 23:* Stamp Act respecting the 13 Colonies passed. *July 16:* Grenville succeeded by Rockingham. *Dec.:* The Dauphin d.; Louis (XVI), his son, becomes heir.	**1765.** Turgot: *Réflexions sur la formation et la distribution des richesses.*	**1765.** Thomas Percy: *Reliques of Ancient English Poetry.* **1765-1769.** W. Blackstone: *Commentaries on the Laws of England.*

I. WESTERN AND SOUTHERN EUROPE	II. CENTRAL, NORTHERN, AND EASTERN EUROPE	III. COUNTRIES OVERSEA
1766. *Feb. 23:* Lorraine definitely incorporated in France.	**1766-1808.** Christian VII, King of Denmark; Struensee, chief Minister.	**1766.** English occupy Falkland Islands. *Nov. 12:* Treaty with Nizam Ali, who cedes Northern Circars to the English.
1767. Jesuits expelled from Spain and France.		**1767-1769.** Bougainville circumnavigates the world.
1768. France buys Corsica from Genoa.	**1768-1774.** War between Russia and Turkey.	**1768.** Gurkhas conquer Nepal. **1768-1773.** Ali Bey, leader of the Mamelukes, Sultan of Egypt.
1769. *Aug. 15:* Napoleon Buonaparte born at Ajaccio. **1769-1774.** Madame Dubarry, mistress of Louis XV.	**1769.** *Aug.:* Josef II and Frederick II meet at Neisse, Silesia.	**1769.** First appointment of a Secretary for the Colonies. Burma made tributary to China. **1769-1770.** James Cook's first voyage round the world; east coast of Australia discovered.
1770. *May 16:* Dauphin marries Marie Antoinette, daughter of Maria Theresa.	**1770.** *July 5-6:* Russians defeat Turks off Tchesme. *Sept.:* Josef II and Frederick II meet at Neustadt, Moravia.	**1770.** *Mar. 5:* Boston Massacre. Marathas bring Shah Alam II, emperor of Delhi, under their control.
	1771-1792. Gustavus III, King of Sweden.	**1771.** *Jan.:* Spain cedes Falkland Islands to Great Britain (unoccupied till **1833**).
	1772. *Aug. 5:* First partition of Poland; Russia obtains the territories east of Duna and Dnieper; Austria: Eastern Galicia and Lodomeria; Prussia: West Prussia, except Danzig, and Ermland.	**1772.** *Feb. 28:* Boston Assembly threatens secession from England unless rights of colonies are maintained. *Apr. 13:* Warren Hastings appointed Governor of Bengal. Parliamentary enquiry into Clive's administration.
1773. *Feb.:* Alliance between France and Sweden renewed. *July 21:* Clement XIV suppresses Jesuit Order. **1773-1796.** Victor Amadeo III, King of Sardinia. **1774.** *May 10:* Louis XV d.; succeeded by Louis XVI.	**1773.** *Oct. 16:* Denmark cedes county of Oldenburg to Russia.	**1773.** Regulating Act concerning East India Company; Hastings appointed Governor-General; Supreme Court established. *Dec. 16:* Boston Tea Party.
	1774. *July 21:* Peace of Kutchuk-Kainardji between Russia and Turkey, which cedes mouth of Dnieper and Crimea.	**1774.** *Sept. 21-Oct. 26:* First Congress of the 13 Colonies except Georgia meets at Philadelphia. Quebec Act establishes rights of French Canadians. *Nov. 22:* Clive d.
1775. England hires 29,000 German mercenaries for war in North America.	**1775.** *May 7:* Austria annexes the Bukovina from Turkey.	**1775.** *Apr. 19:* Battles of Lexington and Concord. *May 10:* Second Congress meets. *June 15:* Washington made commander-in-chief. *June 17:* English victory at Bunker's Hill. Austria acquires Delagoa Bay.

IV. CONSTITUTIONAL HISTORY

1766. *Mar. 11*: Stamp Act repealed; general warrants declared illegal. Declaratory Act, asserting right to tax American colonies. *July 12*: Grafton-Chatham Ministry succeeds Rockingham.

1768. *June 8*: Wilkes sentenced for libel.

1769. *Feb. 4*: Wilkes expelled from Parliament, but re-elected three times. *Letters of Junius* against the Ministry, probably by Sir Philip Francis.

1770. *Jan. 28*: Grafton resigns; succeeded by North; personal rule of George III. Wilkes elected Lord Mayor of London. *Dec. 24*: Fall of Choiseul; D'Aiguillon, French Premier.

1770-1772. Struensee's reforms in Denmark.

1771. Overthrow of French Parlements. Union of Baden-Baden with Baden-Durlach.

1772. Royal Marriage Act. *Aug. 19*: Revolution in Sweden with French support; Gustavus III re-establishes absolutism. *Oct. 28*: Struensee beheaded.

1773-1775. Social revolution in Southern Russia, under Pugachoff.

1774. *Mar. 28*: Coercive acts against Massachusetts which asked for removal of Governor. *June-July*: Maurepas appointed French Premier, Vergennes Foreign Secretary, Turgot Controller-General. *Aug.*: Louis XVI recalls Parlements.

1775. *July 19*: Malesherbes appointed French Minister of the Interior.

V. ECONOMIC HISTORY AND NATURAL SCIENCE

1766. Cavendish discovers hydrogen. Tobacco monopoly in Prussia.

1767. *May*: Townshend taxes American imports of tea, glass, paper, and dye-stuffs.

1768. Ministry for Mines and Forges established in Prussia. Quesnay: *La Physiocratie*.

1769. Prussian Herring Company formed at Emden.

1770. French East India Company dissolved. First public restaurant opened in Paris.

1771. Arkwright founds first spinning-mill in England. Serfdom abolished in Savoy.

1772. Rutherford discovers nitrogen. Carriage traffic begins across Brenner Pass. Bromberg Canal between Oder and Vistula begun (completed **1775**).

1773-1779. First cast-iron bridge built, near Coalbrookdale, Shropshire.

1774. Priestley's discovery of oxygen. Quebec Revenue Act.

1775. *Mar. 19*: Commercial treaty between Prussia and Poland. Watt constructs first efficient steam-engine. Girard invents water-turbine.

VI. CULTURAL LIFE

1766. Goldsmith: *Vicar of Wakefield*. Lessing: *Laocoön*.

1767. Sterne: *Tristram Shandy* (from **1759**). Lessing: *Minna of Barnhelm*. Wieland: *Agathon*. M. Mendelssohn: *Phaedon*.

1768. Sterne: *Sentimental Journey*. Reynolds President of the new Royal Academy. *June 8*: Winckelmann murdered at Trieste.

1769. Lessing: *Hamburgische Dramaturgie*. *Dec. 13*: C. F. Gellert *d.* Oberlin founds first creche, at Steintal, Alsace.

1770. Diderot: *Essai sur la peinture*. First German *Musenalmanach*, at Göttingen. *May 26*: Goldsmith: *The Deserted Village*. Holbach: *Système de la Nature*. *Aug. 25*: Chatterton commits suicide. *Sept. 14*: Censorship abolished in Denmark.

1771. First edition of the *Encyclopedia Britannica*. E. Forcellini: *Totius Latinitatis Lexicon*. Matthias Claudius: *Wandsbek Messenger* (-**1775**).

1772. *Nov. 2*: *Morning Post* appears (-**1937**). Lessing: *Emilia Galotti*. *Sept. 12*: *Hainbund* founded at Göttingen.

1773. Goethe: *Goetz von Berlichingen*. Herder: *Von deutscher Art und Kunst*; *Über Shakespeare*. Klopstock: *Messiah* completed. *German Mercury*, edited by Wieland (-**1789**). Bürger: *Leonore*.

1774. Goethe: *Sorrows of Werther*; *Clavigo*. Wieland: *Abderites*.

1775. Beaumarchais: *Le Barbier de Séville*, performed (written in **1772**). Lavater: *Physiognomy*. *Nov. 7*: Goethe arrives at Weimar. First complete German translation of Shakespeare by Eschenburg (-**1781**).

I. WESTERN AND SOUTHERN EUROPE	II. CENTRAL, NORTHERN, AND EASTERN EUROPE	III. COUNTRIES OVERSEA
	1776. *Apr.*: Provisional treaty of Exchange signed at Copenhagen; Russia cedes claims to Holstein.	**1776.** *Mar.*: Americans driven out of Canada. *July 4*: American Declaration of Independence. Viceroyalty of River Plate (Argentine, Bolivia, Paraguay, Uruguay) established.
1777. *Feb. 24*: Joseph I of Portugal *d*; succeeded by Maria I (**-1792**); fall of Pombal.	**1777.** *Mar. 22*: Oldenburg made dukedom under Frederick Augustus of Holstein-Gottorp. *Dec. 30*: Maximilian III of Bavaria *d.*; Josef II claims Bavaria.	**1777.** *Oct. 3*: Washington defeated at Germantown. *Oct. 17*: Burgoyne capitulates at Saratoga.
1778. *Feb. 6*: Offensive and defensive alliance between France and U.S.A.	**1778.** *Jan. 3*: Convention between Austria and Palatinate about partition of Bavaria. *July 3*: Prussia declares war on Austria on behalf of Bavaria.	**1778.** English take St. Lucia. *Sept.*: French take Dominica. Fernando Po and Annabon become Spanish.
1779. *June 16*: Spain declares war on England; unsuccessful siege of Gibraltar till **1783**.	**1779.** *May 13*: Peace of Teschen; Austria obtains Inn Quarter; Prussia obtains reversionary right to Ansbach and Bayreuth.	**1779.** French lose Senegal and Goree to England. **1779-1781.** First war with Mahrattas in India.
1780. *Nov. 20*: England declares war on Holland.	**1780.** *Mar. 10*: Russia declares armed neutrality between England and U.S.A.; Holland joins in. *June*: Meeting of Josef II and Catherine II. *Nov. 29*: Maria Theresa *d*.	**1780.** *May*: British take Charleston. *Aug. 16*: American defeat at Camden. *Sept. 10*: Hyder Ali conquers Carnatic.
	1781. *May*: Prussia joins League of Armed Neutrality.	**1781.** Portuguese gain Delagoa Bay from Austria. *July 1*: Hyder Ali defeated at Porto Novo. *Oct. 19*: Cornwallis capitulates at Yorktown.
1782. *Feb. 5*: English lose Minorca. *July*: Portugal joins League of Armed Neutrality.	**1782.** Pope Pius VI visits Vienna and Munich. Josef II abrogates Barrier Treaty.	**1782.** *Apr. 12*: French defeat off Les Saintes in West Indies. *May 17*: Treaty of Salbai ends Mahratta war. *Dec. 7*: Hyder Ali *d.*; succeeded by Tippoo Sahib.
1783. *Sept. 3*: Peace of Versailles between England, France, Spain, and U.S.A.; Spain keeps Minorca.	**1783.** Sicily joins League of Armed Neutrality.	**1783.** *Sept. 3*: Peace of Versailles; England recognizes U.S.A., and recovers her West Indian possessions; France recovers her East Indian possessions, St. Lucia, Tobago, Senegal, and Goree, and fishing rights off Newfoundland; Spain recovers Florida. Heraclius II of Georgia recognizes Russian suzerainty.

IV. CONSTITUTIONAL HISTORY

1776. *May 12:* Malesherbes resigns; Turgot dismissed; Necker appointed Director of Finances.

1777. *Feb.:* Habeas Corpus Act suspended. *Nov. 15:* Confederation Articles, first constitution of .U.S.A.; ratified **1781.** Bavaria, the Palatinate, and Jülich-Berg united under Charles Theodore, Elector Palatine.
1778. *May 11:* Earl of Chatham *d.* Relief Act for Roman Catholics in England.

1780. Secretary for the Colonies and Council of Trade abolished.

1781. *Jan.:* Necker publishes his *Compte-rendu. Mar. 20:* Turgot *d. May 19:* Necker dismissed. *Nov. 21:* Maurepas *d.*
1781-1785. Reforms of Josef II in Austria; abolition of serfdom; religious tolerance, freedom of Press (*Oct. 13,* **1781**), abolition of numerous monasteries.
1782. *Mar. 19:* Lord North resigns; succeeded by Rockingham. Ireland obtains legislative independence. *July 1:* Rockingham *d.;* succeeded by Shelburne.

1783. *Apr. 24:* Shelburne resigns; succeeded by Portland, with Fox and North. *July 17:* Besançon Parlement demands convocation of States-General. *Nov. 10:* Calonne appointed French Controller-General. *Dec. 19:* Pitt Ministry.

V. ECONOMIC HISTORY AND NATURAL SCIENCE

1776. Curr perfects construction of iron rails. Torture abolished in Austria. Adam Smith: *Inquiry on the Nature and Causes of the Wealth of Nations.*

1777. A Tailors' Co-operative Workshop formed at Birmingham.

1778. *Feb. 6:* Commercial treaty between France and U.S.A.

1779. First steam-mills in action. Arthur Young: *Political Arithmetic.*

1780. Galvani's important discoveries in electricity. Invention of steel pen by Harrison, water-gas by Fontana, circular saw by Gervinus. Watt constructs letter-copying press, Oliver Evans a lift.
1781. Coffee monopoly in Prussia. Swabian emigration into the Banat.

1783. Cort constructs puddling furnace; Evans, improved flour-mill. Serfdom abolished in Baden. First aerial voyages, by hot-air and hydrogen balloons, invented by the Montgolfier brothers and S. A. C. Charles.

VI. CULTURAL LIFE

1776. Klinger: *Storm and Stress.* Lenz: *Soldiers.* H. L. Wagner: *Child Murderess.* Vienna *Burgtheater* founded.
1776-1788. E. Gibbon: *Decline and Fall of the Roman Empire.*
1776-1786. Somerset House built by Sir Wm. Chambers.
1777. R. B. Sheridan: *School for Scandal.* Geo. Forster: *Journey round the World* (*i.e.* Cook's expedition). Haydn: *C-major Symphony.*

1778. *May 30:* Voltaire *d. July 2:* Rousseau *d.* Herder's collection of folk-songs (-**1779**). Frances Burney: *Evelina.*

1779. Lessing: *Nathan the Wise.* Goethe: *Iphigenia* (in prose). Gluck: *Iphigenia* (opera). Canova: *Orpheus and Eurydice; Dedalus and Icarus* (sculptures).
1780. Frederick the Great: *De la litiérature allemande.* Wieland: *Oberon.*

1781. Rousseau: *Confessions.* Schiller: *The Robbers.* Kant: *Critique of Pure Reason.* J. H. Voss: German translation of Homer's *Odyssey. Feb. 15:* Lessing *d. Mar. 13:* Sir Wm. Herschel discovers Uranus.

1782. Mozart: *Elopement from the Seraglio.*

1783. Schiller: *Fiesco.*

I. WESTERN AND SOUTHERN EUROPE	II. CENTRAL, NORTHERN, AND EASTERN EUROPE	III. COUNTRIES OVERSEA
1784. *May 20:* Peace of Versailles between England and Holland, which cedes Negapatam.	**1784.** Josef II proposes to exchange Bavaria for Belgium.	**1784.** *July 17:* France cedes St. Bartholomew to Sweden. *Aug.:* India Bill puts East India Company under government control.
1785. *Nov. 8:* Treaty of Fontainebleau; abrogates Barrier Treaty of **1715.**	**1785.** *July 23:* North German League against Josef II.	**1785.** *June:* Warren Hastings returns to England. Spanish Philippine Company established. Rajah of Kedah cedes Penang to England. *Sept. 10:* Commercial treaty between Prussia and U.S.A.
1786. Dutch Patriot Party deprives William V of command of army.	**1786.** *Aug. 17:* Frederick the Great *d.*; succeeded by Frederick William II (**-1797**).	**1786-1793.** Lord Cornwallis, governor-general of India.
	1787. Prussia intervenes in Holland in favour of William V against Patriot Party. **1787-1792.** Russia and Austria war against Turkey.	**1787.** *May:* Hastings impeached by Burke. *Sept. 17:* American Constitution passed. France intervenes in Annam. Settlement of Sierra Leone as asylum for negro waifs and slaves. North-West Territory of U.S.A. created.
1788. *Jan. 30:* Charles Edward Stuart *d.* in Rome. *Apr. 15:* Alliance between England and Holland, and (*Aug. 13*) Prussia. *Dec. 14:* Charles III of Spain *d.*; succeeded by Charles IV (**-1808**).	**1788-1790.** War between Russia and Sweden.	**1788.** *Feb.:* Trial of Hastings begins. *Jan. 26:* Penal settlements established near Sydney, Australia. *June 9:* Africa Association founded in London. *June 21:* American Constitution comes into force. *Sept. 13:* New York declared Federal capital and seat of Congress.
1789. *Oct.:* Revolution in Austrian Netherlands. *Dec. 13:* Declaration of their independence under name of Belgium.	**1789.** *Apr. 7:* Selim III succeeds Abdul Hamid as Sultan. Russo-Austrian alliance renewed. *July 31:* Austrians and Russians defeat Turks at Foksani and (*Sept. 22*) on the Rymnik. *Oct. 9:* Austrians take Belgrade.	**1789.** *Apr. 30:* Washington becomes President of U.S.A. *June:* Spaniards attack English at Nootka Sound, west of Vancouver Island. *Dec. 29:* Tippoo attacks Travancore.
1790. *Jan. 9:* Convention of Berlin between England, Prussia, and Holland concerning Belgium. *Dec. 2:* Austrians re-enter Brussels and suppress Belgian revolution.	**1790.** *Feb. 20:* Emperor Josef II *d.*; succeeded by Leopold II, Grand Duke of Tuscany. *July 27:* Treaty of Reichenbach between Austria and Prussia.	**1790.** *June 1:* English alliance with Marathas; *July 4:* with the Nizam. *Oct. 28:* Spain makes reparation for Nootka Sound affair.

IV. CONSTITUTIONAL HISTORY	V. ECONOMIC HISTORY AND NATURAL SCIENCE	VI. CULTURAL LIFE
1784. *Mar. 4:* Parliament dissolved; elections give Pitt large majority. *July 4:* Josef II abrogates Constitution of Transylvania. **1785.** Affair of Diamond Necklace ruins Marie Antoinette's reputation.	**1784.** Goethe discovers intermaxillary bone. **1785.** *Jan. 7:* First Channel crossing by balloon. A. Werner establishes science of geognosy at Freiberg, Saxony. Berthollet invents chemical bleaching, Salsano constructs seismograph, Cartwright power loom.	**1784.** Beaumarchais: *Mariage de Figaro.* Schiller: *Cabal and Love.* Herder: *Ideas toward a Philosophy of a History of Mankind* (**-1791**). **1785.** Mozart: *Marriage of Figaro.* Cowper: *Task.* London Society for the establishment of Sunday Schools founded. T. Reid: *Essays on the intellectual powers of Man* (against Hume).
1786. Consolidating Militia Act, Pitt appoints ' Commissioners for the reduction of the National Debt'. **1787.** *Feb. 13:* Vergennes *d. Feb. 22:* French Notables meet and reject Calonne's reform proposals. *Apr. 17:* Calonne banished and succeeded by Loménie de Brienne. *May 25:* Notables dissolved. **1788.** *Aug. 8:* French States-General summoned for May 5, **1789.** *Aug. 25:* Loménie dismissed. *Aug. 27:* Necker recalled to office. Prussian General Law-Code completed.	**1786.** *Sept. 26:* Commercial treaty between England and France, lowers duties on English clothes, cotton and iron goods, and on French wines, soap, and olive oil. Coal-gas employed as luminant. **1787.** Patrick Miller invents steamboat. Association for Abolition of Slave Trade is formed in England, chiefly by Quakers. **1788.** Tellerships of the Exchequer reduced to fixed salaries. Serfdom abolished in Denmark. Bentham: *Introduction to the Principles of Morals and Legislation.*	**1786.** Robert Burns: *Poems.* *Aug. 25:* Punctation of Ems, congress of German bishops, aiming at a National Catholic Church. **1786-1788.** Goethe's journey to Italy. **1787.** St. Pierre: *Paul et Virginie.* Goethe: *Iphigenia* (in verse). Schiller: *Don Carlos.* Heinse: *Ardinghello.* Mozart: *Don Giovanni. Nov. 15:* Gluck *d.* **1788.** *Jan. 1: The Times* appears. Kant: *Critique of Practical Reason.* Goethe: *Egmont. Aug. 2:* Gainsborough *d.* Linnæan Society founded. **1788-1791.** Brandenburger Tor, Berlin, built by Langhans.
1789. *Feb.:* Gustavus III establishes absolutism in Sweden. *May 5:* French States-General meet at Versailles. *June 17:* Third Estate declares itself National Assembly. *June 27:* Union of the three Estates. *July 14:* Fall of the Bastille. *Aug. 4:* Declaration of Rights of Man. *Oct. 5-6:* Louis XVI forced to move from Versailles to Paris. *Nov. 12:* France divided into 80 Departments. **1790.** *July 12:* Constitution Civile of French clergy. *July 14:* Festival on Champ de Mars. *Sept. 4:* Necker resigns.	**1789.** *July 4:* U.S.A. declare themselves an economic and customs unity. *Aug. 4:* Feudal system abolished in France. *Dec. 21:* Assignats issued in France. **1790.** General prohibition of coalition for employers and employees in England. Oxford - Birmingham canal opened.	**1789.** Goethe: *Tasso.* Lavoisier: *Traité Elémentaire de Chimie.* Blake: *Songs of Innocence.* Pestalozzi: *Lienhard and Gertrud* (begun in **1781**). **1790.** *Nov.:* Edmund Burke: *Reflections on the French Revolution.* Goethe: *Faust, A Fragment.* Kant: *Critique of Judgement.*

I. WESTERN AND SOUTHERN EUROPE	II. CENTRAL, NORTHERN, AND EASTERN EUROPE	III. COUNTRIES OVERSEA
1791. *Apr. 4* : Mirabeau *d. Sept. 4*: France annexes Avignon and Comtat-Venaissin.	**1791.** *Aug. 27*: Declaration of Pillnitz: Austria and Prussia ready to attack France if other sovereigns will join. *Aug. 30*: Peace of Sistova between Austria and Turkey; Turkey cedes Orsova.	**1791.** *May 6*: Canada Constitution Act passed. *Aug. 22*: Negro insurrection in San Domingo. Cornwallis takes Mangalore Vancouver discovers Snake lands, Broughton discovers Ch ham Islands. *Dec. 15*: First ten amendments to U.S.A. Constitution. *Mar. 4*: Vermont created U.S.A. State. Upper and Lower Canada separated. Washington, D.C., founded.
1792. *Apr. 20*: France declares war on Austria. *July 24*: Prussia declares war on France. *July 25*: Duke of Brunswick threatens destruction of Paris in Manifesto of Coblenz. *Aug.*: Prussians and Austrians invade France. *Sept. 20*: Battle of Valmy; Allies retreat. *Oct. 19*: French take Mayence and cross Rhine. *Nov. 6*: Dumouriez defeats Austrians at Jemappes and conquers Austrian Netherlands. *Nov. 27*: France annexes Savoy and Nice.	**1792.** *Jan. 9*: Peace of Jassy between Russia and Turkey; Russia obtains coast of Black Sea. *Jan. 18*: Ansbach and Bayreuth escheat to Prussia. *Feb. 7*: Austro-Prussian alliance against France. *Mar. 1*: Emperor Leopold II *d.*; succeeded by his brother Francis II. *Mar. 29*: Gustavus III of Sweden assassinated; succeeded by Gustavus IV (**-1809**). *May 19*: Russians invade Poland; Polish Constitution abrogated.	**1792.** *Feb. 5*: Tippoo defeated at Seringapatam; cedes half his territory. Charter granted to Sierra Leone Company. *June 1*: Kentucky created U.S.A. State. **1792-1839.** Ranjit Singh, ruler of the Sikhs.
1793. *Feb.*: First Coalition against France, of Britain, Austria, Prussia, Holland, Spain, Sardinia, Tuscany, and Naples. *Feb. 1*: France declares war on Britain and Holland; *Mar. 7*: on Spain. *Mar. 18*: Dumouriez defeated at Neerwinden; French lose Belgium. France annexes bishopric of Basle. *Apr. 4*: Dumouriez and Louis Philippe desert to Austrians. *Aug. 28*: Hood occupies Toulon. *Autumn*: New French offensive into Belgium and Rhineland. *Dec. 19*: French retake Toulon.	**1793.** *Jan. 23*: Russia and Prussia agree upon second partition of Poland. *Mar. 26*: Empire declares war on France. *May 7*: Second partition of Poland: Russia takes Poland east of Duna and Dnieper, Prussia secures Dantzig, Thorn, Posen, Gnesen, and Kalisz. *July 23*: Allies retake Mayence and drive French out of Germany. *Dec. 26*: Allies defeated by French at Weissenburg.	**1793.** British seize French settlements in India. Permanent Settlement of Bengal. *Apr. 23*: U.S.A. proclaim neutrality despite alliance of **1778** with France. *Nov.*: Sunday Islands discovered. Cornwallis reorganizes Indian justice, police, and revenue.
1794. *Apr. 19*: Treaty of the Hague between Britain, Prussia, and Holland. *June 1*: Howe defeats French in the Channel. *June 25*: Austrians defeated at Fleurus, lose Belgium. *Oct. 25*: Prussia denounces Treaty of the Hague and withdraws her troops. *Dec. 27*: French invade Holland.	**1794.** *Mar.*: Polish rising under Kosciusko, suppressed by Russians, who enter Warsaw on *Nov. 9*. *Sept. 28*: Anglo-Russo-Austrian alliance of St. Petersburg.	**1794.** *Feb. 12*: Mahdoji Sindhia, ruler of Central India, *d.* British take Guadaloupe, Martinique, Santa Lucia. French retake Guadaloupe. Aga Mohamad overthrows Send dynasty, and founds Kajar dynasty of Persia (**-1925**). Hamilton suppresses Whisky Rebellion in Pittsburgh.

IV. CONSTITUTIONAL HISTORY	V. ECONOMIC HISTORY AND NATURAL SCIENCE	VI. CULTURAL LIFE
1791. *May 3*: Polish Constitution proclaimed on French model. *June 20*: Flight of Louis XVI stopped at Varennes. *Sept. 3*: French Constitution passed. *Oct. 1*: Legislative Assembly meets at Paris.	**1791.** Inflation of French currency by immense issue of *assignats*. Freedom of trade introduced in France. First general strike in Germany (Hamburg). *July*: First bank of U.S.A. established.	**1791.** Mozart: *The Magic Flute.* J. Boswell: *Life of Johnson. Feb.*: Thos. Paine: *Rights of Man* (2nd part *Feb.* **1792**).
1792. *Mar. 24*: Ministry of the Gironde. *Apr.*: C. Grey founds Friends of the People Society. *June 20*: Mob invades Tuileries. *Aug. 10*: Mob storms Tuileries; massacre of Swiss Guard. Legislative Assembly suspends monarchy. *Aug. 13*: French Royal Family imprisoned in Temple. *Sept. 2*: Massacres in Paris prisons. *Sept. 21*: Convention meets. *Sept. 22*: French Republic proclaimed. *Dec. 5*: Trial of Louis XVI begins.	**1792.** National bankruptcy in France. Maximum prices introduced in France. Illuminating gas used in England for the first time.	**1792.** *Apr. 24*: *La Marseillaise*, by Rouget de l'Isle. *Feb. 23*: Sir Joshua Reynolds *d.* Galvani: *De viribus electricitatis.* The *Observer* begins to appear. James Hoban builds White House, Washington. William Thornton begins Capitol, Washington (completed **1830**). *Mar. 3*: Robert Adam *d.*
1793. *Jan. 21*: Louis XVI executed. *Apr. 6*: Committee of Public Safety set up. *June 2*: Fall of the Gironde; Reign of Terror begins. Civil war in Brittany and La Vendée. *June 24*: Second French Constitution drawn up. *July 13*: Marat murdered by Charlotte Corday. *Aug. 10*: Levée-en-masse. *Oct. 5*: Christianity abolished; new calendar. *Oct. 16*: Marie Antoinette executed. *Nov. 12*: Philippe Egalité executed.	**1793.** English Law concerning free insurance companies against sickness, invalidity and old age. First legal recognition of friendly societies. Board of Agriculture established in England. *Mar.*: Convention between Russia and England to interdict all trade with France in the Baltic.	**1793.** Goethe: *Reineke Fuchs.* Kant: *Religion within the boundaries of reason.* Fichte: *Two pamphlets, concerning the French Revolution.* Anacharsis Cloots: *Base constitutionelle de la république du genre humain.*
1794. *Mar. 24*: Hébertists executed. *Apr. 5*: Danton and followers executed. *July 28*: Robespierre executed. *Nov. 11*: Jacobin Club closed. Habeas Corpus Act suspended for eight years.	**1794.** Abolition of slavery in the French colonies. Foundation of the Ecole Polytechnique at Paris. First telegraph Paris-Lille. Eli Whitney invents cotton gin.	**1794.** *July 14*: Beginning of the friendship between Goethe and Schiller. Coleridge: *Fall of Robespierre*; *Ode on France.* Mrs. Radcliffe: *Mysteries of Udolpho.* Southey: *Wat Tyler* (publ. **1817**). Schiller: *Letters concerning the aesthetic education of mankind.*

I. WESTERN AND SOUTHERN EUROPE	II. CENTRAL, NORTHERN, AND EASTERN EUROPE	III. COUNTRIES OVERSEA
1795. *Feb. 9*: Tuscany makes peace with France. *Apr. 5*: Peace of Basle between France and Prussia: Prussia grants Rhine frontier; line of demarcation secures neutrality of Northern Germany. *June-Oct.*: Risings in Brittany, aided by English. *July 22*: Spain makes peace with France. *Autumn*: Austrians reconquer right bank of Rhine.	**1795.** *Jan. 3*: Secret treaty between Russia and Austria about final partition of Poland; *Aug.*: joined by Prussia. *Oct. 24*: Third partition of Poland: Prussia takes Warsaw and territory between Bug and Niemen, Austria takes Cracow and Western Galicia, Russia the rest. *Nov. 25*: Stanislas of Poland abdicates.	**1795.** *Feb.*: Dutch surrender Ceylon to Britain. *Mar. 11*: Mahrattas defeat Moguls at Kurdla. *Apr. 23*: Warren Hastings acquitted. *June*: French retake Santa Lucia. *Sept.*: British occupy Cape of Good Hope. Spain cedes her half of San Domingo to France.
1796. *May 10*: Bonaparte defeats Austrians at Lodi. *May 15*: Peace of Cherasco; Sardinia cedes Savoy and Nice. *Aug. 19*: Alliance of San Ildefonso between France and Spain. *Oct. 5*: Spain declares war on Britain. *Nov. 15-17*: Bonaparte defeats Austrians at Arcola.	**1796.** *Aug. 5*: Treaty between Prussia and France: Prussia yields possessions on left bank of Rhine in return for ecclesiastical territories. *Nov. 16*: Catherine II of Russia *d.*, succeeded by Paul I.	**1796.** British capture Demerara, Essequibo and Berbice. *June 1*: Tennessee created U.S.A. State. Agha Muhammad of Persia seizes Khorasan.
1797. *Jan. 14*: Bonaparte defeats Austrians at Rivoli. *Feb. 14*: Jervis and Nelson defeat Spaniards off Cape St. Vincent. *Apr. 15-June 16*: Naval mutinies at Spithead and the Nore. *Oct. 11*: Duncan defeats Dutch off Camperdown. *Dec. 16*: Peace Congress opens at Rastatt. *Dec. 29*: French capture Mayence.	**1797.** *Jan. 26*: Final treaty of Polish partition. *Apr. 18*: Preliminary peace between Austria and France, at Leoben. *Oct. 17*: Peace of Campo Formio: Austria cedes Belgium and Lombardy to France, obtains Istria, Dalmatia, and Venice; secret understanding concerning distribution of Germany. *Nov. 16*: Frederick William II of Prussia *d.*; succeeded by Frederick William III.	**1797.** *Feb.*: British take Trinidad and Santa Lucia. *Mar. 4*: John Adams becomes President of U.S.A. Wellesley appointed Governor of India. **1797-1832.** Fetch Ali, Shah of Persia.
1798. *Mar. 9*: France annexes left bank of Rhine. *Aug. 19*: Alliance between France and Helvetian Republic. *Oct. 27*: French attempt to invade Ireland fails. *Nov.*: British capture Minorca. *Nov. 29*: Ferdinand IV of Naples enters Rome. *Dec. 4*: France declares war on Naples.	**1798.** *Sept.*: Turkey declares war on France. *Dec. 24*: Treaty between Russia and England.	**1798.** *May 19*: French expedition to Egypt sets out. *July 21*: Battle of the Pyramids. *Aug. 1*: Nelson destroys French fleet at Aboukir. *Sept. 1*: Treaty of Hyderabad with the Nizam. British take Honduras from Spain. **1798-1800.** George XIII of Georgia.
1799. *Mar. 12*: Austria declares war on France. *June*: Second Coalition against France, of Britain, Russia, Austria, Turkey, Portugal, Naples. *Aug. 15*: French defeat at Novi. *Oct. 9*: Bonaparte lands at Fréjus.	**1799.** *Mar. 25*: Austrians defeat French at Stockach. *Sept. 19*: Anglo-Russian army defeated at Bergen. *Sept. 25-27*: Russians defeated at Zurich. *Oct. 22*: Russia leaves the Coalition.	**1799.** *Feb.*: Bonaparte advances into Syria. *May 4*: Tippoo defeated and killed at Seringapatam. *May 20*: Bonaparte checked at Acre. *July 24*: Bonaparte defeats Turks at Aboukir. *Aug. 22*: Bonaparte leaves Egypt.
1800. *Jan. 17*: Peace of Montluçon pacifies La Vendée. *June 14*: Bonaparte defeats Austrians at Marengo. *Sept. 5*: British capture Malta.	**1800.** *Dec. 3*: French defeat Austrians at Hohenlinden. *Dec. 16*: Northern Confederacy of Russia, Prussia, Sweden, and Denmark, against England.	**1800.** *Mar. 20*: Kleber defeats Turks and Mamelukes at Heliopolis. *June 14*: Kleber assassinated at Cairo. *Oct.*: France buys Louisiana from Spain.

IV. CONSTITUTIONAL HISTORY	V. ECONOMIC HISTORY AND NATURAL SCIENCE	VI. CULTURAL LIFE
1795. *Mar. . 8*: Girondists recalled. *Aug. 22*: Third French Constitution. *Oct. 26*: French Convention dissolved. *Nov. 3*: French Directory installed.	**1795.** Speenhamland Act (Poor Law): wages supplemented by doles.	**1795.** Condorcet: *Esquisse d'un tableau historique des progrès de l'esprit humain.* Foundation of the London Missionary Society. **1795-1827.** Soane builds Bank of England.
1796. *May 16*: Lombardic Republic established. *Oct. 16*: Cispadane Republic established.	**1796.** A. Senefelder invents lithography. E. Jenner vaccinates with lymph from cows for the first time.	**1796.** Goethe: *Wilhelm Meister's Apprenticeship.* de Maistre: *Considérations de la France.* Laplace: *Exposition du système du monde.* Joseph Haydn: *Emperor Quartet.* Burke: *Regicide Peace.*
1797. *May 16*: Venetian Constitution altered. *June 6*: Ligurian Republic established. *July 9*: Cisalpine Republic established. Burke *d. July 15*: Cispadane and Cisalpine Republics united.	**1797.** Bank of England suspends cash payment. *Sept. 30*: Repeated bankruptcy of State in France. England begins to export iron. Maudslay invents the metal lathe. *Oct. 22*: First parachute descent (from a balloon).	**1797.** Goethe: *Hermann und Dorothea.* Hölderlin: *Hyperion.* A. W. Schlegel begins his translation of Shakespeare. Chateaubriand: *Essai sur les révolutions anciennes et modernes.*
1798. *Jan. 22*: Government by Directory established in Holland. *Jan. 24*: Lemanic Republic (Geneva) proclaimed. *Feb. 15*: Roman Republic proclaimed. *Mar. 29*: Helvetian Republic proclaimed. *Dec. 9*: Charles Emmanuel of Sardinia forced to abdicate. **1799.** *Jan. 23–June 19*: Parthenopaean Republic (Naples). *July 12*: Political associations prohibited in England. *Nov. 9*: Bonaparte's *coup d'état*; Directory overthrown, Bonaparte made First Consul. **1800.** *Feb. 17*: French administration thoroughly centralized. *June*: Cisalpine Republic re-established. *July 2*: Act of Union of Great Britain and Ireland, effective *Jan. 1*, **1801.**	**1798.** Malthus: *Essay on the Principle of Population.* Emancipation of peasants on the left bank of the Rhine. England abolishes free coinage of silver. Invention of the voltaic pile. **1799.** Pitt introduces Income Tax (abolished **1802** and **1815-1842**). Russo-American Company obtains monopoly for Alaska. Louis Robert invents paper-machine. **1800.** Robert Owen starts social reforms at New Lanark. Fichte: *The Isolated Commercial State*; advocates state-socialism. Bonaparte begins road over Simplon (completed **1806**).	**1798.** Wordsworth and Coleridge: *Lyrical Ballads.* Journey to Germany of Wordsworth and Coleridge. A. W. and F. Schlegel publish Romantic periodical: *Athenaeum.* **1799.** Thomas Campbell: *Pleasures of Hope.* Schiller: *Wallenstein.* Schleiermacher: *Sermons, concerning Religion.* Church Missionary Society founded. **1800.** R. Burns (*d.* **1796**): *Works.* Schiller: *Mary Stuart.* Beethoven: *First Symphony.* R. College of Surgeons established. R. Institution established.

I. WESTERN AND SOUTHERN EUROPE	II. CENTRAL, NORTHERN, AND EASTERN EUROPE	III. COUNTRIES OVERSEA
1801. *Feb. 9*: Peace of Lunéville between France and Austria; France obtains left bank of Rhine; Tuscany transformed into Kingdom of Etruria under Louis of Parma (*d.* **1803**, *Oct. 9*). *Mar. 28*: Peace between France and Naples. *Oct. 9*: Peace between France and Turkey; Egypt restored to Turkey.	**1801.** *Mar. 23*: Paul I of Russia murdered, succeeded by Alexander I. *Apr. 2*: Nelson destroys Danish fleet off Copenhagen. *Apr.*: Prussia occupies Hanover and Bremen. Northern Confederacy dissolved, Russia reconciled to Britain.	**1801.** *Mar. 4*: Jefferson becomes President of U.S.A. *Mar.*: British capture Danish and Swedish islands in West Indies. *June 6*: Portugal cedes part of Guiana to Spain, by Treaty of Badajoz. *Sept.*: French evacuate Egypt. Rohilcund and Doab ceded to Britain. *Sept. 13*: Georgia annexed by Russia.
1802. *Jan.*: Bonaparte becomes President of Italian Republic. *Mar. 27*: Peace of Amiens between Britain and France; Britain promises to restore her conquests oversea. *Aug.-Sept.*: Bonaparte annexes Elba, Piedmont, Parma, and Piacenza.	**1802.** Russia and France agree on redistribution of Germany.	**1802.** French subdue Negro rebellion in San Domingo. *Oct. 23*: Holkar defeats Peshwa and Sindhia at Poona. *Nov. 29*: Ohio created U.S.A. State. *Dec. 31*: Treaty of Bassein: Peshwa surrenders independence to East India Company.
1803. *May 18*: Britain declares war on France. *July 23*: Insurrection of Robert Emmet in Ireland. *Sept. 19*: Emmet executed.	**1803.** *June*: French occupy Hanover. *Aug. 19*: Mecklenburg acquires Wismar from Sweden. *Oct.*: Russia and Turkey make peace with France.	**1803.** *Apr. 30*: U.S.A. buys Louisiana from France. *June*: British take S. Lucia and Tobago. *Aug. 3*: Second Mahratta War breaks out. *Sept.*: British take Dutch Guiana. *Sept. 23*: Wellesley defeats Sindhia at Assaye. *Dec. 30*: Sindhia submits.
1804. *Mar. 20*: Duke of Enghien executed. *Dec. 2*: Bonaparte crowned Emperor as Napoleon I. *Dec. 12*: Spain declares war on Britain.	**1804.** *Aug. 11*: Francis II assumes title of Emperor for his Austrian possessions.	**1804.** *June*: War breaks out with Holkar. *Nov. 13*: Holkar defeated at Dig. Wahabis capture Mecca and Medina. Hobart, Tasmania, founded.
1805. *Apr. 11*: Treaty of St. Petersburg between Britain and Russia; *Aug. 9*: joined by Austria. *June 4*: Napoleon annexes Genoa. *Oct. 21*: Nelson destroys Franco-Spanish fleet off Trafalgar.	**1805.** *Oct. 19*: Austrians capitulate at Ulm. *Dec. 2*: Napoleon defeats Austrians and Russians at Austerlitz. *Dec. 15*: Franco-Prussian treaty at Schönbrunn: Prussia to cede Cleves, Neuchâtel, and Ansbach in exchange for Hanover. *Dec. 26*: Peace of Pressburg between France and Austria.	**1805.** Wellesley recalled from India; Lord Cornwallis, governor-general (*d. Oct. 5*). *Nov. 23*: Peace treaty with Sindhia.
1806. *Jan. 23*: Pitt *d. Mar. 30*: Joseph Bonaparte created King of Naples; Eliza, Princess of Piombino; Pauline, Princess of Guastalla; Murat, Grand Duke of Berg; Berthier, Prince of Neufchâtel. *June 5*: Louis Bonaparte created King of Holland.	**1806.** *Feb. 15*: Treaty of Paris between France and Prussia against Britain. *Oct. 1*: Prussian ultimatum to Napoleon. *Oct. 14*: Napoleon defeats Prussians and Saxons at Jena and Auerstädt. *Dec. 11*: Peace of Posen between France and Saxony. *Dec.* War breaks out between Russia and Turkey.	**1806.** *Jan.*: British finally occupy Cape of Good Hope. British raids on Buenos Aires and Montevideo fail. Aaron Burr's conspiracy to make Louisiana independent.

IV. CONSTITUTIONAL HISTORY	V. ECONOMIC HISTORY AND NATURAL SCIENCE	VI. CULTURAL LIFE
1801. *Mar. 14*: Pitt resigns; Peace Cabinet of Addington. *Apr. 14*: Habeas Corpus Act again suspended. *July 15*: French Concordat restores Roman Catholicism.	**1801.** Danes occupy Hamburg and Lübeck and exclude English ships from the Elbe.	**1801.** Southey: *Thalaba*. Schiller: *The Maid of Orleans*. Haydn: *Seasons* (Oratorio). Elgin Marbles brought to London. Mir Amman: *Bagh-o-Bahar* (Garden and Spring), establishes modern Hindustani prose.
1802. *Aug. 2*: Bonaparte appointed Consul for life. French educational system reorganized. Legion of Honour instituted. Valais made independent republic.	**1802.** First protective law against child labour in England. J. W. Ritter constructs first accumulator.	**1802.** Chateaubriand: *Génie du Christianisme*. *Nov. 15*: Geo. Romney *d*. John Crome founds Norwich School. University of Dorpat founded. Dalton introduces into chemistry the law of combination and the atomic theory. Freedom of worship established in British Army.
1803. *Feb. 25*: *Reichsdeputationshauptschluss*: Diet of Ratisbon reconstructs Germany; most ecclesiastical princedoms and imperial cities abolished; four new electorates created. *Feb. 29*: Swiss Act of Mediation; Cantons regain their independence.	**1803.** Robert Fulton experiments with a steamboat on the Seine. Bonaparte begins road across Mont Cenis (completed **1810**).	**1803.** Arndt: *Germany and Europe*. Sunday School Union founded.
1804. *May 10*: Pitt forms Cabinet. *Mar. 21*: French *Code Civil* comes into force.	**1804.** Leslie: *On the Nature and Propagation of Heat*. *Oct. 27*: Stein appointed Prussian Minister of Trade.	**1804.** Schiller: *William Tell*. British and Foreign Bible Society founded.
1805. *May 26*: Napoleon becomes King of Italy; Eugene Beauharnais, Viceroy. *June*: Ligurian Republic united with France. *Dec. 26*: Bavaria and Württemberg created kingdoms; Baden, Grand Duchy.	**1805.** Abolition of internal customs duties in Prussia. Congreve reinvents the artillery rocket.	**1805.** Scott: *Lay of the Last Minstrel*. Wordsworth: *Prelude*. Beethoven: *Fidelio* (Opera). British Institution for the Development of the Fine Arts founded. *May 9*: Schiller *d*.
1806. *July 12*: Rhenish Confederation formed. *Aug. 6*: Francis renounces crown of Holy Roman Empire. *Dec. 11*: Saxony made kingdom, joins Rhenish Confederation.	**1806.** First agricultural institute in Germany. Rotation of crops introduced by A. Thaer. *Apr.*: England declares blockade of French coasts. *Nov. 21*: Berlin Decree: Napoleon closes Continental ports against English imports (Continental System).	**1806.** Arnim and Brentano: *Des Knaben Wunderhorn*. Beethoven: *Appassionata* (Sonata). D. Wilkie: *Village Politicians*. H. Davy's memoir on electrochemistry.

I. WESTERN AND SOUTHERN EUROPE	II. CENTRAL, NORTHERN, AND EASTERN EUROPE	III. COUNTRIES OVERSEA
1807. *Aug.*: Jerome Bonaparte created King of Westphalia; Erfurt incorporated in France. *Sept. 2-5*: British bombard Copenhagen and capture Danish fleet. *Oct.*: France and Russia declare war on Britain. *Nov. 13*: Portuguese dynasty of Braganza dethroned by Napoleon, flee to Brazil.	**1807.** *Feb. 7-8*: Napoleon defeats Russians and Prussians at Eylau. *May 29*: Selim III deposed. *June 14*: Battle of Friedland. *July 7*: Peace of Tilsit with Russia. *July 9*: Peace of Tilsit with Prussia; Prussia loses her possessions west of Elbe. *July 28*: Mahmoud II becomes Sultan. *Aug.*: Russians invade Finland. *Sept. 7*: French take Hither Pomerania from Sweden. *Oct.*: Denmark allies with France.	**1807.** Sierra Leone and Gambia organized as Crown colonies.
1808. *Jan.*: Napoleon annexes Etruria and (*Apr.*) Papal Legations. *May 2*: Spanish insurrection against French begins. *May 6*: King and Crown Prince of Spain forced to abdicate. *June 6*: Joseph of Naples made King of Spain; Murat, King of Naples. *Aug. 1*: English expedition lands in Portugal.	**1808.** *Oct.*: Erfurt Congress between Napoleon, Alexander of Russia, and Napoleon's vassals.	**1808.** First British mission to Persia fails. *Jan. 1*: Importation of slaves into U.S.A. prohibited.
1809. *Jan. 16*: Sir John Moore killed at La Coruña. *Apr. 22*: Wellesley takes command in Portugal. *May 1*: Napoleon annexes Papal State; Pius VII prisoner at Savona. *July 28-Dec. 23*: British expedition to Walcheren fails.	**1809.** *Feb. 8*: Austria decides upon war with France. *May 21-22*: Indecisive battle of Aspern. *July 5-6*: Napoleon defeats Austrians at Wagram. *Sept. 17*: Peace of Frederikshamn between Russia and Sweden; Russia obtains Finland. *Oct. 14*: Peace of Vienna: Austria cedes Trieste and Illyria to France, Galicia to Poland and Russia, Salzburg and Inn District to Bavaria.	**1809.** British take Martinique and Gaudaloupe. *Apr. 25*: Treaty of friendship between British and Sikhs.
1810. Napoleon annexes Holland (*July 9*), Valais (*Nov.*), Northern Hanover, Bremen, Hamburg, Lauenburg, Lübeck (*Dec. 10*).	**1810.** *Feb. 10*: Andreas Hofer, leader of Tyrolese rebellion against France and Bavaria, executed at Mantua.	**1810.** Col. Malcolm makes Anglo-Persian treaty. *July*: British capture Ile de Bourbon and Mauritius. Spanish colonies in America refuse to acknowledge Joseph Bonaparte.
1811. *Jan. 22*: Napoleon annexes Oldenburg. *May 8*: British defeat French at Fuentes d'Oñoro. *May 16*: British defeat French at Albuera.	**1811.** *Feb. 10*: Russians take Belgrade and capture a Turkish army.	**1811.** *Mar. 1*: Mehemet Ali massacres Mamelukes at Cairo. *Aug.*: British occupy Java. *Oct. 12*: Paraguay declares her independence of Spain and Argentina. War between Russia and Persia.

IV. CONSTITUTIONAL HISTORY	V. ECONOMIC HISTORY AND NATURAL SCIENCE	VI. CULTURAL LIFE
1807. Stein reforms Prussian administration. *Oct. 9*: Emancipation of Prussian peasants. *Nov. 19*: Town councils instituted in Prussia.	**1807.** Fulton navigates a steamship on the Hudson. Abolition of slave trade in British Empire. *Jan. 7, Nov. 11 and 25*: England declares blockade of coasts of France and her allies. *July 7*: Russia joins Continental System. *July 9*: Prussia joins Continental System. *Aug. 28*: Introduction of commercial law code in France. *Dec. 7*: Napoleon issues the Decree of Milan against British trade. **1808.** Freedom of trade established in Prussia. Co-operation begins between Bentham and James Mill.	**1807.** Byron: *Hours of Idleness.* Moore: *Irish Melodies.* Charles and Mary Lamb: *Tales from Shakespeare.* Turner: *Sun rising in a Mist.* Fichte: *Sermons, Addressed to the German Nation.* Hegel: *Phenomenology of Spirit.* Mme de Staël: *Corinne. Apr. 9*: John Opie *d.* **1808.** Scott: *Marmion.* Goethe: *Faust, Part I.* Kleist: *Penthesilea; Hermannsschlacht; Prince of Homburg; Michael Kohlhaas.* Beethoven: *Fifth Symphony.*
1809. *Mar. 29*: Gustavus IV of Sweden forced to abdicate; followed by Charles XIII. *July*: Metternich appointed chief Minister in Austria (-1848).	**1809.** *Jan. 9*: U.S.A. issues Non-Intercourse Act against British commerce. Sömmering (Munich) invents electric telegraph. *Apr. 26*: England restricts blockade of Europe. *Oct. 14*: Austria joins Continental System. Heathcote invents bobbin net machine.	**1809.** Byron: *English Bards and Scotch Reviewers.* Campbell: *Gertrude of Wyoming. Quarterly Review* founded. John Constable: *Malvern Hall.* Goethe: *The Elective Affinities.* Lamarck: *Système des animaux sans vertèbres.*
1810. Hardenberg continues Stein's reforms in Prussia. *July 1*: Louis, King of Holland, abdicates. *Aug. 18*: Charles XIII of Sweden adopts Bernadotte as heir. **1811.** *Feb. 5*: Regency Bill; Prince of Wales becomes Prince Regent for the insane George III.	**1810.** Founding of Krupp Works at Essen. *Jan. 6*: Sweden adopts Continental System. *Oct. 18 and 25*: Decrees of Fontainebleau, to confiscate and burn English goods. The 'Seehandlung' becomes Bank of Prussia. **1811.** *Feb. 2*: U.S.A. renews Non-Intercourse Act against English commerce. *Feb. 20*: State bankruptcy in Austria. *Mar.*: Luddites begin to destroy machines in England (-1815). *Apr. 1*: Civil Code introduced in Austria. *Dec.*: Secret agreement between Russia and England, aiming at breaking Continental System. Steam power used at Leeds to convey coal on a railway.	**1810.** Scott: *Lady of the Lake. Jan. 23*: John Hoppner *d. Nov. 11*: John Zoffany *d.* Kleist: *Käthchen of Heilbronn.* Mme de Staël: *De l'Allemagne.* Goethe: *Theory of Colours.* Berlin University founded. **1811.** T. MacCrie: *Life of John Knox.* Jane Austen: *Sense and Sensibility.* Niebuhr: *Roman History* (till **1832**). Fouqué: *Undine.* Two-thirds of Welsh Protestants secede from Anglican Church. **1811-17.** Sir John Rennie builds Waterloo Bridge.

I. WESTERN AND SOUTHERN EUROPE

1812. British victories in Spain. *Jan. 19:* Ciudad Rodrigo. *April 6:* Badajoz. *July 22:* Salamanca. *July 18:* Alliance of Örebro between Britain, Russia, and Sweden. *Aug. 12:* Wellington enters Madrid.

1813. *June 14-15:* Britain makes subsidy treaties with Russia and Prussia. *June 21:* Wellington defeats French at Vittoria. *Oct. 7:* Wellington crosses Bidassoa into France. *Nov. 15-17:* Dutch risings against French. *Nov. 30:* William of Orange returns. *Dec. 11:* Treaty of Valençay: Napoleon reinstates Ferdinand VII of Spain.

1814. *Jan. 5:* Murat joins Allies. *Feb. 3-Mar. 19:* Futile peace negotiations at Châtillon. *Mar. 30:* Allies enter Paris. *Apr. 11:* Napoleon abdicates, receives princedom of Elba. *May 30:* First Peace of Paris: France keeps frontiers of **1792;** Louis XVIII, King.

1815. *Mar. 1:* Napoleon lands in France; Louis XVIII flees. *Apr. 10:* Austria declares war on Murat, who had joined Napoleon. *June 8:* Congress of Vienna closes; Britain keeps Malta, Heligoland and most of her conquests oversea; Bourbons, Braganzas, Pope, and minor Italian princes restored; Holland, Belgium, and Luxemburg united; Switzerland neutralized. *June 18:* Wellington and Blücher defeat Napoleon at Waterloo. *June 22:* Napoleon abdicates. *July 7:* Allies enter Paris; Louis XVIII returns; White Terror in Southern France. *Aug. 8:* Napoleon banished to St. Helena. *Oct. 13:* Murat shot. *Nov. 5:* British protectorate over Ionian Islands. *Nov. 20:* Second Peace of Paris: France yields territories to Savoy and Switzerland and gives back captured works of art. *Dec. 7:* Ney shot.

II. CENTRAL, NORTHERN, AND EASTERN EUROPE

1812. *Feb. 24:* Prussia allies with France. *Apr. 9:* Secret treaty of Abo between Sweden and Russia. *May:* Napoleon invades Russia. *May 28:* Treaty of Bucharest between Russia and Turkey; Russia obtains Bessarabia. *Aug. 17:* Russian defeat at Smolensk. *Sept. 7:* Russian defeat at Borodino. *Sept. 14-Oct. 18:* Napoleon in Moscow. *Nov. 26-28:* Disaster to French army on Beresina. *Dec. 30:* Convention of Tauroggen between Russia and Prussia.

1813. *Feb. 28:* Alliance of Kalisz between Russia and Prussia; joined by Sweden. Campaign in Saxony and Silesia. *May 2:* Battle of Lützen. *May 20:* Battle of Bautzen. *June 4-Aug. 10:* Armistice. *Aug. 12:* Austria declares war on Napoleon. *Oct. 8:* Treaty of Ried: Bavaria joins the Allies. *Oct. 16-18:* Battle of Leipzig, Napoleon defeated.

1814. *Jan. 1:* Allies cross Rhine and invade France. *Jan. 14:* Treaty of Kiel between Sweden and Denmark; Denmark cedes Norway. *Nov. 1:* Congress of Vienna opens.

1815. *June 8:* Congress of Vienna closes: Poland placed under Russia; Lombardy and Venice restored to Austria; Prussia gains Rhineland and half Saxony; Hanover obtains East Friesland and Hildesheim; Cracow made independent Republic; organization of the German Confederation under Austrian presidency. *Aug. 26:* Holy Alliance formed by Russia, Austria, and Prussia; joined by the other European countries except Britain, Turkey, and Papal State.

III. COUNTRIES OVERSEA

1812. *Apr. 14:* Louisiana created U.S.A. State. *June 18:* U.S.A. declare war on Britain.

1813. Colombia breaks away from Spain, followed by Uruguay (**1814**), Chile (**1816**), and the other Spanish colonies. Peace of Gulistan: Persia cedes Caucasus district to Russia.

1813-1823. Marquess of Hastings, governor-general of India.

1814. Civil Courts installed in New South Wales. Christianity introduced into New Zealand. *Aug. 13:* Cape of Good Hope made British colony. War with Gurkhas of Nepal. *Dec. 24:* Treaty of Ghent between Britain and U.S.A. (*status quo*).

1814-1840. Francia, dictator of Paraguay.

1815. *Jan. 8:* British defeat at New Orleans. *Jan. 16:* British declare war on King of Kandy, Ceylon. Boer revolt in Cape Colony. *Oct.:* British occupy Ascension Island. *Dec. 16:* Brazil made Empire under John, Prince Regent of Portugal.

IV. CONSTITUTIONAL HISTORY	V. ECONOMIC HISTORY AND NATURAL SCIENCE	VI. CULTURAL LIFE
1812. *Mar. 18*: Spanish Cortes pass liberal Constitution. *June 9*: Conservative Ministry under Liverpool (**-1827**).	**1812.** *Mar. 11*: Emancipation of Jews in Prussia. *June 23*: England revokes Order in Council of *Apr. 26*, **1809,** as concerning American vessels.	**1812.** Byron: *Childe Harold's Pilgrimage* (**-1818**). Grimm: *Fairy Tales.* Baptist Union of Great Britain formed. New Toleration Act repeals Five Mile Act and Conventicle Act.
1813. *Oct*: Rhenish Confederation and kingdom of Westphalia dissolved; Hanover, Brunswick, Oldenburg, Hesse-Cassel restored.	**1813.** *July 1*: Abolition of trade monopoly of East India Company. State bankruptcy in Denmark.	**1813.** Shelley: *Queen Mab.* Jane Austen: *Pride and Prejudice.* Byron: *Giaour; Bride of Abydos.* Chamisso: *Peter Schlemihl.* Robert Owen: *A New View of Society.*
1814. *Apr. 11*: Norwegian Constitution; *Nov. 4*: accepted by Sweden. Louis XVIII grants Charter. *May 4*: Ferdinand of Spain abolishes Constitution. *Aug. 12*: Hanover created a Kingdom.	**1814.** *July 25*: Stephenson uses first effective steam locomotive. Apprenticeship and Wages Act of **1563** repealed.	**1814.** Scott: *Waverley.* Jane Austen: *Mansfield Park.* Wordsworth: *Excursion.* Byron: *Corsair; Lara.* Southey (Poet Laureate from **1813**): *Vision of Judgment.* Dulwich Gallery opened, first collection accessible to the public. Pius VII restores Inquisition, Congregation of the Index, and Jesuit Order.
1815. *May 22*: Frederick William III of Prussia promises Constitution. *June 1*: Napoleon issues liberal Constitution (Champ de Mai). *June 4*: Denmark cedes Pomerania and Rügen to Prussia. *Nov. 27*: Alexander I issues Polish constitution.	**1815.** *Feb.*: Ricardo: *Essay on the Influence of a Low Price of Corn on the Profits of Stock.* Puddling process introduced in England. John Macadam appointed Surveyor-General of British roads. *March*: Corn Law passed.	**1815.** Wordsworth: *White Doe of Rylstone; Laodamia.* Scott: *Guy Mannering.* Byron: *Hebrew Melodies.* Béranger: *Chansons I.* Canova: *Three Graces* (sculpture). D. Stewart: *Progress of Philosophy. Sept. 9*: J. S. Copley *d.*

I. WESTERN AND SOUTHERN EUROPE

1816-1826. John VI, King of Portugal (regent from 1792).

1817. *Sept. 17:* Anglo-Spanish treaty, opens West Indian trade to Britain.

1818. *Sept. 30-Nov. 21:* Congress of Aix-la-Chapelle: Allied troops evacuate France.

1819. *May 24:* Princess Alexandrina Victoria born.

1820. *Jan. 1-Mar. 7:* Revolution in Spain; Constitution restored. *Jan. 29:* George III *d.*, succeeded by George IV. *July 2:* Revolt in Naples. *Aug. 24:* Revolution in Portugal.

1821. Revolutions in Naples (battle of Rieti, *Mar. 7*) and Piedmont suppressed by Austrian troops. Victor Emanuel abdicates in favour of his brother Charles Felix (-1831).

1822. *Oct. 20-Dec. 14:* Congress of Verona discusses Spanish and Greek questions.

1823. *Apr. 7:* War between France and Spain begins. *Aug. 31:* French storm Trocadero and re-establish Ferdinand VII.

1824. *Sept. 16:* Louis XVIII *d.:* succeeded by Charles X (-1830).

II. CENTRAL, NORTHERN, AND EASTERN EUROPE

1817. *Oct. 18:* Wartburg Festival, reveals revolutionary tendencies of German students.

1819. *Mar. 23:* Kotzebue assassinated by a student. *Sept. 20:* Carlsbad decrees to check revolutionary and liberal movements in Germany.

1820. *Oct. 27-Dec. 17:* Congress of Troppau, to discuss concerted policy against revolutionary tendencies in Europe.

1821. *Jan. 26-May 12:* Congress of Laibach; resolves on measures against revolutions in Italy and Greece.

1823. *July 14:* Switzerland refuses right of asylum to foreign refugees.

1824. *Apr. 14:* Frontier Treaty between Russia and U.S.A.

III. COUNTRIES OVERSEA

1816. *Mar. 2:* King of Kandy deposed. *Mar.:* End of war with Nepal. *July 9:* Declaration of Independence of United Provinces of Rio de la Plata. *Dec. 11:* Indiana created U.S.A. State. Java restored to Holland.

1817. *Mar. 4:* Monroe becomes President of U.S.A. *Dec. 10:* Mississippi created U.S.A. State. Third Mahratta War.

1818. *Jan. 6:* Peshwa's dominions annexed, Rajputana States placed under British protection. *Oct. 20:* Frontier between U.S.A. and Canada defined. *Dec. 3:* Illinois created U.S.A. State.

1819. *Feb. 6:* British found Singapore. *Mar. 2:* Alabama created U.S.A. state. *Dec. 17:* Formation of the Republic of Colombia (Venezuela and New Granada) under Bolivar as President.

1820. *Oct. 24:* Spain cedes Floridas to U.S.A. *Mar. 2:* Missouri Compromise on slavery. *Mar. 3:* Maine created U.S.A. State. Egypt subdues Sudan and Kordofan (-**1822**). Washington Colonization Society founds Liberia for repatriation of negroes.

1821. *July 28:* Peru declares its independence of Spain. Republic of San Domingo founded. *Aug. 10:* Missouri made U.S.A. State. *Nov. 28:* Panama declares its independence of Spain and joins Republic of Colombia.

1822. *July 21:* Augustine de Iturbide crowned Emperor of Mexico. *Sept. 7:* Brazil declares itself independent of Portugal. *Oct. 12:* Dom Pedro proclaimed Emperor of Brazil.

1823. *Dec. 2:* President Monroe's message (Monroe Doctrine), closing 'the American continents to colonial settlements by non-American Powers' and excluding 'the European Powers from all interference in the political affairs of the American Republics.'

1824. *Feb. 24:* First Burmese War. *May 11:* British take Rangoon. *Dec. 12:* Last Spanish Army in South America capitulates.

IV. CONSTITUTIONAL HISTORY

1816. *May 5*: Carl August of Saxe-Weimar grants first German Constitution. *Nov. 5*: Diet of German Confederation meets at Frankfort.

1817. Turkey grants autonomy to Serbia.

1818. *May 26*: Bavarian Constitution. Prussia divided into ten provinces. *Aug. 29*: Liberal constitution in Baden.

1819. *Aug. 16*: 'Battle of Peterloo.' *Sept. 25*: Constitution of Württemberg. *Nov. 29*: Six Acts passed to preserve public order. *Dec. 7*: Constitution of Hanover.

1820. *May 24*: 'Final Act' of Vienna authorizing larger German states to interfere in affairs of smaller ones.

1821. *Apr.*: Greeks rise against Turks. *May 5*: Napoleon *d.* on St. Helena.

1822. *Aug. 12*: Castlereagh commits suicide; Canning appointed Foreign Secretary. *Sept. 23*: Portuguese constitution.
1823. Provincial Diets in Prussia.

1824. Charles X subdues growing liberalism in France.

V. ECONOMIC HISTORY AND NATURAL SCIENCE

1816. Gold standard restored in Britain. First protective tariff in U.S.A.

1817. D. Ricardo: *Principles of Political Economy and Taxation.* W. Cobbett: *Paper against Gold: the History and Mystery of the Bank of England.*
1818. *May 26*: Prussian customs law with a tendency to free trade. First steamer (*Savannah*) crosses Atlantic in 26 days. English Board of Agriculture abolished.

1819. Twelve-hour day for young workers in England. Adam Müller: *Necessity of a Theological Foundation of all Political Economics.* Serfdom abolished in Mecklenburg.
1820. First iron steamship in England. Robert Malthus: *Principles of Political Economy.*

1821. St. Simon: *Système industriel.* *May 1*: Bank of England resumes cash payments.

1822. Fourier: *Traité de l'association domestique agricole.*

1823. St. Simon: *Catéchisme des industriels.* Electromotor invented.

1824. Anti-combination laws repealed ; workmen in England allowed to combine.

VI. CULTURAL LIFE

1816. Shelley: *Alastor.* Scott: *The Antiquary.* Jane Austen: *Emma.* Goethe: *Journey to Italy.* Franz Bopp discovers relationship of Indo-European languages. Elgin Marbles bought by British Museum.
1817. Byron: *Manfred.* Thomas Moore: *Lalla Rookh.* John Constable exhibits his landscape paintings for the first time. Hegel: *Encyclopedia of Philosophy.*
1818. Keats: *Endymion.* Jane Austen: *Persuasion*; *Northanger Abbey.* Scott: *Heart of Midlothian.* Mary Wollstonecraft-Shelley: *Frankenstein.* Hazlitt: *Lectures on the English Poets.*
1819. Wordsworth: *Peter Bell.* Keats: *Eve of St. Agnes.* Byron: *Don Juan.* Scott: *Ivanhoe*; *Bride of Lammermoor.* Victor Hugo: *Odes.*
1819-22. H. W. Inwood builds St. Pancras' Church, London.
1820. Keats: *Hyperion.* Shelley: *Prometheus Unbound.* *London Magazine* begins to appear. Lamartine: *Méditations poétiques.*

1821. Manzoni: *The Fifth of May.* Scott: *Kenilworth.* De Quincey: *Confessions of an Opium Eater.* Shelley: *Adonais*; and *Epipsychidion.* Weber: *Freischütz.* Ecole des Chartes, Paris, founded. Hegel: *Philosophy of Right.*
1822. Beethoven: *Missa Solemnis.* Schubert: *A-Minor Symphony.* Heine: *Poems.* First cricket match between Eton and Harrow.
1823. Schleiermacher: *Christian Dogma.* C. Lamb: *Essays of Elia.* Scott: *Quentin Durward.* R. Smirke: British Museum (completed **1847**). *Apr. 23*: J. Nollekens *d.* *July 8*: Sir Henry Raeburn *d.*

1824. *Apr. 19*: Byron *d.* at Missolonghi. Scott: *Redgauntlet.* Landor: *Imaginary Conversations* (-**1829**). Victor Hugo: *Ballads.* Beethoven: *Ninth Symphony.* Ranke: *History of the Romanic and Teutonic Peoples.*

I. WESTERN AND SOUTHERN EUROPE

1825. *Jan. 4*: Ferdinand I of Naples *d.*; succeeded by Francis I (**-1830**). *Aug. 29*: Portugal recognizes independence of Brazil.

1826. *Mar. 10*: John VI of Portugal *d. May 2*: Pedro of Brazil waives claim to Portuguese throne in favour of his daughter Maria da Gloria.

1827. *Apr. 14*: Capodistrias elected President of Greece. *July 6*: Treaty of London between England, Russia, and France, to secure autonomy of Greece.
1828. *Feb. 26*: Dom Miguel takes oath as Regent of Portugal. *June 23*: Dom Miguel proclaimed King of Portugal.

1830. *Feb. 4*: Conference in London: Greece declared independent under protectorate of England, Russia, and France. *June 26*: George IV *d.*; succeeded by William IV. *Nov. 8*: Accession of Ferdinand II of Naples (**-1859**).

1831. *Feb.*: Austria suppresses revolutions in Modena, Parma, and the Papal state. *Oct. 9*: Capodistrias assassinated. *Nov. 15*: Britain and France agree on separation of Belgium from Holland.
1832. *Aug. 8*: Greek National Assembly elects Prince Otto of Bavaria King. *Nov.*: French take Antwerp, to force Holland to recognize independence of Belgium.

II. CENTRAL, NORTHERN, AND EASTERN EUROPE

1825. *Dec. 1*: Nicholas I succeeds Alexander I of Russia.

1826. *Apr. 4*: Protocol of St. Petersburg between Britain and Russia respecting Greek question; France accedes. *Oct.*: Convention of Akkerman between Russia and Turkey.

1827. *Oct. 20*: Turkish Fleet destroyed in bay of Navarino.

1828. *Apr. 27*: Russia declares war on Turkey. *Oct. 11*: Russians take Varna.

1829. *Sept. 14*: Treaty of Adrianople ends Russo-Turkish War; Sultan recognizes independence of Danube princedoms; Russia obtains land south of Caucasus.
1830. Revolutionary risings in Brunswick, Hesse, and Saxony. *Sept.*: Charles of Brunswick dethroned; Saxony receives Constitution. *Nov. 29*: Insurrection breaks out in Poland.

1831. *Sept. 8*: Russians take Warsaw.

1832. *May 4*: Russia accepts decisions of London Conference with regard to Belgium.

III. COUNTRIES OVERSEA

1825. *Feb. 28*: Treaty between Britain and Russia to settle boundaries between British and Russian America. *Aug. 6*: Bolivia declares independence. *Aug. 25*: Uruguay declares independence.
1826. War between Russia and Persia. *Feb. 24*: Treaty of Yandabu ends Burmese War. First Panamerican Congress at Panama, convened by Bolivar.
1826-1863. Dost Muhammad, Amir of Afghanistan.

1827. Russia takes Erivan from Persia. *Jan. 26*: Peru secedes from Colombia.

1828. Second Constitution of New South Wales. *Feb. 22*: Peace of Turkmantchai; Persia cedes part of Armenia to Russia.

1829. Swan River Settlement (Western Australia) founded *Mar. 4*: Jackson, President of U.S.A. *Dec. 4*: Suttee declared illegal in India.
1830. *June*: French conquer Algiers. Mysore and Cachar annexed by East India Company. Colombia divided into republics of New Granada, Venezuela and Ecuador. *Apr. 27*: Bolivar abdicates (*d. Dec. 10*).

1831. *Apr. 7*: Pedro I of Brazil abdicates in favour of his son Pedro II. *Nov. 17*: Venezuela, Colombia and Ecuador dissolve the union of **1819**. Garrison starts abolitionist periodical *The Liberator*.
1832. *Apr. 15*: Turkey declares war on Egypt. British sovereignty proclaimed over Falkland Islands.
1832-1848. Mohamad, Shah of Persia.

IV. CONSTITUTIONAL HISTORY	V. ECONOMIC HISTORY AND NATURAL SCIENCE	VI. CULTURAL LIFE
1825. Trade Unions recognized as legal in Britain. *Dec.*: Revolt in Russian army. James Mill: *Essays on Government* (-1828).	**1825.** First steam-locomotive railway, between Stockton and Darlington. St. Simon: *Nouveau Christianisme. Oct. 26*: Erie Canal opened.	**1825.** Pushkin: *Boris Godunov.* First edition of *Pepys's Diary.* J. Nash: Buckingham Palace; Marble Arch.
1826. *Apr. 26*: Liberal constitution in Portugal. First Parliament in Brazil.	**1826.** First German gasworks at Hanover. Ampère: *Electrodynamics.*	**1826.** Heine: *Reisebilder.* Fenimore Cooper: *Last of the Mohicans.* Disraeli: *Vivian Grey.* Lachmann: Critical edition of *Nibelungenlied.* First vol. of *Monumenta Germaniae Historica,* founded by Freiherr vom Stein. Mendelssohn-Bartholdy: *Overture to Midsummer Night's Dream. Dec. 7*: John Flaxman d.
1827. *Apr.*: Capodistrias elected President of Greek National Assembly. *Aug. 8.*: Canning d. *Sept. 5*: Conservative Ministry under Goderich.	**1827.** Ohm's Law concerning electric currents. Wöhler founds organic chemistry.	**1827.** Keble: *Christian Year.* Heine: *Book of Songs.* Manzoni: *I Promessi Sposi.* Victor Hugo: *Cromwell.* Schubert: *Trout Quintet.*
1828. *Jan. 25*: Wellington forms Conservative Ministry. Test and Corporation Acts repealed. *June*: Miguel revokes Portuguese Constitution.	**1828.** Prusso-Hessian, Bavaro-Württembergian, and Central German customs associations. St. Armand-Bazard: *Exposition de la doctrine de St. Simon* (-1830). Baltimore and Ohio railroad.	**1828.** Lamartine: *Harmonies poétiques et religieuses.* Mickiewicz: *Conrad Wallenrod.* W. Wilkins: University College, London. R. Smirke: King's College, London. Thomas Arnold appointed Headmaster of Rugby.
1829. *March 5*: Roman Catholic Relief Bill passes Commons and (*Apr.*) Lords. *Sept. 29*: Robert Peel remodels London Police ('Bobbies', 'Peelers').		**1829.** Balzac. *Les Chouans.* W. Irving: *Conquest of Granada.* First performance of *Faust* at Brunswick. King's College School founded.
1830. *July 25*: Charles X issues five *ordonnances. July 27-29*: Revolution in France. Charles X abdicates. *Aug. 7*: Louis Philippe of Orleans elected king. *Aug. 25*: Revolution begins in Belgium. *Nov. 16*: Wellington resigns; Grey forms Liberal Ministry. *Nov. 18*: National Council decrees independence of Belgium	**1830.** Liverpool-Manchester railway. Cobbett: *Rural Rides.*	**1830.** Tennyson: *Poems, chiefly Lyrical.* Charles Lyell: *Principles of Geology* (-1833). Pushkin: *Eugene Onegin.* Gautier: *Poésies.* Victor Hugo: *Hernani. Jan. 7*: Sir Thomas Lawrence d.
1831. Constitutions proclaimed in Saxony, Hesse-Cassel, Moldavia, and Wallachia. *Mar. 1*: Russell introduces Reform Bill. *June 4*: Leopold of Saxe-Coburg elected king of Belgium (-1865).	**1831.** Revolts of silk-weavers at Lyons. Faraday discovers electro-magnetism.	**1831.** E. Elliott: *Corn-Law Rhymes.* Victor Hugo: *Notre Dame de Paris.* J. Constable: *Waterloo Bridge.* T. L. Peacock: *Crotchet Castle.*
1832. *Feb. 26*: Polish constitution abolished. *May 27*: Hambach Festival of South German Democrats. *June 4*: Reform Bill passes House of Lords, and becomes law. *Aug. 17*: Irish Reform Bill.		**1832.** *Mar. 22*: Goethe d. Goethe: *Faust II.* Lytton: *Eugene Aram.* Balzac: *La Femme de trente ans; Contes drôlatiques.* Mazzini founds 'Young Italy' and, in Switzerland, 'Young Europe'. **1832-1838.** W. Wilkins builds National Gallery, London.

I. WESTERN AND SOUTHERN EUROPE	II. CENTRAL, NORTHERN, AND EASTERN EUROPE	III. COUNTRIES OVERSEA
1833. *Sept. 27*: Ferdinand VII of Spain *d.*: succeeded by Queen Isabella II (**-1868**).	**1833.** *July 8*: Treaty between Russia and Turkey to close Dardanelles to all but Russian ships. *Sept. 10-20*: Conference of Münchengrätz between Russia, Prussia, and Austria.	**1833.** *May 4*: Turkey recognizes independence of Egypt.
1834. *Apr. 22*: England, France, Spain, and Portugal form Quadruple Alliance in favour of liberal governments in Spain and Portugal. *May 26*: Dom Miguel of Portugal surrenders and abdicates at Evoramonte.	**1834.** *Apr. 3*: Rioting by Democrats at Frankfort. *June 30*: German Confederation forms committee for political investigations.	**1834.** Settlement at Port Phillip Bay (Melbourne), beginning of colony of Victoria. South Australia Act. *May 6*: Sikhs capture Peshawar.
	1835. *Mar. 2*: Francis I of Austria *d.*; succeeded by Ferdinand I.	**1835.** Peru and Bolivia become federal state (**-1839**). Dictatorship of Rosas in Argentina (**-1852**).
1836. *Oct. 29*: Louis Napoleon fails to seize Strasbourg and is exiled to America.		**1836.** Texas breaks away from Mexico and becomes independent (**-1845**). *June 15*: Arkansas made U.S.A. State. *Dec. 26*: Colony founded in South Australia.
1837. *June 20*: William IV *d.*: succeeded by Queen Victoria (**-1901**).	**1837.** *June 20*: Hanover separated from England. King Ernest Augustus suppresses Constitution.	**1837.** Papineau's rebellion in Canada. *Jan. 26*: Michigan made U.S.A. State. Dutch settlers found Natalia Republic.
1838. *Nov. 30*: France declares war on Mexico.	**1838.** Austrians evacuate Papal States except Ferrara.	**1838.** *Jan. 5*: Defeat of Canadian rebels at Toronto. *Oct. 1*: First Afghan War. *Dec. 16*: Boers defeat Zulus on Blood River, Natal.
1839. *Apr. 19*: Treaty of London finally establishes international status of Belgium: Closure of the Scheldt; Luxemburg becomes an independent grand duchy.		**1839.** *July*: Opium War with China; *Aug. 23*: Hong Kong taken. New Zealand proclaimed a colony and incorporated with New South Wales. War between Egypt and Turkey.
1840. *Oct. 10*: William I of Holland resigns in favour of his son, William II (**-1849**).	**1840.** *June 7*: Frederick William III of Prussia *d.*; succeeded by Frederick William IV.	**1840.** *Feb. 6*: Treaty of Waitangi; Maori chiefs hand over sovereignty over New Zealand to Britain. *Feb. 10*: Upper and Lower Canada united. *July 15*: Russo - Anglo - Prusso - Austrian Quadruple Alliance for protection of Turkey.

IV. CONSTITUTIONAL HISTORY

1833. Constitution granted in Hanover. *Sept. 29*: Civil war breaks out in Spain, ends in **1840** with the victory of the constitutional party. Constitution of Chile (in force till **1925**).

1834. *Aug. 14*: Poor Law Amendment Act. *Sept. 24*: Dom Pedro of Portugal *d.*; succeeded by Queen Maria da Gloria (-**1853**).

1835. *Apr. 8*: Peel resigns; *18*: Melbourne, Prime Minister. *Sept. 9*: Municipal Corporation Act.

1836. *Aug. 13*: Tithe Commutation Act.

1837. Struggle between State and Roman Catholic Church in Prussia. Liberal constitution in Spain.

1838. 'People's Charter' issued by Chartists.

1840. *Feb. 10*: Marriage of Queen Victoria to Prince Albert of Saxe-Coburg-Gotha. *Aug.*: Louis Napoleon again attempts to seize power. *Dec. 15*: Burial of Napoleon I in Invalides, Paris.

V. ECONOMIC HISTORY AND NATURAL SCIENCE

1833. *Mar. 22*: German *Zollverein* established. Gauss and Weber invent telegraph. *July*: Factory inspection introduced in England. *Aug. 28*: Act permitting freedom of trade with India and tea trade to China.

1834. New English law of inheritance sets individual before family. Robert Owen: *The Book of the New Moral World.* Revolt of silk weavers at Lyons. *Aug. 1*: Slavery terminated in British possessions.

1835. Baden joins *Zollverein*. *Dec. 7*: First German railway between Nuremberg and Fürth.

1836. Chartist movement (-**1848**). First train in London (to Greenwich). V. Considérant: *Destinée sociale.*

1837. Morse (New York) invents telegraph. Runge discovers aniline dyes in coal-tar. First patent for electric telegraph. First great depression in U.S.A.

1838. Beginning of regular steamship communication between England and America. *July 31*: First Irish Poor Law. *Aug. 1*: Abolition of slavery in India. *Sept. 24*: Anti-Corn-Law-League founded. First State railway (in Brunswick).

1839. *Mar. 9*: First prohibition of child labour in Prussia. Louis Blanc: *L'Organisation du travail.* J. v. Liebig begins researches into problem of diet. Invention of photography by Daguerre and Fox Talbot.

1840. *Jan. 10*: Rowland Hill introduces penny postage. Proudhon: *Qu'est-ce que la propriété?* ('*C'est le vol!*'). Cabet: *Voyage en Icarie.*

VI. CULTURAL LIFE

1833. *July 14*: Keble: *National Apostasy*; starts Oxford Movement. Browning: *Pauline.* Carlyle: *Sartor Resartus.* First public grant for education in England.

1834. Abbé de Lamennais: *Paroles d'un croyant.* Balzac: *Eugénie Grandet.* Wienbarg: *Aesthetische Feldzüge*, creates Young Germany movement. Lytton: *Last Days of Pompeii*, Marryat: *Peter Simple.* Mickiewicz: *Pan Tadeusz.*

1835. Browning: *Paracelsus.* Dickens: *Sketches by Boz.* Georg Büchner: *Danton's Death.* Bettina v. Arnim: *Goethe's Letters to a Child.* Gogol: *Dead Souls.* D. F. Strauss: *Life of Jesus.*

1836. Dickens: *Pickwick Papers.* Marryat: *Midshipman Easy.* Gogol: *Government Inspector.* Ranke: *History of the Popes.* Lamartine: *Jocelyn.*

1837. Carlyle: *French Revolution.* Dickens: *Oliver Twist.* Thackeray: *Yellowplush Papers. Jan. 11*: John Field, composer, *d. Jan. 20*: Sir J. Soane *d. Mar. 31*: John Constable *d.* Durham University refounded.

1838. E. A. Poe: *Arthur Gordon Pym.* Mörike: *Poems.* Schleiden: *Theory of Cellular Development of Plants.* Lamartine: *La chute d'un ange.* Dickens: *Nicholas Nickleby.* Tupper: *Proverbial Philosophy.*

1839. Immermann: *Münchhausen.* Stendhal: *La Chartreuse de Parme.* George Sand: *Spiridion.* W. Turner: *The Téméraire.*

1840. Browning: *Sordello.* Dickens: *Old Curiosity Shop.* Fr. Hebbel: *Judith.* Chas. Barry builds Houses of Parliament (completed **1852**). J. Slowacki: *Lilla Weneda* (Polish tragedy).

I. WESTERN AND SOUTHERN EUROPE

1841. *July 13*: France joins Convention of *July 15, 1840. July 8*: Espartero appointed Regent of Spain.

1843. *July*: Narvaez defeats Espartero, who leaves Spain; *Nov. 8*: Queen Isabella declared of age.

1846. *May 16*: Revolution in Portugal. *June 16*: Pius IX elected Pope (-1878).

1847. *Feb. 22*: Royal troops defeat Portuguese insurgents. *Sept. 3*: Espartero recalled to Spain.

II. CENTRAL, NORTHERN, AND EASTERN EUROPE

1841. *July 13*: Convention of the Straits: Collective guarantee by Europe of Turkish independence. The Porte agrees to close Dardanelles and Bosporus to men-of-war.

1844. *Nov.*: Holstein Estates pass resolution asserting independence of the Duchies of Holstein and Schleswig.

1845. Customs union between Moldavia and Wallachia. *Sept.*: 'Sonderbund' formed by Swiss Roman Catholic cantons.

1846. *July 8*: Christian VIII of Denmark repudiates independence of Schleswig-Holstein by 'open letter'. *Nov. 6*: Austria annexes Cracow.

1847. *May*: Poland made a Russian province. *Oct. 21 - Nov. 29*: Sonderbund war in Switzerland; Roman Catholic Cantons defeated, Sonderbund dissolved.

III. COUNTRIES OVERSEA

1841. *Mar. 4-Apr. 4*: W. H. Harrison, U.S.A. President; succeeded by J. Tyler. *July 15*: Egypt loses Syria to Turkey. Responsible Government established in Canada.

1842. *Jan. 1*: British forces in Afghanistan wiped out. *Aug. 9*: Webster-Ashburton treaty defines frontier between Canada and U.S.A. *Aug. 29*: Treaty of Nanking ends war in China: five ports opened to English merchants, Hong Kong ceded to England. *Aug.-Oct.*: Second Afghan War.

1843. *Feb.-Mar.*: British conquer Sind. *May 12*: Natal proclaimed British colony. Abolition of slavery in India.

1844. *Sept.*: French war in Morocco ends with treaty of Tangiers. Maori risings in New Zealand (-1848).

1845. Anglo-French expedition against Madagascar. *Mar. 3*: Florida and (*Dec. 29*) Texas made U.S.A. States. *Mar. 4*: James Polk becomes U.S.A. President. Mexico at war with U.S.A. (-1848); Mexico loses Arizona, New Mexico, and California. *Dec. 11*: Outbreak of Anglo-Sikh war.

1846. *June 15*: Treaty of Washington defines Oregon frontier. *Dec. 16*: Peace with Sikhs; Punjab brought under British control. *Dec. 28*: Iowa made U.S.A. State.

1847. Straits Settlements become Crown Colony. *Mar. 21*: Union of Central American Republics. *Aug. 24*: Liberia proclaimed independent.

IV. CONSTITUTIONAL HISTORY	V. ECONOMIC HISTORY AND NATURAL SCIENCE	VI. CULTURAL LIFE
1841. *Aug. 10*: Irish Municipal Act passed. *Aug. 28*: Peel succeeds Melbourne as Prime Minister.	**1841.** First law for the protection of workmen in France. F. List: *National System of Political Economy*.	**1841.** Sealsfield: *Kajütenbuch*. Emerson: *Essays*. Carlyle: *Heroes and Hero-Worship*. Browning: *Pippa Passes*. Warren: *Ten Thousand a Year*. *Aug. 26*: Hoffmann von Fallersleben: *Deutschlandlied*. Feuerbach: *Essence of Christianity*. Frederik Paludan-Müller: *Adam Homo* (-1848). *July 17*: Punch started.
1842. *Aug.*: Chartist riots in manufacturing districts.	**1842.** Ashley's Act forbidding child or female labour underground. Peel abolishes prohibition of imports of meat and cattle. James Nasmyth invents steam hammer.	**1842.** Tennyson: *Godiva*; *Locksley Hall*. Auguste Comte: *Cours de philosophie positive*. Robert Mayer: *Law of the conservation of energy*. Macaulay: *Lays of Ancient Rome*. Mudie's Lending Library opened in London.
1843. *May 18*: Disruption of Scottish Church; establishment of Free Church of Scotland.	**1843.** First workmen's Co-operative Societies (Pioneers of Rochdale). Anglo-Chinese commercial treaties. *The Economist* started.	**1843.** J. S. Mill: *System of Logic*. Wagner: *Flying Dutchman*. Macaulay: *Critical and Historical Essays*. Dickens: *Christmas Carol*.
1844. *Mar. 2*: Greek constitution. *July 19*: Bank Charter Act.	**1844.** Graham's Factory Act regulates working hours of women and children. First workmen's union in Germany. Weavers' riots in Silesia and Bohemia.	**1844.** Hebbel: *Mary Magdalen*. Disraeli: *Coningsby*. Heine: *Deutschland, Zeitgedichte*. J. von Liebig: *Letters on Chemistry*.
	1845. F. Engels: *Situation of the Working Classes in England*. *Aug.*: Beginning of potato disease in Ireland. First Roman Catholic journeymen's association, founded by Kolping.	**1845.** Disraeli: *Sybil*. Poe: *Tales of Mystery*; *The Raven*. Carlyle: *Cromwell*. Dumas, sen.: *Monte Cristo*. Wagner: *Tannhäuser*.
1846. Meeting of German professors at Frankfort ('Intellectual Diet of the German People'). *June 30*: Lord John Russell, Prime Minister; Palmerston, Foreign Secretary. **1847.** *Feb. 3*: United Diet summoned in Prussia.	**1846.** *May 23*: Repeal of Corn Laws. Invention of gun-cotton by Schönbein.	**1846.** Grote: *History of Greece* (-1856). Gottfried Keller: *Poems*. George Sand: *La mare au diable*. Mohl discovers protoplasm. Lear: *Book of Nonsense*.
	1847. Hamburg-America Line founded. Helmholtz: *On the Conservation of Energy*.	**1847.** Tennyson: *The Princess*. Ranke: *German History* (from 1839). Charlotte Brontë: *Jane Eyre*. Emily Brontë: *Wuthering Heights*. H. Hoffmann: *Struwwelpeter*.

I. WESTERN AND SOUTHERN EUROPE

1848. *Jan. 12:* Revolution in Sicily. *Feb. 21-24:* Revolution in Paris; Louis Philippe abdicates, Republic proclaimed. *Mar. 12:* Revolution in Venice, *(19)* Parma, and *(22)* Milan. *Mar. 23:* Sardinia declares war on Austria. *Apr. 8:* Austrian defeat at Goito. *Apr. 13:* Sicily declares itself independent of Naples. *Apr. 29:* Pius IX dissociates himself from Italian national movement. *Apr. 30:* Austrian defeat at Pastrengo. *May 15:* Communist riot in Paris. *May 29:* Austrian victory at Curtatone. *June 10:* Austrian victory at Vicenza. *June 23-26:* Cavaignac suppresses rising of Paris workmen. *July 25:* Austrian victory at Custozza. *Aug. 9:* Austro-Sardinian truce at Vigevano. *Sept. 8:* Naples recovers Sicily. *Nov. 15:* Count Rossi, Papal Premier, assassinated. *Nov. 24:* Pius IX flees to Gaeta. *Dec. 10:* Louis Napoleon elected President of the French Republic.

1849. *Feb. 7:* Grand Duke of Tuscany flees. *Feb. 9:* Rome proclaimed Republic under Mazzini. *Mar. 12:* Sardinia terminates truce. *Mar. 23:* Austrian victory at Novara; Charles Albert of Sardinia abdicates in favour of Victor Emanuel II (-**1878**). *Apr. 25:* French expedition lands in Papal State. *May 11:* Garibaldi enters Rome. *May 15:* Sicily submits to Naples. *June 13:* Communist riot in Paris. *July 3:* French take Rome. *July 28:* Austrians restore Grand Duke of Tuscany. *Aug. 6:* Peace of Milan between Austria and Sardinia. *Aug. 22:* Venice submits to Austria, after use of pilotless balloons (first **air-raid** in history).

II. CENTRAL, NORTHERN AND EASTERN EUROPE

1848. *Jan. 20:* Christian VIII of Denmark *d.*, succeeded by Frederick VII (-**1863**). *Mar. 13-15:* Revolution in Vienna; Metternich resigns. *Mar. 18-19:* Revolution in Berlin. *Mar. 23:* Denmark incorporates Schleswig. *Mar. 24:* German government formed in Schleswig-Holstein. *Apr. 23:* Prussians suppress Polish insurrection at Warsaw. *May 2:* Prussians invade Denmark. *May 11:* Austrians suppress revolt in Cracow. *May 15:* Second Revolution in Vienna. *June 17:* Austrians suppress Czech revolt in Prague. *Aug. 12:* Emperor Ferdinand returns to Vienna. *Aug. 26:* Truce of Malmö between Denmark and Prussia. *Sept. 12:* Kossuth proclaimed dictator of Hungary. *Oct. 6:* Third Revolution in Vienna. *Oct. 31:* Prince Windischgrätz takes Vienna. *Dec. 2:* Emperor Ferdinand abdicates in favour of his nephew, Francis Joseph (-**1916**).

1849. *Mar. 28:* Frederick William IV of Prussia elected ' Emperor of the Germans '. *Apr. 3:* Frederick William rejects imperial crown. *Apr. 14:* Hungary declares herself independent of Austria. *May 3-8:* Revolt at Dresden, suppressed by Prussians. *May 11-13:* Military revolt in Baden. *May 26:* Three Kings' League between Prussia, Saxony, and Hanover. *July 23:* Baden insurgents capitulate to Prussian troops at Rastatt. *Aug. 13:* Hungarian insurgents capitulate to Russian troops at Vilagos.

III. COUNTRIES OVERSEA

1848. *Feb. 3:* Sir Harry Smith annexes country between Orange and Vaal. *Mar.:* Second Sikh War breaks out. Liberia established as negro State. *May 29:* Wisconsin made U.S.A. State. *May 30:* United States acquire New Mexico, Texas, California, Nevada, Utah, Arizona, and parts of Colorado and Wyoming from Mexico. *Aug. 29:* Boers defeated at Boomplatz, retire across the Vaal. *Nov. 9:* Ibrahim, Viceroy of Egypt, *d.*; succeeded by Abbas (-**1854**).

1848-1856. Lord Dalhousie, Governor-General of India.

1848-1896. Nasr-ed-Din, Shah of Persia.

1849. Sikhs defeated at Chillianwallah (*Jan. 13*) and Gujerat (*Feb. 21*). *Mar. 4:* Z. Taylor becomes U.S.A. President. *Mar. 12:* Sikhs surrender at Rawal Pindi. *Mar. 30:* Britain annexes Punjab. *Apr.:* Insurrections in Canada. *May 1:* Convention of Balta Liman: joint Russo-Turkish supervision of Danubian principalities for 7 years. *Nov. 22:* Cape Colony forbids landing of convicts.

IV. CONSTITUTIONAL HISTORY	V. ECONOMIC HISTORY AND NATURAL SCIENCE	VI. CULTURAL LIFE
1848. *Feb. 10*: Constitutions in Naples; *Feb. 17*: Tuscany; *Mar. 4*: Piedmont; *Mar. 14*: Rome. *Mar. 31-Apr. 4*: German Ante-Parliament at Frankfurt. *Apr. 10*: Chartists present monster petition to Parliament. *Apr. 25*: Constitution in Austria, repealed *May 15*. *Apr. 27*: French National Assembly meets. *May 18*: German National Assembly meets at Frankfurt. *May 22*: Prussian National Assembly meets. *June 2*: Slavonic Congress meets at Prague. *June 29*: Archduke John elected Regent of the Reich. *July 22*: Habeas Corpus Act suspended. Austrian Reichstag meets. *Nov. 12*: Republican Constitution in France. *Dec. 5*: Prussian National Assembly dissolved, Constitution granted. *Dec. 28*: German National Assembly proclaims Fundamental Rights.	**1848.** *Jan. 24*: Gold discovered in California. *Feb.*: Marx and Engels: *Communist Manifesto. Feb. 25*: National workshops erected in Paris; abolished, *June 21*; Louis Blanc: *Droit au travail. May 1*: Ten-hour day in English textile industry for women and youths. Beginning of Christian Socialism in England. First Peace Congress in Brussels, under Richard Cobden. Labour Congress in Berlin; Labour Association formed. *Sept. 7*: Serfdom in Austria abolished. J. S. Mill: *Principles of Political Economy.* Public Health Act, first sanitary measure on Statute Book. Slavery abolished in French colonies.	**1848.** Thackeray: *Vanity Fair; Book of Snobs*. Pre-Raphaelite Brotherhood founded in London by 7 members, including Holman Hunt, Rossetti, and Millais. Balzac: *Comédie humaine* (complete edition, 100 vols., finished). Murger: *Scènes de la vie de Bohème.* Lowell: *Vision of Sir Launfal.*
1849. *Jan. 23*: Prussia suggests German Union without Austria. *Mar. 4*: Austrian Constitution granted. *Mar. 7*: Austrian Reichstag dissolved. *Mar. 27*: German National Assembly passes Constitution. *May 26*: French National Assembly dissolved. *May 30*: Prussia adopts three-class suffrage (-**1918**). *June 5*: Liberal Constitution in Denmark. *June 6*: German National Assembly moved to Stuttgart. *June 18*: German National Assembly dispersed by troops. *Aug. 27*: Austria rejects Prussian scheme of Union.	**1849.** *May 7*: Navigation Laws of **1651, 1661, 1662,** and **1823** repealed. *Feb. 9*: Prussia again obliges tradesmen to join a guild. Schultze-Delitzsch founds first credit-associations for working classes. Raiffeisen institutes co-operative loan banks in Germany. Prussia prohibits truck system. *Aug. 22*: Universal Peace Congress meets in Paris.	**1849.** Macaulay: *History of England* (-**1861**). A. de Lamartine: *Histoire de la révolution de 1848.* P. J. Proudhon: *Confessions d'un révolutionnaire.* Meyerbeer: *The Prophet.* A. Rethel: *Danse macabre* (series of drawings on the Revolution). Scribe: *Adrienne Lecouvreur.* Tischendorf's edition of the New Testament. *Oct. 17*: Chopin d.

I. WESTERN AND SOUTHERN EUROPE

1850. *Jan.*: British blockade the Piraeus owing to assault on British subject (Don Pacifico). *Apr. 12*: Pius IX re-enters Rome. *Aug. 2*: London convention to maintain integrity of Denmark, between Great Britain, France, Russia, Sweden, and Denmark.

1851. *Dec. 2*: *Coup d'état* of Louis Napoleon. *Dec. 20*: Plebiscite in favour of new French Constitution.

1852. *May 6*: Leopold II of Tuscany abolishes Constitution. *May 8*: Treaty of London guaranteeing integrity of Denmark, by Britain, France, Russia, Austria, Prussia, and Sweden. *Dec. 2*: *Coup d'état* in France: Napoleon III proclaimed Emperor.

1853. *Jan. 30*: Napoleon III marries Eugenia de Montijo. *June 4*: Anglo-French fleet assembled off Dardanelles. *Nov. 15*: Maria II of Portugal *d.*; succeeded by Pedro V (**-1861**). *Dec.*: Anglo-French fleet enters Black Sea.

1854. *Mar. 12*: Alliance between Britain, France, and Turkey. *Mar. 26*: Charles III, Duke of Parma, murdered. *Mar. 27 and 28*: Britain and France declare war on Russia. *May 18*: Western Powers declare blockade of Greece for having attacked Turkey; Greece promises neutrality. *Sept. 14*: Allied armies land in Crimea; battles of Alma (*Sept. 20*), Balaclava (*Oct. 25*), Inkerman (*Nov. 5*); *Oct. 17*: Siege of Sebastopol begins.

II. CENTRAL, NORTHERN, AND EASTERN EUROPE

1850. *July 2*: Peace of Berlin between Denmark and Prussia, which withdraws from Schleswig-Holstein. *July 24*: Schleswig-Holstein insurgents defeated at Idstedt. *Sept.*: Insurrection in Hesse-Cassel; Austria supports the Elector, Prussia the insurgents. *Oct. 26*: Russia intervenes in favour of Austria. *Nov. 28-29*: Convention of Olomuc; Prussia yields to Austria.

1851. *May 15*: Prussia again recognizes German Confederation. *Aug. 23*: German Diet appoints Reaction Committee to control small states, and abolishes Fundamental Rights.

1852. *Mar. 21*: Montenegro made a secular hereditary principality, under Danilo I.

1853. *Apr. 19*: Russia claims protectorate over Christians in Turkey. *May 21*: Turkey rejects Russian ultimatum. *July 2*: Russian army crosses the Pruth. *Oct. 4*: Turkey declares war on Russia. *Nov. 30*: Turkish fleet destroyed off Sinope.

1854. *Apr. 20*: Austro-Prussian defensive alliance against Russia. *June*: Austria occupies Danubian principalities.

III. COUNTRIES OVERSEA

1850. *Apr. 19*: Clayton-Bulwer agreement on a Central American canal. *July 9*: President Taylor *d.*; succeeded by M. Fillmore. *Aug. 5*: Australian Constitution Act: Victoria to be separated from New South Wales; South Australia and Tasmania granted representative government. Eighth Kaffir War breaks out (**-1853**). *Aug. 17*: Denmark sells her possessions on Gold Coast to Great Britain. *Oct.*: Taiping rebellion in China breaks out. *Sept. 9*: California admitted to U.S. as a free State; slave trade forbidden in District of Columbia.

1851. *July 1*: Victoria proclaimed a separate colony. *July 4*: Cuba declares its independence. *Sept.*: Spaniards suppress Cuban revolt. Basuto war breaks out (**-1853**). New Zealand Company dissolved.

1852. *Jan. 17*: Sand River Convention establishes South African Republic. Responsible government in New Zealand. *Dec. 20*: Britain annexes Pegu.

1852-1860. Russia acquires Amur and coastal provinces on Pacific.

1853. Constitution of Cape Colony. F. Pierce (Dem.) becomes U.S.A. President. *June 20*: Peace with Burma. *Dec. 11*: Britain annexes Nagpur. *Dec.*: Russia annexes Khiva. Central American Federation dissolved. France annexes New Caledonia.

1854. *Feb. 23*: Convention of Bloemfontein constitutes Orange Free State. *Mar. 31*: U.S.A. makes first treaty with Japan. *May 2*: Britain declares Monroe Doctrine not binding on European countries. Britain acquires Kuria Muria Islands off Arabia. *July 4*: Abbas, Viceroy of Egypt, *d.*; succeeded by Said. *May 30*: Kansas and Nebraska created territories of U.S.A. Republican Party founded in U.S.A.

IV. CONSTITUTIONAL HISTORY	V. ECONOMIC HISTORY AND NATURAL SCIENCE	VI. CULTURAL LIFE
1850. *Jan. 31:* Prussian Constitution granted (**-1918**). *Mar. 20:* Union Parliament meets at Erfurt. *May 31:* Universal suffrage abolished in France. *July 2:* Sir Robert Peel *d. Sept. 1:* Diet of German Confederation meets again; Prussia holds aloof. *Sept. 26:* Liberty of French Press restricted. *Oct.:* Cavour appointed Minister in Piedmont. Irish franchise extended.	**1850.** Customs union between Austria and Hungary. *Mar. 18:* Insurance for the aged introduced in France. R. W. von Bunsen invents Bunsen burner. Sunday rest introduced in Austria. Bastiat: *Les harmonies économiques.*	**1850.** Dickens: *David Copperfield.* Tennyson: *In Memoriam.* E. B. Browning: *Sonnets from the Portuguese.* Emerson: *Representative Men.* Robert Mayer: *On the Dynamical Equivalent of Heat. Aug. 28:* Wagner: *Lohengrin,* produced by Liszt at Weimar. Menzel: *Round Table of Sanssouci. Aug. 18:* Balzac *d. Apr. 23:* Wordsworth *d.* Tennyson, Poet Laureate. *Sept. 24:* Roman Catholic Church in England reorganized.
1851. *May 12:* Liberty of Prussian Press restricted. *Dec. 19:* Lord Palmerston resigns; Lord Granville appointed Foreign Secretary. *Dec. 31:* Austrian Constitution abolished.	**1851.** *Feb. 12:* Gold discovered in Australia. *May 1-Oct. 15:* Great Exhibition in London. *July 24:* Window tax repealed. *Sept. 7:* Commercial treaty between Prussia and Hanover. *Nov. 13:* First submarine cable from Dover to Calais.	**1851.** Ruskin: *Stones of Venice* (**-1853**). Proudhon: *Idée générale de la révolution au XIXe siècle.* Courbet: *Stonebreakers.* Verdi: *Rigoletto.* Schopenhauer: *Parerga and Paralipomena. Dec. 17:* William Turner *d.* Melville: *Moby Dick.*
1852. *Jan. 14:* French Constitution giving President monarchical power. *Jan. 23:* Orleans family banished from France. *Feb. 22:* Russell Ministry resigns. *Feb. 27:* Conservative Ministry (Lord Derby) (**-Dec. 18**). *Sept. 14:* Duke of Wellington *d. Nov. 4:* Cavour becomes Premier of Piedmont. *Dec. 11:* Disraeli's first budget. *Dec. 28:* Coalition Ministry (Lord Aberdeen).	**1852.** *July 26-27:* First congress of Co-operative Societies in London. Industrial and Provident Societies Act. Crédit Foncier, first great bank, founded in Paris. First airship flight, by Giffard.	**1852.** H. Beecher Stowe: *Uncle Tom's Cabin.* Thackeray: *Henry Esmond.* Dumas (fils): *La Dame aux Camélias.* Th. Storm: *Immensee.* Turgenieff: *A Sportsman's Sketches.* Jhering: *Spirit of Roman Law.* Kuno Fischer: *History of Modern Philosophy* (**-1893**).
1853. *Apr. 18:* Gladstone's first budget. *Aug. 28:* German Navy of **1848** sold by auction. *Nov. 21:* French plebiscite in favour of Imperial Constitution.	**1853.** Hanover and Oldenburg join German *Zollverein.* Prussia prohibits child labour up to age of 12. Telegraph system established in India. Cayley's man-carrying glider.	**1853.** Kingsley: *Hypatia.* Verdi: *Il Trovatore.* Wagner: *Ring des Nibelungen.* Leconte de Lisle: *Poèmes Antiques.* Mrs. Gaskell: *Cranford.* Charlotte Yonge: *The Heir of Redclyffe.*
1854. *June:* Colonial Secretaryship separated from War Secretaryship. *July:* Liberal revolt in Spain; the Regent, Maria Christina, exiled. *Oct. 12:* Prussian *Herrenhaus* (Upper House) established.	**1854.** *Jan. 1:* Commercial treaty between German *Zollverein* and Austria (**-Dec. 31, 1865**). *Mar. 31:* First commercial treaty of Japan (with U.S.). End of Chartist movement. Semmering railway, first railway across Alps. First railways in India and Brazil. Heinrich Goebel invents electric bulbs.	**1854.** Aug. Comte: *Système de politique positive,* completed. G. Freytag: *The Journalists.* H. Berlioz: *Te Deum. Dec. 8:* Dogma of the Immaculate Conception made an article of faith. *Dec. 9:* Tennyson: *Charge of the Light Brigade.* Th. Mommsen: *Roman History* (**-1856**) Thoreau: *Walden.* Working Men's College, London, founded.

I. WESTERN AND SOUTHERN EUROPE	II. CENTRAL, NORTHERN, AND EASTERN EUROPE	III. COUNTRIES OVERSEA
1855. *Jan. 26*: Piedmont joins in Crimean War. *Sept. 11*: Sebastopol capitulates to Allies. *Nov. 28*: Kars surrenders to Russians.	**1855.** *Mar. 2*: Nicholas I of Russia *d.*; succeeded by Alexander II (-**1881**). *Nov. 21*: Sweden allies with England and France against Russia.	**1855.** *Feb.-Mar.*: Chinese government suppress Taiping rebellion. Responsible government in all Australian colonies except Western Australia. Anglo-Afghan treaty against Persia.
1856. *Feb. 25-Mar. 30*: Peace Congress of Paris; Black Sea declared neutral, Danube declared free, integrity of Turkey guaranteed, Russia cedes Bessarabia, Danubian principalities guaranteed by the Great Powers. *Apr. 15*: Britain, France, and Austria guarantee integrity and independence of Turkey. *Apr. 16*: Declaration of Paris abolishes privateering, defines nature of contraband and blockade, recognizes principle of ' free ships, free goods '. *Dec. 2*: Franco-Spanish frontier fixed.	**1856.** *May 27*: Alexander II amnesties Polish insurgents. *July 12*: Austria amnesties Hungarian insurgents of **1848-49**. *Sept. 3*: Unsuccessful rising of Prussian royalists in Neufchâtel, Switzerland.	**1856.** *Feb. 13*: British annex Oudh. *May 7*: Natal made a separate colony. Tasmania made self-governing colony. *Oct. 8*: Arrow War of Britain and France against China. *Nov. 1*: War breaks out between Britain and Persia. *Nov. 3-4*: British fleet bombards Canton.
1857. Irish Republican Brotherhood (Fenians) founded. *Aug.*: Italian National Association founded.	**1857.** *June 19*: Prussia renounces sovereignty over Neufchâtel.	**1857.** *Mar. 4*: Peace of Paris between Britain and Persia. J. Buchanan (Dem.) becomes U.S.A. President. *Mar. 29*: Indian Mutiny breaks out. *May 25-June 1*: Chinese fleet destroyed by British Navy. *June 27*: Massacre of Cawnpore. *Sept. 19*: Delhi, and (*Dec. 6*) Cawnpore recaptured. *Dec. 29*: English and French take Canton. Britain annexes Perim.
1858. *Jan. 14*: Orsini attempts assassination of Napoleon III. *July 21*: Napoleon and Cavour meet at Plombières to prepare unification of Italy.	**1858.** *Feb.-July*: War between Turkey and Montenegro. *Oct. 7*: William, Prince of Prussia, declared Regent for insane King (' New Era '). *Nov. 8*: Boundaries of Montenegro fixed. *Dec.*: Serbian Diet deposes Alexander Karageorgevitch and declares Milan Obrenovitch king.	**1858.** *Mar. 21*: Lucknow captured. *May 12*: Minnesota admitted as U.S.A. State. *June 26*: Treaty of Tientsin; China opens several ports and admits European ambassadors. *Nov. 1*: Powers and territories of East India Company transferred to Crown. *Dec.*: Indian Mutiny finally suppressed. *Dec.*: France begins conquest of Cochin-China (-**1864**). British Columbia organized as Colony. Ottawa declared capital of Canada.

IV. CONSTITUTIONAL HISTORY	V. ECONOMIC HISTORY AND NATURAL SCIENCE	VI. CULTURAL LIFE
1855. *Feb. 6:* Liberal Ministry (Palmerston). *May:* Monasteries and Orders abolished in Piedmont. *Aug. 18:* Austrian Concordat, gives clergy control of education, censorship, and matrimonial law.	**1855.** Paris World Exhibition. Merchant Shipping Act. Hughes invents printing - telegraph. Austrian Creditanstalt, first bank for estate credits, founded. *June 15:* Stamp on newspapers abolished.	**1855.** Kingsley: *Westward Ho!* Longfellow: *Hiawatha.* Gobineau: *Essai sur l'inégalité des races humaines.* J. Burckhardt: *Cicerone.* F. Hebbel: *Agnes Bernauer.* G. Keller: *Der grüne Heinrich.* G. Freytag: *Soll und Haben.* W. Giesebrecht: *History of the Medieval Empire.* L. Büchner: *Force and Matter* (materialistic philosophy). Walt Whitman: *Leaves of Grass.* Trollope: *The Warden.*
	1856. Bessemer invents process of converting iron into steel. Production of aniline dyes begins. *Dec.:* Commercial treaty between Britain and Morocco.	**1856.** Louis Pasteur becomes Professor in University of Paris. *Feb. 17:* H. Heine *d.* Emerson: *English Traits.* Froude: *History of England* (-**1870**).
1857. *June 25:* Prince Albert created Prince Consort. *Aug. 25:* Court of Probate Act. *Aug. 28:* Matrimonial Causes Act.	**1857.** *Mar. 14:* Sound dues abolished by Denmark. *June 14:* Commercial treaty between France and Russia. Monetary convention of Vienna introduces silver standard in Austria and *Zollverein* countries. *Aug. 5:* Atlantic cable completed.	**1857.** Dickens: *Little Dorrit.* Cambridge University Bill. National Portrait Gallery founded. Buckle: *History of Civilization.* Thackeray: *Virginians.* Flaubert: *Mme Bovary.* Baudelaire: *Les fleurs du mal.* Trollope: *Barchester Towers.* **1857-1886.** Migne: *Patrologia Graeca.*
1858. *Feb. 19:* Palmerston resigns. *Feb. 25:* Conservative Ministry (Derby). *July 23:* Jewish Disabilities Bill passed. Property Qualification for Members of Parliament removed.	**1858.** *Jan. 15:* Alexander II begins emancipation of serfs in Russia. *Aug. 26:* Anglo-Japanese commercial treaty. *Sept. 1:* First cable from Britain to America. A. W. Hoffman discovers rosaniline. First European oil-well drilled at Wietze, Hanover.	**1858.** Tennyson: *Idylls of the King.* Carlyle: *Frederick the Great* (-**1865**). E. M. Arndt: *Wanderungen mit Frh. vom Stein.* P. Cornelius: *Barbier von Bagdad.*

I. WESTERN AND SOUTHERN EUROPE

1859. *Apr. 23:* Austrian ultimatum to Piedmont to disarm, rejected by Cavour. *Apr. 27:* Revolutions in Tuscany; *Apr. 28:* Modena; *May 1:* Parma. *Apr. 29:* Austrians cross Piedmont frontier. *May 3:* France declares war on Austria. *June 4:* Austrian defeat at Magenta; *June 24:* at Solferino. *July 11:* Preliminary Peace of Villafranca; Piedmont obtains Lombardy and Parma; Tuscany and Modena restored. *Nov. 10:* Treaty of Zurich, confirms Villafranca Treaty.

1860. *Mar. 11-12:* Plebiscites in Tuscany, Parma, Modena, Romagna in favour of union with Piedmont. *Apr. 15-22:* Plebiscites in Nice and Savoy in favour of union with France. *June 6:* Garibaldi takes Palermo. *Sept. 7:* Garibaldi enters Naples. *Sept. 11:* Victor Emanuel invades Papal State. *Sept. 18:* Defeat of papal troops at Castelfidardo. *Oct. 21-24, Nov. 4-5:* Plebiscites in Naples, Sicily, Umbria, and the Legations in favour of unification.

1861. *Feb. 14:* Francis II of Naples surrenders Gaeta. *Feb. 18:* Victor Emanuel proclaimed King of Italy. *June 6:* Cavour *d.* *Nov. 11:* Peter V of Portugal *d.*; succeeded by Louis I (-1869). *Dec. 14:* Prince Consort *d.*

1862. *Feb.:* France acquires Mentone and Roquebrune. *Aug. 29:* Garibaldi plans to take Rome; captured by royal troops at Aspromonte. *Oct. 26:* Revolution in Athens; King Otho abdicates (*d.* 1867, at Bamberg).

II. CENTRAL, NORTHERN, AND EASTERN EUROPE

1859. *Mar. 11:* Constitution of Holstein abolished. *July 2:* Prussia mobilizes against France. *Sept. 16:* German National Association founded by Bennigsen.

1860. *Aug. 13:* Danilo, Prince of Montenegro, murdered; succeeded by Nicholas (-1918).

1861. *Jan. 2:* Frederick William IV of Prussia *d.*; succeeded by William I (-1888). *Dec. 23:* Moldavia and Wallachia united as the Principality of Rumania, under Alexander Cuza.

III. COUNTRIES OVERSEA

1859. *Feb. 14:* Oregon created U.S.A. State. *May 13:* Queensland separated from New South Wales. *Oct. 16:* John Brown's raid on Harper's Ferry. *Oct. 22:* Spain declares war on Morocco.

1860. *Apr.:* Rising of Maoris in New Zealand. *Apr. 26:* Peace between Spain and Morocco. *May-July:* Massacre of Christians in Syria; Great Powers restore order. *Aug. 21:* Anglo-French troops take Taku forts. *Sept. 21:* Anglo-French troops defeat Chinese at Palikao. *Oct. 24:* Treaty of Pekin; China ratifies treaty of Tientsin. *Nov. 6:* Lincoln (Rep.) elected U.S.A. President. *Dec. 20:* South Carolina secedes from U.S.A. Vladivostok founded.

1861. *Jan. 29:* Kansas created U.S.A. State. *Feb. 4:* Congress of Montgomery; Confederation of 11 Southern States under President Davis. *Mar. 18:* Spain annexes San Domingo. *Mar. 19:* End of Maori rising. *Apr. 12:* Confederates take Fort Sumter; outbreak of American Civil War. *June 25:* Sultan Abdul Mejid *d.*; succeeded by Abdul Aziz (-1876). *July 21:* Victory of Confederates at Bull Run. *Oct. 31:* London Convention of Britain, France, and Spain to recover Mexican debts.

1862. *Apr. 13:* Treaty of Saigon between France and Annam; France annexes Cochin-China. France purchases Obok, opposite Aden. *Sept. 17:* Confederates defeated at Antietam. *Sept. 22:* Lincoln declares all slaves free from *Jan. 1,* 1863.

IV. CONSTITUTIONAL HISTORY	V. ECONOMIC HISTORY AND NATURAL SCIENCE	VI. CULTURAL LIFE
1859. *Mar. 31*: Ministry defeated on Disraeli's Reform Bill. *June 18*: Liberal Ministry (Palmerston). *July 13*: Cavour resigns. *Aug. 16*: Amnesty and extension of political rights in France.	**1859.** De Lesseps begins Suez Canal. First oil well discovered in U.S. First electric lighting plant in New York. *Dec. 24*: First ironclad launched at Toulon. Kirchhoff and Bunsen discover spectrum analysis.	**1859.** Darwin: *Origin of Species by means of Natural Selection.* J. S. Mill: *On Liberty.* G. Meredith: *Ordeal of Rich. Feverel.* Mistral: *Mirèio.* J. Offenbach: *Orpheus in the Underworld.* Gounod: *Faust.* Gontcharov: *Oblomov.* Tischendorf discovers Sinaitic MS. of New Testament.
1860. *Jan. 16*: Cavour recalled to office. *Mar. 5*: Power of Austrian Reichsrat enlarged. *Apr. 2*: First Italian Parliament meets at Turin. *Oct. 20*: Austrian Constitution (' October Diploma'). Turkish law reform, based on Code Napoléon. *Nov. 25*: Constitution of Peru.	**1860.** *Jan. 23*: Anglo - French commercial treaty (' Cobden Treaty'), with most-favourednation clause, abolishes English protective duties.	**1860.** J. S. Mill: *Treatise on Representative Government.* Fr. Spielhagen: *Problematic Natures.* J. Burckhardt: *Civilization of the Renaissance in Italy.* Multatuli: *Max Havelaar.* Ruskin: *Unto this Last.* Collins: *The Woman in White.* George Eliot: *The Mill on the Floss.*
1861. *Feb. 26*: Austrian Constitution centralized (' February Patent'). *Mar. 3*: Emancipation of serfs granted in Russia. *June*: German Progressive Party founded in Prussia. *Aug. 21*: Hungarian Diet dissolved, government by Imperial Commissioners.	**1861.** *Mar. 11*: German Commercial Law Code. *Sept. 2*: Commercial treaty between Prussia and China. *Sept. 16*: Post Office Savings Banks opened. P. Reis constructs telephone. Tariff Act in U.S.A.	**1861.** George Eliot: *Silas Marner.* *Mar. 13*: Wagner: *Tannhäuser*, produced in Paris. Hans Andersen: *Fairy Tales* (begun **1835**). E. Coremans founds Nederduitsche Bond for cultivation of Flemish language.
1862. *Sept. 23*: Bismarck appointed Prussian Premier. *Oct. 7*: Prussian Diet rejects increase of military credits. *Oct. 11*: Prussian Peers pass military budget. *Oct. 13*: Bismarck governs without budget until **1866**; ' blood and iron' speech.	**1862.** London World Exhibition. *Mar. 29*: Commercial treaty between Prussia and France, based on free-trade principles. *July 10*: Central Pacific Railway begun (opened *May 10*, **1869**). Gilbert founds first factory of Liebig's extract of meat in Uruguay. Lassalle: *Working-Class Programme*, advocates State Socialism. Companies Act, introduces Ltd. Liability Co.	**1862.** Henri Dunant: *Souvenirs de Solferino* (inspiration of Red Cross movement). Flaubert: *Salammbô.* Victor Hugo: *Les Misérables.* Turgenieff: *Fathers and Sons.* Scheffel: *Ekkehard.* Hebbel: *Nibelungen.*

I. WESTERN AND SOUTHERN EUROPE

1863. *Mar. 30*: William, Prince of Denmark, recognized as King of Greece; *July 13*: approved by Britain, France, and Russia (George I, -1913). *Nov. 14*: Britain cedes Ionian Islands to Greece.

1864. *Sept. 15*: Franco-Italian Treaty; Italy renounces her claims to Rome, France withdraws troops from Rome, Florence made capital. *Sept.*: Queen Maria Christina returns to Spain.

1865. *Oct.*: Bismarck and Napoleon meet at Biarritz; Napoleon acquiesces in Prussian ascendancy in Germany and a united Italy. *Dec. 9*: Leopold I of Belgium *d.*; succeeded by Leopold II (-1909).

1866. *Apr. 8*: Offensive and defensive alliance between Prussia and Italy. *June 12*: Secret treaty between Austria and France. *June 20*: Italy declares war on Austria. *June 24*: Italian defeat at Custozza. *July 4*: Austria cedes Venetia to Napoleon. *July 20*: Italian fleet destroyed off Lissa. *Oct. 21-22*: Plebiscite in Venetia in favour of Italy.

II. CENTRAL, NORTHERN, AND EASTERN EUROPE

1863. *Jan. 22*: Polish insurrection. *Feb. 8*: Prussia allies with Russia to suppress Polish rising. *Mar. 30*: Denmark incorporates Schleswig. *Oct. 1*: German Diet votes for federal action against Denmark. *Nov. 13*: Schleswig made Danish province. *Nov. 15*: Frederick VII of Denmark *d.*; succeeded by Christian IX (-1906).

1864. *Jan. 16*: Austro-Prussian ultimatum to Denmark. *Feb. 1*: Austro-Prussian troops enter Holstein. *Apr. 18*: Danish defeat at Duppel. *Aug. 1*: Preliminary Peace of Vienna. *Oct. 30*: Peace of Vienna; Denmark cedes Schleswig, Holstein, and Lauenburg.

1865. *Aug. 14*: Convention of Gastein; Austria obtains Holstein, Prussia: Schleswig and Kiel, Lauenburg sold to Prussia.

1866. *Feb. 22-23*: Alexander Cuza of Rumania dethroned; succeeded by Charles, Prince of Hohenzollern (-1914). *June 8*: Prussia annexes Holstein. *June 14*: Prussia declares German Confederation dissolved. *June 16*: Prussians invade Saxony, Hanover, and Hesse. *July 3*: Prussians defeat Austrians at Sadowa. *July 26*: Preliminary peace between Prussia and Austria at Nikolsburg. *Aug. 13, 17, 22, 23*: Peace treaties between Prussia and Württemberg, Baden, Bavaria, and Austria (Austria withdraws from Germany). *Sept. 7*: Prussia annexes Hanover, Cassel, Homburg, Nassau, Frankfort. *Oct. 21*: Peace between Prussia and Saxony.

III. COUNTRIES OVERSEA

1863. *Jan. 30*: Ismail succeeds Said as Viceroy of Egypt. *May 2-4*: Confederate victory at Chancellorsville. *May*: New rising of Maoris. *June 20*: West Virginia created U.S.A. State. *July 1-3*: Confederates defeated at Gettysburg; *4*: at Vicksburg. *Aug. 11*: French protectorate over Cambodia. *Nov. 24-25*: Confederates defeated at Chattanooga.

1864. *Apr. 10*: Archduke Maximilian accepts Mexican crown, supported by a French army. *Sept.*: British, French, and Dutch fleets attack Japan. *Oct. 31*: Nevada created U.S.A. State. *Dec. 22*: Savannah surrenders to Union army.

1865. *Apr. 9*: Lee, Confederate C.-in-C., capitulates at Appomattox; *26*: Last Confederate army capitulates at Durham. *Apr. 14*: Lincoln assassinated; succeeded by A. Johnson (Rep.) as President. *Sept. 2*: End of second Maori war. *Oct.*: U.S.A. demands recall of French troops from Mexico. Transportation of convicts to Australia abolished. Kaffraria incorporated in Cape Colony. Wellington made capital of New Zealand. *Dec. 18*: 13th Amendment to U.S.A. Constitution, abolishes slavery.

1865-1870. Paraguay wages war against Argentina, Brazil, and Uruguay.

1866. *May 21*: Sultan grants right of primogeniture to Ismail of Egypt.

IV. CONSTITUTIONAL HISTORY	V. ECONOMIC HISTORY AND NATURAL SCIENCE	VI. CULTURAL LIFE
1863. *Mar.:* Poland divided into 10 provinces. *Aug. 16 - Sept. 1:* Frankfort meeting of German princes to reform Confederation; Prussia opposes. Thiers forms French party opposed to Napoleon.	**1863.** *June:* Commercial treaty between France and Italy. *July 16:* Scheldt duties abolished. First international postal congress in Paris. *Crédit Lyonnais* founded as deposit bank. First underground railway (Metropolitan line, London). F. Lassalle founds General German Workers' Association; Bismarck discusses social and political reforms with him.	**1863.** J. S. Mill: *Utilitarianism.* Renan: *Vie de Jésus.* Whistler: *Symphony in White.* Longfellow: *Tales of a Wayside Inn.* *Dec. 24:* Thackeray *d.*
1864. *Jan. 13:* Provincial councils instituted in Russia.	**1864.** International Workers' Association founded in London. Right of combination granted to workers in France. Octavia Hill starts movement for housing reform in slum areas. National Bank Act in U.S.A.	**1864.** *Aug. 22:* Geneva Convention for Protection of Wounded (Red Cross). *Dec. 8:* Pius IX issues Syllabus Errorum, condemning Liberalism, Socialism, Rationalism (*Quanta Cura*). Newman: *Apologia pro Vita Sua.* W. Raabe: *Hungerpastor.*
1865. *Sept. 20:* Austrian Constitution temporarily annulled. *Oct. 18:* Palmerston *d.*; Russell becomes Prime Minister; Gladstone, Leader of the House. *Dec.:* Transylvania incorporated in Hungary.	**1865.** First voluntary arbitration in building trade, Wolverhampton. First international telegraph congress in Paris. *May 30:* Commercial treaty between Britain and *Zollverein.* *Dec. 23:* Latin Monetary Union of France, Italy, Belgium, and Switzerland. *Dec. 31:* Commercial treaty between Prussia and Italy.	**1865.** Clerk Maxwell: *Treatise on Electricity and Magnetism.* Wm. Booth founds Salvation Army. Lewis Carroll: *Alice in Wonderland.* Luise Otto-Peters founds German Women's Association. Victor Hugo: *Chansons des rues et des bois.* Tolstoy: *War and Peace.* W. Busch: *Max and Moritz.* *June 10:* Wagner: *Tristan and Isolde,* produced at Munich.
1866. *Feb. 17:* Habeas Corpus Act suspended in Ireland. *June 22:* Swedish Constitution altered; two Chambers instead of four Estates. *June 26:* Russell Ministry defeated on Reform Bill. *July 6:* Conservative Ministry (Derby). *Sept. 3:* Prussian Diet grants indemnity asked for by Bismarck. *Nov.:* National Liberal Party founded in North Germany. Danish Constitution altered in favour of king and Upper House.	**1866.** Submarine cable from Ireland to Newfoundland. W. Siemens invents dynamo. First condensed milk factory in Switzerland. Gothenburg system of State control of sale of spirits in Sweden. The (later Royal) Aeronautical Society founded in London.	**1866.** Huxley: *Elementary Philosophy.* F. A. Lange: *History of Materialism.* Verlaine: *Poèmes Saturniens.* Dostoievsky: *Crime and Punishment.* Ibsen: *Brand.* Thomas: *Mignon.* Smetana: *Bartered Bride.* Liszt: *Christus* oratorio. Mary Baker Eddy founds Christian Science. Haeckel: *General Morphology.* J. G. Whittier: *Snowbound.*

I. WESTERN AND SOUTHERN EUROPE

1867. *May 11:* London Conference guarantees neutrality of Luxemburg; Prussia evacuates the fortress. *Oct. 22:* Garibaldi marches on Rome. *Oct. 28:* French troops arrive in Rome. *Nov. 3:* Garibaldi defeated at Mentana.

1868. *Sept. 17:* Revolution in Spain headed by Marshal Prim. *Sept. 30:* Queen Isabella flees to France.

1869. *May 10:* Alliance between France, Italy, and Austria drawn up.

1870. *July 2:* Leopold, Prince of Hohenzollern, accepts Spanish crown ; *July 12:* withdraws his acceptance. *July 13:* French ultimatum to Prussia ('Ems dispatch'). *July 19:* France declares war on Prussia. French defeats at Weissenburg (*Aug. 4*), Wörth and Spicheren (*Aug. 6*), Vionville and Mars-la-Tour (*Aug. 16*), Gravelotte and St. Privat (*Aug. 18*), Sedan (*Sept. 1*). *Sept. 2:* Napoleon capitulates at Sedan. *Sept. 4:* Revolution in Paris, Republic proclaimed. *Sept. 19:* Siege of Paris begins. *Sept. 21:* Italians enter Rome. *Sept. 28:* Strasbourg and (*Oct. 27*) Metz surrender. *Nov. 16:* Amadeus, Duke of Aosta, elected King of Spain.

1871. *Jan. 17–Mar. 13:* London Conference, abrogates Black Sea neutrality clauses of **1856**. *Jan. 19:* French defeat at St. Quentin. *Jan. 28:* Paris capitulates. *Feb. 1:* French Eastern army crosses Swiss frontier. *July 2:* Rome made Italian capital. *Aug. 31:* Thiers elected French President.

II. CENTRAL, NORTHERN, AND EASTERN EUROPE

1867. *Apr. 17:* North German Confederation formed with Prussia as head; special treaties with South German States. *June 12:* Covenant ('*Ausgleich*') between Austria and Hungary: Dual monarchy with common foreign and military policies.

1868. *Mar.:* Prussia confiscates property of King of Hanover. *June 29:* Michael, King of Serbia, murdered; succeeded by Milan (-**1889**).

1870. *Oct. 3:* Baden asks to join North German Confederation. *Nov. 15 and 23:* Alliance treaties between North German Confederation and South German States.

1871. *Jan. 18:* William I proclaimed German Emperor at Versailles. *Feb. 26:* Preliminary treaty between Germany and France at Versailles. *May 10:* Franco-German peace treaty at Frankfort; France cedes Alsace and Lorraine, and pays 5 milliards of francs.

III. COUNTRIES OVERSEA

1867. *Mar. 1:* Nebraska made U.S.A. State. *Mar.:* Last French troops evacuate Mexico. *Mar. 30:* U.S. buys Alaska from Russia. *June 19:* Emperor Maximilian of Mexico shot. *July 1:* British North America Act establishes Dominion of Canada. *July 26:* Russia forms governor-generalship of Turkestan.

1868. *Jan.-Apr.:* British expedition against Abyssinia. *Feb. 8:* Shogunate abolished in Japan. *Mar. 12:* Basutoland proclaimed British territory. *May:* Russia occupies Samarcand. Third Maori war. *July 28:* 14th Amendment to U.S.A. Constitution, concerning civil rights.

1869. *Mar. 4:* General U. S. Grant (Rep.) becomes President of U.S.A. (-**1877**). *Mar. 9:* Britain buys territories of Hudson Bay Company. *Nov. 16:* Suez Canal opened. Fenian Rising in Western Canada.

1870. Manitoba made Canadian province. Western Australia granted representative government. Diamonds found in Orange Free State; Kimberley founded. *Mar. 30:* 15th Amendment to U.S.A. Constitution, concerning suffrage.

1871. Basutoland united with Cape Colony. *Oct. 27:* Britain annexes diamond-fields of Kimberley, Griqualand West. *Oct. 28:* Livingstone and Stanley meet at Ujiji.

IV. CONSTITUTIONAL HISTORY	V. ECONOMIC HISTORY AND NATURAL SCIENCE	VI. CULTURAL LIFE
1867. *Feb. 18*: Hungarian Constitution of **1848** restored. *Aug. 15*: Parliament Reform Bill passed. *Aug. 31*: First Socialist elected to North German Reichstag. *Dec. 21*: Austrian Constitution.	**1867.** *Jan. 28*: Prussia buys Taxis mail service. *July 8*: Customs treaties between North German Confederation and South Germany. Nobel invents dynamite. Typewriter and collotype process invented. Factory Inspection Act.	**1867.** Gautier, Verlaine, Baudelaire form Les Parnassiens (' *L'art pour l'art*'). Karl Marx: *Capital.* pt. 1. C. de Coster: *Uilenspegel*. Ibsen: *Peer Gynt*. W. Raabe: *Abu Telfan*. Strauss: *Blue Danube* waltz. University Extension courses organized by J. Stuart.
1868. *Feb. 25*: Lord Derby resigns; succeeded by Disraeli. *May*: Freedom of Press and of assembly granted in France. *July 17*: Edo, renamed Tokyo, made capital of Japan. *Sept. 8*: Parliamentary system adopted in France. *Dec. 9*: Gladstone forms Ministry, after Liberal victory at the polls.	**1868.** Bakunin founds *Alliance internationale de la démocratie sociale.*	**1868.** *June 28*: Wagner: *Meistersinger*, produced at Munich. R. Browning: *Ring and the Book*. W. Morris: *Earthly Paradise*. Manet: Portrait of Zola. Brahms: *German Requiem*. Haeckel: *History of Creation.*
1869. *Jan. 2*: Ollivier becomes French Premier. *Mar. 1*: Disestablishment of the Irish Church. *July 1*: Hereditary priesthood abolished in Russia. Wyoming introduces women's suffrage.	**1869.** *Oct. 1*: Austria introduces postcards. German Social Democratic Party founded. J. S. Mill: *Subjection of Women* (furthers feminist movement).	**1869.** *Dec. 8*: Vatican Council meets. Verlaine: *Fêtes galantes*. M. Arnold: *Culture and Anarchy*. College for Women (afterwards Girton College) founded in Cambridge.
1870. *June 25*: Isabella of Spain abdicates in favour of Alfonso XII. *Aug. 1*: Irish Land Bill. *Dec. 13*: German Centre Party (Roman Catholic) formed. *Dec. 30*: Marshal Prim assassinated in Madrid.	**1870.** German Bank founded. Austro-Hungarian Chamber of Commerce in Constantinople, first Chamber of Commerce abroad.	**1870.** Compulsory education in England. Keble College, Oxford, founded. Disraeli: *Lothair*. Schliemann begins to excavate Troy. D. G. Rossetti: *Dante's Dream*. Courbet: *Stormy Sea*. L. Anzengruber: *Pastor of Kirchfeld*. *June 6*: Dickens d. *July 18*: Dogma of Papal Infallibility declared by Vatican Council.
1871. *Feb. 2*: French National Assembly meets at Bordeaux. *Feb. 17*: Thiers elected head of the Executive. *Mar. 18-May 28*: Communist rising in Paris. *May 13*: Italian Law of Guarantees for the Pope. *July 8*: Prussia begins ' Kulturkampf' against Roman Catholic Church. *Aug. 14*: Local Government Board created.	**1871.** *June 29*: Trade Unions legalized. *July 20*: Purchase system in British Army abolished. *Dec. 4*: Germany adopts gold standard. Mont Cenis Tunnel made.	**1871.** Darwin: *Descent of Man*. C. F. Meyer: *Hutten's Last Days*. M. Bakunin: *Dieu et l'état*. First Impressionist exhibition at Paris. *Dec. 24*: Verdi: *Aïda*. **1871-1893.** Zola: *Les Rougon-Macquart*, 20 vols.

I. WESTERN AND SOUTHERN EUROPE

1872. *Apr.*: Don Carlos proclaimed King of Spain as Charles VII; civil war begins.

1873. *Jan. 9*: Napoleon III *d. Feb. 11*: Amadeus of Spain abdicates; Republic proclaimed. *May 24*: Fall of Thiers; MacMahon elected President. *Sept. 15*: Germans evacuate France. *Oct. 27*: French Pretender ('Henry V', Comte de Chambord) refuses to accept tricolour as national flag; destroys hope of restoration of monarchy.

1874. *Jan. 3*: Marshal Serrano becomes dictator of Spain.

1875. *Jan. 9*: Alfonso XII lands at Barcelona, recognized as king. *Jan. 30*: Republican constitution established in France. Britain and Russia intervene to avert Franco-German war.

1876. *Feb. 28*: Charles VII flees from Spain. *May*: Gladstone publishes *Bulgarian Horrors*. *Aug. 12*: Disraeli created Earl of Beaconsfield.

1877. *Jan. 1*: Queen Victoria proclaimed Empress of India. *Mar. 31*: London Protocol of Great Powers demands Turkish reforms. *May 16*: MacMahon appoints monarchist Ministry. *Oct. 14*: French republicans defeat MacMahon's policy at the polls.

II. CENTRAL, NORTHERN, AND EASTERN EUROPE

1872. *Sept.*: Meeting of Emperors of Germany, Russia, and Austria-Hungary in Berlin.

1873. *Oct. 22*: Alliance of Three Empires of Germany, Russia, and Austria-Hungary.

1874. *Jan. 13*: Russia adopts general conscription. *Oct.*: Count Arnim, late German Ambassador in Paris, prosecuted by Bismarck for having favoured monarchism. Iceland obtains self-government from Denmark.

1875. *July–Aug.*: Rising in Bosnia and Herzegovina. *Oct. 2*: Abdul Aziz promises reforms.

1876. *May 9–16*: Bulgarian massacres by Turks. *May 13*: Berlin Memorandum of Germany, Russia, and Austria insists on Turkish reforms. *June 4*: Abdul Aziz murdered. *July 2*: Serbia and Montenegro declare war on Turkey. *Aug. 31*: Abdul Hamid II becomes Sultan (**-1908**). *Oct. 30*: Turkish victory at Alexinatz.

1877. *Feb. 28*: Peace between Turkey and Serbia. *Apr. 12*: Sultan refuses London Protocol. *Apr. 24*: Russia declares war on Turkey. *June 27*: Russians cross Danube. *Nov. 18*: Russians storm Kars. *Dec. 10*: Turks capitulate at Plevna. *Dec. 14*: Serbia declares war on Turkey.

III. COUNTRIES OVERSEA

1872. *Feb. 2*: Holland cedes Gold Coast to Britain. *Feb. 8*: Lord Mayo, Viceroy of India, murdered. *July*: Burghers elected President of South African Republic. *Oct.*: Responsible government established in Cape Colony. West Griqualand annexed to Cape Colony. *Dec.*: San Juan Island assigned to U.S. by arbitration of German Emperor. Universal military service introduced in Japan.

1873. *Aug. 12*: Russia assumes suzerainty of Khiva and Bokhara. *Oct. 18*: Ecuador transformed into theocracy (**-1875**). Prince Edward Island joins Canada. Ashanti war breaks out.

1874. *Mar. 14*: Treaty of Fomena ends Ashanti war. *Mar. 15*: France assumes protectorate over Annam. *Oct. 25*: Britain annexes Fiji Islands.

1875. Delagoa Bay arbitration recognizes Portuguese claims. *Oct. 12*: Provincial Governments in New Zealand abolished. *Nov. 25*: Britain buys Suez Canal shares from Khedive.

1875–1908. Kwang-su, Emperor of China.

1876. *Feb. 26*: China declares Korea independent. *Mar. 5–7*: Abyssinians defeat Egyptians at Gura. New Constitution for New Zealand. Mixed tribunals established in Egypt. *Dec. 23*: Turkish Constitution granted. *Aug.*: Colorado created U.S.A. State. Japan acquires the Bonin Islands.

1877. *Mar. 4*: R. Hayes (Rep.) becomes U.S.A. President. *Apr. 12*: Britain annexes Transvaal. *Aug.*: Last Kaffir war breaks out. *Dec. 12*: Porfirio Diaz becomes President of Mexico (**-1880**).

IV. CONSTITUTIONAL HISTORY	V. ECONOMIC HISTORY AND NATURAL SCIENCE	VI. CULTURAL LIFE
1872. *June 19*: Jesuits expelled from Germany. *July 18*: Ballot Act. *July 28*: France adopts general conscription. Constitutional dispute begins in Denmark (**-1894**).	**1872.** *Nov.*: Anglo-French commercial treaty. National Union of Agricultural Workers founded. Union for Social Politics (*Kathedersozialisten*) founded in Germany.	**1872.** H. Spencer: *Study of Sociology*. D. F. Strauss: *The Old Faith and the New*. Daudet: *Tartarin de Tarascon*. *May 1*: Strasbourg University opened.
1873. *Mar. 13*: Gladstone defeated on Irish University Bill; Cabinet reshuffled. *Apr. 2*: Reform of Austrian franchise in favour of Germans. *May 11-14*: *Kulturkampf* Laws in Prussia. *Dec*: Papal Nuncio expelled from Switzerland. Italy abolishes monasteries in Rome and closes theological faculties. Flemish language admitted in courts in Flanders.	**1873.** Severe economic crisis in Europe, America, and Australia. Germany adopts Mark coinage. Drainage of Het Y, Amsterdam, begun (**-1877**). U.S.A. adopts gold standard. *Dec.*: National Federation of Employers formed.	**1873.** W. Pater: *Essays on the Renaissance*. P. Heyse: *Children of the World*. Jules Verne: *Round the World in 80 Days*. Ibsen: *Emperor and Galilean*. Brahms: *German Requiem*. W. Wundt: *Physiological Psychology*.
1874. *Feb. 2*: Conservative Ministry (Disraeli). *Aug. 7*: Public Worship Regulation Act; Endowed Schools Act. *May*: Austrian Concordat abolished. *May 29*: Swiss Constitution revised and centralized. Prussia dissolves Social Democratic Party.	**1874.** *Aug. 30*: Factory Act, institutes working week of 56½ hours. *Oct. 9*: *Union générale des postes* formed at Berne. France introduces factory inspectors and prohibits women working underground and child labour.	**1874.** Victor Hugo: *Ninety-Three*. J. Strauss: *Die Fledermaus*. Stubbs: *Constitutional History of England*.
1875. *May*: Prussia abolishes all Roman Catholic Orders and Congregations. *May*: Marxians and Lassalleans unite in German Socialist Labour Party at Congress of Eisenach.	**1875.** *July 1*: Universal Postal Union founded. *Aug. 13*: Agricultural Holdings Act, Land Transfer Act, Artisans' Dwellings Act. German Reichsbank founded. National bankruptcy in Turkey.	**1875.** Mme Blavatsky founds Theosophical Society. H. Taine: *Origines de la France Contemporaine*. Dictionary of German Biography begun. Bizet: *Carmen*. Mark Twain: *Adventures of Tom Sawyer*. Mrs. Eddy: *Science and Health*.
1876. *Jan.-Feb.*: Final victory of French republicans in elections. *Nov. 1*: Appellate Jurisdiction Act. German Conservative Party formed. Socialist People's Party formed in Russia.	**1876.** First International dissolved. Industrial and Provident Societies Act. Graham Bell invents telephone. Enclosure of Commons Act.	**1876.** F. Dahn: *Struggle for Rome*. C. F. Meyer: *George Jenatsch*. Bayreuth Festspielhaus opened: *Ring of the Nibelung*.
1877. Administration and procedure of justice unified in Germany. *Mar. 17*: First Turkish parliament meets.	**1877.** *Mar. 23*: Switzerland introduces factory inspection. Edison invents phonograph. First great railway strikes in U.S.A.	**1877.** J. P. Jacobsen: *Fru Marie Grubbe*. Ibsen: *Pillars of Society*. Tolstoy: *Anna Karenina*. Carducci: *Odi Barbare*. Gobineau: *La Renaissance*. Brahms: *1st and 2nd Symphonies*.

I. WESTERN AND SOUTHERN EUROPE	II. CENTRAL, NORTHERN, AND EASTERN EUROPE	III. COUNTRIES OVERSEA
1878. *Jan. 9*: Victor Emanuel of Italy *d.*; succeeded by Humbert (**-1900**). *Feb. 7*: Pope Pius IX *d.*; succeeded by Leo XIII (**-1903**). *June 4*: Britain acquires Cyprus from Turkey.	**1878.** *Jan. 9*: Turks capitulate at Shipka Pass. *Jan. 20*: Russians take Adrianople. *Mar. 3*: Preliminary Treaty of San Stefano. *June 13-July 13*: Berlin Congress: Bosnia and Herzegovina under Austrian administration, Russia gains Bessarabia, Rumania gains Dobrudja, Montenegro gains Antivari, Rumania and Serbia become independent, Eastern Rumelia semi-independent, of Turkey.	**1878.** *Mar.*: Britain annexes Walvis Bay. *Sept.*: War breaks out with Afghanistan. U.S.A., Germany, and Britain make commercial treaties with Samoa.
1879. *Jan. 30*: MacMahon resigns; Grévy elected French President. *June 1*: Prince Imperial killed in Zululand. *Nov. 27*: French Chamber removed from Versailles to Paris; amnesty for Communards.	**1879.** *Apr. 29*: Alexander of Battenberg elected Prince of Bulgaria. *Aug. 4*: Alsace-Lorraine declared *Reichsland* (Territory) under Governor-General. *Oct. 7*: Austro-German Dual Alliance.	**1879.** *Jan.-July*: Zulu war. *May 26*: Treaty of Gandamak fixes Indo-Afghan frontier. *Sept. 3*: British envoy murdered at Kabul. *Oct.*: British invade Afghanistan. *Dec. 16*: Transvaal Republic proclaimed. **1879-1883.** Saltpetre war of Chile against Bolivia and Peru.
	1880. *Nov. 26*: Montenegro occupies Dulcigno.	**1880.** *June 29*: France annexes Tahiti. *Sept.*: Afghan war ends. *Oct. 13*: Transvaal declares itself independent. *Oct. 16*: War breaks out with Transvaal.
1881. *Apr. 19*: Beaconsfield *d.*	**1881.** *Mar. 13*: Alexander II of Russia murdered; succeeded by Alexander III (**-1894**). *Mar. 26*: Prince of Rumania proclaimed king. *June 18*: Alliance of the Three Emperors renewed. *June 28*: Austro-Serbian alliance. *July 3*: Britain induces Turkey to cede Thessaly and Epirus to Greece.	**1881.** *Jan. 28*: British defeat at Laing's Nek. *Feb. 26*: British defeat at Majuba Hill. *Mar. 4*: J. Garfield (Rep.), U.S.A. President. *May 12*: France assumes protectorate of Tunis. *July 2*: President Garfield shot (*d. Sept. 19*). *Aug. 8*: Pretoria Convention restores South African Republic under British suzerainty. *Sept. 9*: Nationalist rising in Egypt under Arabi. *Sept. 19*: C. A. Arthur (Rep.), U.S.A. President.
1882. *May 6*: Phoenix Park murders of Lord Frederick Cavendish, Chief Secretary for Ireland, and his secretary, T. H. Burke. *May 20*: Italy joins Austro-German Alliance (Triple Alliance). *June 6*: Hague Convention fixes three-mile limit for territorial waters. *Dec. 31*: Léon Gambetta *d.*	**1882.** *Jan 6*: Milan of Serbia assumes title of king. *Apr. 4*: Prussian legation at Vatican restored.	**1882.** *July 11*: British bombard Alexandria. *Sept. 13*: British victory at Tel-el-Kebir, followed by occupation of Egypt and Sudan. Afrikander Bond formed in Cape Colony. *May*: Royal Charter for North Borneo Company. Italy occupies Assab and establishes colony of Eritrea.
1883. *Aug. 24*: Henry (V), Comte de Chambord, French Pretender, *d.*	**1883.** *Oct. 30*: Alliance between Austria and Rumania.	**1883.** *May*: Kruger, President of South African Republic. *Aug. 25*: French protectorate over Annam and Tonkin. *Sept.*: Stellaland Republic founded. *Oct. 20*: Peace of Ancón; Peru cedes saltpetre provinces to Chile. *Nov. 5*: British defeat at Kordofan.

IV. CONSTITUTIONAL HISTORY	V. ECONOMIC HISTORY AND NATURAL SCIENCE	VI. CULTURAL LIFE
1878. *May 11* and *June 2*: Attempts to murder Emperor William I. *Oct. 11*: Austria and Prussia annul clause in the Peace of Prague concerning plebiscite in Schleswig. *Oct. 18*: German Socialists outlawed. Flemish made official language in Flanders.	**1878.** *Feb. 28*: Bland-Allison Bill; U.S.A. re-introduces silver standard. Germany introduces factory inspection. Mannlicher invents repeating rifle. D. Hughes invents microphone. Factory and Workshop Act, regulating hours and conditions of employment.	**1878.** Sully-Prudhomme: *La Justice*. Th. Fontane: *Before the Storm*. G. Keller: *Züricher Novellen*. Millais: *Yeoman of the Guard*.
1879. *June 1*: Belgium introduces secular education (**-1884**). *June*: French laws against Jesuits. Taaffe becomes Premier of Austria-Hungary; end of German predominance in favour of Slavs.	**1879.** *July 12*: German protectionist laws. British Chamber of Commerce established in Paris. De Lesseps founds Panama Company. Edison constructs electric bulb. Henry George: *Progress and Poverty* (agrarian reform, single tax on land).	**1879.** G. Meredith: *The Egoist*. E. Arnold: *Light of Asia*. Zola: *L'Assommoir*. Strindberg: *The Red Room*. Ibsen: *Doll's House*. H. v. Treitschke: *History of Germany in the 19th cent.* (**-1894**). F. Th. Vischer: *Auch Einer*. St. Thomas Aquinas proclaimed Doctor Ecclesiae. Tchaikovsky: *Eugene Onegin*.
1880. *Apr. 28*: Liberal Ministry (Gladstone). *June 29*: Papal Nuncio expelled from Belgium. *Oct.-Nov.*: Roman Catholic Orders expelled from France.	**1880.** *Aug. 2*: Relief of Distress Act for Ireland. *Sept. 7*: Employers' Liability Bill. Switzerland suggests international legislation for protection of workmen. ' Boycotting ' in Ireland.	**1880.** L. Wallace: *Ben Hur*. J. P. Jacobsen: *Niels Lyhne*. Dostoevsky: *Brothers Karamazov*.
1881. *Nov. 14*: Gambetta forms ' Grand Ministry ' (*-Jan. 1882*).	**1881.** Canadian Pacific Railway Co. formed. *Feb. 1*: De Lesseps begins Panama Canal. Federation of Labor Unions of U.S.A. and Canada founded. Rockefeller founds Standard Oil Co. (first trust). *Aug. 22*: Irish Land Law Act.	**1881.** Revised Version of New Testament. P. Verlaine: *Sagesse*. E. Pailleron: *Le Monde où l'on s'ennuie*. Ibsen: *Ghosts*. Carmen Sylva: *Roumanian Poems*. A. France: *Le Crime de Sylvestre Bonnard*. L. Ranke: *History of the World* (**-1888**). Vatican Archives opened to historians. Henry James: *Portrait of a Lady*.
1882. Municipal Corporations Act. Consolidation (Militia) Act. Primrose League founded. *Jan. 22*: Italian Electoral Reform.	**1882.** Immigration of Chinese labourers prohibited in California. Cotton duties abolished in India. *Jan. 25*: First meeting of London Chamber of Commerce. *Aug. 18*: Married Women's Property Act.	**1882.** Mallarmé: *L'Après - Midi d'un Faune*. Wagner: *Parsifal*. Nietzsche: *Joyful Wisdom*. Mark Twain: *Adventures of Huckleberry Finn*.
1883. *Jan. 6*: Pendleton Act, reforms U.S.A. Civil Service. Secondary schools in Flanders made bilingual.	**1883.** First skyscraper built in Chicago (ten storeys). Benz and Daimler factories established.	**1883.** R. L. Stevenson: *Treasure Island*. Seeley: *Expansion of England*. Nietzsche: *Zarathustra*. W. Dilthey: *Einleitung in die Geisteswissenschaften*.

I. WESTERN AND SOUTHERN EUROPE	II. CENTRAL, NORTHERN, AND EASTERN EUROPE	III. COUNTRIES OVERSEA
1884. *Aug. 4*: Members of former dynasties excluded from French presidency; life senatorships abolished.	**1884.** *Mar. 27*: Three Emperors' Alliance renewed.	**1884.** *Jan. 31*: Russians take Merv. *Feb. 18*: Gordon sent to Sudan. *Feb. 27*: London Convention regulates status of Transvaal. *Apr. 4*: Bolivia cedes her coast to Chile. *Apr.-Aug.*: Germany occupies South-West Africa, Togoland, and Cameroons. Basutoland (*Mar. 13*), Somali Coast, Nigeria, and New Guinea made British protectorates. *Oct. 13*: Mahdi takes Omdurman. *Nov. 15*: Congo Conference meets in Berlin. *Nov.*: Britain annexes St. Lucia Bay. *Dec. 10*: Diaz again President of Mexico (-*May 4*, **1911**).
1885. *Dec. 28*: Grévy re-elected French President.	**1885.** *Sept. 18*: Revolution in Eastern Rumelia, which is united with Bulgaria. *Nov. 13*: Serbians invade Bulgaria. *Nov. 17*: Serbian defeat at Slivnitza.	**1885.** *Jan. 22*: Treaty of friendship between Germany and South African Republic. *Jan. 26*: Mahdi takes Khartoum; Gordon d. *Feb. 6*: Italy occupies Massawah. *Feb. 25*: Germany annexes Tanganyika and Zanzibar. *Feb. 26*: Congo State under Leopold II of Belgium established. *Mar. 4*: G. Cleveland (Dem.) becomes U.S.A. President. *Mar.*: British protectorate over North Bechuanaland proclaimed; end of Stellaland Republic. *Mar. 30*: Russia occupies Penjdeh, Afghanistan. *May 17*: Germany annexes Northern New Guinea and Bismarck Archipelago. *Aug.-Dec.*: German-Spanish dispute over Carolines, settled by papal arbitration.
1886. *June 23*: Bonaparte and Orléans families banished from France.	**1886.** *Mar. 3*: Peace of Bucharest between Serbia and Bulgaria on *status quo*. *Aug. 20-21*: Military *coup d'état* at Sofia. *Sept. 7*: Alexander of Bulgaria abdicates.	**1886.** *Jan. 1*: British annex Upper Burma. Royal Charter for Niger Company. *Oct. 30*: British protectorate proclaimed over Sokotra. Anglo-German agreement about East Africa.
1887. *Apr. 4*: First Colonial Conference meets in London. *June 21*: Golden Jubilee of Queen Victoria. *Dec. 2*: President Grévy resigns owing to financial scandals. *Dec. 12*: Triple Alliance between Britain, Austria, and Italy to maintain *status quo* in Near East.	**1887.** *June 18*: Reinsurance treaty between Germany and Russia. *July 7*: Ferdinand, Prince of Coburg, becomes Prince of Bulgaria (-**1918**).	**1887.** *Jan. 20*: New Zealand annexes Kermadec Islands. *June 21*: Zululand annexed. *July*: Anglo-Russian agreement about Afghanistan. *Oct. 1*: Baluchistan united with India. *Nov. 16*: Anglo-French condominium over New Hebrides.

IV. CONSTITUTIONAL HISTORY	V. ECONOMIC HISTORY AND NATURAL SCIENCE	VI. CULTURAL LIFE
1884. *July:* Imperial Federation League founded. Democratic reforms of Norwegian Constitution.	**1884.** *Jan.:* Russia abolishes Poll Tax, last relic of serfdom. First labour bureaux in Washington. French trade unions recognized by legislation. **St.** Gotthard Tunnel opened. *Jan.:* Fabian Society founded. First practical airship, by Renard and Krebs.	**1884.** *Feb. 1:* Oxford English Dictionary begins to appear. G. d'Annunzio: *Terra Vergine.* Ibsen: *Wild Duck.* A. Bruckner: *Seventh Symphony.* E. Burne-Jones: *King Cophetua and the Beggar Maid.*
1885. *June:* Redistribution Bill. *July 24:* Conservative Ministry (Salisbury). *Aug. 14:* Office of Secretary for Scotland created. *Aug. 14:* Irish Land Bill passed. Belgian Labour Party founded. *Dec.:* A. O. Hume founds Indian National Congress.	**1885.** First public labour bureaux in England. Gold discovered in Transvaal.	**1885.** W. Pater: *Marius the Epicurean. Dictionary of National Biography* begun. Guy de Maupassant: *Bel Ami.* Zola: *Germinal.* **Tolstoy:** *My Religion.*
1886. *Jan. 7:* Boulanger becomes French Minister of War. *Feb. 1:* Liberal Ministry (Gladstone). *June 7:* Government defeated on Home Rule Bill. *July 26:* Conservative Ministry (Salisbury).	**1886.** *Apr. 26:* Prussian law expropriating Polish landowners in Western Prussia and Posen. *Dec. 8:* American Federation of Labor founded.	**1886.** Pierre Loti: *Pêcheur d'Islande.* Ibsen: *Rosmersholm.* Nietzsche: *Beyond Good and Evil. English Historical Review* founded. Froude: *Oceana.*
1887. Independent Labour Party formed. *Aug. 1:* Crispi becomes Italian Premier. *Oct.:* Boulanger's *coup d'état* fails.	**1887.** *Feb. 4:* Interstate Commerce Act, regulates U.S.A. railways. *Sept. 16:* Allotments Act. Copyhold Act.	**1887.** Tolstoy: *Powers of Darkness.* Strindberg: *Son of a Servant.* Théâtre Libre, Paris, opened. Sudermann: *Frau Sorge.* C. F. Meyer: *Temptation of Pescara.*

I. WESTERN AND SOUTHERN EUROPE	II. CENTRAL, NORTHERN, AND EASTERN EUROPE	III. COUNTRIES OVERSEA
1888. *Aug. 13*: Imperial Defence Act passed.	**1888.** *Mar. 9*: Emperor William I *d. June 15*: Emperor Frederick III *d.*; succeeded by William II (**-1918**).	**1888.** *May 12*: British protectorate over North Borneo, Brunei, and Sarawak established. Royal Charter for East Africa Company. *May 13*: Serfdom abolished in Brazil. *Sept.*: Arab rising in German East Africa. *Oct.*: Rudd Concession granted by Lobengula. Kruger re-elected President of Transvaal.
1889. *Feb. 1*: General Boulanger flees from France. **1889-1908.** Charles, King of Portugal.	**1889.** *Mar. 7*: Milan of Serbia abdicates in favour of his son Alexander.	**1889.** *Feb. 22*: North and South Dakota, Montana, and Washington created States. *Mar. 4*: B. Harrison (Rep.), U.S.A. President. *May 2*: Treaty of Ucciali, implying Italian protectorate over Abyssinia. *June 4*: Condominium of Britain, U.S.A., and Germany over Samoa. *Oct. 29*: Royal Charter for South Africa Company. *Oct. 29*: Treaty of Constantinople internationalizes and neutralizes Suez Canal.
1890. *July 1*: Anglo-German Convention; Britain exchanges Heligoland for Zanzibar and Pemba. *Nov. 23*: Grand Duchy of Luxemburg separated from Netherlands.	**1890.** *Mar. 20*: Bismarck dismissed; Caprivi appointed Reich Chancellor (**-1894**).	**1890.** *July 1 and 8*: Idaho and Wyoming created U.S.A. States. *Aug. 5*: Anglo-French agreement on Nigeria. *Aug.*: Anglo-Portuguese agreement on Zambesi and Congo. *Oct. 22*: Responsible government set up in Western Australia. *Dec. 26*: Britain occupies Sikkim, Uganda, and Mashonaland.
1891. *Mar. 24* and *Apr. 15*: Anglo-Italian agreements over Abyssinia. *July 23*: French squadron visits Kronstadt. *Aug. 27*: Franco-Russian alliance. *Sept. 30*: Boulanger commits suicide. **1892.** *Aug. 17*: Franco-Russian military convention. *Oct. 15*: Anglo-German agreement over Cameroons.	**1891.** *Apr. 14*: Field-Marshal von Moltke *d. May 6*: Triple Alliance renewed for 12 years. **1892.** *Feb. 1*: Commercial treaties of Germany with Austria-Hungary, Italy, Switzerland, and Belgium. *Sept.*: Witte appointed Russian Minister of Finance.	**1891.** *Apr. 1*: Constitution of United States of Brazil. Charter of British South Africa Company extended to north of Zambesi; Nyasaland proclaimed British Protectorate. **1892.** *Jan. 7*: Abbas succeeds Tewfik as Khedive of Egypt. *Nov. 8*: Cleveland re-elected President of U.S.A.
1893. *Mar. 8-21*: Panama Trial in Paris; de Lesseps fined. *Oct. 13-29*: Russian squadron visits Toulon. *Nov. 15*: Anglo-German agreement over Shari district. *Dec. 4*: Anglo-French agreement over Siam. *Dec. 27*: Franco-Russian military convention comes into force.	**1893.** *Apr. 13*: Alexander of Serbia declares himself of age. *July 13*: German Army Bill.	**1893.** Kruger re-elected President of Transvaal. *May 10*: Responsible government in Natal. *July*: Matabele War; British occupy Buluwayo. War between France and Siam. *Nov. 17*: Dahomey made French Protectorate.

IV. CONSTITUTIONAL HISTORY	V. ECONOMIC HISTORY AND NATURAL SCIENCE	VI. CULTURAL LIFE
1888. *Aug. 9*: Local Government Act, establishes County Councils. Panama scandal in France.	**1888.** *Oct.*: France floats Russian loan. *Oct. 14-15*: Hamburg and Bremen join German Customs Union. *Nov. 24*: First railway in China. Baghdad railway scheme. Rhodes amalgamates Kimberley Diamond Companies. Pasteur Institute, Paris, established. Hertz detects electromagnetic waves.	**1888.** Kipling: *Plain Tales from the Hills.* A. France: *La Vie littéraire.* Rodin: *Burghers of Calais.* Bellamy: *Looking Backward.*
1889. *Feb. 11*: Japanese Constitution granted. *May 31*: Naval Defence Act passed. *July 23*: Board of Agriculture created. *Nov. 15*: Pedro II of Brazil abdicates; Republic proclaimed.	**1889.** *Aug. 19-Sept. 14*: London Dockers' Strike. Belgium introduces factory inspection. Gustave Eiffel builds Eiffel Tower, Paris. Panama Canal Company bankrupt.	**1889.** Bernard Shaw: *Fabian Essays.* W. James: *Principles of Psychology.* Björnson: *In God's Way.* G. Hauptmann: *Before Dawn.* Sudermann: *Honour.* Liliencron: *Poems.* B. v. Suttner: *Lay down your Arms.*
1890. *Mar. 27*: Spain adopts universal suffrage. *Oct. 1*: German anti-Socialist law expires. *Oct. 21*: Congress of Erfurt of German Social Democrats adopts new programme. *Nov. 29*: First Japanese Diet opened.	**1890.** *Mar. 15-28*: First international congress for protection of workers, in Berlin. *July 2*: Anti-slavery congress in Brussels. *July 14*: Sherman Bill, regulates silver coinage in U.S.A. *Oct. 1*: McKinley Tariff in U.S.A. Housing of the Working Classes Act, begins slum clearance.	**1890.** Wilde: *Dorian Gray.* Tolstoy: *Kreutzer Sonata.* Mahan: *Influence of Sea Power, 1660-1783.* Free elementary education established in England. Stefan George founds ' *Blätter für die Kunst* '. Knut Hamsun: *Hunger.* Langbehn: *Rembrandt als Erzieher.* Mascagni: *Cavalleria Rusticana.* *July 29*: van Gogh d.
1891. *Jan. 31*: Crispi resigns. *Apr. 9*: Pan-German League founded. *Oct. 6*: Parnell d.	**1891.** *May 25*: Papal Encyclical on Labour. *May 31*: Siberian Railway begun (completed **1904**). Lilienthal starts gliding (killed **1896**).	**1891.** Lagerlöf: *Gösta Berling.* Ibsen: *Hedda Gabler.* Aulard: *Histoire politique de la révolution française.* Lamprecht: *German History* (**-1909**). Wedekind: *Frühlings Erwachen.*
1892. *Jan.-Mar.*: Dispute about Prussian Education Bill, which is ultimately withdrawn. *Aug. 18*: Gladstone's fourth Ministry. Leo XIII orders French Catholics to accept the Republic. *Dec. 12*: Pan-Slav Congress at Cracow.	**1892.** Income-tax adopted in Netherlands. *Feb. 1*: Gold standard adopted in Austria-Hungary. *June 14*: National bankruptcy in Portugal. Commercial treaty between Austria-Hungary and Serbia (**-1905**).	**1892.** Hardy: *Tess of the D'Urbervilles.* Kipling: *Barrack-Room Ballads.* Zola: *La Débâcle.* Hauptmann: *The Weavers.* Léoncavallo: *Pagliacci.* *Oct. 6*: Tennyson d.
1893. *Jan. 13*: First meeting of Independent Labour Party. *Sept.*: Commons pass, Lords reject Home Rule Bill. *Oct. 29*: Taaffe, Austro-Hungarian Premier, resigns. Reform of suffrage in Belgium, Spain, and New Zealand (Women's Suffrage).	**1893.** *June*: Franco-Russian commercial treaty. *Aug. 6*: Corinth Canal opened. *Nov. 1*: Cleveland repeals Sherman Bill. German commercial treaties with Rumania, Serbia, and Spain. Customs war between France and Switzerland (**-1895**).	**1893.** Sardou: *Mme Sans-Gêne.* Sudermann: *Magda.* Wilde: *Salome.* Verdi: *Falstaff.* Tchaikovsky: *Pathetic Symphony.* Puccini: *Manon Lescaut.*

I. WESTERN AND SOUTHERN EUROPE

1894. *May 5*: Anglo-Italian agreement over Eastern Africa. *May 12*: Anglo-Belgian agreement over Bahr-el-Ghazal. *June 24*: Carnot, French President, murdered; succeeded by Casimir-Périer. *Dec.*: Trial of Dreyfus in Paris.

1895. *Jan. 13*: Casimir-Périer resigns. *Jan. 17*: Faure elected French President (-*1899*). *Aug. 1-8*: Emperor William II in England; Salisbury suggests partition of Turkey.

1896. *Jan. 5*: Anglo-French agreement over spheres of influence in Siam. *Sept. 30*: Franco-Italian agreement about Tunis. *Oct.*: Nicholas II visits London and Paris.

1897. *June 22*: Diamond Jubilee of Queen Victoria. *June-July*: Second Colonial Conference in London. *Sept. 18*: Anglo-French agreement about Tunisia. *Nov. 5*: Italo-Austrian agreement over Albania. *Nov.*: Government inquiry into the Dreyfus case.

1898. *Feb.*: Chamberlain suggests Anglo-German alliance. *May 19*: Gladstone *d. June 14*: Anglo-French agreement over Nigeria and Gold Coast. *July 30*: Bismarck *d. Aug. 30*: Anglo-German agreements over Portuguese African colonies. *Aug. 31*: Wilhelmina, Queen of Netherlands, comes of age.

II. CENTRAL, NORTHERN, AND EASTERN EUROPE

1894. *Aug.*: First organized massacres of Armenians. *Nov. 1*: Alexander III of Russia *d.*; succeeded by Nicholas II (-*1917*). **1894-1897.** Christian risings in Crete against Turks.

1895. *June 19*: Kiel Canal opened. *July 15*: Stambuloff, Bulgarian Premier, murdered; subsequent rapprochement between Russia and Bulgaria.

1896. *Jan. 3*: 'Kruger telegram' of William II. *Mar.*: Ferdinand of Bulgaria recognized by Great Powers. *Oct. 24*: Bismarck publishes Russo-German Reinsurance Treaty.

1897. *Mar. 18*: Crete proclaims union with Greece. *Apr. 18*: Greece declares war on Turkey. *Apr. 28*: Austro-Russian agreement over Macedonia. *May 12*: Turks defeat Greeks in Thessaly; Powers intervene. *Dec. 16*: Peace of Constantinople between Greece and Turkey.

1898. *Mar. 28*: First German Navy Bill passed. *Apr. 30*: German Navy League founded by von Tirpitz. *Oct.-Nov.*: William II visits Palestine and Syria.

III. COUNTRIES OVERSEA

1894. *Jan.*: British occupy Matabeleland. *Apr. 11*: Uganda declared British Protectorate. *July 17*: Italians take Kassala from the Dervishes. German rapprochement with Boers. *July 25*: Japan attacks China. *Aug. 1*: Japan declares war on China.

1895. *Apr. 17*: Peace of Shimonoseki; China cedes Formosa and Liaotung to Japan. *Apr. 22*: Russia, France, and Germany intervene against Japan. *May 8*: Final treaty of Shimonoseki. *June 28*: Nicaragua, Honduras, and Salvador united. *Dec. 29*: Jameson Raid into Transvaal.

1896. *Jan. 2*: Jameson capitulates. *Jan. 4*: Utah becomes U.S.A. State. *Mar. 1*: Abyssinians defeat Italians at Adowa. *May 1*: Nasr ed Din of Persia murdered. *Aug. 18*: France annexes Madagascar. *Sept. 30*: Cassini Convention between Russia and China concerning Manchuria. *Oct. 18*: Treaty of Addis Ababa; Italian Protectorate over Abyssinia withdrawn.

1897. *Mar. 4.*: McKinley (Rep.) becomes U.S.A. President (-*1901*). *Oct.*: King of Korea proclaims himself Emperor. *Nov. 14*: Germany occupies Kiaochow. *Dec. 13*: Russia occupies Port Arthur.

1898. *Feb. 9*: Kruger re-elected President. *Mar.-Apr.*: Germany, Russia, Britain, and France obtain leases of Kiaochow, Port Arthur, Weihaiwei, and Kwangchow respectively. *Apr. 24*: War between Spain and U.S.A. breaks out. *July 7*: U.S.A. annexes Hawaii. *July 10*: France occupies Fashoda, causing Franco-British tension. *Sept. 2*: Kitchener defeats Dervishes at Omdurman. *Nov. 4*: French evacuate Fashoda. *Dec. 10*: Treaty of Paris between U.S.A. and Spain, which cedes Cuba, Porto Rico, Guam, and Philippines.

IV. CONSTITUTIONAL HISTORY	V. ECONOMIC HISTORY AND NATURAL SCIENCE	VI. CULTURAL LIFE
1894. *Mar. 3*: Gladstone resigns; succeeded by Lord Rosebery. *Oct. 26*: Reich Chancellor Caprivi resigns, succeeded by Prince Hohenlohe. Dutch Labour Party formed.	**1894.** *Feb. 10*: Commercial treaty between Russia and Germany. Goldfields discovered in Transvaal. Riots of agricultural labourers in Sicily. First railway over Andes. Compulsory arbitration adopted in New Zealand.	**1894.** Kipling: *Jungle Book.* Tchekhoff: *In the Twilight. Historische Zeitschrift* founded by Sybel. Lord Halifax starts Anglo-Catholic movement. S. and B. Webb: *History of Trade-Unionism. June 20*: Encyclic *Praeclara gratulationis*, on world peace.
1895. *May 15*: Goluchowski appointed Austrian Foreign Secretary. *June 22*: Rosebery Ministry defeated; succeeded by Lord Salisbury (Cons.); J. Chamberlain (Unionist), Colonial Secretary.	**1895.** French Trade Unions form Confédération Générale du Travail. Röntgen discovers X-rays. Lumière brothers invent cinematograph. Marconi invents wireless telegraphy.	**1895.** W. B. Yeats: *Poems.* Balfour: *Foundations of Belief.* Seeley: *Growth of British Policy.* Verlaine: *Confessions.* Sienkiewicz: *Quo Vadis.* Fontane: *Effie Briest.*
1896. *Jan. 6*: Rhodes resigns Premiership of Cape Colony. *July 1*: German Reichstag passes Civil Law Code. *July*: 40th Land Bill for Ireland passed.	**1896.** *July 28*: Anatolian railway opened as far as Konia. First electric submarine built in France.	**1896.** National Portrait Gallery opened. Björnson: *Beyond Our Powers.* Hauptmann: *Florian Geyer*; *Versunkene Glocke.* Puccini: *La Bohème.* William Morris: Kelmscott *Chaucer.*
1897. *April 5*: Czech language granted equal rights with German in Bohemia. *June 15*: Tirpitz appointed German Naval Secretary. *Oct. 20*: Bülow appointed German Foreign Secretary. Austro-Hungarian Socialist Party split into six national parties.	**1897.** *Mar. 1*: Gold standard in Japan. *Mar. 31*: Dingley Bill increases U.S.A. protective tariff. Marconi founds Wireless Telegraph Company. Goldfields discovered in Klondyke. *Aug. 5*: Workmen's Compensation Act. Ramsay discovers helium.	**1897.** A. France: *Le Jardin d'Epicure.* Rostand: *Cyrano de Bergerac.* Tolstoy: *Resurrection.* D'Annunzio: *Trionfo della Morte.* Ratzel: *Political Geography.*
1898. *July 30*: Delcassé becomes French Foreign Secretary. *Aug. 12*: Irish Local Government Act. *Sept. 21*: Dowager Empress seizes supreme power in China.	**1898.** *Apr.-May*: Labourers' and peasants' riots in Italy. *Nov. 26*: Franco-Italian commercial treaty. Gold standard in Russia. Zeppelin invents his airship. M. and Mme Curie discover radium. Diesel motor first used.	**1898.** D'Annunzio: *Il Fuoco.* Bismarck: *Reflections and Reminiscences.* M. Barrès: *L'Energie nationale* (completed **1901**). Strindberg: *To Damascus.*

I. WESTERN AND SOUTHERN EUROPE	II. CENTRAL, NORTHERN, AND EASTERN EUROPE	III. COUNTRIES OVERSEA
1899. *Feb. 18*: Loubet elected French President (-**1906**). *Mar. 21*: Anglo-French agreement over Wadai and Darfur. *May 18-July 29*: First Peace Conference at The Hague. *Aug.*: Franco-Russian Alliance extended. Second trial and pardon of Dreyfus. *Oct. 14*: Anglo-Portuguese treaty of Windsor, renews treaties of **1642** and **1661**. *Nov. 14* and *Dec. 2*: Agreement between Britain, U.S.A., and Germany over Samoa. *Nov. 19-25*: William II in England, discusses Anglo-German alliance.	**1899.** *Feb. 12*: Germany buys Marianne, Caroline, and Pelew Islands from Spain. *Feb. 15*: Nicholas II suppresses liberties of Finland. *Mar.*: Prince George of Greece appointed High Commissioner of Crete by Great Powers. *Dec. 23*: Germany secures Baghdad railway concession.	**1899.** *Aug. 9*: Britain buys possessions of Niger Company. *Oct. 3*: Frontier settled between British Guiana and Venezuela. *Oct. 10*: Boer war breaks out; British defeated at Stormberg (*Dec. 10*), Magersfontein (*Dec. 11*), and Colenso (*Dec. 15*). *Dec. 18*: Roberts and Kitchener appointed C.-in-C. and Chief of Staff respectively.
1900. *July 29*: Humbert, King of Italy, murdered; succeeded by Victor Emanuel III. *Oct. 16*: Anglo-German agreement over Yangtze basin. *Dec. 14-16*: Franco-Italian agreement over Mediterranean.	**1900.** *July 27*: William II's 'Huns' speech at Bremerhaven. *Oct. 17.* Bülow appointed German Chancellor.	**1900.** *Feb. 27*: Cronje capitulates at Paardeberg. *May 19*: Britain annexes Tonga Islands. *May 24*: Britain annexes Orange Free State. Boxer rising in China; *June 20*: German Ambassador murdered; *Aug. 14*: International army enters Pekin. *July 9*: Commonwealth of Australia Constitution proclaimed. *Sept. 1*: Britain annexes Transvaal. *Oct.*: Russia completes occupation of Manchuria.
1901. *Jan. 19-30*: William II of Germany visits England. *Jan. 22*: Queen Victoria d.; succeeded by Edward VII. *Oct. 25*: Anti-German speech by Chamberlain at Edinburgh. *Dec. 27*: Britain breaks off negotiations on Anglo-German alliance.	**1901.** *Feb. 27*: Bogolyepoff, Russian Minister of Propaganda, murdered. *Nov. 11*: Turkey accepts French ultimatum concerning violation of treaties.	**1901.** *Sept. 7*: Peace of Pekin between China and Great Powers. *Sept. 6*: President McKinley assassinated; *Sept. 14*: succeeded by Theodore Roosevelt (-**1909**). *Nov. 18*: Hay-Pauncefote treaty concerning Panama Canal.
1902. *Jan. 30*: Anglo-Japanese treaty. *June 30-Aug. 11*: Second Colonial Conference in London. *July 12*: Balfour Ministry (Conservative). *Nov. 1*: Franco-Italian agreement over North Africa.	**1902.** *Apr. 15*: Sipyagin, Russian Minister of Interior, murdered; Plehve suppresses peasants' revolt. *June 28*: Triple Alliance renewed. *Dec. 31*: Austro-Hungarian *Ausgleich* renewed.	**1902.** *Mar. 26*: Cecil Rhodes d. *May 31*: Peace of Vereeniging ends Boer War.
1903. *Apr.-May*: Edward VII visits Lisbon, Rome, and Paris. *July 6-9*: Loubet and Delcassé visit London. *July 20*: Pope Leo XIII d.; succeeded by Pius X (-**1914**). *Aug. 31*: Edward VII visits Vienna.	**1903.** *June 11*: King Alexander of Serbia and his Queen murdered; succeeded by Peter Karageorgevitch (-**1921**). *Oct. 1-3*: Austro-Russian agreement of Mürzsteg over Macedonia.	**1903.** *Jan. 22*: Hay-Herran pact concerning Panama Canal territory. *July*: Russo-Japanese negotiations over Manchuria fail. *Oct. 20*: Alaska frontier settled between Canada and U.S.A. *Nov. 3*: Panama makes herself independent of Colombia.

IV. CONSTITUTIONAL HISTORY	V. ECONOMIC HISTORY AND NATURAL SCIENCE	VI. CULTURAL LIFE
1899. *Aug. 9:* Board of Education and London Borough Councils created. *Oct. 17:* Bohemian language ordinances repealed.	**1899.** *June 26:* International Women's Congress in London. Revisionist movement in German Social Democracy abandons strict Marxism. Pupin invents inductance coils for telephone. *Dec.:* International economic crisis.	**1899.** Zola: *La Vérité en marche.* H. S. Chamberlain: *Foundations of the 19th Century.* A. Holz: *Phantasus.* Haeckel: *Riddle of the Universe. Action française* appears.
1900. Waldeck-Rousseau Ministry adopts strong anti-clerical policy in France. Giolitti begins financial and social reforms in Italy. *Jan. 1:* German Civil Law Code comes into force. *Feb. 27:* British Labour Party founded. *July 14:* Second German Navy Bill.	**1900.** *Mar. 14:* Gold standard in U.S.A. *June 1:* Private postal services abolished in Germany. *July 2:* First trial flight of Zeppelin. *Aug. 8:* Agricultural Holdings Act. *Oct. 26:* Belgium adopts Old Age Pensions. Browning revolver invented.	**1900.** Pinero: *Gay Lord Quex.* Ellen Key: *Century of the Child.* Conrad: *Lord Jim.* G. B. Shaw: *Three Plays for Puritans.* Spitteler: *Olympic Spring* (-**1905**). Wundt: *Comparative Psychology* (-**1920**). Harnack: *Nature of Christianity.* Puccini: *Tosca. Jan. 20:* Ruskin *d. Aug. 25:* Nietzsche *d. Nov. 30:* Oscar Wilde *d.*
1901. *May 20:* Polish school strike in Prussian province of Posen. *Aug. 17:* Royal Titles Act.	**1901.** *Feb. 23:* Morgan founds Steel Trust. Miners' Eight Hours Bill. *Dec. 13:* First wireless communication between America and Europe. Labour riots in Spain.	**1901.** Th. Mann: *Buddenbrooks.* Strindberg: *Dance of Death.* Maeterlinck: *Life of the Bee.* Gooch: *Annals of Politics and Culture.* Hardy: *Poems of the Past and Present.* Kipling: *Kim.*
1902. *June:* Combes Ministry continues anti-clerical policy in France. *July 12:* Balfour, Prime Minister. *Dec. 18:* Education Act, for elementary schools in England and Wales.	**1902.** *Mar. 5:* Brussels sugar convention. *May 10:* National bankruptcy in Portugal. *June 28:* U.S.A. buys rights of French Panama Company. *Dec. 25:* German protectionist tariff.	**1902.** Kipling: *Just So Stories.* Belloc: *Path to Rome.* Doyle: *Hound of the Baskervilles.* A. Gide: *L'Immoraliste.* Maeterlinck: *Monna Vanna.* Gorky: *Night's Lodging.* B. Croce: *Estetica.* Mereshkovsky: *Leonardo da Vinci. Sept. 29:* Zola *d.*
1903. *Mar. 18:* French religious orders dissolved. *July 10:* Firth of Forth made naval base of Home Fleet. *Nov.:* Russian Labour Party split into Menshevists (Plechanoff) and Bolshevists (Lenin, Trotsky). *Aug. 29:* Witte, Russian Minister of Finance, dismissed. *Sept. 18:* Chamberlain resigns to conduct Tariff Reform campaign.	**1903.** *Feb.:* Anti-trust law in U.S.A. re-enforced. *Aug. 14:* Employment of Children Act. *Dec. 17:* First powered flight of Wright brothers at Kitty Hawk, N.C. Krupp Company founded.	**1903.** Butler (*d.* **1902**): *Way of All Flesh.* Shaw: *Man and Superman.* Hofmannsthal: *Electra.* Dehmel: *Zwei Menschen.* Schnitzler: *Reigen.* O. Weininger: *Sex and Character.*

I. WESTERN AND SOUTHERN EUROPE	II. CENTRAL, NORTHERN, AND EASTERN EUROPE	III. COUNTRIES OVERSEA
1904. *Apr. 8*: *Entente cordiale* between France and Britain; agreement over Morocco, followed by agreements over Siam, Newfoundland, and Egypt. *Oct. 3*: Franco-Spanish agreement over Morocco. *Oct. 21-22*: Dogger Bank incident between Britain and Russia.	**1904.** *July 28*: Plehve, Russian Minister of Interior, murdered. *Oct. 27*: Germany suggests to Russia continental *bloc* against Britain.	**1904.** *Jan.*: Herrero rising in German S.W. Africa. *Feb. 8*: Japan declares war on Russia; Russians defeated. *Sept.*: Hottentot rising in German S.W. Africa.
1905. *Mar. 31*: William II lands at Tangier. *Apr. 30*: Anglo-French military convention. *June 6*: Delcassé, French Foreign Minister, resigns under German pressure. *Aug. 12*: Anglo-Japanese Alliance. *Dec. 5*: Campbell-Bannerman Ministry (Liberal): Grey, Foreign Secretary; Haldane, Secretary for War.	**1905.** *Jan. 22*: Revolt in St. Petersburg. *Feb. 17*: Grand Duke Sergius murdered. *June 7*: Norwegian Diet decides upon separation from Sweden. *July 23-24*: Treaty of Bjoerkoe between William II and Nicholas II. *Sept. 27*: Norway becomes independent. *Nov. 18*: Prince Charles of Denmark elected King Haakon VII of Norway.	**1905.** *Jan. 1*: Port Arthur surrenders to Japanese. *Mar. 1-9*: Japanese defeat Russians at Mukden. *May 27-28*: Japanese naval victory off Tsushima. *Sept. 5*: Treaty of Portsmouth; Russia cedes Port Arthur and Talienwan to Japan. *Nov. 18*: Japan establishes protectorate over Korea.
1906. *Jan. 16-Mar. 31*: Algeciras Conference on Morocco. *Apr. 8*: Algeciras Act signed. *July 12*: Dreyfus rehabilitated. *Dec. 13*: Anglo-Italian agreement over Abyssinia.	**1906.** *Jan. 1*: Moltke appointed Chief of German General Staff. *Apr. 5*: Holstein dismissed. *Apr. 27*: Pashitch, Serbian Premier. *May 11*: Isvolsky, Russian Foreign Secretary. *Oct. 24*: Aehrenthal, Austro-Hungarian Foreign Secretary.	**1906.** *Dec. 6*: Transvaal and Orange Colonies granted self-government. Aga Khan founds All Indian Moslem League. *Aug.*: Anglo-Chinese convention on Tibet.
1907. *Feb.-Apr.*: Edward VII visits Paris, Madrid, and Rome. *Apr. 15-May 14*: Third Imperial (Colonial) Conference in London. *May 16*: Anglo-Spanish agreement over Mediterranean. *June 15-Oct. 18*: Second Peace Conference at The Hague. *Aug. 31*: Anglo-Russian Convention on Persia, Afghanistan and Tibet.	**1907.** *Aug. 3-6*: William II and Nicholas II meet at Swinemünde. *Dec. 8*: King Oscar of Sweden *d.*; succeeded by Gustavus V.	**1907.** *July 19*: Emperor of Korea abdicates. *Sept. 21*: Risings in German S.W. Africa suppressed. *Nov. 16*: Oklahoma admitted as State of U.S.A.
1908. *Feb. 1*: King Carlos and Crown Prince of Portugal murdered. *Apr. 8*: Asquith Ministry (Liberal); Lloyd George, Chancellor of Exchequer.	**1908.** *July 24*: Rising of Young Turks. *Oct. 5*: Austria annexes Bosnia and Herzegovina; Bulgaria annexes Eastern Rumelia and becomes Tsardom. *Oct. 12*: Crete proclaims union with Greece. *Oct. 28*: *Daily Telegraph* interview with William II published. *Dec. 2*: Revolt in Bohemia.	**1908.** *Aug. 20*: King Leopold hands Congo State over to Belgium. *Sept. 25*: Casablanca incident between Germany and France.

IV. CONSTITUTIONAL HISTORY	V. ECONOMIC HISTORY AND NATURAL SCIENCE	VI. CULTURAL LIFE
1904. *Mar. 8*: German anti-Jesuit law revised.	**1904.** Canadian protectionist tariff. Ten Hours' Day in France. *May 4*: Panama Canal begun. New German commercial treaties with Belgium, Russia (*July 28*), Switzerland, Serbia, and Austria-Hungary.	**1904.** Barrie: *Peter Pan.* Chesterton: *Napoleon of Notting Hill.* London: *Sea Wolf.* W. Reymont: *Polish Peasants* (-**1909**). Puccini: *Madam Butterfly.* Rolland: *Jean Christophe* (**1912**).
1905. *Mar. 3*: Tsar issues reform programme. *Oct.*: Mutiny on board battleship *Potemkin. Nov. 16*: Witte appointed Russian Premier. *Nov. 28*: Sinn Fein party founded in Dublin. *Dec. 6*: State and Church separated in France.	**1905.** Sunday labour further reduced in England. International Agricultural Institute founded in Rome. German commercial treaties with Bulgaria and Abyssinia.	**1905.** Wilde: *De Profundis.* Shaw: *Major Barbara.* Wells: *Modern Utopia.* Unamuno: *Vida de Don Quijote y Sancho.* Rilke: *Livre d'heures.* Strindberg: *Historical Miniatures.* Dilthey: *Experience and Poetry.* R. Strauss: *Salome.* Einstein's special relativity theory.
1906. *May 5*: Fall of Witte, succeeded by Goremykin. *May 6*: Russian Constitution promulgated. *May 10*: First Duma meets; *July 22*: dissolved; Stolypin, Prime Minister. *June 5*: Third German Navy Bill. *Dec. 13*: German Reichstag opposes Colonial war expenses; dissolved.	**1906.** Night work by women internationally forbidden. Austro-Serbian customs war. Confederazione Generale del Lavoro founded in Italy. Norway adopts Unemployment Insurance. *Nov. 22*: Russian village communities (Mir) abolished. *May 19*: Simplon tunnel opened. Zuider Zee drainage begun.	**1906.** Galsworthy: *Man of Property.* Sinclair: *The Jungle.* Andersen-Nexö: *Pelle, the Conqueror. Oct. 22*: Cézanne *d.*
1907. Haldane's Territorial and Reserve Forces Act. *Jan. 10*: Reform of Austrian suffrage. *Mar. 19-June 16*: Second Duma. *June 14*: Women's suffrage in Norway. *Nov. 14*: Third Duma meets.	**1907.** Small Holdings Bill in England. Shell Oil Trust founded. Immigration into U.S.A. restricted. Lumière invents colour photography. *Oct. 21*: Economic panic in U.S.A.	**1907.** Bergson: *L'Evolution créatrice.* Gorky: *Mother.* Kolbenheyer: *Paracelsus.* Stefan George: *The Seventh Ring.* Rilke: *New Poems* (2nd part, 1908).
1908. *June 14*: Fourth German Navy Bill. *July*: Pan-Slav Congress in Prague. *Sept. 13-18*: German Social Democratic rally at Nuremberg; Revisionists defeat Marxists. *Nov. 10-11*: German Reichstag debate on *Daily Telegraph* interview.	**1908.** Old Age Pensions Bills in Britain and Australia. *May 1*: Hejaz railway opened as far as Medina. *Aug.-Dec.*: Wilbur Wright flies in France, revolutionizes European aviation.	**1908.** Meinecke: *Cosmopolitanism and Nation State.* Kolbenheyer: *Amor Dei.* Picasso founds Cubism. Chesterton: *The Man Who Was Thursday.* Hardy: *Dynasts* (completed).

I. WESTERN AND SOUTHERN EUROPE	II. CENTRAL, NORTHERN, AND EASTERN EUROPE	III. COUNTRIES OVERSEA
1909. *Feb. 9:* Franco-German agreement over Morocco. *Dec. 17:* Leopold II of Belgium *d.*; succeeded by Albert (**-1934**).	**1909.** *Feb. 28:* Austro-Turkish agreement over Bosnia. *Mar. 31:* Serbia yields in Bosnian dispute. *Apr. 27:* Young Turks depose Abdul Hamid; Muhammad V, successor (**-1918**). *July 14:* Beth-mann-Hollweg, German Chancellor (**-1917**).	**1909.** *Mar. 4:* Taft (Rep.), U.S.A. President. *July 15:* Mahommed Ali, Shah of Persia, deposed; succeeded by Ahmed Mirza (**-1925**). *Oct. 25:* Prince Ito murdered; Japanese dictatorship established in Korea. Spanish war in Morocco.
1910. *May 6:* Edward VII *d.*; succeeded by George V (**-1936**). *Oct. 4:* Revolution in Portugal; King Manuel flees to England.	**1910.** *Aug. 28:* Montenegro proclaimed kingdom. *Oct.:* Sazonov, Russian Foreign Secretary; Isvolsky, Ambassador in Paris. *Nov. 4-5:* William II and Nicholas II meet at Potsdam.	**1910.** *July 1:* Union of South Africa becomes Dominion. *July 4:* Russo-Japanese agreement over Manchuria and Korea. *Aug. 24:* Japan annexes Korea.
1911. *Aug. 18:* Portuguese Republican Constitution voted. *Aug. 31:* Franco-Russian military convention. *Sept. 29:* Italy declares war on Turkey and seizes Tripoli. *Dec. 12:* Canalejas, Spanish Premier, murdered.	**1911.** *Sept. 14:* Stolypin, Russian Premier, murdered. *Nov. 4:* Franco-German agreement over Morocco and Congo.	**1911.** *May:* Revolution in Mexico. *July 1:* German gunboat *Panther* arrives at Agadir, Morocco, creates international tension. *July 13:* Anglo-Japanese alliance renewed for four years.
1912. *Jan. 14:* Poincaré, French Premier and Foreign Secretary. *Feb. 8-11:* Haldane's mission to Berlin. *July 16:* Franco-Russian naval convention. *Aug. 9-16:* Poincaré visits St. Petersburg. *Sept.:* Anglo-French naval convention. *Nov. 22-23:* Grey-Cambon correspondence strengthens *Entente*.	**1912.** *Feb. 17:* Berchtold, Austro-Hungarian Foreign Secretary (**-1915**). *Feb. 29:* Balkan Alliance between Serbia and Bulgaria, joined by Greece (*May*) and Montenegro (*June*). *Oct. 17-Dec. 3:* First Balkan War. *Oct. 28:* Treaty of Ouchy between Turkey and Italy, which obtains Tripoli. *Dec. 5:* Triple Alliance renewed till **1918**.	**1912.** *Feb. 12:* China proclaimed Republic. *Mar. 30:* French Protectorate established over Morocco. *Nov. 6:* Woodrow Wilson (Dem.) elected U.S.A. President (**-1921**). *Jan. 5:* New Mexico and (*Feb. 14*) Arizona created States of U.S.A.
1913. *Jan. 17:* Poincaré elected French President (**-1920**). *Feb. 1:* Delcassé, French Ambassador to Russia. *Mar. 28:* Belgian Army Bill. *Aug. 7:* French Army Bill, 3 years' service. *Dec. 13:* Britain and France oppose German-Turkish military convention.	**1913.** *Feb. 3-Apr. 23:* Second Balkan War. *May 19-Aug. 10:* Third Balkan War of Bulgaria against her allies and Rumania; *Aug. 10:* Treaty of Bucharest. *Oct. 28:* German-Turkish military convention. *Nov. 1:* Naval convention of Triple Alliance.	**1913.** *May 31:* Seventeenth amendment to U.S.A. Constitution concerning popular election of Senators. *Oct. 6:* Yuan Shi Kai elected Chinese President.
1914. *June 15:* Anglo-German agreement over Baghdad railway. *July 15-23:* Poincaré visits Nicholas II. *July 26:* Irish rising in Dublin.	**1914.** *June 23-25:* Enlarged Kiel Canal opened. *June 28:* Francis Ferdinand murdered at Sarajevo.	**1914.** *Jan. 11:* Yuan Shi Kai dissolves Chinese National Assembly and governs without Parliament. *Apr. 21-22:* U.S.A. fleet shell and take Vera Cruz, Mexico.

IV. CONSTITUTIONAL HISTORY	V. ECONOMIC HISTORY AND NATURAL SCIENCE	VI. CULTURAL LIFE
1909. *Mar. 12*: British Navy Bill. *July 26-Sept. 26*: Revolutionary rising in Catalonia. *Nov. 30*: Lords reject Lloyd George's Finance Bill; Parliament dissolved.	**1909.** *July 25*: Blériot makes first crossing of Channel by aeroplane. *Aug. 5*: Payne-Aldrich Tariff in U.S.A.	**1909.** Meredith: *Last Poems*. Bergson: *Matière et Mémoire*. Rolland: *Théâtre de la Révolution*. Thos. Mann: *Royal Highness*. Kandinsky founds Absolute Painting.
1910. *Feb. 10*: Revision of Swedish Constitution. *Apr. 28*: Finance Bill passed. *May 27*: Prussian Diet rejects any reform of suffrage. *July 3*: Self-government in Finland abolished.	**1910.** International Motor-Car Convention. *July*: Commercial treaty between Austria-Hungary and Serbia. *Oct.*: French railway strike. Swiss railways nationalized. Old Age Pensions in France.	**1910.** Newbolt: *Songs of the Fleet*. G. Hauptmann: *Emanuel Quint*. H. Löns: *Wehrwolf*. Freud: *Psychoanalysis*.
1911. *Feb. 24*: German Army Act. *Apr. 21*: State and Church separated in Portugal. *May 26*: Constitution granted to Alsace-Lorraine. *June 11*: Revision of Greek Constitution. *July 6*: Parliament Act; reduces power of Lords.	**1911.** National Insurance Act. Japanese commercial treaties with Britain (*Apr. 3*), France, and Germany (*June 28*). Buenos Aires-Valparaiso railway opened. *Dec. 15*: Amundsen reaches South Pole.	**1911.** Brooke: *Poems*. Wells: *The New Macchiavelli*. Masefield: *The Everlasting Mercy*. Gundolf: *Shakespeare in Germany*. Vaihinger: *Philosophy of 'As If'*. Strauss and Hofmannsthal: *Rosenkavalier*. Galsworthy: *The Patrician*.
1912. *May 21*: German Army and Navy Bills passed. *June 16*: Austro-Hungarian Army Bill. *June 19*: Russian Navy Bill. *Nov. 12*: Belgian Army Bill.	**1912.** French *Code du Travail* issued. Russia adopts Workmen's Insurance.	**1912.** R. Tagore: *Gitanjali*. Karin Michaelis: *The Dangerous Age*. H. G. Wells: *Marriage*.
1913. *Jan. 16* and *June 10*: Commons vote, and (*Jan. 30* and *July 24*) Lords reject, Home Rule for Ireland. *Mar. 7*: Hungarian suffrage altered in favour of Magyars. *June 30*: German Army Bill. *July 26*: Bohemian Constitution abolished. *Oct. 30*: Austro-Hungarian Army Bill. *Nov. 1*: Ernest Augustus, Duke of Cumberland, becomes Duke of Brunswick. *Nov.*: Zabern incident in Alsace-Lorraine.	**1913.** *Feb. 25*: Federal Income-tax; *Oct. 3*: Underwood Tariff; *Dec. 23*: Federal Reserve Bank in U.S.A. Netherlands and Switzerland adopt Old Age and Sickness Insurance.	**1913.** Gooch: *History and Historians*. Lawrence: *Sons and Lovers*. Walpole: *Fortitude*. Thos. Mann: *Death in Venice*. Husserl: *Phenomenology*. Einstein's general relativity theory. Bohr discovers atom structure.
1914. *Mar. 10*: Suffragette riots in London. *Mar. 10*: Fall of Giolitti; Salandra, Italian Premier. *Mar. 30*: Asquith appointed Secretary for War. *May 10*: Conservatives and Liberal Unionists united. *May 25*: Commons pass Home Rule Bill for third time. *July 3*: Norwegian Army Bill.	**1914.** *Apr. 7*: Canadian Grand Trunk Pacific Railway completed. Belgium adopts Old Age, Sickness, and Disablement Insurance. Switzerland extends measures against Female and Child labour. *Aug. 15*: Panama Canal opened. *Oct. 15*: Clayton Anti-Trust Act in U.S.A.	**1914.** Holme: *Lonely Plough*. Walpole: *Wooden Horse*. Masefield: *Philip the King*. H. Mann: *Der Untertan*. Ric. Huch: *The Great War in Germany*. Hugh Walpole: *The Duchess of Wrexe*.

I. POLITICAL EVENTS

1914

July 23: Austrian ultimatum to Serbia. *25*: Serbian reply; Austrian envoy leaves Belgrade. *28*: Austria-Hungary declares war on Serbia. *30*: Jaurès murdered in Paris. *Aug. 1*: Germany declares war on Russia. *2*: German ultimatum to Belgium. *3*: Germany declares war on France. *4*: Britain and Belgium declare war on Germany. U.S.A. declares neutrality. *5*: Montenegro declares war on Austria. *6*: Austria declares war on Russia (posted on *4th*), Serbia on Germany. *12*: Britain and France declare war on Austria. *23*: Japan declares war on Germany. *Sept. 4*: London Treaty; Britain, France and Russia agree not to make separate peace. *Oct. 10*: Charles I of Rumania *d.*; succeeded by Ferdinand I (**-1927**). *Nov. 5*: Britain declares war on Turkey and annexes Cyprus. *12*: Turkey declares war on Britain, France and Russia. *Dec. 17*: British protectorate proclaimed over Egypt; Abbas II deposed, succeeded by Husein. *25*: Italy occupies Valona, Albania.

1915

Jan. 12: Burian succeeds Berchtold as Austro-Hungarian Foreign Secretary. *25*: Germany introduces bread-cards. *Feb. 4*: Germany declares blockade of Great Britain from *Feb. 18*. *23*: Britain closes North Sea and declares blockade of Germany, *Mar. 1*. *Mar. 6*: Gounaris succeeds Venizelos as Greek Premier. *Apr. 26*: Secret treaty of London between Italy and Allies. *May 4*: Italy leaves Triple Alliance. *23*: Italy declares war on Austria. *25*: China accepts Japanese ultimatum. *26*: British Coalition Government formed under Asquith. *June 9*: Ministry of Munitions Bill passed. *23*: Lansing appointed U.S.A. Secretary of State. *24*: First big American loan to Allies. *July 26*: Reprisals of Allies against Greece. *Aug. 20*: Italy declares war on Turkey. *23*: Venizelos again appointed Greek Premier. *Sept. 6*: German-Bulgarian military convention and Turko-Bulgarian alliance. *Oct. 5*: Russia and (*6*) other Allies break off relations with Bulgaria. *5*: Zaimis succeeds Venizelos. *14*: Serbia and (*15-20*) other Allies declare war on Bulgaria. *19*: Japan accedes to Treaty of London of *Sept. 4, 1914*. *29*: Briand, French Premier. *Nov. 21*: Italy accedes to Treaty of London. *Dec. 21*: Robertson appointed Chief of Imperial General Staff.

II. WESTERN FRONT

1914

Aug. 2: Germans occupy Luxembourg. *3*: Germans invade Belgium. *9*: British Expeditionary Force lands in France. *16*: Germans take Liège. *20*: Germans occupy Brussels. *22-23*: Battles of Namur and Mons. British retreat from Mons, ends *Sept. 7*. *25*: Germans take Namur and destroy Louvain. *26-28*: Germans cross Meuse. *30*: Germans take Amiens. *31*: Germans take Givet and Montmédy, cross Oise. *31-Sept. 2*: Battle of the Aisne. *Sept. 3-4*: Germans cross Marne, advance between Aisne and Marne, Meuse and Argonne. *6-9*: Battle of the Marne. *9-15*: German retreat. *14*: Falkenhayn succeeds Moltke as German C.-in-C. *Oct. 9*: Germans take Antwerp, *12*: Ghent and Lille, *14*: Bruges, *15*: Ostend. *17-30*: Battle of the Yser. *30-Nov. 18*: First Battle of Ypres. *Nov. 14*: Lord Roberts *d.*

1915

Jan. 8-14: Battle of Soissons. *Feb. 16-Mar. 19*: Battle in Champagne. *Mar. 10-20*: Battle of Neuve Chapelle. *30-Apr. 14*: Battle of St. Mihiel. *Apr. 22*: Germans first use poison gas. *20-May 24*: Second battle of Ypres. *May 9-July 18*: Battle between Arras and Armentières. *June 4*: Allies take Souchez and (*8*) Neuville. *20-July 14*: Battle of the Argonne. *23-July 7*: First battle of Isonzo. *July 18-Aug. 3*: Second battle of Isonzo. *Sept. 22-Oct. 13*: Battle in Artois. *22-Oct. 19*: Battle in Champagne. *Oct. 11*: Nurse Cavell shot in Brussels. *18-Nov. 4*: Third battle of Isonzo. *Nov. 10-Dec. 3*: Fourth battle of Isonzo. *Dec. 3*: Joffre appointed French C.-in-C. *19*: Haig succeeds French as British C.-in-C.

III. EASTERN FRONT	IV. ORIENT AND COLONIES	V. NAVAL AND AIR WAR

III. EASTERN FRONT

1914

Aug. 12-24: Austrian offensive against Serbia. *22*: Hindenburg appointed Commander in East Prussia, Ludendorff Chief of Staff. *26-31*: Battles of Tannenberg, East Prussia, and Komarov, Galicia. *Sept. 6-Dec. 15*: Second Austrian invasion of Serbia. *9-14*: Battle of Masurian Lakes. *27*: Russians invade Hungary. *28*: Germans and Austrians advance towards Warsaw-Ivangorod and river San. *Oct. 27*: Germans and Austrians retreat from Poland. *Nov. 1*: Hindenburg appointed C.-in-C. on Eastern front. *Dec. 2*: Austrians take Belgrade. *3-9*: Serbian victory south of Belgrade. *6*: Germans take Lodz. *15*: Austrians evacuate Belgrade.

1915

Jan. 23: Austro-German offensive in Carpathians. *Feb. 7-27*: Battle in Masuria; Russians evacuate East Prussia. *Mar. 22*: Russians take Przemysl. *Apr. 27-Oct. 30*: German offensive in Lithuania and Courland. *May 1-3*: Austro-German break-through at Gorlice-Tarnów. *June 3*: Austro-Germans recover Przemysl and (*23*) Lemberg. *July. Middle*: Austro-German offensive in central Poland. *Aug. 1*: Germans take Mitau and Cholm, (*4*) Ivangorod, (*5*) Warsaw, (*19*) Kaunas and Novo-Georgievsk, (*26*) Brest-Litovsk. *27-Sept. 15*: Austrian offensive in Eastern Galicia and Volhynia. *Sept. 3*: Germans take Grodno, (*16*) Pinsk, (*18*) Vilna. *8*: Grand Duke Nicholas Nicholaievitch, Russian C.-in-C., dismissed. *Oct. 6-9*: Austro-German offensive against Serbia begins. *9*: Belgrade taken. *14*: Bulgarian offensive against Serbia begins. *Nov. 24-29*: Battle of Kossovo. *Dec. 9-13*: Anglo-French offensive towards Serbia checked on Greek frontier.

IV. ORIENT AND COLONIES

1914

Aug. 5: Turkey closes Dardanelles. *10*: German cruisers *Goeben* and *Breslau* escape into Dardanelles. *26*: Togoland capitulates to British and French. *29*: New Zealanders occupy Samoa. *Sept. 9*: British take Lüderitz Bay, S.W.A. *11*: British seize New Pomerania. *12*: Japanese occupy German possessions in the Pacific. *21*: German New Guinea capitulates. *27*: British take Duala, Cameroons. *Oct. 7*: Japanese take island of Yap. *Nov. 7*: Japanese take Tsingtao. *14*: Turkey proclaims Holy War. *22*: British occupy Basra. *Dec. 9*: Turkish garrison of Kurna, Mesopotamia, surrenders. *14-Jan. 17*: Turkish attack in Caucasus fails.

1915

Feb. 2-4: Battle on Suez Canal; Turks repulsed. *Mar. 3*: British fleet in Dardanelles. *18*: Anglo-French naval attack on Dardanelles fails. *20*: Botha invades South-West Africa. *Apr. 12-14*: British repel Turkish attack on Basra. *20*: Anglo-French troops take Mandera, Cameroons. *25-29*: Anglo-French expedition lands on Gallipoli. *May 12*: South Africans take Windhoek, capital of S.W. Africa. *16*: British fail to land at Smyrna. *June 3*: British take Amara, Mesopotamia. *July 9*: South-West Africa capitulates to British. *29*: French occupy Mitylene. *Sept. 28*: British take Kut el Amara, Mesopotamia. *Oct. 5*: British and French land at Salonika. *Nov. 22-24*: British defeat at Ctesiphon. *Dec. 7*: Townshend besieged in Kut el Amara. *19-20*: British evacuate Anzac and Suvla, Gallipoli.

V. NAVAL AND AIR WAR

1914

Aug. 2: British fleet mobilized. *27*: *Kaiser Wilhelm der Grosse* sunk off Rio de Oro. *Sept. 5*: *Pathfinder* sunk. *10*: German raiding cruiser *Emden* in Bay of Bengal. *12*: German cruiser *Hela* sunk. *14*: German cruiser *Cap Trafalgar* sunk. *22*: *Cressy, Hogue* and *Aboukir* sunk by U. *29*. *Emden* shells Madras. *Oct. 23*: German raiding cruiser *Karlsruhe* in Atlantic. *27*: *Audacious* mined. *30*: *Emden* at Penang. *Nov. 1*: Cradock defeated by von Spee off Coronel, Chile. *2*: Britain declares North Sea war-zone; blockade of Germany begins. *9*: *Emden* sunk off Sumatra. *Dec. 8*: Sturdee destroys von Spee's squadron off Falkland Islands.

1915

Jan. 1: *Formidable* sunk. *Mar. 19-20*: German air raid on Yarmouth and King's Lynn. *24*: Dogger Bank action; *Blücher* sunk. *Feb. 11*: British air raid on Ostend and Zeebrugge. *18*: Germany begins submarine warfare against merchantmen. *22*: German air raid on Essex. *Mar. 15*: *Dresden* sunk in Pacific. *18*: French and British warships sunk in Dardanelles. *24-26*: British raid Schleswig air base. *31-Apr. 5*: Zeppelins raid southern counties. *Apr. 27*: *Léon Gambetta* sunk in Adriatic by Austrians. *May 7*: Cunard liner *Lusitania* sunk. *12*: *Goliath* and *26*: *Triumph* sunk in Dardanelles. *27*: Lord Fisher resigns as First Sea Lord. *June 1*: German air raid on London. *July 4*: *Königsberg* sunk off East African coast. *Aug. 9*: Five Zeppelins raid London. *18*: *Moltke* sunk. *Sept. 8*: Zeppelins raid London and East Counties. *18*: German submarines restricted to cruiser warfare.

I. POLITICAL EVENTS

1916

Jan. 27: 'Spartacus group' (Communist party) founded in Berlin. *Feb. 2*: Stürmer appointed Russian Premier. *Mar. 9*: Germany and (*15*) Austria declare war on Portugal. *15*: Admiral von Tirpitz resigns. U.S.A. troops invade Mexico. *Apr. 23*: Easter rebellion in Dublin. *May 16*: Sykes-Picot arrangement on partition of Turkey. *17*: Daylight Saving Act. *24*: Conscription in Great Britain. *June 6-24*: Allies blockade Greece. *28*: First political strike at Berlin. *July 6*: Lloyd George, Secretary for War. *23*: Sazonov, Russian Foreign Minister, resigns. *Aug. 3*: Casement executed. *26*: Italy declares war on Germany. *27*: Rumania declares war on Austria. *28*: Germany declares war on Rumania. *Sept. 6*: Supreme War Council of Central Powers established. *Oct. 11*: Allied ultimatum to Greece; Greek fleet surrendered. *18*: Venizelos establishes government at Salonika. *21*: Stürgkh, Austrian Premier, assassinated. *Nov. 5*: Central Powers proclaim Kingdom of Poland. *7*: Wilson re-elected President. *21*: Emperor Francis Joseph *d.*; succeeded by Charles, his grandnephew. *26*: Venizelos declares war on Germany. *Dec. 5*: Asquith resigns. *7*: Coalition Ministry under Lloyd George. *10*: War Cabinet instituted. *12*: Peace offer of Central Powers. *22*: Czernin, Austro-Hungarian Foreign Minister. *30*: Allies refuse peace offer of Central Powers.

1917

Feb. 2: Bread-cards in England. *3*: U.S.A. breaks off diplomatic relations with Germany. *Mar. 8-14 (Feb. 23-Mar. 1, old style)*: February Revolution in Russia. *16*: Nicholas II abdicates; Lvov, Miliukov, and Kerensky form Cabinet. *19*: Ribot, French Premier, *31*: Poincaré receives peace offer from Emperor Charles (Prince Sixtus letter). *Apr. 6*: U.S.A. declares war on Germany. *7*: William II promises universal suffrage in Prussia. *11*: German Independent Labour Party founded. *May 18*: Kerensky, Minister for War. *June 3*: Albania proclaimed independent under Italian protectorate. *12*: Constantine of Greece abdicates; Alexander succeeds. *27*: Venizelos, Greek Premier, joins Allies. *July 13*: Bethmann-Hollweg succeeded by Michaelis as Chancellor. *19*: Reichstag passes motion for peace. *22*: Kerensky, Russian Premier. *14*: China declares war on Germany. *Sept. 7*:

II. WESTERN FRONT

1916

Feb. 21- Dec. 16: Battle of Verdun. *Mar. 15-20*: Fifth battle of Isonzo. *May 15-31*: Austrian offensive between Adige and Brenta. *June 25*: Austrians evacuate positions gained in South Tirol. *July 1-Nov. 18*: Heavy fighting on the Somme. *Aug. 4-16*: Sixth battle of Isonzo. *29*: Hindenburg appointed Chief of General Staff, Ludendorff Quartermaster-General. *Sept. 14-17*: Seventh battle of Isonzo. *15*: British use tanks for the first time. *Oct. 9-12*: Eighth battle of Isonzo. *24-Nov. 5*: French offensive east of Verdun. *Nov. 1-7*: Ninth battle of Isonzo. *Dec. 3*: Nivelle succeeds Joffre as French C.-in-C. *9*: Castelnau appointed French Chief of General Staff. *15-17*: French offensive between Meuse and Woëvre Plain.

1917

Feb. 4: German retreat from Arras-Péronne-Soissons front. *Mar. 16-19*: Germans take stand on Siegfried line. *17-18*: British take Bapaume, Péronne, Nesle, Chaulnes. *Apr. 4*: British offensive in Artois, *9*: French offensive in Champagne begun. *9-21*: Battle of Vimy Ridge. *16-18*: Great battle in Champagne. *23-26*: Battle of Arras. *28-29*: Battle between Lens and Cambrai. *May 3-5*: Battle of Arras. *5-9*: Great battle on Chemin des Dames. *11-20*: Battle of Arras. *14-June 5*: Tenth battle of Isonzo. *15*: Pétain appointed French C.-in-C. *20*: Mutinies begin in French army. *20-27*: Battle of Prosnes. *June 7*: Battle of Messines. *26*: First American troops in France. *July 22-Nov. 10*: 100 days' battle in Flanders. *Sept. 7-11*: Battle east of river Meuse. *20*: British offensive near Ypres resumed. *Oct. 4*: British take Poelcappelle and Zonnebeke. *23*: French take Laffaux, Chemin des Dames. *24-*

III. EASTERN FRONT	IV. ORIENT AND COLONIES	V. NAVAL AND AIR WAR

1916

Jan. 14: Austrians take Cettinje and (*23*) Scutari. *Feb.*: Austrians conquer Albania north of Valona. *March 19-26*: Russian offensive between Jakobstadt and Beresina. *June 4-7*: Russian offensive towards Luck, west of Tarnopol, and north of Czernowitz. *7*: Russians take Luck. *10*: Russians cross Dniester. *13-July 29*: Russian offensive at Baranovici. *16*: Russians take Czernowitz. *July*. General Russian offensive. *28*: Russians take Brody. *Aug. 7-10*: Russian break-through at Zalosce. *Sept. 1-30*: Russian offensive in Carpathians. *1-Dec. 9*: Austro-German-Bulgarian offensive against Rumania. *Dec. 6*: Central Powers enter Bucharest.

1916

Jan. 6-8: Allies evacuate Gallipoli Peninsula. *11*: Russian offensive in Armenia begins. *Feb. 6-15*: German troops leave Cameroons for Spanish Rio Muni. *10*: Smuts takes over command in East Africa. *16*: Russians take Erzerum. *18*: Last German troops in Cameroons surrender. *Mar. 2*: Russians take Bitlis and (*19*) Ispahan *Apr. 18*: Russians take Trebizond. *29*: Townshend capitulates at Kut-el-Amara. *June 21*: Grand Sherif takes Mecca. Turkish offensive towards Persia begins. *July 1*: Turks take Kermanshah. *7*: Smuts occupies Tanga. *25*: Russians take Ersingian. *Aug. 7*: Turks take Bitlis. *10*: Turks take Hamadan. *Sept. 4*: British take Dar-es-Salaäm. *12*: Bulgarians take Kavalla. *Oct. 15*: Allies occupy Athens. *Nov. 19*: French take Monastir. *Dec. 13*: British offensive begins in Mesopotamia. *23*: British take El Arish, Palestine.

1916

Feb. 8: French cruiser *Amiral Charner* sunk. *29*: Germans resume submarine warfare. *Mar. 25*: British raid Zeppelin base in Schleswig. *May 4*: German submarine warfare restricted. *31-June 1*: Battle of Jutland; heavy British losses, but naval supremacy definitely established. *June 6*: *Hampshire* sunk; Kitchener drowned. *22*: Air raids on Karlsruhe, Cologne, and Trier. *July 10*: German submarine *Deutschland* reaches Baltimore. *24*: German submarine *Bremen* reaches New York; sunk on return voyage.

1917

Jan. 4-8: Russo-Rumanians defeated at Focsani. *5*: Austro-Germans take Braila and (*8*) Focsani and mouth of Danube. *Mar. 1*: Arz succeeds Conrad as Austrian C.-in-C. *June 26*: Kerensky launches Russian offensive. *July 1-11*: Russians break through at Zborov and on Dniester. *19-27*: Russian offensive at Smorgon. *22-25*: Russo-Rumanian offensive on Sereth. *24*: Russians take Nardworna, Stanislau, Tarnopol. *Aug. 3*: Russians take Czernowitz. *6*: German offensive at Focsani fails. *Sept. 3*: Germans take Riga, (*4*) Dünamünde, (*22*) Jakobstadt. *Oct. 12-21*: Ger-

1917

Feb. 24: Turks defeated, evacuate Kut-el-Amara and Sanna-i-Yat. *Mar. 11*: British take Baghdad. Turks retreat from Persia. *26-28*: First battle of Gaza, British victory. *Apr. 13*: Further Turkish retreat in Mesopotamia. *18-19*: Second battle of Gaza, British victory. *May 7-17*: Battle between Doiran and Lake Presba, Macedonia. *June 29*: Allenby in command in Palestine. *July 19*: Russians leave Mesopotamian front. *Aug. 30*: Turks take Merivan, Persia. *Sept. 28*: Anglo-Indian forces capture Ramadieh, Mesopotamia. *Oct. 15-18*: Battle of Mahiva, East Africa. *Nov. 7*: British take Gaza. *17*:

1917

Jan. 31: Germany proclaims unrestricted submarine warfare. *Feb. 1*: Submarine warfare begins with 103 boats. *Mar. 16*: *Danton*, French Dreadnought, sunk. *July 19-Aug. 2*: Mutiny in German fleet. *Oct. 19-20*: Zeppelins raid English industrial areas; four airships brought down. *Nov. 17*: Light cruiser fight off Heligoland. *21-24*: Zeppelin 59 flies from Adrianople to Khartum and back. *Dec. 10*: Italians torpedo Austrian battleship *Wien* in Trieste harbour.

I. POLITICAL EVENTS	II. WESTERN FRONT

1917

Painlevé, French Premier. *15*: Kerensky proclaims Russian Republic. *Oct. 30*: Orlando, Italian Premier. *Nov. 1*: Hertling, German Chancellor. *2*: Balfour Declaration on Palestine. *5-7*: Conference of Rapallo establishes Supreme War Council of Allies. *7* (*Oct. 26, old style*): Bolshevist Revolution in Russia. *10-12*: Counter-revolution of Kerensky and Kornilov fails. *17*: Clemenceau, French Premier. *Dec. 6*: Finland proclaims its independence. *7*: U.S.A. declares war on Austria-Hungary. *22*: Peace conference begins at Brest-Litovsk.

1918

Jan. 8: Wilson issues Fourteen Points. *16*: Strikes in Vienna and (*28-Feb. 3*) Berlin. *Feb. 9*: Peace between Central Powers and Ukraine. *Mar. 3*: Treaty of Brest-Litovsk between Central Powers and Russia. *7*: Treaty between Germany and Finland. *12*: Moscow proclaimed capital of Russia. *23*: Lithuania proclaimed independent. *Apr. 9*: Latvia and (*10*) Estonia proclaimed independent. Bessarabia proclaims union with Rumania. *May 7*: Treaty of Bucharest between Central Powers and Rumania. *July 3*: Sultan Muhammad V *d.*; succeeded by Muhammad VI. *16*: Nicholas II of Russia and family murdered. *Sept. 14*: Austria-Hungary offers peace to Allies; *20*: refused. *29*: Hindenburg demands immediate offer of armistice and peace. *Oct 3*: Prince Max of Baden, Chancellor. Ferdinand of Bulgaria abdicates; succeeded by Boris. *3-4*: Germany asks Wilson for armistice. *27*: Austria-Hungary offers separate peace. *28*: William II issues democratic reform of constitution. *30*: Czechoslovak State proclaimed in Prague. *31*: Revolution in Austria-Hungary. Tisza, Hungarian Premier, assassinated. *Nov. 3*: Revolution at Kiel. *8*: Bavarian Republic proclaimed at Munich. *9*: Revolution in Berlin; German Republic proclaimed; Prince Max resigns in favour of Ebert. *10*: William II flees to Holland; Council of People's Delegates assumes power. Emperor Charles abdicates in Austria and (*13*) Hungary. *12*: Austria proclaims union with Germany. *13*: Russia cancels peace of Brest-Litovsk. *14*: Masaryk elected Czechoslovak president. *28*: William II abdicates. *29*: Nicholas of Montenegro deposed and country united with Serbia under King Peter. *30*: Transylvania proclaims union with Rumania. *Dec. 1*: Yugoslav Kingdom proclaimed. *13*: Wilson arrives in Paris. *14*: General Election: Coalition 484, Opposition 222.

1917

Nov. 14: Austro-German offensive on Isonzo. *Oct. 24-27*: Battle of Caporetto; Austro-Germans break through. *28*: Austro-Germans take Gorizia and Udine. *Nov. 2*: German retreat beyond Aisne-Oise and Ailette Canals. *2-5*: Austro-Germans cross Tagliamento. *4*: British troops arrive on Italian front. *6*: British take Passchendaele. *10*: Italians take stand on river Piave. *20-30*: British offensive at Cambrai; Hindenburg Line broken. *30-Dec. 7*: German counter-attack at Cambrai. *Dec. 3*: Austro-German operations in Italy definitely stopped.

1918

Mar. 21-Apr. 6: German offensive towards Amiens. *26*: Foch appointed C.-in-C. of Allied forces in France. *Apr. 12*: Germans take Armentières, (*14*) Bailleul, (*25*) Mount Kemmel. *24-26*: British victory at Villers-Bretonneux. *May 27-June 5*: Second German offensive; battle of Soissons and Reims. *27*: Germans storm Chemin des Dames, (*30*) reach Marne at Dormans and Château-Thierry. *July 15-17*: Last German offensive; second battle of Marne; unsuccessful attack on Reims. *18*: French and Americans attack from Villers-Cotterêts Forest. *20*: Germans evacuate left bank of Marne. *22*: Allies cross Marne. *Aug. 2*: Germans evacuate Soissons and left banks of Vesle and Aisne. *20*: British offensive begins. *Sept. 1*: British take Péronne and Mount Kemmel. *4*: Germans retreat to Siegfried line. *12-14*: Americans take St. Mihiel salient. *26*: General offensive of Allies begins. *Oct. 1*: French take St. Quentin. *9-10*: British take Cambrai and Le Cateau. *13*: French take Laon. *17*: British in Ostend. *19*: Belgians take Zeebrugge and Bruges. *26*: Allied offensive across Piave begins. Ludendorff dismissed. *28*: Austro-Hungarian front broken through at Vittorio Veneto. *Nov. 3*: Armistice signed with Austria-Hungary. *4*: Germans retreat to Antwerp-Meuse line. *7*: French and Americans take Sedan. German Armistice Commission crosses front line. *11*: Armistice signed at Compiègne (*6 a.m.*), comes into force (*11 a.m.*). *Dec. 6*: Allies occupy Cologne and (*9*) Mainz.

III. EASTERN FRONT	IV. ORIENT AND COLONIES	V. NAVAL AND AIR WAR

1917

mans occupy islands of Ösel, Moon, and Dagö. *Nov. 26*: Soviets offer armistice to Central Powers. *Dec. 2*: Hostilities suspended on Russian and (*4*) Rumanian fronts. *5*: Armistices with Russia and (*9*) Rumania.

1918

Jan. 28: Bolshevists occupy Helsinki. *Feb. 18*: Germans resume hostilities on Russian front; occupy Dünaburg and Luck; (*21*) Minsk, (*22*) Dubno, (*24*) Dorpat, (*25*) Reval. *Mar. 1*: Germans occupy Kiev (*2*) Narva, (*5*) Aaland islands, (*13*) Odessa, (*20*) Cherson. *Apr. 4*: Germans invade Finland; occupy Ekaterinoslav, (*8*) Charkov, (*14*) Helsinki. *May 1*: Germans occupy Sebastopol and (*8*) Rostov. *July 6-10*: Allies break through in Albania. *Sept. 15*: Allies break through Bulgarian front between Cerna and Vardar. *25*: Bulgaria asks for armistice. *29*: Bulgaria capitulates. *Oct*: Allies expel Austro-Germans from Serbia and Albania. *Nov. 3*: Armistice signed with Austria-Hungary. *14*: Germans evacuate Finland. *Dec. 5*: Blockade of Germany extended over Baltic. *8*: Bolshevist rule in Estonia, (*20*) Lithuania and (*22*) Latvia. *27*: Poles occupy Poznan.

1917

British take Jaffa. *25*: East African Germans enter Mozambique. *Dec. 9*: Allenby enters Jerusalem.

1918

Feb. 14: Turks take Ersingian and (*24*) Trebizond. *21*: Australians take Jericho. *Mar. 12*: Turks take Baku. *Apr. 5*: Japanese occupy Vladivostok. *7*: Turks take Van, (*13*) Batum, (*26*) Kars. *May 14*: Turks evacuate Baku. *June 16*: Turks enter Tabriz, Persia. *July 13*: Last Turkish offensive in Palestine to recover Jericho; *14*: checked by Australians. *Aug. 2*: Japanese advance in Siberia begins. *Sept. 15*: Turks recapture Baku. *19*: British break through in Palestine. *Oct. 1*: Australians enter Damascus. *6*: French occupy Beirut. *18*: British occupy Aleppo, French occupy Alexandretta. *30*: Turkey surrenders unconditionally. *Nov. 1*: Anglo-French occupy Constantinople. *2*: East African Germans invade Northern Rhodesia. *14*: Germans capitulate in Northern Rhodesia.

1918

Jan 14: Naval battle at Imbros: *Breslau* sunk and *Goeben* driven ashore. *Apr. 22-23*: British raid on Zeebrugge. *May 9*: British fleet attacks Ostend and (*10*) obstructs Bruges Canal by sinking H.M.S. *Vindictive*. *Aug. 11*: British fleet attacks German coast. *Oct. 14*: Wilson demands suspension of submarine warfare. *20*: Germany suspends submarine warfare; total tonnage sunk since *1914*: 14.5 million gross tons. *28*: German attack on England delayed because of mutiny aboard *Markgraf*. *30*: Attack definitely abandoned because of mutiny in several ships. *Nov. 3*: General mutiny in German fleet. *14*: German fleet surrenders at sea to British Navy.

I. INTERNATIONAL AFFAIRS	II. BRITISH EMPIRE	III. AMERICA
1919. *Jan. 18*: Peace Conference meets in Paris. *Mar. 29*: Shantung assigned to Japan; Chinese leave Peace Conference. *June 28*: Treaty of Versailles signed. *July 12*: Blockade of Germany terminated. *Sept. 2*: Ultimatum against Austro-German union. *10*: Austria signs Treaty of St. Germain. *Oct. 17*: Austria ratifies St. Germain Treaty. *29*: International Labour Conference meets in Washington; *Nov. 23*: adopts 8-hour day. *27*: Bulgaria signs Treaty of Neuilly. *Dec. 16*: Germans evacuate Latvia and Lithuania.	**1919.** *Apr. 5*: De Valera elected President of Sinn Fein Executive. *Aug. 8*: Imperial Preference Provisions Act. *22*: Botha d. *Oct. 27*: Curzon succeeds Balfour as Foreign Secretary. *28*: War Cabinet ends. *Dec. 1*: Viscountess Astor, first woman M.P.	**1919.** *Jan. 6*: Theodore Roosevelt d. *June 14-15*: First direct crossing of the Atlantic by aeroplane (Alcock and Brown).
1920. *Jan. 10*: Versailles Treaty and League Covenant come into force. *Feb. 11*: League takes over Danzig. *15*: Allies take over Memel district. *26*: League takes over Saar district. *Apr. 18-26*: Allied conference at San Remo; Anglo-French agreement on Mesopotamia. *June 4*: Hungary signs Treaty of Trianon. *15*: Denmark takes over North Slesvig. *July 24*: Treaty of St. Germain comes into force. *Aug. 9*: Treaty of Neuilly comes into force. *10*: Constantinople government signs Treaty of Sèvres. *Sept. 20*: League Council assigns Eupen and Malmédy to Belgium. *Nov. 15-Dec. 18*: First League Assembly: mandates allotted, International Court established. *Dec. 3*: Austria joins League. *15-22*: Brussels Conference: Germany to pay £13,450 million in 42 years. *16*: Bulgaria joins League.	**1920.** *Apr. 30*: Conscription abolished. *July 1*: Sir Herbert Samuel, High Commissioner of Palestine. *6*: British troops evacuate Batum. *8*: East Africa Protectorate transformed into Kenya Colony. *Dec. 23*: Home Rule Act.	**1920.** *Jan. 16*: U.S.A. Senate votes against joining League of Nations. Prohibition comes into force. *Feb. 15*: Lansing, Secretary of State, resigns. *Mar. 19*: U.S.A. Senate refuses ratification of Versailles Treaty. *Apr. 9*: U.S.A. Congress decides upon terminating state of war with Germany. *May 20*: Carranza, President of Mexico, assassinated. *24*: Huerta elected President of Mexico. *Aug. 26*: Women's suffrage adopted in U.S.A. *Nov. 2*: Harding (Rep.) elected U.S.A. President.

IV. WESTERN AND SOUTHERN EUROPE	V. CENTRAL AND EASTERN EUROPE	VI. RUSSIA AND ASIA
1919. *Feb. 23*: Mussolini founds Fasci del Combattimento. *June 21*: Nitti Cabinet in Italy. *Sept. 12*: D'Annunzio seizes Fiume from Yugoslavia. *Nov. 17*: Belgo-Dutch agreement on Scheldt question.	**1919.** *Jan. 5-13*: Communist revolt in Berlin. *5*: National Socialist Party founded. *10-Feb. 4*: Soviet Republic of Bremen. *19*: Election of German National Assembly. *Feb. 11*: Ebert elected Reich President. *13*: Scheidemann Ministry. *Mar. 3-10*: Communist revolt in Berlin. *21-Aug. 1*: Hungary proclaimed Soviet Republic. *Apr. 3*: Hapsburg dynasty exiled from Austria. *7-May 2*: Soviet Republic of Bavaria (from *13* Munich only). *June 20*: German fleet scuttled at Scapa Flow. *21*: Bauer Ministry. *July 3*: Supreme War Command dissolved. *7*: Black-red-gold made German national flag. *Aug. 4-Nov. 13*: Rumanians occupy Budapest. *Aug. 11*: German Constitution signed.	**1919.** *Jan. 20*: Habibullah, Amir of Afghanistan, assassinated succeeded by (*Feb. 19*) Amanullah. *Feb. 21*: Blockade of Turkey ceases. *Mar. 4*: Third International founded at Moscow. *May 3-Aug. 8*: War between Britain and Afghanistan. *22*: Riga freed from Bolsheviks. *28*: Armenia proclaims its independence. *June 9*: Red Army takes Ufa; beginning of White defeat. *Aug. 5*: Mustafa Kemal declares himself independent of Istanbul. *8*: Anglo-Afghan Treaty of Rawalpindi. *Sept. 15*: China terminates war with Germany. *Oct. 12*: British evacuate Murmansk. *22*: Yudenitch defeated by Red Army near Petersburg. *Nov. 14*: Yudenitch's Army dissolved. *15*: Red Army takes Omsk, Siberia.
1920. *Jan. 17*: Deschanel elected French President; Millerand, Premier. *May 1*: Customs union between Belgium and Luxemburg. *16*: Joan of Arc canonized. *Sept. 7*: Franco-Belgian military convention. *16*: Deschanel resigns. *23*: Millerand elected French President. *24*: Leygues, French Premier. *Oct. 25*: King Alexander of Greece d. *Nov. 12*: Treaty of Rapallo between Italy and Yugoslavia; Italy obtains Zara, renounces Split and Sebenico; Fiume made independent. *Dec. 19*: King Constantine restored in Greece.	**1920.** *Feb. 10*: Plebiscite in first zone of North Slesvig (74 per cent. for Denmark). *28*: Hungarian Constitution. *29*: Czechoslovak Constitution. *Mar. 1*: Horthy elected Regent of Hungary. *13-17*: Kapp Revolt in Germany. *14*: Plebiscite in second zone of Slesvig (80 per cent. for Germany). *Apr. 25*: Polish offensive against Russia. *May 1*: Union of eight Thuringian republics. *June 21*: Fehrenbach, German Chancellor. *July 6*: Russian offensive against Poland. *11*: Plebiscite in East and West Prussia (97 per cent. for Germany). *Aug. 14-16*: Poles defeat Russians at Warsaw. *14*: Czechoslovakia and Yugoslavia form Little Entente; *17*: joined by Rumania. *Oct. 1*: Austrian Constitution. *9*: Poland annexes Vilna. *10*: Plebiscite in Carinthia (57 per cent. for Austria). Southern Tirol incorporated in Italy.	**1920.** *Feb. 2*: Treaty of Tartu between Russia and Estonia. *7*: Admiral Koltchak executed. *Mar. 11*: Feisal proclaimed King of Syria. *16*: Allies occupy Constantinople. *Apr. 27*: Russians take Baku. *May 11*: Turkish National Assembly meets at Ankara. *July 12*: Treaty of Moscow between Russia and Lithuania. *24*: French occupy Damascus. *Aug. 11*: Treaty of Riga between Russia and Latvia. *Oct. 12*: Preliminary Treaty of Riga between Russia and Poland. *14*: Treaty of Tartu between Russia and Finland. *20*: Treaty of Ankara between France and Turkey. *Nov. 16*: Wrangel expelled from Crimea; end of Russian counter-revolution. *Dec. 2*: Peace of Alexandropol; Armenia cedes half her territory to Turkey.

I. INTERNATIONAL AFAIRS	II. BRITISH EMPIRE	III. AMERICA
1921. *Jan. 24-29*: Paris Conference; Germany to pay £11,300 million in 42 years. *Feb. 21-26*: Near East Conference of Allies in London. *Mar. 15-Sept. 30*: French occupy Ruhr district. *20*: Plebiscite in Upper Silesia; 63 per cent. for Germany. *May 5*: London Ultimatum; Germany to pay £6,600 million. *10*: Germany accepts Ultimatum. *Oct. 12*: League Council suggests partition of Upper Silesia; *26*: accepted by Germany. *Nov. 12-Feb. 6*, **1922**: Disarmament Conference in Washington. *Dec. 13*: Four Power Pacific Treaty signed in Washington. *14*: Plebiscite at Ödenburg; 65 per cent. for Hungary.	**1921.** *Jan. 3*: First Indian Parliament meets. *Mar. 16*: Anglo-Russian trade agreement. *24*: Reparation Recovery Act imposes 50 per cent. duties on German goods. *May 20*: Recovery Act duties reduced to 26 per cent. *July 1*: Safeguarding of Industries Act. *Dec. 6*: Irish Peace Agreement signed. Liberals win Canadian elections. *29*: MacKenzie King, Premier.	**1921.** *Feb. 18*: U.S.A. representative recalled from Reparation Commission. *Mar. 4*: Harding becomes U.S.A. President. *Apr. 24*: German petition for U.S. mediation in Reparations refused. *May 19*: Emergency Quota Immigration Act. *Aug. 24*: Peace treaties of U.S.A. with Austria, (*25*) Germany, and (*29*) Hungary. *Oct. 28*: Treaty between U.S.A. and Liberia.
1922. *Jan. 4-13*: Conference of Cannes; postpones German payments. *Apr. 10-May 19*: Conference of Genoa. *Oct. 4*: Geneva Protocol; Austria renounces *Anschluss*, receives loan. *Nov. 2-7*: Conference of experts on German currency at Berlin. *Dec. 26*: Reparation Commission declares ' deliberate default ' of Germany.	**1922.** *Feb. 6*: Anglo-Japanese alliance lapses. *28*: Britain abolishes Protectorate over Egypt. *Mar. 15*: Britain recognizes independence of Egypt under King Fuad. *Sept. 10*: Commercial treaty between Britain and Russia. *Oct. 19*: Lloyd George Coalition Cabinet overthrown. *23*: Bonar Law (Cons.), Premier. *Nov. 17*: General Election; 344 Cons., 138 Lab., 117 Lib.	**1922.** *Feb. 6*: Washington Naval Agreement between U.S.A., Britain, and Japan. *Sept. 20*: U.S.A. Protectionist Tariff comes into force.
1923. *Jan. 7*: Reparation Commission declares another ' deliberate default ' by Germany. *10*: French occupy Ruhr district, (*Feb. 4*) Offenburg and Appenweier, (*Mar. 3-6*) Darmstadt, Mannheim, and Karlsruhe. *Feb. 16*: Allies assign Memel territory to Lithuania. *Mar. 14*: Allies assign Vilna and Eastern Galicia to Poland. *Nov. 29*: Reparation Commission appoints Committee of Experts to examine German economic conditions.	**1923.** *Feb. 2*: Bruce, Australian Premier. *Apr. 20*: Egyptian Constitution. *May 22*: Baldwin succeeds Bonar Law as Premier. *25*: Britain proclaims independence of Transjordan under Amir Abdullah. *Sept. 29*: Palestine mandate comes into force. *Oct. 26-Nov. 8*: Empire Conference in London. *Nov. 10*: Reparation Recovery Act suspended. *Dec. 6*: General election; 258 Cons., 191 Lab., 158 Lib., 8 Indep.	**1923.** *Jan. 6*: U.S.A. Senate decides on recalling occupation forces from Rhineland. *Apr. 26*: Mexico recognizes oil concessions granted before **1917**. *June 19*: Anglo-American war debt convention signed by Baldwin and Mellon. *Aug. 2*: President Harding d.; succeeded by C. Coolidge (Rep.). *Sept. 3*: U.S.A. resumes relations with Mexico. *Dec. 18*: Commercial treaty between U.S.A. and Germany.

IV. WESTERN AND SOUTHERN EUROPE	V. CENTRAL AND EASTERN EUROPE	VI. RUSSIA AND ASIA
1921. *Feb. 19*: Franco-Polish alliance. *Mar. 8*: Dato, Spanish Premier, murdered. *May 14*: General election in Italy; 29 Fascists elected. *July 25*: Economic agreement for fifty years between Belgium and Luxemburg.	**1921.** *Mar. 3*: Polish-Rumanian alliance. *17*: Polish Constitution. *27*: *Coup d'état* of Emperor Charles in Hungary fails. *Apr. 23*: Czecho-Rumanian alliance. *May 10*: Wirth, German Chancellor. *28*: Rathenau, German Minister for Reparations. *June 7*: Alliance between Rumania and Yugoslavia. *Aug. 26*: Erzberger, German Minister of Finance, assassinated. *29-Dec. 16*: State of Emergency in Germany conflict between Reich and Bavaria. *Oct. 21-25*: Second *coup d'état* of Emperor Charles in Hungary fails. *Nov. 1*: Braun Ministry in Prussia (-*July 20, 1932*). *6*: Hapsburg dynasty exiled from Hungary.	**1921.** *Feb. 26*: Treaty between Russia and Persia. *28*: Treaty between Russia and Afghanistan. *Mar. 1*: Treaty between Turkey and Afghanistan. *11*: French agreement with Turkey; France renounces Cilicia. *16*: Treaty between Russia and Turkey. *18*: Final Treaty of Riga between Russia and Poland. *May 20*: Agreement between China and Germany. *June 27*: Treaty between Persia and Afghanistan. *Oct. 20*: Franco-Turkish agreement signed. *Dec. 21*: Russo-Turkish agreement.
1922. *Jan. 12*: Poincaré succeeds Briand as Premier. *Feb. 26*: Facta, Italian Premier. *May 24*: Commerical treaty between Italy and Russia. *Sept. 13*: Franco-Polish military convention for ten years. *27*: Constantine of Greece abdicates. *Oct. 28*: Mussolini's march on Rome.	**1922.** *Jan. 31*: Rathenau, German Foreign Minister. *Apr. 1*: Emperor Charles d. *June 16*: Germany cedes East Upper Silesia to Poland. *24*: Rathenau murdered. *26*: Emergency decree for Protection of Republic; new conflict between Reich and Bavaria (-*Aug. 20*). *Oct. 24*: Ebert elected Reich President. *Nov. 22*: Cuno, German Chancellor. *Dec. 1*: Pilsudski, Polish President, resigns.	**1922.** *Feb. 6*: Nine-Power-Treaty secures independence of China; Japan restores Shantung. *Apr. 16*: Treaty of Rapallo between Russia and Germany; diplomatic and economic relations resumed. *Sept. 13*: Turks take Smyrna from Greeks. *Oct. 10*: Turco-Greek armistice. *Nov. 1*: Kemal Pasha proclaims Turkish Republic.
1923. *Apr. 24*: Popular Party leaves Italian Government. *May 10*: Vorovski, Russian delegate, murdered at Lausanne; relations between Russia and Switzerland broken off. *June 10*: Customs union between Switzerland and Liechtenstein. *July 10*: Non-Fascist parties dissolved in Italy. *Sept. 13-27*: Italy occupies Corfu. *14*: Primo de Rivera assumes Spanish dictatorship. *Dec. 18*: Agreement on Tangier signed by Britain, France, and Spain.	**1923.** *Jan. 10*: Lithuanians occupy Memel territory. *19*: Germany proclaims Passive Resistance. *Aug. 6*: Stresemann, Chancellor and Foreign Minister. *Sept. 26*: Passive Resistance abandoned. *Oct. 1*: *Coup d'état* of Black Reichwehr fails. *Oct. 21-Nov. 30*: Separatist riots in Rhineland and Palatinate. *Nov. 8-9*: Hitler's *coup d'état* fails, in Munich. *20*: German currency stabilized. *30*: Marx, Chancellor; Stresemann, Foreign Minister.	**1923.** *Jan. 1*: Union of Soviet Socialist Republics established. *Feb. 10*: Alliance between Turkey and Afghanistan. *July 6*: Russian Constitution comes into force. *July 26*: Peace of Lausanne between Turkey and Allies. *Sept. 1*: Terrible earthquake in Japan. *Oct. 29*: Turkish Republican Constitution; Kemal Pasha, President.

I. INTERNATIONAL AFFAIRS	II. BRITISH EMPIRE	III. AMERICA
1924. *Apr. 18*: League reorganizes Hungarian finances. *May 8*: Memel Statute issued. *July 16-Aug. 16*: London Reparations Conference, accepts Dawes Report. *Aug. 18*: French evacuate Offenburg and Appenweier. *Sept. 1*: Dawes Plan comes into force. *30*: Naval control abolished in Germany. *Oct. 2*: Geneva Protocol on wars of aggression.	**1924.** *Jan. 23*: Labour Ministry (MacDonald). *Feb. 1*: Britain recognizes Soviet government. *Feb. 23*: Reparation Recovery duties reduced to 5 per cent. *June 30*: Hertzog, South African Premier. *July 15*: Britain cedes Jubaland to Italy. *Oct. 29*: General Election; 413 Cons., 151 Lab., 40 Lib. *Nov. 6*: Conservative Ministry (Baldwin); Austen Chamberlain, Foreign Secretary. *19*: Sir Lee Stack murdered in Cairo. *Dec. 2*: Anglo-German commercial treaty.	**1924.** *Feb. 3*: Wilson d. *28*: U.S.A. troops land in Honduras. *July 6*: Calles elected President of Mexico. *Nov. 4*: Coolidge elected U.S.A. President.
1925. *Jan. 20*: Costa Rica leaves League. *Mar. 10*: Britain rejects Geneva Protocol. *May 4-June 17*: Geneva Conference on trade in arms. *July 20*: French evacuate Westphalia and (*31*) Ruhr district. *Aug. 19-29*: Oecumenical Church Conference in Stockholm. *Oct.5-16*: Locarno Conference. *Dec. 1*: Locarno treaties signed in London.	**1925.** *Jan. 20*: Anglo-Chinese treaty of Pekin. *Apr. 3*: Reparation Recovery Act repealed. *May 20*: Lord Lloyd High Commissioner for Egypt. *21*: Field-Marshal Plumer succeeds Sir H. Samuel as High Commissioner for Palestine. *Oct. 30*: E. Wood (Lord Irwin), Viceroy of India. *Dec. 3*: Irish Boundary Agreement. *6*: Agreement on Cyrenaica between Italy and Egypt.	**1925.** *Jan. 11*: Kellogg appointed U.S.A. Secretary of State. *Feb. 10*: Fishing agreement between U.S.A. and Canada. *Mar. 9*: Coolidge arbitrates in Tacna-Arica conflict between Chile and Peru. *Aug. 18*: Agreement on war debts between U.S.A. and Belgium and (*Nov. 12*) Italy.
1926. *Jan. 31*: First Rhineland zone evacuated. *Mar. 17*: Brazil prevents Germany's admission to League. *May 18*: Preparatory Disarmament Conference (until *Dec. 9 1930*). *June 12*: Brazil leaves League. *Sept.* 8: Germany joins League. *11*: Spain leaves League.	**1926.** *May 1-Nov. 27*: Strike of coal-miners. *May 3-12*: General strike. *June 5*: Anglo-Turkish agreement on Mosul. *Oct. 19-Nov. 23*: Empire Conference in London.	**1926.** *May 24*: Mexico nationalizes minerals and oil. *July 2*: Anti-Church legislation in Mexico. *28*: Alliance between U.S.A. and Panama.
1927. *Jan. 31*: Military control of Germany abolished. *May 2-23*: World Economic Conference at Geneva. *June 20-Aug. 4*: Naval Disarmament Conference in Washington. *Aug. 22*: Military control of Hungary abolished *Dec. 17*: Pact for the renunciation of war suggested by Kellogg, U.S.A. Secretary of State.	**1927.** *May 20*: Britain recognizes Ibn Saud by treaty of Jeddah. *27*: Britain breaks off diplomatic relations with Russia. *July 28*: Trade Union Bill passed. *Dec. 14*: Treaty between Britain and Iraq.	**1927.** *Apr. 11*: Ibañez assumes dictatorship in Chile; *May 22*: elected President. *May 20-21*: First solo aeroplane crossing of the Atlantic, by Lindbergh. *Aug. 7*: International Peace Bridge between U.S.A. and Canada opened.

IV. WESTERN AND SOUTHERN EUROPE	V. CENTRAL AND EASTERN EUROPE	VI. RUSSIA AND ASIA
1924. *Jan. 24*: Non-Fascist Trade-Unions dissolved in Italy. *25*: Alliance between France and Czechoslovakia. *Mar. 9*: Fiume incorporated with Italy. *24*: Greece proclaimed Republic. *May 11*: Left Cartel defeats National Bloc at French elections. *June 10*: Matteotti murdered; Opposition leaves Italian Chamber. Millerand resigns. *13*: Doumergue elected French President. *15*: Herriot, French Premier.	**1924.** *Feb. 17*: Separatists overthrown in Palatinate. *Apr. 1*: Hitler sentenced to five years' confinement (released *Dec. 20*). *May 4*: Nationalists and Communists successful in German elections. *Aug. 29*: Reichstag passes Dawes Acts. *Oct. 25*: State of Emergency abolished in Germany. *Dec. 7*: Nationalists and Communists defeated at German elections.	**1924.** *Jan. 21*: Lenin *d. Feb. 2*: Turkish National Assembly abolishes Caliphate. *3*: German-Turkish treaty of friendship. *19*: Ahmad, Shah of Persia, dethroned; Reza Khan appointed Regent. *Oct. 2*: Amir Ali succeeds Husain as King of Hedjaz. *Nov. 5*: Civil war breaks out in China.
1925. *Jan. 31*: Ahmad Zogu elected President of Albania. *Apr. 10*: Painlevé, French Premier. *23*: Franco-Spanish war against Kabyles breaks out in Morocco. *July 18*: Treaty of Nettuno between Italy and Yugoslavia concerning Dalmatia. *Aug. 15*: Norway annexes Spitsbergen.	**1925.** *Jan. 15*: Luther, Chancellor. *Feb. 28*: President Ebert *d. Apr. 26*: Hindenburg elected President. *Aug. 29*: Kapp conspirators amnestied.	**1925.** *Jan. 20*: Russo-Japanese Treaty. *Mar. 12*: Sun Yat Sen *d. Apr. 4*: Japan evacuates Saghalein. *Oct. 12*: Commercial treaty between Russia and Germany. *18-20*: French bombard Damascus. *31*: Reza Khan becomes Shah of Persia. *Dec. 17*: Treaty of security between Russia and Turkey.
1926. *Jan. 3-Aug. 22*: Pangalos, Greek dictator. *May 26*: Abd-el-Krim submits to France. *31*: *Coup d'état* in Portugal. *July 23*: Poincaré, French Premier. *Aug. 17*: Treaty of friendship between Greece and Yugoslavia. *Nov. 27*: Treaty of friendship between Italy and Albania.	**1926.** *Jan. 20*: Luther, Chancellor. *May 12*: *Coup d'état* of Pilsudski in Poland. *17*: Marx, Chancellor. *Sept. 25*: Pilsudski, Polish Premier. *Oct. 12*: Sudeten Germans join Czechoslovak Cabinet. *Dec. 17*: Woldemaras, dictator of Lithuania.	**1926.** *Jan. 8*: Ibn Saud becomes King of Hedjaz. *Apr. 24*: Berlin treaty of reassurance between Russia and Germany. *Dec. 25*: Emperor Yoshohito *d.*; succeeded by Hirohito.
1927. *Apr. 5*: Treaty of friendship between Italy and Hungary. *15*: Diplomatic relations resumed between Russia and Switzerland. *21*: Italian Labour Charter issued. *June 2*: Greek Constitution. *Nov. 11*: Treaty of friendship between France and Yugoslavia. *22*: Alliance between Italy and Albania.	**1927.** *Jan. 29*: Marx, Chancellor. *May 13*: Black Friday; breakdown of German economic system. *27*: Masaryk re-elected Czechoslovak President. *July 15-16*: Socialist riots at Vienna; Palace of Justice burnt. *20*: Ferdinand of Rumania *d.*; succeeded by Michael, his grandson.	**1927.** *Jan. 1*: Chinese Nationalist Government established at Hankow. *Apr. 15*: Chiang Kai-Shek organizes government at Nanking. *Oct. 1*: Russo-Persian Non-aggression pact. *Dec. 14*: Relations between Russia and China broken off. Chiang Kai-Shek overthrows Hankow government.

I. INTERNATIONAL AFFAIRS	II. BRITISH EMPIRE	III. AMERICA
1928. *Jan. 13:* Military control of Bulgaria abolished. *June 11:* Reparations Agent demands final settlement of German liabilities. *July 25:* Italy adheres to Tangier Statute. *Aug. 27:* Kellogg Pact signed in Paris. *Dec. 22:* Commission of Experts for reparations appointed.	**1928.** *Feb. 20:* Britain recognizes independence of Transjordan. *May 7:* Parliament passes Women's Suffrage Bill. *July 5:* Sir J. Chancellor appointed High Commissioner of Palestine. *19: Coup d'état* of King Fuad of Egypt.	**1928.** *Apr. 1:* Irigoyen, President of Argentina. *July 1:* Obregon, President of Mexico; *17:* assassinated. *Sept. 10:* Argentina nationalizes oil. *Nov. 7:* H. Hoover (Rep.) elected U.S.A. President. *Dec. 6:* War breaks out between Bolivia and Paraguay.
1929. *Feb. 11:* Young Committee meets. *June 7:* Young Report on German reparations. *July 24:* Kellogg Pact comes into force. *Aug. 6-31:* Reparation Conference at Hague; settles evacuation of Rhineland. *Nov. 13:* Bank for International Payments, Basle, founded. *30:* Second Rhineland zone evacuated.	**1929.** *May. 30:* General Election; 287 Lab., 261 Cons., 59 Lib., 8 others. *June 5:* Labour Ministry (MacDonald). *Aug. 8:* Sir P. Loraine, High Commissioner of Egypt. Unrest between Jews and Arabs in Palestine. *Oct. 3:* Anglo-Russian relations resumed.	**1929.** *Jan. 5:* Inter-American treaty of arbitration. *May 17:* Chile and Peru settle Tacna-Arica conflict. *June 21:* Agreement between State and Church in Mexico. *Sept. 14:* U.S.A. join International Court. *16:* Peace between Bolivia and Paraguay. *Oct. 28:* Collapse of New York Stock Exchange; beginning of world economic crisis. *Nov. 17:* Ortez Rubio elected President of Mexico.
1930. *Jan. 3-20:* Second Reparation Conference at Hague: Germany to pay 38 milliard gold marks in 59 years. *21-Apr. 22:* Naval Disarmament Conference in London. *Feb. 18-Mar. 24:* Tariff conference at Geneva. *Apr. 22:* Five-Power Treaty on Naval Disarmament. *May 17:* Young Plan comes into force. Briand Memorandum on United States of Europe. *June 30:* Third Rhineland zone evacuated. *Nov. 17-28:* Economic Conference at Geneva.	**1930.** *Mar. 12:* Gandhi opens civil disobedience campaign. *June 24:* Simon Report on India. *30:* Britain recognizes independence of Iraq. *Aug. 7:* Conservative Ministry (Bennett) in Canada. *Oct. 1:* Britain restores Weihai-wei to China. *1-Nov. 14:* Empire Conference; Statute of Westminster defines status of Dominions. *Nov. 12-Jan. 19:* Round Table Conference on India in London. *Dec. 19:* Lord Willingdon, Viceroy of India.	**1930.** *Jan. 20:* War breaks out between Bolivia and Paraguay. *June 17:* New tariff comes into force in U.S.A. *Sept. 5-8:* Revolution in Argentina; Irigoyen deposed; succeeded by Uriburu. *Oct. 4-Nov. 3:* Revolution in Brazil; Vargas becomes President.
1931. *Jan. 12:* Allied military control committee dissolved. *Mar. 17:* Failure of Tariff Truce convention. *June 20:* Hoover plan of moratorium for one year on reparations and war debts. *Aug. 11:* London Protocol on Hoover Plan. *Sept. 12:* Mexico joins League. *17:* Stand-still agreement with creditors of Germany. *Nov. 1:* Armaments Truce for one year comes into force.	**1931.** *Mar. 4:* Agreement between Gandhi and Lord Irwin; end of civil disobedience campaign. *Aug. 1:* Franco-U.S.A. loan to Britain. *25:* National Government (MacDonald) formed. *Sept. 7-Dec. 1:* Second India Conference in London, attended by Gandhi. *Sept. 21:* Britain abandons gold standard. *Oct. 27:* General Election; 558 Government, 56 Opposition. *Nov. 5:* Second National Government (MacDonald).	**1931.** *July 25:* Ibañez, President of Chile, resigns. *Oct. 4:* Montero elected President of Chile. *Nov. 8:* Justo elected Argentine President.

IV. WESTERN AND SOUTHERN EUROPE	V. CENTRAL AND EASTERN EUROPE	VI. RUSSIA AND ASIA
1928. *Apr. 22* and *29*: Left parties win French elections. *Aug. 2*: Italo-Abyssinian treaty of friendship. *Sept. 1*: Ahmad Zogu (Zog) proclaimed King of Albania. *23*: Italo-Greek treaty of friendship.	**1928.** *May 20*: Left parties win German elections. *June 28*: H. Müller, Chancellor. *27*: Bartel, Polish Premier. *Oct. 4-16*: Plebiscite against new battleships fails in Germany. *Dec. 5*: Miklas elected President of Austria.	**1928.** *Apr. 19*: Japan occupies Shantung. *May 10*: Persia abolishes capitulations. *July 19*: China annuls all ' unequal treaties '. *Oct. 6*: Chiang Kai-Shek elected President of China. *Nov. 1*: Turkey adopts Latin alphabet.
1929. *Feb. 11*: Italian Concordat and Treaty of Lateran (creates Vatican City). *Mar. 24*: Italian elections (99.4 per cent. for Fascist list). *July 27*: Briand succeeds Poincaré as Premier. *Sept. 12*: Grandi appointed Italian Foreign Minister. *Nov. 3*: Tardieu, French Premier. *24*: Clemenceau *d.*	**1929.** *Jan. 5*: King Alexander establishes dictatorship in Yugoslavia. *June 27*: Reichstag repeals Protection of Republic Act. *Aug. 8-29*: Airship *Graf Zeppelin* flies round the world. *Sept. 19*: Dictatorship of Woldemaras overthrown in Lithuania. *Oct. 3*: Stresemann *d.*	**1929.** *Jan. 31*: Trotsky expelled from Russia. *Feb. 9*: Eastern Pact between Russia, Estonia, Latvia, Poland, Rumania; *27*: joined by Turkey; *Apr. 3*: Persia; *5*: Lithuania. *May 20*: Japanese evacuate Shantung. *22*: Amanullah flees from Afghanistan; succeeded by Habibullah. *26*: Soviet Congress passes Five Years Plan. *Oct. 15*: Nadir Khan, King of Afghanistan. *23*: Habibullah executed. *Dec. 6*: Turkey adopts women's suffrage.
1930. *Jan. 28*: Dictatorship of Primo de Rivera ends. *Feb. 6*: Treaty of friendship between Italy and Austria. *Mar. 20*: Inland customs duties abolished in Italy. *Apr. 3*: Ras Tafari becomes Emperor Haile Selassie of Abyssinia. *June 27*: Treaty of arbitration between Denmark Norway, Sweden, Finland, and Iceland. *Sept. 30*: Economic pact between Holland and Scandinavian countries.	**1930.** *Jan. 23*: Frick, first Nazi minister in Thuringia. *Mar. 30*: Brüning forms ' Presidential Cabinet ' without Reichstag majority. *June 6*: Crown Prince Charles returns to Rumania; *8*: elected King. *Aug. 25*: Pilsudski Ministry in Poland. *Sept. 14*: German elections (107 Nazis).	**1930.** *Jan. 1*: Extraterritoriality abolished in China. *July 21*: Litvinov succeeds Tchitcherin as Foreign Minister. *Oct. 30*: Treaty of friendship between Turkey and Greece.
1931. *Jan. 27*: Laval, French Premier. *Apr. 14*: Revolution in Spain; King Alfonso flees abroad. *May 13*: Doumer elected French President. *Oct. 20*: ' Protection of Republic ' Law in Spain. *Dec. 9*: Spanish Republican Constitution; Alcalá Zamora elected President.	**1931.** *Mar. 21*: Austro-German customs union announced; France, Italy, and Czechoslovakia protest. *May 11*: Austrian *Creditanstalt* bankrupt. *July 13*: German *Danatbank* bankrupt; banks closed till *Aug. 5*. *Sept. 3*: Germany and Austria renounce customs union. *13*: Austrian Heimwehr *coup d'état* fails. *Oct. 11*: Hitler-Hugenberg alliance at Harzburg.	**1931.** *Mar. 8*: Russia and Turkey agree on naval reduction in Black Sea. *26*: Treaty of friendship between Iraq and Transjordania. *June 15*: Russo-Polish treaty of friendship and commerce. *24*: Russo-Afghan treaty of neutrality. *Sept. 18*: Japan begins military operations in Manchuria. *Dec. 11*: Japan abandons gold standard.

I. INTERNATIONAL AFAIRS	II. BRITISH EMPIRE	III. AMERICA
1932. *Feb. 2:* Disarmament Conference opened at Geneva. *June 16-July 9:* Reparation Conference of Lausanne; final conditional payment of 3 milliard marks accepted by Germany. *15:* Geneva Protocol on Austrian loan; Austria again renounces *Anschluss.* *18:* Turkey joins League. *Sept. 5-20:* Conference of Stresa on Central and South-East European problems. *14:* Germany leaves Disarmament Conference. *Oct. 3:* Iraq joins League. *Dec. 11:* Geneva Protocol on Germany's equality of rights; Germany returns to Disarmament Conference. *15:* Mexico leaves League.	**1932.** *Jan. 4:* Gandhi arrested; Indian Government receives special powers for six months. *Feb. 16:* Irish elections; 72 Fianna Fail, 89 others. *Mar. 1:* Protectionist tariff in Britain 9: De Valera, Irish Premier. *July 13:* Anglo-French Pact of Friendship signed at Lausanne. *July 21-Aug. 20:* Imperial Economic Conference at Ottawa. *Oct. 3:* British mandate over Iraq terminates. *Nov. 19-Dec. 24:* Third India Conference in London. *Nov. 29:* Persia cancels concession of Anglo-Persian Oil Co. of **1901.**	**1932.** *Feb. 27:* Federal Reserve system reorganized. *June 6-18:* Revolution in Chile; Socialist government established. *July 11-Oct. 3:* Revolution in Brazil. *Sept. 1:* War breaks out between Peru and Colombia for Leticia harbour. *July 31:* War breaks out between Bolivia and Paraguay. *Sept. 4:* Ortez Rubio re-elected Mexican President. *14:* Military *coup d'état* in Chile. *Oct. 3:* Strife between Church and State renewed in Mexico. *Nov. 8:* Democrats win U.S.A. elections; Roosevelt elected President.
1933. *Feb. 24:* **League** adopts Lytton Report on Manchuria. *Mar. 16:* British Disarmament Plan. *19:* Mussolini suggests Four-Power Pact. *27:* Japan leaves League. *June 12-July 27:* World Monetary and Economic Conference in London. *July 3:* Roosevelt rejects Currency Stabilisation Plans of World Conference. *3:* London Convention defining the aggressor, signed by Afghanistan, Estonia, Latvia, Persia, Poland, Rumania, Russia, Turkey; *(5)* Czechoslovakia and Yugoslavia. *15:* Four-Power Pact signed in Rome. *Oct. 14:* Germany leaves Disarmament **Conference** and League.	**1933.** *Jan. 24:* Irish elections (Fianna Fail 77, others 76). *Feb. 3:* Anglo-Persian oil conflict settled. *Mar. 30:* Hertzog and Smuts form Coalition Cabinet. *Apr. 16-July 1:* Embargo on Russian imports. *Apr. 25:* Canada abandons gold standard. *27:* Anglo-German trade pact. *May 3:* Oath of Allegiance removed from Irish Constitution. *17:* South African elections (138 Government, 12 Opposition). *26:* Australia claims one third of Antarctic Continent. *July 1:* London Passenger Transport Board comes into existence. *Sept. 3:* Irish opposition parties form United Ireland Party. *Oct. :* Unrest in Palestine. *Nov. 16:* Liberals go into opposition. *Dec. 18:* Newfoundland Constitution suspended owing to economic mismanagement.	**1933.** *Jan. 2:* U.S.A. troops leave Nicaragua. *13:* U.S.A. Congress votes independence of Philippines. *Feb. 14:* U.S.A. bank crisis. *Mar. 4:* Roosevelt inaugurated. *6-9:* Banks closed throughout U.S.A. *9:* Congress grants Roosevelt dictatorial powers over credit and currency. *31:* Terra assumes dictatorship in Uruguay. *Apr. 30:* U.S.A. abandons gold standard. *May 1:* President Cerro of Peru assassinated; succeeded by Benavides. *10:* Paraguay declares war on Bolivia. *June 16:* National Industrial Recovery Act. *Oct. 5:* 20th Amendment advances date of Inauguration of President to *Jan. 20* and meeting of Congress to *Jan. 3. 11:* Non-aggression pact between South American countries signed at Rio. *Nov. 16:* Brazilian Constitutional Assembly grants dictatorial powers to Vargas. *Dec. 5:* 21st Amendment repeals 18th (Prohibition) Amendment.

IV. WESTERN AND SOUTHERN EUROPE	V. CENTRAL AND EASTERN EUROPE	VI. RUSSIA AND ASIA

1932. *Feb. 21*: Tardieu Ministry. *Mar. 7*: Briand d. *May 1* and *8*: Left parties win French elections. *6*: President Doumer murdered. *10*: Lebrun elected French President. *26*: Zuider Zee drainage completed. *June 4*: Herriot Ministry. *Nov. 4*: Tsaldaris, Greek Premier. *29*: Franco-Russian non-aggression pact. *Dec. 18*: Paul-Boncour Ministry.

1932. *Feb. 6*: Lithuanian *coup d'état* in Memel territory. *29-Mar. 3*: Nazi revolt in Finland. *Apr. 10*: Hindenburg re-elected President. *24*: Nazis win elections in Prussia, Bavaria, Württemberg, Hamburg. *May 20*: Dollfuss, Austrian Chancellor. *June 1*: von Papen Ministry. *July 20*: Prussian Cabinet removed by threat of force. *31*: German elections; 230 Nazis. *Nov. 6*: German elections, 196 Nazis. *Dec. 4*: von Schleicher Ministry.

1932. *Jan. 2*: Manchukuo Republic proclaimed. *22*: Second Russian Five Years Plan issued. *25*: Russo-Polish non-aggression pact. *28*: Japanese occupy Shanghai. *Mar. 9*: Chinese ex-Emperor Pu Yi installed as President of Manchukuo. *May 16*: Inukai, Japanese Premier, murdered. *June 27*: Siam receives Constitution. *Sept. 22*: Hedjaz and Nejd renamed Saudi Arabia. *Nov. 27*: Russo-Polish non-aggression pact. *Dec. 9*: Japanese invade Jehol province.

1933. *Jan. 2-12*: Left revolt in Spain. *15*: Venizelos, Greek Premier. *25*: Liberal Ministry (Mowinckel) in Norway. *31*: Daladier Ministry. *Feb. 7*: Mutiny on Dutch battleship in the Netherlands Indies. *Mar. 6*: *Coup d'état* of General Plastiras fails. *10*: Tsaldaris, Greek Premier. *26*: New Constitution in Portugal. *May 31*: Colijn forms Dutch National Cabinet. *Sept. 14*: Greco-Turkish pact of mutual security and cooperation. *Oct. 16*: Labour wins Norwegian elections. *23*: Sarraut Ministry. *Nov. 19*: Right parties win Spanish elections. *22*: Chautemps Ministry.

1933. *Jan. 28*: Fall of Schleicher. *30*: Hitler appointed Chancellor. *Feb. 16*: Reorganization of Little Entente. *27*: Reichstag fire. *Mar. 5*: German elections (44 per cent. Nazis, 8 per cent. Nationalists). *6-16*: Poland occupies port of Danzig. *7*: Dollfuss suspends Parliamentary government in Austria. *23*: Enabling Law for Hitler. *May 2*: German Trade Unions suppressed. *8*: Moscicki re-elected Polish President. *28*: Nazis win Danzig elections. *June 27*: Hugenberg resigns. *July 14*: German parties other than Nazis forbidden. *Sept. 5*: Outbreak of Church struggle in Germany. *Nov. 12*: German elections (95 per cent. Nazis). *14*: Duca Ministry (Liberal) in Rumania. *Dec. 30*: Duca murdered by Iron Guard.

1933. *Feb. 23-Mar. 12*: Japanese occupy China north of Great Wall. *May 5*: Russo-German treaties of 1926 and 1929 prolonged. *July-Aug.*: Assyrian Christians massacred by Iraqis. *Sept. 8*: King Feisal of Iraq d.; succeeded by Ghazi. *Nov. 8*: Nadir Shah of Afghanistan murdered.

I. INTERNATIONAL AFFAIRS	II. BRITISH EMPIRE	III. AMERICA
1934. *June 15*: Germany announces suspension of all cash transfers on debts abroad from *July 1*. *Sept. 18*: Russia admitted to League. *Oct. 23-Dec. 19*: London Naval Disarmament Conference fails; *Dec. 29*: Japan denounces Washington Treaty.	**1934.** *Feb. 11*: Treaty of friendship between Britain, India and Yemen. *16*: Anglo-Russian trade agreement. *Apr. 7*: Gandhi suspends civil disobedience. *June 12*: Cape Parliament passes South Africa Status Bill. *July 20*: Frontier between Sudan and Libya defined. *Sept. 17*: United Australia Party wins Australian elections. *Oct. 2*: Royal Indian Navy inaugurated. *Nov. 7*: Lyons forms Australian Coalition Cabinet. *13*: Sedition Bill passed. *Dec. 5*: Transvaal National Party and Free State South African Party fused into United Party. *21*: Anglo-Irish Coal-Cattle pact.	**1934.** *Mar. 24*: Philippines declared independent from **1945**. *May 24*: Peru and Colombia settle Leticia conflict. *29*: Cuba abrogates U.S.A. right of intervention. *July 16*: Brazilian Constitution promulgated. *17*: Vargas elected President of Brazil. *Nov. 30*: Cardenas succeeds Rodriguez as President of Mexico.
1935. *Jan. 13*: Saar plebiscite in favour of Germany. *Mar. 7*: Saar district restored to Germany. *16*: Germany repudiates military clauses of Versailles Treaty. *Apr. 11-14*: Stresa Conference of Britain, France, and Italy. *Nov. 18*: League applies economic sanctions against Italy. *Dec. 9*: Hoare-Laval proposals on Abyssinia. Naval Conference meets in London.	**1935.** *Jan. 14*: Iraq-Mediterranean pipe-line inaugurated. *June 7*: Baldwin reconstructs National Government. *18*: Anglo-German Naval Agreement on ratio 3:1. *Aug. 2*: Government of India Act passed. *Oct. 14*: Liberals win Canadian elections; *23*: Mackenzie King, Premier. *Nov. 14*: General election (428 Government, 184 Opposition). *27*: Labour wins New Zealand elections; *29*: Savage, Premier. *Dec. 10*: United front of all Egyptian parties. *18*: Sir S. Hoare resigns; *23*: Eden, Foreign Secretary.	**1935.** *Jan. 7* and *May 27*: Supreme Court declares parts of National Industrial Recovery Act unconstitutional. *June 12*: Armistice between Bolivia and Paraguay. *Aug. 14*: Roosevelt signs Social Security Act. *20*: President Ibarra, of Ecuador, deposed, succeeded by Pons. *Nov. 14*: Commonwealth of Philippines inaugurated. *Dec. 17*: Gomez, President of Venezuela since 1908, d.; succeeded by Contreras. *27*: Uruguay breaks off relations with Russia.
1936. *Jan. 15*: Japan leaves Naval Conference. *Mar. 7*: Germany denounces Locarno Treaty and occupies demilitarized Rhineland zone. *25*: London Naval Convention signed by Britain, U.S.A., and France. *Apr. 1*: Britain sends 'letters of reassurance' to France and Belgium. *July 15*: League raises sanctions against Italy. *20*:	**1936.** *Jan. 20*: King George V d.; succeeded by Edward VIII. *Apr. 1*: Sind and Orissa become separate provinces. *7*: Cape Parliament passes Native Representative Bill. *28*: King Fuad of Egypt d.; succeeded by Farouk. *May 10*: Nahas Pasha forms all-Wafdist Cabinet in Egypt. *28*: Irish Senate abolished. *June 19*: Irish Republican Army pro-	**1936.** *Jan. 21*: Peace between Bolivia and Paraguay. *Feb. 18*: Franco assumes dictatorship in Paraguay. *Mar. 2*: Treaty between U.S.A. and Panama. *Oct. 11*: Benavides assumes dictatorship in Peru. *Nov. 3*: Roosevelt re-elected President. *Dec. 1-16*: Pan-American Peace Conference in Buenos Aires; *16*: Non-intervention Protocol signed.

IV. WESTERN AND SOUTHERN EUROPE	V. CENTRAL AND EASTERN EUROPE	VI. RUSSIA AND ASIA
1934. *Jan. 30*: Daladier Ministry. *Feb. 5*: Italian Corporations Act promulgated. *9*: Doumergue forms Ministry of National Union. *17*: King Albert of Belgium *d.*; succeeded by Leopold III. *21-Mar. 16*: French subdue Berber tribes in S.W. Morocco. *Mar. 16*: Protocols of Rome between Italy, Austria, and Hungary. *June 14-15*: Mussolini and Hitler meet in Venice. *Oct. 9*: King Alexander of Yugoslavia and Barthou assassinated at Marseilles. *15*: Poincaré *d.* *30*: Greek-Turkish Mixed Commission of 1923 dissolved. *Nov. 9*: Flandin Ministry. *10*: Italian Corporations installed. *Dec. 14*: Zaimis re-elected Greek President.	**1934.** *Jan. 26*: German-Polish non-aggression pact for ten years. *Feb. 1-16*: Civil war in Austria; Socialists suppressed. *9*: Balkan pact between Rumania, Greece, Yugoslavia, and Turkey. *May 15*: Ulmanis establishes dictatorship in Latvia. *24*: Masaryk re-elected Czechoslovak President. *June 6*: *Coup d'état* of Woldermaras fails in Lithuania. *30*: Nazi ' Purge '. *July 25*: Nazi revolt in Austria; Dollfuss murdered; Schuschnigg, Chancellor. *Aug. 2*: Hindenburg *d.* *19*: Hitler made ' Leader and Chancellor '. *Sept. 12*: Treaty of Agreement and Collaboration between Latvia, Estonia, and Lithuania. *Oct. 24*: German Labour Front constituted.	**1934.** *Mar. 1*: Pu Yi assumes title of Emperor Kang Te of Manchukuo. *Apr. 7*: Russo-Finnish non-aggression pact prolonged for ten years. *May 5*: Russo-Polish non-aggression pact for ten years. *June 9*: Russo-Czech relations resumed. *10*: Russo-Rumanian relations resumed. *19*: Peace between Ibn Saud and Yemen after six weeks' war. *Nov. 26*: Turkey abolishes titles.
1935. *Jan. 7*: Franco-Italian agreement at Marseilles; France cedes part of her East African possessions. *Mar. 1-11*: Rising in Greece, headed by Venizelos, suppressed. *19*: Van Zeeland Ministry in Belgium. *20*: Socialist Cabinet (Nygaardsvold) in Norway. *May 2*: Franco-Russian treaty of mutual assistance. *31*: Bouisson Ministry. *June 4*: Laval Ministry. *Oct. 2*: Italians invade Abyssinia. *28*: Greece proclaimed monarchy. *Nov. 3*: Greek plebiscite in favour of King George II.	**1935.** *Apr. 23*: New Polish Constitution comes into force. *May 12*: Pilsudski *d.* *19*: Czechoslovak elections; Nazis become strongest German party. *June 23*: Stoyadinovitch, Yugoslav Premier. *July 4*: Austria abolishes anti-Hapsburg laws. *Sept. 15*: Nuremberg Laws make Swastika official Reich flag, and outlaw Jews. *17*: Schuschnigg's *coup d'état*, drops Heimwehr. *Nov. 4*: German-Polish economic agreement. *5*: Hodza, Czechoslovak Premier. *Dec. 18*: Beneš elected Czechoslovak President.	**1935.** *Mar. 21*: Persia renamed Iran. *23*: Russia sells Chinese Eastern Railway to Japan. *May 16*: Russo-Czech pact of mutual assistance. *July 13*: Russo-U.S.A. trade agreement. *Nov. 7*: Russo-Turkish treaties extended for ten years. *Dec. 1*: Chiang Kai-Shek elected President of Chinese Executive.
1936. *Feb. 16*: Spanish elections (265 Popular Front, 142 Right, 66 Centre); Azaña elected Premier, re-establishes 1931 Constitution. *Mar. 18*: Venizelos *d.* *19*: Twelve economic agreements between Italy and Albania. *Apr. 10*: Cortes dismiss President Zamora. *13*: General Metaxas, Greek Premier. *May 3*: French elections (387 Popular Front,	**1936.** *Mar. 10*: Austro-Czech trade agreement. *23*: Three Power Pact of Rome signed by Italy, Austria, and Hungary. *29*: German elections (99 per cent. Nazis). *Apr. 1*: Austria re-introduces conscription. *11*: Ulmanis elected President of Latvia. *May 21*: Schuschnigg made autocratic leader of Fatherland Front. *July 11*: Austro-German	**1936.** *Feb. 26*: Japanese officers murder several ministers and generals; Hirota forms cabinet of militarists. *Apr. 8*: Treaty of mutual assistance between Russia and Mongolia. *Aug. 11*: Chiang-Kai-Shek enters Canton; unity of China almost restored. *25*: Zinoviev and Kamenev sentenced to death. *Sept. 9*: Treaty of friendship and alliance between France

I. INTERNATIONAL AFFAIRS	II. BRITISH EMPIRE	III. AMERICA
Convention of the Straits signed at Montreux; Turkey recovers sovereignty over Dardanelles and Bosphorus. *Aug. 2*: France suggests non-intervention in Spain. *Sept. 9*: Non-intervention Committee of all European Powers meets in London. *Oct. 1*: Russia accedes to London Naval Convention. *Nov. 14*: Germany denounces treaty clauses relative to internationalization of waterways.	claimed illegal. *Aug. 26*: Anglo-Egyptian treaty; terminates military occupation, forms alliance of 20 years (ratified *Dec. 22*). *Nov. 14*: Berar Agreement with Nizam of Hyderabad; Berar accedes to Indian Federation. *Dec. 10*: Edward VIII abdicates. *11*: Accession of Duke of York as King George VI. *12*: Irish Constitution (Amendment) and Executive Authority Acts, abolish chief functions of Governor-General and retain King for external relations only.	
1937. *Jan. 24*: France and Turkey agree on Sanjak of Alexandretta. *Feb. 20*: Paraguay withdraws from League. *Apr. 24*: Britain and France release Belgium from Locarno Treaty obligations. *May 8*: Montreux convention abolishes capitulations in Egypt. *26*: Egypt joins League of Nations. *28*: Trade pact of Oslo signatories signed at The Hague. *June 23*: Germany and Italy withdraw from Non-intervention Committee. *July 8*: Non-aggression Pact between Afghanistan, Iran, Iraq, and Turkey signed at Teheran. *Nov. 3-24*: Conference of Nine Powers, on the Sino-Japanese war, at Brussels. *Dec. 16*: Italy withdraws from International Labour Office.	**1937.** *Jan. 2*: Anglo-Italian agreement signed. *Feb. 20*: Congress Party wins majority of seats in six Indian provinces. *Apr. 1*: Indian Constitution comes into force; Burma and Aden separated from India. *May 12*: Coronation of King George VI. *14-June 15*: Imperial Conference in London. *May 28*: Baldwin resigns, succeeded by N. Chamberlain. *June 14*: Dail passes Constitution of Eire. *July 7*: Plan for partition of Palestine published. *17*: Anglo-Russian and Anglo-German naval agreements signed. *22*: De Valera re-elected Irish Premier. *Aug. 10 and 30*: Reorganization of Army service. *Oct. 1*: Higher Arab Committee declared illegal in Palestine.	**1937.** *Mar. 2*: President Cardenas assumes control of Mexican oil resources. *May 1*: Roosevelt signs U.S. Neutrality Act. *6*: German airship *Hindenburg* destroyed at Lakehurst. *26*: Diplomatic relations resumed between Bolivia and Paraguay. *July 13*: Military *coup d'état* in Bolivia. *Aug. 6*: Trade pact between U.S.A. and Russia. *13*: Dictatorship of Franco overthrown in Paraguay. *Oct. 30*: Ortiz elected President of Argentina. *Nov. 10*: New Constitution of Brazil promulgated. *Dec. 14*: All parties dissolved in Brazil.
1938. *July 12*: Venezuela withdraws from League. *31*: Bulgaria signs non-aggression pact with Balkan Entente; demilitarized zones abolished. *Aug. 23*: Little Entente acknowledges Hungary's right to rearm. *Sept. 15*: Chamberlain meets Hitler at Berchtesgaden. *18*: Anglo-French proposals on Czech question. *22-23*: Chamberlain meets	**1938.** *Feb. 20*: Eden resigns; *25*: succeeded by Lord Halifax. *Apr. 25*: Agreement between Britain and Eire signed. *May 17*: Turco-British agreements signed. *18*: Election in South Africa; United Party 111, Opposition 38 seats. *June 17*: Election in Eire; Fianna Fail 77, Opposition 61 seats. *July 25*: Lord Runciman's mission to	**1938.** *Mar. 19*: Mexico expropriates British and U.S. oil properties. *21 and 28*: U.S. Congress passes Reorganization Bill. *May 11*: Nazi revolt suppressed in Brazil. *June 14*: U.S. Congress passes Wages and Hours Bill. *Sept. 5*: Nazi plot fails in Chile. *Oct. 10*: Frontier between Bolivia and Paraguay fixed by international arbitration. *24*:

IV. WESTERN AND SOUTHERN EUROPE	V. CENTRAL AND EASTERN EUROPE	VI. RUSSIA AND ASIA

IV. WESTERN AND SOUTHERN EUROPE

231 others). *9*: Italy proclaims annexation of Abyssinia; King takes title of Emperor of Ethiopia. *10*: Azaña elected Spanish President. *June 4*: Blum Ministry (Soc. and Radicals); decrees 40-hour week and collective labour agreements. *9*: Count Ciano, Italian Foreign Minister. *July 18*: Army insurrection under Mola and Franco in Spain. *24*: Junta de Defesa Nacional set up at Burgos. *Aug. 4*: Greek Chamber dissolved. *Sept. 27*: Switzerland and Holland abandon gold standard. *Oct. 1*: Franco appointed ' Chief of the Spanish State '. *Nov. 18*: Germany and Italy recognize Franco Government.

1937. *Feb. 8*: Spanish insurgents take Malaga. *27*: French Chamber passes defence plan (Schneider-Creusot factory nationalized, Maginot line extended, Ministry of Defence created). *Mar. 18*: Italian legionaries defeated at Brihuega; insurgent attack on Madrid checked. *Apr. 27*: Spanish insurgents destroy Guernica. *May 31*: German fleet bombards Almeria. *June 21*: Blum Ministry resigns; succeeded by Chautemps (Rad. and Soc.). *Aug. 26*: Spanish Nationalists take Santander, *Oct. 21*: Gijon, and *22*: Oviedo. *Nov. 6*: Italy joins German-Japanese Anti-Comintern Pact. *23*: Fascist plot discovered in Paris.

1938. *Feb. 18*: French Chamber cancels Labour Code. *Mar. 13*: Blum Ministry (Soc. and Radicals). *27*: Spanish Nationalists enter Catalonia. *Apr. 10*: Daladier Ministry (Radicals). *May 3-9*: Hitler meets Mussolini in Rome. *Oct. 25*: Libya declared part of Italy. *Nov. 9*: France recognizes Italian conquest of Abyssinia. *10*: Anti-Jewish legis-

V. CENTRAL AND EASTERN EUROPE

understanding; Germany acknowledges Austrian independence. *13*: Smigly-Ridz appointed ' second citizen ' of Poland after President. *Aug. 24*: Germany adopts two years' compulsory military service. *Oct. 10*: Schuschnigg drops last Heimwehr ministers and dissolves Heimwehr. *19*: German Four Year Plan promulgated. *Nov. 1*: Mussolini proclaims Rome-Berlin axis. *10*: Smigly-Ridz appointed Marshal of Poland.

1937. *Jan. 7*: Polish-Danzig agreement. *15*: Amnesty for Austrian Nazis. *Feb. 1*: Kallio elected President of Finland. *15-18*: Balkan Conference at Athens, joined by Bulgaria. *Mar. 26*: Italo-Yugoslav pact of Belgrade. *Apr. 22*: Schuschnigg meets Mussolini in Venice. *Sept. 14*: Masaryk d. *Oct. 17*: Riots in Sudeten German part of Czechoslovakia. *Nov. 17-21*: Lord Halifax visits Hitler. *23*: Pact between Italy, Austria and Hungary extended till *June 30, 1938*. *Dec. 10*: Property of Hapsburg family restored in Austria. *28*: Goga, leader of Anti-Semites, appointed Rumanian Premier.

1938. *Jan. 9-12*: Conference at Budapest reaffirms Protocols between Italy, Austria, and Hungary. *Feb. 4*: Hitler assumes supreme command; Ribbentrop appointed Foreign Minister. *Mar. 11*: German troops enter Austria. *12*: Austria declared part of German Reich. *Apr. 23*: Henlein demands full autonomy for Sudeten Germans. *Aug. 12*: Ger-

VI. RUSSIA AND ASIA

and Syria and (*Nov. 13*) Lebanon. *Oct. 29*: General Sidqi seizes power in Iraq. *Nov. 24*: German-Japanese agreement against Communism.

1937. *Jan. 4*: Lebanese Constitution of 1926 again put into force. *15*: Russian Congress adopts new Constitution. *23-30*: Moscow trial of seventeen political leaders; thirteen sentenced to death. *Apr. 30*: Japanese Government defeated at general election (41 seats out of 516). *June 1*: Prince Konoye, Japanese Premier. *12*: Eight Russian army chiefs executed. *July 7*: Incident near Pekin leads to Japanese aggression on China. *Aug. 8*: Japanese take Pekin. *11*: General Sidqi, Dictator of Iraq, murdered. *Nov. 9*: Japanese capture Shanghai. *Dec. 12-13*: Japanese take Nanking. *16*: Franco-Syrian convention signed.

1938. *Jan. 10*: Japanese enter Tsingtao. *Apr. 27*: Greco-Turkish treaty of friendship. *May 12*: Manchukuo recognized by Germany. *July 3-Aug. 11*: Russo-Japanese hostilities on border of Manchukuo. *Sept. 5*: Sanjak of Alexandretta renamed Hatay Republic. *Oct. 21*: Japanese enter Canton and (*25*) Hankow. *29*: Arita, Japanese

I. INTERNATIONAL AFFAIRS	II. BRITISH EMPIRE	III. AMERICA
Hitler at Godesberg. *27-28*: League pronounces Japan to be aggressor and invites members to support China. *29*: Munich conference of Chamberlain, Daladier, Mussolini, and Hitler; agreement on transfer of Sudeten territory. *Oct. 1*: League separates Covenant from Peace Treaties. *Nov. 2*: Japan withdraws from technical organizations of the League. *29*: Belgium withdraws from Non-intervention Committee.	Prague; reports in favour of Nazi claims. *Sept. 27*: British fleet mobilized. *Oct. 1*: Duff Cooper resigns as First Lord; *26*: succeeded by Earl Stanhope. *15*: Election in New Zealand; Labour 54, Opposition 26 seats. *Nov. 16*: Anglo-Italian pact put into force.	Labor Standards Act becomes effective in U.S.A. *25*: Cerda (Popular Front) elected President of Chile. *Nov. 8*: U.S.A. elections: Senate, 69 Dem. 23 Rep.; Representatives, 261 Dem., 168 Rep. *Dec. 9-26*: Eighth Pan-American Conference in Lima; issues 'Declaration of Lima' against ' all foreign intervention or activity '.
1939. *Apr. 16*: Russia proposes alliance with Britain and France against German aggression. *May 8*: Spain leaves League of Nations. *Dec. 14*: Russia expelled from League of Nations.	**1939**. *Mar. 14*: Cabinet Menzies in Australia. *24*: British guarantee to Poland; *Apr. 13*: to Rumania and Greece. *May 17*: Palestine White Paper (3 zones; independence within 10 years). *July 11*: Ministry of Supply set up. *Aug. 24*: Emergency Powers Bill carried by both Houses. *25*: Anglo-Polish pact of mutual assistance.	**1939**. *Mar. 20*: U.S. Ambassador recalled from Berlin. *Apr. 15*: Roosevelt's ' peace plea' to Hitler; refused *28*. *July 26*: U.S.A. denounces trade pact of **1911** with Japan. *Sept. 22-Oct.*: Pan-American conference in Panama.

IV. WESTERN AND SOUTHERN EUROPE	V. CENTRAL AND EASTERN EUROPE	VI. RUSSIA AND ASIA
lation in Italy. *21-Dec. 12*: Political strike in France. *30*: Italian deputies claim Tunisia, Nice and Corsica. *Dec. 14*: Last session of Italian Chamber of Deputies; institutes Chamber of Fasci and Corporations. *22*: Italy denounces agreement with France of *Jan. 7*, **1935.**	many mobilizes. *Sept. 7*: Clash between Czechs and Sudeten Germans at Moravska Ostrava; negotiations break down. *Oct. 1*: Czechs accept Polish ultimatum on cession of Teschen. *1-10*: German troops occupy Sudeten territory. *5*: Beneš resigns Presidency. *21*: Czechs terminate pact with Russia. *Nov. 8-14*: Violent pogroms in Germany. *10*: Hungarians occupy areas ceded by Czechoslovakia. *21*: Autonomy granted to Slovakia and Ruthenia. *30*: Hacha elected Czech President. Fourteen leaders of Rumanian Iron Guard shot.	Foreign Minister. *Nov. 10*: Kemel Atatürk *d.* *11*: Ismet Inönü elected Turkish President. *26*: Russo-Polish declaration of friendship. *Dec. 28*: Iran severs diplomatic relations with France.
1939. *Feb. 28*: Britain recognizes Franco. *Mar. 29-30*: Franco occupies Madrid. *Apr. 7*: Italy invades Albania. *16*: Victor Emanuel accepts crown of Albania. *May 22*: German-Italian alliance for 10 years.	**1939.** *Jan. 13*: Hungary joins anti-Comintern pact. *Mar. 14*: Slovakia proclaims independence under German protection. *15*: German troops occupy Czechoslovakia. *16*: Bohemia and Moravia declared German protectorate. *22*: Lithuania cedes Memel to Germany. *Apr. 28*: Hitler denounces non-aggression pact with Poland. *Aug. 25*: Croatian autonomy agreed. *29*: German ultimatum to Poland.	**1939.** *Feb. 10*: Japanese occupy Hainan. *Apr. 4*: King Ghazi of Iraq *d.*; succeeded by Faisal II. *June 23*: France cedes Alexandrette to Turkey. *Aug. 23*: Russo-German non-aggression pact. *Sept. 16*: Russo-Japanese armistice. *30*: Russo-German treaty of friendship. *28*: Russia obtains naval and air bases in Estonia, (*Oct. 5*) Latvia and (*Oct. 10*) Lithuania. *Oct. 19*: Anglo-French-Turkish pact of mutual assistance. *Nov. 24*: Japanese sever China from French Indo-China. **30:** Russia invades Finland.

I. POLITICAL EVENTS

1939

Sept. 3: Britain, Australia, New Zealand and France declare war on Germany. *4*: Hertzog's neutrality motion defeated; Smuts, South African Premier. *28*: Poland partitioned by Germany and Russia. *Oct. 19*: Anglo-Turkish pact. *Nov. 4*: U.S.A. neutrality act, repeals arms embargo.

1940

Mar. 20: Reynauld French Premier. *May 10*: Churchill forms coalition government. *June 10*: Italy declares war on Britain and France. *14*: Spain occupies Tangier. *16*: British offer of Anglo-French union rejected; Pétain, French premier. *22*: France capitulates. *23*: De Gaulle starts Free French movement. *July 1*: Rumania renounces Anglo-French guarantee. *5*: Vichy breaks off relations with Britain. *10*: Pétain, chief of the French state. *Aug. 30*: Vienna award transfers Transylvania to Hungary. *Sept. 16*: U.S.A. introduces compulsory military service. *27*: Tripartite pact between Germany, Italy and Japan ('New Order'). *Nov. 5*: Roosevelt re-elected for third term.

1941

Feb. 10: Britain breaks off relations with Rumania. *17*: Turco-Bulgarian non-aggression pact. *Mar. 1*: Bulgaria joins Axis. *5*: Britain breaks off relations with Bulgaria. *11*: Roosevelt signs Lend-Lease Bill. *27*: Pro-Axis government of Yugoslavia overthrown. *Apr. 18*: France withdraws from League of Nations. *May 10*: Hess lands in Scotland. *June 4*: William II *d.* at Doorn. *18*: Non-aggression pact between Germany and Turkey. *30*: Vichy breaks off relations with U.S.S.R. *July 2*: China breaks off relations with Axis. *Aug. 11*: Roosevelt and Churchill issue Atlantic Charter. *Sept. 16*: Shah of Persia abdicates. *29*: Three-power conference in Moscow. *Dec. 11*: Germany and Italy declare war on U.S.A. *19*: Hitler assumes command of German army.

1942

Jan. 1: Washington pact of 26 United Nations. *Feb. 6*: Roosevelt and Churchill appoint Combined Chiefs of Staff. *May 26*: Anglo-Soviet treaty for 20 years. *June 10*: Nazis wipe out Lidice, Czechoslovakia.

II. WAR IN THE WEST

1939

Sept. 4: *Athenia* sunk. *17*: Aircraft-carrier *Courageous* sunk. *Oct. 14*: *Royal Oak* sunk in Scapa Flow. *Nov. 25*: *Rawalpindi* sunk.

1940

Apr. 9: Germans invade Denmark and Norway. *May 10*: Germans invade Holland, Belgium and Luxemburg. *15*: Dutch capitulate; French front penetrated. *28*: Belgians capitulate; Germans capture Narvik. *30–June 3*: Dunkirk evacuation. *9*: Norwegian resistance ends. *10*: British evacuate Norway. *14*: Germans enter Paris. *30*: Germans occupy Channel Islands. *Aug. 8–Sept. 6*: Battle of Britain. *Sept. 7–Oct. 31*: London Blitz. *Nov. 14*: Raid on Coventry. *Dec. 29*: Raid on London.

1941

Jan. 20: Mussolini places Italy under German control. *April 9*: U.S.A. occupy Greenland. *May 10–11*: Heavy raid on London; House of Commons destroyed. *24*: *Hood* sunk by *Bismarck*. *27*: *Bismarck* sunk. *July 7*: U.S.A. occupy Iceland. *Sept. 4*: 'Shoot on sight' order to U.S. naval patrols.

1942

May 30: First 1000-bomber raid on Cologne. *June 25*: Eisenhower, C.-in-C., U.S.A. forces, European Theatre. *Aug. 19*: Raid on Dieppe. *Nov. 11–12*: Germans occupy Vichy France. *27*: French navy scuttled in Toulon.

III. WAR IN THE EAST

1939

Sept. 1: Germany invades Poland. *17*: Russia invades Poland. *Nov. 28*: Russia denounces non-aggression pact with Finland. *30*: Russia invades Finland.

1940

Mar. 12: Finland signs peace with Russia. *June 26*: Russian ultimatum to Rumania; *28*: Bessarabia and Northern Bukovina ceded. *Aug. 3*: Lithuania, *5*: Estonia and Latvia incorporated in Soviet Union. *Oct. 7*: Germans occupy Rumania. *28*: Italy attacks Greece; *29*: British troops land in Greece. *Nov. 11*: Raid on Italian navy in Taranto.

1941

Feb. 9: Germans occupy Bulgaria. *Mar. 28*: Battle of Cape Matapan. *Apr. 6*: Germans invade Yugoslavia and Greece. *13*: Germans take Belgrade. Russo-Japanese neutrality pact. *27*: Germans take Athens. *May 19-June 1*: Battle for Crete. *June 22*: Germans invade Russia. *July 12*: Anglo-Russian alliance. *Sept. 4*: Siege of Leningrad begins (*-27 Jan.*, **1944**). *19*: Germans take Kiev. *Oct. 5-Dec. 6*: Battle for Moscow. *Nov. 26*: Russian counter-offensive; recapture of Rostov (*Nov. 28*) and Kertch (*Dec. 29*). *Dec. 7*: Britain declares war on Finland, Hungary and Rumania.

1942

Jan. 10: German offensive in the Crimea. *May 12-17*: Russian offensive on Kharkov front smashed. *June 10*: German offensive in the Ukraine. *July 2*: Sevastopol capitulates. *Sept. 5*: Germans enter Stalingrad. *23*: Russian counter-offensive near Stalingrad begins. *Nov. 10*: Germans reach Ordshonikidze. *Dec. 29*: German relief-army defeated at Kotelnikovo.

IV. WAR OVERSEAS

1939

Dec. 13: Battle of River Plate; *17*: *Graf Spee* scuttled.

1940

July 3: British cripple French fleet at Oran and Mers el-Kebir. *4*: Italians invade Sudan. *18*: Britain closes Burma Road. *Aug. 4*: Italians invade British Somaliland. *17*: British evacuate Somaliland. *Sept. 2*: Exchange of 50 U.S. destroyers for lease of British bases in West Indies. *13*: Italians invade Egypt. *23-25*: British and Free French attempt at Dakar fails. *Oct. 18*: Burma Road reopened. *Dec. 8-Feb. 8*, **1941**: Wavell offensive in Libya as far as El Agheila.

1941

Jan. 19: British retake Kassala (Sudan). *Feb. 26*: Mogadishu (Italian Somaliland) taken. *Mar. 24*: British Somaliland regained. Axis offensive in Lybia starts. *Apr. 3*: Pro-Axis coup in Iraq. *5*: Addis-Abeba occupied. *26*: Axis troops take Sollum. *May 19*: Italian surrender at Amba Alagi. *June 8-July 14*: British and French occupy Syria. *Aug. 25*: British and Russians secure Persia. *Nov. 18-Dec. 28*: British offensive in Lybia as far as El Agheila. *Nov. 27*: Last Italian troops surrender at Gondar, Abyssinia. *Dec. 7*: Japanese attack on Pearl Harbour; Britain and U.S.A. declare war on Japan. *8*: Japanese occupy Siam. *10*: *Prince of Wales* and *Repulse* sunk. *11*: Japanese take Guam, *23*: Wake. *25*: Hong Kong surrenders.

1942

Jan. 2: Japanese occupy Manila. *23-25*: Battle of Macassar Straits. *Feb. 8*: Japanese invade Burma. *15*: Singapore surrenders. *Mar. 9*: Java and Rangoon surrender. *Apr. 4-9*: Japanese raids on Ceylon. *18*: Raid on Tokyo. *May 6*: Corregidor capitulates. *7-11*: Battle of the Coral Sea. *26-July 1*: German offensive in Lybia as far as El Alamein. *June 3-6*: Battle of Midway. *June 3*: Japanese invade Aleutians. *Aug. 1*: Montgomery takes over Eighth Army. *7*: Americans land on Guadalcanal. *Oct. 23-Nov. 3*: Battle of El Alamein. *Nov. 8*: Allied landings in Morocco and Algeria. *11-Dec. 28*: First Battle of Tunisia. *Dec. 13*: Germans evacuate El Agheila.

I. POLITICAL EVENTS	II. WAR IN THE WEST

1943

Jan. 14-26: Casablanca conference: Roosevelt demands 'unconditional surrender'. *June 18*: Wavell, Viceroy of India. *July 25*: Mussolini resigns. Badoglio signs secret armistice. *26*: Fascist Party dissolved. *Aug. 11-24*: Quebec meeting plans Allied strategy. *24*: Himmler appointed Reich Minister of the Interior. *28*: Tsar Boris III of Bulgaria died. *Oct. 12*: Agreement with Portugal for use of Azores. *13*: Italy declares war on Germany. *Nov. 22-26*: Cairo meeting of Roosevelt, Churchill and Chiang Kai-shek. *Nov. 26-Dec. 2*: Teheran meeting of Roosevelt, Churchill and Stalin.

1944

Jan. 11: Count Ciano executed. *June 5*: Prince Humbert appointed Lieutenant-General of the Realm *9*: Badoglio resigns, succeeded by Bonomi. *July 20*: Attempt on Hitler fails. *Aug. 23*: King Michael of Rumania overthrows Antonescu dictatorship. *25*: Rumania declares war on Germany. *Sept. 5*: Russia declares war on Bulgaria. *8*: Bulgaria declares war on Germany. *12*: Armistice with Rumania. *Oct. 9-19*: Moscow conference between Churchill and Stalin. *19*: Armistice with Finland. *23*: De Gaulle's Provisional Government recognized. *28*: Armistice with Bulgaria. *Dec. 30*: Hungary declares war on Germany.

1945

Jan. 20: Armistice with Hungary. *Feb. 23*: Turkey declares war on Germany and Japan. *Mar. 22*: Pact of Union of Arab States signed in Cairo. *Apr. 12*: President Roosevelt d. *24-June 26*: San Francisco Conference of United Nations. *Apr. 28*: Mussolini executed. *30*: Hitler's suicide. *May 26*: Churchill Government without Labour Party. *June 26*: U.N. Charter signed. *28*: Polish Government of National Unity. *July 5*: General Election (Labour 393, Cons. 189). *17-Aug. 2*: Three-power conference at Potsdam. *July 27*: Attlee Government. *Sept. 2*: U.S.A. terminates Lend-Lease.

1943

Jan. 30: First daylight bombing of Berlin. *Feb. 6*: Eisenhower, Allied C.-in-C., North Africa. *July 9-Aug. 17*: Conquest of Sicily. *Sept. 3*: Allied landing in Italy. Italy surrenders unconditionally. *9*: Allies land at Salerno. *Oct. 7*: Allies occupy Naples. *Dec. 24*: Allied invasion chiefs appointed; Eisenhower, Supreme Commander; Tedder, Deputy. *26*: *Scharnhorst* sunk.

1944

Jan. 22: Landings at Nettuno and Anzio. *Feb. 1-May 18*: Battle for Montecassino. *Feb. 20*: Strategic bombing of Germany begins. *May 11*: Attack on Gustav and Hitler lines opened. *June 4*: Allies enter Rome. *6*: Allied landings in Normandy. *15*: Flying bomb attacks on London begin. *27*: Cherbourg taken. *July 9*: Caen taken. *27*: Break-through at St. Lô. *30-31*: Battle of Avranches. *Aug. 7-23*: Battle of Falaise. *11*: Allies enter Florence. *15*: Allied landings between Toulon and Cannes. *23*: Marseille, *26*: Toulon occupied. *25*: Paris surrenders. *Sept. 3*: Brussels, *9*: Luxemburg liberated. *11*: German frontier crossed. *17-26*: Battle of Arnhem. *24*: British airborne landings in Greece. *Oct. 14*: Athens liberated. *21*: Aachen captured. *Nov. 1*: British land on Walcheren. *12*: *Tirpitz* sunk. *Dec. 16-22*: Last German offensive in the Ardennes.

1945

Feb. 4: Belgium liberated. *Mar. 6*: Cologne taken. *7*: Rhine crossed at Remagen, *23*: at Wesel. *27*: Last rocket on England. *30*: Dutch frontier crossed. *Apr. 9*: Allied offensive in Italy. *16*: *Lützow* sunk. *26*: Russians and Americans link up near Torgau. Milan taken. *29*: Unconditional surrender of Germans in Italy. Munich and Venice captured. *May 3*: Hamburg captured. *5*: Unconditional surrender of German forces in N.W. Germany, Holland and Denmark. *7*: Unconditional surrender of all German fighting forces.

III. WAR IN THE EAST	IV. WAR OVERSEAS

1943

Jan. 25: Russians take Voronesh. *Feb. 2*: Last Germans in Stalingrad surrender. *8*: Russians take Kursk. *Aug. 4*: Russians take Orel, *23*: Kharkov, *30*: Taganrog. *Sept. 16*: Russians take Novorossisk, *17*: Bryansk, *25*: Smolensk. *Oct. 7*: Russians cross Dnieper. *8-9*: Germans evacuate Kuban. *Nov. 6*: Russians take Kiev. *Dec. 20*: U.S.A. and Britain decide to give military aid to Tito. *31*: Russians take Zhitomir.

1944

Jan. 15-Feb. 21: Russian offensive from Leningrad to Pskov. *Feb. 4-19*: Russians dislodge Germans from Upper Dnieper; battle of Korsun. *Feb. 8-Mar. 13*: Russians clear lower Dnieper. *Apr. 2*: Russians enter Poland and Rumania. *10*: Odessa taken. *May 9*: Sevastopol taken. *June 10*: Offensive against Finland starts; *20*: Viborg taken. *22*: Offensive in White Russia. *July 11*: Offensive against Latvia and Estonia; *13*: Vilna captured. *14*: Offensive in Poland; *28*: Lvov taken. *Aug. 1-Oct. 2*: Polish rising in Warsaw. *Aug. 17*: Russians reach East Prussia. *20*: Offensive in Rumania. *31*: Bucharest taken. *Sept. 22*: Tallinn captured. *Oct. 6*: Russians invade Hungary. *13*: Riga captured. *19*: Russians invade East Prussia. *20*: Belgrade liberated. *25*: Kirkenes taken.

1945

Jan. 11: Russians enter Warsaw. *Feb. 13*: Budapest taken. *Mar. 30*: Danzig and Küstrin taken. *Apr. 13*: Vienna liberated. *21*: Russians reach Berlin. *May 2*: Berlin surrendered. *10*: Prague liberated. *Aug. 17*: Russo-Polish frontier treaty.

1943

Jan. 23: Eighth Army enters Tripoli. *Feb. 9*: Guadalcanal cleared of Japanese. *Mar. 1-3*: Battle of the Bismarck Sea. *21-29*: Break through Mareth Line. *May 7*: Tunis and Bizerta taken. *11-30*: Attu recaptured. *13*: Axis forces in Tunisia surrender. *June 11*: Pantelleria, *12*: Lampedusa surrender. *Aug. 25*: Mountbatten, supreme Allied commander, South-east Asia. *Sept. 11*: Australians take Salamaua. *Nov. 1*: Americans land on Bougainville. *21-25*: Capture of Tarawa.

1944

Feb. 1-6: **Capture** of Kwajalein. *Mar. 13-June 30*: Manipur campaign. *June 15-July 9*: Battle of Saipan. *June 15-16*: Strategic bombing of Japan begins. *July 20-Aug. 3*: Guam reconquered. *Sept. 15-Oct. 13*: Palau islands occupied. *Oct. 5*: Japanese take Foochow, last seaport in Chinese hands. *20*: Philippines invaded. *23-25*: Battle of the Philippine Sea; decisive defeat of Japanese navy.

1945

Jan. 9: U.S. forces land on Luzon. *Feb. 5-24*: Manila occupied. *Apr. 5* : Russia denounces neutrality pact with Japan. *May 3*: Rangoon recaptured. *June 21*: Okinawa captured. *July 1*: Australians land at Balikpapan. *5*: Philippines liberated. *Aug. 6*: Atomic bomb on Hiroshima, *9*: on Nagasaki. *8*: Russia declares war on Japan. *14*: Japan's unconditional surrender (signed *Sept. 2*). *23*: Russians complete occupation of Manchuria. *Sept. 8*: MacArthur enters Tokyo. *9*: Japanese surrender in China. *12*: Japanese surrender in S.E. Asia.

I. INTERNATIONAL AFFAIRS	II. AMERICA	III. ASIA AND OCEANIA
1946. *Feb. 1:* Lie elected secretary of U.N. *Mar. 5:* Churchill advocates Anglo-U.S. 'fraternal association' against Soviet expansion (Fulton, Mo.). *July 1:* First atomic test over Bikini. *Sept. 19:* Churchill advocates European Union (Zürich). *Oct. 1:* Nazi war criminals sentenced at Nürnberg. *Nov. 19:* Afghanistan, Iceland, Sweden, Thailand admitted to U.N.	**1946.** *Jan. 31:* Dutra, President of Brazil. *Feb. 24:* Perón, President of Argentina. *Dec. 1:* Valdés, President of Mexico.	**1946.** *Jan. 5:* China recognizes independence of Mongolia. *Apr. 1:* Malayan Union established. *May 17:* Sarawak ceded to British Crown. *July 4:* Philippine Republic inaugurated. *Nov. 3:* Japanese constitution promulgated. *Dec. 19:* Vietminh forces open hostilities in Indo-China.
1947. *Feb. 10:* Paris peace treaties with Bulgaria, Finland, Hungary, Italy, Rumania. *Mar. 4:* Anglo-French treaty of Dunkirk (50-year alliance). *June 5:* Marshall suggests European Recovery Programme. *Sept. 22:* Marshall Plan accepted by 16 nations. *30:* Pakistan and Yemen admitted to U.N.	**1947.** *July 19:* U.S.A. takes over trusteeship of former Japanese mandates. *Aug. 24:* President Ibarra of Ecuador deposed.	**1947.** *Feb. 20:* Lord Mountbatten, Viceroy of India. *Mar. 25:* Netherlands recognizes independence of Indonesia. *June 3:* Partition of India and Pakistan announced. *Aug. 15:* India and Pakistan become British dominions. *Sept. 24:* Constitution of Burma passed. *Oct. 17:* Anglo-Burmese treaty; Burma leaves Commonwealth.
1948. *Mar. 17:* Brussels treaty organization of U.K., France, Benelux. *Apr. 7:* World Health Organization established. *16:* Organization for European Economic Co-operation established. *19:* Burma admitted to U.N. *Aug. 23:* World Council of Churches constituted at Amsterdam.	**1948.** *Apr. 30:* Charter of Organization of (21) American States signed in Bogotá. *June 3:* President Morinigo of Paraguay deposed. *Oct. 30:* Gen. Odria seizes power in Peru. *Nov. 2:* Truman re-elected President of U.S.A. *Dec. 1:* Costa Rican army dissolved.	**1948.** *Jan. 4:* Union of Burma inaugurated. *30:* Gandhi assassinated. *Feb. 1:* Malayan Union becomes Federation of Malaya. *4:* Ceylon becomes British dominion. *May 1:* North Korea proclaimed people's republic. *July 17:* South Korean constitution passed; *20:* Syngman Rhee elected President. *Sept. 11:* Jinnah d. *13-18:* Indian troops occupy Hyderabad.
1949. *Apr. 4:* North Atlantic Treaty signed; *Aug. 24:* comes into force. *May 11:* Israel admitted to U.N. *July 13:* Roman Catholic Church excommunicates Communists.	**1949.** *Jan. 30:* Lopez seizes power in Paraguay. *Mar. 31:* Newfoundland becomes the tenth Canadian province. *Aug. 11:* U.S.A. Department of Defence established.	**1949.** *Mar. 8:* France recognizes independence of Vietnam within French union (*July 19:* Laos; *Nov. 8:* Cambodia). *May 11:* Name of Siam changed to Thailand. *June 19:* Chandernagor referendum for union with India. *Sept. 21:* Chinese People's Republic proclaimed in Peking. *Dec. 28:* Netherlands transfers sovereignty to Indonesia.

IV. AFRICA AND MIDDLE EAST	V. EUROPE
1946. *Mar. 22*: Jordan independence recognized by Britain. *May 25*: Amir Abdullah of Jordan assumes title of king.	**1946.** *Jan. 2*: King Zog of Albania deposed; *12*: republic proclaimed. *20*: De Gaulle resigns French Premiership. *25*: Council for Mutual Economic Aid (Comecon) established in Moscow. *Feb. 1*: Hungary proclaimed republic. *Mar. 1*: Bank of England nationalized. *9*: Paasikivi elected President of Finland. *May 9*: Victor Emmanuel III of Italy abdicates in favour of Umberto II. *June 2*: Italian plebiscite on republic (12·7m. for, 10·7m. against, 1·5m. invalid); *10*: Republic proclaimed. *Sept. 1*: Greek plebiscite in favour of monarchy; *28*: George II returns. *Oct. 13*: French plebiscite on constitution of Fourth Republic (9·3m. for, 8·2m. against, 8·5m. invalid).
1947. *Sept. 26*: Britain announces withdrawal from Palestine.	**1947.** *Jan. 1*: British coal industry nationalized. *16*: Auriol elected French President. *Feb. 5*: Bierut, President of Poland. *Apr. 1*: George II of Greece *d.*, succeeded by Paul I. *20*: Christian X of Denmark *d.*, succeeded by Frederik IX. *May 4*: Communists excluded from French and (*28*) Italian cabinets. *Oct. 5*: Cominform established in Belgrade. *29*: Benelux customs union established. *Dec. 22*: Italian constitution passed. *30*: King Michael of Rumania abdicates; republic proclaimed.
1948. *Jan. 1*: East Africa High Commission established. *Feb. 17*: Imam Yahya of Yemen assassinated; *Mar. 14*: succeeded by Ahmad. *May 14*: Israel proclaimed independent state. *15*: Arab League invade Palestine. *26*: South African elections; *June 3*: Malan (National) Prime Minister. *Sept. 17*: Count Bernadotte assassinated by Jewish terrorists.	**1948.** *Jan. 1*: British inland transport nationalized. *Feb. 25*: Communist rule established in Czechoslovakia. *Apr. 1*: British electricity industry nationalized. *28*: Luxembourg constitution abandons disarmed neutrality. *May 10*: Einaudi elected President of Italy. *June 7*: Beneš resigns as President of Czechoslovakia; *9*: new constitution; *14*: Gottwald elected President. *18*: Soviet blockade of West Berlin; relieved by Anglo-U.S. airlift (*-6 Oct. 1949*). *28*: Yugoslavia expelled from Cominform. *July 5*: British National Health Service comes into operation. *Sept. 4*: Queen Wilhelmina of Netherlands abdicates in favour of Juliana. *Nov. 30*: Soviet administration set up in East Berlin.
1949. *Feb. 16*: Weizmann elected President of Israel. *14*: Israeli-Egyptian armistice (*Mar. 23*: Lebanon; *Apr. 3*: Jordan).	**1949.** *Apr. 18*: Eire leaves Commonwealth. *27*: British king recognized as 'head of the Commonwealth'. *May 1*: British gas industry nationalized. *5*: Council of Europe established. *23*: Basic Law of Federal German Republic comes into force. *Aug. 9*: Greece and Turkey join Council of Europe. *Sept. 12*: Heuss elected Federal German President; *15*: Adenauer Chancellor. *Oct. 7*: German Democratic Republic established; *11*: Pieck elected President.

I. INTERNATIONAL AFFAIRS	II. AMERICA	III. ASIA AND OCEANIA
1950. *July 1*: European Payments Union set up. *Sept. 28*: Indonesia admitted to U.N. *Dec. 18*: Eisenhower appointed Supreme Commander, NATO.	**1950.** *Jan. 20*: Netherlands colonies in Latin America obtain self-government. *Nov. 13*: Arbenz Guzmán elected President of Guatemala.	**1950.** *Jan. 26*: India proclaimed republic; Rajandra Prasad, President. *Mar. 1*: Chiang Kai-shek proclaimed President of Nationalist China in Taiwan. *June 25*: North Korean forces invade South Korea. *Aug. 14*: Unitary Constitution of Indonesia. *Oct. 7*: Chinese invade Tibet.
1951. *Apr. 18*: European Coal and Steel treaty signed. *Sept. 8*: Japanese peace treaty with Allies signed at San Francisco. *Oct. 10*: Mutual Security Act approved by U.S.A. Congress.	**1951.** *Oct. 3*: Vargas elected President of Brazil. *Nov. 11*: Perón re-elected President of Argentina. *Dec. 16*: Uruguay referendum replaces Presidency by Council of Government.	**1951.** *May 23*: Tibet placed under Chinese suzerainty. *July 1*: Colombo Plan comes into force. *Sept. 1*: New Zealand elections (National 50, Labour 30). *Oct. 16*: Liaqat Ali Khan assassinated.
1952. *Feb. 18*: Greece and Turkey join NATO. *Aug. 23*: Arab League Security Pact comes into force.	**1952.** *Mar. 10*: Gen. Batistá seizes power in Cuba. *Apr. 9*: Nationalist Revolutionary Party seizes power in Bolivia. *May 16*: Hector Trujillo elected President of Dominican Republic. *June 1*: Ibarra elected President of Ecuador. *July 6*: Ruiz Cortines elected President of Mexico. *25*: Constitution of Puerto Rica comes into force. *Nov. 4*: Gen. Eisenhower (Rep.) elected President of U.S.A. *Dec. 3*: Col. Pérez seizes power in Venezuela.	**1952.** *Oct. 3*: First British atomic explosion, off Monte Bello islands, Western Australia.
1953. *Apr. 7*: Hammarskjöld elected Secretary-General of U.N.	**1953.** *June 13*: Gen. Rojas seizes power in Colombia.	**1953.** *July 27*: Armistice in Korea.

IV. AFRICA AND MIDDLE EAST	V. EUROPE
1950. *Mar. 13*: Customs union of Syria and Lebanon dissolved. *Sept. 11*: Field Marshall Smuts *d*.	**1950.** *Feb. 14*: 30-year alliance between China and U.S.S.R. *24*: U.K. elections (Lab. majority 6); *28*: Attlee, Prime Minister. *Mar. 7*: Iceland joins Council of Europe. *May 22*: Bayar elected President of Turkey. *July 6*: Frontier treaty between German Democratic Republic and Poland. *22*: Leopold III of Belgium returns from exile; *Aug. 11*: Prince Baudouin appointed regent. *Oct. 29*: Gustaf V of Sweden *d*., succeeded by Gustaf VI Adolf.
1951. *Jan. 1*: Gold Coast constitution comes into force. *Apr. 28*: Musaddiq, Persian Premier. *May 2*: Persia nationalizes oil industry. *July 20*: King Abdullah of Jordan assassinated. *Oct. 8*: Egypt abrogates 1936 treaty with Britain. *Dec. 24*: Kingdom of Libya established.	**1951.** *Apr. 27*: Danish-U.S. agreement on defence of Greenland. *May 2*: Federal Germany joins Council of Europe. *July 16*: Leopold III of Belgium abdicates in favour of Baudouin. *Sept.*: U.S.S.R. explodes atomic bomb. *Oct. 25*: U.K. elections (Cons. majority 16); *26*: Churchill, Prime Minister, Eden, Foreign Secretary.
1952. *Jan. 1*: Nigeria constitution comes into force. *July 23*: Gen. Neguib seizes power in Egypt; *26*: King Farouk abdicates in favour of Fuad II. *Sept. 15*: Eritrea united Ethiopia.	**1952.** *Feb. 6*: George VI *d*.; succeeded by Elizabeth II. *July 22*: Polish constitution. *Aug. 10*: European Coal and Steel Community inaugurated.
1953. *Feb. 12*: Anglo-Egyptian agreement on Sudan. *Mar. 28*: Libya joins Arab League. *June 18*: Gen. Neguib proclaims republic of Egypt. *Aug. 1*: Federation of Rhodesia and Nyasaland inaugurated. *19*: Musaddiq régime overthrown in Persia. *20*: Sultan Sidi Mohammed of Morocco deposed. *Nov. 9*: King Abdul Aziz of Saudi Arabia *d*., succeeded by Saud.	**1953.** *Jan. 13*: Constitution of Federal People's Republic of Yugoslavia. *Mar. 5*: Stalin *d*. *June 5*: New constitution and law of succession in Denmark. *17*: Anti-Communist riots in German Democratic Republic. *Dec. 23*: Beria shot. *24*: Coty elected French President.

I. INTERNATIONAL AFFAIRS	II. AMERICA	III. ASIA AND OCEANIA
1954. *Mar. 8*: U.S.-Japan defence pact. *July 21*: Armistice in Indo-China signed at Geneva. *Sept. 8*: South-East Asia Collective Defence Treaty signed at Manila. *Oct. 23*: Paris agreements establish Western European Union and terminate occupation of Western Germany.	**1954.** *May 5*: Army deposes President Chaves of Paraguay. *17*: Supreme Court declares racial segregation in U.S. schools unconstitutional. *June 18-27*: President Arbenz of Guatemala overthrown. *Aug. 24*: President Vargas of Brazil commits suicide; succeeded by Vice-President Café Filho.	**1954.** *Aug. 10*: Indonesia leaves Netherlands Union. *Sept. 20*: New Chinese Constitution. *Oct. 18*: French settlements in India vote for union with India (effective *Nov. 1*). *Dec. 29*: France transfers sovereignty to Cambodia.
1955. *July 18-23*: Geneva conference of heads of state.	**1955.** *Sept. 19*: Perón régime overthrown in Argentina. *Dec. 2*: American Federation of Labor and Congress of Industrial Organizations merge into one trade union (AFL–CIO).	**1955.** *Apr. 18-24*: Bandung Conference of Asian and African states. *Oct. 26*: South Vietnam proclaimed republic.
1956. *June 18*: Britain evacuates Suez Canal zone. *July 26*: Egypt nationalizes Suez Canal. *Oct. 29*: Israel attacks Egypt; *Nov. 5-Dec. 22*: Anglo-French intervention between Egypt and Israel; *Nov. 15*: U.N. forces take over in Egypt. *Dec. 18*: Japan admitted to U.N.	**1956.** *Nov. 6*: Eisenhower re-elected President of U.S.A.	**1956.** *Feb. 29*: Pakistan proclaimed Islamic Republic. *May 28*: India takes over French possessions.
	1957. *June 10*: Canadian elections. Diefenbaker Prime Minister. *Sept. 24*: U.S. federal troops sent to Little Rock, Ark., to maintain law and order against State Governor's segregation policy.	**1957.** *Aug. 31*: Federation of Malaya attains independence. *Nov. 30*: New Zealand elections (41 Labour, 39 National); Nash, Prime Minister.
1958. *July 15*: U.S.A. troops called in by Lebanese government; *17*: British troops by Jordan government, to protect independence. *Dec. 28*: European Payments Union replaced by European Monetary Agreement.		

IV. AFRICA AND MIDDLE EAST	V. EUROPE
1954. *Jan. 9*: First all-Sudanese government appointed. *Aug. 31*: International agreement on Persian oil. *Oct. 19*: Agreement on withdrawal of British troops from Suez Canal. *Nov. 1*: National revolt against French rule in Algeria. *14*: President Neguib of Egypt deposed.	**1954.** *July 3*: Food rationing ends in U.K. *Aug. 9*: Alliance between Greece, Turkey, Yugoslavia. *30*: France rejects European Defence Community. *Oct. 5*: Italo-Yugoslav understanding on Trieste.
1955. *Apr. 22*: Agreement on home rule for Tunisia.	**1955.** *Feb. 8*: Bulganin succeeds Malenkov as U.S.S.R. Premier. *Apr. 6*: Churchill resigns; Eden, U.K. Prime Minister. *9*: U.S.S.R. denounces treaties with Britain (1942) and France (1944). *29*: Gronchi elected President of Italy. *May 6*: Western European Union inaugurated. *14*: East-European Defence Treaty signed in Warsaw. *15*: Austrian state treaty signed in Vienna. *26*: U.K. elections (345 Cons., 277 Lab.). *Oct. 23*: European statute of Saar territory rejected by referendum.
1956. *Jan. 1*: Sudan attains independence. *Mar. 2*: France recognizes independence of Morocco and Tunisia (*20*). *June 23*: Nasser, President of Egypt.	**1956.** *Jan. 26*: U.S.S.R. withdraws forces from Finland. *Feb. 25*: Khrushchev denounces Stalin's policy. *Apr. 17*: Cominform dissolved. *Oct. 21*: Gomulka, Polish Premier, after bloodless overthrow of Stalinist régime. *23*: Anti-Stalinist revolution in Hungary; *Nov. 4-22*: suppressed by Soviet forces.
1957. *Mar. 6*: Ghana attains independence. *13*: Anglo-Jordan treaty of 1948 terminated. *July 25*: Tunisia proclaimed a republic.	**1957.** *Jan. 1*: Saar Territory incorporated with Federal Germany. *17*: Macmillan, U.K. Prime Minister. *Sept. 21*: Haakon VII of Norway d. *Oct. 4 and Nov. 3*: First earth satellites (Sputniks I and II) placed in orbit.
1958. *Feb. 1*: Egypt and Syria combine in United Arab Republic; Yemen accedes (*Mar. 9*). *14*: Iraq and Jordan form Arab Federation. *July 14*: King Faisal of Iraq assassinated; Iraq proclaimed a republic, withdraws from Arab Federation and Bagdad Pact.	**1958.** *Jan. 1*: Treaty of Rome comes into force establishing the European Economic Community. *Mar. 27*: Krushchev, U.S.S.R. Premier. *June 1*: Gen. de Gaulle, Premier of France. *Sept. 28*: Referendum in French Union approves constitution of Fifth Republic (36·5m. for, 5·4m. against); *Dec. 21*: De Gaulle elected President of the Republic.

I. INTERNATIONAL AFFAIRS	II. AMERICA	III. ASIA AND OCEANIA
1959. *March 5*: U.S.A. adheres to Bagdad Pact. *Oct. 9*: Bagdad Pact renamed Central Treaty Organization (Cento), with headquarters in Ankara.	**1959.** *Jan. 1-3*: Batistá régime in Cuba overthrown by Fidel Castro. *3*: Alaska 49th U.S. state. *Apr. 25*: St. Lawrence Seaway opened. *Aug. 21*: Hawaii 50th U.S. state.	**1959.** *Mar.*: Unsuccessful rising in Tibet against Chinese; Dalai Lama flees to India. *June 3*: Singapore becomes self-governing state. *July 31*: President of India dismisses Communist cabinet in Kerala. *Sept. 25*: Premier Bandaranaike of Ceylon assassinated.
1960. *May 3*: European Free Trade Association comes into force. *July 15*: U.N. intervention in Congo.	**1960.** *July-Aug.*: Cuba expropriates U.S. firms. *Nov. 4*: Kennedy (Dem.) elected U.S. President. *Dec. 13*: Central American Common Market established.	**1960.** *Apr. 27*: Syngman Rhee resigns as President of Korea. *July 21*: Mrs. Bandaranaike, Premier of Ceylon.
1961. *Sept. 18*: Hammarskjöld, U.N. Secretary-General, killed in air crash. *30*: Organization for European Economic Co-operation replaced by Organization for Economic Co-operation and Development. *Nov. 3*: U Thant (Burma) elected acting Secretary-General of U.N.	**1961.** *Feb. 18*: Latin American Free Trade Association established. *May 17-20*: Unsuccessful attempt to overthrow Castro régime in Cuba. *30*: Trujillo, dictator of Dominican Republic, assassinated.	**1961.** *Dec. 18*: Indian troops annex Goa.
1962. *July 10*: Telstar launched by U.S.A. (transatlantic television). *Oct. 11*: Vatican Council opened. *Oct. 22-Nov. 20*: U.S.-Soviet crisis over Soviet missile bases in Cuba. *Nov. 30*: U Thant elected U.N. secretary-general.	**1962.** *Jan. 31*: Cuba expelled from Organization of American States. *Mar. 29*: President Frondizi of Argentina deposed. *July 18*: President Prado of Peru deposed. *Aug. 6*: Jamaica independent. *31*: Trinidad and Tobago independent.	**1962.** *Jan. 1*: Western Samoa independent. *Mar. 1*: Pakistan adopts presidential constitution. *May 13*: Radhakrishnan elected President of India. *Oct. 20-Nov. 21*: China invades India.
1963. *Aug. 5*: Nuclear test ban treaty between U.S.A., U.S.S.R. and Britain.	**1963.** *Apr. 22*: Pearson Prime Minister of Canada. *Nov. 22*: President Kennedy assassinated; succeeded by Vice-President Lyndon B. Johnson.	**1963.** *Sept. 16*: Federation of Malaysia (Malaya, Singapore, Sabah, Sarawak). *Nov. 1*: Dictatorship of the Diem family overthrown in Vietnam. *30*: Menzies (Australia) and Holyoake (New Zealand) governments returned.

IV. AFRICA AND MIDDLE EAST	V. EUROPE

1959. *Feb.*: Greek-Turkish-British agreement on Cyprus. *June 17*: De Valera elected President of Eire. *July 1*: Lübke elected President of Federal Germany. *Oct.*: Russian satellite Lunik III obtains photographs of hidden side of moon. *8*: U.K. elections (365 Cons., 258 Lab.).

1960. *Feb. 3*: Macmillan's 'wind of change' speech in Cape Town. *Mar. 21*: Blacks massacred by South African police in Sharpeville. *Apr. 27*: French Togoland independent. *June 30*: Belgian Congo independent. *July 1*: Ghana becomes republic. Somalia becomes republic. *3*: Anarchy in Congo. *Aug. 21*: Federation of Mali breaks up into Mali and Senegal. *Oct. 1*: Nigeria independent.

1960. *May 8*: L. I. Brezhnyov, President of U.S.S.R. *27*: Army takes over government of Turkey. *Aug. 16*: Cyprus independent; Makarios, President.

1961. *Mar. 15*: Prime Minister of South Africa withdraws from Commonwealth. *16*: Tanganyika, fully self-governing. *Apr. 27*: Sierra Leone independent. *May 31*: Union of South Africa becomes republic. *June 1*: Northern Cameroons joins Federation of Nigeria. *Oct. 1*: Southern Cameroons joins Republic of Cameroun. *Dec. 9*: Tanganyika independent.

1961. *Jan. 1*: Farthing ceases to be legal tender in Britain. *Apr. 12*: Gagarin in first manned satellite orbits the earth. *Aug. 13*: German Democratic Republic seals off Berlin border. *Oct. 25*: Gen. Gursel elected President of Turkey. *31*: Stalin's body removed from Lenin mausoleum in Moscow; all cities. etc. named after Stalin renamed. *Nov. 7*: Adenauer re-elected German chancellor. *20*: Russian Orthodox Church joins World Council of Churches. *Dec. 9*: U.S.S.R. breaks off relations with Albania; Albania expelled from Comecon.

1962. *Mar. 19*: Cease-fire in Algeria. *28*: Army seizes power in Syria. *July 1*: Burundi and Rwanda independent. *3*: France relinquishes Algeria. *Aug. 16*: Algeria joins Arab League. *Sept. 25*: Ferhat Abbas, President of Algeria; Ben Bella, Prime Minister. *27*: Revolution in Yemen, monarchy abolished. *Oct. 9*: Uganda independent. *Dec. 9*: Tanganyika becomes republic; Nyerere, President.

1962. *Apr. 14*: Pompidou succeeds Debré as French Premier. *May 6*: Segni elected President of Italy.

1963. *Feb. 9*: President Qasim of Iraq overthrown and executed. *Mar. 1*: Aden joins South Arabian Federation. *May 25*: Organization of African Unity set up in Addis Ababa. *Sept. 9*: Ben Bella, President of Algeria. *Oct. 1*: Nigeria becomes republic. *4-Nov. 2*: War between Morocco and Algeria. *Dec. 9*: Zanzibar independent. *12*: Kenya independent. *31*: Federation of Rhodesia and Nyasaland dissolved.

1963. *Jan. 29*: De Gaulle vetoes Britain's entry into European Economic Community. *Apr. 7*: New constitution of Socialist Federal Republic of Yugoslavia. *Oct. 15*: Erhard succeeds Adenauer as German chancellor. *19*: Lord (Sir Alec Douglas-) Home, U.K. Prime Minister. *Dec. 22*: Fighting between Greeks and Turks in Cyprus; Makarios calls in British and U.N. forces and U.N. mediator.

1964—1966

I. INTERNATIONAL AFFAIRS	II. AMERICA	III. ASIA AND OCEANIA
	1964. *Mar. 31*: President Goulart of Brazil deposed; *Apr. 15*: succeeded by Marshal Castelo Branco. *July 2*: Civil Rights Bill signed by President Johnson. *Nov. 3*: Johnson re-elected U.S. President (486 electoral votes against 52 for Senator Goldwater). *4*: President Estenssoro of Bolivia deposed.	**1964.** *May 27*: Nehru *d.*, Shastri, Indian Premier (*June 2*). *Aug. 2*: North Vietnamese attack U.S. warships; retaliatory bombing of North Vietnam begins. *Sept. 2*: Indonesian regular troops begin raids on Malaysia. *Oct. 16*: China explodes atomic bomb in Sinkiang.
1965. *Jan. 7*: Indonesia withdraws from U.N. *Dec. 8*: Vatican Council closed. *10*: U.N. Security Council enlarged from 11 to 15 members. *16*: Security Council votes mandatory sanctions against Rhodesia.	**1965.** *Apr. 24-Sept. 3*: Civil war in Dominican Republic; *Apr. 30*: U.S. troops land. *July 30*: Medical Care for the Aged Bill signed by President Johnson.	**1965.** *Mar. 3*: U.S. Marines begin landing in force in Vietnam. *25*: D. Senanayake, Ceylon Premier. *Apr. 9-June 30*: India-Pakistan fighting on Kutch-Sind border. *May 14*: China explodes second atomic bomb. *June 8*: U.S. troops in Vietnam authorized to take offensive action. *20*: Army takes over government in South Vietnam. *July 26*: Maldive Islands independent. *Aug. 9*: Singapore secedes from Malaysia. *Sept. 1-22*: India-Pakistan war over Kashmir. *Oct. 16*: Afghanistan becomes parliamentary democracy.
1966. *Jan. 10*: Tashkent declaration to end confrontation between Pakistan and India.	**1966.** *Feb. 6*: Dr. José Joaquín Trejos elected President of Costa Rica. *May 26*: British Guiana attains independence as Guyana. *June 29*: President Illia of Argentina deposed; Juan Carlo Ongania, President. *July 1*: President Mendez Montenegro of Guatemala returns to democratic government. Medicare comes into operation in U.S.A. *2*: Dr. Joaquín Balaguer elected President of Dominican Republic. *Nov. 27*: Uruguay returns to presidential system.	**1966.** *Jan. 11*: Shastri *d*; *24*: Mrs Gandhi, Prime Minister of India. *Feb. 14*: Australia introduces decimal currency. *Mar. 21*: Re-election of Chiang Kai-shek as President of Taiwan. *Apr. 30*: Great Proletarian Cultural Revolution launched in China. *May 2*: Tibet made autonomous region of China. *9*: China's third nuclear bomb test. *Aug. 11*: Confrontation between Indonesia and Malaysia ends. *Sept. 11*: Elections for National Assembly of South Vietnam.

IV. AFRICA AND MIDDLE EAST	V. EUROPE

1964. *Jan. 12*: Zanzibar sultan exiled; People's Republic. *Apr. 8*: Ian Smith, Premier of Rhodesia. *27*: Tanganyika and Zanzibar united as Tanzania. *June 15*: Last French forces leave Algeria. *July 6*: Malawi (Nyasaland) independent. *9*: Tshombe, Congo Premier. *Oct. 24*: Zambia (Northern Rhodesia) independent. *Nov. 2*: King Saud of Saudi Arabia deposed by his brother Faisal. *Dec. 12*: Kenya republic.

1964. *Mar. 6*: Paul of Greece *d.*; succeeded by Constantine XIII. *Apr. 1*: Unified U.K. Ministry of Defence. *July 15*: Mikoyan, President of U.S.S.R. *Sept. 21*: Malta independent. *Oct. 14*: Premier Khrushchev replaced by Kosygin; Brezhnyov, First Secretary of Party. *15*: U.K. elections (317 Lab., 304 Cons., 9 Lib.); Harold Wilson, Prime Minister. *Nov. 12*: Charlotte of Luxembourg abdicates; succeeded by Grand Duke Jean.

1965. *Feb. 18*: Gambia independent. *May 7*: Smith wins all white seats in Rhodesia. *June 19*: President Ben Bella of Algeria deposed by Col. Boumédienne. *Oct. 13*: Kasavubu dismisses Tshombe in Congo. *Nov. 11*: Unilateral declaration of independence in Rhodesia; Smith régime proclaimed illegal. *25*: Gen. Mobuto deposes Kasavubu.

1965. *Jan. 24*: Churchill *d. Apr. 1*: Greater London Council established. *May 12*: Federal Republic of Germany establishes diplomatic relations with Israel. *Nov. 9*: Abolition of death penalty in U.K. *Dec. 9*: Podgorny, President of U.S.S.R. *14*: Free trade pact U.K.-Eire. *19*: De Gaulle re-elected French President. *31*: Common Market Commission, Coal and Steel Authority and Euratom merged into one authority.

1966. *Jan. 15*: Military *coup* in Nigeria; Prime Minister Sir Abubakar Tafawa Balewa assassinated. *Feb. 2*: British withdraw from Libya. *22*: President Obote suspends constitution of Uganda. *24*: Army *coup* deposes President Nkrumah of Ghana. *Mar. 30*: South African general elections. *July 6*: Malawi becomes republic. *8*: King of Burundi deposed by his son. *Aug. 1*: Lt.-Col. Gowan succeeds Gen. Ironsi as Head of State, Nigeria. *Sept. 6*: Assassination of South African Prime Minister Verwoerd. *13*: Vorster, Prime Minister of South Africa. *30*: Bechuanaland attains independence as republic of Botswana. *Oct. 4*: Basutoland attains independence as kingdom of Lesotho. *13*: South African apartheid laws extended to South West Africa. *Nov. 28*: Burundi becomes republic.

1966. *Jan. 15*: Treaty of friendship between U.S.S.R. and Mongolia. *Mar. 31*: U.K. elections, Labour increases majority. *Apr.*: U.S.S.R. five-year plan 1966-70. *June 2*: De Valera re-elected President of Eire. *25-July 2*: 23rd Communist Party Congress of U.S.S.R. *July 7*: European Nuclear Energy Agency created at Mol. *Sept. 6-15*: London Commonwealth Conference. *Nov. 9*: Lynch, Prime Minister of Eire.

I. INTERNATIONAL AFFAIRS	II. AMERICA	III. ASIA AND OCEANIA
1967. *Mar. 28*: *Encyclia Popularum Progressio. Dec. 3*: World's first heart transplant carried out in South Africa.	**1967.** *Feb. 10*: U.S. Presidential Disability and Succession bill passed. *Mar. 15*: Brazil gets new constitution under President Artur da Costa e Silva. *Oct.*: Che Guevara *d.*	
1968. *June 12*: Nuclear Non-Proliferation Treaty adopted by U.N. *Sept.*: Abu Simbal Nile temples re-erected.	**1968.** *Apr. 4*: Martin Luther King assassinated. *11*: Civil rights bill passed in U.S.A. *20*: Trudeau Prime Minister of Canada. *May 20*: Rio de la Plata Basin Development signed. *Oct. 3*: Military *coup* in Peru, Gen. J. Velasco Alvarado President. *Nov. 5*: President Nixon (Rep.) elected in U.S.A. (302 electoral votes against 191 for Hubert H. Humphrey).	**1968.** *Jan. 31*: Nauru independent republic. *Feb. 19*: Rann of Kutch dispute between India and Pakistan settled. *Mar. 27*: Gen. Suharto, President of Indonesia. *Nov. 11*: Maldives becomes republic.
1969. *July 20*: Man first lands on moon.	**1969.** *Apr. 27*: President Barrientos of Bolivia *d.*	**1969.** *Mar. 24*: President Ayub Khan of Pakistan resigns. *31*: President Yahya Khan proclaims martial law. *Sept. 3*: Ho Chi Minh *d. Oct. 3*: Bhutan becomes democratic monarchy.
1970. *Apr. 13*: American Apollo 13 explodes before moonlanding. *24*: China launches first satellite.	**1970.** *Feb. 23*: Guyana becomes republic in British Commonwealth. *June 18*: Robert Marcello Levingston, President of Argentina. *20*: U.S.A. lowers voting age to 18. *22*: President Ibarra assumes dictatorial powers in Ecuador. *July 5*: Luis Echeverrin Alvarer elected President of Mexico. *Aug. 31*: Desegregation law for schools comes into force in 11 southern U.S. states. *Oct. 7*: Gen. Juan José Torres of Bolivia proclaims himself President. *Nov. 3*: Salvadore Allende Gossens elected President of Chile.	**1970.** *Mar. 18*: Prince Norodom Sihanouk of Cambodia deposed by General Lon Nol. *June 4*: Tonga becomes independent. *27-July 4*: General election in Ceylon; Mrs. Bandaranaike forms leftwing coalition. *Oct. 10*: Fiji becomes independent.

IV. AFRICA AND MIDDLE EAST	V. EUROPE

1967. *Mar. 27*: Col. Andrew Juxon Smith assumes power in Sierra Leone, suspends constitution. *May 27*: Nigeria divided into 12 states. *30*: Biafra, under Lt.-Col. Ojukwu, secedes from Nigeria; civil war. *June 5*: 6-day war between Israel and Egypt, Syria and Jordan. *Sept. 8*: Uganda becomes republic under new constitution. *Nov. 5*: Egypt withdraws from Yemen. President Abdulla-al-Sallal of Yemen deposed. *30*: Kuria Maria islands revert to Muscat and Oman. *Dec. 1*: Inauguration of East African Community, replacing East African Common Services Organization.

1968. *Mar. 12*: Mauritius gains independence. *24*: Senegal River Basin Development agreement signed. *Apr. 2*: Union of Central African States. *26*: Constitutional government restored in Sierra Leone; Siaka Stevens, Prime Minister. *Sept. 6*: Swaziland independent. *Oct. 12*: Equatorial Guinea independent. *Nov. 29*: British leave Aden; People's Republic of South Yemen proclaimed (*30*).

1969. *Jan.*: Kenya and Uganda withdraw citizenship of British Asians. *Mar. 17*: Golda Meir, Prime Minister of Israel. *May 25*: Sudan taken over by revolutionary council; Chairman M. al Nemery dissolves all parties. *Aug. 29*: Democratic elections in Ghana. *Sept. 1*: King Idris of Libya deposed. *3*: K. A. Busia, Prime Minister of Ghana. *Oct. 21*: Somali President assassinated, military *coup*. *30*: Kenya becomes one party state.

1970. *Jan. 12*: Biafra surrenders to Nigeria, Ojukwu flees country. *Mar. 2*: Smith declares Rhodesia a republic. *31*: King Moshoeshoe II exiled from Lesotho. *Apr. 24*: Gambia becomes a republic in the British Commonwealth. *Sept. 28*: President Nasser of Egypt *d.*

1967. *Apr. 21*: Military coup in Greece. *Dec. 13*: Constantine XIII leaves Greece.

1968. *Mar. 8-9*: Student unrest in Poland. *Apr.*: Action programme in Czechoslovakia overthrows Stalinists. *Aug. 20-21*: Warsaw Pact countries invade Czechoslovakia and overthrow government. *Sept. 26*: President Salazar of Portugal released from appointment. Portugal grants franchise to all literate women. *29*: New constitution for Greece.

1969. *Jan. 1*: New constitution of Czechoslovakia; *Apr. 17*: Anti-Soviet disturbances. *28*: French referendum; De Gaulle resigns. *June 15*: Georges Pompidou elected President of France. *Sept. 28*: Willy Brandt forms government in Federal Republic of Germany.

1970. *Jan. 1*: Age of majority lowered to 18 in Britain. *Mar. 20*: Treaty of Friendship between U.S.S.R. and Czechoslovakia. *21-22*: Lenin centenary celebrations in Moscow. *May 14*: Creation of Comecon Investment Bank. *June 18*: U.K. elections (330 Cons., 287 Lab., 6 Lib.). *19*: Federal Republic of Germany lowers voting age to 18. *July 8*: Dubček dismissed from Czech Communist Party. *17-20*: 20 years extension of Soviet-Finnish Treaty of Friendship and Mutual Assistance. *Aug. 12*: Signing of Treaty of Renunciation of Force between U.S.S.R. and Federal Republic of Germany. *Nov. 9*: De Gaulle *d. Dec. 7*: Federal Republic of Germany and Poland sign treaty recognizing Oder-Neisse line. *14-18*: Riots in Polish Baltic ports.

1971–1972

I. INTERNATIONAL AFFAIRS	II. AMERICA	III. ASIA AND OCEANIA
1971. *Feb. 11*: Treaty banning sea-bed atomic weapons signed in Moscow by 40 nations (excluding France and China). *Oct. 1*: Joseph Luns succeeds Manlio Brosio as Secretary-General of NATO. *25*: China becomes member of U.N., Taiwan vacates Security Council seat. *Dec. 9*: Federated United Arab Emirates join U.N. *21*: Bhutan joins U.N. *31*: U Thant resigns as Secretary-General of U.N., succeeded by Kurt Waldheim.	**1971.** *Feb. 5*: Second moon landing. Apollo 14. *Mar. 23*: President Levingston of Argentina overthrown by army junta. *Apr. 21*: President Duvalier of Haiti *d.*, succeeded by son, Jean-Claude. *24*: Washington peaceful demonstration of 200,000 against Vietnam war. *July 1*: Andean Subregional Integration Agreement. *15*: Chile nationalizes mining industry. *26*: Apollo 15 moon landing. *Aug. 15*: U.S. suspends conversion of dollars into gold. *22*: Hugo Banzer deposes President Torres of Bolivia.	**1971.** *Mar. 10*: McMahon becomes Prime Minister of Australia following Gorton. *11*: Mrs Gandhi of India returned with clear majority. *26*: Shaikh Mujibur Rahman declares republic of Bangladesh; civil war. *June 17*: Riots in Japan; U.S.A. agrees to return Okinawa to Japan. *Aug. 9*: India signs friendship treaty with U.S.S.R. *Dec. 3*: India mobilizes following weeks of fighting on Pakistan border; *6*: Recognizes Bangladesh. *14*: Government of Pakistan resigns. *16*: Pakistan forces surrender to India. *17*: President Yahya Khan resigns, succeeded by Bhutto. *22*: Shaikh Mujibur Rahman released.
1972. *Apr. 10*: Britain and U.S.S.R. sign agreement to outlaw biological weapons. *May 26*: U.S.A. and U.S.S.R. sign agreement to limit nuclear weapons. *June 3*: Signing of Berlin agreement by four powers. *5-16*: First World Conference on the Human Environment meets in Stockholm.	**1972.** *Feb. 15*: President Ibarra of Ecuador deposed by Brig-Gen. Guillermo Rodriguez Lara, sworn in as President. *16. Mar. 1*: Juan Marie Bordaberry President of Uruguay. *May 15*: American Pacific Islands Ryukyu and Okinawa revert to Japan. *18-25*: President Nixon of U.S.A., state visit to China (and to U.S.S.R., *May 22-30*). *Apr. 16-27*: Apollo 16 (and *Dec. 7-19* Apollo 17) explore surface of moon. *June 29*: Supreme Court of U.S.A. declares death penalty contrary to Constitution. *Nov. 7*: Nixon re-elected U.S.A. President (521 electoral votes against 17 for Senator McGovern). *Dec. 4*: President Ramon Ernesto Crux of Honduras overthrown in military *coup*, succeeded by Oswaldo López Arellano.	**1972.** *Jan. 12*: Shaikh Mujibur Rahman, Prime Minister of Bangladesh. *30*: Pakistan withdraws from Commonwealth (and *July 14* from SEATO). *31*: King Mahendra of Nepal *d.*, succeeded by his son Bir Bikram Shah Deva. *Apr. 18*: Bangladesh admitted to Commonwealth. *21*: Bhutto becomes President of Pakistan under new constitution. *May 22*: Ceylon becomes republic as Sri Lanka. *July 21*: King of Bhutan *d.*, succeeded (*24*) by Crown Prince Jigme Singhi Wangchuk. *Nov. 25*: Norman Kirk, Prime Minister of New Zealand. *Dec. 2*: Gough Whitlam, Prime Minister of Australia.

IV. AFRICA AND MIDDLE EAST	V. EUROPE

1971. *Jan. 15:* Aswan High Dam inaugurated. *25:* President Obote of Uganda deposed by Idi Amin. *May 27:* Egypt and Soviet Union sign treaty of friendship. *June 21:* Vorster rejects ruling of International Court of Justice for withdrawal of South Africa from South West Africa. *Aug. 27:* Bahrain independent. *Sept. 1:* Qatar independent. *Oct. 4:* Federation of Egypt, Libya and Sudan; Syria joins *27 Nov. 7:* Oman independent. *27:* Congo (Kinshasa) renamed Republic of Zaïre. *Nov. 28:* Wasfi Tal, Prime Minister of Jordan, assassinated in Cairo. *30:* Libya nationalizes British Petroleum Company; Libya and Iraq break off relations with Britain. *Dec. 2:* Britain leaves Gulf States.

1972. *Jan. 13:* Busia deposed by military *coup* in Ghana; Lt-Col. Ignatius Kuto Acheampong, chairman of National Redemption Council. *Feb. 28:* Sudan signs agreement on the future of southern Sudan. *Mar. 28:* First parliamentary elections in the Gambia. *Apr. 7:* President Karume of Zanzibar assassinated; *12:* Aboud Jumbe elected President. *May 18:* Maj.-Gen. Gabriel Ramanatsoa, Prime Minister of military government in Madagascar. *June 1:* Iraq nationalizes Iraq Petroleum Company. *Aug. 9:* President Amin of Uganda orders expulsion of Asians holding British passports. *Oct. 26:* Military *coup* in Dahomey. *Dec. 13:* Zambia becomes one party state.

1971. *Feb. 14:* Ninth Russian five-year plan. *15:* United Kingdom adopts decimal currency system. *Mar. 23:* Faulkner Prime Minister of Northern Ireland. *May 3:* Walter Ulbricht of German Democratic Republic succeeded by Erich Honecker. *19:* Russia launches spacecraft Salyut. *June 17:* Mintoff Prime Minister of Malta. *Aug. 19:* NATO forces leave Malta. *Sept. 11:* Khrushchev *d. Oct. 31:* First women elected to Swiss Parliament. *Dec. 2:* Russian Mars 3 makes soft landing on moon. *24:* Giovanni Leone, sixth President of Italy.

1972. *Jan. 14:* Frederik IX of Denmark *d.,* succeeded by his daughter Margrethe II. *Mar. 21:* Papadopoulos succeeds Zoitakis as Regent of Greece. *26:* Malta signs defence agreement with Britain. *30:* British government suspends Stormont and assumes direct rule in Northern Ireland. *May 16:* Opening of the Danube dam system constructed by Rumania and Yugoslavia. *July 5:* Messmer succeeds Chavan-Delmas as French Premier. *Sept. 26:* Norway withdraws application from E.E.C. Treaty of Accession, following referendum. *Dec. 7:* Eire vote, in referenda, for reduction in voting age to 18 and on place of Roman Catholic church in the constitution.

I. INTERNATIONAL AFFAIRS	II. AMERICA	III. ASIA AND OCEANIA
	1973. *Mar. 11*: Argentine general elections confirmed Peronists. *June 27*: Military *coup* in Uruguay. *Sept. 11*: President Allende of Chile overthrown by armed forces. *23*: Gen. Perón elected Argentinian President, Senõra Perón Vice-President (sworn in *Oct. 12*).	**1973.** *Jan. 27*: Peace agreement for Vietnam signed. *July 17*: King of Afghanistan deposed by Gen. Daud; republic proclaimed. *Aug. 12*: Elahi elected President of Pakistan. Bhutto Prime Minister. *Oct. 14*: Military régime in Thailand resigns after student revolt.
	1974. *Jan. 15*: Geisel, President of Brazil. *Feb. 7*: Grenada independent within British Commonwealth. *July 1*: Perón *d.*, succeeded by Senõra Perón as President of Argentina. *Aug. 8*: Nixon resigns as President of U.S.A. following Watergate affair, succeeded by Vice-President Gerald Ford. *Sept. 4*: U.S.A. establishes formal relations with German Democratic Republic. *9*: Proclamation of pardon for Nixon by Ford.	**1974.** *Feb. 22*: Pakistan recognizes Bangladesh. *Mar. 2*: U Ne Win appointed Chairman of the Council of State.
1975. *June 5*: Suez Canal reopens to international shipping. *July 1*: Ramphal succeeds Arnold Smith as Commonwealth Secretary-General.	**1975.** *Jan 1*: Watergate conspirators convicted in U.S.A. *Mar. 9*: Work begins on the Alaskan pipeline. *Apr. 22*: President López of Honduras overthrown. *Aug 29*: President Alvardo of Peru overthrown, replaced by Gen. Francisco Morales Bermúdez. *Oct 18*: Signature in Panama by 23 countries of treaty establishing new Latin American Economic System (SELA). *Nov. 25*: Surinam independent.	**1975.** *Jan. 17*: China replaces 1954 constitution. *Apr. 5*: Chiang Kai-shek, President of Taiwan, *d.*, succeeded by Yen Chia-kan. *30*: Vietnamese war ends; President Thieu resigns. *May 16*: Sikkim becomes twenty-second state of the Indian Union. *Aug. 15*: Shaikh Mujibur Rahman assassinated. *Sept. 16*: Papua New Guinea independent. *Nov. 11*: Governor-General of Australia dismisses Prime Minister Whitlam; Fraser forms caretaker government. *29*: Muldoon, Prime Minister of New Zealand. *Dec. 1-2*: King Savang Vatthana of Laos abdicates. *7*: Indonesia invades East Timor. *13*: General elections in Australia confirm Fraser as Prime Minister.

IV. AFRICA AND MIDDLE EAST	V. EUROPE
1973. *Mar 20*: Shah nationalizes foreign-operated oil industry in Iran. *July 5*: Military *coup* in Rwanda. *Sept. 4*: Guinea-Bissau proclaimed independent. *Oct. 6*: Fourth Arab-Israeli war begins. *14-16:* Military régime overthrown in Thailand by student revolt. *Nov. 11*: Arab-Israeli cease-fire agreement signed.	**1973.** *Jan. 1*: U.K., Denmark and Eire become members of E.E.C. *June 1*: Greece becomes a republic. *3*: Soviet supersonic airliner, TU 144, crashes at Paris air show. *Sept. 16*: Gustaf VI Adolf of Sweden *d.*, succeeded by his grandson, Carl XVI Gustaf.
1974. *Apr. 11*: Golda Meir resigns; Gen. Rabin appointed Prime Minister of Israel (*26*). *15*: Military *coup* in Niger. *May 2*: Organization for the Development of the Senegal River adopts 40-year development plan. *June 13*: Military *coup* in Yemen Arab Republic. *Sept. 12*: Emperor Haile Selassie of Ethiopia deposed. *26*: Guinea-Bissau gains independence.	**1974.** *Feb. 13*: Alexander Solzhenitsyn expelled from U.S.S.R. after publication of *The Gulag Archipelago*. *28*: U.K. general elections with no overall majority. *Mar. 4*: Heath resigns as U.K. Prime Minister, Wilson appointed. *Apr.*: President Pompidou of France *d. 25*: Portuguese government overthrown by military; President Tomás and Prime Minister Caetano detained; Spinola heads government. *May 6*: Federal German Chancellor Brandt resigns and Schmidt appointed. *19*: Giscard d'Estaing elected French President. *July 15*: Makarios of Cyprus overthrown in military *coup*. *20*: Turkish invasion of Cyprus. *Nov. 17*: Democratic elections in Greece, Karamanlis Prime Minister. *23*: Military dictatorship ends in Greece. *Dec. 8*: Greece rejects monarchy in referendum.
1975. *Mar. 25*: King Faisal of Saudi Arabia assassinated; succeeded by King Khaled. *Apr. 13*: President of Chad assassinated. *May 26-28*: Creation of Economic Community of West African States (ECOWAS). *June 16*: Simonstown (naval) agreement between U.K. and the Republic of South Africa ends. *25*: Mozambique independent. *July 5*: Cape Verde Islands independent. *6*: Unilateral declaration of independence from France by Comoro Islands. *29*: Gen. Gowan overthrown as Nigeria's Head of State in bloodless *coup*; Gen. Mohammed appointed. *Aug. 27*: Haile Selassie *d. Nov. 11*: Angola independent.	**1975.** *Feb 13*: Turkish Cypriot Federated State proclaimed. *Apr 25*: Constituent Assembly elections held in Portugal. *May 29*: Husák, President of Czechoslovakia. *June 5*: U.K. votes to remain within E.E.C. *7*: New Greek constitution. *Aug. 29*: De Valera of Eire *d. Oct. 7*: 20-year Treaty of Friendship, Co-operation and Mutual Assistance between German Democratic Republic and U.S.S.R. signed in Moscow. *Nov 1*: Catalan and Basque languages legalised in Spain. *20*: Gen. Franco of Spain *d.* Inauguration of King Juan Carlos I.

I. INTERNATIONAL AFFAIRS	II. AMERICA	III. ASIA AND OCEANIA
1976. *July*: Vatican suspends Mgr. Marcel Lefèbre because of opposition to Second Vatican Council teachings.	**1976.** *Jan. 11*: Military *coup* in Ecuador. *Mar. 24*: President Isobel Perón of Argentina overthrown. Gen. Videla, President (*29*). *June 12*: President Bordaberry deposed in Uruguay. *Oct. 10*: Free elections held in Cuba. *26*: Trinidad and Tobago becomes republic. *Nov. 2*: Carter elected President of U.S.A. *15*: *Parti Quebécois* win 69 out of 110 seats in Quebec provincial elections. *Dec. 1*: López Portillo, President of Mexico.	**1976.** *Jan 2*: Ellice Islands become Tuvalu. *8*: Chou En-lai *d.*, succeeded by Hua Kuo-Feng on *Feb. 8*. *June 29*: Seychelles becomes independent. *July 2*: Reunification of Vietnam proclaimed. *Sept. 9*: Mao Tse-tung *d.* *Oct. 6*: Military *coup* in Thailand overthrows coalition government.
1977. *Nov. 5*: U.S.A. withdraws from I.L.O.	**1977.** *Mar. 1*: U.S.A. extends fishing rights to 200 miles. *Sept. 7*: U.S.A. and Panama sign Panama Treaties dealing with defence and permanent neutrality until 1999.	**1977.** *Mar. 22*: Mrs. Gandhi resigns as Prime Minister of India; replaced by Desai (*24*). *July 5*: Gen. Mohammad Zia, President of Pakistan after military *coup*. *21*: Jayawardere, Prime Minister of Sri Lanka after general elections. *Oct. 20*: Military *coup* in Thailand and formation of Revolutionary Council.
1978. *Aug. 6*: Pope Paul VI *d. 27*: John Paul I elected Pope (*d. Sept. 28*). *Oct. 16*: John Paul II elected Pope, first non-Italian Pope for 450 years.	**1978.** *July 4*: Turbay Ayala elected President of Colombia (Proclaimed *16*). *21*: Juan Pereda Asbún, President of Bolivia (deposed by Gen. David Padilla Arancibia *Nov. 24*). *Aug. 16*: Guizmán Fernández sworn in as President of Dominican Republic (elected *May 16*). *Nov. 3*: Dominica independent.	**1978.** *Apr. 27*: President Daud of Afghanistan overthrown in *coup*; Democratic Republic established. *June 29*: Vietnam admitted to Comecon. *July 7*: Solomon Islands gain independence. *Sept. 16*: Mohammed Zia-ul-Haq, President of Pakistan. *Oct. 1*: Tuvalu gains independence.

IV. AFRICA AND MIDDLE EAST	V. EUROPE

1976. *Feb. 13:* Gen. Mohammed of Nigeria assassinated in attempted *coup*; Lt.-Gen. Obasanjo appointed Head of State. *26:* Western Sahara handed over to Morocco and Mauritania by Spain. *Sept. 13:* Sarkis, President of Lebanon. *Oct. 26:* Transkei independent. *Nov. 1:* President Micombero overthrown in Burundi; 30-member Supreme Council of Revolution assumes power.

1976. *Feb. 24-Mar. 5:* 25th Congress of Communist Party of the U.S.S.R. held in Moscow. *Mar. 5:* Direct rule from Westminster for Northern Ireland. *Apr. 5:* Callaghan, Prime Minister of U.K. *Sept. 4:* Peace march by Irish women. *Oct. 13:* Charter 77 manifesto published in Czechoslovakia. *22:* President O Dalaigh of Eire resigns; Patrick Hillery elected.

1977. *Feb. 3:* Benti, Ethiopian Head of State, assassinated. *Mar. 18:* President Ngouabi of Congo assassinated. *June 27:* Republic of Djibouti, formerly French Territory of the Afars and Issas, independent. *Sept. 12:* Biko *d.* in Republic of South Africa. *Oct. 11:* Assassination of Head of State of Yemen Arab Republic; assumption of power by Presidential Council. *Nov. 19:* President Sadat of Egypt arrives in Israel on peace mission. *Dec. 4:* Bokassa crowned Emperor of the Central African Empire. *6:* Bophuthatswana independent. *25:* Prime Minister Begin of Israel visits Egypt on continued peace mission.

1977. *Apr. 9:* Communist Party legalised in Spain. *May 14:* Don Juan de Bourbon renounces all claims to the Spanish throne. *June 16:* Leonid Brezhnev elected President of U.S.S.R. Supreme Soviet. *Aug. 3:* Makarios of Cyprus *d.*, succeeded by Kyprianou. *Sept. 29:* Catalans granted autonomy within Spanish state.

1978. *Apr. 19:* Navon elected President of Israel. *Aug. 22:* Jomo Kenyatta *d. Sept. 5-17:* The Camp David Summit: Sadat, Begin and Carter. *Oct. 10:* Daniel Arap Moi President of Kenya. John Vorster President of the Republic of South Africa. *Dec. 8:* Golda Meir, *d. 10:* Begin and Sadat receive Nobel peace prize. *17:* New Constitution approved in referendum, Rwanda. *27:* Hourari Boumedienne, President of Algeria, *d.*

1978. *Oct. 31:* New Spanish Constitution replaces the Fundamental Laws. *Nov. 27:* Gorbachov becomes Secretary of the Central Committee of the Communist Party of U.S.S.R.

I. INTERNATIONAL AFFAIRS	II. AMERICA	III. ASIA AND OCEANIA
1979. *June 18* SALT II Treaty signed by Presidents Carter and Brezhnev in Geneva. *July 11* Whaling banned in Red Sea, Arabian Sea and most of the Indian Ocean. *Oct. 17*: The Nobel Peace Price awarded to Mother Teresa.	**1979.** *Feb. 8*: U.S. withdraws support from President Somoza in Nicaragua. *22*: St. Lucia becomes independent. *Mar. 12*: Campins sworn in as President of Venezuela. *15*: Gen. da Figueiredo takes office as President of Brazil. *July 17*: Somoza Debayle resigns as President of Nicaragua and goes into exile. *20*: Sandinista government in Nicaragua sworn in. *Aug. 10*: Jaime Roldós Aguilera President of Ecuador. *Oct. 15*: Military *coup* overthrows Romero of El Salvador. *27*: St. Vincent and the Grenadines becomes independent. *Nov. 1*: President Walter Guevera Arce of Bolivia overthrown in *coup*. *4*: U.S.A. establishes formal relations with German Democratic Republic. *9*: Proclamation of pardon for Nixon by Ford.	**1979.** *Jan. 1*: China adopts Phonetic Alphabet (pinyin). *6*: Vietnamese invasion of Cambodia and fall of Phnom-Penh (*7*). *Feb. 17*: China invades Vietnam, withdraws (*Mar. 16*). *Mar. 29*: Supreme Head of State of Malaysia, the Sultan of Kelantan, d. *July 4*: Zulfikar Ali Bhutto executed in Pakistan. *12*: The Gilbert Islands become an independent republic within the Commonwealth as Kiribati. *Oct. 26*: President Park of South Korea assassinated. *Dec. 27*: Soviet troops airlifted into Afghanistan.
1980. *July 19*: Olympic Games XXII Olympiad opens in Moscow, boycotted by over 30 countries as protest against U.S.S.R. invasion of Afghanistan.	**1980.** *Mar. 24*: Archbishop Romero of El Salvador murdered. *May 20*: Quebec votes against giving the *Parti Québécois* government a mandate to negotiate sovereignty-association with the rest of Canada. *July 28*: Fernando Belaúndo Terry President of Peru. Return to civilian rule. *Sept. 11*: New constitution in Chile. *17*: Ex-President Somoza of Nicaragua assassinated in Paraguay. *Oct. 30*: Peace and Border Treaty between El Salvador and Honduras. Edward Seaga's Jamaican Labour Party wins general election. *Nov. 4*: Ronald Reagan elected President of the U.S. (sworn in *Jan. 20*, **1981**). *24*: Tobago holds first parliamentary election.	**1980.** *Mar. 30*: President Ton Duc Thang of Vietnam, d. *June 12*: Masayoshi Ohira, Japanese Prime Minister, d. *23*: Sanjay Gandhi killed in plane accident in India. *July 30*: The New Hebrides becomes independent as Vanuatu. *Sept. 7*: Zhao Ziyang becomes Chinese Prime Minister. *11*: Sirimavo Bandaranaike expelled from the Sri Lanka Parliament, for her abuse of power. *Oct. 18*: General elections in Australia confirm Malcolm Fraser as Prime Minister for second term. *Nov. 20*: Trial opens of the 'Gang of Four' in Beijing (concluded *Dec. 29*).

IV. AFRICA AND MIDDLE EAST

1979. *Jan. 16:* The Shah and his family leave Iran. *31:* Col. Chadli Bendjedid, President of Algeria. *Feb. 1:* The Ayatollah Khomeini returns to Iran from exile in France. *Mar. 14-15:* Israeli invasion of southern Lebanon. *26:* Egypt and Israel sign peace treaty, ending the state of war which had existed between the two countries since 1948. *31:* Arab League denounces Egypt for concluding peace treaty with Israel. *May 31:* Bishop Abel Muzorewa, Prime Minister of Zimbabwe-Rhodesia. *June 4:* President B. J. Vorster of the Republic of South Africa resigns. *20:* President Lule of Uganda ousted, Geoffrey Binaisa installed. *July 4:* Ben Bella released from house arrest in Algeria. *10:* Hilla Limann, President of Ghana. *23:* Ayatollah Khomeini bans music in Iran. *Aug. 11:* Morocco formally annexes Tiris el-Gharbia in Western Sahara. *16:* Nigeria elects Shenhu Shagari as President. *Sept. 10:* Rhodesian constitutional conference at Lancaster House, London (ends *Dec. 15*). *20:* Emperor Jean Bedel Bokassa of the Central African Empire deposed. *Nov. 4:* Occupation of the American Embassy in Tehran, by Islamic Revolutionary 'students' (hostages released *Jan. 20,* **1981**). *Dec. 3:* Iran adopts Islamic Constitution.

1980. *Jan. 25:* Abolhassan Bani-Sadr becomes first President of the Islamic Republic of Iran. *Mar. 4:* Rhodesia election results give 57 seats to Mugabe's ZANU party, 3 to supporters of Joshua Nkomo and 3 to Bishop Muzorewa's supporters. *Apr. 12:* Military *coup* in Liberia, and death of President Tolbert. *18:* Republic of Zimbabwe independent. *July 10:* Military *coup* foiled in Iran. *13:* Sir Seretse Khama, President of Botswana, *d. 27:* The Shah of Iran, *d. 30:* Israel makes Jerusalem its capital. *Sept. 22:* Conflict escalates between Iran and Iraq. *Oct. 26:* Julius Nyerere President of Tanzania for fifth term. *Nov. 14:* President Cabral of Guinea-Bissau overthrown. *25:* President Lamizana of Upper Volta overthrown in bloodless *coup. Dec. 13:* Milton Obote declared President of Uganda.

V. EUROPE

1979. *Jan. 1:* Jura, a new canton of the Swiss Confederation established. *Mar. 1:* Referendum held on the implementation of the Wales and Scotland Acts, which were rejected. *13:* European Monetary System inaugurated. *18:* The Greek Party for Democratic Socialism inaugurated. *31:* British military presence in Malta ends. *May 3:* The Conservative Party wins the U.K. general election. *June 7 and 10:* First direct elections to the European Parliament. *July 6:* The Statute of Limitations in the Federal Republic of Germany abolished. *Aug. 27:* Earl Mountbatten of Burma murdered by I.R.A. *Oct. 7:* NATO reaffirms its decision to deploy long-range nuclear weapons into Europe.

1980. *Jan. 12-14:* The Federal German Green Party formally constituted as a national political party. *Mar. 2:* In a Swiss national referendum, separation of the church and state rejected. *Apr. 30:* Queen Juliana of the Netherlands abdicates in favour of her daughter Princess Beatrix. *May 4:* President Tito of Yugoslavia *d. Aug. 1:* Vigdis Finnbogadottir, President of Iceland. *Sept. 17:* Solidarity founded in Poland. *Dec. 4:* Francisco Sá Carneiro, the Portuguese Prime Minister, killed. Antonio Ramalho Eanes re-elected President (7). *18:* Aleksey N. Kosygin *d.*

I. INTERNATIONAL AFFAIRS	II. AMERICA	III. ASIA AND OCEANIA
	1981. *Jan. 28*: Outbreak of hostilities between Peru and Ecuador over a disputed border area. *Mar. 11*: Pinochet of Chile confirmed as President for further eight-year term. *29*: Gen. Roberto Eduardo Viola assumes the Presidency of Argentina. *30*: Assassination attempt on President Reagan. *Apr. 12*: First space shuttle launched from Cape Canaveral. *May 24*: President Jaime Roldós Aguilera of Ecuador killed in air crash, succeeded by Osvaldo Hurtado Larrea. *Aug. 1*: Omar Torrijos Herrera of Panama killed in air crash. *Oct. 21*: Belize gains independence. *Dec. 11*: Gen. Leopoldo Galtieri President of Argentina.	**1981.** *Jan. 25*: China sentences 'Gang of Four'. Widow of Mao Tse-tung sentenced to death, later commuted to life imprisonment. *May 30*: Unsuccessful military *coup* in Bangladesh; President Ziaur Rahman assassinated. *June 16*: President Marcos of Philippines re-elected. *Nov. 9*: U San Yu elected President of Burma. *15*: Abdus Sattar, President of Bangladesh.
1982. *Jan. 1*: Javier Perez de Cuellar, Secretary-General of the U.N. *June 29*: The Strategic Arms Reduction Talks (START) open in Geneva.	**1982.** *Jan. 21*: Argentina abrogates the 1972 Arbitration Agreement with Chile over the Beagle Channel. *27*: Honduras ends military rule and installs President Roberto Suazo Córdova. *Mar. 15*: Nicaragua suspends Constitution. *29*: Canada Bill passes the British Houses of Parliament and gains Royal Assent. *Apr. 2*: Argentina invades the Falkland Islands. *May 2*: Britain lands on East Falklands and on *June 15* Argentinian troops surrender the Falkland Islands. *June 9*: Rios Montt assumes total power in Guatemala. *17*: President Galtieri of Argentina replaced by Bignone. *July 19*: Gen. G. Vildoso Caldéron President of Bolivia. *Sept. 1*: Mexican banks nationalized.	**1982.** *Jan 29*: Referendum in Guam, which chooses to become a commonwealth of the U.S. *Feb. 9*: Chan Si, Cambodian President of the Council of Ministers. *Mar. 24*: Armed forces seize power in Bangladesh and on *27* Ahsanuddin sworn in as President. *July 9*: The Maldives join the Commonwealth as a special member. *15*: Zail Singh elected President of India. *30*: State of Emergency declared in Sri Lanka. *Dec. 4*: China ratifies new Constitution.

IV. AFRICA AND MIDDLE EAST	V. EUROPE

1981. *Jan. 1*: Abdou Diouf President of Senegal. *20*: Iran releases U.S. hostages after 444 days. *June 22*: President Bani-Sadr of Iran deposed. *July 24*: Mohammed Ali Rajai elected President of Iran (assassinated *Aug. 30*). *Sept. 1*: President Dacko of the Central African Republic overthrown, replaced by Gen. André Kolingba. *Oct. 5*: Sayyed Ali Khamensi elected President of Iran. *6*: President Sadat of Egypt assassinated and Hosni Mubarak confirmed as President on *13*. *Nov. 14*: Gambia announces a new confederation with Senegal to be known as Senegambia. *24*: Attempted mercenary *coup* in the Seychelles. *Dec 3*: 'Independence' given to the Ciskei Black Homeland, South Africa. *14*: Israel annexes Golan Heights. *31*: Jerry L. Rawlings ousts Ghanaian President Hilla Limann in a *coup*.

1981. *Jan. 1*: Greece joins European Communities. *29*: González resigns as Spanish Prime Minister. *Feb. 4*: Mrs G. Harlem Bruntland elected as Norway's first woman Prime Minister. *9*: Gen. Wojciech Jaruzelski Polish Prime Minister. *23*: Right wing *coup* fails in Spain. *Mar. 26*: Social Democratic Party established in U.K. *Apr. 12*: Serious inner city violence and rioting in U.K. *May 10*: Giscard d'Estaing defeated by Mitterand in French presidential election. *13*: Assassination attempt on the Pope. *June 14*: Referendum on Equal Rights for Women in Switzerland succeeds. *16*: Political and electoral alliance between the Liberals and the Social Democratic Party in U.K. *Dec. 13*: Martial law declared in Poland.

1982. *Feb. 17*: Joshua Nkomo dismissed from the Zimbabwe government. *Apr. 25*: Israel completes withdrawal from the Sinai. *May 5*: President Sir Dawda Jawara re-elected President of the Gambia. *June 13*: King Khaled of Saudi Arabia, *d.*, accession of King Fahd. *Aug. 31*: First phase of withdrawal of PLO and Syrian forces from Beirut. *Sept. 14*: President Bashir Gemayel of Lebanon assassinated in Beirut (elected *Aug. 23*), succeeded by Amin Gemayel (*Sept. 23*). *16*: Massacre of Palestinians in Beirut refugee camps.

1982. *Jan. 27*: Mauno Koivisto President of Finland. *June 30*: Spain joins NATO. *Aug. 8*: Corsica granted own Assembly. *Sept. 14*: Princess Grace of Monaco *d*. *Nov. 10*: President L. Brezhnev *d*. Yuri Andropov appointed as General Secretary of the Communist Party of the U.S.S.R. (*12*). *Dec. 2*: Felipe González Spanish Prime Minister. *18*: Poland suspends martial law.

I. INTERNATIONAL AFFAIRS	II. AMERICA	III. ASIA AND OCEANIA
1983. *Jan 18*: International Monetary Fund increased for emergencies. *June 13*: Pioneer 10, the unmanned spacecraft, crosses the orbit of Neptune and travels beyond the solar system.	**1983.** *Feb. 28*: Argentina agrees timetable for the return to civilian rule. *Apr. 28*: Documents on the 'dirty war' in Argentina. *Aug. 8*: Rios Montt overthrown in Guatemala. *Sept. 19*: St. Christopher (Kitts)–Nevis becomes independent. *Oct. 14*: Prime Minister Bishop of Grenada overthrown and murdered on *Oct. 19*, followed by military intervention by U.S. with Caribbean forces on *Oct. 25*. *Dec. 5*: The military junta dissolved in Argentina, new civilian government under President Alfonsín takes office on *Dec. 10*. *10*: Raúl Alfonsín sworn in as civilian President of Argentina and announces (*13*) that the junta face criminal charges.	**1983.** *Jan. 20*: State of Emergency lifted in Sri Lanka. *Mar. 10*: President Suharto of Indonesia re-elected for a further five-year term. *11*: Robert Hawke forms Australian Labor Party government. *June 18*: Li Xiannian of China elected President. *Aug. 21*: Benigno Aquino shot on his return to Philippines from exile.
1984. *Jan. 10*: The Vatican establishes full diplomatic relations with the U.S. *July 8*: The Olympic Games XXIII Olympiad opens in Los Angeles, boycotted by 17 countries. *Oct. 27*: World reacts to famine in Africa. *Nov. 29*: Treaty settles the Beagle Channel dispute between Argentina and Chile, after Vatican mediation. *Dec. 11*: U.N. Law of the Sea finally signed by 159 nations, abstentions include U.K., U.S.A. and the Federal Republic of Germany. *31*: U.S. withdraws from UNESCO.	**1984.** *Feb. 29*: Pierre Trudeau resigns as Canadian Prime Minister and leader of the Liberal Party. *May 6*: Leon Febres Cordero President of Ecuador. *16*: Nicolás Ardito Barletta sworn in as President of Panama. *Nov. 4*: Sandinistas led by Daniel Ortega win elections in Nicaragua. *25*: Uruguay returns to civilian rule.	**1984.** *Jan. 3*: Brunei gains independence. *June 5*: Indian troops attack Sikh militants in the Golden Temple, Amritsar. *Sept. 26*: Initialling of the Joint Declaration on Hong Kong by China and the U.K. Ratified by the British Parliament (*Dec. 5, 10*) and signed in Beijing (*Dec. 19*). *Oct. 31*: Indian Prime Minister Indira Gandhi assassinated, succeeded by her youngest son, Rajiv. *Dec. 3*: Chemical plant disaster in Bhopal, India, leaves 1,745 dead and 200,000 injured. *22*: General elections in Singapore, the People's Action Party win 77 of the 79 seats.

IV. AFRICA AND MIDDLE EAST	V. EUROPE

1983. *Jan. 17*: Nigeria expels 2,000,000 illegal aliens. *Mar. 9*: Joshua Nkomo flees Zimbabwe (returns on *Aug. 16*). *June 24*: Yasir Arafat expelled from Syria. *Sept. 15*: President Begin resigns, replaced by Yitzhak Shammir on *Oct. 10*. *Oct. 27*: President Kaunda of Zambia re-elected for fifth term. *Dec. 20*: Yasir Arafat leaves Lebanon. *31*: The Shagari government in Nigeria overthrown.

1984. *Feb.*: Libyan People's Bureau in London taken over by 'revolutionary students'. Killing outside the Bureau (*Apr. 17*); U.K. severs diplomatic relations (*Apr. 22*). *Mar. 16*: Non-aggression pact signed by Mozambique and the Republic of South Africa. *26*: Ahmed Sékou Touré, President of Guinea, *d*. *Apr. 12*: Edward Sokoine, President of Tanzania, killed in accident. *July 26*: Liberia restores political activities. *Aug. 4*: Upper Volta renamed Burkina Faso. *Sept. 10*: Ethiopia becomes communist state. *14*: P. W. Botha became State President of South Africa. *Oct. 27*: Beginning of famine relief to Ethiopia. *Nov. 12*: Morocco leaves Organization of African Unity. *Dec. 3*: President Khouna Ould Haydalla of Mauritania deposed.

1983. *Jan. 11*: N. Podgorny of Russia *d*. *Mar. 18*: Ex-king Umberto of Italy *d*. *Apr. 22*: 'Hitler Diaries' acquired, proved to be forgeries (*May 6*). *June 9*: Conservatives incease majority in the U.K. general election. *16*: Yuri Andropov President of U.S.S.R.

1984. *Jan. 1*: The U.S. deploys missiles into northern Europe. *Feb. 9*: Yuri Andropov *d*: *18*: Italy signs a new Concordat with the Vatican. *Apr. 11*: Konstantin U. Chernenko, President of the U.S.S.R. *May 26*: Danube–Black Sea Canal opens. *July 31*: Greater autonomy granted to New Caledonia and French Polynesia by France. *Oct. 12*: Bombing attempt on British cabinet in Brighton. *19*: Jercy Popieluszko, Polish priest, kidnapped and murdered.

I. INTERNATIONAL AFFAIRS	II. AMERICA	III. ASIA AND OCEANIA
	1985. *Jan. 10*: Daniel Ortega sworn in as President of Nicaragua. *15*: Tancredo Neves elected first civilian President of Brazil since 1964. *20*: Ronald Reagan begins his second term as U.S. President. *Mar. 5*: Norman Saunders of Turks and Caicos Islands arrested on drugs charge, resigns as Prime Minister *22*. *Apr. 21*: Tancredo Neves, Brazilian President-elect *d*. José Sarney sworn in *22*. *May 1*: U.S. trade embargo against Nicaragua. *July 14*: Victor Paz Estensuoro elected President of Bolivia. *28*: Alan García sworn in as President of Peru. *Sept. 19*: Massive earthquake destroys large areas of Mexico City. *28*: Eric Arturo de Valle President of Panama. *Nov. 14*: Volcano engulfs Armero in Colombia.	**1985.** *Jan. 14*: Hun Sen, Cambodian President of the Council of Ministers. *Mar. 10*: Pakistan's 1973 Constitution restored. *28*: President Devan Nair of Singapore resigns. *Apr. 10*: China ratifies agreement with U.K. on future of Hong Kong. *May 24*: Cyclone at mouth of the Ganges causes 10,000 deaths in Bangladesh. *June 20*: Agreement reached between North and South Korea on economic co-operation. *July 10*: *Rainbow Warrior*, ship owned by Greenpeace, sunk in Auckland Harbour, New Zealand. *Sept. 1*: Wee Kim Wee sworn in as President of Singapore. *9*: Unsuccessful military *coup* in Thailand.

IV. AFRICA AND MIDDLE EAST	V. EUROPE

1985. *Jan. 3*: 20,000 Falasha Jews airlifted from Ethiopia to Israel since *Nov. 1984*. *25*: Tri-racial and tri-cameral parliament inaugurated in the Republic of South Africa. *31*: President Botha of South Africa offers Nelson Mandela freedom if violence renounced. The offer is refused. *Apr. 24*: Israel completes second phase of withdrawal from southern Lebanon *June 14*: South African security forces hunting members of the African National Congress raids houses in Gaborone, Botswana. *17*: Legislative power and executive authority return to 'transitional' government of Namibia (South West Africa) after two years of direct rule from Pretoria. *July 13*: 'Live Aid' charity concerts raise money for African famine relief. *20*: State of Emergency declared in 36 areas of the Transvaal and eastern Cape provinces of South Africa following unrest in Soweto. *27*: President Obote of Uganda deposed and Tito Okello sworn in on *29*. *Aug. 15*: President Botha rejects the concept of 'one man one vote'. *27*: President Buhari of Nigeria deposed, Maj.-Gen. Ibrahim Babangida sworn in as President *30*. *Sept. 11*: Proposed restoration of South African citizenship to citizens of the independent black homelands. *Oct. 15*: Samuel Doe of Liberia reelected Head of State. *23*: Morocco announces ceasefire in Western Sahara and the holding of a referendum under U.N. auspices.

1985. *Feb. 1*: Greenland withdraws from European Communities. *4-5*: Gibraltar frontier with Spain fully opened. *Mar. 10*: President Chernenko *d*. Mikhail Gorbachov appointed as CPSU General Secretary in U.S.S.R. (*11*). *Apr. 11*: Enver Hoxha of Albania *d.*, succeeded (*13*) by Ramiz Alia. *July 2*: Gromyko elected President of the U.S.S.R. *Nov. 15*: Anglo-Irish agreement on Northern Ireland. *Dec. 17*: Resignation of 15 Ulster Unionist M.P.s over Anglo-Irish accord.